T0189096

Lecture Notes in Computer Science 12665

More information about this subseries at http://www.springer.com/series/7412

Alberto Del Bimbo · Rita Cucchiara ·
Stan Sclaroff · Giovanni Maria Farinella ·
Tao Mei · Marco Bertini ·
Hugo Jair Escalante · Roberto Vezzani (Eds.)

Pattern Recognition

ICPR International Workshops and Challenges

Virtual Event, January 10–15, 2021
Proceedings, Part V

 Springer

Editors
Alberto Del Bimbo ⓘ
Dipartimento di Ingegneria
dell'Informazione
University of Firenze
Firenze, Italy

Stan Sclaroff ⓘ
Department of Computer Science
Boston University
Boston, MA, USA

Tao Mei
Cloud & AI, JD.COM
Beijing, China

Hugo Jair Escalante ⓘ
Computational Sciences Department
National Institute of Astrophysics,
Optics and Electronics (INAOE)
Tonantzintla, Puebla, Mexico

Rita Cucchiara ⓘ
Dipartimento di Ingegneria "Enzo Ferrari"
Università di Modena e Reggio Emilia
Modena, Italy

Giovanni Maria Farinella ⓘ
Dipartimento di Matematica e Informatica
University of Catania
Catania, Italy

Marco Bertini ⓘ
Dipartimento di Ingegneria
dell'Informazione
University of Firenze
Firenze, Italy

Roberto Vezzani ⓘ
Dipartimento di Ingegneria "Enzo Ferrari"
Università di Modena e Reggio Emilia
Modena, Italy

ISSN 0302-9743   ISSN 1611-3349   (electronic)
Lecture Notes in Computer Science
ISBN 978-3-030-68820-2   ISBN 978-3-030-68821-9   (eBook)
https://doi.org/10.1007/978-3-030-68821-9

LNCS Sublibrary: SL6 – Image Processing, Computer Vision, Pattern Recognition, and Graphics

This Springer imprint is published by the registered company Springer Nature Switzerland AG
The registered company address is: Gewerbestrasse 11, 6330 Cham, Switzerland

Foreword by General Chairs

It is with great pleasure that we welcome you to the post-proceedings of the 25th International Conference on Pattern Recognition, ICPR2020 Virtual-Milano. ICPR2020 stands on the shoulders of generations of pioneering pattern recognition researchers. The first ICPR (then called IJCPR) convened in 1973 in Washington, DC, USA, under the leadership of Dr. King-Sun Fu as the General Chair. Since that time, the global community of pattern recognition researchers has continued to expand and thrive, growing evermore vibrant and vital. The motto of this year's conference was *Putting Artificial Intelligence to work on patterns*. Indeed, the deep learning revolution has its origins in the pattern recognition community – and the next generations of revolutionary insights and ideas continue with those presented at this 25th ICPR. Thus, it was our honor to help perpetuate this longstanding ICPR tradition to provide a lively meeting place and open exchange for the latest pathbreaking work in pattern recognition.

For the first time, the ICPR main conference employed a two-round review process similar to journal submissions, with new papers allowed to be submitted in either the first or the second round and papers submitted in the first round and not accepted allowed to be revised and re-submitted for second round review. In the first round, 1554 new submissions were received, out of which 554 (35.6%) were accepted and 579 (37.2%) were encouraged to be revised and resubmitted. In the second round, 1696 submissions were received (496 revised and 1200 new), out of which 305 (61.4%) of the revised submissions and 552 (46%) of the new submissions were accepted. Overall, there were 3250 submissions in total, and 1411 were accepted, out of which 144 (4.4%) were included in the main conference program as orals and 1263 (38.8%) as posters (4 papers were withdrawn after acceptance). We had the largest ICPR conference ever, with the most submitted papers and the most selective acceptance rates ever for ICPR, attesting both the increased interest in presenting research results at ICPR and the high scientific quality of work accepted for presentation at the conference.

We were honored to feature seven exceptional Keynotes in the program of the ICPR2020 main conference: David Doermann (Professor at the University at Buffalo), Pietro Perona (Professor at the California Institute of Technology and Amazon Fellow at Amazon Web Services), Mihaela van der Schaar (Professor at the University of Cambridge and a Turing Fellow at The Alan Turing Institute in London), Max Welling (Professor at the University of Amsterdam and VP of Technologies at Qualcomm), Ching Yee Suen (Professor at Concordia University) who was presented with the IAPR 2020 King-Sun Fu Prize, Maja Pantic (Professor at Imperial College UK and AI Scientific Research Lead at Facebook Research) who was presented with the IAPR 2020 Maria Petrou Prize, and Abhinav Gupta (Professor at Carnegie Mellon University and Research Manager at Facebook AI Research) who was presented with the IAPR 2020 J.K. Aggarwal Prize. Several best paper prizes were also announced and awarded, including the Piero Zamperoni Award for the best paper authored by a student, the BIRPA Best Industry Related Paper Award, and Best Paper Awards for each of the five tracks of the ICPR2020 main conference.

The five tracks of the ICPR2020 main conference were: (1) Artificial Intelligence, Machine Learning for Pattern Analysis, (2) Biometrics, Human Analysis and Behavior Understanding, (3) Computer Vision, Robotics and Intelligent Systems, (4) Document and Media Analysis, and (5) Image and Signal Processing. The best papers presented at the main conference had the opportunity for publication in expanded format in journal special issues of *IET Biometrics* (tracks 2 and 3), *Computer Vision and Image Understanding* (tracks 1 and 2), *Machine Vision and Applications* (tracks 2 and 3), *Multimedia Tools and Applications* (tracks 4 and 5), *Pattern Recognition Letters* (tracks 1, 2, 3 and 4), or *IEEE Trans. on Biometrics, Behavior, and Identity Science* (tracks 2 and 3).

In addition to the main conference, the ICPR2020 program offered workshops and tutorials, along with a broad range of cutting-edge industrial demos, challenge sessions, and panels. The virtual ICPR2020 conference was interactive, with real-time live-streamed sessions, including live talks, poster presentations, exhibitions, demos, Q&A, panels, meetups, and discussions – all hosted on the Underline virtual conference platform.

The ICPR2020 conference was originally scheduled to convene in Milano, which is one of the most beautiful cities of Italy for art, culture, lifestyle – and more. The city has so much to offer! With the need to go virtual, ICPR2020 included interactive **virtual tours** of Milano during the conference coffee breaks, which we hoped would introduce attendees to this wonderful city, and perhaps even entice them to visit Milano once international travel becomes possible again.

The success of such a large conference would not have been possible without the help of many people. We deeply appreciate the vision, commitment, and leadership of the ICPR2020 Program Chairs: Kim Boyer, Brian C. Lovell, Marcello Pelillo, Nicu Sebe, René Vidal, and Jingyi Yu. Our heartfelt gratitude also goes to the rest of the main conference organizing team, including the Track and Area Chairs, who all generously devoted their precious time in conducting the review process and in preparing the program, and the reviewers, who carefully evaluated the submitted papers and provided invaluable feedback to the authors. This time their effort was considerably higher given that many of them reviewed for both reviewing rounds. We also want to acknowledge the efforts of the conference committee, including the Challenge Chairs, Demo and Exhibit Chairs, Local Chairs, Financial Chairs, Publication Chair, Tutorial Chairs, Web Chairs, Women in ICPR Chairs, and Workshop Chairs. Many thanks, also, for the efforts of the dedicated staff who performed the crucially important work behind the scenes, including the members of the ICPR2020 Organizing Secretariat. Finally, we are grateful to the conference sponsors for their generous support of the ICPR2020 conference.

We hope everyone had an enjoyable and productive ICPR2020 conference.

Rita Cucchiara
Alberto Del Bimbo
Stan Sclaroff

Preface

The 25th International Conference on Pattern Recognition Workshops (ICPRW 2020) were held virtually in Milan, Italy and rescheduled to January 10 and January 11 of 2021 due to the Covid-19 pandemic. ICPRW 2020 included timely topics and applications of Computer Vision, Image and Sound Analysis, Pattern Recognition and Artificial Intelligence. We received 49 workshop proposals and 46 of them have been accepted, which is three times more than at ICPRW 2018. The workshop proceedings cover a wide range of areas including Machine Learning (8), Pattern Analysis (5), Healthcare (6), Human Behavior (5), Environment (5), Surveillance, Forensics and Biometrics (6), Robotics and Egovision (4), Cultural Heritage and Document Analysis (4), Retrieval (2), and Women at ICPR 2020 (1). Among them, 33 workshops are new to ICPRW. Specifically, the ICPRW 2020 volumes contain the following workshops (please refer to the corresponding workshop proceeding for details):

- CADL2020 – Workshop on Computational Aspects of Deep Learning.
- DLPR – Deep Learning for Pattern Recognition.
- EDL/AI – Explainable Deep Learning/AI.
- (Merged) IADS – Integrated Artificial Intelligence in Data Science, IWCR – IAPR workshop on Cognitive Robotics.
- ManifLearn – Manifold Learning in Machine Learning, From Euclid to Riemann.
- MOI2QDN – Metrification & Optimization of Input Image Quality in Deep Networks.
- IML – International Workshop on Industrial Machine Learning.
- MMDLCA – Multi-Modal Deep Learning: Challenges and Applications.
- IUC 2020 – Human and Vehicle Analysis for Intelligent Urban Computing.
- PATCAST – International Workshop on Pattern Forecasting.
- RRPR – Reproducible Research in Pattern Recognition.
- VAIB 2020 – Visual Observation and Analysis of Vertebrate and Insect Behavior.
- IMTA VII – Image Mining Theory & Applications.
- AIHA 2020 – Artificial Intelligence for Healthcare Applications.
- AIDP – Artificial Intelligence for Digital Pathology.
- (Merged) GOOD – Designing AI in support of Good Mental Health, CAIHA – Computational and Affective Intelligence in Healthcare Applications for Vulnerable Populations.
- CARE2020 – pattern recognition for positive teChnology And eldeRly wEllbeing.
- MADiMa 2020 – Multimedia Assisted Dietary Management.
- 3DHU 2020 – 3D Human Understanding.
- FBE2020 – Facial and Body Expressions, micro-expressions and behavior recognition.
- HCAU 2020 – Deep Learning for Human-Centric Activity Understanding.
- MPRSS - 6th IAPR Workshop on Multimodal Pattern Recognition for Social Signal Processing in Human Computer Interaction.

- CVAUI 2020 – Computer Vision for Analysis of Underwater Imagery.
- MAES – Machine Learning Advances Environmental Science.
- PRAConBE - Pattern Recognition and Automation in Construction & the Built Environment.
- PRRS 2020 – Pattern Recognition in Remote Sensing.
- WAAMI - Workshop on Analysis of Aerial Motion Imagery.
- DEEPRETAIL 2020 - Workshop on Deep Understanding Shopper Behaviours and Interactions in Intelligent Retail Environments 2020.
- MMForWild2020 – MultiMedia FORensics in the WILD 2020.
- FGVRID – Fine-Grained Visual Recognition and re-Identification.
- IWBDAF – Biometric Data Analysis and Forensics.
- RISS – Research & Innovation for Secure Societies.
- WMWB – TC4 Workshop on Mobile and Wearable Biometrics.
- EgoApp – Applications of Egocentric Vision.
- ETTAC 2020 – Eye Tracking Techniques, Applications and Challenges.
- PaMMO – Perception and Modelling for Manipulation of Objects.
- FAPER – Fine Art Pattern Extraction and Recognition.
- MANPU – coMics ANalysis, Processing and Understanding.
- PATRECH2020 – Pattern Recognition for Cultural Heritage.
- (Merged) CBIR – Content-Based Image Retrieval: where have we been, and where are we going, TAILOR – Texture AnalysIs, cLassificatiOn and Retrieval, VIQA – Video and Image Question Answering: building a bridge between visual content analysis and reasoning on textual data.
- W4PR - Women at ICPR.

We would like to thank all members of the workshops' Organizing Committee, the reviewers, and the authors for making this event successful. We also appreciate the support from all the invited speakers and participants. We wish to offer thanks in particular to the ICPR main conference general chairs: Rita Cucchiara, Alberto Del Bimbo, and Stan Sclaroff, and program chairs: Kim Boyer, Brian C. Lovell, Marcello Pelillo, Nicu Sebe, Rene Vidal, and Jingyi Yu. Finally, we are grateful to the publisher, Springer, for their cooperation in publishing the workshop proceedings in the series of Lecture Notes in Computer Science.

December 2020   Giovanni Maria Farinella
                                                              Tao Mei

Challenges

Competitions are effective means for rapidly solving problems and advancing the state of the art. Organizers identify a problem of practical or scientific relevance and release it to the community. In this way the whole community can contribute to the solution of high-impact problems while having fun. This part of the proceedings compiles the best of the competitions track of the *25th International Conference on Pattern Recognition (ICPR)*.

Eight challenges were part of the track, covering a wide variety of fields and applications, all of this within the scope of ICPR. In every challenge organizers released data, and provided a platform for evaluation. The top-ranked participants were invited to submit papers for this volume. Likewise, organizers themselves wrote articles summarizing the design, organization and results of competitions. Submissions were subject to a standard review process carried out by the organizers of each competition. Papers associated with seven out the eight competitions are included in this volume, thus making it a representative compilation of what happened in the ICPR challenges.

We are immensely grateful to the organizers and participants of the ICPR 2020 challenges for their efforts and dedication to make the competition track a success. We hope the readers of this volume enjoy it as much as we have.

November 2020

Marco Bertini
Hugo Jair Escalante

ICPR Organization

General Chairs

Rita Cucchiara   Univ. of Modena and Reggio Emilia, Italy
Alberto Del Bimbo   Univ. of Florence, Italy
Stan Sclaroff   Boston Univ., USA

Program Chairs

Kim Boyer   Univ. at Albany, USA
Brian C. Lovell   Univ. of Queensland, Australia
Marcello Pelillo   Univ. Ca' Foscari Venezia, Italy
Nicu Sebe   Univ. of Trento, Italy
René Vidal   Johns Hopkins Univ., USA
Jingyi Yu   ShanghaiTech Univ., China

Workshop Chairs

Giovanni Maria Farinella   Univ. of Catania, Italy
Tao Mei   JD.COM, China

Challenge Chairs

Marco Bertini   Univ. of Florence, Italy
Hugo Jair Escalante   INAOE and CINVESTAV National Polytechnic Institute of Mexico, Mexico

Publication Chair

Roberto Vezzani   Univ. of Modena and Reggio Emilia, Italy

Tutorial Chairs

Vittorio Murino   Univ. of Verona, Italy
Sudeep Sarkar   Univ. of South Florida, USA

Women in ICPR Chairs

Alexandra Branzan Albu   Univ. of Victoria, Canada
Maria De Marsico   Univ. Roma La Sapienza, Italy

Demo and Exhibit Chairs

Lorenzo Baraldi   Univ. Modena Reggio Emilia, Italy
Bruce A. Maxwell   Colby College, USA
Lorenzo Seidenari   Univ. of Florence, Italy

Special Issue Initiative Chair

Michele Nappi   Univ. of Salerno, Italy

Web Chair

Andrea Ferracani   Univ. of Florence, Italy

Corporate Relations Chairs

Fabio Galasso   Univ. Roma La Sapienza, Italy
Matt Leotta   Kitware, Inc., USA
Zhongchao Shi   Lenovo Group Ltd., China

Local Chairs

Matteo Matteucci   Politecnico di Milano, Italy
Paolo Napoletano   Univ. of Milano-Bicocca, Italy

Financial Chairs

Cristiana Fiandra   The Office srl, Italy
Vittorio Murino   Univ. of Verona, Italy

Contents – Part V

IUC 2020 - The 1st International Workshop on Human and Vehicle Analysis for Intelligent Urban Computing

**IWBDAF 2020 - International Workshop on Biometric Data Analysis
and Forensics**

**MADiMa 2020 - 6th International Workshop on Multimedia Assisted
Dietary Management**

IMTA VII - Workshop on Image Mining Theory and Applications

IMTA-VII-2020: Workshop on Image Mining Theory and Applications

Workshop Description

The primary purpose of the IMTA-VII-2020 workshop has been to provide the fusion of modern mathematical approaches and techniques for image analysis/pattern recognition with the requests of applications.

Image mining methods are able to extract knowledge and to highlight patterns, enabling very important applications such as medical diagnosis, robotics, technical diagnosis and non-destructive testing, precision agriculture, novel industrial support system, remote sensing, anthropogenic and ecological forecasting and monitoring, and many others. The mathematical foundations, means and tools are of the first importance for the field. In essence, the mathematical foundations and instrumentation of image analysis and pattern recognition, mainly of image mining –a leading line of the modern mathematical theory of image analysis– is the subject of IMTA-VII-2020.

The technological advances and the increase of storage capability support the growth of large and detailed, but possibly noisy, image datasets. Hence, IMTA-VII-2020 topics are of utmost relevance being the perfect humus for giving rise to significant cross-contamination with other emerging fields, both theoretical and applied.

An example of how the main subject of Image-Mining may merge profitably with other fields, such as computational topology, algebraic lattice methods, or machine learning, is the rise of new concepts and trends, such as topological features and invariants and their computation for digital images, representations and compression of nD images based on topology, Descriptive Image Algebras and Descriptive Image Models and Representations and, based on them multi-level multiple image classifiers, lattice-based learning from time-series, images by video/image mining, applications of fuzzy lattices in pattern recognition, and many others.

The main goals of IMTA-VII-2020 have been:

i) to unite the Algebraic, Discrete Mathematics and otherwise mathematically inspired scientists, engineers, researchers, IT-people involved in Pattern Recognition and Image Analysis for providing them new opportunities to know and understand each other better and to communicate;

ii) to provide an event for discussing actual and prospective lines of research and to exchange recent advances in Algebraic and Discrete Mathematics and other Mathematical Problems and Techniques inspired by Image Analysis and Pattern Recognition.

The IMTA-VII-2020 has continued the successful series of workshops devoted to modern mathematical techniques of image-mining and to corresponding applications (2008, Funchal, Madeira, Portugal; 2009, Lisboa, Portugal; 2010, Angers, France; 2013, Barcelona, Spain; 2015, Berlin, Germany, 2018, Montreal, Canada). The IMTA-VII-2020 has been conducted by the Technical Committee No. 16 "Algebraic and

Discrete Mathematical Techniques in Pattern Recognition and Image Analysis" of the International Association for Pattern Recognition (IAPR) and by the National Committee for Pattern Recognition and Image Analysis of the Russian Academy of Sciences.

The workshop has consisted of invited talks, contributed talks, informal discussions and a wrap-up session. This year we received 34 submissions for reviews from authors belonging to 11 different countries. After the review process, 31 papers were accepted and, eventually, 27 regular papers were included in the workshop program for oral presentation. The review process, based on a minimum of two reviews for each paper, focused both on paper quality and prospective interest in the themes of IMTA workshop. A number of invited talks further enriched the program. Notably, the lecture titled "Basic Models of Descriptive Image Analysis" has been delivered by Dr.-Eng. I. Gurevich and Dr. V. Yashina (Federal Research Center "Computer Sciences and Control" of the Russian Academy of Sciences, Moscow, the Russian Federation) while "Learning topology: bridging computational topology and machine learning" has been presented by Dr. M. A. Pascali and Dr. D. Moroni (ISTI-CNR, Italy). The corresponding invited papers are included in this collection.

We are also grateful to all the members of the Scientific Committee that, besides helping in the review process, have provided useful comments and remarks contributing to the success of the workshop. Last but not least, we thank ICPR Organisers and Workshop Chairs for having hosted our workshop, for the patience in answering to all our questions and, finally, for the courage and determination in continuing to organize such a complex event despite the difficult times.

Organization

IMTA Chairs

Igor Gurevich   Federal Research Center "Computer Sciences and Control", Russian Academy of Sciences, Moscow, the Russian Federation

Davide Moroni   ISTI, National Research Council (CNR), Italy

Dietrich Paulus   University Koblenz-Landau, Germany

Vera Yashina   Federal Research Center "Computer Sciences and Control", Russian Academy of Sciences, Moscow, the Russian Federation

Scientific Committee

Sergey Ablameyko   Belarusian State University, Belarusian Academy of Sciences, Belarus Republic

Sara Colantonio   ISTI, National Research Council (CNR), Italy

Daniela Giorgi   ISTI, National Research Council (CNR), Italy

Manuel Grana   Universidad del Pais Vasco, Spain

Vassilis Kaburlasos   Eastern Macedonia and Thrace Institute of Kavala, Greece

Claudia Landi   University of Modena and Reggio Emilia, Italy

Anatoly Nemirko   St. Petersburg Electrotechnical University "LETI", the Russian Federation

Heinrich Niemann   Friedrich-Alexander-University of Erlangen-Nuremberg, Germany

Maria Antonietta Pascali   ISTI, National Research Council (CNR), Italy

Bernd Radig   Munich Technical University, Germany

Gerhard Ritter   University of Florida, USA

Ovidio Salvetti   ISTI, National Research Council (CNR), Italy

Humberto Sossa   Instituto Polytechnico National (IPN), Mexico

The Study of Improving the Accuracy of Convolutional Neural Networks in Face Recognition Tasks

Nikita Andriyanov[2]([⊠]) [iD], Vitaly Dementev[1] [iD], Alexandr Tashlinskiy[1],
and Konstantin Vasiliev[1] [iD]

[1] Ulyanovsk State Technical University, Severny Venets st., h. 32, 432027 Ulyanovsk, Russia
[2] Financial University under the Government of the Russian Federation,
Leningradsky av., h. 49, 125167 Moscow, Russia
nikita-and-nov@mail.ru

Abstract. The article discusses the efficiency of convolutional neural networks in solving the problem of face recognition of tennis players. The characteristics of training and accuracy on a test set for networks of various architectures are compared. Application of weight drop out methods and data augmentation to eliminate the effect of retraining is also considered. Finally, the transfer learning from other known networks is used. It is shown how, for initial data, it is possible to increase recognition accuracy by 25% compared to a typical convolutional neural network.

Keywords: Recognition · Convolutional neural networks · Regularization · Drop out · Augmentation · Learning transfer · Cats vs Dogs · Federer vs Nadal

1 Introduction

Nowdays one of the typical applications of computer vision is face recognition [1–4]. The application of face recognition can be found in various access control systems, for example, to mobile devices [5], to the territory of the organization [6], etc. In addition, a new application for face recognition is the accounting system in stores without sellers. In such a system the user is authenticated at the entrance and special program is tracking his actions in the store, counting taken goods, etc. It is clear that this is already a more complex task, also associated with the recognition of goods. Although private algorithms, such as SURF [7], are often used for face recognition, the general task in recognition is to extract features characteristic of an object. In this case, a more general algorithms based on convolutional neural networks are of interest [8–11]. Moreover, the operation of such networks is similar to the correlation algorithm, which is often used in mathematical modeling in image processing [12–15].

However, the main advantage of convolutional neural networks is their performance, i.e. a trained neural network in recognition is able to produce a response much faster compared to the correlation-extreme algorithm. Another feature is also high accuracy

© Springer Nature Switzerland AG 2021
A. Del Bimbo et al. (Eds.): ICPR 2020 Workshops, LNCS 12665, pp. 5–14, 2021.
https://doi.org/10.1007/978-3-030-68821-9_1

or probability of correct recognition, which greatly depends on the training data and the methods used in the training. So in this work, recognition of Roger Federer and Rafael Nadal is investigated. Using the example of two tennis players face recognition, it is shown how, using general methods of increasing recognition accuracy, it is possible to achieve a significant increase in accuracy compared to conventional convolutional neural networks. Moreover, the proposed regularization methods, such as drop out of weights, data augmentation, and learning transfer, are applicable to recognition tasks using other data.

2   Data Preparation and Problem Statement

By randomly searching for images in the public domain, a database of images was collected, which represented either Roger Federer or Rafael Nadal. Then, using Haar cascades [16], images containing only the faces of the players were obtained from the original images. Figure 1 shows examples of some images. At the same time, tennis players alternate in order from left to right and from top to bottom, i.e. Federer is represented in the upper left corner and Nadal is in the lower right corner.

Fig. 1. Examples of images for face recognition

However, manual data collection did not allow a sufficiently large representative sample to be created. The initial data set consisted of 440 images in the training set (226 images of Roger Federer and 214 images of Rafael Nadal) and 54 images in the test sample (28 images of Roger Federer and 26 images of Rafael Nadal). Despite the fact that for such a small data set there were general trends in increasing the recognition accuracy based on the training methods described in the next section, sometimes the accuracy decreased. This is probably due, firstly, to the small volume of the training sample, from which it is more difficult to extract common features, especially for faces, and secondly, due to the small volume of the test sample, on which even one error costs almost 2%.

But much more interesting results were obtained when working with a database augmented in various ways. Moreover, Fig. 2 shows examples of transformations applied to source face images. Augmentation models are described in more detail in [17]. The extra images was also obtained by using doubly stochastic model [18, 19]. It should be noted that a lot of augmentations were used with small probabilities of their appearance ($p = 0.15 - 0.2$), which in most cases provided completely different received augmented images due to a combination of different random factors, and their difference from the initial ones. Thus, the database further investigated consisted of 10557 images in the training set (5406 images of Roger Federer and 5151 images of Rafael Nadal) and 2244 images of the test sample (1173 images of Roger Federer and 1071 images of Rafael Nadal). This volume can be considered sufficient for further experiments with learning.

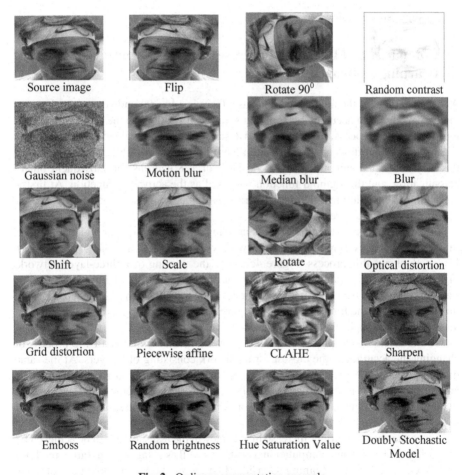

Fig. 2. Ordinary augmentation example

Images presented on Fig. 2 confirm the assumption about the possibility of a strong volume increase in the original database using the presented augmentation methods. Figure 3 shows the example of combining different augmentation methods.

Fig. 3. Combinations of different augmentation

So augmentation allows to get much more images in dataset.

3 Comparison of Learning Processes and the Accuracy of Different Learning Approaches

As noted earlier for the augmented database, there is a logical and general tendency to increase recognition accuracy by applying some modifications to the network architecture and learning process. All the networks described below are trained using the method of simple gradient descent (SGD), with a learning rate $lr = 0.001$. For all networks, the fully connected smoothing layer consisted of 128 neurons for subsequent binary classification, and the sigmoid function was used as the activation function. At first, a conventional convolutional neural network was trained, consisting of one layer of 32 neurons to extract features.

Figure 4a shows the training process in terms of loss accuracy for a given network. Similar dependences were obtained for a two-layer network (32 neurons + 64 neurons). Figure 4b shows this process. Figure 4c shows the training of a three-layer network. Figure 4d shows the training process for four-layer network, and Fig. 4e shows the training process for five-layer network. The learning took place over 25 epochs. The red line characterizes the training sample, the green is for test sample. Top graphs present loss and bottom graphs present accuracy.

The analysis of the presented graphs shows that the similarity of the process of changing the accuracy is the closest for a network consisting of 5 layers. At the same time, it provides the greatest accuracy compared to networks consisting of a smaller number of layers. It is also obvious that all the networks considered lead to significant retraining. At the same time, an increase in accuracy in the training sample occurs almost in the first 5 epochs.

Given the above, a further increase in accuracy in the test sample can be achieved by increasing the layers (and computational costs), as well as using regularization methods to weaken the effect of retraining. Consider first the method of dropping out of some network neurons. Let us establish the probability of a drop out during a training epoch as $p_{do1} = 0.2$ for convolutional layers and $p_{do2} = 0.5$ for a fully connected layer.

Figure 5a shows the training processes with weight dropping out (0.5). Then it is also possible to use the augmentation methods for increasing training sample examples

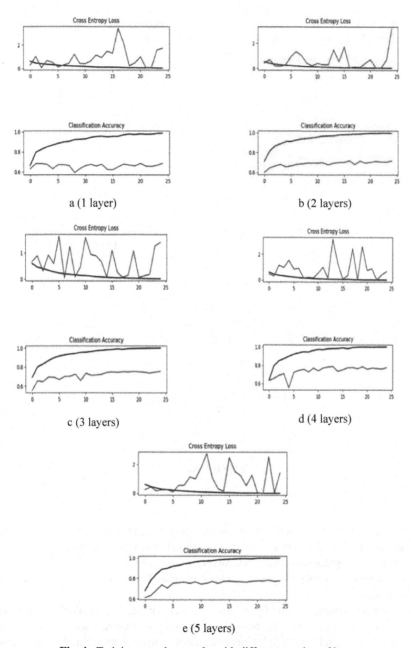

Fig. 4. Training neural networks with different number of layers

in the training batch. Since the great number of augmentation was already implement in source data set this time the augmentation methods will only use shift and rotation by 90°. Figure 5b shows the process of learning a network with augmentations. Figure 5c shows the learning process with a combination of dropping weights out (0.5) and augmentation. Research was being done for a five-layer convolution network.

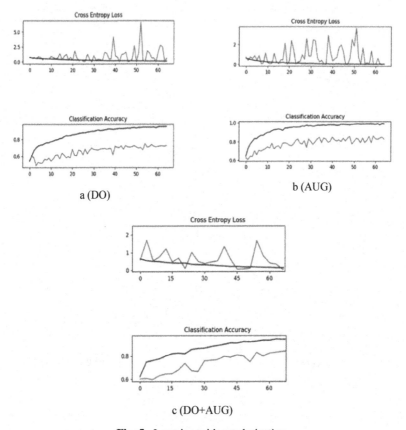

a (DO)

b (AUG)

c (DO+AUG)

Fig. 5. Learning with regularization

From the presented curves it is seen that the use of weight drop out and data augmentation allowed to slow down the speed of the network retraining. Moreover, it provided an increase in recognition accuracy. However, it should be noted that for the study of regularizations, the number of epochs has been increased to 65 due to a slowdown in the retraining rate.

However, a maximum result of just over 80% is not enough to consider the developed network effective. Therefore, the transfer of training was chosen as the last step in transforming the model. The VGG16 network model with weights trained for ImageNet dataset was used as feature extraction layers. The fully connected layer also consisted of 128 neurons, and training took place only for this layer, which significantly reduced the time spent on training. Moreover, subject to the need for training only in a fully connected layer, the number of learning epochs was reduced to 10. Figure 6a shows the learning process of such a network without regularization. Figure 6b shows the learning process with the use of dropping out of weights (0.5). Figure 6c shows the learning process with data augmentation. Figure 6d shows the learning process when a combination of weight dropping out (0.5) and image augmentation was used.

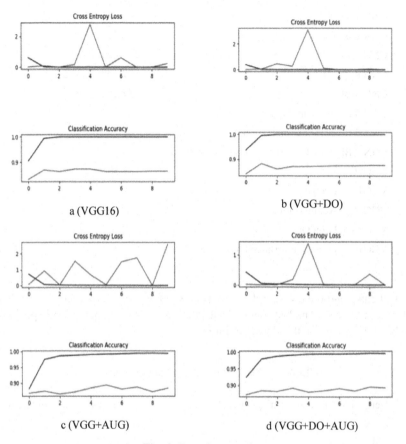

a (VGG16)

b (VGG+DO)

c (VGG+AUG)

d (VGG+DO+AUG)

Fig. 6. Learning transfer

From the graphs presented, it can be seen that network training starts immediately from sufficiently high values and quickly reaches maximum accuracy for the training sample. At the same time, augmentations and its combinations with weight dropping out lead to increased accuracy in the test sample.

Table 1 presents all the obtained accuracy on the test sample for the described models of neural networks and learning processes for Roger Federer and Rafael Nadal identification. The last row indicates the case when augmentation is performed at the batch level (on the fly) during training.

An analysis of the data presented shows that neural networks can be improved by several methods. Moreover, it is not enough to simply transfer the already trained network to obtain the maximum result. Augmentation and weight drop out also works better. Table 2 presents the similar results for training on the Kaggle [20] data set "Dogs vs Cats". The training sample consists of 16 000 images (8 000 images of dogs and 8000

Table 1. Face recognition accuracy of Federer and Nadal

№	Network model and learning methods	Accuracy on test sample, %
1	CNN 1 Block	68.627
2	CNN 2 Block	71.791
3	CNN 3 Block	75.490
4	CNN 4 Block	77.496
5	CNN 5 Block	77.852
6	CNN 5 Block + drop out	73.727
7	CNN 5 Block + Augmentation	82.709
8	CNN 5 Block + Drop out + Augmentation	83.645
9	VGG16	86.586
10	VGG16 + Drop out	87.522
11	VGG16 + Augmentation	88.102
12	VGG16 + Drop Out + Augmentation	89.362
13	VGG16 + Drop Out + Batch level augmentation	87.543

images of cats), and the test sample consists of 8000 images (4000 images of dogs and 4000 images of cats). The last row indicates the case when augmentation is performed at the batch level (on the fly) during training.

Table 2. Dogs and cats recognition accuracy

№	Network model and learning methods	Accuracy on test sample, %
1	CNN 1 Block	71.942
2	CNN 2 Block	73.814
3	CNN 3 Block	76.910
4	CNN 4 Block	80.879
5	CNN 5 Block	80.954
6	CNN 5 Block + Drop out	84.523
7	CNN 5 Block + Augmentation	87.64
8	CNN 5 Block + Drop out + Augmentation	89.982
9	VGG16	97.654
10	VGG16 + Drop Out	97.680
11	VGG16 + Augmentation	97.803
12	VGG16 + Drop Out + Augmentation	97.878
13	VGG16 + Drop Out + Batch level augmentation	97.614

The results obtained indicate the possibility of generalizing the use of augmentation and dropping weights out when training fully-connected layers of pre-trained models to increase recognition accuracy.

Figure 7 shows the VGG-16 network architecture because this network provides the best results of recognition.

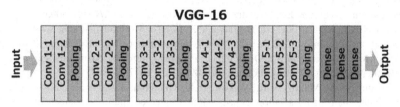

Fig. 7. VGG-16 architecture

As for other architectures, they are not the subject of interest because the recognition accuracy for such architectures much less than accuracy for VGG-16.

4 Conclusion

Thus, the article discusses the methods of regularization used in the training of neural networks, which allow to increase the recognition accuracy both in the identification of individuals and in the classification of other data. The most effective leap in the recognition accuracy comes from the use of a pre-trained model. However, increases in percentages or fractions thereof can be achieved by dropping weights out and augmentation. In particular, for the face recognition task of Federer and Nadal, accuracy was increased by 2.8% compared to the pre-trained VGG16 model and by 20.7% compared to the simplest convolutional neural network. Similar results are confirmed by the study of recognition of dogs and cats.

Acknowledgement. The study was funded by RFBR, Project № 19-29-09048, RFBR and Ulyanovsk Region, Project № 19-47-730011.

References

1. Shilpi, S., Prasad, S.V.: Techniques and challenges of face recognition: a critical review. Proc. Comput. Sci. **143**, 536–543 (2018)
2. Zhang, Y., Lv, P., Lu, X.: A deep learning approach for face detection and location on highway. In: IOP Conference Series: Materials Science and Engineering, vol. 435, p. 012004 (2018). https://doi.org/10.1088/1757-899x/435/1/012004
3. Ye, L., Ying, W., Liu, H., Hao, J.: Expression-insensitive 3D face recognition by the fusion of multiple subject-specific curves. Neurocomputing **275**, 1295–1307 (2018)
4. Logan, A.J., Gordon, G.E., Loffler, G.: Contributions of individual face features to face discrimination. Vis. Res. **137**, 29–39 (2017)

5. Guillaume, D., Chao, X., Kishore, S.: Face recognition in mobile phones. Depart. Electr. Eng. Stanford Univ. (2010)
6. Guillaume, D.: Facial recognition tech secures enterprise access control. Biometric Technol. Today **2017**(10), 2–3 (2017). https://doi.org/10.1016/S0969-4765(17)30145-5
7. Geng, D., Fei, S., Anni, C.: Face recognition using SURF features. Proc. SPIE – Int. Soc. Optic. Eng. **2**, 6–12 (2009). https://doi.org/10.1117/12.832636
8. Chen, Z., Lam, O., Jacobson, A., Milford, M.: Convolutional Neural Network-based Place Recognition. Access mode: https://arxiv.org/ftp/arxiv/papers/1411/1411.1509.pdf
9. Boubacar, B.T., Kamsu-Foguem, B., Tangara, F.: Deep convolution neural network for image recognition. Ecol. Inform. **48**, 257–268 (2018). https://doi.org/10.1016/j.ecoinf.2018.10.002
10. Coşkun, M., Uçar, A., Yıldırım, O., Demir, Y.: Face recognition based on convolutional neural network. MEES (2017). https://doi.org/10.1109/MEES.2017.8248937
11. Andriyanov, N.A., Volkov, Al.K., Volkov, An.K., Gladkikh, A.A. Danilov, S.D.: Automatic x-ray image analysis for aviation security within limited computing resources. In: IOP Conference Series: Materials Science and Engineering, vol. 862, p. 052009 (2020). https://doi.org/10.1088/1757-899x/862/5/052009
12. Vasil'ev, K.K., Dement'ev, V.E., Andriyanov, N.A.: Application of mixed models for solving the problem on restoring and estimating image parameters. Pattern Recogn. Image Anal. **26**(1), 240–247 (2016). https://doi.org/10.1134/S1054661816010284
13. Andriyanov, N.A., Vasiliev, K.K., Dementiev, V.E.: Anomalies detection on spatially inhomogeneous polyzonal images. CEUR Workshop Proc. **1901**, 10–15 (2017). https://doi.org/10.18287/1613-0073-2017-1901-10-15
14. Vasiliev, K.K., Andriyanov, N.A.: Synthesis and analysis of doubly stochastic models of images. CEUR Workshop Proc. **2005**, 145–154 (2017)
15. Andriyanov, N.A., Dementiev, V.E.: Developing and studying the algorithm for segmentation of simple images using detectors based on doubly stochastic random fields. Pattern Recogn. Image Anal. **29**(1), 1–9 (2019). https://doi.org/10.1134/S105466181901005X
16. Tanwir, K.: Computer Vision - Detecting objects using Haar Cascade Classifier. Electronic resource. Access mode: https://towardsdatascience.com/computer-vision-detecting-objects-using-haar-cascade-classifier-4585472829a9 (2019)
17. Buslaev, A., Parinov, A., Khvedchenya, E., Iglovikov, V., Kalinin, A.: Albumentations: fast and flexible image augmentations. arXiv:1809.06839v1 [cs.CV] (2018)
18. Andriyanov, N.A., Dement'ev, V.E.: Application of mixed models of random fields for the segmentation of satellite images. CEUR Workshop Proc. **2210**, 219–226 (2018)
19. Andriyanov, N.A.: Software complex for representation and processing of images with complex structure. CEUR Workshop Proc. **2274**, 10–22 (2018)
20. Electronic resource. Access mode: https://www.kaggle.com/c/dogs-vs-cats

Estimate of the Neural Network Dimension Using Algebraic Topology and Lie Theory

Luciano Melodia$^{(\boxtimes)}$ ⓘ and Richard Lenz ⓘ

Chair of Computer Science 6 Friedrich-Alexander University Erlangen-Nürnberg,
91058 Erlangen, Germany
{luciano.melodia,richard.lenz}@fau.de

Abstract. In this paper we present an approach to determine the smallest possible number of neurons in a layer of a neural network in such a way that the topology of the input space can be learned sufficiently well. We introduce a general procedure based on persistent homology to investigate topological invariants of the manifold on which we suspect the data set. We specify the required dimensions precisely, assuming that there is a smooth manifold on or near which the data are located. Furthermore, we require that this space is connected and has a commutative group structure in the mathematical sense. These assumptions allow us to derive a decomposition of the underlying space whose topology is well known. We use the representatives of the k-dimensional homology groups from the persistence landscape to determine an integer dimension for this decomposition. This number is the dimension of the embedding that is capable of capturing the topology of the data manifold. We derive the theory and validate it experimentally on toy data sets.

Keywords: Embedding dimension · Parameterization · Persistent homology · Neural networks · Manifold learning

1 Motivation

Since the development of deep neural networks, their parameterization, in particular the smallest possible number of neurons in a layer, has been studied. This number is of importance for auto-encoding tasks that require extrapolation or interpolation of data, such as blind source separation or super-resolution. If this number is overestimated, unnecessary resources are consumed during training. If the number is too small, no sufficiently good estimate can be given. To solve this problem, we make the following contribution in this paper:

- We study topological invariants using statistical summaries of persistent homology on a filtered simplicial complex on the data.
- Using the theory of Lie groups, we specify the smallest possible embedding dimension so that the neural network is able to estimate a projection onto a space with the determined invariants.

© Springer Nature Switzerland AG 2021
A. Del Bimbo et al. (Eds.): ICPR 2020 Workshops, LNCS 12665, pp. 15–29, 2021.
https://doi.org/10.1007/978-3-030-68821-9_2

2   Related Work

We present relevant work on neural networks from a differential geometric perspective. Further, we summarize earlier attempts to determine depth and width of a neural network, depending on the data to be processed.

2.1   Differential Geometry in Neural Networks

The manifold of a dense neural network is in most cases Euclidean. Nevertheless, it does often approximate a manifold with different structure. Recently there have been results in the direction of other manifolds on which neural networks can operate and that fit more the nature of data, such as spherical neural networks [6]. They operate on a model of a manifold with commutative group structure. Manifolds induce a notion of distance, with symmetric properties, also referred to as metric. A Riemannian metric describes the geometric properties of a manifold. The change of coordinate systems and the learned metric tensor of a smooth manifold during back propagation was formalized [14], which shows, that we often operate on a model of a Lie group. Further, it has been shown that dense neural networks can't approximate all functions arbitrarily precisely [15]. Thereupon, neural networks with residual connections were investigated. Residual networks add the output of one layer to a deeper one, bypassing some of the layers in between. Indeed, they are universal function approximators [19]. Inspired by finite difference methods, such a residual layer was defined as a forward or backward difference operator on a partition of layers. Its state space dimension with residual connections is homeomorphic to $\mathbb{R}^{k \cdot n}$, where $n = \dim M$ and k is the number of times the difference operator was used [13]. Such a layer is able to embed into $(k \cdot n)$-dimensional Euclidean space. The smooth manifold perspective inspired us to investigate its invariants.

2.2   Embedding Dimension of Neural Networks

Cybenko showed that dense neural networks with one hidden layer can approximate any continuous function with a bounded domain with arbitrarily small error [7]. Raghu et al. [22] quantified the upper bound for ReLU and hard tanh networks considering the length of activation patterns – a string of the form $\{0, 1\}^k$ for ReLU-networks and $\{-1, 0, 1\}^k$ for hard tanh-networks – with k being the number of neurons. They gave a tight upper bound for both in the context of dense networks. The activation pattern for ReLU-networks is bounded by $\mathcal{O}(k^{mn})$ and the one for hard tanh is bounded by $\mathcal{O}((2k)^{mn})$, with $m = \dim \mathbb{R}^m$ being the dimension of input space, n being the number of hidden layers and k being their width, respectively. Bartlett et al. show an almost tight bound for VC dimensions. A neural network with W weights and L layers is bounded by $\mathcal{O}(WL \log W)$ VC dimensions but has $\Omega(WL \log W/L)$ VC dimensions [2]. Its depth was determined as a parameter depending on the moduli of continuity of the function to be approximated [19]. To these fundamental results we contribute a topological approach to the parameterization of the minimal amount of neurons within a layer, such that the topology of the data manifold can be represented. Similar to Futagami et al. [10], we investigate the manifold on which we suspect the data. Our approach is applicable to topological spaces in general and is based on persistent homology. We look for the dimension of a space with the same topological properties that the data indicates and which can be approximated. We assume a simple decomposition into a product space of real planes and 1-spheres to get the same homology groups as the persistent ones on a filtration of data. The dimension of the decomposition is a lower bound.

3   The Manifold Assumptions

The assumption that a set of points lies on a manifold is more accurate than the treatment in Euclidean space. A topological manifold M is a Hausdorff space, which means that any two points $x, y \in M$ always have open neighborhoods $U_x, U_y \subset M$, so that their intersection is empty. This behaviour may give an intuitive feeling for the position of points in space. The topology (M, ν) is a set system that describes the structure of a geometric object. Here M itself and the empty set $\emptyset$ must be contained in ν and any union of open sets from ν and any finite intersection of ν must be contained in ν. If this set system has a subset which generates the topology ν by any unions, then this subset is a basis of the topology. We demand of a manifold that the basis is at most countable. In addition, M is locally Euclidean, i.e. each point has a neighborhood which can be mapped homeomorphically to a subset of $\mathbb{R}^n$. The natural integer n is the dimension of the manifold M.

3.1   Smooth Manifolds

A smooth structure is a stronger condition than a topological manifold which can be described by a family of continuous functions. The assumption to operate on a smooth manifold when processing data is justified by the theorem of Stone-Weierstrass which proves that every continuous function can be approximated arbitrarily exactly by a specific smooth one, namely a polynomial [23]. Smooth manifolds are described by a family of local coordinate maps $\varphi : U \to \varphi(U) \subseteq \mathbb{R}^n$ which are homeomorphic to a subset of $\mathbb{R}^n$ and cover an open neighborhood (U_i, φ_i) in M. A family of charts $\mathcal{A} = (U_i, \varphi_i)_{i \in I}$ is an atlas on M [18]. $x_1, \cdots, x_n : U \to \mathbb{R}$ are local coordinates $\varphi(p) = (x_1(p), \cdots, x_n(p))$. If the atlas is maximal in terms of inclusion, then it is a differentiable structure. Each atlas for M is included in a maximal atlas. Due to the differentiable structure, the maps in $\mathcal{A}$ are also compatible with all maps of the maximal atlas. Thus, it is sufficient to use a non maximal atlas. As long as the activation functions of a neural network are of the same differentiable structure, they also are compatible with each other, and the manifold does not change as the data propagates through the layers. Only the coordinate system changes.

3.2 Lie Groups

The study of group theory deals with symmetries which can be expressed algebraically. A pair $(M, \bullet)$, consisting of a map $\bullet : M \times M \rightarrow M$ is called group if the map is associative, i.e. $x \bullet (y \bullet z) = (x \bullet y) \bullet z$ and has a neutral element so that $x \bullet e_M = x$. We also require an inverse element to each element of the group, i.e. $x \bullet x^{-1} = e_M$. A Lie group is a smooth manifold which is equipped with a group structure such that the maps $\bullet : M \times M \rightarrow M, (x, y) \mapsto xy$, and $\imath : M \rightarrow M, x \mapsto x^{-1}$ are smooth. A space is connected if it can't be divided into disjoint open neighbourhoods. A group is commutative if all elements commute under the group operation. We apply a theorem from Lie theory, which states that each connected abelian Lie group $(M, \bullet)$ of dimension $\dim M = n$ is isomorphic to a product space $\mathbb{R}^p \times \mathbb{T}^q$ with $p + q = n$, for a proof we refer to [21, p. 116]. The q-torus $\mathbb{T}^q$ is a surface of revolution. It moves a curve around an axis of rotation. These curves are given by 1-spheres, such that the q-torus is a product space $\mathbb{T}^q = S_1^1 \times \cdots \times S_q^1$. The initial decomposition of connected commutative Lie groups can be further simplified into $M \cong \mathbb{R}^p \times S_1^1 \times \cdots \times S_q^1$. Recall, that the $(n-1)$-sphere is given by $S^{n-1} := \{x \in \mathbb{R}^n \mid \|x\|_2 = 1\}$. Thus, S^1 can be embedded into $\mathbb{R}^2$. Next, we derive how many dimensions are at least needed for a suitable embedding. For each 1-sphere we count two dimensions and for each real line accordingly one. Finally, we have to estimate from data how the decomposition may look like to yield the topology of the data manifold.

4 Persistent Homology

Algebraic topology provides a computable tool to study not the topology of a set of points themselves, but an abelian group attached to them. The core interest in this discipline lies in homotopy equivalences, an equivalence class to which objects belong that are continuously deformable into one another. This is much broader than homeomorphism. For two topological spaces X and Y we seek for a function $h : X \times I \rightarrow Y$, which gives the identity at time $h_0(X) = X$ and for $h_1(X) = Y$ a mapping into another topological space. If this mapping is continuous with respect to its arguments, it is called homotopy. Consider two functions $f, g : I \rightarrow X$ so that $f(1) = g(0)$. Then there is a composition of product paths $f \cdot g$, which pass first through f and then through g and which is defined as $f \cdot g(s) = f(2s)$ for $0 \leq s \leq 1/2$ and $g(2s - 1)$, for $1/2 \leq s \leq 1$. We first run f at double speed up to $1/2$ and from $1/2$ to 1 we run the function g at double speed. In addition, suppose that a family of functions $f : I \rightarrow X$ is given which have the same start and end point $f(0) = f(1) = x_0 \in X$. They intuitively form a loop. The set of all homotopy classes $[f]$ of loops $f : I \rightarrow X$ at base point x_0 is noted as $\pi_1(X, x_0)$ and is called first homotopy group or fundamental group. The group operation is the product of equivalence classes $[f][g] = [f \cdot g]$. If we do not look at the interval I, but at mappings considering the unit cube I^n, we obtain the n-th homotopy group $\pi_n(X, x_0)$ by analogy. With the help of homotopy groups we study connected components of a topological space for the 0-th group, the loops for the 1-st group, the cavities for the 2-nd and so forth. Since homotopy groups are difficult to compute, we resort to an algebraic variant, the homology groups.

4.1   Simplices

In data analysis, we do not study the topological spaces themselves, but points that we assume are located on or near this space. In machine learning we mostly deal with the investigation of closed surfaces, which can always be triangulated, i.e. completely covered with simplices. For a proof with excellent illustrations we refer to [12, p. 102]. The concept of a triangle is too specific for our purpose, thus we'll define the n-simplices as a generalization. They are the smallest convex set in Euclidean space with $(n + 1)$-points $v_0, v_1, \cdots, v_n$, having no solutions for any system of linear equations in n-variables. Thus, we say they lie in general position with respect to $\mathbb{R}^n$, because they do not lie on any hyperplane with dimension less than n [12, p. 103]. We define the n-simplex as follows:

$$\sigma = [v_0, ..., v_n] = \left\{ v_i = \sum_{j=0}^{n} \lambda_j v_j \;\middle|\; \sum_{j=0}^{n} \lambda_j = 1 \text{ and } \lambda_j \geq 0 \text{ for all } j \right\}. \quad (1)$$

Removing a vertex from σ results in a $(n - 1)$-simplex called face of σ. A 0-simplex is a point, a 1-simplex is a path between two 0-simplices, a 2-simplex is a surface enclosed by three 1-simplices and so on. Therefore, they follow the intuition and generalize triangles to polyhedra, including points by definition.

4.2   Simplicial Complexes

A finite simplicial complex K is a set of simplices, such that any face of a simplex of K is a simplex of K and the intersection of any two simplices of K is either empty or a common face of both [3, p. 11]. This defines the simplicial complex as a topological space. Illustrations for simplicial complexes can be found in Fig. 2 b). Its properties ensure that simplices are added to the complex in a way, such that they are 'glued' edge to edge, point to point, and surface to surface. Thus, every n-simplex has $n + 1$ distinct vertices and no other n-simplex has the same set of vertices. This is a unique combinatorial description of vertices together with a collection of sets $\{\sigma_1, \sigma_2, \cdots, \sigma_m\}$ of k-simplices, which are $k + 1$ element subsets of K [12, p. 107]. This set system can be realized geometrically with an injective map into Euclidean space or any other metric space.

We would like to explain in brief, using a plain example, how we can create a simplicial complex from a set of points. For this purpose, we will not use the Delaunay complex, which will be utilised in the subsequent experiments, but will base our remarks on the Vietoris-Rips complex, which fulfils the explanatory purposes. Let $X = \{x_0, x_1, \cdots, x_n\}$ be a set of points in general position sampled from $\mathbb{R}^{n+1}$. Then the Vietoris-Rips complex contains all points $\{x_0, x_1, \cdots, x_k\} \in \text{Rips}^\epsilon(X)$ for which $||x_i - x_j|| \leq \epsilon$. The simplicial complexes for increasing ϵ are connected by inclusion and form a filtration, see Sect. 4.4.

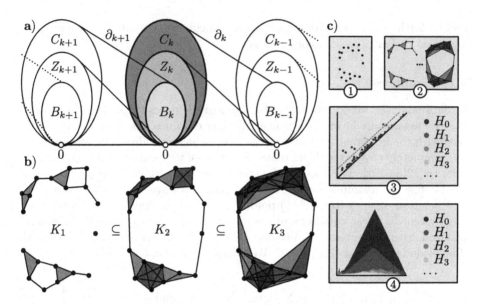

Fig. 1. a) Illustration of the chain complex following Zomorodian et al. [25]. **b)** Sublevel sets of a simplicial complex connected by inclusion. **c)** Pipeline for persistent homology: **c)**1. Loading point sets. **c)**2. Computation of a filtration. **c)**3. Computation of persistent homology with confidence band. **c)**4. Computation of persistence landscapes.

4.3   Associated Abelian Groups

Algebraically, the simplices can be realized as a system of linear combinations as $\sum_i \lambda_i \sigma_i$ following Eq. 1. Together with addition as an operation, they form a group structure called k-th chain group $(C_k, +)$ for the corresponding dimension of the k-simplices used. The group is commutative or abelian. The used coefficients λ_i induce an orientation, intuitively a direction of the edges, by negative and positive signs, such that $\sigma = -\tau$, iff $\sigma \sim \tau$ and σ and τ have different orientations. The objects of the chain group are called k-chains, for $\sigma \in C_k$. The groups are connected by a homomorphism, a mapping which respects the algebraic structure, the boundary operator:

$$\partial_k : C_k \to C_{k-1}, \tag{2}$$

$$\partial_k \sigma \mapsto \sum_i (-1)^i [v_0, v_1, \cdots, \hat{v}_i, \cdots, v_n]. \tag{3}$$

The i-th face is omitted, alternatingly. Using the boundary operator we yield the following sequence of abelian groups, which is a chain complex (cf. Fig. 1 a):

$$0 \xrightarrow{\partial_{k+1}} C_k \xrightarrow{\partial_k} C_{k-1} \xrightarrow{\partial_{k-1}} \cdots \xrightarrow{\partial_2} C_1 \xrightarrow{\partial_1} C_0 \xrightarrow{\partial_0} 0. \tag{4}$$

For the calculation of homology groups we have to choose some algebraic structure from which to obtain the coefficients λ_i. Since, according to the Universal Coefficient Theorem, all homology groups are completely determined by homology groups with integral coefficients, the best choice would be the ring of integers $(\mathbb{Z}, +, \cdot)$, see the proof in [11]. A certain field, however, has more favourable arithmetic properties, so by convention $\mathbb{Z}_p := \mathbb{Z}/(p\mathbb{Z})$ is chosen for a prime p. For our experiments we have therefore chosen $\mathbb{Z}_2$. The k-th chain groups contain two different abelian subgroups that behave normal to it. First, the so-called cycle groups $(Z_k, +)$, which are defined as

$$Z_k := \ker \partial_k = \{\sigma \in C_k \mid \partial_k \sigma = \emptyset\}. \tag{5}$$

This follows the intuition of all elements that form a loop, i.e. have the same start and end point. Some of these loops have the peculiarity of being a boundary of a subcomplex. These elements form the boundary group $(B_k, +)$, defined by

$$B_k := \operatorname{im} \partial_{k+1} = \{\sigma \in C_k \mid \exists \tau \in C_{k+1} : \sigma = \partial_{k+1}\tau\}. \tag{6}$$

The connection of these groups is illustrated in Fig. 1 a). Now we define the homology groups as quotients of groups. Homology – analogous to homotopy theory – gives information about connected components, loops and higher dimensional holes in the simplicial complex:

$$H_k(K) := \frac{\ker \partial_k C_k(K)}{\operatorname{im} \partial_{k+1} C_{k+1}(K)} = \frac{Z_k(K)}{B_k(K)}. \tag{7}$$

4.4 Homological Persistence

Examining the homology groups of a set of points gives little information about the structure of a data set. Instead, we are interested in a parameterization of the simplicial complex as geometric realization in which the homology groups appear and disappear again. For this purpose we consider all possible subcomplexes that form a filtration, a nested sequence of subcomplexes, over the point set X. We denote $K^\epsilon := K^\epsilon(X)$. Depending on how we vary the parameter ϵ_i of the chosen simplicial complex, the following sequence is generated, connected by inclusion:

$$\emptyset = K^{\epsilon_0} \subset K^{\epsilon_1} \subset \cdots \subset K^{\epsilon_{n+1}} = K, \tag{8}$$

$$K^{\epsilon_{i+1}} = K^{\epsilon_i} \cup \sigma^{\epsilon_{i+1}}, \quad \text{for } i \in \{0, 1, \cdots, n-1\}. \tag{9}$$

An example of a filtration is given in Fig. 1 b). The filtration has in our case a discrete realization with a heuristically fixed $\epsilon = \epsilon_{i+1} - \epsilon_i = \min(||x - y||_2)$ for all $x, y \in X$. Through filtration we are able to investigate the homology groups during each step of the parameterization. We record when elements from a homology group appear and when they disappear again. Intuitively speaking, we can see when k-dimensional holes appear and disappear in the filtration. We call this process birth and death of topological features. Recording the Betti numbers of the k-th homology group along the filtration, we obtain the k-dimensional persistence diagram (see Fig. 1 c)3). The Betti numbers β_k are defined by rank H_k.

We write $H_k^{\epsilon_i}$ as k-th homology group on the simplicial complex K with parameterization ϵ_i. Then $H_k^{\epsilon_i} \to H_k^{\epsilon_{i+1}}$ induces a sequence of homomorphisms on the filtration, for a proof we refer to [9]:

$$0 = H_k^{\epsilon_0} \to H_k^{\epsilon_1} \to \cdots \to H_k^{\epsilon_n} \to H_k^{\epsilon_{n+1}} = 0. \tag{10}$$

The image of each homomorphism consists of all k-dimensional homology classes which are born in K^{ϵ_i} or appear before and die after spanning $K^{\epsilon_{i+1}}$. Tracking the Betti numbers on the filtration results into a multiplicity

$$\mu_k^{\epsilon_i,\epsilon_j} = (\beta_k^{\epsilon_i,\epsilon_{j-1}} - \beta_k^{\epsilon_i,\epsilon_j}) - (\beta_k^{\epsilon_i-1,\epsilon_{j-1}} - \beta_k^{\epsilon_i-1,\epsilon_j}), \tag{11}$$

for the k-th homology group and index pairs $(\epsilon_i, \epsilon_{j+1}) \in \overline{\mathbb{R}_+^2} := \mathbb{R}_+^2 \cup \{\infty, \infty\}$ with indices $i \leq j$. The Euclidean space is extended, as the very first connected component on the filtration remains connected. Thus, we assign to it infinite persistence, corresponding to the second coordinate ϵ_{j+1}. The first term counts elements born in $K^{\epsilon_{j-1}}$ and which vanish entering K^{ϵ_j}, while the second term counts the representatives of homology classes before K^{ϵ_j} and which vanish at K^{ϵ_j}. The k-th persistence diagram is then defined as

$$\mathrm{Ph}_k(X) := \left\{ (\epsilon_i, \epsilon_{j+1}) \in \overline{\mathbb{R}_+^2} \,\middle|\, \mu_k^{\epsilon_i,\epsilon_{j+1}} = 1, \, \forall\, i,j \in \{0,1,\cdots,n-1\} \right\}. \tag{12}$$

4.5   Persistence Landscapes

Persistence landscapes give a statistical summary of the topology of a set of points embedded in a given topological manifold [4]. Looking at the points $(\epsilon_i, \epsilon_{j+1}) \in \overline{\mathbb{R}_+^2}$ on the k-th persistence diagram $\mathrm{Ph}_k(X)$, one associates a piecewise linear function $\lambda_{\epsilon_{j+1}}^{\epsilon_i} : \mathbb{R} \to [0, \infty)$ with those points:

$$\text{If } x \notin (\epsilon_i, \epsilon_{j+1}), \ \lambda_{\epsilon_{j+1}}^{\epsilon_i}(x) = 0, \tag{13}$$

$$\text{if } x \in \left(\epsilon_i, (\epsilon_i + \epsilon_{j+1})/2\right], \ \lambda_{\epsilon_{j+1}}^{\epsilon_i}(x) = x - \epsilon_i \text{ and} \tag{14}$$

$$\text{if } x \in \left((\epsilon_i + \epsilon_{j+1})/2, \epsilon_{j+1}\right), \ \lambda_{\epsilon_{j+1}}^{\epsilon_i}(x) = \epsilon_{j+1} - x. \tag{15}$$

The summaries for the general persistence diagram are the disjoint union of the k-th persistence diagrams $\mathrm{Ph}(X) := \coprod_{i=0}^{k} \mathrm{Ph}_i(X)$. A persistence landscape $\mathrm{Pl}(X)$, contains the birth-death pairs $(\epsilon_i, \epsilon_{j+1})$, for an $i, j \in \{1, \cdots, n\}$ and is the function sequence $\Lambda_k : \mathbb{R} \to [0, \infty)$ for a $k \in \mathbb{N}$, where $\Lambda_k(x)$ denotes the k-th greatest value of $\lambda_{\epsilon_{j+1}}^{\epsilon_i}(x)$ (see Fig. 1 c) 4). Thus, $\Lambda_k(x) = 0$ if $k > n$. $\mathrm{Pl}(X)$ lies in a completely normed vector space, suited for statistical computations.

5   Neural Networks

Neural networks are a composition of affine transformations with a non-linear activation function. This transformation obtains collinearity. It also preserves parallelism and partial relationships. The projection onto the $(l+1)$-th layer of such a network can be written as

$$\mathbf{x}^{(l+1)} = f(\mathbf{W}^{(l+1)} \cdot \mathbf{x}^{(l)} + \mathbf{b}^{(l+1)}). \tag{16}$$

The composition of multiple such maps is a deep neural network. The linear map $\mathbf{x} \mapsto \mathbf{W}\mathbf{x}$ and the statistical distortion term $\mathbf{x} \mapsto \mathbf{x} + \mathbf{b}$ are determined by stochastic gradient descent. Note, that the linear transformation $\mathbf{x} \mapsto \mathbf{W} \cdot \mathbf{x}$ can be interpreted as the product of a matrix $\mathbf{W}_{ij} = \delta_{ij} \mathbf{W}_i$ with the input vector $\mathbf{x}$ using the Kronecker-δ, while $(\cdot)$ denotes element-wise multiplication. Commonly used are functions from the exponential family. As a result a neural network is a map $\varphi^{(l)} : \mathbf{x}^{(l)}(M) \to (\varphi^{(l)} \circ \mathbf{x}^{(l)})(M)$. Learning by back propagation can in this way be considered as a change of coordinate charts of a smooth manifold. For a detailed formulation of back propagation as a shift on the tangent bundle of this manifold we refer to Hauser et al. [14]. In practice, neural networks are used with a different number of neurons per layer. However, a layer can represent the manifold of the previous one. Manifolds can always be immersed and submersed as long as the rank of the Jacobian of the respective map does not change. Thus, the dimension of the data manifold is equal to the width of the smallest possible layer of a neural network that is able to represent it [14]. In other words, the layer with minimal width which does not loose topological structure.

6   Counting Betti Numbers

According to our main assumption, we seek a decomposition of the data manifold into a product of the real plane and tori. We refer to this Lie group as $G \cong \mathbb{T}^q \times \mathbb{R}^p$. Thus, there is also an isomorphism of the homology groups of G with those of $\mathbb{R}^p \times \mathbb{T}^q$, so that

$$H_k(G) \cong H_k(S_1^1 \times \cdots \times S_q^1 \times \mathbb{R}^p), \tag{17}$$

with $p + q = \dim G$. We demand from a neural network that these homology groups can all be approximated, i.e. that all topological structure of the input space can be represented sufficiently well, by means of its topological invariants. Using Künneth's theorem, we know that the k-th singular homology group of a topological product space is isomorphic to the direct sum of the tensor product of k-th homology groups from its factors, for a proof we refer to [12, p. 268]:

$$H_k(X \times Y) \cong \bigoplus_{i+j=k} H_i(X) \otimes H_j(Y). \tag{18}$$

This applies to all fields, since modules over a field are always free. If we apply the theorem to the decomposition, we get for the space we are looking for

$$H_k(S_1^1 \times \cdots \times S_q^1 \times \mathbb{R}^p) \cong \tag{19}$$

$$\bigoplus_{i_1+\cdots+i_r=k} H_{i_1}(S_1^1) \otimes \cdots \otimes H_{i_{r-1}}(S_q^1) \otimes H_{i_r}(\mathbb{R}^p). \tag{20}$$

One might wonder to what extent homology groups of a simplicial complex can be used to estimate homology groups of smooth manifolds. Through construction of continuous maps from a simplex into a topological space, so-called singular simplices, the singular homology groups $H_k(X)$ are obtained. We refer to Hatcher [12, p. 102] for a proof. This allows to assign abelian groups to any trianguliable topological space. If one constructs smooth mappings instead of continuous ones, one gets smooth singular homology groups $H_k^\infty(X)$, consider [18, pp. 473] for a proof. Finally a chain complex can be formed on a smooth manifold over the p-forms on X and from this the so-called de Rham cohomology can be defined $H_{\mathrm{dR}}^k(X)$, for a proof we refer to [18, pp. 440]. In summary, we have homology theories for simplicial complexes, topological spaces and for smooth manifolds. Simplicial homology is determined by a simplicial complex, which is merely a rough approximation of the triangulation of the underlying topological space. However, we can draw conclusions about a possible smooth manifold, since the discussed homology groups all have isomorphisms to each other known as the de Rham Theorem, see [12, 18, pp. 106, pp. 467]. By the isomorphism of simplicial, singular, smooth singular and de Rham cohomology, our approach is legitimized. We count the representatives of homology classes in the persistence landscapes to derive the dimension of the sought manifold. We get for S^1:

$$H_0(S^1) \cong H_1(S^1) \cong \mathbb{Z}, \tag{21}$$

$$H_i(S^1) \cong 0, \text{ for all } i \geq 2. \tag{22}$$

Note, in Eq. 19 terms remain only for indices $i_j \in \{0, 1\}$. Thus, we get

$$H_0(\mathbb{R}^p) \cong \mathbb{Z}, \tag{23}$$

$$H_k(\mathbb{T}^q) \cong H_k(S_1^1 \times \cdots \times S_q^1) \cong \mathbb{Z}^{\binom{q}{k}}, \tag{24}$$

where p indicates the number of connected components. The persistence landscape functions $\lambda_{\epsilon_{j+1}}^{\epsilon_i}(x)$ are in general not differentiable for an x yielding a maximum value. For a smooth approximation $\tilde{\lambda}$, of each specific λ, the number of local maxima for a homology group in the persistence landscape is the cardinality of the set of points $(\epsilon_i, \epsilon_{j+1})$ with derivatives $d\tilde{\lambda}_{\epsilon_{j+1}}^{\epsilon_i}(x) = 0$ and $d^2\tilde{\lambda}_{\epsilon_{j+1}}^{\epsilon_i}(x) < 0$, for an example of these maximum values within a persistence landscape (see Fig. 2 b), c)). Also, it is the solution for the binomial coefficient:

$$\binom{q}{k} = \frac{q}{1} \cdot \frac{q-1}{2} \cdots \frac{q-(k-1)}{k} = \prod_{i=1}^{k} \frac{q+1-i}{i}. \tag{25}$$

We count in $\mathrm{Pl}(X)$ the elements of the 0-th homology group. The amount of elements from higher homology groups correspond to q (Eq. 24) and are computed using brute force for an (approximate) integer solution (see Table 1).

7   Experimental Setting

We train an auto-encoder using as input heavily noisy images and map them to their noiseless original. We perturb each input vector $\mathbf{x}^{(0)}$ with Gaussian noise

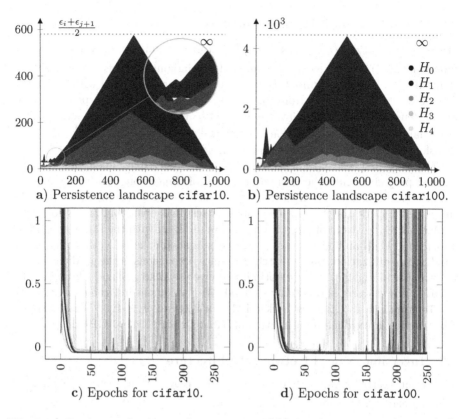

Fig. 2. a) Persistence landscape for `cifar10` and b) for the `cifar100` dataset [17]. Persistence landscapes are computed up to a resolution of 10^3. c) and d) show the MSE loss function on the validation dataset using a $7 : 3$ split on training and test data.

$\epsilon \sim \mathcal{N}(0, \sigma^2 \mathbf{I})$, such that the input is weighted $0.5 \cdot \mathbf{x}^{(0)} + 0.5 \cdot \epsilon$. The layer size is increased for each experiment by 2, i.e. $2, 4, 6, \cdots, 784$. 392 neural networks have been trained around a hundred times each. Each line of Fig. 2 c), d) represents one neural architecture as averaged loss function.

7.1 Persistence Landscapes Hyperparameters

We use the Delaunay complex for the filtration, according to Melodia et al. [20]. The maximum α-square is set to e^{12}. The maximal expansion dimension of the simplicial complex is set to 10. The maximal edge length is set to one. The persistent landscapes are smoothened by a Gaussian filter $G(x) = 1/\sqrt{2\pi\sigma^2} \cdot e^{-x^2/2\sigma^2}$ with $\sigma = 2$ for visualization purposes. We implement the persistence diagrams and persistence landscapes using the GUDHI v.3.0.0 library – Geometry Understanding in Higher Dimensions – with its Python-bindings [24]. Persistent homology is computed on Intel Core i7 9700K processors.

7.2   Neural Network Hyperparameters

We use $L(\mathbf{x}^{(0)}, \mathbf{y}) = 1/n \sum_{i=1}^{n} (\mathbf{x}_i^{(0)} - \mathbf{y}_i)^2$ as loss function. The sigmoid activation function $\sigma(\mathbf{x}^{(l)}) = 1/(1 + e^{-\mathbf{x}^{(l)}})$ is applied throughout the network to yield the structure of a smooth manifold. Dense neural networks are used with bias term. The data sets are flattened from $(32, 32, 3)$ into (3072) for the purpose of fitting into a dense layer. The first layer is applied to the flattened data set, which is also adapted by back propagation, i.e. $\varphi^{(0)}(x^{(0)}) = \sigma(\sum_{i=1}^{n-k} \mathbf{W}_{ji}^{(1)} \mathbf{x}_i^{(0)} + \mathbf{b}_i^{(1)})$. It transfers the data to the desired embedding dimension.

The very first and last dense layers are not invertible. Their purpose is a learned projection into the desired subspace of dimension $(n - k)$ for some k and afterwards projecting into the original space in an encoding fashion. The subsequent layers are then implemented as residual invertible layers following Dinh et al. [8].[1] A total of 5 hidden layers are used, all with the same embedding dimension. The batch size is set to 128, which should help to better recognize good parameterization. Higher batch size causes explosions of the gradient, which we visualize in Fig. 2 c), d). For optimization we use ADAM [16] and a learning rate of 10^{-4}. The data set is randomly shuffled. We implement in Python v.3.7. We use Tensorflow v.2.2.0 as backend [1] with Keras v.2.4.0 [5] as wrapper. The training is conducted on multiple NVIDIA Quadro P4000 GPUs.

7.3   Invertible Neural Network Architecture

The input vector of any other layer l is given by $\varphi^{(l)} := \mathbf{x}^{(l)} = (\mathbf{u}_1^{(l)}, \mathbf{u}_2^{(l)})$, splitting the l-th layer into $\mathbf{u}_1^{(l)}$ and $\mathbf{u}_2^{(l)}$ [8]:

$$\mathbf{u}_1^{(l)} = \left(\mathbf{v}_1^{(l)} - \psi_2 \left(\mathbf{u}_2^{(l)} \right) \right) \cdot \exp \left(-\xi_2 \left(\mathbf{u}_2^{(l)} \right) \right), \tag{26}$$

$$\mathbf{u}_2^{(l)} = \left(\mathbf{v}_2^{(l)} - \psi_1 \left(\mathbf{v}_1^{(l)} \right) \right) \cdot \exp \left(-\xi_1 \left(\mathbf{v}_1^{(l)} \right) \right). \tag{27}$$

We apply batch normalization after the activation function. The partition of the vector is still an open research question [8]. We divide the flattened vector precisely into two halves, since the samples are square matrices:

$$\mathbf{x}^{(l)} = (\mathbf{u}_1^{(l)}, 0, \cdots, 0) + (0, \cdots, 0, \mathbf{u}_2^{(l)}). \tag{28}$$

The weights are initialized uniformly distributed and the bias term is with zeros. Leaky ReLU is used as activation function. Batch normalization can be written for a batch k at the l-th layer as

$$\mathrm{BN}(\mathbf{x}_{(k)}^{(l)})_{\gamma_{(k)}^{(l)}, \beta_{(k)}^{(l)}} = \frac{\gamma_{(k)}^{(l)}}{\sqrt{\mathrm{Var}[\mathbf{x}_{(k)}^{(l)}] + \epsilon_{(k)}^{(l)}}} \mathbf{x}_{(k)}^{(l)} + \left(\beta_{(k)}^{(l)} - \frac{\gamma_{(k)}^{(l)} \mathrm{E}[\mathbf{x}_{(k)}^{(l)}]}{\sqrt{\mathrm{Var}[\mathbf{x}_{(k)}^{(l)}] + \epsilon_{(k)}^{(l)}}} \right), \tag{29}$$

---

[1] Invertible architectures guarantee the same differentiable structure during learning. Due to the construction of trivially invertible neural networks the embedding dimension is doubled, see [8].

where $\gamma_{(k)}^{(l)}, \beta_{(k)}^{(l)}$ and $\epsilon_{(k)}^{(l)}$ are parameters updated during back propagation. The two input vectors $\mathbf{v}_1^{(l)}$ and $\mathbf{v}_2^{(l)}$ of the layer ensure that the output is trivially invertible. The multiplication is to be understood element-wise:

$$\mathbf{v}_1^{(l)} = \mathbf{u}_1^{(l)} \cdot \exp\left(\xi_2\left(\mathbf{u}_2^{(l)}\right) + \psi_2\left(\mathbf{u}_2^{(l)}\right)\right), \tag{30}$$

$$\mathbf{v}_2^{(l)} = \mathbf{u}_2^{(l)} \cdot \exp\left(\xi_1\left(\mathbf{v}_1^{(l)}\right) + \psi_1\left(\mathbf{v}_1^{(l)}\right)\right). \tag{31}$$

The changes of coordinate charts are Lie group actions from $GL(n, \mathbb{R})$ on the representation of the first layer. The functions ξ_1, ξ_2 and ψ_1, ψ_2 are implemented as neural subnetworks themselves and also parameterized during learning. These networks do not have to be invertible in general. Each function is a $\mathcal{C}^1$-residual network with a total of 3 dense layers [13]. Leaky ReLU has been selected for each layer such that $\text{LReLU}(\mathbf{x}_i^{(l)}) = \mathbf{x}_i^{(l)}$ if $\mathbf{x}_i^{(l)} \geq 0$ and $-5.5 \cdot \mathbf{x}_i^{(l)}$ otherwise.

7.4 Experimental Results

We want to represent all invariants of the persistence landscape. This yields the embedding dimensions $\dim U_1 = 92 \pm 44$ for cifar10 and $\dim U_2 = 97 \pm 50$ for cifar100 (see Table 1). According to our assumption, a suitable embedding in an Euclidean space of dimension $2 \cdot \dim U_1 \in [184, 272] \subset \mathbb{N}$ and $2 \cdot \dim U_2 \in [194, 294] \subset \mathbb{N}$ should be chosen. We interpret, by the similarity of the persistence landscapes (see Fig. 1) and the likewise extremely similar numbers of representatives of the persistent homology groups (see Table 1), that the larger data set does differ slightly from a topological viewpoint, i.e. is located in a similar topological space as its smaller counterpart. In Fig. 2 c) d) we colored the neural networks according to the chosen embedding, such that the lines show the training of an architecture with the following bottleneck dimensions:

$$\text{cifar10:} \quad \in [2, 148], \bullet \in [150, 198], \bullet \in [200, 270] \text{ and } \bullet \in [272, 784], \tag{32}$$

$$\text{cifar100:} \quad \in [2, 148], \bullet \in [150, 198], \bullet \in [200, 292] \text{ and } \bullet \in [294, 784]. \tag{33}$$

All models below our dimensional tresholds $\dim U_i$ – colored $\bullet$ – show drastic explosions of the gradient (see Fig. 2 c), d)). The models above the treshold remain stable. A neural network still shows an explosive gradient in Fig. 2 d). It is close to our threshold, identified as 270 and 292 dimensional embedding for cifar10 and cifar100, respectively. The closer we come to the treshold, the sparser are the fluctuations of loss.

Table 1. Counts of the representatives per homology group from $\mathrm{Pl}(X)$.

Data	Features										
	Homology groups					$\approx$ Embedding dimension					
	H_0	H_1	H_2	H_3	H_4	p	$q\|H_1$	$q\|H_2$	$q\|H_3$	$q\|H_4$	$\dim U$
cifar10	12	16	40	59	50	12	16	$9_{\pm 4}$	$8_{\pm 3}$	$7_{\pm 15}$	$92_{\pm 44}$
cifar100	13	18	34	46	48	13	18	$9_{\pm 2}$	$8_{\pm 10}$	$7_{\pm 13}$	$97_{\pm 50}$

8   Conclusion

Based on the theory of Lie groups and persistent homology, a method for neural networks has been developed to parameterize them using the assumption that the data lies on or near by some connected commutative Lie group. This forms an approximate solution for a special case of learning problems. Applying Künneth's theorem, the homology groups of the topological factor spaces could be connected with the ones of their product space. Using persistence landscapes, the elements originating from some homology groups on the filtration were estimated. With numerical experiments we predicted near ideal embedding dimensions and could confirm that a neural embedding above the treshold delivers a loss function on the validation data set with small fluctuations and best reconstruction results (see Fig. 2). We pose following open research questions:

- The neural layers do not have the explicit structure of an abelian Lie group. How can spherical CNNs [6] be used to always represent a product space $\mathbb{R}^p \times \mathbb{T}^q$ from layer to layer in order to operate on the proposed Lie group?
- This approach can be applied to any kind of manifold, as far as its minimal representation is known. Using decompositions, one may generalize this result. What decomposition allows to neglect the connectedness? For example, the persistence diagrams could be used to identify connected components. These in return could be represented as independent connected manifolds.
- Questions come up considering approximations using points from a knotted manifold. How would our method perform in such a case? Can this theory be extended to estimates of embedding dimensions for knotted manifolds?

Acknowledgements. We thank Christian Holtzhausen, David Haller and Noah Becker for proofreading and anonymous reviewers for their constructive criticism and corrections. This work was partially supported by Siemens Energy AG.

Code and Data. The implementation, the data sets and experimental results can be found at: https://github.com/karhunenloeve/NTOPL.

References

1. Abadi, M., et al.: TensorFlow: large-scale machine learning on heterogeneous systems (2015). https://www.tensorflow.org/, software available from tensorflow.org

2. Bartlett, P., Harvey, N., Liaw, C., Mehrabian, A.: Nearly-tight VC-dimension and pseudodimension bounds for piecewise linear neural networks. J. Mach. Learn. Res. **20**, 1–17 (2019)
3. Boissonnat, J.D., Chazal, F., Yvinec, M.: Geometric and Topological Inference. Cambridge University Press, Cambridge (2018)
4. Bubenik, P.: Statistical topological data analysis using persistence landscapes. J. Mach. Learn. Res. **16**, 77–102 (2015)
5. Chollet, F., et al.: Keras (2015). https://keras.io
6. Cohen, T.S., Geiger, M., Köhler, J., Welling, M.: Spherical cnns. In: 6th International Conference on Learning Representations (2018)
7. Cybenko, G.: Approximation by superpositions of a sigmoidal function. Math. Control, Signals Syst. **5**(4), 455 (1992)
8. Dinh, L., Sohl-Dickstein, J., Bengio, S.: Density estimation using real NVP. In: 5th International Conference on Learning Representations (2017)
9. Edelsbrunner, H., Harer, J.: Persistent homology - a survey. Contemp. Math. **453**, 257–282 (2008)
10. Futagami, R., Yamada, N., Shibuya, T.: Inferring underlying manifold of data by the use of persistent homology analysis. In: 7th International Workshop on Computational Topology in Image Context, pp. 40–53 (2019)
11. Gruenberg, K.W.: The universal coefficient theorem in the cohomology of groups. J. London Math. Soc. **1**(1), 239–241 (1968)
12. Deo, S.: Algebraic Topology. TRM, vol. 27. Springer, Singapore (2018). https://doi.org/10.1007/978-981-10-8734-9
13. Hauser, M., Gunn, S., Saab Jr., S., Ray, A.: State-space representations of deep neural networks. Neural Comput. **31**(3), 538–554 (2019)
14. Hauser, M., Ray, A.: Principles of riemannian geometry in neural networks. Adv. Neural Inf. Process. Syst. **30**, 2807–2816 (2017)
15. Johnson, J.: Deep, skinny neural networks are not universal approximators. In: 7th International Conference on Learning Representations (2019)
16. Kingma, D., Ba, J.: Adam: a method for stochastic optimization. In: 3rd International Conference on Learning Representations (2015)
17. Krizhevsky, A.: Learning multiple layers of features from tiny images (2009)
18. Lee, J.: Smooth manifolds. Introduction to Smooth Manifolds. Springer, New York (2013)
19. Lin, H., Jegelka, S.: Resnet with one-neuron hidden layers is a universal approximator. Adv. Neural Inf. Process. Syst. **31**, 6172–6181 (2018)
20. Melodia, L., Lenz, R.: Persistent homology as stopping-criterion for voronoi interpolation. In: Lukić, T., Barneva, R.P., Brimkov, V.E., Čomić, L., Sladoje, N. (eds.) IWCIA 2020. LNCS, vol. 12148, pp. 29–44. Springer, Cham (2020). https://doi.org/10.1007/978-3-030-51002-2_3
21. Onischtschik, A.L., Winberg, E.B., Minachin, V.: Lie Groups and Lie Algebras I. Springer (1993)
22. Raghu, M., Poole, B., Kleinberg, J., Ganguli, S., Dickstein, J.S.: On the expressive power of deep neural networks. In: 34th International Conference on Machine Learning, pp. 2847–2854 (2017)
23. Stone, M.H.: The generalized weierstrass approximation theorem. Math. Mag. **21**(5), 237–254 (1948)
24. The GUDHI Project: GUDHI user and reference manual (2020). https://gudhi.inria.fr/doc/3.1.1/
25. Zomorodian, A., Carlsson, G.: Computing persistent homology. Discrete Comput. Geom. **33**(2), 249–274 (2005)

On the Depth of Gestalt Hierarchies in Common Imagery

Eckart Michaelsen[✉]

Fraunhofer-IOSB, Gutleuthausstr. 1, 76275 Ettlingen, Germany
eckart.michaelsen@iosb.fraunhofer.de

Abstract. Apart from machine learning and knowledge engineering, there is a third way of challenging machine vision – the Gestalt law school. In an interdisciplinary effort between psychology and cybernetics, compositionality in perception has been studied for at least a century along these lines. Hierarchical compositions of parts and aggregates are possible in this approach. This is particularly required for high-quality high-resolution imagery becoming more and more common, because tiny details may be important as well as large-scale interdependency over several thousand pixels distance. The contribution at hand studies the depth of Gestalt-hierarchies in a typical image genre – the group picture – exemplarily, and outlines technical means for their automatic extraction. The practical part applies bottom-up hierarchical Gestalt grouping as well as top-down search focusing, listing as well success as failure. In doing so, the paper discusses exemplarily the depth and nature of such compositions in imagery relevant to human beings.

Keywords: Hierarchical pattern composition · Gestalt-laws · Perceptual grouping

1 Introduction

Perceptual grouping is long known to contribute significantly to human vision. We may assume that it has developed evolutionary, and conclude that it probably provides advantages for the survival and reproduction of seeing animals. In the field of machine vision, several important approaches based on perceptual grouping are known as well (see below in Sect. 1.1). However, interest in this kind of work has been buried a bit under the huge pile of recent machine vision publications on what is called "artificial intelligence" today, i.e. machine learning models in the fashion of deep and convolutional neural networks (CNNs).

Standard perceptual grouping composes an aggregate out of its parts utilizing Gestalt laws, such as good continuation, parallelism, repetition, reflection symmetry, etc. That is only a very shallow hierarchy. However, everyone in the field has been aware that such aggregates may often be parts of larger scaled Gestalten, and that the parts themselves may be further decomposed into yet smaller scaled parts. An obvious way of modelling such hierarchies are various picture grammars discussed in the literature (see Sect. 1.2 below). Most of such endeavors are from long time ago, and they were apparently not

© Springer Nature Switzerland AG 2021
A. Del Bimbo et al. (Eds.): ICPR 2020 Workshops, LNCS 12665, pp. 30–43, 2021.
https://doi.org/10.1007/978-3-030-68821-9_3

Fig. 1. A typical group picture, 20 million Pixel (image source: IAPR-TC7)

very successful. However, there is a recent approach, which is less syntactic and more algebraic: The Gestalt algebra [1] (a brief self-contained introduction on it is given in Sect. 2 below).

The paper at hand uses the tools and structure given by this approach on one example case in particular – the group picture seen in Fig. 1. We regard such imagery as typical, important and frequent. The goal is to get some experience on the expectable depth of Gestalt hierarchies in such imagery. Some readers may doubt that working with only one image can create sufficient empirical evidence. However, bear in mind that such images have a very high resolution. In fact, as first step the paper analyses the behavior of the perceptual grouping on the eleven people in the front row separately. This set of parts of the image already gives a quite divers probe of how persons may appear in such data. Followed by that is an analysis of the behavior on the previous results combined. That adds a twelves case on a different scale, as well as different nature. For those who still doubt, the same grouping method was also applied to a public symmetry recognition benchmark, so that a quantitative result can be reported.

This introduction would not be complete without an important distinction: Gestalt composition must not be confused with knowledge-based composition. The latter requires machine-interpretable knowledge specific to the field and task at hand – such as medical imagery of a particular body-part and sensing mode, or remotely sensed imagery of urban terrain and a particular sensor type. Instead, standard perceptual grouping works universally on any kind of imagery and claims to help for any task. A further distinction is also helpful: Neither knowledge-based vision nor perceptual grouping have anything to do with machine learning. Both are more "pattern recognition" in its common sense, not in today's technical sense.

The contribution of this paper is claimed as follows: Compositionality is studied along the lines of Gestalt-laws only, deliberately avoiding any machine-learning, machine-knowledge application, or other semantics. Such separation allows assessments on the prospective contribution of Gestalt laws to the performance of seeing machines. Such contribution is assumed to be independent of the contribution of machine learning as well as knowledge utilization. The depth of decomposition hierarchies is analyzed exemplarily with high-resolution imagery of common use at hand, namely a typical group picture.

1.1 Related Work on Perceptual Grouping

The scientific issue of perceptual grouping has opened up with physicists such as Helmholtz and Mach taking interest in the process of perception. A little later Psychology was scientifically mature enough to challenge seeing in particular, and publish their results and theories – the most well-known example being *Wertheimer* [2]. A hundred years ago things where preferably published in German, so that the term Gestaltgesetze or Gestalt-laws became the technical key-term of this field, along with other technical terms such as "Prägnanz" and "gute Fortsetzung". Some of them are a bit cloudy and fuzzy.

With the advent of powerful computing machinery, some researchers, aware of the preceding psychological work, started coding the Gestalt-laws in an effort to build machines that see, like humans do. Whilst working on this they had to give the Gestalt-laws a sounder mathematical foundation, based in particular on probability calculus. Most elaborate is here the work of *A. Desolneux* et al. [3, 4], defining the "maximal meaningful aggregation" by means of the a-contrario test. She has to make some uniformity assumptions on the distribution of elements in an image before quantifing, when configurations violate such randomness. This is called the *Helmholtz* principle – things are salient if they cannot have happened by chance with reasonable probability. In detail, such estimations can be quite complicated, with *Desolneux* being the leading master in the field.

A real interdisciplinary working group has gathered around Z. *Pizlo* [5], comprising expertise about empirical psychological experiments with human subjects, statistical modelling, coding vision algorithms, as well as deep knowledge of the vast body of literature, which is in parts quite old, and distributed over remote fields. One main point raised by *Pizlo* is, that symmetry and Gestalt actually hold in 3D, and that they are most often destroyed by projection to 2D imagery. He argues, that humans perceive such structure immediately and readily in 3D, and directed the machine coding in his group in that direction.

1.2 Related Work on Aggregation of Parts

So-called *picture languages* were a popular topic when machine vision was in its infancy [6]. In a way, the analogy to parsing text or code was too tempting. It appeared self-evident to many that image understanding must use hierarchies of parts and compositions, where spatial relations replace the concatenations used in string grammars. However, these approaches were not particularly successful on the long run. At least, the ideas remained alive in the golden days of classical artificial intelligence, e.g. with semantic nets or production rule systems for aerial image understanding, such as *SIGMA* [7].

A quite natural way of describing part-aggregate relations in images is by use of graphs. Following a segmentation step, an adjacency graph of the segments is easily constructed. Graph grammars constructing hierarchies by replacing sub-graphs with other graphs are however very cumbersome in coding as well as in run-complexity. Therefore, usually no hierarchies are proposed today. Instead, contemporary work focusses on learning relations in *scene graphs* [8].

This is a part of the science of meaning – often referred to as semantics. Each node of the graph has a label assigned to it, or a set of possible meanings with associated probabilities. Then a relaxation is required, because the relations – i.e., links of the graph – alter the probabilities, basically along Bayes law.

In this living branch of structural pattern recognition, like in almost any other branch, machine-learning approaches such as CNNs prevail today. The old artificial intelligence engineering approaches – such as *semantic nets* [9] – are not much studied anymore. That used to be logical approaches.

The approach of hierarchical perceptual grouping presented in the paper at hand can be regarded as a third path between machine learning and knowledge engineering. The resulting view on the issue is closer to the common sense meaning of 'pattern recognition' then to its contemporary meaning as technical term: A pattern is regarded as a law of mutual spatial relations forming an aggregate in an algebraic manner. Most important is repetition of similar parts in patterns.

2 Gestalt Algebra

Here a brief introduction is given. More details can be obtained from [1]. It turned out useful to work on a continuous domain instead of the pixel-matrix, which is often the basis of machine vision. Main feature of a Gestalt is its *location* in the 2D-plane (no raster, no margins). Gestalten also have a *scale* feature, which is a positive and continuous feature and an *orientation* in the additive angular group. The Gestalt laws are actually coded in functions giving an *assessment* of saliency for each Gestalt. This continuous feature between zero and one is compulsory and most important as well for the theory as for practical applicability.

2.1 Operations

Six operations aggregate larger scale composite-Gestalten from smaller scaled part-Gestalten. Figure 2 shows these operations, where the smaller circles indicate location and scale of the parts p or q, and the larger circles for the aggregates s. The orientation is indicated by lines from the center to the periphery of the circle. Table 1 lists the six operations on the Gestalt-domain. It gives the algebraic notation as well as the corresponding Gestalt-law. Such laws are a combination of relations which the parts must fulfill mutually in order to be grouped as Gestalt.

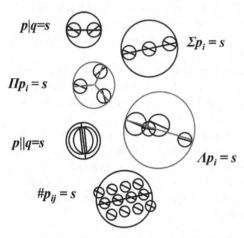

$p|q=s$

$\Sigma p_i = s$

$\Pi p_i = s$

$p\|q=s$

$\Lambda p_i = s$

$\#p_{ij} = s$

Fig. 2. The six operations of Gestalt-algebra

If these mutual relations are fulfilled the resulting aggregate s will gain a good assessment close to one. If they are less well given the resulting assessment will be mediocre. If they are completely violated the worst assessment zero will result. The assessment functions are continuous and differentiable. And their fusion is multiplicative (corresponding to logic conjunction). Figure 2 displays the corresponding preferred geometric configurations for each of these operations.

For the details we refer to [1]. However, it is important for the topic of this paper that all operations contain the law of proximity (some weaker some stronger). The assessment of an aggregate Gestalt can only be close to one if the parts are not too far away from each other – as well as not too close. For any Gestalt with two parts having the same location assessment zero results mandatory.

Moreover, proximity depends linearly on scale. If all the parts of an aggregate are of double scale, and all the mutual distances between them double as well, the same proximity assessment will result.

Table 1 also lists in the last column the commutativity laws on the part indices. This is trivial for the operations | and ||. But it is more sophisticated for the larger aggregations. Here an index re-enumeration according to the specific groups does not change the aggregate. Such algebraic properties are very important in practice.

Table 1. The six Gestalt-operations, their respective laws, and algebraic properties

Notation	Gestalt-laws	Commutativity
$p|q = s$	Mirror reflection, proximity	Pairwise commutative
$\Sigma p_1...p_n$	Frieze in good continuation (rows), proximity	Enumeration reversion
$\Pi p_1...p_n = s$	Rotational symmetry, proximity	Finite rotational index group
$p\|q = s$	Parallelism, strong proximity	Pairwise commutative
$\Lambda\{p_1...p_n\} = s$	Good linear continuation, minor gaps, weak proximity along the line	Complete index permutation group
$\#p_{ij} = s$	Lattice, proximity	Reversing enumeration in i and j, flipping i and j

2.2 Search

The domain and operations outlined above may as well be used for rendering. However, the main intended use is in machine perception. In this task the given input-datum is usually a digital image, i.e. a matrix of digitized intensity values or color vectors. Prerequisite is therefore an extraction method with such image as input and a set of primitive Gestalten as output that fit into the domain as outlined above. There are several possibilities, but a kind-of default method is *super-pixel segmentation* in its fast *SLIC* implementation [10]. Figure 3 upper line shows an example image (cropped from Fig. 1), and the super-pixel primitives obtained from it. Each is displayed as an ellipse at the corresponding location (1st moment of its pixel-set), and orientation, scale, and eccentricity, respectively (from 2nd moments). The assessment of each super-pixel primitive Gestalt is given by its dissimilarity in color with respect to its neighbors. They are displayed as leftmost frame, good instances being dark, and meaningless ones white, so that they disappear on white background. Let the set of these primitives be called L_0.

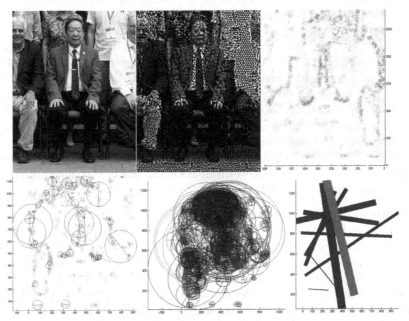

Fig. 3. Section from the center of the group picture, primitives obtained from it and bottom-up grouping results. Upper line: 1 million Pixel section, super-pixels displayed as ellipses with corresponding color, and primitives displayed according to Gestalt format (gray-tone coding assessment); lower line: Λ-Gestalten obtained from primitives, all non-primitivel-Gestalten entering the final symmetry-clustering Λ-step, and the ten dominating axis clusters found – the best assessed one in red color) (Color figure online)

Bottom-Up: The standard search method is the stratified search. This constructs the strata L_i by successive application of the operations:

$$L_{i+1} = \{s = o(p_1 \cdots p_n) | p_i \in L_i\}$$

$$o \in \{|, \Sigma, \Pi, \Lambda, \|\#\} \tag{1}$$

We already mentioned the commutativity laws for each operation. Very often, a Gestalt can be constructed in multiple ways from the same set of primitives. Obviously, definition (1) is combinatorial, and the size of these sets will be huge and exponentially growing with i. Therefore, a minimal assessment $\alpha > 0$ will be set and we add $a(s) \geq \alpha$ to definition (1). *Michaelsen & Meidow* give a theorem stating that for each such α there exists an i_{max} so that L_i is empty for all $i > i_{max}$ [1]. Therefore, under this condition search for Gestalten is at least a finite problem that holds – in the sense of theoretical cybernetics.

However, some of the intermediate strata will still be of practically intractable size. A quite drastic way of handling this is restricting the size of any stratum, e.g. to the number of primitives $N_0 = |L_0|$. Once a particular level is listed, the elements in it are sorted with respect to their assessment, and only the best N_0 are accepted for the next level, hoping that the desired Gestalten, related to something meaningful, are still contained. This resembles the well-known *constant-false-alarm-rate* approach to pattern recognition.

It is advisable to be still greedier: E.g., the best Gestalt that can be aggregated from a set of parts may suppress all sub-optimal other possibilities. Accordingly, in Fig. 3 the very well assessed vertical Λ-Gestalten along the tie of the person suppress all other Σ-Gestalten or|-Gestalten that may be aggregated from the same primitives. These primitives are removed also from the corresponding figure.

The example result displayed in Fig. 3 is rather typical. It is on the margin between success and failure. Such behavior is often encountered in "images in the wild" using *Liu's* terms [13]. Gestalt grouping behaves much better than tossing the dice. However, more precision in locating and orienting the symmetry axis, which is instantaneously perceived as very salient by human subjects, would be nice. Also, the assessing of the best axis is not far from other axes, which are not in accordance with human perception, indicating a certain lack of stability.

Top Down: Additionally, to bottom-up search, more can be done. In the golden days of artificial intelligence smart and goal driven search rationales were proposed and analyzed in detail (see, e.g. [9]). First of all, there is goal-directed focus of attention. I.e., the analysis of the image – whether automatic or manual – is undertaken with a certain purpose, and seen from that purpose a subset of relations and objects are more important, while others are too irrelevant for assigning search efforts to them. E.g., for the analysis of group pictures the purpose might be to count the people, or to search for a particular person, or to determine the message of the picture in terms of social rank-orders etc. Each such purpose would require different methods in different sequences from the toolbox presented here, as well as additional relations and object recognition methods from beyond Gestalt science.

And secondly, there will often be incomplete instantiations, where parts are missing that would complete more perfect aggregate Gestalten. This may result from failures of the primitive extraction method, or something may have been lost due to the greedy decisions in the bottom-up search. This can be fixed subsequently, by focusing attention to such areas and re-parametrize the search there, based on the higher-level aggregations as a kind of prior.

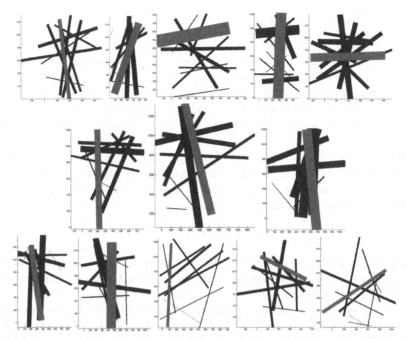

Fig. 4. Gestalt-grouping results on the 13 persons in the first row of the group picture displayed in Fig. 1 (Color figure online)

3 Application to Example Imagery

The popular image repositories for benchmarking proposed machine vision methods today contain mostly small image formats – a few hundred lines and columns for each image. This results from the fact that deep learning CNNs, which constitute the large majority of the proposals today, are limited and rigid in their input layer. A 20 million Pixel image, such as the example used here, can only be processed by scanning it, or down-scaling it. Therefore, the benchmarks rarely contain such imagery.

Of course, there are benchmark data-sets with high resolution available in the remote sensing community. Gestalt algebra approaches to such data have been investigated lately by *Michaelsen et al.* [11, 12]. However, such imagery is not the topic here.

While the common low-resolution imagery of the machine vison community can only contain shallow hierarchies, we are living in a world, where every smartphone has cameras with several million Pixels resolution. A decent professional camera has around forty million, with twelve-bit dynamic resolution per pixel color. I.e., high-resolution imagery is quite common in our everyday life.

We reckon the most important pictorial stimulus for human beings is other human beings – if not self. Therefore, for this work we base the empirical part on high-resolution pictures containing humans. From few or even a single such image more can be learned than from dozens of low-quality images. Yet, for comparison with other approaches we also tested the method at hand on the symmetry recognition benchmarks known in the community [13, 14].

3.1 Bottom-Up Analysis of Sections of the Image

A socially very important genre of photography is the group picture, for which an example is given in Fig. 1. For such imagery, smooth ambient lighting is preferred, and focus is set on the faces, which may well be distributed a bit in depth. Accordingly, a certain depth of focus is required, so that tiny details appear on the clothes of the persons as well. Thus, a fairly deep hierarchy of Gestalten is established on such imagery. Figure 3 lower row shows exemplarily the Gestalten aggregated around the central person in the front row:

As long as the primitives are obtained by super-pixel segmentation, operation Λ is important on the first level in order to compensate for over-segmentation at elongated structures. Parallelism captured by operation‖ as second level gives strong results usually on long structures yielding Gestalten of the algebraic form

$$(\Lambda p_1 \ldots p_n) \| (\Lambda q_1 \ldots q_m), \tag{2}$$

where usually $n \neq m$. Here we find Gestalten of this algebraic structure on the tie with high assessment – see Fig. 3 lower row right frame. Salient things like that appear in many image genres frequently.

Rows – in symmetry recognition literature often referred to as friezes – appear here for instance at the hands, where the fingers are repeated in fairly good continuation and similarity. The example person presents his reflection symmetry almost perfectly to the camera, so that the reflection of friezes yields Gestalten of the form

$$(\Sigma p_1 \ldots p_4) \mid (\Sigma q_1 \ldots q_4), \tag{3}$$

which is a balanced term (in the terminology of [1]), so that correspondence between the fingers can be established in a top down manner, and adjustments can be enforced accordingly. What restrains the assessment of this Gestalt from being perfect is the distance between the friezes, which is definitely larger then in perfect proximity.

Of course, there is reflection symmetry in the face of the example person as well. E.g. both eye regions manifest as super-pixel primitives, so that a well assessed level-one $p|q$ Gestalt is established precisely on the center of the face. It contributes together with the Gestalten (2) and (3) to the overall reflection symmetry cluster. However, on its own, it is not very dominant within the set of other such level-one aggregates found all over that part of the image, and in fact all over the whole image. Most important for reflection symmetry recognition is cluster formation from multiple reflection symmetry cues to the same axis. Written as Gestalt-term the form

$$\overset{n}{\underset{i=1}{\Lambda}} (p|q)_i \tag{4}$$

results, where the parts can be taken from different strata. All such non-primitive Gestalten going into the cluster-process for the example section are displayed in the middle frame of the lower line of Fig. 3. The ten most salient clusters of reflection symmetries constitute the local result, and are given in the rightmost frame.

For most reflection symmetry recognition methods, axis-clustering of this kind constitutes the core functionality [13], often implemented in Hough-like accumulators.

Using the prolongation operation Λ, problems with raster parameter choice, and spatial range limiting are avoided. Moreover, more flexibility is provided concerning the inclusion of objects of different sizes and structure, such as reflection pairs of primitives, pairs of prolonged primitives, reflection pairs of friezes, reflection pairs of reflection pairs, etc. Since the operation ‖ yields symmetric aggregates as well – with the axis running in the middle, and a re-assessing punishing skewed‖ -Gestalten – these can also contribute to the reflection symmetry cluster.

Figure 4 shows such result for each of 13 cutouts cropped from the group picture, each in its own coordinate system. The red axes indicate the best one in each cutout, while the other nine are given in blue, with the thickness indicating assessment respectively. The central instance of the middle row corresponds to the central person, and thus to Fig. 3. It is scaled a little larger for saliency.

3.2 Performance Assessment of the Application to a Set of Image Sections

The results given above provide evidence on the perceptive performance of the bottom-up Gestalt search alone. Properly coded and with reasonable default setting of parameters, it will perform as good as this, i.e. much better than tossing the dice. There may be room for smaller improvements. However, we do not expect pure bottom-up Gestalt search to become substantially stronger.

As of 2013, this would have been a competitive performance in reflection symmetry recognition – compare [13]. Up to eight best axis results out of thirteen are roughly vertical and correspond to the persons' main symmetry in location and size. The details depend on the person marking the ground-truth and the tolerances on angular and positional deviations. The CVPR competition [13] had 10° on the orientation and 10% on the locations of the endpoints of the axis. We might well lose one or two of the true-positives with such setting.

As of 2017 [14], such performance might not be state-of-the-art anymore. However, the leading performance in 2017 obtained by *Funk&Liu* with a deep-learning-CNN, incorporates elements of object recognition, that cannot be separated from the pure symmetry-recognizing parts of the machine. We tested the method used in this paper for the thirteen sections also on the 100 images used for the 2017 competition [14]. 31 instances reproduced the ground-truth correctly as best axis-cluster. For another 12 instances we found an axis-cluster corresponding to the ground-truth not as best, but among the first few in rank order. In our view, this is still a reasonable performance for a non-learning machine with no object recognition capabilities. The leading reflection symmetry recognition CNN of 2017 outperforms our method on the 100 real-world images. However, it later performed remarkably low on simple synthetic data that contain a lot of symmetry but no objects [15].

3.3 Larger-Scale Gestalten on Global Image Level

Up to this stratum grouping was only on a local level with the largest Gestalten covering roughly one Mega-pixel. However, the 130 reflection symmetry clusters can be further aggregated in a bottom-up manner constructing larger frieze-Gestalten using operation Σ. Many of such objects fill seven thousand Pixels in width, which is the larger part of the image. Three of these Gestalten are depicted in Fig. 5.

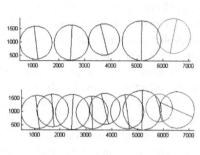

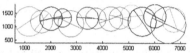

Fig. 5. Global frieze Gestalten from all 130 reflection cluster axes displayed in Fig. 4.: upper – best assessed; lower – most parts; center – compromise between assessment and part number

The upmost one is the best assessed found on this level (assessment 0.9606). Comparing it to what would be the ground-truth, the 1st part corresponds to the best (and correct) axis of the 1st person. The 2nd part corresponds to best axis on the 4th person, which is a little displaced to the left. The 3rd part is on the central person discussed in detail above. The 4th incorporates and affirms the good result on the 10th person. The last part of the frieze picks the best it can find on the rightmost man in the first row, correcting the bad bottom-up detection result there.

Default parameters for proximity are used here, preferring a distance similar to the scale of the objects. Thus, the best row only picks every third person. Friezes with more components of this scale only fit into the 7k-pixel, when they are less well assessed. Still, such objects exist, and one of the longest is displayed at the bottom of Fig. 5. It is made of 14 parts, overestimating the number of people in the first row. However, that is probably accidental. The aggregate has a very low assessment of 0.5656, and must be regarded as quite meaningless. Often, a good trade-of can be found balancing assessment against number of parts, i.e. complexity. This would be somehow in accordance with *Desolneux's Helmholtz*-principle [3]. E.g. if one multiplies assessment with the root of the number of parts the optimal frieze has nine parts and an assessment of 0.8618. It is given in the center of Fig. 5. This one agrees with the best one on four of the five correct instances (namely 1st 4th 7th and 10th). For the rightmost person it pics a rather oblique choice. It also incorporates clusters on the 2nd 6th 12th person. On the 2nd instance its choice fits better than the bottom-up best. On the 6th it agrees with the bottom-up result, which is substantially displaced to the left, and thus only marginally correct. On the 12th person it again corrects the wrong bottom-up result, and decides for the best possibility there.

3.4 Top-Down Constraint Enforcement

As first step of top-down analysis for such well-assessed high-level aggregates chapter 5.3 of [1] recommends enforcing the Gestalt-laws as constraints, and adjusting the location, scale and orientation attributes of the parts accordingly. Figure 6 displays

Fig. 6. The frieze constraints enforced on the middle frieze of Fig. 4 (best according to Helmholtz-principle)

the result for the top-scoring five-element frieze, and the best-compromise nine-element frieze, respectively, overlaid over a brighter version of the group image.

The same chapter of [1] defines the term "balanced term" for Gestalt-algebra terms: The part-trees of the same depth of the term-tree must have the same structure, i.e., symmetry in the algebraic structure. When such property is given, correspondence or association can be constructed between very small details very far apart from each other – such as in this example the left eye of the left-most person to the right eye of the right-most person, or the index finger of one hand of one person, to the corresponding finger of other persons, etc. For the frieze displayed above such things are not possible without object-recognizing components in the processing lines. Here all parts of the frieze have similar term-trees, but they differ in many details, so that the overall frieze recognition gives not a balanced tree below that level. On a picture where all people wear the same uniform or team-outfit there may well be better chances for deeper Gestalt-term balance. The deeper the balance is, the more constraints can be exploited, and the more can be gained.

With further adjustment to the parameters, the results can be improved. In particular, the proximity law and parallelism can be better tuned to fit this particular image, or a set of representative group images. This may well be done manually or automatically using machine learning.

Gap-handling in friezes is not implemented as yet. Note, friezes such as the ones presented in Fig. 5, come in harmonic hierarchies – the two friezes presented in Fig. 6 being an octave apart, and in phase on three instances. This gives prospects for further development of the method.

4 Discussion and Conclusion

Common sense holds that the images, we encounter in our world, are compositions of parts in meaningful arrangements. The paper at hand analyzes how deep such hierarchies are, and of what structure. In the example a large frieze is found of structure

$$\sum_{k=1}^{m} \left(\mathop{\Lambda}_{i=1}^{n_k} \left(p_{ki} | q_{ki}, \left[\sum_j p_{kij} | \sum_j q_{kij} \right], [p_{ki1} | q_{ki1}] | [p_{ki2} | q_{ki2}] \right) \right), \tag{5}$$

which has hierarchical depth four.

Deliberately, we avoided semantic decomposition, since this is the topic of other working groups, such as [8]. Instead, the rules of our compositions and aggregations are taken from the old and successful branch of psychology known as Gestalt-laws. It turns out that the moderate recognition performance of bottom-up perceptual grouping on standard-sized imagery can be significantly improved by top-down focus of attention setting and constraint enforcement on larger scale imagery.

We expect that the cooperation between such perceptual grouping on one side, and pattern recognition based on machine-learning methods on the other side, or also machine-knowledge-application as a third mode, will be superior to any of these three modes alone. They are mutually very different. E.g., perceptual grouping should still be working if completely new items are encountered, that neither resemble anything in the training sets, nor fit to any knowledge rules. On the other hand, well trained CNNs outperform any such methods, when applied to data fitting the training base. E.g., in this example a state-of-the-art face or person detector will outperform any Gestalt-law method.

This paper reports on experiments with very limited imagery. Further evidence is required from other genres and application fields. The algebraic approach to hierarchical perceptual grouping is not mature yet. The top-down search mechanisms, any-time deep search, and gap-handling require further investigation. Further theoretical, i.e. probabilistic, backing of the detailed choice of the Gestalt-laws is required, e.g. building on the *Desolneux* theory [3, 4].

References

1. Michaelsen, E., Meidow, J.: Hierarchical Perceptual Grouping for Object Recognition. Springer, Advances in Computer Vision and Pattern Recognition, Heidelberg (2019)
2. Wertheimer, M.: Untersuchungen zur Lehre der Gestalt. Psychologische Forschung **4**, 301–350 (1923)
3. Desolneux, A., Moisan, L., Morel, J.-M.: From Gestalt Theory to Image Analysis: A Probabilistic Approach. Springer, Heidelberg (2008)
4. Mumford, D., Desolneux, A.: Pattern Theory. CRC Press, A K Peters Ltd. Natick MA (2010)
5. Pizlo, Z., Li, Y., Sawada, T., Steinman, R.M.: Making a Machine that Sees Like Us. Oxford University Press, Oxford (2014)
6. Rosenfeld, A.: Picture Languages. Academic Press, New York (1979)
7. Matsuyama, T., Hwang, V.S.-S.: SIGMA, A Knowledge-based Aerial Image Understanding System. Springer, Heidelberg (1990)

8. Chen, V.S., Varma, P., Krishna, R., Bernstein, M,. Re, C., Fei-Fei, L.: Scene graph prediction with limited labels. ICCV 2019. arXiv:1904.11622. (2019)

9. Niemann, H.: Pattern Analysis and Understanding. Springer, Heidelberg (1990)

10. Achanta, R., Shaji, A., Smith, K., Lucchi, A., Fua, P., Susstrunk, S.: SLIC superpixels compared to state-of-the-art superpixel methods. IEEE-PAMI **34**(11), 2274–2281 (2012)

11. Michaelsen, E., Münch, D., Arens, M.: Searching remotely sensed images for meaningful nested Gestalten. XXIII ISPRS Congress 2016, ISPRS, 2016 (ISPRS Archives XLI-B3), 899–903 (2016)

12. Michaelsen, E., Meidow, J.: Design of orientation assessment functions for Gestalt-grouping utilizing labeled sample-data. PIA 2019 + MRSS 2019, ISPRS, 2019 (ISPRS Archives XLII-2/W16), 169–173 (2019)

13. Liu, J., et al.: Symmetry detection from real-world images competition 2013: summary and results. In: CVPR 2013, Workshops, Portland (2013)

14. Funk C., et al.: 2017 ICCV challenge: detecting symmetry in the wild. In: ICCV 2017, Workshops, Venice (2017)

15. Michaelsen, E., Vujasinovic, S.: Estimating efforts and success of symmetry-seeing machines by use of synthetic data. Symmetry, **11**(2), 227 (2019)

Image Recognition Algorithms Based on the Representation of Classes by Convex Hulls

Anatoly Nemirko$^{(\boxtimes)}$ (iD)

Saint Petersburg Electrotechnical University "LETI", Saint Petersburg 197376, Russia
apn-bs@yandex.ru

Abstract. Various approaches to the construction of pattern recognition algorithms based on the representation of classes as convex hulls in a multidimensional feature space are considered. This trend is well suited for biometrics problems with a large number of classes and small volumes of learning samples by class, for example, for problems of recognizing people by faces or fingerprints. In addition to simple algorithms for a point hitting a convex hull, algorithms of the nearest convex hull with different approaches to assessing the proximity of a test point to the convex hull of classes are investigated. Comparative experimental results are given and the advantages and disadvantages of the proposed approach are formulated.

Keywords: Intelligent systems · Computational geometry · Pattern recognition · Nearest convex hull classification · Linear programming · Automatic medical diagnostics

1 Introduction

Algorithms of k-nearest neighbors (kNN) [1] due to their simplicity and efficiency are successfully used in many multiclass problems of pattern recognition and image analysis. The kNN rule is that it assigns a test object to the most common class among its k nearest neighbors. Despite the great success achieved in many applied problems, its application is limited by the well-known drawbacks: the limitation of the dimension of the feature space and the number of objects in the training set. For kNN, the problems of the influence of noise and small training sets remain.

Another well-known method in machine learning is the support vector machines (SVM) [2]. Designed for binary classification, it is widely used in all kinds of pattern recognition problems. SVM is highly generalizable and handles high-dimensional data easily. However, it does not directly solve multiclass problems.

In this paper, we consider the nearest convex hull (NCH) classifier, which is conceptually related to both kNN and SVM. NCH is an intuitive geometric classification method that assigns a test point to the class whose convex hull is closest to it. The useful properties of NCH are:

© Springer Nature Switzerland AG 2021
A. Del Bimbo et al. (Eds.): ICPR 2020 Workshops, LNCS 12665, pp. 44–50, 2021.
https://doi.org/10.1007/978-3-030-68821-9_4

1. NCH classifies multi-class problems easily in a straightforward way.
2. NCH is well suited for biometrics problems with a large number of classes and small volumes of learning samples by class: problems of recognizing people by faces [7] or fingerprints.
3. Since, NCH is resistant to the problems of small learning samples and noise, since the elimination of one point of an element of the convex set does not affect or only locally affects the entire convex hull.

This article is organized as follows. First, we give a definition of a convex hull, then a classifier is formulated based on the description of classes in the form of convex hulls in general, approaches to determining the proximity of a test point to the convex hull of a class are given, which are used in classification algorithms for the nearest convex hull. These approaches include: the SVM-based method used in [3], the Lightweight nearest convex hull method (LNCH), based on calculating the projection of the class onto the direction from the test point to the centroid of the class [4] and the method [6] based on the application of linear programming [5]. All of the above approaches provide only an approximate estimate of the proximity parameter. At the end of the article, a classification algorithm based on the use of linear programming is described, the results of experimental studies are given, and a conclusion is formulated, thanks and a list of references are given.

2   The Definition of a Classifier Based on the Convex Hull Representation of Classes

Let the learning set of one class have the form $X = \{x_i, \ x_i \in R^n, \ i = 1, 2, \ldots, k\}$. Then the convex hull generated by this set is defined as

$$conv\,(X) = \left\{ v : v = \sum_{i=1}^{k} a_i x_i, \quad 0 \le a_i, \quad \sum_{i=1}^{k} a_i = 1, \quad x_i \in X \right\}$$

where a_i - are scalar non-negative coefficients. For m classes, we have m sets of X_i, $i = 1, 2, \ldots, m$ and, accordingly, m convex hulls $conv(X_i)$, $i = 1, 2, \ldots, m$. The simplest classifier for an arbitrary requested point x will use the following rule.

Rule A:
If x is inside $conv(X_p)$, then it belongs to class p, otherwise it belongs to another class or its affiliation is undefined.

Leaving aside the question of how to determine the location of x "inside $conv(X_p)$", you need to decide what to do if x is inside several convex hulls at the same time (the case of their intersection) or x is not in any convex hull. In these cases, a way out can be found by introducing the concept of the distance from x to the convex hull of the i-th class $d_i(x, conv(X_i))$. Then the classification algorithm can be formulated as follows.

Rule B

- If x is inside only one convex hull $conv(X_p)$, then it belongs to class p.

- If **x** is outside the convex hulls of all classes, then it belongs to the class i, distance $d_i(\mathbf{x}, conv(X_i))$ to which is less.
- If **x** is inside several convex hulls, then its membership is undefined.

In this case, two points present difficulties. It is necessary to determine how to check the location of the test vector **x**: inside $conv(X)$ or outside it. In addition, it is necessary to remove the uncertainty of the membership of the vector **x** in the case when it enters into two or more convex hulls.

3 Determining the Distance from the Test Point to the Convex Hull

If **x** is not inside $conv(X)$, the minimum distance $d(\mathbf{x}, conv(X))$ can be determined as in [3], using the support vector machines (SVM). In the case when **x** is inside $conv(X)$, the SVM method does not give an exact solution due to the dependence of the obtained weight vector on classification errors.

In papers [4, 6], approaches to the approximate definition of $d(\mathbf{x}, conv(X))$ are proposed regardless of the location of the test point.

3.1 Lite Distance Determination Method

The paper [4] describes a lightweight method for determining the distance regardless of the location of **x** in relation to $conv(X)$. For data **x** and $conv(X)$, the method consists in analyzing the projections of nodes $conv(X)$ onto the unit vector **u**, directed from test point **x** to centroid **c** of class X, i.e. $\mathbf{u} = (\mathbf{c} - \mathbf{x}) / norm(\mathbf{c} - \mathbf{x})$. The analysis is carried out by the following algorithm.

DISTANCE algorithm

Input: $\mathbf{u}, \mathbf{x}, X_i$ {direction vector, test point, set of elements of the i-th class}

Output: F_i, $d_i(\mathbf{x}, conv(X_i))$ {intersection mark, distance to the convex hull of the i-th class}. Distance $d_i(\mathbf{x}, conv(X_i))$ is defined along the direction vector **u**.

1. For the set X_i, form the matrix $\mathbf{X}_i$

2. If $\min(\mathbf{u}^T \mathbf{X}_i) \le \mathbf{u}^T \mathbf{x} \le \max(\mathbf{u}^T \mathbf{X}_i)$

$$F_i = 1; \; d_i(\mathbf{x}, conv(X_i)) = \left| \mathbf{u}^T \mathbf{x} - \min(\mathbf{u}^T \mathbf{X}_i) \right|$$

   else if $\mathbf{u}^T \mathbf{x} \le \min(\mathbf{u}^T \mathbf{X}_i)$

$$F_i = 0; \; d_i(\mathbf{x}, conv(X_i)) = \left| \mathbf{u}^T \mathbf{x} - \min(\mathbf{u}^T \mathbf{X}_i) \right|$$

   else $F_i = 0; \; d_i(\mathbf{x}, conv(X_i)) = \left| \mathbf{u}^T \mathbf{x} - \max(\mathbf{u}^T \mathbf{X}_i) \right|$

   end

As a result of executing this algorithm for a given test point and m classes we obtain m pairs (F_i, d_i), $i = 1, 2, \ldots, m$, where F_i – is the i-th class intersection mark with $\mathbf{x}$ ($F_i = 0$, if $\mathbf{x}$ is outside $conv(X_i)$, and $F_i = 1$, if $\mathbf{x}$ is inside $conv(X_i)$), d_i - parameter of distance to $conv(X_i)$. Further, the following rule is used for classification.

Rule B

- If $\mathbf{x}$ is inside only one convex hull $conv(X)$, then it belongs to this class,
- otherwise, if it is inside several convex hulls, then it belongs to the class into which it entered most deeply, i.e. for which $d(\mathbf{x}, conv(X))$ is maximum,
- otherwise ($\mathbf{x}$ is outside the convex hulls of all classes) it belongs to the class for which $d(\mathbf{x}, conv(X))$ is minimal

3.2 A Method Based on Linear Programming

In paper [5], the optimal solution z^* of the following LP1 linear programming problem was considered. Given set $X = \{\mathbf{x}_i, \mathbf{x}_i \in R^n, i = 1, 2, \ldots, m\}$ and point $\mathbf{b} \in R^n$, and the origin must be inside $conv(X)$ ($P = conv(X)$).

LP1

$$z = \min \sum_{i=1}^{m} \lambda_i$$

Provided that

$$\sum_{i=1}^{m} \lambda_i \mathbf{x}_i = \mathbf{b},$$

$$\lambda_i \geq 0, \ i = 1, \ldots, m,$$

where $\mathbf{b}$ is an arbitrary nonzero vector.

For this problem, the following statement was formulated and proved [5].

If z^* is an optimal solution to LP1 problem for some $\mathbf{b} \neq 0$, then

1. $z^* < 1$, if and only if $\mathbf{b}$ is inside P
2. $z^* = 1$, if and only if $\mathbf{b}$ is on the boundary of P
3. $z^* > 1$, if and only if $\mathbf{b}$ is outside P

This can be illustrated with the help of Fig. 1. The above statement creates the prerequisites both for determining that the vector $\mathbf{x}$ is inside the convex hull and for estimating the proximity of a given point to the convex hull of the class based on solving a linear programming problem [6]. Theoretical considerations and experiments show that the ratio of the distance from a point to the convex hull D (along the ray from the origin to the test point $\mathbf{b}$) to the length of the vector $\mathbf{b}$ is equal to the ratio $|z^* - 1|$ to z^*. That is, it is true regardless of the location of the test point ($F = 1$ or $F = 0$)

$$\frac{D}{\|\mathbf{b}\|} = \frac{|z^* - 1|}{z^*}$$

whence follows

$$D = \|\mathbf{b}\| \cdot |z^* - 1| / z^*$$

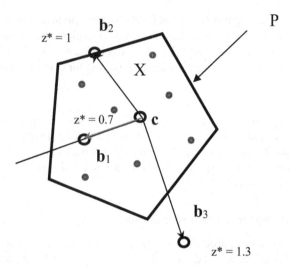

Fig. 1. The figure shows: a set of points X in a multidimensional space, P is a convex hull, **c** is the origin, b_1, b_2, b_3 are test points (vectors), z^* are the optimal values of the objective function z for these points (examples).

Since the ray used is not perpendicular to the facet it "pierces", the determined distance D is an approximation of the true distance to the convex hull. In order to increase the accuracy of such approximation, it is advisable to align the origin of coordinates with the centroid of the set X before measuring.

4   The Nearest Convex Hull Algorithm Based on the Linear Programming Method

The principle of measuring the distance from the tested (test) point **x** to the convex hull described above can be used to construct a multi-class classifier of the nearest convex hull. Before solving the LP1 problem for each class of points X_i, it is necessary to place the origin at the centroid point of this class. After finding the optimal solution to LP1 problem, we introduce a label F, which shows the location of **x**: inside or outside the given convex hull. $F = 0$ if $z^* \geq 1$ (point outside or on the boundary of the convex hull), and $F = 1$ if $z^* < 1$ (point inside the convex hull). Then for a given **x** and X_i we get a pair (F, D_i).

For a given **x** and m classes X_i, $i = 1, 2, \ldots, m$ we get m pairs (F_i, D_i), $i = 1, 2, \ldots, m$. Further, the classification is carried out according to the following decision rule.

1. If no pair contains $F = 1$, then the number of the recognized class is given by formula
   $$class(\mathbf{x}) = \underset{i=1,2,\ldots m}{\arg\min}\ d_i(\mathbf{x},\ conv(X_i)).$$
2. If only one pair contains $F = 1$, then the number of the recognized class is equal to the index of this pair.

3. If several pairs (possibly all) contain F = 1 and the indices of these pairs form a set G, then the number of the recognized class is chosen from these classes so that $class(\mathbf{x}) = \arg\max_{i \in G} d_i(\mathbf{x}, conv(X_i))$. The penetration of the test point into this class turns out to be the greatest.

As a description of classes, it is better to use not the original sets X_i, but only the vertices of their convex hulls. To do this, it is necessary to calculate the set of vertices of the convex hulls of the classes from the initial learning set. This is an easier task. This significantly reduces the running time of the linear programming algorithm. Using the vertex list at the learning stage makes it more accurate to determine the center of the convex hull, which can affect the accuracy of determining the distance D.

5 Experimental Research

The described algorithm for the classification of the nearest convex hull using linear programming was tested on a two-class problem of medical diagnostics of breast cancer [8]. A sample of 683 people was used (444 cases of healthy and 239 cases of sick). To form the control sample, the classes were divided in half. Convex hulls were constructed from the first halves of the samples. The second half of the samples were used as test samples. The average classification error on test samples was 2.15%, which is better than the same indicator when solving this problem with other classification algorithms [6].

6 Conclusion

This paper discusses approaches to pattern recognition algorithms based on the representation of classes as convex hulls in a multidimensional feature space. For classification algorithms based on the nearest convex hull, different approaches to assessing the proximity of a test point to a convex hull are considered: based on the analysis of the directed penetration depth and based on the use of linear programming. Both approaches estimate the distance from the test point to the convex hull along the ray from the class centroid to the test point. As shown by the results of experiments, the method using linear programming is characterized by high recognition quality. It is easy to implement, does not require any parameter setting, and can be easily used to solve multiclass problems, especially biometrics problems with a large number of classes and small volumes of learning samples by class.

Acknowledgments. The study is performed with partial support from the Russian Foundation for Basic Research (RFBR), grants 19-29-01009 and 18-29-02036.

References

1. Cover, T.M., Hart, P.E.: Nearest neighbor pattern classification. IEEE Trans. Inf. Theory **13**(1), 21–27 (1967)

2. Burges, C.J.C.: A tutorial on support vector machines for pattern recognition. Knowl. Discov. Data Min. **2**, 121–167 (1998)
3. Nalbantov, G., Smirnov, E.: Soft nearest convex hull classifier. In: Coelho, H. et al. (eds.) Proceeding of the 19th European Conference on Artificial Intelligence (ECAI-2010), (IOS Press, 2010), pp. 841–846 (2010). https://doi.org/10.3233/978-1-60750-606-5-841
4. Nemirko, A.P.: Lightweight nearest convex hull classifier. Pattern Recogn. Image Anal. **29**(3), 360–365 (2019). https://doi.org/10.1134/s1054661819030167
5. Dulá, J.H., Helgason, R.V.: A new procedure for identifying the frame of the convex hull of a finite collection of points in multidimensional space. Eur. J. Oper. Res. **92**(2), 352–367 (1996). https://doi.org/10.1016/0377-2217(94)00366-1
6. Nemirko, A., Dulá, J.: Machine learning algorithm based on convex hull analysis. In: 14th International Symposium «Intelligent System» , INTELS 2020, 14–16 December 2020, Moscow, Russia (in press) (2020)
7. Zhou, X., Shi, Y.: Nearest neighbor convex hull classification method for face recognition. In: Allen, G., Nabrzyski, J., Seidel, E., van Albada, G.D., Dongarra, J., Sloot, P.M.A. (eds.) ICCS 2009. LNCS, vol. 5545, pp. 570–577. Springer, Heidelberg (2009). https://doi.org/10.1007/978-3-642-01973-9_64
8. Breast Cancer Wisconsin (Original) Data Set. UCI Machine Learning Repository. https://archive.ics.uci.edu/ml/datasets/breast+cancer+wisconsin+(original)

Tire Surface Segmentation in Infrared Imaging with Convolutional Neural Networks

Rodrigo Nava[1]([✉])[iD], Duc Fehr[2], Frank Petry[2], and Thomas Tamisier[1][iD]

[1] Luxembourg Institute of Science and Technology (LIST),
Belvaux, Grand Duchy, Luxembourg
rodrigo.nava@list.lu
[2] Goodyear Innovation Center Luxembourg,
Avenue Gordon Smith, Colmar-Berg 7750, Luxembourg

Abstract. Tire modeling is a fundamental task that experts must carry out to ensure optimal tire performance in terms of stability, grip, and fuel consumption. In addition to the major forces that act on the tire, the temperature changes that occur during test handling provide meaningful information for an accurate model. However, the analysis of the temperature in a rolling tire is not a trivial task due to the interactions of the tire and the pavement. A non-invasive technique, such as thermal infrared inspection, allows analyzing temperature changes on the surface of the tire under dynamic rolling conditions. Thus, the accurate segmentation of the tire is the first objective towards a better understanding of its performance. To this aim, we propose a novel approach that combines image processing techniques with convolutional neural networks. First, the handcrafted features extracted from the infrared images are used to build a dataset; then, a convolutional neural network is trained with the labeled images. Finally, the network makes predictions of the tire surface under different test conditions. The results have shown that our proposal achieves a segmentation accuracy >0.98 and a validation error <0.05.

Keywords: Convolutional neural networks · Image segmentation · Inception · Tire tread · Thermal infrared imaging.

1 Introduction

Tire performance analysis under nearly real driving conditions is a key task that provides an insight into the way tire components should be optimized. The distribution of the temperature is particularly important, because it has a significant impact on many performances (e.g. grip or cornering stiffness) [5].

Many studies include the thermal effect as an additional variable. Ferroni et al. [9] analyzed the distribution of the temperature of the tire to estimate local grip, whereas Büttner et al. [1] proposed a model to explain the relationship between vehicle handling characteristics and the surface temperature of the tire. Recent articles suggest that, in addition to the lateral forces and moments, the accurate characterization of the tire must include temperature as a key indicator [2,12,13].

© Springer Nature Switzerland AG 2021
A. Del Bimbo et al. (Eds.): ICPR 2020 Workshops, LNCS 12665, pp. 51–62, 2021.
https://doi.org/10.1007/978-3-030-68821-9_5

High-resolution thermal infrared imaging (IR) is a powerful technique that allows capturing the temperature of the tire surface under dynamic rolling conditions. However, the temperature is not distributed uniformly. Typically, expert tire engineers identify different regions in the tire surface (e.g. shoulders, grooves, rib, and tread blocks) to perform a subsequent local analysis. This process constitutes a laborious and time-consuming task that can be automated.

Traditional segmentation algorithms for IR can be summarized into three categories: threshold-based segmentation, edge detection, and region-based methods [7]. To the extent of our knowledge, very little literature has been dedicated to tire surface segmentation, but there have been efforts to segment objects under IR. Gauci et al. [11] segmented fingers captured with a FLIR SC7200M IR camera. The method is based on an adaptive threshold followed by morphology operations. The authors used temperature as a prior feature and assumed that the temperature of the body lies between 30–36 °C, while the room temperature is close to 25 °C.

Beyond the difficulties in data acquisition and sensing the correct temperature, the segmentation algorithms grouped in the aforementioned categories are tailored to specific problems and use prior information to reduce complexity.

On the other hand, with the increasing complexity of the algorithms needed to solve relevant problems in image processing, machine learning –specifically deep learning– has emerged and improved the state-of-the-art in many fields and is changing the paradigm of the image processing community. Tire industry is not an exception, especially since it generates large volumes of data during the design and development of tires [23].

Among the articles found in the literature that use deep learning under IR modality, we highlight Jangblad [17] who presented an introduction to deep convolutional networks. The author used RetinaNet [18] as backbone to detect objects in images taken from an airborne airplane, whereas Ivašić et al. [16] conducted experiments with YOLOv3 [20] for human detection under different weather conditions. Their network was trained with COCO [19] and the infrared images were captured with a FLIR ThermaCam P10 camera. The authors' assumption is that the frequency bands of RGB images resemble thermal images.

We must point out that most of the available convolutional networks are designed for classification tasks. However, segmentation requires to preserve spatial information to produce an explicit partition of the scene. Our interest is to design and exploit a small and efficient convolutional network that does not require many training parameters to segment the tire surface in IR. Due to the lack of labeled data, we designed a heuristic method to segment the tire surface, and subsequently, by data augmentation, trained our network to predict the tire surface under extended conditions. This approach is equivalent to weak supervision techniques [6].

We included in our proposal an inception module [24] to improve the accuracy of the segmentation. Inception allows analyzing images at various scales similarly to multi-scale analysis.

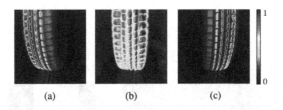

(a)　　　　　(b)　　　　　(c)

Fig. 1. Three IR images were captured on a test stand. The snapshot shows the distribution of the temperature on the tire surface during the acquisition of the IR videos. Red represents the hottest area, whereas blue represents the coolest region. (a) and (c) Moderate cornering maneuvers are performed. (b) The tire rolls straight while braking or driving torque is applied.

2 Methodology

The data were recorded in our laboratory using a test stand and the FLIR X8400sc IR camera, which captures the infrared band in the range of [1.5 – 5.5] μm. The IR videos were collected under two conditions: **Condition A** - the tire rolls straight and only braking or driving torque is applied (Fig. 1b) and **Condition B** - the tire rolls, but moderate cornering maneuvers are also performed (Fig. 1a and Fig. 1c).

2.1 Building a Dataset with a Heuristic Method

Even though the temperature of the tire changes abruptly due to the interactions with the surface of the test stand, the temperature of the background is quasi-constant during the acquisition of the videos. We consider such information and propose a heuristic method to segment the tire surface as follows:

First, column-wise mean temperature is computed over time and the maximum value per column is projected onto a line. Then, a polynomial P_c is fit to the projection, so that, P_c describes the average temperature per column throughout the IR video V as follows:

$$P_c(i) = \max\{mean\{f_j(i)|j = 1, \ldots, N\}\} \tag{1}$$

where i indicates the ith-column, j is the jth-frame, and N is the number of frames in V. Similarly, a polynomial P_r is adjusted to the average temperature in the direction of the image's rows (Fig. 2a).

Due to the laboratory air conditions, we can assume that the tire surface is always warmer than the mean temperature of the room. So, it is possible to detect such differences by finding the local minima of the polynomials P_c and P_r around the largest slopes. We define a bounding box to calculate the threshold T and refine the segmentation of the tire surface (Fig. 2b):

$$T = mean(B_{out}) + \sigma(B_{out}) \tag{2}$$

where B_{out} represents the pixels outside the bounding box. We included σ to bring the segmentation closer to the shoulders of the tire. Values larger than σ lead to mis-segmentation.

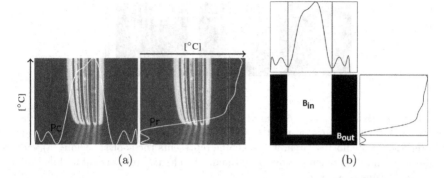

Fig. 2. (a) Two polynomials P_c (left) and P_r (right) are fit to the average temperature of the tire surface while the tire is rolling in the test stand. There is a noticeable difference between the temperature of the background and the temperature of the tire. (b) Once the polynomials P_c and P_r are fit to the average temperature of the tire throughout the IR video V, the transitions between the background and the tire surface (red lines) are calculated and the bounding box is defined. (Color figure online)

Finally, the jth binary mask $M_j \in V$ under the Condition A is defined as:

$$M_j(x,y) = \begin{cases} 1 & \text{if } f_j(x,y) \geq T \text{ and} \\ & \quad f_j(x,y) \in B_{in} \\ 0 & \text{otherwise} \end{cases} \qquad (3)$$

where B_{in} are the pixels inside the bounding box.

This methodology represents a simple yet efficient way to distinguish and segment the tire surface from the background under the straight condition.

Unfortunately, the cornering maneuvers cause the distribution of the temperature on the tire surface to change dramatically. This leads the algorithm to fail sometimes in finding the correct bounding box or the need to adjust parameters. Therefore, we are interested in the use of a convolutional neural network to address the segmentation in a more general way.

This segmentation task falls into the category of weakly-supervised segmentation, where the labeled data are incomplete [3]. Nevertheless, the conditions A and B share a few characteristics: background temperature, tire model, and temperature distribution before the cornering maneuvers.

We assume that both conditions belong to the same manifold, so we use data augmentation extensively to generate synthetic observations that are close to the Condition B (Fig. 3). The idea is that close instances will have similar predictions.

We collected 150 IR videos from 11 different tire models. Every tire was recorded under three different pressure conditions and 6 different maneuvers. The image format is 1280×1024×1 px. with a dynamic range of 16 bits. The number of images varies per IR video. We further divided the dataset into training (77,870 images), validation (25,950 images), and test (12,990 images) sets.

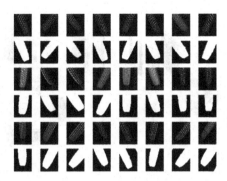

Fig. 3. Training dataset. We used data augmentation to generate new images. Geometric transformations such as rotations between 1 and 20°, horizontal and vertical translations, and scaling were applied to the labeled images. In summary, 77,870 images were used for training.

2.2   Proposed Architecture

Some of the earliest semantic segmentation models are originally based on neural networks designed for image classification. The idea was to take advantage of dense predictions to infer pixel-wise labels [10]. However, this solution generates usually very large networks and requires thousands of images for training.

We are interested in proposing a compact segmentation architecture that only requires few training parameters.

An encoder-decoder architecture with skip connections is the most suitable option. U-Net [21] and UNet++ [25] are two examples of fully convolutional networks originally proposed for medical image segmentation, but currently, they have been used successfully in other domains.

U-Net defines an encoder that captures information through four downsampling operations. Each level is composed of two convolutional layers (3×3) followed by max pooling (2×2). The decoder recovers the resolution of the image by a deconvolutional layer with stride 2 followed by two convolutional layers (3×3). Encoder and decoder are connected by concatenations (Fig. 4a).

UNet++ redefines the skip pathways and includes nested convolutions and dense blocks to reduce the semantic gap between the feature maps at every level. All the convolutional layers on the skip pathways use (3×3) kernels (Fig. 4b).

A common drawback is that the optimal depth of the network depends on the specific problem to be solved. The more depth there is, the larger the number of the training parameters required. Although a very deep network can improve the training error, it often causes the test error to increase, namely, it is prone to overfitting. It also demands more computational resources. Another issue associated with the depth of the network is that very low resolution images often mislead context information.

An additional characteristic of a network is the selection of the adequate kernel size for a convolutional layer. Szegedy et al. [24] proposed the technique called inception that is a combination of three kernel filters (1×1, 3×3, and 5×5) with their outputs concatenated to improve network performance.

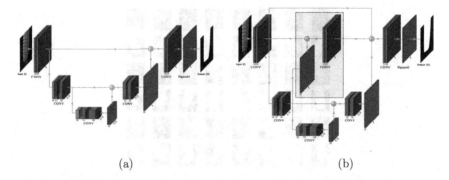

(a)   (b)

Fig. 4. Two convolutional networks used originally for medical image segmentation. (a) U-Net [21] defines an encoder-decoder scheme with 4 levels. We only illustrate two levels for simplicity here. This model is commonly named U-Net L^2. (b) UNet++ [25] uses nested pathways to generate a more accurate segmentation. We also show only two levels, UNet++ L^2. The numbers below the blocks indicate the number of filters used in our experiments. Blue box is a convolutional layer with an activation, green box is a max pooling layer, red box is deconvolution, and purple box is an activation layer. We use PlotNeuralNet package to draw the networks [15].

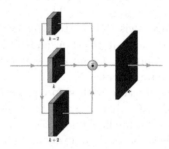

Fig. 5. We included inception [24] in our network. The output of the three kernel filters is averaged to minimize the error caused by the size of the individual receptive fields. $K = 5$ is the size of the receptive field. The max pooling block was removed to keep spatial coherence. A blue box represents a convolutional layer with an activation. This module replaces every block "CONV" in U-Net.

We propose to replace the basic "CONV" block in U-Net (see Fig. 4b) with the modified inception module shown in Fig. 5, while the depth of the networks is fixed at only two levels. The size of the receptive field is $k = 5$. In this article, we refer to our proposal as Inception U-Net L^2. We adapted Inception V1 [24] by removing the max pooling block to keep spatial coherence and the output is defined as the average response of the three kernels. In this way, Inception U-Net L^2 is rather wide than deep.

Our proposal resembles multi-scale analysis, the process of averaging the filter responses allows us to reduce mis-segmentation caused by the size of the individual receptive fields.

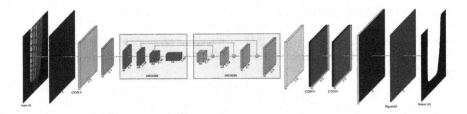

Fig. 6. LinkNet [4] defines a light pixel-wise semantic segmentation architecture. Every encoder is linked to its corresponding decoder by a skip connection to recover spatial information. The numbers below the blocks are the number of filters used in our experiments.

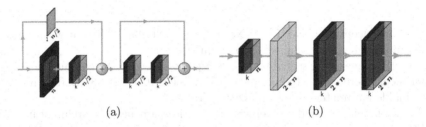

(a)   (b)

Fig. 7. LinkNet modules. The main feature is that the encoder uses residual blocks. The numbers below the blocks are the number of filters used in our experiments. (a) Encoder. (b) Decoder.

2.3   Validation and Optimization

We want to produce a single convex segmentation of the tire surface and penalize holes and disconnected segmentations. We use intersection-over-union (IoU) as the validation loss as follows: $VL\left(A,B\right) = 1 - IoU\left(A,B\right)$:

$$VL\left(A,B\right) = 1 - \frac{A \cap B + \delta}{A \cup B + \delta} \tag{4}$$

where A is the ground truth, B is the prediction, and δ is a parameter to avoid dividing by zero.

We chose AdaGrad as the optimizer [8] with a learning rate of 10^{-3} during the training stage. Early-stop is called after two epochs with decrease in performance. The accuracy used is the binary accuracy.

3   Experiments and Results

We compared our proposal, Inception U-Net L^2, against three different convolutional networks: U-Net with three levels (Fig. 4a), UNet++ with three levels (Fig. 4b), and LinkNet [4] (Fig. 6). According to [25], three levels of decomposition is the best trade-off between accuracy and inference time. Another reason

Table 1. Comparison of the number of trainable parameters required for a forward pass. Even though our proposal consists of >1M parameters, it is considered a small network compared to ResNet [14] >25M or VGG16 [22] >138M. The format of the input image for all the experiments is $320 \times 256 \times 1$. L^i denotes the number of levels used in the architecture.

CNN model	Parameters
LinkNet	11,545,093
U-Net L^3	1,488,849
UNet++ L^3	1,724,689
Inception U-Net L^2	1,146,593

to compare Inception U-Net L^2, U-Net L^3, and UNet++ L^3 is that we are interesting in studying wide against deep architectures.

The IR images were scaled to 320×256 px to speed up the computation. The experiments were conducted on an NVIDIA GTX 1080 with 8GB. The number of trainable parameters is summarized in Table 1.

LinkNet defines a light pixel-wise semantic segmentation architecture. We included it in the comparisons because we are interested in assessing the performance of residual blocks, which is the main characteristic of LinkNet (Fig. 7). However, it shows the poorest performance among the four networks. The residual blocks introduced overfitting; hence, LinkNet fails in predicting segmentation where the distribution of the temperature is not close to the Condition A.

U-Net L^3 and UNet++ L^3 sometimes predict mis-segmentations at the center of the tire surface when an extreme maneuver is presented. When the tire is cornering, most of the pressure is concentrated on one of the shoulders, this makes it extremely hot compared to the center of the tire surface. Figure 8 compares U-Net L^3, UNet++ L^3, LinkNet, and Inception U-Net L^2 in terms of validation error and prediction accuracy.

Although there are no evident differences in terms of validation error and accuracy between UNet++ L^3 and Inception U-Net L^2, our proposal is smaller and minimizes the validation error faster. Our proposal takes advantage of multiple responses from the receptive fields to improve its performance. (Table 2 shows examples of the tire surface segmentation). Since the inception module averages the responses of the kernel filters, a larger receptive field can reduce the effects of local temperature changes. In addition, the validation loss used in Eq. 4 penalizes the non-convex segmentation.

Another advantage is that our proposal achieved better performance with fewer number of epochs.

Our proposal, Inception U-Net L^2, successfully predicts the tire surface under conditions that are not considered into the training set (e.g. cornering maneuvers). From the results, we can say that it is better to use a wide architecture than a deep network to avoid introducing overfitting.

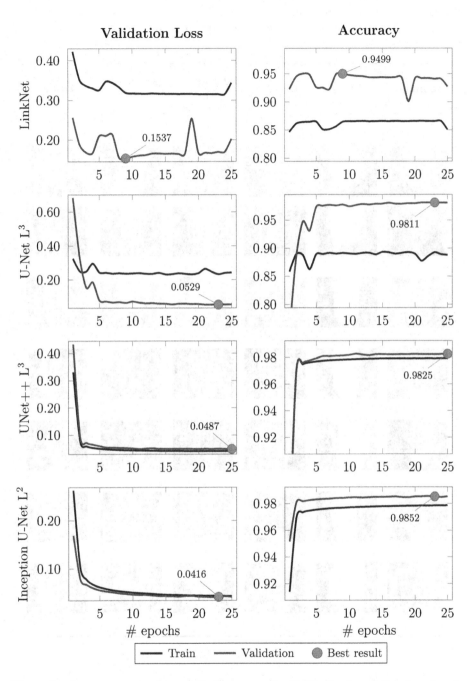

Fig. 8. Performance comparison of the four networks. Validation loss (left column) and accuracy (right column). Green circle shows the best epoch results for every network. (Color figure online)

Table 2. Tire surface segmentation comparison. The images were taken randomly from the test set and enhanced for a better visualization. Line in cyan shows the contour of the segmentation.

IR image	Mask	LinkNet	U-Net L^3	UNet++ L^3	Inception U-Net L^2

4   Conclusions

It is common in deep learning methods that the dataset is already present or is labeled manually. However, the absence of a database is often the biggest issue when using supervised methods. In this paper, we have addressed such a problem by designing a method to generate a dataset under a specific condition and exploited the concept of inception and data augmentation to explain extreme cases not considered during the training stage. Our article presents both, a novel problem and a novel solution.

The results show that a wide architecture is more suitable than a deep network for tire tread segmentation in IR imaging.

Inception U-Net L^2 is able to segment the tire surface even under different temperature distributions. The performance achieved is similar to the state-of-the-art U-Net and UNet++ segmentation networks, but it needs fewer number of epochs. Future work contemplates data drift to detect when the model degrades.

References

1. Büttner, F., Unterreiner, M., Bortolussi, P.: An effective method to identify thermodynamic tire characteristics through driving maneuvers. In: Bargende, M., Reuss, H.-C., Wiedemann, J. (eds.) 15. Internationales Stuttgarter Symposium. P, pp. 921–936. Springer, Wiesbaden (2015). https://doi.org/10.1007/978-3-658-08844-6_62

2. Calabrese, F., Bäcker, M., Gallrein, A.: Evaluation of different modeling approaches for the tire handling simulations – analysis and results. In: Pfeffer, P. (ed.) 6th International Munich Chassis Symposium 2015. P, pp. 749–773. Springer, Wiesbaden (2015). https://doi.org/10.1007/978-3-658-09711-0_48

3. Chan, L., Hosseini, M.S., Plataniotis, K.N.: A Comprehensive Analysis of Weakly-Supervised Semantic Segmentation in Different Image Domains. Int. J. Comput. Vis. 1–24 (2020). https://doi.org/10.1007/s11263-020-01373-4

4. Chaurasia, A., Culurciello, E.: Linknet: exploiting encoder representations for efficient semantic segmentation. In: IEEE Visual Communications and Image Processing (VCIP), pp. 1–4 (2017)

5. Corollaro, A.: Essentiality of temperature management while modeling and analyzing tires contact forces. Ph.D. thesis, Universitá degli studi di Napoli Federico II (2014)

6. Dehghani, M., Severyn, A., Rothe, S., Kamps, J.: Avoiding your teacher's mistakes: training neural networks with controlled weak supervision. arXiv preprint arXiv:1711.00313 (2017)

7. Duarte, A., et al.: Segmentation algorithms for thermal images. Procedia Technology **16**, 1560–1569 (2014)

8. Duchi, J., Hazan, E., Singer, Y.: Adaptive subgradient methods for online learning and stochastic optimization. J. Mach. Learn. Res. **12**, 2121–2159 (2011)

9. Farroni, F., Giordano, D., Russo, M., Timpone, F.: TRT: thermo racing tyre a physical model to predict the tyre temperature distribution. Meccanica **49**, 707–723 (2014)

10. Garcia-Garcia, A., Orts-Escolano, S., Oprea, S., Villena-Martinez, V., Martinez-Gonzalez, P., Garcia-Rodriguez, J.: A survey on deep learning techniques for image and video semantic segmentation. Appl. Soft Comput. **70**, 41–65 (2018)

11. Gauci, J., et al.: Automated region extraction from thermal images for peripheral vascular disease monitoring. J. Healthc. Eng. **2018**, 1–14 (2018)
12. Gil, G., Park, J.: Physical handling tire model incorporating temperature and inflation pressure change effect. In: SAE Technical Paper. SAE International (2018)
13. Harsh, D., Shyrokau, B.: Tire model with temperature effects for formula SAE vehicle. Appl. Sci. **9**(24), 5328 (2019)
14. He, K., Zhang, X., Ren, S., Sun, J.: Deep residual learning for image recognition. In: IEEE Conference on Computer Vision and Pattern Recognition (CVPR), pp. 770–778 (2016)
15. Iqbal, H.: Harisiqbal88/plotneuralnet v1.0.0 (2018). https://doi.org/10.5281/zenodo.2526396
16. Ivašić-Kos, M., Krišto, M., Pobar, M.: Human detection in thermal imaging using YOLO. In: Proceedings of the 2019 5th International Conference on Computer and Technology Applications. ICCTA 2019, Association for Computing Machinery, pp. 20–24 (2019)
17. Jangblad, M.: Object detection in infrared images using deep convolutional neural networks. Master's thesis, Uppsala University (2018)
18. Lin, T., Goyal, P., Girshick, R., He, K., Dollár, P.: Focal loss for dense object detection. IEEE Trans. Pattern Anal. Mach. Intell. **42**(2), 318–327 (2020)
19. Lin, T.-Y., et al.: Microsoft COCO: common objects in context. In: Fleet, D., Pajdla, T., Schiele, B., Tuytelaars, T. (eds.) ECCV 2014. LNCS, vol. 8693, pp. 740–755. Springer, Cham (2014). https://doi.org/10.1007/978-3-319-10602-1_48
20. Redmon, J., Divvala, S., Girshick, R., Farhadi, A.: You only look once: unified, real-time object detection. In: IEEE Conference on Computer Vision and Pattern Recognition (CVPR), pp. 779–788 (2016)
21. Ronneberger, O., Fischer, P., Brox, T.: U-Net: convolutional networks for biomedical image segmentation. In: Navab, N., Hornegger, J., Wells, W.M., Frangi, A.F. (eds.) MICCAI 2015. LNCS, vol. 9351, pp. 234–241. Springer, Cham (2015). https://doi.org/10.1007/978-3-319-24574-4_28
22. Simonyan, K., Zisserman, A.: Very deep convolutional networks for large-scale image recognition. arXiv preprint arXiv:1409.1556 (2014)
23. Singh, K., Sarvari, P., Petry, F., Khadraoui, D.: Application of machine learning & deep learning techniques in the context of use cases relevant for the tire industry. In: VDI Wissensforum, pp. 1–24 (2019–10)
24. Szegedy, C., et al.: Going deeper with convolutions. In: IEEE Conference on Computer Vision and Pattern Recognition (CVPR), pp. 1–9 (2015)
25. Zhou, Z., Rahman Siddiquee, M.M., Tajbakhsh, N., Liang, J.: UNet++:a nested U-net architecture for medical image segmentation. In: Stoyanov, D., et al. (eds.) DLMIA/ML-CDS -2018. LNCS, vol. 11045, pp. 3–11. Springer, Cham (2018). https://doi.org/10.1007/978-3-030-00889-5_1

Human Action Recognition Using Recurrent Bag-of-Features Pooling

Marios Krestenitis[1(✉)], Nikolaos Passalis[1], Alexandros Iosifidis[2], Moncef Gabbouj[3], and Anastasios Tefas[1]

[1] Department of Informatics, Aristotle University of Thessaloniki,
Thessaloniki, Greece
{mikreste,passalis,tefas}@csd.auth.gr

[2] Department of Engineering Electrical and Computer Engineering,
Aarhus University, Aarhus, Denmark
ai@eng.au.dk

[3] Faculty of Information Technology and Communication, Tampere University,
Tampere, Finland
moncef.gabbouj@tuni.fi

Abstract. Bag-of-Features (BoF)-based models have been traditionally used for various computer vision tasks, due to their ability to provide compact semantic representations of complex objects, e.g., images, videos, etc. Indeed, BoF has been successfully combined with various feature extractions methods, ranging from handcrafted feature extractors to powerful deep learning models. However, BoF, along with most of the pooling approaches employed in deep learning, fails to capture the temporal dynamics of the input sequences. This leads to significant information loss, especially when the informative content of the data is sequentially distributed over the temporal dimension, e.g., videos. In this paper we propose a novel stateful recurrent quantization and aggregation approach in order to overcome the aforementioned limitation. The proposed method is inspired by the well-known Bag-of-Features (BoF) model, but employs a stateful trainable recurrent quantizer, instead of plain static quantization, allowing for effectively encoding the temporal dimension of the data. The effectiveness of the proposed approach is demonstrated using three video action recognition datasets.

1 Introduction

Computer vision is one of the most active and continuously expanding research fields, while with the advent of deep learning (DL) many powerful visual information analysis methods for high dimensional data have been recently proposed [8]. The typical pipeline of a visual information analysis approach involves at least the following two steps: a) feature extraction, in which lower level information is extracted from small spatial or temporal segments of the data, and b) feature aggregation, in which the extracted information is fused into a compact representation that can be used for the subsequent tasks, e.g., classification, retrieval, etc. DL unified, to some extent, these two steps by employing deep trainable feature extraction layers, e.g., convolutional layers, that are combined with naive

© Springer Nature Switzerland AG 2021
A. Del Bimbo et al. (Eds.): ICPR 2020 Workshops, LNCS 12665, pp. 63–76, 2021.
https://doi.org/10.1007/978-3-030-68821-9_6

pooling operators, e.g., max or average pooling, to lower the complexity of the model and provide translation invariance. Indeed, the outstanding performance of Convolutional Neural Networks (CNNs) in complex and challenging image analysis tasks, has confirmed their ability to extract meaningful feature vectors with high discriminative power [8]. However, these powerful feature vectors are crushed through the pooling layers of the network, that usually implement the pooling operation in a less sophisticated manner. As we will demonstrate through this paper, this can lead to significant information loss, especially in cases where the informative content of the data is sequentially distributed over the spatial or temporal dimension, e.g., videos, which often requires extracting fine-grained temporal information, which is discarded by these pooling approaches.

The aforementioned limitations can be better understood through the following example. Consider the task of activity recognition in videos, where the action of *sitting down* must be distinguished from the action of *standing up*. Feature vectors can be extracted from every video frame or a sequence of them by using a deep CNN. However, the pooling layers, as the weak point of the network, dull the expressiveness of the extracted feature vectors and produce less discriminative representations by pooling over the time dimension. For example, assume that a sequence of feature vectors is extracted from a given video instance of action *sitting down*. Let that sequence, notated as $S_1 = [a_1, a_2, a_3]$, be composed of three feature vectors $a_1 = [0, 0, 1]^T$, $a_2 = [0, 1, 0]^T$, and $a_3 = [1, 0, 0]^T$, which are the feature vectors that correspond to the sub-actions *standing above a chair*, *bending knees* and *sitting on a chair*, respectively. Similarly, consider the same feature vector sequence, but in reverse order, i.e., $S_2 = [a_3, a_2, a_1]$, that represents a video instance of the activity *standing up*. Also, let s_i denote the aggregated representation extracted for the i-th video. Note that when average or max pooling is applied over both sequences, then the same representation is extracted for both videos, i.e., $s_1 = s_2 = [\max_i[a_i]_1, \max_i[a_i]_2, \max_i[a_i]_3]^T = [1, 1, 1]^T$ for max pooling (where the notation $[x]_i$ is used to refer to the i-th element of vector x) or $s_1 = s_2 = \frac{1}{3} \sum_{i=1}^{3} a_i = [\frac{1}{3}, \frac{1}{3}, \frac{1}{3}]^T$ for average pooling. Therefore, even though the employed CNN was capable of perfectly recognizing the fundamental sub-actions from still frames, the resulting deep model cannot discriminate between the two actions due to the employed pooling layer. Therefore average and max pooling layers are not capable of capturing the fine-grained spatial or temporal interactions between the feature vectors extracted from a given sequence. Note that in other cases, instead of employing a pooling layer, the extracted feature map may be flatten to a vector and fed to the subsequent fully connected layer. However, this approach makes it impossible for the network to handle inputs of arbitrary size, while it significantly reduces the invariance of the network to temporal shifts (the features must always arrive at the exact same moment).

In this paper, we propose a novel stateful recurrent pooling approach that is capable of overcoming these limitations. The proposed method builds upon the well-known Bag-of-Feature (BoF) model [11], which is capable of creating a constant-length representation of a multimedia object, e.g., video, audio, etc., by compiling a histogram over its quantized feature vectors. Therefore, every object is represented using a fixed-length histogram over the learned codewords. The codewords/dictionary can be either learned using generative/reconstruction approaches [11], or by employing discriminative dictionary learning methods [4], which usually better fit classification tasks. This scheme found application in numerous computer vision tasks, including scene recognition [7], texture classification [16], etc. BoF can be also combined with deep neural networks to provide more powerful trainable pooling layers that can better withstand distribution shifts, while handling inputs of various sizes [9]. Despite its remarkable success in various tasks and its ability to handle variable size inputs, the main drawback of BoF-based methods is the loss of spatial and temporal information, as well as their inability to capture the geometry of input data [7].

These drawbacks severely limit the ability of BoF to process temporal or sequential data, such as video data, since it is not capable of capturing the temporal succession of events. To overcome this limitation, we suggest that the quantization process should take into account the order in which the features arrive, allowing for forming temporal codewords that also capture the interrelation between the feature vectors. As a result, a BoF method employing a stateful recurrent quantizer would be able to quantize the vector a_2 - "bending knees" (given in the previous examples) into a different codeword depending on whether it was following the vector a_1 - "standing above a chair" or the vector a_3 - "sitting on a chair". In this way, it would be possible to extract a representation that can discriminate the standing up action from the sitting down action.

The proposed method is inspired by the BoF model, but employs a stateful trainable recurrent quantizer, instead of a plain static quantization approach to overcome the limitation of existing BoF formulations. In this way, the proposed method harness the power of a novel powerful recurrent quantization formulation in order to capture the temporal information of input data, which is crucial in classification tasks, such as activity recognition, while still maintaining all the advantages of the BoF model. In this work, the proposed Recurrent BoF (abbreviated as "ReBoF") layer is used between the last feature extraction layer and the fully connected layer of a network. Therefore, instead of using other naive pooling layers, that can lead to significant loss of temporal information, the extracted feature vectors are quantized to a number of codewords in a recurrent manner, enabling us to encode the fine-grained temporal information contained in the original feature vectors. The resulting network can be trained in an end-to-end fashion using plain gradient descent and back-propagation, since the proposed ReBoF formulation is fully differentiable.

This allows for building powerful deep learning models for various visual information analysis tasks, as thoroughly demonstrated in this paper, while at the same time keeping the overall space and time complexity low compared to competitive approaches. In this way, the proposed method holds the credentials for providing fast and efficient human-centric perception methods for various embedded and robotics applications [6]. To the best of our knowledge, in this paper we propose the first stateful recurrent Bag-of-Features model that is capable of effectively modeling the temporal dynamics of video sequences. It is also worth noting that existing BoF formulations, e.g., [9], merely provide models that fully ignore the temporal information.

The rest of the paper is structured as follows. In Sect. 2 the proposed Recurrent BoF (ReBoF) method is analytically derived. Then, the experimental evaluation of the ReBoF method is provided in Sect. 3. A thoroughly discussion on how ReBoF could be used for practical applications, along with its limitations, are provided in Sect. 4, while conclusions are drawn and future work is discussed in Sect. 5.

2   Proposed Method

In this Section, we first briefly introduce the regular (non-recurrent) Bag-of-Features model. Then, we derived the proposed Recurrent Bag-of-Features formulation, draw connections with the regular Bag-of-Features model and discuss how it can be used for video classification tasks.

2.1   Bag-of-Features

Let $\mathcal{X} = \{x_i\}_{i=1}^{N}$ be a set of N videos to be represented using the standard BoF model. From each video N_i feature vectors are extracted: $\mathbf{x}_{ij} \in R^D (j = 1, ..., N_i)$, where D is the dimensionality of each feature vector. BoF provides a way to efficiently aggregate these features into a fixed-length histogram. To this end, each feature vector is first quantized into a predefined number of codewords, by employing a codebook $\mathbf{V} \in R^{N_K \times D}$, where N_K is the number of codewords. This codebook is usually learned by clustering all feature vectors into N_K clusters [11]. Clustering algorithms, such as k-means, can be used to this end, with each centroid, $\mathbf{v}_k \in R^D (k = 1, ..., N_K)$, corresponding to a codeword. Then, the quantized feature vectors of each object are accumulated to form the final histogram. Even though several feature quantization approaches have been proposed [11], this work focuses on using a soft quantization approach that allows for learning the codebook using regular back-propagation, along with the rest of the parameters of the model [10]. This can significantly improve the discriminative power of the model, since the codebook is adapted for the task at hand.

More specifically, each feature vector $\mathbf{x}_{ij}$, extracted from the i-th object, is quantized by measuring its similarity with each of the N_k codewords as:

$$[\mathbf{d}_{ij}]_k = \exp\left(\frac{-\|\mathbf{v}_k - \mathbf{x}_{ij}\|_2}{\sigma}\right) \in [0, 1],\tag{1}$$

where σ controls the fuzziness of the quantization process. Then, for each feature vector we obtain a fuzzy membership vector, after normalizing the observed similarities as:

$$\mathbf{u}_{ij} = \frac{\mathbf{d}_{ij}}{\|\mathbf{d}_{ij}\|_1} \in R^{N_K}.\tag{2}$$

Finally, the final histogram is extracted by accumulating all the normalized membership vectors as:

$$\mathbf{s}_i = \frac{1}{N_i} \sum_{j=1}^{N_i} \mathbf{u}_{ij} \in R^{N_K}. \tag{3}$$

The histogram $\mathbf{s}_i$ has unit l_1 norm, regardless the number of the extracted feature vectors, and provides an efficient representation of the feature vectors extracted from the corresponding video. This histogram is then fed to a multilayer perceptron (MLP) to classify the video. Note that the extracted histogram can be also used in other tasks, such as regression or retrieval.

2.2   Proposed Recurrent BoF

The histogram extracted using the regular BoF formulation, as described previously, discards any spatial or temporal information encoded by the feature vectors. To overcome this limitation, in this work we propose using a recurrent stateful quantizer, which allows for capturing and effectively encoding the temporal information expressed by the order in which the feature vectors arrive to the model. Note that in the case of video, we assume that the feature vector $\mathbf{x}_{ij}$ corresponds to the j-th timestep of the i-th video sequence. Before deriving the proposed recurrent quantization approach, it is worth examining, from a probabilistic perspective, the quantization process involved in the BoF model. Using Kernel Density Estimation [1], we can estimate the probability of observing the feature vector $\mathbf{x}_{ij}$, given an input object x_i, as:

$$p(\mathbf{x}_{ij}|x_i) = \sum_{k=1}^{N_K} [\mathbf{s}_i]_k K(\mathbf{x}_{ij}, \mathbf{v}_k) \in [0, 1], \tag{4}$$

where the histogram $\mathbf{s}_i \in \mathbb{R}^{N_K}$ separately adjust the density estimation, while $K(\cdot)$ is a kernel function. Then, a maximum likelihood estimator can be used to actually calculate the histogram:

$$\mathbf{s}_i = \arg\max_{\mathbf{s}} \sum_{j=1}^{N_i} \log \left(\sum_{k=1}^{N_K} [\mathbf{s}]_k K(\mathbf{x}_{ij}, \mathbf{v}_k) \right). \tag{5}$$

The involved parameters (histogram) can be estimated as $\mathbf{s}_i = \frac{1}{N_i} \sum_{j=1}^{N_i} \mathbf{u}_{ij}$, as shown in [1], where

$$[\mathbf{u}_{ij}]_k = \frac{K(\mathbf{x}_{ij}, \mathbf{v}_k)}{\sum_{l=1}^{N_K} K(\mathbf{x}_{ij}^{(t)}, \mathbf{v}_l)} \in [0, 1]. \tag{6}$$

Using this formulation, we can re-derive the regular BoF with soft-assignments. Also, note that we can also replace the Gaussian kernel used in (1), which typically requires tuning the width σ, with an easier to use hyperbolic kernel, which does not require tuning any hyper-parameter. The hyperbolic kernel also proved to be stabler and easier to use when the proposed method was combined with deep neural networks. Therefore, we can now measure the similarity between each feature vector and the codewords in order to quantize the feature vectors as:

$$[\mathbf{d}_{ij}]_k = \sigma(\mathbf{x}_{ij}^T \mathbf{v}_k) \in \mathbb{R}^{N_K}, \tag{7}$$

where

$$\sigma(x) = \frac{1}{1 + \exp(-x)}, \tag{8}$$

is the logistic sigmoid function. Note that this formulation still ignores the temporal information, since it provides no way to encode the current *state* of the quantizer. Therefore, we extend (7) in order to take into account the temporal information, as expressed by the histogram extracted until the current step, as:

$$[\mathbf{d}_{ij}]_k = \sigma(\mathbf{V}\mathbf{x}_{ij} + \mathbf{V}_h(\mathbf{r}_t \odot \mathbf{s}_{i,j-1})) \in \mathbb{R}^{N_K}, \tag{9}$$

where $\mathbf{V}_h \in \mathbb{R}^{N_K \times N_k}$ is a weight matrix that is used to transfer the gated histogram vector into the quantization space, $\mathbf{s}_{i,j-1}$ is the histogram extracted from previous quantizations (state) and $\mathbf{r}_j \in \mathbb{R}^{N_K}$ is the output of a reset gate, introduced to ensure the long-term stability of the model. The additional parameters introduced in this formulation are learned during the training process using back-propagation. The proposed method also employs a reset gate, inspired by the GRU model [2], to further increase the stability of the learning process. Therefore, the reset gate is defined as:

$$\mathbf{r}_{ij} = \sigma(\mathbf{W}_r \mathbf{x}_{ij} + \mathbf{U}_r \mathbf{s}_{i,j-1}) \in \mathbb{R}^{N_K}, \tag{10}$$

where $\mathbf{W}_r \in \mathbb{R}^{N_K \times D}$ and $\mathbf{U}_r \in \mathbb{R}^{N_K \times N_K}$ are the weight matrices used to implement the reset gate.

Then, the l_1 normalized membership vector is computed similarly to the regular BoF model as:

$$\mathbf{u}_{ij} = \frac{\mathbf{d}_{ij}}{\|\mathbf{d}_{ij}\|_1}. \tag{11}$$

Note that the initial state $\mathbf{s}_{i,0}$ is initialized to:

$$\mathbf{s}_{i,0} = \frac{1}{N_K}\mathbf{1}, \tag{12}$$

where N_K is the number of codewords and $\mathbf{1} \in \mathbb{R}^{N_K}$ is a vector of all ones. This ensures that quantizer's output will be always a properly normalized membership vector. Therefore, the histogram is recurrently updated as:

$$\mathbf{s}_{i,j} = (\mathbf{1} - \mathbf{z}_{ij}) \odot \mathbf{s}_{i,j-1} + \mathbf{z}_j \odot \mathbf{u}_{ij} \in \mathbb{R}^{N_K}. \tag{13}$$

The update gate $\mathbf{z}_{i,j}$, which controls how much the current histogram will be updated, is defined as:

$$\mathbf{z}_{ij} = \sigma(\mathbf{W}_z \mathbf{x}_{ij} + \mathbf{U}_z \mathbf{s}_{i,j-1}) \in \mathbb{R}^{N_K}, \tag{14}$$

where $\mathbf{W}_z \in \mathbb{R}^{N_K \times D}$ and $\mathbf{U}_z \in \mathbb{R}^{N_K \times N_K}$ are parameters of the update gate. Finally, to compile the final histogram we average all the intermediate histograms as:

$$\mathbf{s}_i = \frac{1}{N_i} \sum_{j=1}^{N_i} \mathbf{s}_{i,j} \in \mathbb{R}^{N_K}. \tag{15}$$

Back-propagation can be directly used to learn all the parameters of the proposed ReBoF model. Note that ReBoF allows for capturing their temporal information, since it is capable of recursively processing the input feature vectors. First, the proposed recurrent stateful quantizer is employed to quantize the input feature vectors, as described by (9) and (11). Then, these vectors are employed to update the state of the quantizer, as descibed by (13), and allowing for compiling the resulting histogram. It is worth noting that ReBoF, similarly to all BoF-based models, is capable of processing varying-length input sequences.

ReBoF provides a significant advantage over existing BoF formulations, since it allows to capture the temporal information of sequential input data. This alows the ReBoF model to effective tackle challenging video analysis problems, e.g., video retrieval, activity recognition, etc. Therefore, to apply ReBoF we: a) use a convolutional neural network to extract a feature vector $\mathbf{x}_{ij}$ from each frame of a video, and b) feed the extracted feature vectors to the ReBoF model in order to extract a compact representation for each video. This allows ReBoF to process videos of arbitrary duration, while creating fixed-length compact representations of them. Note that the whole architecture can be trained in an end-to-end fashion, since the proposed ReBoF formulation is fully differentiable.

3   Experimental Evaluation

The proposed method was evaluated using three video activity recognition datasets, the UTKinect-Action3D [15] dataset, the UCF101 dataset [12] and a more challenging dataset, the Complex UCF101, which was designed to evaluate the ability of the methods to capture the temporal dimension of video sequences, as it will be described below. The UTKinect-Action3D [15] consists of 10 types of human activities in indoor settings. Samples for each action are collected from 10 different people that perform every activity two times. The provided RGB frames were used for all of the conducted experiments. Since there is no official training/testing split provided, a 50%–50% subject-based split strategy was employed, i.e., the videos of the first five subjects were included in the training set and the rest of them were used to form the testing set. Hence, a quite challenging setup was created, as the activities belonging in the testing set were performed from unseen subjects. The UCF101 dataset [12] is widely used for benchmarking action recognition models. The dataset contains $13,320$ action instances belonging in 101 classes, that can be grouped in five generic categories. For all the experiments conducted in this paper, the first evaluation split of the dataset was used.

We also created a challenging and more complex dataset based on the UCF101 dataset to better demonstrate the ability of the proposed method to capture the temporal dynamics of video data. To this end, we compiled a dataset by mixing instances from different activities of the UCF101 dataset together. More specifically, 10 activities of UCF101 (split 1) were selected to be joined together. Every action of this subset was joined with each one of the remaining, leading to 90 complex actions. One can further understand the significance of encoding the temporal information of these instances by considering that a sample of action "A" combined with one of action "B" (let name this complex activity class "AB") must be separated from samples of complex activities from class "BA". Note that "AB" and "BA" videos contain the same set of frames (for a specific instance of "A" and "B"), but in a different order. Hence, 114 samples were selected for each class, as this was the minimum number of instances contained in the selected initial classes. The selected 10 action classes were the following: *ApplyEyeMakeup, ApplyLipstick, Billiards, BoxingPunchingBag, BoxingSpeedBag, Haircut, Hammering, TableTennisShot, TennisSwing,* and *Typing*. Then, the i-th sample of initial class "A" is combined with the i-th sample of initial class "B" and so on, leading to 7, 380 training and 2, 880 testing data equally balanced among the 90 classes. The compiled dataset is called "Complex UCF" in the rest of this paper.

Table 1. UTKinect-action3D evaluation

Method	# Codewords/ GRU Units	Test Accuracy (%)
Average pooling	–	40.83
GRU	512	47.71
ReBoF	512	**54.64**

Table 2. UCF101 evaluation

Method	# Codewords/ GRU Units	Test Accuracy (%)
Avg. Pooling	–	70.32 ± 0.43
GRU	2048	71.04 ± 0.20
ReBoF	1024	$\mathbf{72.02 \pm 0.68}$

For the UTKinect-Action3 and UCF101 datasets, every video instance was uniformly sampled in time in order to extract a predefined number of frames, denoted by N_f. The number of extracted frames was set to $N_f = 30$ for the UTKinect-Action3D dataset and to $N_f = 40$ for the UCF101 dataset. Shorter videos were looped over as many times as necessary to ensure that each video contains at least N_f frames, following the methodology described in the relevant literature [3]. Then, an Inception V3 model [13], pretrained in ImageNet, was

Table 3. Complex UCF101 evaluation

Method	# Codewords/ GRU Units	Test Accuracy (%)
Average pooling	–	48.95
GRU	512	88.86 ± 2.04
ReBoF	512	89.25 ± 1.08
GRU	1024	88.62 ± 1.02
ReBoF	1024	**89.29** ± 0.89

used to extract a feature representation from each frame from the last average pooling layer of the network. Therefore, from each video, a sequence of N_f feature vectors was extracted. This sequence was then fed to the proposed ReBoF layer, followed by a hidden fully connected layer with 512 neurons and dropout with rate 0.5, as well as by the final classification layer. The ReLU activation function was used for the hidden layer, while the cross-entropy loss was used for training the model. The network was trained using the Adam optimizer and a learning rate of 10^{-5}, apart from the pretrained feature extractors which were kept frozen. Furthermore, note that we also experimentally found out that scaling the extracted histogram by N_K significantly improved the convergence of the proposed method, especially when training from scratch. This scaling ensures that the gradients from the fully connected layers will not diminish as they are back-propagated to the previous layers. The network was trained for 800 epochs for the UTKinect-Action3D dataset and for 500 epochs for the UCF101 (the training/evaluation procedure was also repeated 3 times and the mean and standard deviation is reported). For the Complex UCF101 a slightly different setup was used. First, a 16-frame sliding window, with overlap of 4 frames, was applied on every activity instance of UCF101 dataset, while a pretrained 3D ResneXt-101 [3] was used to extract a feature vector from each window. The features were extracted from the last average pooling layer of the network. Therefore, a 32-length sequence ($N_f = 32$) of 2048-dimensional feature vectors were extracted for each video action. The training process stopped when 99.9% accuracy was achieved in training set (for the average pooling baseline, the network was trained for 50 epochs). The evaluation of ReBoF and GRU methods was repeated 3 times and the mean accuracy and standard deviation on the test set are reported.

The performance of the proposed method was also compared to two other established pooling methods. The same feature extractors and classification block was used to ensure a fair comparison between the methods. First, global average pooling (denoted by "Average Pooling" in the rest of the paper), over the temporal dimensions of the input sequence, was used instead of the proposed ReBoF method. Furthermore, a more powerful recurrent aggregation model, a GRU [2], was also employed to aggregate the extracted features.

First, the proposed method was evaluated on the UTKinect-Action3D, while the results are reported in Table 1. The proposed method greatly outperforms the other two evaluated methods, leading to the highest accuracy (54.64%) using 512 codewords. For the GRU also 512 units were employed, since at this point GRU achieved its best accuracy, which is however significantly lower (47.71%) compared to the proposed ReBoF method. Both ReBoF and GRU outperform the plain Average Pooling, since they are capable of effectively modeling the temporal dynamics of the input video sequences allowing for better discriminating between similar activities, such as *stand up* and *sit down*.

Moreover, in Fig. 1 the effect of using a wider range of codewords and number of GRU units in the classification accuracy on the UTKinect-Action3D dataset is evaluated using the two methods that achieve the highest performance (GRU and ReBoF). In all cases, the proposed method leads to higher accuracy compared to the GRU method. Furthermore, the proposed method allows for reducing the size of the extracted representation, since it outperforms the best GRU model (512 units) using just 128 codewords. This allows for reducing the size of the extracted representation and, as a result, the number of parameters in the subsequent fully connected layer. Both methods achieve their best performance for 512-dimensional representations. After this point, the accuracy for both models drops, mainly due to overfitting phenomena.

Again, similar conclusions can be drawn from the evaluation results on the UCF101 dataset, which are reported in Table 2. Note that even though UCF101 is a less challenging dataset, in terms of temporal dependence, the proposed method still outperforms the rest of the evaluated methods, achieving the highest accuracy (72.02%) for 1024 codewords. Again, all the methods were tuned to use the best number of codewords/representation length to ensure a fair comparison. Note that the proposed method outperforms the GRU while using representations with half the size of the ones used by the GRU. The effect of using different number of codewords and recurrent units is also evaluated in Fig. 2. Again, the proposed method outperforms the GRU method regardless the number of used codewords, while it achieves comparable accuracy using 2 to 4 times smaller representations.

Finally, the proposed method was also evaluated on the Complex UCF dataset. The results are provided in Table 3. As expected, Average Pooling fails to overpass the 50% test accuracy, since "AB" activities cannot be distinguished from those of "BA", due to employing global averaging, which completely discards the temporal information. On the other hand, ReBoF again achieves the highest accuracy (89.29% when 1024 codewords are used). It is worth noting that even though spatio-temporal information is already encapsulated in the extracted feature vectors, since 3D kernels were used in feature extraction block, GRU again achieves lower accuracy compared to the ReBoF for both representation sizes.

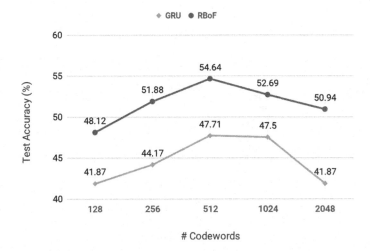

Fig. 1. UTKinect-Action3D Evaluation: Effect of using different number of codewords/recurrent units for the ReBoF and GRU methods

4   Discussion

In this section, some further practical details regarding the employment of ReBoF method are presented, providing more insight into the proposed method compared to our previous works, e.g., [5]. A more thorough inspection of equations (9), (10), (13) and (14) implies that ReBoF shares some similarities with GRU units [2], since both ReBoF and GRUs use a similar update-reset gate structure. Therefore, the RBoF method can be implemented by modifing an existing (and optimized) GRU implementation by a) replacing the output activation function (in order to ensure the quantization of the feature vectors), b) setting the initial state $s_{i,0}$ (to ensure that the histogram vector will maintain a unit l^1 norm) and c) appropriately initializing the codebook. This allows us to simply modify existing and highly optimized GRU implementations to provide highly efficient ReBoF implementations. As far as the number of employed codeworks, a rule of thumb, based on the current work's analysis, could be to initialize ReBoF with 512 codewords, since it can provide a balanced trade-off among feature space dimensionality and model accuracy.

Furthermore, the advantages of employing ReBoF architecture in the corresponding framework for video analysis might be limited under certain circumstances. In case that temporal information is not crucial to distinguish different video instances, the employment of ReBoF is not guaranteed that will lead to significantly higher performance compared to a simpler architecture designed to analyze video instances by a single or a small set of frames. Yet, any method that discards temporal information is incapable to cope with tasks where crucial information is contained over temporal dimension of data. This is clearly demonstrated via the experimental results on UCF101 and Complex UCF101 datasets. In the first case, the employment of ReBoF slightly improves the model

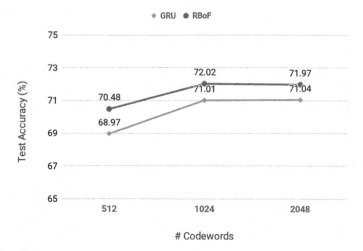

Fig. 2. UCF101 Evaluation: Effect of using different number of codewords/recurrent units for the ReBoF and GRU methods

accuracy, since performing classification of the videos of UCF101 can considered a not so challenging task in terms of temporal dependence, given that in many cases we can achieve quite high recognition accuracy just using one frame from the videos. On the contrary, in the second case of Complex UCF101, enclosing temporal information is crucial to distinguish different video activities and thus, the employment of ReBoF leads to significant performance improvements compared to methods that discard temporal information. Finally, it should be noted that feeding to the ReBoF layer feature vectors that a priori enclose temporal information might lead to improvements to some extent however, this could also disproportionately increase overall the complexity of the models.

5 Conclusions

A novel stateful Recurrent Bag-of-Features (ReBoF) model was proposed in this paper. ReBoF employs a stateful trainable recurrent quantizer, instead of a plain static quantization approach, as the one used in existing BoF formulations. This allows ReBoF to capture the temporal information of the input data, which is crucial in classification tasks, such as activity recognition, while still maintaining all the advantages of the BoF model. ReBoF can be directly used in DL models and the resulting architecture can be trained in an end-to-end fashion using backpropagation, allowing for building powerful deep learning models for various visual information analysis tasks.

ReBoF opens several interesting future research directions. First, ReBoF can be also used for encoding the spatial information, instead of merely the temporal one. For example, the spatial information encoded in the feature vectors extracted from static images can be encoded by manipulating the extracted feature map as a sequence of feature vectors. This allows for overcoming one long-standing limitation of regular BoF formulation that led to the need of using complicated spatial segmentation schemes [7]. Furthermore, activity recognition can be further enhanced by combining a ReBoF layer over the spatial dimension, followed by a ReBoF layer over the temporal dimension. In this way, the spatio-temporal information can be more properly encoded by creating a spatiotempo-ral histograms. Finally, using ReBoF for other tasks, such as video retrieval and hashing [14], is expected to further boost the performance of existing methods by extracting compact, yet more discriminative representations.

References

1. Bhattacharya, S., Sukthankar, R., Jin, R., Shah, M.: A probabilistic representation for efficient large scale visual recognition tasks. In: Proceedings of the IEEE Conference on Computer Vision and Pattern Recognition, pp. 2593–2600 (2011)
2. Cho, K., et al.: Learning phrase representations using RNN encoder-decoder for statistical machine translation. arXiv preprint arXiv:1406.1078 (2014)
3. Hara, K., Kataoka, H., Satoh, Y.: Can spatiotemporal 3d CNNs retrace the history of 2d CNNs and ImageNet? In: Proceedings of the IEEE Conference on Computer Vision and Pattern Recognition, pp. 6546–6555 (2018)
4. Iosifidis, A., Tefas, A., Pitas, I.: Discriminant bag of words based representation for human action recognition. Pattern Recogn. Lett. **49**, 185–192 (2014)
5. Krestenitis, M., Passalis, N., Iosifidis, A., Gabbouj, M., Tefas, A.: Recurrent bag-of-features for visual information analysis. Pattern Recogn. **106**, 107380 (2020)
6. Lane, N.D., Bhattacharya, S., Mathur, A., Georgiev, P., Forlivesi, C., Kawsar, F.: Squeezing deep learning into mobile and embedded devices. IEEE Pervasive Comput. **16**(3), 82–88 (2017)
7. Lazebnik, S., Schmid, C., Ponce, J.: Beyond bags of features: spatial pyramid matching for recognizing natural scene categories. In: Proceedings of the IEEE Computer Society Conference on Computer Vision and Pattern Recognition, vol. 2, pp. 2169–2178 (2006)
8. LeCun, Y., Bengio, Y., Hinton, G.: Deep learning. Nature **521**(7553), 436 (2015)
9. Passalis, N., Tefas, A.: Learning bag-of-features pooling for deep convolutional neural networks. In: Proceedings of the IEEE International Conference on Computer Vision, pp. 5755–5763 (2017)
10. Passalis, N., Tefas, A.: Neural bag-of-features learning. Pattern Recogn. **64**, 277–294 (2017)
11. Sivic, J., Zisserman, A.: Video google: A text retrieval approach to object matching in videos. In: Proceedings of the International Conference on Computer Vision, p. 1470 (2003)
12. Soomro, K., Zamir, A.R., Shah, M.: UCF101: A dataset of 101 human actions classes from videos in the wild. arXiv preprint arXiv:1212.0402 (2012)
13. Szegedy, C., Vanhoucke, V., Ioffe, S., Shlens, J., Wojna, Z.: Rethinking the inception architecture for computer vision. In: Proceedings of the IEEE Conference on Computer Vision and Pattern Recognition, pp. 2818–2826 (2016)

14. Tang, J., Lin, J., Li, Z., Yang, J.: Discriminative deep quantization hashing for face image retrieval. IEEE Trans. Neural Netw. Learn. Syst. **29**(12), 6154–6162 (2018)
15. Xia, L., Chen, C., Aggarwal, J.: View invariant human action recognition using histograms of 3d joints. In: Proceedings of the IEEE Conference on Computer Vision and Pattern Recognition Workshops, pp. 20–27 (2012)
16. Zhang, J., Marszałek, M., Lazebnik, S., Schmid, C.: Local features and kernels for classification of texture and object categories: a comprehensive study. Int. J. Comput. Vis. **73**(2), 213–238 (2007)

Algorithms Based on Maximization of the Mutual Information for Measuring Parameters of Canvas Texture from Images

Dmitry M. Murashov[1](✉), Aleksey V. Berezin[2], and Ekaterina Yu. Ivanova[3]

[1] FRC CSC RAS, Moscow, Russia
d_murashov@mail.ru
[2] State Historical Museum, Moscow, Russia
berezin_aleks@mail.ru
[3] Glazunov Academy, Moscow, Russia
ivanova-e-u@yandex.ru

Abstract. This work deals with the problem of canvas threads counting in images of paintings. Counting of threads is necessary for measuring canvas density and a number of other parameters used by art historians for dating the artworks. We propose to use raking light in the image acquisition process in order to emphasize canvas texture. We improve known techniques developed for inspecting fabrics in the textile industry. Two new threads counting algorithms based on filtering in the Fourier domain and mutual information maximization thresholding techniques are proposed and tested. These algorithms for measuring the canvas density from images taken in raking light are efficient in cases when the analysis of canvas images acquired in X-rays and transmitted light is ineffective. The results of the experiment show that the accuracy of the proposed threads counting algorithms is comparable to the accuracy of known techniques. The analysis of the characteristics of canvases of paintings by F.S. Rokotov allowed obtaining an informative feature that can be used by art historians and experts for dating the artworks.

Keywords: Canvas support · Threads counting · Raking light · Mutual information

1 Introduction

One of the components of technical and technological research of painting layers is the analysis of canvas support. An important characteristic of canvas used in the attribution of paintings is the density of the fabric in warp and weft directions. To determine the density of the fabric, it is necessary to count the number of threads in the sample. Traditionally, this operation was carried out manually [1].

In the past ten years, automated algorithms for calculating the characteristics of canvases using X-ray images have been developed (see [2–4]). The X-ray images show the "imprint" of the canvas in the ground, and the ground relief corresponding to the

© Springer Nature Switzerland AG 2021
A. Del Bimbo et al. (Eds.): ICPR 2020 Workshops, LNCS 12665, pp. 77–89, 2021.
https://doi.org/10.1007/978-3-030-68821-9_7

threads is clearly visible due to the rather noticeable absorption of radiation by the ground material [4].

In works [5–7], a mathematical model of weave patterns was proposed, and a semi-automatic algorithm was developed for measuring the canvas density of Van Gogh paintings from X-ray images. The algorithm is based on filtering in the Fourier domain and analyzing the Fourier spectrum peaks. In [7] the authors reported that the best of several spectrum-based algorithms achieved 84% of canvas density measurements within ±0.5 thread/cm and 95% of measurements within ±1 thread/cm in images of 1.8 by 1.4 cm swatches.

If lead white paint has been used for creating the painting, then X-rays may not provide the required information for analysis. In this case, it is necessary to use images taken in other spectral ranges. To overcome this obstacle, in [3] van der Maaten et al. proposed to analyze terahertz canvas images. But they pointed out the impossibility of obtaining a required spatial resolution of canvas images.

To control the density of the fabric in textile production, a number of algorithms based on image analysis methods have been developed [8, 9]. In this works, the transmitted light source was used to illuminate the fabric samples. In [8], the image was fixed by a CCD camera with a 2-megapixel matrix mounted on a microscope. The authors analyzed woven fabric samples of the size of about 1.2 by 1.2 cm. They proposed an algorithm that included the steps of sample image filtering in the Fourier-domain and thresholding using local Niblack's technique. The binary objects representing canvas threads were counted along the selected baseline, and the fabric density was calculated. The error obtained in the experiment with 15 fabric samples of three types with different densities did not exceed one percent. In [9], the authors proposed an algorithm comprising the steps of Wiener filtering in the spatial domain and Otsu thresholding method [11]. In the tests, 512×512 pixels images of six fabric samples fixed by a CCD camera were used. The error of threads counting in fabric samples of plain structure did not exceed 5%. In paper [12] Aldemir et al. proposed a method for measuring fabric density based on Gabor filters. The method allowed measuring the fabric density with an accuracy of about 90%. Despite the fact that the considered methods developed for analyzing images of fabrics obtained in a transmitted light provide acceptable results, they cannot be applied to analyze painting canvases, because the paint layer of paintings is opaque.

This work is aimed at developing an efficient automatic technique for measuring painting canvas density from images fixed by a digital camera in a visible spectral band. To emphasize canvas texture, we propose to use raking light in the image acquisition process and modify methods developed for measuring fabric density in textile production. We experimentally estimate the effectiveness of the proposed technique by applying it to canvases of paintings created in the 18th–19th centuries. Finally, we evaluate the characteristics of canvases of six fine-art paintings of the 18th century by F.S. Rokotov to obtain a feature that can be used in attribution.

2   Algorithms for Counting Threads

The images used in this work are taken from a distance of approximately 28 cm at the position of the illuminator, providing the incidence of light in the range of angles from

10 to 30° relative to the plane of the painting from below, above, left and right. We use Nikon D 7100 digital camera with a Nikon AF-S Micro NIKKOR 40 mm 1: 2.8 G lens.

The following features of painting canvases should be noted: threads of different thicknesses in one sample, variations of thread thickness, presence of contaminants, ground penetration, and thread damages. The uneven tension of the canvas creates a significant curvature of the threads and a significant unevenness of the gaps between the threads. These features of canvas generate artifacts in the processed images. These artifacts create obstacles for applying canvas density measurement methods designed to control fabrics quality in textile production [8, 9]. To overcome the difficulties caused by the above-mentioned features of canvas images, it is necessary to modify the methods [8, 9] by including a number of image processing operations and choosing the appropriate thresholding algorithm. An image fragment of a canvas dated to the 18th century obtained in raking light is shown in Fig. 1.

In this section, four algorithms for counting the number of threads in canvas samples are proposed basing on the approach developed in [8, 9]. The proposed algorithms are designed using the assumption that the canvas image has a periodic texture in the warp and weft directions. The main idea of these algorithms is to emphasize texture elements oriented in a certain direction in the sample image, to segment image, and count the segmented objects. For thresholding filtered image, four algorithms are applied: global Otsu algorithm [11], adaptive local Niblack algorithm [10], global and local algorithms based on the maximum of the mutual information (MIMax) criterion [13].

(a)   (b)

Fig. 1. An image fragment of a canvas dated to the 18th century: (a) the light falls from above; (b) the light falls from the left.

2.1 Filtering

In [4], a mathematical model of the texture of an X-ray image of the canvas was proposed. The model includes a periodic component describing the structure of the canvas, and a component describing other X-ray visible layers of the painting (paint layer, stretcher, and others). For grayscale images obtained in raking light, we will use a similar model:

$$I(\mathbf{x}) = I_0 + a \cdot \sin(2\pi \mathbf{k}^T \mathbf{x} - \varphi(\mathbf{x})) + n(\mathbf{x}), \tag{1}$$

where $I(\mathbf{x})$ is a grayscale value at image point $\mathbf{x}$ with coordinates (x, y); I_0 is a shift of grayscale value; a is an amplitude of the gray level; $\mathbf{k} = (k_1, k_2)^T$ is a vector of wave numbers; φ is a phase; $n(\mathbf{x})$ is a periodic function that simulates weaves of threads. To obtain an image that can be used for counting threads number, it is necessary to perform operations to suppress the component $n(\mathbf{x})$ of the model (1).

In the canvas image (see Fig. 1), a periodic texture is visible. This texture can be roughly described by the model (1). It seems reasonable to use frequency filtering methods to suppress the component $n(\mathbf{x})$. As in [8], filtering in the Fourier domain is applied to highlight threads with the desired orientation and spatial frequency range:

$$I_F(\mathbf{x}) = \mathcal{F}^{-1}\{\mathcal{F}\{I(\mathbf{x})\}I_M(\mathbf{x})\}, \qquad (2)$$

where $I(\mathbf{x})$ is an input image, $I_F(\mathbf{x})$ is filtered image, $\mathcal{F}$ and $\mathcal{F}^{-1}$ are the direct and inverse Fourier transform, and $I_M(\mathbf{x})$ is a filter mask. To select the horizontal threads in the sample image $I(\mathbf{x})$, we use the mask in the form of a strip of size $(H/4 + 1) \times 3$ pixels for warp and $H \times 3$ for weft threads. The mask is blurred by a Gaussian filter with a small σ value. Here, H is the image height. Before Fourier filtering, operations of the input image histogram equalization are performed. Filtering operation is illustrated in Fig. 2. In Fig. 2 (a)–(d), the sample image obtained in raking light, filter mask, the result of filtering, and filtered image histogram are shown.

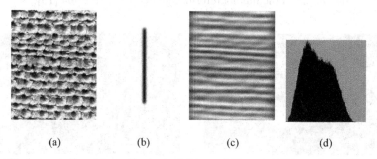

(a)   (b)   (c)   (d)

Fig. 2. Filtering operation: (a) equalized sample image; (b) inverted filter mask; (c) filtered image; (d) filtered image histogram.

2.2 Thresholding

Next, it is necessary to outline objects corresponding to canvas threads in the filtered image. For this purpose, we use four thresholding algorithms: the global Otsu algorithm [11], the local Niblack algorithm [10], global and local algorithms based on the mutual information criterion [13].

The Otsu global thresholding method [11] was successfully used in work [9]. The Otsu method imposes a threshold value that minimizes intraclass variance. The method shows good results on images with a bimodal intensity histogram, but in the case of a unimodal histogram (see Fig. 2 (d)), it can give an incorrect result. This method is very fast and does not require parameter tuning. In order to remove small objects that appeared after thresholding and capable of distorting the result of thread counting, morphological erosion by a 5 by 5 square structuring element is performed. The thresholded image after erosion is shown in Fig. 3(a).

The second thresholding method we apply to the filtered image of the canvas sample is the local adaptive Niblack method. The method finds the threshold value in a sliding window:

$$T_N = m + k_N \sigma_N, \tag{3}$$

where T_N is a threshold value, m is the mean value, σ_N is the standard deviation of image I_F gray values in a sliding window, k_N is a coefficient. Here, we used a 30 by 30 sliding window size and $k_N = 0.2$. Thresholded image after erosion by a 5 by 5 square structuring element is shown in Fig. 3(b). The result of the Niblack method depends on the ratio of the sizes of the sliding window and image texture elements.

Another thresholding algorithm is based on the optimization of information criterion. For segmenting the filtered image, it is preferable to apply an algorithm that would not require parameter settings and is also independent of the gray level histogram shape of the analyzed images. In this paper, we propose to use a method, which allows obtaining the maximum informational similarity between the input and thresholded images. Such a method was presented in [13]. The method is based on the criterion of the maximum of the mutual information, which the authors called the "maximum segmented image information thresholding criterion". In this method, the mutual information is used as a measure of image similarity. Since the method will use the global threshold value, in order to provide the correct segmentation, the processing of the filtered image $I_F(\mathbf{x})$ is required. For this, an uneven illumination is corrected using the morphological closing operation [14] with a square structuring element of size 11 by 11 pixels. Then, to remove small valleys, a morphological closing operation is performed with a structuring element of size 3 by 3 pixels:

$$I_{proc} = \phi_{3B}([\phi_{11B}(I_F) - I_F]/\phi_{11B}(I_F)), \tag{4}$$

where I_{proc} is the processed image; ϕ_{3B} and ϕ_{11B} denote closing operations with square structuring elements of size 3 and 11, respectively; "/" denotes the point-wise division.

Consider the following model of the thresholding system:

$$I_{Bin} = T(I_{proc}, t), \tag{5}$$

where I_{proc} and I_{Bin} are the discrete random variables describing the processed image (see formula (4)) and binary image (see (5)); T is a function describing image transformation; t is a threshold value. The variables I_{proc} and I_{Bin} are stochastically dependent. Here we present a more simple way of obtaining the optimal threshold value than in paper [13]. Mutual information is determined by the expression [15]:

$$MI(I_{proc}; I_{Bin}) = H(I_{Bin}) - H(I_{Bin}|I_{proc}), \tag{6}$$

where $MI(I_{proc}; I_{Bin})$ is the mutual information between images I_{proc} and I_{Bin}, $H(I_{Bin})$ is the entropy of image I_{Bin}, $H(I_{Bin}|I_{proc})$ is the conditional entropy of I_{Bin} under the condition that the input of system (5) is the image I_{proc}. Since the output of the system is the binary image, then $H\left(I_{Bin}|I_{proc}\right) = 0$. In this case, the maximum of (6) is reached at the maximum value of the entropy of the output $H(I_{Bin})$. Maximum of $H(I_{Bin})$ is taking place in the case of equal probability of the values 0 and 255 in the binary image I_{Bin}:

$$P(0) = P(255) = 0.5 \tag{7}$$

Thereby, the threshold value t in the model (5, 6) should be chosen to satisfy condition (7). This result is consistent with those of other thresholding methods based on entropy criteria (see review [16]).

To remove small artifacts confusing thread counting, after thresholding we use dilation with 3 by 3 structuring element, erosion with 5 by 5 pixels structuring element, and the "Fillhole" operation [14]. The result of applying this algorithm to the filtered image of the canvas sample is given in Fig. 3(c).

The fourth thresholding algorithm is a modification of the algorithm based on the maximum criteria of mutual information. The threshold value in each pixel of the image is calculated from the condition (7) in the sliding window. We chose a window size of 36 by 36 pixels. In this case, the image obtained after the filtering operation (2) is processed in the same way as in the case of the global MIMax algorithm. After thresholding, a morphological closing operation is performed with the structuring element of size 3 by 3 pixels. The output of the algorithm is given in Fig. 3 (d).

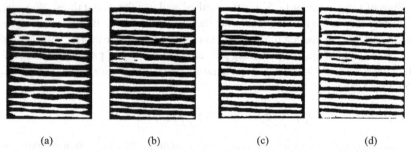

(a)	(b)	(c)	(d)

Fig. 3. Results of processing filtered canvas image: (a) after applying the Otsu method; (b) after applying the Niblack method; (c) after applying the MIMax method; (d) after applying local MIMax method.

2.3 Thread Counting

In this section, we propose the procedure for counting the number of objects in the binary images corresponding to the threads. In [8], counting the number of threads is performed along a given standard line. In this paper, we propose to use the voting procedure. For this purpose, it is necessary to perform counting of threads in all columns of the image matrix and obtain a histogram. The number of threads will be determined by the maximum of the histogram, which will correspond to the maximum number of votes. Each object is characterized by the presence of brightness transitions from 0 to

255 and from 255 to 0 (with the exception of objects containing pixels in the first and last rows of the image matrix). If the indicated combination of brightness transitions occurs when scanning a matrix column, then the number of objects in the column increases by one. After scanning the column, the number of threads found is recorded in a histogram, which corresponds to a vote for this result. The proposed voting procedure improves the reliability of the result since the features of images of old canvases generate objects of complex shape in binary images (see Fig. 3).

In the following section we present the results of testing the algorithms for counting threads in photographs of the canvases of paintings created in the 18th–19th centuries.

3 Experiment

To estimate the effectiveness of the described above algorithms, a computational experiment is carried out. The experiment includes two stages. At the first stage, the spatial resolution of the sample images, at which the highest accuracy of counting the threads can be achieved, is determined. In this case, images with highlighted warp threads are used. At the second step, the described above algorithms are applied to the images of the canvas samples obtained at the selected optimal spatial resolution. At this stage, images with highlighted both warp and weft threads are used.

In the experiment, fragments of images obtained by photographing canvases of paintings in raking light, directed from below or from above and from left or right are analyzed. Images are fixed at angles of incidence of light ranging from 15 to 30° relative to the plane of the canvas. Three samples are taken from each image of the painting.

To estimate the accuracy of the algorithms, the obtained values of the number of threads are compared with the results of counting performed by experts. Then we build histograms of relative error values calculated by the formula:

$$\delta = \frac{N_a - N_e}{N_e}, \tag{8}$$

where δ denotes the value of the relative error of counting the number of threads; N_a is the number of threads in the sample found by the algorithm, N_e is the number of threads counted by the experts.

The first stage of the experiment involves 30 samples taken from ten images of canvases. Samples contain from 50 to 110 threads. The width of the canvas samples is in the range from 0.7 to 1.7 cm, and the height is in the range from 4.8 to 8.7 cm. The spatial resolution of the sample images covers a range from 390 to 675 pixels per centimeter. For each sample image, three algorithms are used to calculate warp threads. Thread counting is performed at three values of scale: 1, 0.75, and 0.5. The obtained thread numbers are compared with the results of counting performed by experts, and relative error values (8) are computed. Mean values and standard deviations of δ obtained at various image scales are given in Table 1. From data presented in Table 1, it follows that the algorithms are efficient at images scale value equal to 0.75, which corresponds to the special resolution in the range from 292.5 to 506.25 pixels per centimeter. The thread counting algorithms based on Niblack and MIMax methods show the best accuracy. MIMax-based counting technique appears to be more stable to changing image size, than others.

Table 1. Mean values/standard deviation of the relative error δ obtained at various image scale values.

Algorithm	Scale value		
	1	0.75	0.5
Otsu-based	−0.26/0.345	−0.045/0.049	−0.066/0.178
Niblack-based	−0.064/0.083	0.0044/0.047	0.093/0.141
MIMax-based	−0.055/0.09	−0.00095/0.024	0.012/0.028

At the second stage of the experiment, the described above algorithms were used to count the warp and weft threads. The counting of warp threads was carried out in images of samples with the spatial resolution in the range from 292.5 to 506.25 pixels per centimeter, which was determined at the first stage of the experiment. Measurements of warp threads number were carried out in 33 images, partially different from those used in the previous step. Figure 4 shows the resulting histogram of relative errors of threads counting. The algorithm based on the local Niblack method showed the counting error within 5% for 90% of the samples. The algorithm based on the Otsu method showed the relative error in counting threads within 5% in 76% of images. The algorithm based on MIMax thresholding technique for 94% of canvas samples gave the error limited to 5%. The threads counting method based on local MIMax technique for 90% of the samples produced the relative error within 5%.

Weft threads counting was performed in 42 sample images. The resulting histogram of relative errors of counting the threads is shown in Fig. 5.

The algorithm based on the Otsu method calculated the number of threads with the error not exceeding 5% in 4% of sample images. The algorithm based on the local Niblack thresholding method counted the number of threads with the error within 5% in 35% of cases. The method based on the maximum of the mutual information criterion in 73% of cases showed accuracy within 5%, and in 100% of cases the error was less than 10%. The method based on the local MMI technique produced the error less than 5% for 95% of analyzed images.

Mean values and standard deviations of δ obtained at this stage of the experiment are given in Table 2.

In practice, the density of the canvas is measured by experts in the number of threads per unit length in the direction of the warp or weft [14]. When estimating the density of canvases in the direction of the warp threads, the algorithm based on the Otsu method in 92.8% of cases showed the error within one thread per centimeter, the algorithm based on the Niblack method – in 83%, the algorithm based on the mutual information maximization - in 100%, and the method using the local MIMax technique – in 97% of cases.

When estimating the canvas density in the direction of weft threads, the algorithm based on the Otsu method always showed the error of more than one thread per centimeter, and the algorithm based on the Niblack method - for 60% of samples. The method based

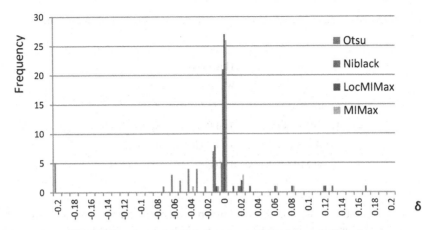

Fig. 4. Histogram of the relative error of counting warp threads.

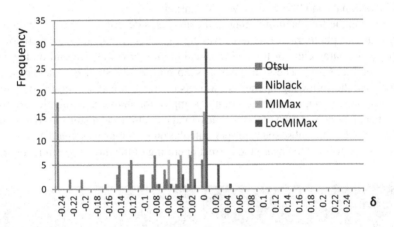

Fig. 5. Histogram of the relative error of counting weft threads.

on the global MIMax criterion in 88% of cases provided the error not exceeding one thread per centimeter, and the method using the local MIMax technique – in 95% cases.

From the results of the experiment, one can conclude that the technique based on the global MIMax method is more efficient for counting warp threads, and the technique based on the local MIMax method is more accurate for counting the weft threads.

4   Application of the Proposed Algorithms to Canvas Images of Paintings by F.S. Rokotov

This section describes the application of the presented above algorithms to the study of canvases of paintings by F.S. Rokotov. This study made it possible to identify the peculiarities of the fabric support of the portraits he painted and to present to art historians accurate data that can be used as a criterion for attribution of the artist's paintings. The

Table 2. Mean values/standard deviation of the relative error δ obtained when counting warp and weft threads.

Algorithm	Thread type	
	Warp	Weft
Otsu-based	−0.15/0.32	−0.33/0.31
Niblack-based	0.009/0.042	−0.076/0.046
MIMax-based	0.003/0.019	−0.032/0.025
Local MIMax-based	0.0067/0.025	−0.01/0.021

study examined the canvases of six paintings by Rokotov and his workshop from the State Historical Museum (Moscow) collection: "Portrait of V.I. Streshnev", "Portrait of F.N. Rzhevskaya", "Portrait of E.P. Voeikova", "Portrait of an Unknown", "Portrait of V.A. Naryshkina", and "Portrait of M.V. Gagarina".

The technique for obtaining images of canvases is described in Sect. 2. Figure 6(a) shows a digital photograph of the canvas taken under illumination from below. For measuring the parameters of the canvas, a calibration grid was overlaid on the canvas surface (see Fig. 6 (b)). The grid spacing is 2.5 mm. At the stage of image processing and analysis, the following operations were performed: image rotation and distortion compensation, scaling, manual selection of samples for analysis, automatic counting of the number of threads in each of the samples. Image rotation and distortion compensation are necessary for the subsequent proper calculation of the canvas characteristics. The scaling was performed to ensure the correct operating of the thread counting algorithm.

(a)   (b)

Fig. 6. An image of an 18th-century canvas: (a) canvas image taken under illumination from below; (b) a calibration grid overlaid on the canvas.

In the canvas image, from three to six samples (usually four) were selected. The length of the fragments ranges from 2.1 to 14.9 cm, and the width is from 0.6 to 1.6 cm. Images of masks of the selected samples on the canvas of the portrait of E.P. Voeikova to determine the characteristics of the warp and weft threads are shown in Fig. 7.

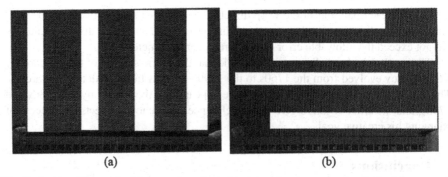

(a)   (b)

Fig. 7. Image of the mask of the samples selected to determine the parameters in the (a) warp and (b) weft directions.

Table 3. Characteristics of canvases of portraits by F. Rokotov.

Name	Date	Mean canvas density in the warp direction, threads/cm	Mean canvas density in the weft direction, threads/cm	Mean thickness of warp threads, mm	Mean thickness of weft threads, mm
Portrait of V.I. Streshnev	1760s	9.16	14.78	1.09	0.68
Portrait of F.N. Rzhevskaya	The first half of the 1770s	10.45	14.89	0.957	0.67
Portrait of E.P. Voeikova	1780s	11.4	13.54	0.877	0.74
Portrait of an Unknown	1790s	13.47	16.508	0.742	0.606
Portrait of V.A. Naryshkina	1790s	12.8	16.47	0.781	0.607
Portrait of M.V. Gagarina	1794	13.84	22.6	0.722	0.448

Using the proposed algorithms and the images of the canvas and sample masks, we counted the number of threads in the selected samples in the warp and weft directions. Then from the images of sample masks and calibration grid, we measured the following characteristics: (a) the spatial resolution of the sample images; (b) the size of the samples in centimeters; (c) the density of the canvas in the warp and weft directions; (d) the mean thread thickness in millimeters. The mean values of the characteristics over the whole canvas image are computed by averaging the corresponding values from all of the considered fragments. The results of measuring the numerical parameters of the canvases of six paintings are given in Table 3. To check the correctness of the obtained values of the canvas density, we counted manually the number of threads in one sample image from each painting in the warp direction and on one sample image in the weft direction. The difference in the number of threads counted automatically and manually did not exceed the allowable error of one thread per centimeter.

The results obtained allow us to conclude that the fabric support of the portraits by F.S. Rokotov evolved from the 1760s to the 1790s towards fabric with thinner threads. This kind of canvases with smoother facture appeared on the market by the 1780s and 1790s, and the artist began to give them preference. This choice reflects the process of changing his creative goals.

5   Conclusions

In this work, the problem of threads counting in images of canvases of paintings was considered. We proposed to use canvas images taken in raking light to emphasize the warp and weft threads. We used the known approach based on filtering in the Fourier domain and thresholding techniques. Threads counting algorithms were modified and improved taking into account the features of images of canvases of paintings. For segmenting threads, we proposed to use global and local thresholding algorithms based on mutual information maximization. The voting procedure for counting threads was proposed.

To evaluate the effectiveness of the threads counting algorithms, a computational experiment was carried out. The results of the experiment showed that the accuracy of the proposed algorithms is comparable to the accuracy of known techniques. The proposed thread counting algorithms based on the mutual information maximization thresholding technique demonstrated the highest accuracy at various values of the spatial resolution of canvas images.

The presented thread counting technique can be used in technical and technological research in attribution. The results of the analysis of the characteristics of the canvases by F.S. Rokotov 1770–1790s provides art historians and experts with an informative feature that can be used for dating fine-art paintings.

The future research will be aimed at improving the accuracy of counting threads, developing methods for analyzing weave patterns and measuring other parameters of canvases of paintings.

Acknowledgements. The research was supported in part by the Foundation (grants No 18-07-01385 and No 18-07-01231).

References

1. Cornelis, B., Dooms, A., Cornelis, J., Leen, F., Schelkens, P.: Digital painting analysis, at the cross section of engineering, mathematics and culture. In: 19th European Signal Processing Conference, pp. 1254–1258. IEEE (2011)
2. Johnson, D.H., Johnson, Jr.C.R., Erdmann, R.G.: Weave analysis of paintings on canvas from radiographs. IEEE Signal Process. Mag. **93**(3), 527–540 (2013)
3. Van der Maaten, L., Erdmann, R.G.: Automatic thread-level canvas analysis: a machine-learning approach to analyzing the canvas of paintings. IEEE Signal Process. Mag. **32**(4), 38–45 (2015)

4. Yang, H., Lu, J., Brown, W.P., Daubechies, I., Ying, L.: Quantitative canvas weave analysis using 2-D synchrosqueezed transforms: application of time-frequency analysis to art investigation. IEEE Signal Process. Mag. **32**(4), 55–63 (2015)
5. Klein, A., Johnson, D., Sethares, W.A., Lee, H., Johnson, C.R., Hendriks, E.: Algorithms for old master painting canvas thread counting from X-rays. In: Proceedings of the 42nd Asilomar Conference on Signals, Systems and Computers, pp. 1229–1233. IEEE (2008)
6. Johnson, D.H., Johnson, C., Klein, A.G., Sethares, W.A., Lee, H., Hendriks, E.: A thread counting algorithm for art forensics. In: 13th IEEE Digital Signal Processing Workshop and 5th IEEE Signal Processing Education Workshop, pp. 679–684. IEEE (2009)
7. Johnson, Jr.C.R., Hendriks, E., Noble, P., Franken, M.: Advances in computer-assisted canvas examination: thread counting algorithms. In: 37th Annual Meeting of American Institute for Conservation of Historic and Artistic Works, Los Angeles, CA (2009)
8. Pan, R., Gao, W., Li, Z., Gou, J., Zhang, J., Zhu, D.: Measuring thread densities of woven fabric using the Fourier transform. Fibres Text. Eastern Eur. **23**, 35–40 (2015)
9. Shady, E., Qashqary, K., Hassan, M., Militky, J.: Image processing based method evaluating fabric structure characteristics. Fibres Text. Eastern Eur. **6A**, 86–90 (2012)
10. Niblack, W.: An Introduction to Digital Image Processing, vol. 34. Prentice-Hall, Englewood Cliffs (1986)
11. Otsu, N.: A threshold selection method from gray-level histograms. IEEE Trans. Syst. Man Cybern. **9**(1), 62–66 (1979)
12. Aldemir, E., Ozdemir, H., Sari, Z.: An improved gray line profile method to inspect the warp–weft density of fabrics. J. Text. Inst. **110**(1), 105–116 (2019)
13. Leung, C.K., Lam, F.: Maximum segmented image information thresholding. Graph. Models Image Process. **60**(1), 57–76 (1998)
14. Soille, P.: Morphological Image Analysis: Principles and Applications. Springer, Heidelberg (2013)
15. MacKay, D.J.: Information Theory, Inference, and Learning Algorithms. Cambridge University Press, Cambridge (2003)
16. Sezgin, M., Sankur, B.: Survey over image thresholding techniques and quantitative performance evaluation. J. Electron. Imaging **13**(1), 146–166 (2004)

Machine Learning Approach for Contactless Photoplethysmographic Measurement Verification

Ivan Semchuk[✉], Natalia Muravskaya, Konstantin Zlobin, and Andrey Samorodov

Bauman Moscow State Technical University, Moscow, Russia
ivan7chuk@gmail.com

Abstract. Contactless heart rate measurement techniques can be applied in medical and biometrical tasks such as vital signs measurement and vitality detection. Incorrect measurement result can cause serious consequences. In this paper a method for contactless heart rate measurement result verification is proposed. A binary classifier is used in order to identify whether a contactless photoplethysmogram (PPG) signal is reliable. Experimental setup used for signal dataset acquisition consists of contact plethysmograph, web-camera and contactless plethysmography device. Feature vector containing various signal and signal's spectral density metrics as classification algorithms input is used. The highest classification accuracy is shown by classifier based on logistic regression (99.94%). The classification results demonstrate that the proposed method can be used in further contactless methods research.

Keywords: Contactless vital signs measurement · Videoplethysmography · Measurement result verification

1 Introduction

Photoplethysmography as a method for registration of cardiovascular system activity can be used to measure various physiological parameters, such as heart rate and breath rate [1], heart rate variability [2]. The analysis of these parameters is widely used in clinical practice in screening and diagnosing diseases of the cardiovascular system [3], in sports medicine [4], neonatology [5] and psychology [6].

Contactless methods for pulse curve registration do not require attaching sensitive elements to the patient's skin surface, which enables application of such systems in subspecialities of medicine where direct contact of measuring equipment with the skin surface is undesirable (such as neonatology, injury medicine, sport).

However the presence of noise components in the signal, such as irregularity of the light source radiation pattern, inconstancy of the spectral composition and intensity of light sources, artifacts associated with the movements of the biological object, criticality to the distance from the surface of the biological object to the photosensor plane, etc. impose additional requirements to the measurement system and cause difficulties in subsequent processing. Incorrect measurement result can be crucial in use cases where it

© Springer Nature Switzerland AG 2021
A. Del Bimbo et al. (Eds.): ICPR 2020 Workshops, LNCS 12665, pp. 90–96, 2021.
https://doi.org/10.1007/978-3-030-68821-9_8

can be applied such as medical care and biometrics vitality detection. This problem can be solved by introducing additional algorithms for assessing the reliability of physiological values calculated using the received signal.

The first step towards contactless measurement result verification is development of a binary signal classifier, which assigns a signal (or its fragment) to class "1" (reliable) or to class "0" (unreliable). Such an approach can further be applied in clinical practice and in scientific research of the characteristics of contactless photoplethysmographic systems.

2 Materials and Methods

2.1 Experimental Setup

Figure 1 shows the experimental setup for simultaneous contact and contactless PPG signals acquisition, which includes a web-camera, contactless plethysmograph and contact plethysmograph connected to personal computer with specific application pre-installed [7].

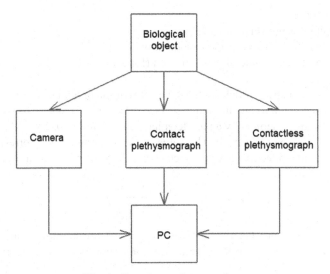

Fig. 1. Experimental setup scheme

The application functions are simultaneous grabbing of data from all three devices, its visualization and saving to files for further processing. Multithreading approach is implemented to ensure the high accuracy of the sampling rate (25 Hz) for each device and provide the synchronous reception of the data.

The device for contactless plethysmography consists of optical unit, analog signal processing unit and embedded software. The optical scheme of the device is shown on the Fig. 2. Lenses (pos. 1 and pos. 2) are used as a collimator for parallel beam narrowing. Beam splitter (pos. 3) divides the beam into two each of which passes through the

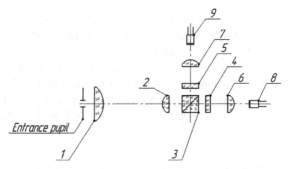

Fig. 2. Optical scheme of the contactless plethysmograph

corresponding band-pass filter (pos. 4–540 nm, pos. 5–700 nm) and focuses on the photodiode (pos. 8 and 9) [7].

The second contactless technique used in the experimental setup is videoplethys-mography. It is based on videostream processing obtained with web-camera. Image processing algorithm for plethysmogram signal extraction consists of:

1. Image grabbing.
2. Face detection using Haar cascade.
3. Skin areas detection using color segmentation.
4. Calculation of mean value of pixels of ROI (for each RGB channel separately).

The area of color space which contains the distribution of human skin colors is quite limited. Thus segmentation of the required face area can be reduced to sifting pixels belonging to a cluster defined by a parallelepiped with borders (0, 133, 77), (255, 173, 127) in the YCrCb color space [8]. The value of the VPG amplitude corresponding to the i-th frame of the video image of the face is calculated using the formula:

$$VPG_i = \frac{\sum_{j,k} G_{j,k}}{\sum_{j,k} R_{j,k} + \sum_{j,k} B_{j,k}} \tag{1}$$

Where i is the frame number of the video image; j, k are the coordinates of pixels belonging to the selected area; R, G, B are the color coordinates of the corresponding pixels.

For reference signal registration a contact plethysmograph sensor connected to microcontroller's ADC was used.

2.2 Data Processing

To assess the reliability of contactless heart rate measurement results, it was decided to develop a binary signal classifier that divides the input data into two classes: "1" is a reliable signal, "0" is an unreliable signal. Various characteristics of the signal and its spectral density used in the initial composition of the feature vector are presented in the Table 1.

Table 1. Extracted signal features

Symbol	Description	Formula
f_c	Frequency which corresponds to the highest peak of spectral density of the signal	
k_{freq}		$\frac{f_c}{f_{c2}}$, where f_{c2} – frequency corresponding to the second highest peak of spectral density of the signal
$S(f_c)$	Spectral density highest peak value	
N_{peak}	Number of local maximums of spectral density in range from 0.5 Hz to 4 Hz	
μ_{peak}	Mean value of local maximums of spectral density in range from 0.5 Hz to 4 Hz	
σ_{peak}	Standard deviation of local maximums of spectral density in range from 0.5 Hz to 4 Hz	
k_{peak}		$\frac{\left\| S(f_c) - \mu_{peak} \right\|}{\sigma_{peak}}$
$k_{integral}$		$\frac{S(f_c)}{\sum_i S(f_i)}$
r	Dickson criteria for maximums of spectral density in range from 0.5 Hz to 4 Hz	
μ_{signal}	Mean value of contactless PPG signal	
σ_{signal}	Standard deviation of contactless PPG signal	

Target variable is calculated as a result of the following boolean expression:

$$target = f_c contactless = f_c contact \& f_{c2} contactless = f_{c2} contact \qquad (2)$$

where $f_c^{contactless}$ and $f_c^{contact}$ - frequencies which correspond to the highest peak of spectral density of contactless PPG (VPG) and contact PPG respectively, $f_{c2}^{contactless} =$ and $f_{c2}^{contact}$ – frequencies which correspond to the second highest peak of spectral density of contactless PPG (VPG) and contact PPG respectively.

Pairs of signals obtained synchronously with contact and contactless devices were used to form an input dataset. According to the algorithm signals are divided into separate sections with a size of 256 points (which corresponds to a duration of 10 s), the feature vector is calculated for each of the sections of the contactless PPG (VPG) signal. The target variable is calculated comparing the relevant areas of contactless and contact PPG signals using expression (2).

The dataset was randomly divided into training and test datasets of 2,654 objects in size (the ratio between classes in each of the datasets was reduced to 1:1 using undersampling technique). The following algorithms were used for classification and compared:

- Decision tree (varying tree depth)
- Radom forest (varying number of trees)
- k-nearest neighbors (varying number of neighbors)
- Logistic regression (varying regularization parameter)

Following metrics were used in order to estimate model effectiveness:

- Accuracy:

$$accuracy = \frac{TruePositive + TrueNegative}{TruePositive + TrueNegative + FalsePositive + FalseNegative} \tag{3}$$

- Precision:

$$precision = \frac{TruePositive}{TruePositive + FalsePositive} \tag{4}$$

- Recall:

$$recall = \frac{TruePositive}{TruePositive + FalseNegative} \tag{5}$$

- F1-score:

$$F_1 = \frac{precision \cdot recall}{precision + recall} \tag{6}$$

3 Results

Feature importance (I_f) of each element of input vector were estimated using decision tree algorithm for dimensionality reduction. According to the results the most informative features are f_c, k_{freq}, $k_{integral}$ and σ_{signal}, which allows to use a vector consisting only of these features for further analysis.

Table 2 shows the values of the estimated metrics and the varied parameter for the case of the maximum value of the F1-score (as the most balanced metric) for each of the classification model. The analysis of the table shows that in terms of the F1-score maximization the classification algorithm based on logistic regression has shown itself in the best way.

Table 2. Models accuracy estimation

Model	Accuracy,%	Precision,%	Recall.%	F1-score,%	Parameter
Decision tree	89, 51	89, 72	89, 34	89, 53	8
Random forest	91, 25	89, 72	91, 825	90, 48	38
k-nearest neighbors	99, 62	99, 24	99, 94	99, 62	189
Logistic regression	99, 94	99, 89	99, 98	99, 94	0,6250

4   Conclusions

The paper presents a method for verifying the results of contactless photopletsmographic heart rate measurements based on the binary classification of a contactless PPG signal. Classifiers training was carried out on a dataset of signals that were synchronously obtained using contactless and contact methods. Two contactless measurement methods were included in the experimental setup: videoplethysmography and contactless photoplethysmography using specialized device. Classification accuracy estimation confirms the informativeness of the developed feature vector. Among the selected classification algorithms, the best results are obtained using logistic regression model. Proposed method can be used for further research on real-time analysis of contactless PPG signals and measurement systems.

References

1. Elgendi, M.: On the analysis of fingertip photopletismograph signals. Curr. Cardiol. Rev. **8**(1), 14–25 (2012)
2. Bockeria, L.A., Bockeria, O.L., Volkovskaya, I.V.: Cardiac rhythm variability: methods of measurement, interpretation, clinical use. Ann. Arythmol. **6**(4), 21–32 (2009)
3. Task force of the European society of cardiology and the North American society of pacing and electrophysiology. heart rate variability: standards of measurement, physiological interpretation, and clinical use. Circulation, **93**, 1043–1065 (1996)
4. Dong, J.G.: The role of heart rate variability in sports physiology (review). Exper. Ther. Med. **11**, 1531–1536 (2016)
5. Javorka, K., et al.: Heart rate variability in newborns. Physiol. Res. **66**(2), 203–214 (2017)
6. Appelhans, B.M., Luecken, L.J. Heart rate variability as an index of regulated emotional responding. Rev. Gen. Psychol. **10**(3), 229–240 (2006)

7. Semchuk, I.P., Zmievskoy, G.N., Muravskaya, N.P., Volkov, A.K., Murashko, M.A., Samorodov, A.V.: An experimental study of contactless photoplethysmography techniques. Biomed. Eng. **53**, 1–5 (2019)
8. Kaur, A., Kranthi, B.V.: Comparison between YCbCr color space and CIELab color space for skin color segmentation. Int. J. Appl. Inf. Syst. **4**(3), 30–33 (2012)

On New Kemeny's Medians

Sergey Dvoenko$^{(\boxtimes)}$ (iD) and Denis Pshenichny

Tula State University, Lenin Ave. 92, 300012 Tula, Russia
dvsrge@gmail.com

Abstract. The Kemeny's median is the well-known method to get a coordinated decision representing a group opinion. This ranking is the least different from experts' orderings of alternatives. If rankings are immersed in a metric space, the median should be an average ranking from the mathematical point of view. As a result, the correct median should be the center of the set of rankings as points in a metric space. In this case it should be the median denoted as the Kemeny's metric median. In this paper we propose also a new median denoted as the Kemeny's weighted median as another type of the metric one. A new procedure is developed for the linear combination of experts' rankings to build the weighted median.

Keywords: Kemeny's median · Ranking · Metrics

1 The Classic Kemeny's Median

The most popular aggregation principle is the majority rule. It is proved, if the majority relation is transitive then it appears to be the median. For a set of rankings, this median is the ranking too with the least distance to others. This median is known as the Kemeny's median. There are different algorithms to find the Kemeny's median. One version of the locally optimal algorithm calculates the special loss matrix.

Let $A = \{a_1, \ldots a_N\}$ be some unordered set of alternatives. Let a ranking P be defined as an ordering of alternatives with a preference ($\succ$) or indistinguishability ($\sim$) relations between them. Therefore, the ranking P can be presented by the relation matrix $M(N, N)$ with elements

$$m_{ij} = \begin{cases} 1, & a_i \succ a_j \\ 0, & a_i \sim a_j \\ -1, & a_i \prec a_j . \end{cases}$$

Let two rankings P_u and P_v be presented by relation matrices M_u and M_v with the distance between them under the same numeration in A:

$$d(P_u, P_v) = \frac{1}{2} \sum_{i=1}^{N} \sum_{j=1}^{N} |m_{ij}^u - m_{ij}^v|. \tag{1}$$

It is known, this is the metric value for binary relations in (quasi)ordinal scales, i.e. for rankings [1].

© Springer Nature Switzerland AG 2021
A. Del Bimbo et al. (Eds.): ICPR 2020 Workshops, LNCS 12665, pp. 97–102, 2021.
https://doi.org/10.1007/978-3-030-68821-9_9

Let n individual preferences (rankings) be given. It needs to find a group relation P coordinated in a certain way with relations $P_1, \ldots P_n$. Methods to find a group relation are usually denoted as concordance principles. It is proved, the group transitive relation (or transformed to it) is the median, specifically, the Kemeny's one. The median P^* is the ranking with the least distance to other rankings

$$P^* = \arg\min_P \sum_{u=1}^{n} d(P, P_u). \qquad (2)$$

There are different algorithms to find the Kemeny's median. One version of the locally optimal algorithm to find the Kemeny's median calculates the loss matrix $Q(N, N)$ for N alternatives [2].

Let some ranking P and experts' rankings $P_1, \ldots P_n$ be presented by relation matrices M and $M_1, \ldots M_n$. The total distance from P to all other rankings is defined by

$$\sum_{u=1}^{n} d(P, P_u) = \frac{1}{2} \sum_{i=1}^{N} \sum_{j=1}^{N} \sum_{u=1}^{n} d_{ij}(P, P_u)$$

with partial distances defined under conditions $m_{ij} = 1$ as

$$d_{ij}(P, P_u) = |m_{ij} - m_{ij}^u| = \begin{cases} 0, & m_{ij}^u = 1 \\ 1, & m_{ij}^u = 0 \\ 2, & m_{ij}^u = -1 \end{cases}.$$

The loss matrix element $q_{ij} = \sum_{u=1}^{n} d_{ij}(P, P_u)$ defines the total mismatch losses of the preference $a_i \succ a_j$ in the unknown ranking P relative to corresponding preferences in rankings $P_1, \ldots P_n$.

The Kemeny's algorithm finds the ordering of alternatives to minimize the sum of elements above the main diagonal of the loss matrix Q, and consists of the follows.

The matrix Q is reduced step-by-step by eliminating the line (and corresponding column) with the minimal sum of losses in the line. The corresponding alternative takes the last place in the ordered line of alternatives. The result is the so-called ranking P_{I}. In a sequential reverse scan, it is checked the correspondence between preferences in the ranking ($a_i \succ a_j$) and penalties in the loss matrix ($q_{ij} \leq q_{ji}$). In a case of violation, the current pair of alternatives is reversed. The final result is the so-called ranking P_{II}, i.e. the Kemeny's median [2].

2   The Kemeny's Metric Median

Let the distance matrix $D(n, n)$ be calculated between all pairs of rankings according to (1). According to it, the set $P_1, \ldots P_n$ of rankings is considered like points immersed into Euclidean space as an unordered set.

If metric violations have not occurred in the set configuration, then it is known, the scalar product matrix calculated relative to some origin appears to be the positive definite or nonnegative definite at least [3].

According to the Torgerson's method of principal projections [4], it is suitable to use the center element of the given set as the origin. This center element P_0 can be presented by distances to other rankings

$$d^2(P_0, P_i) = d_{0i}^2 = \frac{1}{n} \sum_{p=1}^{n} d_{ip}^2 - \frac{1}{2n^2} \sum_{p=1}^{n} \sum_{q=1}^{n} d_{pq}^2, \quad i = 1, \ldots n. \tag{3}$$

The central element P_0 is the least distant from other elements in the set like the median P^* and needs to satisfy (2) as well as a ranking. Nevertheless, the median P^* is represented both by distances (1) to other rankings and by the ranking itself, while the central element P_0 is represented only by distances (3) and it doesn't exist as a ranking.

From the mathematical point of view, these points must coincide with each other $P^* = P_0$. In this case, the well-known clustering and machine learning algorithms (for example, k-means, etc.) developed for pair comparisons [5, 6] can be correctly used instead of discrete optimization ones for ordinal scales.

The monotonic transformation is correct for ordinal scales and consists in reallocations of alternatives on a numerical axis without changing their ordering relative to each other. In general, the center P_0 and the ranking P^* are both presented by their own distances to other elements $P_1, \ldots P_n$. Based on the monotonic transformation, we can show that the ranking P^* is equivalent by distances to the center P_0.

We denote as the Kemeny's metric median P_0^* the Kemeny's median P^* with the same distances to other rankings like the center P_0 has. We use the Kemeny's algorithm to find it.

Let points P_u, P_0, and P^* be given, where $\delta = d(P_0, P_u) - d(P^*, P_u) \neq 0$. There are two cases of the δ value, if P_0 and P^* are similar each other as rankings [7].

1. The case of $\delta > 0$. To compensate this difference, it is necessary to uniformly distribute this value between all nonzero elements of M_u and to calculate the new relation matrix $\tilde{M}_u$ with elements

$$\tilde{m}_{ij}^u = \begin{cases} +1 + 2\delta/k, & a_i \succ a_j \\ 0, & a_i \sim a_j \\ -1 - 2\delta/k, & a_i \prec a_j, \end{cases}$$

where $k = N^2 - N - N_0$ is the general number of nonzero elements in M_u without the main diagonal, N_0 is the number of zero non-diagonal elements $m_{ij}^u = 0$ in M_u. This new relation matrix $\tilde{M}_u$ doesn't change the expert's ranking P_u.

The value $2\delta/k$ is used, since in (1) all differences are used twice. It is necessary to correct nonzero elements only, since each zero element indicates two alternatives are on the same place in the expert's ranking. Hence, the distance between the modified median and the other ranking increases to compensate $\delta > 0$. In this case, for $m_{ij} = 1$ the preference $a_i \succ a_j$ in the unknown ranking P is penalized by the expert's ranking P_u to form partial distances

$$d_{ij}(P, P_u) = \begin{cases} 0 + 2\delta/k, & \tilde{m}_{ij}^u = +1 + 2\delta/k \\ 1, & \tilde{m}_{ij}^u = 0 \\ 2 + 2\delta/k, & \tilde{m}_{ij}^u = -1 - 2\delta/k. \end{cases}$$

2. The case of $-1 < 2\delta/k' < 0$. To remove this difference, it is necessary to uniformly distribute this value between nonzero elements in M_u too. Additionally, the number of modified elements in M_u is decreased to $k' = k - \Delta k$, where Δk is the number of coinciding elements $m_{ij}^u = m_{ij}^*$ in relation matrices M_u and M^*. Indeed, the partial distance is zero $d_{ij}(P^*, P_u) = 0$ in this case and any negative additive to m_{ij}^u obligatory increases the distance between P_u and P^*.

To get the unchanged expert's ranking P_u, it is necessary to calculate the new relation matrix $\tilde{M}_u$ with elements

$$\tilde{m}_{ij}^u = \begin{cases} +1 - |2\delta/k'|, & a_i \succ a_j \\ 0, & a_i \sim a_j \\ -1 + |2\delta/k'|, & a_i \prec a_j \\ m_{ij}^*, & m_{ij}^u = m_{ij}^*. \end{cases}$$

For $m_{ij} = 1$ the preference $a_i \succ a_j$ in the unknown ranking P is penalized by the expert's ranking P_u to form partial distances

$$d_{ij}(P, P_u) = \begin{cases} 0, & \tilde{m}_{ij}^u = 1 \\ 1, & \tilde{m}_{ij}^u = 0 \\ 0 + |2\delta/k'|, & \tilde{m}_{ij}^u = +1 - |2\delta/k'| \\ 2 - |2\delta/k'|, & \tilde{m}_{ij}^u = -1 + |2\delta/k'|. \end{cases}$$

As a result, the metric median has the following main properties. In general case, the Kemeny's metric median isn't obligatory coincides with the classic Kemeny's median as the binary relation. There is not a contradiction, since the metric median only clarifies the classic median. Namely, previously indistinguishable alternatives usually become distinguishable, while positions of previously distinguishable alternatives are not changed relative to each other.

The metric median as the ranking P_0^* can be finally presented by its relation matrix M_0^* with distances (1) to other rankings presented by their relation matrices M_u, $u = 1, \ldots n$. Unfortunately, such distances differ again from distances of the center P_0 to other rankings. In order to preserve "metric" distances, it is necessary to remember all modified experts' relation matrices $\tilde{M}_u$, $u = 1, \ldots n$.

It isn't so convenient sometimes. Moreover, changes in the expert group (for example, a reduction by one) change the Kemeny's median and, consequently, change the modified relation matrices of the remaining experts.

3   The Kemeny's Weighted Median

Usually, weights are considered as experts' competences and determine the proportion of taking their opinions into account in the group decision. Different techniques are developed to determine a competence level, for example in [8].

Let $w_1 \geq 0, \ldots w_n \geq 0$, where $\sum_{u=1}^{n} w_u = 1$, be weights of expert opinions. An element q_{ij} is defined as $q_{ij} = \sum_{u=1}^{n} w_u d_{ij}(P, P_u)$ for the weighted loss matrix

$Q(N, N) = \sum_{u=1}^{n} w_u Q_u(N, N)$. In this case, the problem (2) is solved actually with weighted partial distances defined under conditions $m_{ij} = 1$ as

$$\tilde{d}_{ij}(P, P_u) = w_u d_{ij}(P, P_u) = w_u |m_{ij} - m_{ij}^u| = \begin{cases} 0, & m_{ij}^u = 1 \\ w_u, & m_{ij}^u = 0 \\ 2w_u, & m_{ij}^u = -1 \end{cases}.$$

It is possible to find any ranking within the convex hull of a given set $P_1, \ldots P_n$ by a linear combination of individual rankings as elements of a discrete set. In particular, any individual ranking can be found as the Kemeny's median $P^* = P_i$ for weights $w_i = 1$, $w_{j \neq i} = 0, j = 1, \ldots n$.

The classic Kemeny's median can be found with weights $w_i = 1/n, \quad i = 1, \ldots n$. Moreover, it is the same Kemeny's median with any $w_i = const > 0$, and the inverted one with $w_i = const < 0, \quad i = 1, \ldots n$.

The problem to find the Kemeny's weighted median is formulated as follows. Let rankings be presented by the distance matrix $D(n, n)$, the center P_0 be presented by distances $d(P_0, P_u)$, $u = 1, \ldots n$, and the Kemeny's median be presented by distances $d(P^*, P_u)$, $u = 1, \ldots n$. Such distances define deviations $\delta_u = d(P_0, P_u) - d(P^*, P_u)$, $u = 1, \ldots n$.

4 Weights Searching

It needs to solve the optimization problem under constraints:

$$\sum_{u=1}^{n} \delta_u^2 \to \min, \quad \sum_{u=1}^{n} w_u = 1, \quad w_u \geq 0, \quad u = 1, \ldots n.$$

This procedure is based on the Gauss-Seidel coordinate descent algorithm, where each expert determines a "coordinate" axis. The changing in the weight of the expert's individual loss matrix $Q_u(N, N)$ in the range from 0 to 1 is considered as a variation of the correspondent coordinate axis.

At the beginning, all n experts' weights are changed from $1/(n-1), \ldots 0, \ldots 1/(n-1)$ for completely excluded loss matrix Q_u, till weights $0, \ldots 1, \ldots 0$ for the loss matrix Q_u only. Each step ends after weight variations for all experts with selecting the "optimal" expert with the number u^* for the total deviation $\sum_{u=1}^{n} \delta_u^2 \to \min$.

At the next step, the weight of the loss matrix Q_u varies in the interval $0 \leq p \leq 1$. It defines the normalized weight $w_u = p$. Other loss matrices have constant weights $q_i, \quad i = 1, \ldots n, i \neq u$ with the constant sum $V = \sum_{i=1}^{n} q_i, \quad i \neq u$.

The normalized weights of the loss matrices for other rankings vary in the range from $w_i = q_i/V$ to $w_i = 0$, taking values $w_i = q_i(1 - p)/V$ within the range of variation. Initial weights $p = q_u, q_i, \quad i = 1, \ldots n, i \neq u$ correspond to the inner point of the variation interval $w_i = q_i, \quad i = 1, \ldots n$. The Kemeny's median is calculated for the linear combination of losses $Q(N, N) = \sum_{u=1}^{n} w_u Q_u(N, N)$, and deviations $\delta_u, \quad u = 1, \ldots n$ are defined.

In such problem statement, the solution does not guarantee that the distance difference from the center P_0 and the weighted median P_0^w to other rankings becomes zero. In this case, it is required to take this weighted median as the original one, and find the metric median by modifying the experts' relation matrices.

5 Conclusion

The considered types of Kemeny's median allow correct solving of important tasks appeared in the problem of rank aggregation: coordination of individual rankings, identifying of conflicting opinions, and reaching consensus.

The classical Kemeny's median is one of relevant methods for solving the problem of ranks aggregation. However, rankings are discrete objects and after immersion in a continuous metric space, they form a set of isolated points (there is nothing between them). In this situation, the metric and weighted Kemeny's medians allow refinement of the group ranking relative to the correct arithmetic mean of the set of points representing individual rankings.

In the case of conflicting opinions, the classical Kemeny's median often contains many indistinguishable alternatives. Using of metric medians reduces the number of such alternatives, i.e. improves the quality of a group ranking. Immersion of rankings in the metric space allows identifying of groups of experts with very different opinions as a solution of the clustering problem. For this purpose, it is convenient to apply, for example, the well-known k-means algorithm (in the appropriate metric form) in contrast to usually complex discrete optimization algorithms. Then, for average objects of each cluster the group ranking is defined as the metric or weighted Kemeny's median.

Finally, to rich a consensus, it is necessary to determine weights of individual opinions or groups as a solution of the problem of opinion competence. Using of the weighted Kemeny's median allows more accurate taking into account of conflicting opinions in the right proportion. It is also improves the quality of the group decision compared to the case, when only the most competent individual or group opinions are used.

Acknowledgments. This work is supported by the Russian Foundation for Basic Research (RFBR) under Grants 20-07-00055, 18-07-01087, 18-07-00942.

References

1. Kemeny, J., Snell, J.: Mathematical Models in the Social Sciences. Blaisdell, New York (1963)
2. Litvak, B.G.: Expert Information: Methods of Acquisition and Analysis. Radio i Svyaz, Moscow (1982). In Russian
3. Young, G., Housholder, A.: Discussion of a set of points in terms of their mutual distances. Psychometrica **3**(1), 19–22 (1938)
4. Torgerson, W.: Theory and methods of scaling. John Wiley, NY (1958)
5. Dvoenko, S.D.: Clustering and separating of a set of members in terms of mutual distances and similarities. Trans. MLDM **2**(2), 80–99 (2009)
6. Dvoenko, S., Owsinski, J.: The permutable k-means for the bi-partial criterion. Informatica **43**, 253–262 (2019). https://doi.org/10.31449/inf.v43i2.2090
7. Dvoenko, S., Pshenichny, D.: On a metric Kemeny's median. In: Strijov, V.V., Ignatov, D.I., Vorontsov, K.V. (eds.) IDP 2016. CCIS, vol. 794, pp. 44–57. Springer, Cham (2019). https://doi.org/10.1007/978-3-030-35400-8_4
8. Mirkin, B.G.: The Problem of a Group Choice. Nauka, Moscow (1974). In Russian

Image Decomposition Based on Region-Constrained Smoothing

Pavel A. Chochia$^{(\boxtimes)}$ (iD)

Institute for Information Transmission Problems Russian Academy of Sciences,
Bolshoy Karetny per. 19, Moscow 127051, Russia
chochia@iitp.ru

Abstract. The task of image decomposition is to split an image into piecewise smooth structural and difference texture-noise components. It is used in many tasks of video information processing and analyzing. The problem of decomposition is to provide independent smoothing in each of the structural regions of the image and to preserve the signal structure. Most of the known methods of decomposition and smoothing are based on analysis of measurable parameters of the local image area, for example, the distribution of signal values. These data does not reflect image area characteristics well enough. Obvious criterion for spatial limiting of the analyzed area is the belonging of the target and surrounding points to the same image spatial area. A sufficient criterion for the connectivity of the points in a region is the absence of contour edges between them. The article proposes an approach to the construction of a decomposition algorithm based on a preliminary delineation of image areas by detecting contours between them and subsequent contour-limited smoothing inside each of the areas. The concept of *similarity* of points in the image is introduced, on the basis of which the smoothing algorithm is built. Experimental comparisons of the proposed algorithm with other well-known smoothing algorithms are carried out.

Keywords: Image decomposition · Image smoothing · Structure preservation · Region-constrained smoothing · Similarity factor

1 Introduction

The decomposition operation aims at dividing an image signal into smoothed and difference components. As an operation of signal filtering, it is used to solve many problems of processing and analyzing of video information. Its purpose, as a rule, is to suppress noise and texture while extracting the structure of the image, i.e. contained objects, their shape, average brightness and edge differences. Most of the known methods and algorithms focused on smoothing within extended objects do not use direct data on the spatial structure of the image, which carries information about the position and characteristics of contour steps, but are limited to indirect information, for example, a change in the type of distribution of signal values. Typically, such an analysis is performed during the smoothing process and using the same data to be smoothed.

© Springer Nature Switzerland AG 2021
A. Del Bimbo et al. (Eds.): ICPR 2020 Workshops, LNCS 12665, pp. 103–111, 2021.
https://doi.org/10.1007/978-3-030-68821-9_10

The problem of image smoothing while preserving its structure is close to the segmentation problem and is essentially related to the issue of drawing the boundaries between regions in the image. In some sense, the tasks of segmentation and drawing contour lines are dual to each other, from which it follows, that one of them can be solved with the helps of solving the other. If no strict fulfillment of topological conditions is required, such as: closeness, minimum thickness, and others, then the detection of contour steps in the image in most cases do not cause difficulties. As shown below, this information is very useful in solving the decomposition.

2 Filtering Methods Preserving Image Structure

Recently, it is ordinarily to consider an image as a sum of *structural* and *textural* components. In this case, it is assumed that the structural component carries the main brightness and contour information, and the texture component contains the difference information. This repeats the well-known point of view [1], according to which image smoothing is interpreted as removing the texture component [2], and enhancement as strengthening the texture [3]. This approach corresponds to the image model [3], according to which the received signal is described by the formula

$$f(z) = s(z) + t(z) + \xi(z), \tag{1}$$

which consider the image $f(z)$ in the space of coordinates $z \in Z \subset \mathbb{R}^2$ (for simplicity, we will omit the two-coordinate indexing). Here $f(z)$ is represented by the sum of components: piecewise-smooth $s(z)$, defining extended objects of the image, texture $t(z)$ and noise $\xi(z)$ ones. The problem of decomposition of the signal $f(z)$ can be formulated as separation the mixture to components $s(z)$ and $t(z) + \xi(z)$ [3]. Representation (1) is typical for classification problems using statistical models. In many cases, they are solved based on the distribution of element values over the analysis area.

An important step in solving the problem of image smoothing was the appearance of the sigma filter Lee [5, 6]:

$$s(x) = \int_Z f(z) D(x - z) B(f(x) - f(z)) dz \bigg/ \int_Z D(x - z) B(f(x) - f(z)) dz. \tag{2}$$

Here $f(z)$ is the signal value at the point z, $D(d)$ and $B(b)$ are the spatial (distance) and brightness analysis windows: $D(d) = 1$, if $|d| \leq \delta$, and $D(d) = 0$ otherwise; $B(b) = 1$, if $|b| \leq \sigma$, and $B(b) = 0$ otherwise. 2δ and 2σ are the sizes of the analysis windows in the spatial domain and in the range of values, respectively.

The evolution of the sigma filter was an algorithm of two-scale decomposition [3, 7] into the components $s(z)$ and $t(z) + \xi(z)$ according to (1). It differs in that it uses spatial and brightness analysis windows of several scales and has a parameter for assigning image details to a structural or texture-noise component.

The bilateral filtering algorithm [8] was also a development of the sigma filter (2). Its difference is that the functions of the analysis windows $D(d)$ and $B(b)$ can have any values in the range [0,1]. As a rule, the larger d and b, the smaller the values of $D(d)$ and

$B(b)$. Most often, Gaussian functions are used for this:

$$D(x-z) = k \exp\{-\|x-z\|^2 / 2\delta^2\},$$
$$B(f(x)-f(z)) = k \exp\{-\|f(x)-f(z)\|^2 / 2\sigma^2\}.$$

(3)

By the choice of the averaging set, the closest to the approach proposed below are the methods of smoothing along geodesic lines [9], that consider the signal $f(z)$ as a surface in the region Z. For each $z \in Z$, in the analysis window on the surface $f(z)$, a geodetic line $G(x, z)$ from the target point x is found, which has the length $L(G(x,z))$. To set the weight, the function $\psi(t)$, $t \geq 0$, is selected rapidly decreasing with increasing t, for example, $\psi(t) = \exp\{-kt\}$. The smoothing filter then looks like:

$$s(x) = \int_Z f(z)\psi(L(G(x, z)))\, dz \Big/ \int_Z \psi(L(G(x, z)))\, dz.$$

(4)

The main difficulty of methods based on geodesics is finding those for each of the possible pairs of points. The presence of noise makes it difficult to find the optimum. For grayscale images, the task is complicated by the need to combine the distances in the spatial domain and in the brightness domain.

Among other smoothing methods focused on preserving contour steps, we note the mean shift algorithm [10], based on Parzen smoothing [11] and using an iterative calculation scheme. Also interesting is the approach [4], in which a transformation is found that reduces the dimension of the data space, but preserves the distance between the characteristics of the image details. In [12], to limit the range of smoothing, it is proposed to use contours for constructing binary indicator functions.

3 An Approach to Region-Constrained Smoothing

The problem of smoothing preserving the object boundaries can be formulated as the choice of the variety of points over which the averaging will be performed. According to the model [3], such a set should be constrained by the boundaries of the region containing the target point. In most number of smoothing methods, spatial constraints are overridden by range constraints. But the criterion for limiting the averaging area should not be the difference in the values of the target point and its surroundings, but the fact that these points belong to the same connected area of the image.

Assessment of the belonging of points to one area requires the choice of some parameter of their "connectivity". For this, below we will enter the *similarity factor* for a pair of points. The evaluation criterion should be the presence or absence of contour steps between the points. The presence and magnitude of such steps will make it possible to assess the degree of interrelation of the points.

Therefore, a new approach to solving the problem of smoothing is proposed, in which the *averaging area* is constrained by contour lines (boundaries) between image areas. At the same time, the boundaries are not subject to the requirements of topological correctness, continuity, closure, etc. As such a partition, it is proposed to use a *contour steps map*, which can be formed from the smoothable image itself using gradient operators, or in another way.

4 Similarity Factor

The image $f(z)$ is considered as a surface in the coordinate space $\{z_v, z_h\} \equiv \{z\}$ with a gradient $\mathbf{g}(z)$ at the point z. The characteristics of the gradient are the amplitude $g(z) \geq 0$ and the direction $\varphi(z)$ of the vector:

$$g(z) = \left((g_v(z))^2 + (g_h(z))^2\right)^{1/2}, \quad \varphi(z) = \text{arctg}\{g_v(z)/g_h(z)\}, \tag{5}$$

where $g_v(z)$ and $g_h(z)$ are the gradients of $f(z)$ in the vertical and horizontal directions. The amplitude $g(z)$ serves as a criterion for the belonging of the point z to contour step or to inner part of the object and is the basis for formation of the *control signal* in the smoothing algorithm.

Let us introduce the "similarity" characteristic of a pair of points, determined by the proximity of their values and the presence of contour steps between them. Let us define the *similarity factor* of points x and y, mediated to the segment $[x,y]$ connecting them as the value $A[x,y]$, $(0 \leq A \leq 1)$, depending on the gradients $f(z)$ on the segment $z \in [x, y]$, and equal to 1 in the case of $f(z) = $ const. The value $A[x,y]$ is defined as the product of individual similarity factors a_n $(0 \leq a_n \leq 1)$ on successive n sections of the segment $[x,y]$:

$$A[x, y] = a_1 \cdot a_2 \cdot \ldots \cdot a_N. \tag{6}$$

The similarity factor $A[x,y]$ in its meaning corresponds to the transmittance of the medium in the segment $[x,y]$, and the dependence (6) coincides with the law of attenuation of light when passing through an absorbing medium. In discrete space, we can talk about the *similarity factor at a point* $a(z)$, which satisfies the relation:

$$A[x, z] = a(z)A[x, z - 1], z \in [x, y]. \tag{7}$$

Consider a section of the function $f(z)$ on the segment $z \in [x, y]$. Assuming that the necessary conditions of continuity and smoothness are satisfied, the similarity factor $a(z)$ should decrease with increasing modulus of the gradient $g(z) = |f'(z)|$ at the point. We choose the following relation as a simple model for $a(z)$:

$$a(z) = 1 - g(z)/g_{Max} \text{ if } g(z) \leq g_{Max}, \text{ and } a(z) = 1 \text{ if } g(z) > g_{Max}, \tag{8}$$

where g_{Max} is the maximum allowable level for the gradient values $g(z)$.

Thus, having found the values of $a(z)$ at each point z of the image, it is easy to calculate the similarity factor $A[x,y]$ in (6) for any segment $[x,y]$. Note that $A[x,y]$ is a commutative function, that is, $A[x,y] = A[y,x]$. From (6)–(8) one can see the importance of the structure of gradients $g(z)$ in the image, on the basis of which the set of similarity factors $A[x,y]$ is formed.

According to the image model [3], the distribution $P\{|g|\}$ reflects the sum of two sets. It contains a peak in the region of small values of $|g|$, corresponding to the interior points of the image regions and generated by the mixture $t(z) + \xi(z)$ in (1). Long "tail" in the region of large $|g|$ reflects the $g_C(z)$ gradients at the contour steps. For our task, the parameters of this distribution are important. First, we find the point of maximum of

$P\{|g|\}$, which we denote by v_{Max}. Assuming that the distribution $|g|$ for the components $t(z) + \xi(z)$ is close to symmetric, we take the point $(2v_{Max} + \varepsilon)$ as its right margin. The values of $P\{|g|\}$ on the segment $[0, v_{Max}]$ are set to zero, and in the range $[v_{Max}, 2v_{Max} + \varepsilon]$, are replaced by linearly increasing values from 0 to $P\{2v_{Max} + \varepsilon\}$. According to the obtained approximate graph of the probability density $|g_C(z)|$ we construct the distribution function of the modulus of contour component gradient $F_C\{x\} = P\{|g_C| < x\}$.

To determine the correction range $[v_L, v_R]$, the values of lower and upper boundaries of the distribution range are set a priori as $M_{Bot} = 0.2$ and $M_{Top} = 0.9$. Then, the values of v_L and v_R are found from the distribution function $F_C\{x\}$ as:

$$v_L = F_C\{M_{Bot}\} \text{ and } v_R = F_C\{M_{Top}\}.$$

Based on v_L and v_R, the grayscale transformation function $\gamma(v)$ is constructed:

$$\gamma(v) = 0 \text{ for } v < v_L, \ \gamma(v) = 1 \text{ for } v > v_R, \text{ and } \gamma(v) = (v-v_L)/(v_R-v_L) \text{ otherwise.}$$

$\gamma(v)$ is used to correct the gradient map:

$$g_C(z) = \gamma(g(z)).$$

Thus, $0 \leq g_C(z) \leq 1$, and the similarity (7) at a point z is calculated as

$$a(z) = 1 - g_C(z).$$

Knowing $a(z)$ for all $z \in Z$, according to formulas (6)–(8) find $A[x,y]$ for the required segment $[x,y]$.

5 Filtering Based on Similarity Factor

The filtering problem is to find the value of the piecewise smooth component $s(z)$ in (1). For a point that at the moment of analysis is target and denoted by 0, local analysis is carried out over the surrounding fragment Ω. Point 0 will also be called the *center* point of the fragment.

We introduce the weight function $q(d) = q(d(0,z))$, $z \in \Omega$, where $d = d(0,z)$ is the distance from point 0 to point z. As such, it is convenient to take the Gaussian function: $q(d) = \exp\{-d^2/2\delta^2\}$. The weight coefficient of the point $z \in \Omega$ is defined as the product of the similarity indicator and the weight function:

$$w(z) = A(0, z)q(d(0, z)).$$

The value $f(z)w(z)dz$ is the contribution of the neighborhood dz of the point z to the total sum.

The total weight of the elements of the fragment Ω surrounding the central point is

$$W(\Omega) = \int_{\Omega} w(z)dz.$$

Then the resulting smoothed value $s(0)$ written to point 0 is calculated as:

$$s(0) = \int_{\Omega} f(z)w(z)dz \Big/ W(\Omega). \qquad (9)$$

6 Experiments

To compare the quality of smoothing algorithms that preserve the contour steps, the test signal was generated, which contains three horizontal stripes of constant and linearly varying brightness values with a vertical contour in the middle. An additive Gaussian noise with variance of $\sigma = 20$ gradations was added to this signal.

The noisy signal was smoothed out by different filters with approximately equal parameters. Comparison of the results of smoothing demonstrates that almost all algorithms (except for the contour-constrained one) one iteration is completely insufficient to suppress such a strong noise. Three iterations almost always reveal acceptable smoothing of extended areas (except for a sigma filter with an unsatisfactory result), but in some cases the contour boundaries are noticeably distorted and blurred.

Table 1. Signal noise level estimates (in gray scales).

Smoothing filter	1 iteration			3 iterations		
	RMS	Tonelli	Kronrod	RMS	Tonelli	Kronrod
Source signal with noise	19.88	11641	386.3	–	–	–
Sigma filter	11.16	8642	289.3	3.74	896	23.09
Bilateral filter	11.50	6526	216.9	4.72	457	7.83
Two-scale decomposition	9.29	4220	111.0	3.10	298	4.23
Geodetic filter	9.34	4077	107.8	3.59	302	2.24
Contour-constrained filter	3.38	601	6.87	2.27	203	0.96

Table 1 demonstrates the numerical values of residual distortions measured by the difference between the original undistorted and noisy signals filtered by smoothing algorithms. The data are presented after one and three iterations. The following values were measured: root-mean-square deviation (RMS), two-dimensional variation of Tonelli [13, 15] and the first Kronrod variation (W_1) [14, 15]. The experiments demonstrate that the known filters do not suppress noise well enough in the case of one iteration: the worst parameters are for the sigma filter and bilateral filter; the decomposition algorithm and geodesic filter have twice better values compared to them. The contour-constrained smoothing has significantly higher characteristic. It is easy to see that three iterations can significantly improve the results of all smoothing filters, but the qualitative relationships between the algorithms have changed little. As one can see, the proposed contour-constrained smoothing algorithm (9) demonstrates significantly better performance compared to other filters.

Figure 1 and 2 demonstrate examples of image decomposition using the contour-constrained smoothing algorithm (9) after one iteration. Versions: 'a' – original images; 'b' – contour-constrained smoothing with the analysis window size of 11 × 11 elements, 'c' – enlarged fragments of smoothed images. One can see the preservation of the smallest details with almost complete noise suppression.

Fig. 1. a) Original image "Girl"; b) smoothed image; c) fragment of smoothed image.

Fig. 2. a) Original image "Kremlin"; b) smoothed image; c) fragment of smoothed image.

7 Conclusion

Unlike most smoothing methods, in which for the restriction of the averaging set the difference in signal values is used, in our case, a similarity factor for a pair of points is introduced, which depends only on the presence and magnitude of contour steps at the line between points. Based on the concept of the similarity factor and the method for its calculation, a new algorithm for contour-constrained image smoothing has been developed, which preserves the signal structure. It is shown that in comparison with other known smoothing algorithms, the efficiency of the proposed algorithm is the highest. The results are demonstrated on test and real data.

The developed algorithm is applicable to images with any number of channels — monochrome, color, or multispectral ones, the statistical characteristics of the channels of which may differ significantly. The stages of diagnostics and smoothing are separated, therefore diagnostics, i.e. the calculation of the similarity factor $A(0,z)$ can be carried out over any combination of color or multispectral image channels, or even on the basis of other data substantially related with the processed image. The resulting factor $A(0,z)$ is then applied to all image channels.

It is also possible to transform the components of a color image into another color space (for example, from *RGB* to *HSI*, *Lab* or other ones), obtain the general contour picture (more often over the brightness component), independently smooth each of the components, and convert the aggregate back to *RGB* format. The proposed approach avoids the problem of differences in the characteristics of individual channels, which requires changes in the smoothing parameters from channel to channel. Another possible option may be an application to the analyzed image some independently obtained contour picture, for example, from another image combined with it, or, moreover, from a map.

References

1. Nishikawa, S., Massa, R.J., Mott-Smith J.C.: Area properties of television pictures. IEEE Trans. IT **11**(3), 348–352 (1965)
2. Jeon, J., Lee, H., Kang, H., Lee, S.: Scale-aware structure-preserving texture filtering. Comput. Graph. Forum **35**(7), 77–86. Eurographs Association & John Wiley, GBR, Chichester (2016)
3. Chochia, P.A.: Methods for Processing of Video Information on the Basis of Two-Scale Image Model. Lambert Academic Publ., Saarbrucken, LAP (2017). [in Russian]
4. Gastal E.S.L., Oliveira M.M. Domain transform for edge-aware image and video processing. In: Proceedings of SIGGRAPH, ACM Transaction on Graphics vol. 30, no. 4, pp. 1–12 (2011)
5. Lee, J.-S.: Digital image smoothing and the sigma filter. Comput. Vis. Graph. Image Process. **24**(2), 255–269 (1983)
6. Mastin, G.A.: Adaptive filters for digital image noise smoothing: an evaluation. Comput. Vis. Graph. Image Process. **31**(1), 103–121 (1985)
7. Chochia, P.A.: Image enhancement using sliding histograms. Comput. Vis. Graph. Image Process. **44**(2), 211–229 (1988)
8. Tomasi, C., Manduchi, R.: Bilateral filtering for gray and color images. In: Proceeding IEEE 6th International Conference on Computer Vision, pp. 839–846. IEEE, Bombay, India (1998)
9. Criminisi, A., Sharp, T., Blake, A.: Geos: geodesic image segmentation. In: Computer Vision – ECCV 2008, pp. 99–112. Springer (2008)

10. Comaniciu, D., Meer, P.: Mean shift analysis and applications. In: Proceeding 7th IEEE International Conference on Computer Vision, vol. 2, pp. 1197–1203. Kerkyra, Greece (1999)
11. Parzen, E.: On estimation of a probability density function and model. Ann. Math. Statistics **33**, 1065–1076 (1962)
12. Abiko, R., Ikehara, M.: Fast edge preserving 2D smoothing filter using indicator function. IEICE Trans. Inf. Syst. **E102D**(10), 2025–2032 (2019)
13. Mathematical Encyclopedia. vols. 1–5. Sov. Entsiklopediya, Moscow (1977). [in Russian]
14. Kronrod, A.S.: On functions of two variables. Uspehi Matematicheskih Nauk **5**(1), 24–134 (1950). [in Russian]
15. Chochia, P.A., Milukova, O.P.: Comparison of two-dimensional variations in the context of the digital image complexity assessment. J. Commun. Technol. Electron. **60**(12), 1432–1440 (2015)

Machine Learning Based on Minimizing Robust Mean Estimates

Zaur M. Shibzukhov[1,2]([⊠]) and Timofey A. Semenov[2]

[1] Moscow Institute of Physics and Technology, Moscow, Russia
intellimath@mail.ru
[2] Institute of Mathematics and Informatics MPSU, Moscow, Russia

Abstract. The article considers the approach to the construction of robust methods and machine learning algorithms, which are based on the principle of minimizing estimates of average values that are insensitive to outliers. Proposed machine learning algorithms are based on the principle of iterative reweighting. Illustrative examples show the ability of the proposed approach and algorithms to overcome the influense of outliers.

Keywords: Machine learning · Robust estimate · Image analysis · Data analysis

1 Introduction

Machine learning tasks are often formulated as tasks of minimizing the weighted sums of parameterized functions:

$$Q(\mathbf{w}) = \sum_{k=1}^{N} v_k \ell_k(\mathbf{w}), \tag{1}$$

where Q is the objective function, $\mathbf{w}$ is unknown parameter vector of the model to be optimized, $v_1, \ldots, v_N$ are sample weights, $\ell_k(\mathbf{w})$ $(1 \leqslant k \leqslant N)$ is a parameterized basic function that evaluate the contribution of the k-th object of the training sample.

Usually $\ell_k(\mathbf{w}) = \varrho(r_k(\mathbf{w}))$, where $r_k(\mathbf{w})$ is the value of the model inconsistency for the k-th object, $\varrho(r)$ is a function that calculates the contribution of the residual to the value of the objective function. For example:

1) in the regression problem $r_k(\mathbf{w})$ is the error value for k-th object;
2) in the 2-class classification problem $r_k(\mathbf{w})$ is the margin value for k-th object;
3) in the centers based clusterization problem $r_k(\mathbf{w})$ is the distance value from the k-th object to nearest center.

If the sample weights are not specified, then $v_1 = \cdots = v_N = 1/N$ is usually selected. In this case

$$Q(\mathbf{w}) = \frac{1}{N} \sum_{k=1}^{N} \ell_k(\mathbf{w}). \tag{2}$$

This work was supported by grant RFBR 18-01-00050.

The optimal parameter vector $\mathbf{w}^*$ should minimize the objective function $\mathcal{Q}$:

$$\mathbf{w}^* = \arg\min_{\mathbf{w}} \mathcal{Q}(\mathbf{w}) + \tau\mathcal{R}(\mathbf{w}), \tag{3}$$

where $\mathcal{R}(\mathbf{w})$ is a regularizer, $\tau > 0$ is a regularization parameter.

1.1 Outliers Problem

In the standard setting with minimizing the *arithmetic mean* (AM) (2), a problem may arise if the empirical distribution of the values of the basis functions $\{z_1, \ldots, z_N\}$, where $z_k = \ell_k(\mathbf{w})$ $(1 \leqslant k \leqslant N)$, contains outliers. This can usually happen for the following reasons:

1) the training sample contains highly distorted data, which makes them inadequate in relation to the problem being solved;
2) the training sample contains data that are substantially inadequate for the selected models.

Under these conditions, minimization of the objective function $\mathcal{Q}(\mathbf{w})$, constructed over the entire training sample, usually leads to a distortion of the desired model parameters. This is due to the fact that the AM is sensitive to outliers.

If we minimize $\mathcal{Q}(\mathbf{w})$ for the part of the training sample that does not contain inadequate data corresponding to outliers, then we can obtain adequate assessment of the optimal values of the model parameters. However, it is not always possible to identify outliers before solving the problem. This is especially true for case 2), since sometimes the adequacy of the data in relation to the training model can be detected only in the process of solving the problem.

The problem of outliers could be solved if we could choose the sample weights $v_1, \ldots, v_N$ so that outliers will correspond to very small values that would «suppress» the contribution of the outliers to the objective function $\mathcal{Q}$. However, this task is almost equivalent in complexity to the problem of identifying outliers.

There are some classic approaches to overcome influence of the outliers on the base of robust statistics [1, 2]. As a rule, a the function $\rho(r)$ is chosen here so that it grows slowly enough to limit the influence of outliers that appear among the residual values $r_1(\mathbf{w}), \ldots, r_N(\mathbf{w})$. But it doesn't always work.

Here we propose a different approach.

2 The Principle of Minimizing Robust Average Estimates

In situations where there are a large number of outliers in the training set (up to 40–50%), it's almost impossible to select the $\varrho(r)$ function with which to suppress the effect of outliers. In this situation, it becomes quite obvious that the main cause of the distortion $\mathbf{w}^*$ is the instability of the arithmetic mean with respect to the outliers in data. To overcome this issue, it is advisable to use estimates of the average value, which are insensitive to outliers. Moreover, it is highly desirable that such estimates be differentiable. Otherwise, it becomes impossible to use gradient minimization procedures for the function $\mathcal{Q}$.

Let $\mathsf{M}\{z_1,\ldots,z_N\}$ be one of such estimates of the average value, insensitive to outliers. The function $\mathcal{Q}$ is defined as follows:

$$\mathcal{Q}(\mathbf{w}) = \mathsf{M}\{\ell_1(\mathbf{w}),\ldots,\ell_N(\mathbf{w})\}. \tag{4}$$

The solution of (3) satisfies the system of equations:

$$\nabla\mathcal{Q}(\mathbf{w}) = \sum_{k=1}^{N} \frac{\partial \mathsf{M}}{\partial z_k}\nabla\ell_k(\mathbf{w}) + \tau\nabla\mathcal{Q}(\mathbf{w}) = 0,$$

where $z_k = \ell_k(\mathbf{w})$. Computing $\partial\mathsf{M}/\partial z_k$ is usually not cheap. Therefore, it is advisable to use the method of *iterative reweighting*.

It builds the sequence $\mathbf{w}^t$ ($t = 0, 1, 2, \ldots$). At the beginning, $\mathbf{w}^0$ is selected. The rest $\mathbf{w}^t$ ($t > 0$) are calculated according to the following rule:

$$\mathbf{w}^{t+1} = \arg\min_{\mathbf{w}}\left\{\sum_{k=1}^{N} v_k^t \ell_k(\mathbf{w}) + \tau\mathcal{Q}(\mathbf{w})\right\},$$

where $v_k^t = \partial\mathsf{M}\{z_1^t,\ldots,z_N^t\}/\partial z_k$, $z_k^t = \ell_k(\mathbf{w}^t)$.

3   Outliers Insensitive Average Estimates

Almost all known functions for estimating the average value can be defined as the solution to the problem of minimizing the penalty function:

$$\bar{z} = \mathsf{M}\{z_1,\ldots,z_N\} = \arg\min_{u} \mathcal{S}(z_1 - u,\ldots,z_N - u), \tag{5}$$

where $\mathcal{S}(x_1,\ldots,x_N)$ is a convex penalty function (penalty for deviation from the average value). It should be noted that in the general case, the set of values of u at which the minimum is reached in (5) can be a connected set with the boundaries $a < b$. In such cases, by convention, the value $(a + b)/2$ is taken as the value $\mathsf{M}\{z_1,\ldots,z_N\}$.

One can use the iterative procedure to find the value $\bar{z}$:

$$u^{t+1} = \sum_{k=1}^{N} v_k(z_1 - u^t,\ldots,z_N - u^t)z_k,$$

where $v_k = v_k(x_1,\ldots,x_N)$,

$$v_k(x_1,\ldots,x_N) = \frac{\varphi_k(x_1,\ldots,x_N)}{\sum_{l=1}^{N}\varphi_l(x_1,\ldots,x_N)},$$

$\varphi_k(x_1,\ldots,x_N) = \frac{1}{x_k}\frac{\partial\mathcal{S}(x_1,\ldots,x_N)}{\partial x_k}$. Usually $\varphi_k(x_1,\ldots,x_N) \geqslant 0$.
This procedure converges if

$$\left|\sum_{k=1}^{N} \frac{d}{du}\varphi_k(z_1 - u,\ldots,z_N - u)(z_k - u)\right| < \sum_{k=1}^{N}\varphi_k(z_1 - u,\ldots,z_N - u).$$

As a result, the average value $\bar{z}$ can be represented as a weighted arithmetic mean:

$$\bar{z} = \sum_{k=1}^{N} v_k(z_1, \ldots, z_N) z_k.$$

Based on this view, we can construct another version of the iterative reweighting method to minimize $\mathcal{Q}$:

$$\mathbf{w}^{t+1} = \arg\min_{\mathbf{w}} \left\{ \sum_{k=1}^{N} v_k^t \ell_k(\mathbf{w}) + \tau \mathcal{Q}(\mathbf{w}) \right\},$$

where

$$v_k^t = \frac{\varphi_k(z_1^t - \bar{z}_t, \ldots, z_N^t - \bar{z}_t)}{\sum_{l=1}^{N} \varphi_l(z_1^t - \bar{z}_t, \ldots, z_N^t - \bar{z}_t)},$$

$z_k^t = \ell_k(\mathbf{w}_t)$, $\bar{z}_t = \mathsf{M}\{z_1^t, \ldots, z_N^t\}$.

Next, we consider various presentation options for estimating arithmetic mean insensitive to outliers.

3.1 M-Averages

Let $z_1, \ldots, z_N$ be a finite set of real numbers. The center point $\bar{z}_\rho = \mathsf{M}_\rho\{z_1, \ldots, z_N\}$ is defined as follows:

$$\mathsf{M}_\rho\{z_1, \ldots, z_N\} = \arg\min_{u} \sum_{k=1}^{N} \rho(z_k - u), \tag{6}$$

where $\varrho(r)$ is a convex function such that $\min \rho(r) = \rho(0) = 0$.

For example,

1) if $\rho(r) = r^2$, then $\bar{z}_\rho$ is arithmetic mean value;
2) if $\rho(r) = |r|$, then $\bar{z}_\rho$ is median value;
3) if $\rho(r) = (\alpha - [\![r < 0]\!])r$, then $\bar{z}_\rho$ is value of α-quantile[1] (median for $\alpha = 0.5$).

If $\varrho(r)$ is twice differentiable, then $\mathsf{M}_\rho\{z_1, \ldots, z_N\}$ has partial derivatives:

$$\frac{\partial \mathsf{M}_\rho}{\partial z_k} = \frac{\rho''(z_k - \bar{z})}{\rho''(z_1 - \bar{z}) + \cdots + \rho''(z_N - \bar{z})}.$$

Wherein,

$$\frac{\partial \mathsf{M}_\rho}{\partial z_1} + \cdots + \frac{\partial \mathsf{M}_\rho}{\partial z_N} = 1.$$

Since $\varrho(r)$ is convex, then also $\partial \mathsf{M}_\rho / \partial z_k \geqslant 0$ for all $k = 1, \ldots, N$. If $\varrho(r)$ is strictly convex, then $\partial \mathsf{M}_\rho / \partial z_k > 0$ for all $k = 1, \ldots, N$.

---

[1] If the logical expression S is true, then $[\![S]\!] = 1$, otherwise $[\![S]\!] = 0$.

An estimate of the average value $\bar{z}_\rho$ can be calculated using the Newton method or using the following iterative scheme:

$$u^{t+1} = \frac{\sum\limits_{k=1}^{N} \varphi(z_k - u^t) z_k}{\sum\limits_{k=1}^{N} \varphi(z_k - u^t)},$$

where $\varphi(z) = \rho'(z)/z$, $t = 0, 1, 2, \ldots$, $\min\{z_1, \ldots, z_N\} \leqslant u_0 \leqslant \max\{z_1, \ldots, z_N\}$ is initial approximation (can also be taken equal to the arithmetic mean). This scheme converges if

$$\left| \sum_{k=1}^{N} \varphi'(z_k - \bar{z}_\rho)(z_k - \bar{z}_\rho) \right| < \sum_{k=1}^{N} \varphi(z_k - \bar{z}_\rho). \tag{7}$$

Smoothed Analogs of the Median and Quantile. Using a median instead of AM helps to cope with the problems of fitting linear regression with a large number of outliers (up to 50%) in the data. Gradient-type algorithms are not applicable in this case, since the partial derivatives of the median have properties unsuitable for gradient algorithms. Smoothed versions of the median with continuous partial derivatives can be defined using the parameterized functions $\rho_\varepsilon(z)$, such that:

1) $\lim\limits_{\varepsilon \to 0} \rho_\varepsilon(z) = |z|$;
2) $\lim\limits_{\varepsilon \to 0} \rho'_\varepsilon(z) = \operatorname{sign} z$;
3) $\lim\limits_{\varepsilon \to 0} \rho''_\varepsilon(z) = \delta(z)$.[2]

For example, $\rho_\varepsilon(r) = \sqrt{\varepsilon^2 + r^2} - \varepsilon$.

In order to define smoothed variants of α-quantiles let's define

$$\rho_{\varepsilon,\alpha}(r) = \alpha \rho_\varepsilon(r) [\![r \geqslant 0]\!] + (1 - \alpha) \rho_\varepsilon(r) [\![r < 0]\!]. \tag{8}$$

3.2   Smoothly Winsorized Averages

Winzorized AM is a variant of the AM, which is less sensitive to outliers. Since the values of the basic functions are non-negative and large residual values are associated with outliers, in this case it can be considered as the AM, when calculating which values exceeding $\bar{z}_\alpha$ ($\alpha > 0.5$) are replaced by $\bar{z}_\alpha$. We will replace the value of the α-quantile $\bar{z}_\alpha$ with a smoothed analogue:

$$\mathrm{WM}_{\rho_\alpha}\{z_1, \ldots, z_N\} = \frac{1}{N} \sum_{k=1}^{N} \min\{z_k, \bar{z}_{\rho_\alpha}\},$$

---

[2] Dirac's δ-function.

where ρ_α is the dissimilarity function for constructing a smoothed version of the α-quantile. Partial derivatives are of the form:

$$\frac{\partial \mathsf{WM}_{\rho_\alpha}}{\partial z_k} = \frac{1}{N}[\![z_k \leqslant \bar{z}_{\rho_\alpha}]\!] + \frac{m}{N}\frac{\partial \mathsf{M}_{\rho_\alpha}}{\partial z_k},$$

where m is the number value $z_k > \bar{z}_{\rho_\alpha}$.

3.3 Smoothly Truncated Averages

Let's define

$$\tilde{z}_\alpha = \arg\min_u \Big\{ \sum_{|z_k - u| \leqslant c_\alpha} (z_k - u)^2 + \sum_{|z_k - u| > c_\alpha} c_\alpha^2 \Big\},$$

where $C_\alpha = c_\alpha^2 = \mathsf{M}_{\rho_\alpha}\{(z_1 - u)^2, \ldots, (z_N - u)^2\}$.

From the definition we get a recurrence relation for calculating $\tilde{z}_\alpha$:

$$u^{t+1} = \frac{1}{N}\sum_{k=1}^{N}\Big([\![|z_k - u^t| \leqslant c_\alpha^t]\!] + m^t\frac{\partial \mathsf{M}_{\rho_\alpha}}{\partial v_k}\Big)z_k,$$

where $C_\alpha^t = \mathsf{M}_{\rho_\alpha}\{(z_1 - u^t)^2, \ldots, (z_N - u^t)^2\}$, $m^t = |\{k\colon |z_k - u^t| > c_\alpha^t\}|$.

In the limit, we obtain the weighted AM

$$\tilde{z}_\alpha = \frac{1}{N}\sum_{k=1}^{N}\Big([\![|z_k - \tilde{z}_\alpha| \leqslant \tilde{c}_\alpha]\!] + m\frac{\partial \mathsf{M}_{\rho_\alpha}}{\partial v_k}\Big)z_k,$$

where $\tilde{C}_\alpha = \tilde{c}_\alpha^2 = \mathsf{M}_{\rho_\alpha}\{(z_1 - \tilde{z}_\alpha)^2, \ldots, (z_N - \tilde{z}_\alpha)^2\}$, $m = |\{k\colon |z_k - \tilde{z}_\alpha| > \tilde{c}_\alpha\}|$.

In this situation, to minimize the objective function (4), it is advisable to use the following version of the iterative reweighting method:

$$\mathbf{w}^{t+1} = \arg\min_{\mathbf{w}} \sum_{k=1}^{N}\Big(\frac{1}{N}[\![|z_k^t - \tilde{z}_\alpha^t| \leqslant \tilde{c}_\alpha^t]\!] + \frac{m^t}{N}\frac{\partial \mathsf{M}_{\rho_\alpha}}{\partial v_k}\Big)\ell_k(\mathbf{w}),$$

where $\tilde{C}_\alpha^t = (\tilde{c}_\alpha^t)^2 = \mathsf{M}_{\rho_\alpha}\{(z_1^t - \tilde{z}_\alpha^t)^2, \ldots, (z_N^t - \tilde{z}_\alpha^t)^2\}$, $m^t = |\{k\colon |z_k^t - \tilde{z}_\alpha^t| > \tilde{c}_\alpha^t\}|$, $z_k^t = \ell_k(\mathbf{w}^t)$.

4 Illustrative Examples

All examples are use «smoothed» quantile averaging function with (8) and $\rho_\varepsilon(r) = \sqrt{\varepsilon^2 + r^2} - \varepsilon$.

Linear Regression

The data sets correspond to almost the dependence $y = 4x + 1$ with little noise. In addition, outliers are added, so that they are 29%, 38%, 49% of the total number of points, respectively. Outliers are added so that the classic robust linear regression methods will obviously produce distorted results.

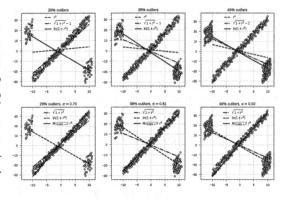

Classification

Two classes are generated in such a way that the standard SVC method obviously leads to the rotation of the line separating the classes. A robust version of the SVC using a smoothed quantile, instead of the arithmetic mean allows you to get a line that confidently separates the classes.

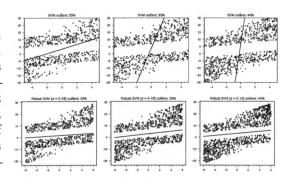

Clustering Example

Consider datasets S3–S4 for clustering from [6,7]. They contain 5000 points, 15 clusters. On each figure, on the left side there is the result of the robust algorithm, and on the right side there is the classical one. During the training, a robust mean estimate was used with $\tilde{z}_\alpha$, $\varepsilon = 0.001$, $\alpha = 0.96 - 0.97$, $h = 0.95$. It is easy to see that the robust algorithm allows one to find more adequate positions of the centers of clusters and the shape of the variance matrices.

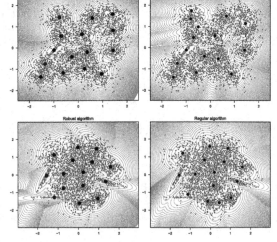

5   Conclusion

Thus, a new approach to the construction of robust machine learning algorithms is proposed, which is based on replacing the arithmetic mean in the objective function with a differentiable estimate of the average value that is insensitive to outliers. Illustrative examples of the problems of regression, classification, and clustering convincingly show the stability of this approach to large volumes of outliers.

This work was supported by grant RFBR 18-01-00050.

References

1. Maronna, R., Martin, R., Yohai, V.: Robust Statistics: Theory and Methods. Wiley, New York (2006)
2. Huber, P.J.: Robust Statistics. John Wiley and Sons, NY (1981)
3. Shibzukhov, Z.M.: On the principle of empirical risk minimization based on averaging aggregation functions. Doklady Math. **96**(2), 494–497 (2017). https://doi.org/10.1134/S106456241705026X
4. Shibzukhov, Z.M., Kazakov, M.A.: Clustering based on the principle of finding centers and robust averaging functions of aggregation. In: Proceedings of V International Conference Information Technology and Nanotechnology - ITNT 2019. Journal of Physics: Conference Series (2019). https://iopscience.iop.org/article/10.1088/1742-6596/1368/5/052010/pdf
5. Davies, P.L.: Asymptotic behavior of S-estimates of multivariate location parameters and dispersion matrices. Ann. Statist. **15**, 1269–1292 (1987)
6. Fränti, P., Sieranoja, S.: K-means properties on six clustering benchmark datasets. Appl. Intell. **48**(12), 4743–4759 (2018). https://doi.org/10.1007/s10489-018-1238-7
7. Clustering basic benchmark. http://cs.joensuu.fi/sipu/datasets/

The Use of Machine Learning Methods to Detect Defects in Images of Metal Structures

Vitalii E. Dementev[✉], Maria A. Gaponova, Marat R. Suetin, and Anastasia S. Streltzova

Ulyanovsk State Technical University, 32 Severni Venets Street, Ulyanovsk 432027, Russian Federation
vitawed@mail.ru

Abstract. The work is devoted to the study of the possibilities provided by modern neural networks in image processing for solving the problem of monitoring the state of steel and reinforced concrete structures. The paper presents a method for solving problems of such monitoring based on the use of a combination of several neural networks focused on recognizing a fragment of a structure and parts of a structure. Methods for training neural networks on small training samples are proposed. The results of algorithms on real images that show the consistency and efficiency of the proposed solution are presented.

Keywords: Prediction · Anomaly detection · Recognition · Adaptive algorithm · Neural networks · Deep learning

1 Introduction

Machine learning methods that have emerged in recent years made it possible to solve a number of problems related to the processing of various types of data at a significantly new level. The tasks of the image processing take up a special place among these tasks. This is connected with wide capabilities that modern algorithms of machine vision provide for the automatic search and identification of objects, assessment of their parameters, image segmentation, etc. The results of the leading research groups [1–8] indicate that the errors of such algorithms can be even less insignificant than the errors made by a person engaged in expert processing. At the same time, the practical application of digital processing methods for images is connected with overcoming a number of difficulties. These difficulties are largely determined by one of the two selected strategies for processing real material. The first strategy is associated with the search for some formalized patterns in images which make it possible to identify certain objects in these images and to assess their parameters. For example, when searching for fires in satellite imagery, a search is made for compact bright objects that correspond to open fires. This specified strategy is usually associated in the literature with model-oriented groups of methods. The disadvantages of this strategy are the difficulties in identifying and formalizing the generalizing signs and errors that arise if the characteristics of the real material differ from the expected ones. The second strategy is based on the automatic

© Springer Nature Switzerland AG 2021
A. Del Bimbo et al. (Eds.): ICPR 2020 Workshops, LNCS 12665, pp. 120–128, 2021.
https://doi.org/10.1007/978-3-030-68821-9_12

training of algorithms as a result of processing a large amount of real data. The most famous example of the implementation of such a strategy is neural network procedures that assume the preliminary training of a hierarchical computational graph with the help of the error back propagation algorithm [7]. An obvious disadvantage of this approach is the requirements for the volume and quality of the training sample which should be sufficient for training a neural network, which usually includes tens and hundreds of billions of weight parameters.

The authors of this paper consider the issues of the synthesis of image processing algorithms for steel and reinforced concrete structures that are intended for finding various visually detectable defects: cracks, fractures, rust, etc. The topicality of applying such algorithms is determined by the importance of prompt detection of these defects. For example, the growth rate of a crack in a railway bridge pier under intense loads can reach several centimeters per day. In practice, this often means that monthly expert inspection of a structure often leads to an acknowledgment that the entire pier is defective and it may entail a temporary stop of railway traffic and significant financial losses. In this regard, new technological solutions are required that make it possible to identify defects more efficiently and with high accuracy. One of such solutions can be the use of an unmanned aerial vehicle which can help to obtain a large amount of photo and video material depicting structural elements in the framework of daily flight routes. In this case, additional tasks arise that are associated with the processing of such images, namely, the identification and assessment of parameters (length, width of the opening, dynamics) of cracks, the identification and assessment of the area of defects after painting, and the assessment of the deformation degree of structural elements.

2 Features of Steel Structure Monitoring Tasks

The complexity of solving such problems is determined by the necessity to use some a priori information about the nature and characteristics of possible defects and training samples that are very limited in volume. Indeed, in reality, when the same crack is detected in the structure, there is no way to collect information about it and record its development. It is necessary within a short period of time to carry out measures to identify it and, if required, replace a structural element. In this regard, the volume of photographic materials with defects in testing laboratories is measured in no more than thousands of pieces. Moreover, all these photographic materials were obtained under different conditions from different structures and at different times. This creates objective difficulties in the formation of full-fledged training samples and does not allow one to apply the known approaches to training directly. Significant processing problems are also associated with the features of the images of defects. In Fig. 1 a typical image of a steel structure fragment is shown depicting a crack that starts at the junction of the steel beam and bridge pier.

It is obvious that the use of classical methods on the basis of color (brown tint) and morphological (elongated shape) features of the detected object can lead to a significant number of false positives. Indeed, in Fig. 1a, one can see several large objects and a large number of small ones that meet these criteria. Figure 1b shows the identified areas that potentially contain a defect. The results were obtained using a simple color-morphological detector [13].

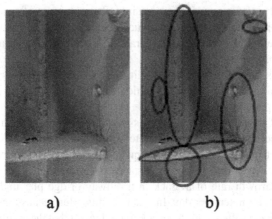

a)   b)

Fig. 1. An example of an image containing a defect (crack) and the results of applying a color-morphological detector

3 Recognition of Structural Elements

One of the options to overcome these difficulties is to use the fact that the design of a real structure (for example, a bridge span) is known and typical. This, firstly, makes it possible to form a three-dimensional photorealistic model of the structure and to perform preliminary training of algorithms on images that do not contain any defects. And secondly, to build an auxiliary algorithm that allows one to identify the location of taking pictures of the structure from a photo and highlight areas of greatest interest. For instance, the most common place for cracks to appear is the area at the junction of load-bearing beams in which the static loads are the highest. This, in particular, is confirmed by visual studies carried out by the authors of the paper at the bridge crossings of the Kuibyshev Russian Railroads. Out of more than 60 cracks identified by experts, 58 were in the same typical locations.

Under these conditions, it seems reasonable to synthesize a procedure that makes it possible to select similar areas in a photo or video image for subsequent deep processing. For the purpose of determining the possibility of such detection, a 3D model of a typical bridge was developed, the areas of potential location of defects were determined, and a great number of training multi-angle photorealistic images were formed. Examples of such images with the areas of possible location of defects are shown in Fig. 2.

The sets of images arranged in this way were used to train the UNET network [1–3], consisting of 19 convolutional layers alternating with subsampling layers, in the framework of solving the image segmentation problem. The number of epochs during training was 100 pieces. An example of applying a trained network to an image from a control sample is shown in Fig. 3.

Analysis of Fig. 3 shows that the neural network quite confidently determines the areas with the highest probability of defect concentration which gives grounds for further use of this approach. During this stage of work, the influence of augmentation on the quality of training was also investigated. For this, the network was sequentially trained on an unaugmented set of training images and an augmented one. At the same time, the standard KERAS algorithms and the original augmentation algorithms were used as augmentation algorithms [14].

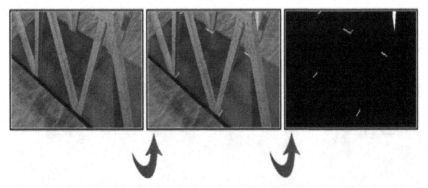

Fig. 2. Areas that contain a potential defect

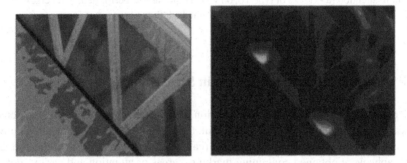

Fig. 3. Result of identifying the areas that require attention

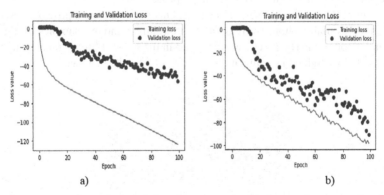

Fig. 4. Convergence of neural network learning processes with the use of augmentation (Fig. 4b) and without it (Fig. 4a).

As a result, the data scattering slightly increased, but the convergence of the results to the training sample increased significantly. This allows us to recommend augmentation to train neural networks in the framework of this project.

Additional training [9] of the obtained neural network was also carried out on the images of fragments of components obtained during the inspection of the bridge. Figure 5 shows such fragments with the corresponding markings.

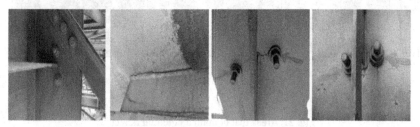

Fig. 5. Fragments of images used for additional training in the problem of recognizing the areas that require attention (a - cracks of type T6, on which training was performed; b–d - cracks of type T1, T9, T10, on which the neural network was trained additionally)

4 Synthesis Detection of Defects in Steel Structures

Let us now consider in more detail the solution to the problem of identifying the defects (cracks) themselves in the images. In general, to solve the problem of detecting defects in the elements of the span structures of a real bridge during the visit to the site, 212 photographs were obtained containing markings, areas of attention and various defects in the elements of steel structures. The volume of the obtained training sample turned out to be insufficient to obtain an acceptable training result, which led to the need to resort to some tricks associated with image preprocessing.

To organize the training process of the neural network for the purpose of subsequent validation, all available photos were divided into training and test samples (in the ratio of 175 and 37 photos). The cracks were marked in the form of binary images, in which the cracks are highlighted in white and the background in black (Fig. 6).

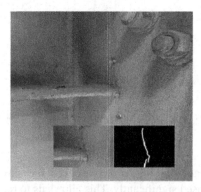

Fig. 6. Formation of a training sample when recognizing defects

To carry out an experiment related to the study of the influence of the training sample volume on the result of training, the regions containing fracture fragments were cut from the original photographs and, on their basis, three sets of images were prepared containing 342/509/842 images, respectively. The training of the neural network was carried out on the original and on the amplified sets of images; in addition, augmentation was used [10–12, 14] to introduce maximum diversity into the training set. The training results were checked on a test set of images that did not participate in training and are presented in Table 1 in the form: the minimum value of the error function/the number of epochs that passed until the minimum value of the error function was obtained.

Table 1 .

A set of images (number of images)	Unaugmented	Augmented
Initial (175)	0.43	0.37
Accentuated №1 (342)	0.56	0.49
Accentuated №2 (509)	0.6	0.55
Accentuated №3 (842)	0.62	0.6

To obtain the best result, a technology was applied associated with a sequential decrease in the step of gradient descent during training. Seventy-five epochs were trained with a step of 10–2, 30 epochs - with a step of 10–3, and another 30 epochs with a step of 10–4.

Figure 7 shows the relationship between the loss function and the number of epochs for the cases of using the original (Fig. 7a) and augmented samples (Fig. 7b). It is noticeable that the second option provides a more controlled version of convergence.

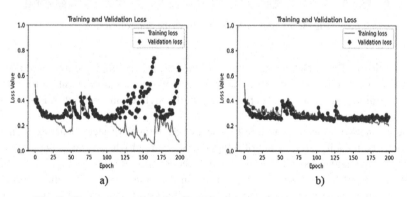

a)   b)

Fig. 7. Convergence of the loss function when training a neural network

To reduce the number of false positives and improve the segmentation accuracy, a second approach to defect detection was proposed which consists in preliminary identifying the areas of attention by the Darknet neural network [4–6], followed by their

Table 2 .

	Augmentation	Control sample of the bridge images			Control sample obtained from the Russian Railroads		
		% of actual successful detection of a defect	% of false positives	Sørensen coefficient	% of actual successful detection of a defect	% of positives	Sørensen coefficient
U-Net only	Not provided	0,76	0,06	0,16	0,7	0,06	0,11
	Provided	0,59	0,07	0,09	0,5	0,07	0,06
Darknet + U-Net	Not provided	0,81	0,01	0,71	0,75	0,01	0,5
	Provided	0,76	0,01	0,57	0,77	0,02	0,4
Model image processing method		0.68	0.78	0.36	0.69	0.75	0.28

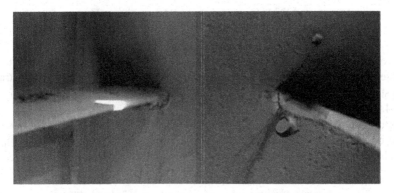

Fig. 8. Examples of images from the control sample

segmentation by the U-Net neural network trained during the implementation of the first approach. To train the Darknet neural network to highlight areas of attention for images from the training set, markup was performed in the style of an open set of Pascal VOC images.

Neural networks were tested on two sets of 37 images of steel structure elements with defects in each. The first set of images was obtained when visiting the site of the railway bridge, and the second - directly from the Russian Railroads (Fig. 8).

Images from the test sets were not used in the neural network training process. During testing, the percentage of actual successful defect detection, the percentage of false positives, and the Sorensen coefficient were evaluated as a measure of the similarity between the detection results and the manually made markup. As an example, in Table 2, in addition to the results obtained using neural networks, the results of defect detection using model image processing methods [13] are presented.

5 Conclusions

The results obtained testify to the practical possibility of applying the developed procedures in tasks of automatic or automated monitoring of the state of steel structures based on the results of processing photographic images of these structures. A relatively low number of false positives of the developed algorithm is a very important outcome. Also, in the course of the work, the results were obtained, indicating a good susceptibility of the obtained neural networks to additional training on new data blocks. This gives reasonable hope that the algorithm will be in demand in practical applications.

Acknowledgements. The reported study was funded by the Russian Fund for Basic Researches according to the research projects № 18–47-730009 and № 19–29-09048.

References

1. Ronneberger, O., Fischer, P., Brox, T.: U-Net: convolutional networks for biomedical image segmentation. In: Navab, N., Hornegger, J., Wells, W.M., Frangi, A.F. (eds.) MICCAI 2015. LNCS, vol. 9351, pp. 234–241. Springer, Cham (2015). https://doi.org/10.1007/978-3-319-24574-4_28
2. Huang, H., et al.: Unet 3+: a full-scale connected Unet for medical image segmentation. arXiv preprint arXiv:2004.08790 (2020)
3. Li, R., et al.: DeepUNet: A deep fully convolutional network for pixel-level sea-land segmentation. arXiv preprint arXiv:1709.00201 (2017)
4. Redmon, J., Divvala, S., Girshick, R., Farhadi, A.: You Only Look Once: unified, real-time object detection. arXiv preprint arXiv:1506.02640 (2016)
5. Redmon, J., Farhadi, A.: YOLO9000: better, faster, stronger arXiv preprint arXiv:1612.08242 (2016)
6. Sermanet, P., Eigen, D., Zhang, X., Mathieu, M., Fergus, R., LeCun, Y.: OverFeat: Integrated recognition, localization and detection using convolutional networks arXiv preprint arXiv: 1312.6229 (2014)
7. LeCun, Y., et al.: Handwritten digit recognition with a backpropagation neural network. In: Advances in Neural Information Processing Systems, vol. 2, pp. 396–404 (1990)
8. LeCun, Y., Huang, F.-J., Bottou, L.: Learning methods for generic object recognition with invariance to pose and lighting. In: Proceedings of Computer Vision and Pattern Recognition, vol. 2, pp. 97–104 (2004)
9. Tang, Y.: Deep learning using linear support vector machines. arXiv preprint arXiv:1306.0239 (2015)
10. Zhong, Z., Zheng, L., Kang, G., Li, S., Yang, Y.: Random erasing data augmentation. arXiv preprint arXiv:1708.04896 (2017)
11. Biau, G., Cadre, B., Rouviere, L.: Accelerated gradient boosting. arXiv preprint arXiv:1803.02042 (2018)
12. Ye, L., Liu, Z., Wang, Y.: Learning semantic segmentation with diverse supervision. arXiv preprint arXiv:1802.00509 (2018)

13. Krasheninnikov, V., Vasil'ev, K.: Multidimensional image models and processing. In: Favorskaya, M.N., Jain, L.C. (eds.) Computer Vision in Control Systems-3. ISRL, vol. 135, pp. 11–64. Springer, Cham (2018). https://doi.org/10.1007/978-3-319-67516-9_2
14. Andrianov, N.A., Dementev, V.E., Vasilev, K.K.: Use of images augmentation and implementation of doubly stochastic models for improving accuracy of recognition algorithms based on convolutional neural networks. In: 2020 Systems of Signal Synchronization, Generating and Processing in Telecommunications (SYNCHROINFO) (2020). 4 p. DOI: https://doi.org/10.1109/SYNCHROINFO49631.2020.9166000

Multiregion Multiscale Image Segmentation with Anisotropic Diffusion

V. B. Surya Prasath[1,2,3,4], Dang Ngoc Hoang Thanh[5(✉)],
Nguyen Hoang Hai[6], and Sergey Dvoenko[7]

[1] Department of Electrical Engineering and Computer Science,
University of Cincinnati, Cincinnati, OH 45221, USA
surya.iit@gmail.com
[2] Division of Biomedical Informatics, Cincinnati Children's Hospital Medical Center,
Cincinnati, OH 45229, USA
[3] Department of Biomedical Informatics, College of Medicine,
University of Cincinnati, Cincinnati, OH 45267, USA
[4] Department of Pediatrics, University of Cincinnati College of Medicine,
Cincinnati, OH 45257, USA
[5] Department of Information Technology, School of Business Information Technology,
University of Economics Ho Chi Minh City, Ho Chi Minh City, Vietnam
thanhdnh@ueh.edu.vn
[6] Department of Computer Science, Vietnam-Korea University of Information
and Communication Technology – The University of Danang, Danang, Vietnam
nhhai@vku.udn.vn
[7] Department of Information Security, Institute of Applied Mathematics
and Computer Science, Tula State University, Tula city, Russia
dvsrge@gmail.com

Abstract. We present a multiregion image segmentation approach which utilizes multiscale anisotropic diffusion based scale spaces. By combining powerful edge preserving anisotropic diffusion smoothing with isolevel set linking and merging, we obtain coherent segments which are tracked across multiple scales. A hierarchical tree representation of the given input image with progressively simplified regions is used with intra-scale splitting and inter-scale merging for obtaining multiregion segmentations. Experimental results on natural and medical images indicate that multiregion, multiscale image segmentation (MMIS) approach obtains coherent segmentation results.

Keywords: Image segmentation · Multiregion · Multiscale · Anisotropic diffusion · Vectorial diffusion · Linking · Pruning

1 Introduction

Image segmentation has been studied for many years now and forges the first step in many computer vision and pattern recognitions systems. Among a wide variety of techniques available we mention the variational or energy minimization methods which encompass boundary regularity along with regional properties

© Springer Nature Switzerland AG 2021
A. Del Bimbo et al. (Eds.): ICPR 2020 Workshops, LNCS 12665, pp. 129–140, 2021.
https://doi.org/10.1007/978-3-030-68821-9_13

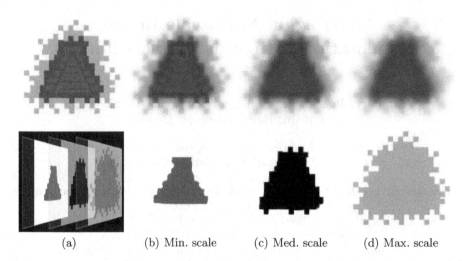

(a)   (b) Min. scale   (c) Med. scale   (d) Max. scale

Fig. 1. Our proposed MMIS approach obtains coherent multiscale segmentations of images. Top row: Input color image (ICPR 2016 logo) of size 125×118, and the result of vectorial PDE smoothing (2) at iterations $T = 20, 50, 60$. Bottom row: (a) scale space of segmentations with objects at three different scales (minimum, medium, maximum) shown as layers, and segmentations at iterations of vectorial diffusion PDE, (b) 20 (red), (c) 50 (black), and (d) 60 (orange). We show the average value of each segment to highlight the segmented part. As the scale increases number of segmented regions are reduced by merging across scales. (Color figure online)

of objects to be segmented in images. One of the cornerstone variational minimization is due to Mumford and Shah [9] and we refer to the monograph [6] for theoretical details. An efficient level set based implementation of Mumford-Shah variational energy minimization was undertaken by Chan and Vese [3] who derived an active contour without edges model. However, these active contours require careful initializations, constant re-initialization to signed distance function, and computationally heavy iterative steps. In contrast, the clustering type algorithms avoid the issue boundary regularization by grouping similar pixels with some affinity criteria. However, determining cluster centers automatically from a given image data require careful consideration.

In parallel to the development of variational methods, nonlinear partial differential equations (PDEs) based smoothing and filtering has seen used for low level image processing [2]. This PDE based filters belong to the scale space paradigm where the artificial time parameter now takes the place of scale of objects in images. In this work, we consider an application of anisotropic diffusion filters for obtaining a nonlinear scale space of progressively simplified images which are used to segment multiple objects via tracking across scales. Our motivation comes from the scale space theory and multiresolution methods [4,5,11,12]. Unlike the linear scale space based on Gaussian smoothing (equivalently using a heat equation) which progressively obtains blurrier images, anisotropic diffusion filters obtain a sequence of piecewise constant images with edges preserved intact [10,17]. By using the nonlinear scale spaces and coarse to fine linking approach, we obtain a hierarchical tree representation which is then pruned based on intra-scale splitting and inter-scale merging for obtaining multiregion segmentations. For gray scale images we utilize the Perona and Malik PDE and for color images, we utilize the unified vectorial anisotropic diffusion approach of Tschumperle and Deriche [17] and test color distance metric in the inter-scale merging stage. Our multiregion, multiscale image segmentation (MMIS) framework is general in the sense that, various image smoothing operators can be utilized depending upon the application domain. Further, the segmentation stack is generated only once and provides the possibility of different segmentation results based on appropriate stopping parameter, see for e.g. Fig. 1. In this case, our MMIS segmentation approach obtained 3 objects at based on the chosen stopping time of the PDE filtering (scale levels). Experimental results on gray scale and color image segmentation with natural (Berkeley segmentation dataset - BSDS500[1]), and medical (heart CT, brain MRI, and dermoscopic skin lesion) are undertaken to show the applicability of our proposed approach.

We organized the paper as follows. Section 2 introduces the proposed MMIS method based on anisotropic diffusion filters with intra-scale splitting and inter-scale linking procedure. Section 3 provides experimental segmentation results on natural and medical imagery. Finally, Sect. 4 concludes the paper.

2   Anisotropic Diffusion Based Multiregion Multiscale Image Segmentation

2.1   Anisotropic Diffusion Filters

Grayscale Images. Anisotropic diffusion filters are widely used for image denoising, smoothing and simplification [2]. The iterative method is based on continuous domain partial differential equation, where the artificial time t here takes the meaning of scale. The general formulation of anisotropic diffusion can be written as (for a given grayscale image $u_0 : \Omega \subset \mathbb{R}^2 \to \mathbb{R}$)

$$\begin{cases} \dfrac{\partial u(x,t)}{\partial t} = div(D(u(x,t), \nabla u(x,t)) \nabla u(x,t)), & \text{in} \quad \Omega \\ u(x,0) = u_0, & \text{in} \quad \partial\Omega. \end{cases} \tag{1}$$

The diffusion coefficient D controls the smoothing of the image function u, for e.g. Perona-Malik functions,

$$D_{pm1} = \exp\left(-\frac{|\nabla u|^2}{K^2}\right), \quad D_{pm2} = \left(1 + \frac{|\nabla u|^2}{K^2}\right)^{-1},$$

with $K > 0$ is known as the contrast parameter. By using gradient ($|\nabla u|$) based diffusion coefficients the smoothing is done along edges and not across them along with effective noise removal.

---

[1] https://www2.eecs.berkeley.edu/Research/Projects/CS/vision/grouping/resources.html.

Vectorial Images. For vectorial (multichannel) images, $\mathbf{u} = (u^1, u^2, \ldots, u^N)$: $\Omega \subset \mathbb{R}^2 \to \mathbb{R}^N$, we consider the unified variational - PDE common framework Tschumperlé and Deriche [17]. Their unified approach which is trace-based can be written, for example in color images $N = 3$,

$$\frac{\partial u^i(x,t)}{\partial t} = trace\left(\mathbf{TH}^i(\mathbf{x},t)\right), \quad (i = 1, 2, 3). \tag{2}$$

where $\mathbf{H}^i$ is the Hessian matrix of the vector component u^i and $\mathbf{T}(x)$ is the tensor field defined pointwise. To define the tensor field let us consider the smoothed multigradient structure tensor,

$$J_\sigma = G_\sigma \star \sum_{i=1}^{3} \nabla u^i (\nabla u^i)^T \tag{3}$$

where

$$G_\sigma(\mathbf{x}) = (2\pi\sigma^2)^{-1} \exp\left(-|\mathbf{x}|/2\sigma^2\right) \tag{4}$$

the normalized 2D Gaussian kernel, $\star$ denotes the convolution operator and superscript T the transpose. Let the eigenvalues of J_σ be (λ_+, λ_-), with eigenvectors (θ_+, θ_-). Using $\mathcal{N} = \sqrt{\lambda_+ + \lambda_-}$ as an edge indicator in vector images leads to the tensor field in (2) as,

$$\mathbf{T} = f_-(\mathcal{N})\,\theta_-\theta_-^T + f_+(\mathcal{N})\,\theta_+\theta_+^T \tag{5}$$

where $f_-(\mathcal{N}) = (1+(\mathcal{N})^2)^{-1/2}$ and $f_+(\mathcal{N}) = (1+(\mathcal{N})^2)^{-1}$. Due to the use of the multigradient structure tensor J_σ and its eigenvectors [7], the overall geometric structure of the input vector image $\mathbf{u}$ is captured and preserved in the PDE flow.

2.2   Intra-scale Splitting and Inter-scale Linking

We create nonlinear scale spaces corresponding to the PDEs (1) (for grayscale) or (2) (for color) up-to a termination time T, i.e, $\{u(x,t)\}_{t=0}^T$ with $u(x,0) = u_0$ the initial input image. These scale space representation can be used for various image processing tasks [5], and in this work we utilize it to partition and merge multiple regions to obtain segmentations of the given image. We first consider partitioning the regions in each scale image $u(x,t)$ using the connected components $\mathcal{R}_t$ obtained by isolevel sets, that is based on constant valued isophotes [2]. Due to the discrete maximum-minimum principle of anisotropic filters [20,21], the coarse to fine linking is inclusive, that is, each region in coarse scales can be traced towards finer levels and the linking is guaranteed to connect the regions enclosed by level lines across scales. For linking the regions across the scale space we chose all the nodes belonging to a certain scale level and these selected nodes are then fully linked across the hierarchical tree. Thus, for our final segmentation we consider regions which are fully linked to a node in the scale space tree structure. There are other involved selection mechanisms for inter-scale linking, which require deeper analysis of scale space tree pruning along with complex seed nodes selection [18, 19, 22].

For merging the regions across scales (which are overlapping) we need an efficient distance metric. There exists various color distance metrics depending upon the color space utilized [1]. For example, in this work, CIE-La*b* color space the traditional L^2 distance metric that captures the perceptually uniform color distances,

$$\|u - v\|_2^2 = (u_L - v_L)^2 + (u_{a*} - v_{a*}) + (u_{b*} - v_{b*}). \tag{6}$$

All connected regions of initial regions computed using the isolevel sets can then be linked to the same region at the end scale T. Other color spaces and distance metrics can also be used depending upon the application domains and in this work for natural images (BSDS500) the CIE-La*b* color space with L^2 metric obtained good results. To summarize, we obtain a multiregion, multiscale image segmentation (MMIS) method with anisotropic diffusion which is robust to noise and respects object edges.

2.3   Overall Scale Space Segmentation Method

The overall flow of our proposed MMIS is given as follows:

(1) Compute the scale space $\{u(x,t)\}_{t=0}^T$ with a maximum iteration number T using a nonlinear PDE ((1) or (2)) of a given input image $u(x, t = 0) = u_0$.
(2) Partition $u(x,t)$ at each t by connected components $\{\mathcal{C}_t^r\}_{r=0}^{\mathcal{R}_t}$ (using isolevel sets) to obtain the multiregions $\mathcal{D}_t$, where $\mathcal{R}_t$ the total number of distinct regions at scale t:

$$\mathcal{C}_t^r = \{x \in \Omega : u(x,t) = r\} \quad \text{and} \quad \mathcal{C}_t^r \cap_{r \neq l} \mathcal{C}_t^l = 0, \quad \mathcal{D}_t = \cup_{r=0}^{\mathcal{R}_t} \mathcal{C}_t^r.$$

Thus, we have at each time t, a partitioned $\mathcal{D}_t$ of the image domain Ω.
(3) Link two subsequent scale regions (t, and $t + 1$) if they overlap,

$$\mathcal{L}_t^{t+1} = \left\{ arg \min_{\mathcal{C}_{t+1}^k, k=0,\dots,\mathcal{R}_{t+1}} \left\| u(\mathcal{C}_{t+1}^k, t+1) - u(\mathcal{C}_t^r, t) \right\| : \mathcal{C}_{t+1}^k \cap \mathcal{C}_t^r \neq 0 \right\}$$

Here the minimum is taken to obtain minimal graylevel/color distance among all overlapping regions. The injective linking operator $\mathcal{L}_t^{t+1} : \mathcal{C}_t^r \to \mathcal{C}_{t+1}^k$ uses the minimal absolute value (grayscale) or color distance (see Eq. (6)) and overlapping regions across scales. This inter-scale linking works in general as well, i.e., $\mathcal{L}_{t_1}^{t_2} : \mathcal{C}_{t_1}^r \to \mathcal{C}_{t_2}^k$ with $t_1 < t_2$.
(4) Final segmentation is obtained at scale level T:

$$\mathcal{S}_T^k = \cup_{r=0}^{\mathcal{R}_0} \mathcal{C}_0^r \quad \text{and} \quad \mathcal{C}_0^r \to \mathcal{C}_T^k$$

That is, we aggregate all connected regions at time $t = 0$ (input image) that are linked to the same region at termination time T (coarse image).

The final obtained segments $\{\mathcal{S}_T^k\}$ represent multiregion segmentation of the given input image u_0 with intra-scale splitting respecting object boundaries and inter-scale linking with final merging connecting the coarse to fine levels.

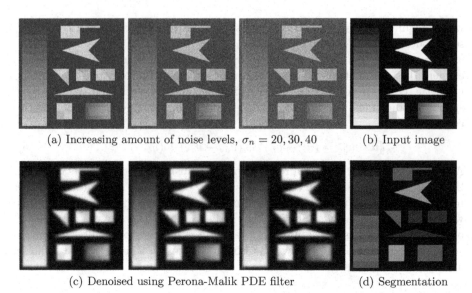

(a) Increasing amount of noise levels, $\sigma_n = 20, 30, 40$ (b) Input image

(c) Denoised using Perona-Malik PDE filter   (d) Segmentation

Fig. 2. Our proposed MMIS segmentation is robust to noise due to the edge preserving smoothing property of PDE filter. (b) Increasing amount of additive Gaussian noise added images obtained from the (b) input synthetic grayscale *Shapes* image. (c) Corresponding scale space images obtained with Perona-Malik diffusion filter (1) with D_{pm1} diffusion coefficient function with the terminal time $T = 40$, and (d) our proposed MMIS segmentation result. We show the individual regions as colored segments overlayed on top of the original image. (Color figure online)

3 Experimental Results

We implemented the anisotropic diffusion filters considered here using standard finite differences [21] and further optimizations can be undertaken [13] without compromising the smoothing quality of these filters. For grayscale images we used the absolute value L^1 distance and color images we utilized the CIE-La*b* color space with the L^2 color distance metric at linking step (see step (3) in Sect. 2.3). The parameters of the Perona-Malik (1) (contrast parameter $K = 40$, discrete time step size $\Delta t = 0.025$) and Tschumperlé and Deriche vectorial diffusion PDE (2) (Gaussian smoothing $\sigma = 2$) were fixed for all the experiments reported here. The final iteration time T is an important user defined parameter, with higher values (corresponding to bigger scale) reduces the number of segments (see Fig. 1(b-d) bottom row), and comprises of the bulk of the computational complexity of proposed MMIS method. The scale space $\{u(x, t)\}_{t=0}^{T}$ is formed only once and the segmentations for any time ($T^* < T$) can be easily obtained. In our experiments the maximum terminal time utilized is under 50 in general and it is known that running for longer times $T \to \infty$ the PDE filters converge to the mean value of the input image. For a $512 \times 512 \times 3$ image our algorithm takes on average 0.5 s for 40 iterations (for the scale space with PDE (2)) based on

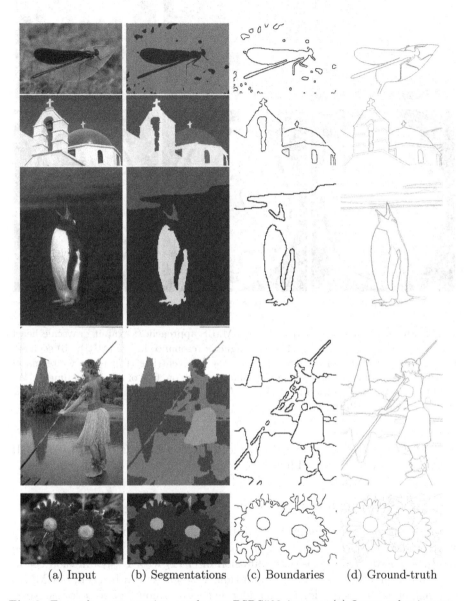

(a) Input   (b) Segmentations   (c) Boundaries   (d) Ground-truth

Fig. 3. Example segmentation results on BSDS500 images. (a) Input color images, (b) obtained MMIS segmentations, (c) borders of computed segments (using Canny edge detector with default setting), and (d) ground-truth aggregated from 5 human observers. No pre or post-processing was applied to these results. (Color figure online)

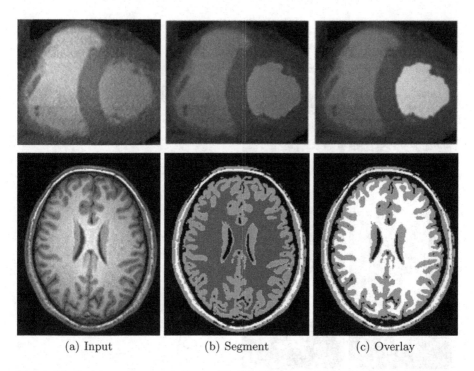

(a) Input   (b) Segment   (c) Overlay

Fig. 4. Medical image segmentations with MMIS approach. (a) Input grayscale heart computed tomography (CT) and brain magnetic resonance image (MRI), (b) segmentation obtained with our MMIS capturing the left ventricle (top row), white mater (bottom row), and (c) super-imposing the segment on top of the input image. We used Perona-Malik diffusion filter (1) with D_{pm1} diffusion coefficient function with the terminal time $T = 40$ in both cases.

MATLAB implementation in a MacBook Pro laptop 2.3 GHz Intel Core i7, 8 GB RAM. The results presented here are obtained with no pre or post-processing.

3.1 MMIS Segmentation Results

Figure 2 shows some examples of MMIS segmentations on synthetic *Shapes* input image (size 256×256) with increasing amount of additive Gaussian noise levels. We used the Perona-Malik diffusion filter (1) with D_{pm1} diffusion coefficient function, and chose the terminal time $T = 40$. As can be seen, our MMIS obtains robust segmentations even under increasing amount of noise levels. Next, in Fig. 3 shows some example BSDS500 natural images segmentation obtained with our proposed MMIS method. We used the Tschumperlé and Deriche vectorial diffusion PDE filter (2) based results with terminal time chosen as $T = 40$. We show the borders of detected regions (using Canny edge detector with default parameters) corresponding to each segmentation result and compared with the

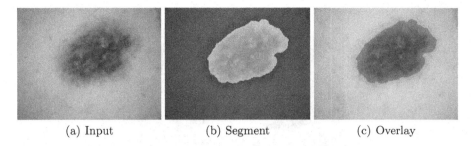

(a) Input   (b) Segment   (c) Overlay

Fig. 5. Melanoma image segmentations with MMIS approach. (a) Input color dermo-scopic image, (b) segmentation obtained with our MMIS capturing the lesion, and (c) super-imposing the segment on top of the input image. We used Tschumperlé and Deriche vectorial diffusion PDE (2) with the terminal time $T = 40$.

human annotated (aggregated from 5 different humans), we see that our seg-mentations contain some of the salient object boundaries. Moreover, the bound-aries of the segments are smoother indicating the inherent regularity of PDE based filters which respect to object boundaries and smoother enclosed regions. The merging of the penguin body with the background in Fig. 3 (third row) is unavoidable as the PDE filtering (2) was not able to capture the faint edge on the back of the penguin. Higher level context or semantic boundaries are required in this case and defines one of our current works.

3.2 Medical Image Segmentation and Comparisons

Medical Image Segmentations. Figure 4 shows a couple of examples of med-ical images (heart CT of size 152×128 and brain MRI of size 169×207) and our MMIS segmentations of regions of interest required by medical experts. We note that no a prior knowledge of the CT or MRI imaging is utilized and the segmenta-tion is shown for the left ventricle (CT) and white mater (MRI) respectively. We obtained good coherent segments that delineate regions of interest in biomedical imagery. Figure 5 shows the segmentation of melanoma skin images [16] with our MMIS model. As can be seen, overall we obtain good segmentation that also preserves the low intensity regions around the skin lesion. This shows the poten-tial applicability of our approach to other imaging domains wherein the object of interest can be segmented if the particular scales are known. Including an auto-matic scale detector [15] within our MMIS segmentation is an interesting future work where we can utilized the structure tensor based robust indicators [14].

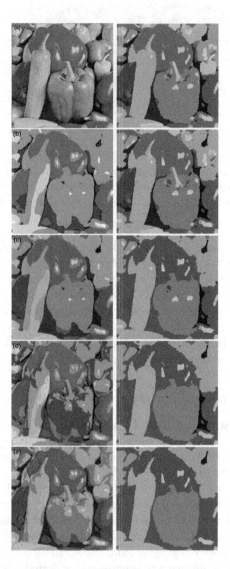

Fig. 6. Comparison of our proposed MMIS with color categorization models [1] based segmentation. Left column: (a) Input color *Peppers* image, and segmentation results obtained with, (b) estimation of "C" attribute, (c) representation of the result using the average RGB color information in each segment of the image in (b), (d) estimation of "S" given "C", (e) representation of the result using the average RGB color information in each segment of the image in (d). Right column: Our proposed MMIS at different terminal times of the PDE (2), $T = 10, 15, 25, 30, 40$. (b-e) utilize the color categorization model approach [1] with "C" $\in$ [red, green, blue, yellow, purple, orange, gray, black, white, pink, brown] and "S" $\in$ [light, dark] are the color and intensity attributes respectively. (Color figure online)

Comparison Results. Finally, in Fig. 6 we show a comparison of segmentations on a natural color image *Peppers* with color categorization models considered in Alarcon and Dalmau [1]. In their method, each extracted color region in the color image has a descriptor ⟨"C", "S"⟩, where "C" ∈ [red, green, blue, yellow, purple, orange, gray, black,white, pink, brown] and "S" ∈ [light, dark] the color and intensity attributes respectively. Estimation of the color attribute "C" is based on an optimization approach, namely the generalized entropy-controlled quadratic Markov measure field model and attribute "S" is computed as a refinement of "C". We refer to [1] for more details regarding these linguistic color image segmentation models. As can be seen from Fig. 6(bottom row), our proposed MMIS segmentation with the Tschumperlé and Deriche vectorial diffusion PDE filter (2) at various terminal times $T = 10, 15, 25, 30, 40$ obtains coherent segments. Both green peppers at the front are segmented well in our approach (Fig. 6(right column)) compared to the color categorization models (Fig. 6(left column)) which all obtained spurious segments.

4   Conclusions

In this work, we considered a multi-region and multiscale image segmentation using isolevel set linking with anisotropic diffusion filters based nonlinear scale space. By simplifying images with anisotropic diffusion with edge preservation we obtained coherent structures which can be traced across multiple scales. Our proposed method relies on the edge preserving anisotropic diffusion filters and a multiscale merging method for obtaining scale controlled segmentations. Experimental results showed that we obtained robust segmentations in natural and medical imagery. Future works include testing and benchmarking the proposed approach with other related scale space segmentation methods, applying different chromatic diffusion methods and different color spaces (such as HSV [8]), distance metrics.

Acknowledgments. This research was funded by University of Economics Ho Chi Minh City, Vietnam.

References

1. Alarcon, T., Dalmau, O.: Color categorization models for color image segmentation. In: Celebi, M.E., Smolka, B. (eds.) Advances in Low-Level Color Image Processing. LNCVB, vol. 11, pp. 303–327. Springer, Dordrecht (2014). https://doi.org/10.1007/978-94-007-7584-8_10
2. Aubert, G., Kornprobst, P.: Mathematical Problems in Image Processing: Partial Differential Equation and Calculus of Variations. Springer-Verlag, New York, USA (2006)
3. Chan, T.F., Vese, L.A.: Active contours without edges. IEEE Trans. Image Process. **10**(2), 266–277 (2001)
4. Koepfler, G., Lopez, C., Morel, J.-M.: A multiscale algorithm for image segmentation by variational method. SIAM J. Numer. Anal **31**(1), 282–299 (1994)

5. Lindeberg, T.: Scale-Space Theory in Computer Vision. Kluwer (1994)
6. Morel, J.-M., Solimini, S.: Variational Methods in Image Processing. Birkhauser, Boston, MA, USA (1994)
7. Moreno, J.C., Prasath, V.B.S., Neves, J.C.: Color image processing by vectorial total variation with gradient channels coupling. Inverse Prob. Imaging **10**(2), 461–497 (2016)
8. Mousavi, S.M.H., Vyacheslav, L., Prasath, V.B.S.: Analysis of a robust edge detection system in different color spaces using color and depth images. Comput. Opt. **43**(4), 632–646 (2019)
9. Mumford, D., Shah, J.: Optimal approximations by piecewise smooth functions and associated variational problems. Commun. Pure Appl. Math. **42**(5), 577–685 (1989)
10. Perona, P., Malik, J.: Scale-space and edge detection using anisotropic diffusion. IEEE Trans. Pattern Anal. Mach. Intell. **12**(7), 629–639 (1990)
11. Petrovic, A., Escoda, O.D., Vandergheynst, P.: Multiresolution segmentation of natural images: from linear to nonlinear scale-space representations. IEEE Trans. Image Process. **13**(8), 1104–1114 (2004)
12. Prasath, V.B.S.: Color image segmentation based on vectorial multiscale diffusion with inter-scale linking. In: Chaudhury, S., Mitra, S., Murthy, C.A., Sastry, P.S., Pal, S.K. (eds.) PReMI 2009. LNCS, vol. 5909, pp. 339–344. Springer, Heidelberg (2009). https://doi.org/10.1007/978-3-642-11164-8_55
13. Prasath, V.B.S., Moreno, J.C.: On convergent finite difference schemes for variational - PDE based image processing. Comput. Appl. Math. **37**(2), 1562–1580 (2018)
14. Prasath, V.B.S., Thanh, D.N.H.: Structure tensor adaptive total variation for image restoration. Turk. J. Electr. Eng. Comput. Sci. **27**(2), 1147–1156 (2019)
15. Prasath, V.B.S., Thanh, D.N.H., Hai, N.H.: On selecting the appropriate scale in image selective smoothing by nonlinear diffusion. In: 7th International Conference on Communications and Electronics (ICCE), Hue, Vietnam, June 2018
16. Thanh, D.N.H., Prasath, V.B.S., Hieu, L.M., Hien, N.N.: Melanoma skin cancer detection method based on adaptive principal curvature, color normalization and features extraction with the ABCD rule. J. Digit. Imaging (2020)
17. Tschumperle, D., Deriche, R.: Vector-valued image regularization with PDE's: a common framework for different applications. IEEE Trans. Pattern Anal. Mach. Intell. **27**(4), 506–517 (2005)
18. Vincken, K.L.: Probabilistic multiscale image segmentation by the hyperstack. PhD thesis, Utrecht University, The Netherlands (2001)
19. Vincken, K.L., Koster, A.S.E., Viergever, M.A.: Probabilistic multiscale image segmentation. IEEE Trans. Pattern Anal. Mach. Intell. **19**(2), 109–120 (1997)
20. Weickert, J.: Anisotropic diffusion in image Processing. B.G. Teubner-Verlag, Stuttgart, Germany (1998)
21. Weickert, J., Romeny, B.M.H., Viergever, M.A.: Efficient and reliable schemes for nonlinear diffusion filtering. IEEE Trans. Image Process. **7**(3), 398–410 (1998)
22. Ziliani, F., Jensen, B.: Unsupervised image segmentation using the modified pyramidal linking approach. In: International Conference on Image Processing, pp. 303–307. IEEE (1998)

The Test of Covariation Functions of Cylindrical and Circular Images

Victor Krasheninnikov[(✉)], Yuliya Kuvayskova, Olga Malenova, and Alexey Subbotin

Ulyanovsk State Technical University,
32 Severny Venets Street, Ulyanovsk 432027, Russian Federation
kvrulstu@mail.ru, u.kuvaiskova@mail.ru, nika-lilu@yandex.ru,
ashkael@gmail.com

Abstract. Nowadays, image processing problems are becoming increasingly important due to development of the aerospace Earth monitoring systems, radio and sonar systems, medical devices for early disease diagnosis etc. But the most of the image processing works deal with images defined on rectangular two-dimensional grids or grids of higher dimension. In some practical situations, images are set on a cylinder (for example, images of pipelines, blood vessels, parts during turning) or on a circle (for example, images of the facies (thin film) of dried biological fluid, an eye, cut of a tree trunk). The peculiarity of the domain for specifying such images requires its consideration in their models and processing algorithms. In the present paper, autoregressive models of cylindrical and circular images are considered, and expressions of the correlation function depending on the autoregression parameters are given. The spiral scan of a cylindrical image can be considered as a quasiperiodic process due to the correlation of image rows. To represent inhomogeneous images with random heterogeneity, «doubly stochastic» models are used in which one or more controlling images control the parameters of the resulting image. Given the resulting image, it is possible to estimate parameters of the model of controlling images. But it is not enough to identify hidden images completely. It is necessary to investigate the covariation function of given image. Does it match the hypothetical one? The test for covariation functions of cylindrical and circular images is proposed with investigation its power relative to parameters of image model.

Keywords: Cylindrical and circular images · Quasiperiodic process · Autoregressive model · Covariation function · Test · Power

1 Introduction

At the present time, the methods of image analysis are applied in aerospace Earth monitoring systems, navigation, radio and sonar systems, medical diagnostics and computer vision systems, for example, [1–4]. The vast majority of works on image processing

© Springer Nature Switzerland AG 2021
A. Del Bimbo et al. (Eds.): ICPR 2020 Workshops, LNCS 12665, pp. 141–154, 2021.
https://doi.org/10.1007/978-3-030-68821-9_14

deal with images defined on rectangular grids [5–9]. There are much fewer works on images defined on curved surfaces, for example, [10, 11]. Sometimes images are set on a cylinder, for example, images of a pipeline, worm, snake, round building, etc. Some of cylindrical images are shown in Fig. 1. Besides, there are images on a circle with radial or radial-circular structure, for example, images of the facies (thin film) of dried biological, an eye, etc. Some of cylindrical images are shown in Fig. 2.

In Sect. 2, we show that well known Habibi model [5] of flat image is not good for cylinder images description. We use a single autoregressive equation to represent the whole homogeneous cylindrical or circular image using special grids of pixels. The expressions of covariance function is given relative to parameters of the model.

In Sect. 3, to represent inhomogeneous images with random heterogeneity, «doubly stochastic» models are used. In these models one or more images (controlling ones) set the parameters of the resulting image [12, 13]. The controlling images affect the properties of observed resulting image but they are unobserved. So the problem of hidden controlling images identification (evaluation of their parameters) erases. This problem was considered in [15, 16].

Fig. 1. Examples of cylindrical images.

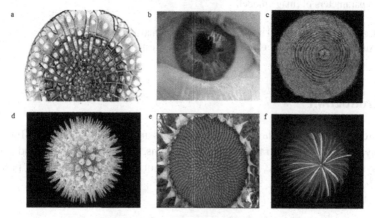

Fig. 2. Examples of circular images.

The criterion for covariation function of cylindrical and circular images is proposed in Sect. 4 with investigation its power relative to parameters of image model.

2 Models of Homogeneous Images on a Cylinder and a Circle

We first consider the well-known autoregressive model Habibi of a flat image [5],

$$x_{k,l} = a\,x_{k,l-1} + b\,x_{k-1,l} - a\,b\,x_{k-1,l-1} + \beta\,\xi_{k,l}, \tag{1}$$

where k is the number of the row; l is the number of the column, $\xi_{k,l}$ are independent standard random variables. The generated image has zero mean and covariance function (CF)

$$V(m,n) = M[x_{k,l}\,x_{k+m,l+n}] = \frac{\beta^2 a^{|m|} b^{|n|}}{(1-a^2)(1-b^2)}, \tag{2}$$

the graph view of which is shown in Fig. 3.

Fig. 3. CF graph of the model in (1).

Correlation of image elements decreases along rows and columns. Therefore, the elements of this image located at the beginning and end of the row are weakly dependent. When connecting the image into the cylinder, there will be a large jump in brightness at the junction, that is not characteristic of the image on a cylinder. The adjacent rows of the rectangular image with $b \approx 1$ have a high correlation. Therefore, when combining the rows into a sequence, we can obtain a model of a quasiperiodic process. However, the beginning and end of each row, being at a considerable distance from each other, are practically independent of each other, so there will be sharp jumps at the junction of the quasi-periods of the process, which are unusual for relatively continuous processes. Thus, rectangular images do not give acceptable representations of cylindrical images and quasiperiodic processes. In this paper, for this purpose, we use images defined on a cylinder, the values of which along the spiral do not have undesirable sharp jumps.

Let us consider a spiral grid on the cylinder (Fig. 4a). Rows of this grid are turns of a cylindrical spiral. The turns of this image can also be considered as closed circles on the cylinder with the same numbering (Fig. 4b).

To describe the image defined on a cylindrical grid, we use an analog [10] of the autoregressive model (1):

$$x_{k,l} = a\,x_{k,l-1} + b\,x_{k-1,l} - a\,b\,x_{k-1,l-1} + \beta\,\xi_{k,l}, \tag{3}$$

where k is a spiral turn number and l is a node number ($l = 0, ..., T - 1$) in the turn, T is the period, i.e. the number of points in one turn.

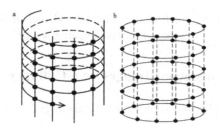

Fig. 4. (a) cylindrical grid; (b) circular grid.

1. This model can be represented in equivalent form

$$x_n = a\,x_{n-1} + b\,x_{n-T} - ab\,x_{n-T-1} + \beta\,\xi_n \tag{4}$$

as a scan of the image along a spiral, where $n = kT + l$ is end-to-end image point number. It can be shown that the CF of this model is

$$V(n) = \beta^2 \left(\frac{1}{(1-b^2)T} \sum_{k=0}^{T-1} \frac{z_k}{(1 - a z_k)(z_k - a)} z_k^n + \frac{s}{(1-a^2)(1-bs)(s-b)} \rho^n \right), \tag{5}$$

where $z_k = \sqrt[T]{b}\exp(i 2\pi k/T)$ and $s = a^T$. The graph view of such a CF is shown in Fig. 5. In particular, when $n = kT$ we obtain

$$V(kT) = \frac{\beta^2}{(1-a^2)(1-b^2)(1-sb)(b-s)} \left((1-s^2)b^{k+1} - (1-b^2)s^{k+1} \right)$$

and the variance $\sigma^2 = \frac{c^2(1+bs)}{(1-a^2)(1-b^2)(1-bs)}$, when $k = 0$.

A cross-section of the image obtained using this model is shown in Fig. 6.

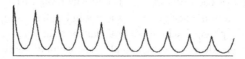

Fig. 5. The graph of CF process given by model in (3).

The characteristic feature of CF (5) is continuity at the junction of periods, in contrast to Fig. 3. The image in Fig. 6 is also continuous along the cut line, which is noticeable in the first few columns (Fig. 6b) attached to this image. As a result, the process described by model in Eq. 4, that is, the scan of the cylindrical image along a spiral, does not have sharp jumps at the junction of periods (Fig. 7). The examples of simulating cylindrical images at various values of this model parameters are shown in Fig. 8.

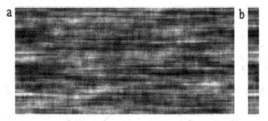

Fig. 6. (a) section of a cylindrical image; (b) it's the first columns.

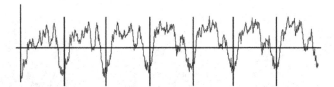

Fig. 7. Schedule of a simulation of a process by the model in Eq. 4.

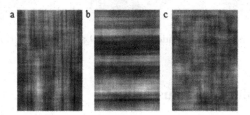

Fig. 8. Simulated image on a cylinder with parameters: (a) $a = 0.95$, $b = 0.99$; (b) $a = 0.99$, $b = 0.95$; (c) $a = b = 0.95$.

A polar coordinate system (r, φ) is convenient for circular images representation. To do this, we will consider circle grid showed in Fig. 9a. In other words, index k is converted into a polar radius, and index l into a polar angle. Thus, $x_{k, l}$ is the value of the circular image in the pixel with coordinates $(k\Delta r,\ l\Delta\varphi)$. It is also convenient to use a spiral grid (Fig. 9b). Note, this representation in the form of a spiral is made conditionally to facilitate analysis. In the image, a sequence of turns of a conditional spiral is a sequence of expanding circles. In this case, it is possible to represent values $x_{k, l}$ as a sequence of values x_1, x_2, x_3, ... Let us use the autoregressive model (4) of this sequence, where T is the period, i.e. the number of points in one turn.

The examples of simulating cylindrical images at various values of this model parameters1 are shown in Fig. 10. The parameters a and b set the degree of correlation in the circular and radial directions. If the autoregressive coefficient b from the previous coil of the spiral prevail, the image will be more correlated in radial direction (Fig. 10a). If the autoregressive coefficient a of the previous pixel is relatively large, then the image will have a high circular correlation (Fig. 10b). If $a \approx b$ then the image is equally correlated in both directions (Fig. 10c).

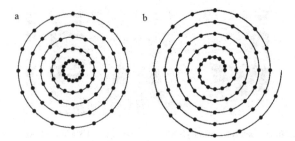

Fig. 9. (a) a circular grid; (b) a spiral grid.

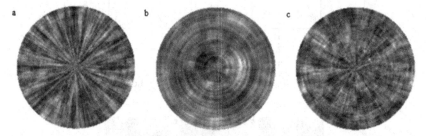

Fig. 10. (a) The parameters of simulation are $a = 0.9$ and $b = 0.95$; (b) $a = 0.98$, $b = 0.9$; (c) $a = b = 0.9$.

3   Models of Inhomogeneous Images

The images generated by model in (4) are homogeneous, which limits the scope of their application, since many images and signals have significant and random heterogeneity. In [13], it was proposed to represent the heterogeneity of images in the form of «doubly stochastic» model. In this view, several common «controlling» images set random parameters for a «managed» resulting image. The heterogeneity of the resulting image is determined by the local features of the controlling images. In [13], controlling and managed images were autoregressive given on rectangular grids.

To represent inhomogeneous cylindrical images, we apply the doubly stochastic model similar to those considered in [13]. To do this, let us take some two images and as controlling ones. The managed image is set by Eq. 1 but with variable parameters and given by

$$x_n = a_n x_{n-1} + b_n x_{n-T} - a_n b_n x_{n-T-1} + \beta \xi_n. \tag{6}$$

Figure 11 shows the examples of cylindrical images generated with two controlling images $A = \{a_n\}$(Fig. 11a) and $B = \{b_n\}$(Fig. 11b). Figures 11c, 11d and 11e show three variants of managed images. If $a_n < b_n$, then the managed images are more correlated vertically (top part of images). If $a_n > b_n$, then the managed images are more correlated in horizon direction (bottom part of images). These three images are different because of different random ξ_n in (4), but have common structure because of the same controlling images.

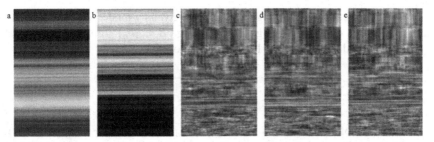

Fig. 11. The simulation using controlling images: (a) controlling image A; (b) controlling image B; (c, d, e) managed images.

Figure 12 shows the examples of circular images generated with two controlling images (Fig. 12a and 12b). Figures 12c-12f show 4 variants of managed images. If $a_n < b_n$, then the managed images are more correlated in radial direction. If $a_n > b_n$, then the managed images are more correlated in circular direction.

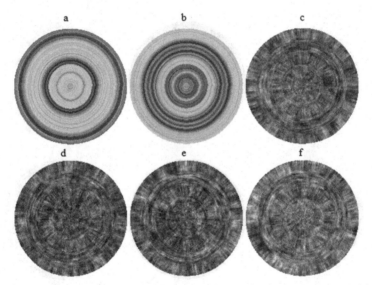

Fig. 12. The simulation using controlling images: (a) controlling image A; (b) controlling image B; (c, d, e, f) managed images.

4 The Test of Covariation Functions of Cylindrical and Circular Images

It is very important to have an adequate description of images in order to successfully solve the problems of their processing. This explains the large number of publications on image models, for example, [1–9]. The problem of identifying models of cylindrical and circular images was considered in [15, 16].

Let the observed managed image $X = \{x_n\}$ be given by model in (4). It is required to evaluate hidden controlling images $A = \{a_n\}$ and $B = \{b_n\}$. To solve this problem, we apply the pseudo-gradient [10, 14] adaptive algorithm

$$\hat{a}_{n+1} = \hat{a}_n + h\text{sgn}[\Delta_n(x_{n-1} - \hat{b}_n x_{n-T-1})],$$
$$\hat{b}_{n+1} = \hat{b}_n + h\text{sgn}[\Delta_n(x_{n-T} - \hat{a}_n x_{n-T-1})] \tag{7}$$

for minimization of squared errors $\Delta_n^2 = [x_n - (\hat{a}_n x_{n-1} + \hat{b}_n x_{n-T} - \hat{a}_n\hat{b}_n x_{n-T-1})]^2$, where $(\hat{a}_{n+1}, \hat{b}_{n+1})$ is the next estimate of (a_n, b_n) following estimate $(\hat{a}_n, \hat{b}_n)$, h is the step value of the algorithm. Thus, components of $(\hat{a}_{n+1}, \hat{b}_{n+1})$ differ of $(\hat{a}_n, \hat{b}_n)$ by $\pm h$. Numerical experiments have shown high accuracy in estimating the parameters a_n and b_n. Figure 13 shows an example controlling images estimation. Figures 13a and 13b show hidden controlling images $A = \{a_n\}$ and $B = \{b_n\}$, Fig. 14c shows managed image X using model (4). Figures 13d and 13e show obtained estimates $\hat{A}$ and $\hat{B}$ of A and B. Figure 13f shows image Y simulated using (4) with $\hat{A}$ and $\hat{B}$ as the controlling images. Note, it is visually very common to X.

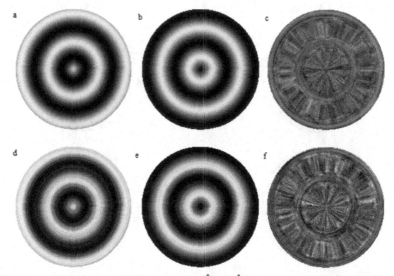

Fig. 13. (a) and (b) are A and B; (d) and (e) are $\hat{A}$ and $\hat{B}$; (c) image X managed by A and B; f) image Y managed by $\hat{A}$ and $\hat{B}$.

One can see good visual estimation $\hat{A}$ and $\hat{B}$ of A and B. But is it good enough to be considered a well-identified model? In our opinion, the main characteristic of an image is its CF. From this currents of view, the adequacy of the model should be assessed. An analysis of the proximity of CF images of X and Y was not done in [15, 16]. Now let us consider the problem of constructing a test for hypothesis about the form of CF of cylindrical and circular images.

Let X be a cylindrical or circular image, which is reduced to a model of the form (4), that is, it is considered as a stationary Gaussian centered discrete random process

$x_1, x_2, \ldots$ With unknown CF $V_n = M[x_i x_{i+n}]$. Required to test the simple hypothesis

$$H_0 : V_n = c_n, \ n \in N_r, \tag{8}$$

against the complex hypothesis

$$H_1 : \exists n(V_n \neq c_n) \tag{9}$$

with significance level α for the available sample $\bar{x} = (x_1, \ x_3, \ \ldots, \ x_N)^T$, where N_r is a set of r parameter n values; and (9) means that $V_n \neq c_n$ for at least one value n from N_r.

Note, in (9) there are covariance values only for values from a given set, and not for all integer values. This was done for two reasons. First, covariance values for a limited set of argument values are usually of interest. Second, it is possible to estimate the process covariance only at limited distances in time using a limited data. Thus, the hypothesis is that the sample values of the covariance and their theoretical values do not statistically contradict each other on the set N_r.

Let us first construct an estimate of the maximum likelihood (ML) of the values V_n. The likelihood function (LF) in our case has the form

$$L(\bar{x}|\{V_n\}) = \frac{1}{(2\pi)^{n/2}|V|^{1/2}} \exp\left(-\frac{1}{2}\bar{x}^T V^{-1} \bar{x}\right), \tag{10}$$

where V is the symmetric covariance matrix. The inverse matrix $U = V^{-1} = (u_{ij})$ is also symmetric. We will use the following CF estimate:

$$\hat{V}_n = \frac{1}{N-n} \sum_{k=1}^{N-n} x_k x_{k+n}, \tag{11}$$

which is not biased, consistent, and asymptotically normal. Let us construct a criterion for distinguishing between CF hypotheses based on statistics

$$S_n = \frac{1}{N-n} \sum_{k=1}^{N-n} x_k x_{k+n}, n \in N_r. \tag{12}$$

Let us consider the criterion [17] for testing the hypothesis (8) against (9), based on statistics (12), that is, on statistics

$$\overline{S} = \{S_n, n \in N_r\}. \tag{13}$$

Let the hypothesis H_0 be true, then (13) will be an unbiased estimate of the vector of parameters

$$\bar{c} = \{c_n, n \in N_r\}.$$

It is known [18] that for $N \to \infty$ random variables

$$\varphi_n = \sqrt{N-n}(S_n - c_n) \tag{14}$$

are asymptotically normal with zero mean and covariance

$$v\psi_{hg} = \sum_{k=-\infty}^{\infty} (c_{k+h}c_{k+g} + c_{k+h}c_{k-g}), \tag{15}$$

that is, the vector

$$\overline{\varphi} = \{\varphi_n, n \in N_r\}$$

has zero mean and covariance matrix

$$\Psi = \{\psi_{h,g}\}, h, g \in N_r.$$

Thus, the likelihood function (LF) for the hypothesis H_0 is

$$L(\overline{S}|H_0) = L(\overline{\varphi}|H_0) \frac{1}{(2\pi)^{r/2}|\psi|^{1/2}} \exp\left(-\frac{1}{2}\overline{\varphi}^T \psi^{-1}\overline{\varphi}\right). \tag{16}$$

Let us consider first a simple competing hypothesis

$$\tilde{H}_1 : V_n = d_n, \ n \in N_r, \tag{17}$$

with LF

$$L(\overline{S}|\tilde{H}_1) = L(\overline{\mu}|\tilde{H}_1) \frac{1}{(2\pi)^{r/2}|G|^{1/2}} \exp\left(-\frac{1}{2}\overline{\mu}^T G^{-1}\overline{\mu}\right). \tag{18}$$

The best critical region (BCR) for the hypothesis H_0 against $\tilde{H}_1$ is

$$\frac{L(\overline{S}|H_0)}{L(\overline{S}|\tilde{H}_1)} = \frac{L(\overline{\varphi}|H_0)}{L(\overline{\mu}|\tilde{H}_1)} \leq k_\alpha, \tag{19}$$

where k_α depends on the given level of significance α. Substituting (16) and (18) into (19) and taking the logarithm, we obtain

$$\overline{\mu}^T G^{-1}\overline{\mu} - \overline{\varphi}^T \Psi^{-1}\overline{\varphi} \leq l_\alpha = \ln\left(\frac{k_\alpha|G|^{1/2}}{|\Psi|^{1/2}}\right), \tag{20}$$

where

$$\overline{\varphi} = \left\{\sqrt{N-n}(S_n - c_n), n \in N_r\right\}, \ \overline{\mu} = \left\{\sqrt{N-n}(S_n - d_n), n \in N_r\right\}, \tag{21}$$

therefore, the expressions on the left side of (20) are ordinary (reduced to the origin of coordinates) quadratic forms, in relation to $\overline{\mu}$ and $\overline{\varphi}$, and relative to $\overline{S}$ are displaced quadratic forms with centers at points $\overline{c}$ and и $\overline{d}$ of r-dimensional space. Except in the degenerate cases when $|\Psi| = 0$ and/or $|G| = 0$, these quadratic forms are positively defined with hyperellipsoids of equal values. However, the difference of two quadratic forms can be a quadratic form with any rank and any signature, that is, with any number of negative, positive and zero squares in canonical form. Therefore, the surface defining the BCR in (20) can be very diverse. The BCR analysis is significantly complicated by the fact that the shape matrix depends on the CF values d_n.

The dependence of BCR on the parameters of a simple hypothesis means that there is no uniformly most powerful (UMP) criterion for a complex hypothesis (9). Therefore, one can only accept some kind of compromise criterion. For this purpose, we transform expression (20). Using (21), we have:

$$\mu_n = \sqrt{N - n}(S_n - d_n) = \sqrt{N - n}((S_n - c_n) - (d_n - c_n)) =$$
$$= \sqrt{N - n}(S_n - c_n) - \sqrt{N - n}(d_n - c_n) = \varphi_n - \sqrt{N - n}\delta_n = \varphi_n - \Delta_n,$$

where

$$\delta_n = d_n - c_n, \quad \Delta_n = \sqrt{N - n}\delta_n.$$

Further,

$$\overline{\mu}^T G^{-1} \overline{\mu} = \left(\overline{\varphi} - \overline{\Delta}\right)^T G^{-1}\left(\overline{\varphi} - \overline{\Delta}\right) = \overline{\varphi}^T G^{-1}\overline{\varphi} - 2\overline{\Delta}^T G^{-1}\overline{\varphi} + \overline{\Delta}^T G^{-1}\overline{\Delta}. \quad (22)$$

Substituting (22) into (20), we obtain

$$\overline{\varphi}^T G^{-1}\overline{\varphi} - \overline{\varphi}^T \Psi^{-1}\overline{\varphi} - 2\overline{\Delta}G^{-1}\overline{\varphi} \le l_\alpha - \overline{\Delta}^T G^{-1}\overline{\Delta}. \quad (23)$$

Let the hypothesis H_0 be true. Then, $M[\overline{\varphi}] = 0$, $M\left[\overline{\Delta}^T G^{-1}\overline{\varphi}\right] = 0$, $M\left[\overline{\varphi}^T G^{-1}\overline{\varphi}\right]$ и $M\left[\overline{\varphi}^T \Psi^{-1}\overline{\varphi}\right]$ and are limited and tend to their limit values as $N \to \infty$. The value $\overline{\Delta}^T G^{-1}\overline{\Delta}$ is not random, it is a positively defined quadratic form of variables $\Delta_n = \sqrt{N - n}(d_n - c_n)$ that increase with increasing N if $d_n \ne c_n$:

$$\lim_{N \to \infty} |\Delta_n| = \infty, \ if \ d_n \ne c_n.$$

Thus, if the hypothesis H_0 is true, we have:

$$\lim_{N \to \infty} \overline{\Delta}^T G^{-1}\overline{\Delta} = +\infty. \quad (24)$$

It follows from (23) and (24) that, for any simple alternative $\tilde{H}_1$, the BCR for H_0 is infinitely canceled out (for continuous distributed $\overline{\varphi}$). Let us rewrite (23) as:

$$\overline{\varphi}^T \psi^{-1}\overline{\varphi} \ge \overline{\Delta}^T G^{-1}\overline{\Delta} - l_\alpha - 2\overline{\Delta}G^{-1}\overline{\varphi} + \overline{\varphi}^T G^{-1}\overline{\varphi}. \quad (25)$$

Considering that the right-hand side of (25) increases infinitely with growth N, we can conclude that for any simple hypothesis $\tilde{H}_1$ and a sufficiently large sample size, the BCR for H_0 contains points at which $\overline{\varphi}^T \Psi^{-1}\overline{\varphi}$ t has large values. Therefore, it is advisable to include only such points in the critical area of the hypothesis H_0 with a complex hypothesis (9):

$$\overline{\varphi}^T \Psi^{-1}\overline{\varphi} \ge b_\alpha,$$

where the threshold b_α corresponds to the significance level α. Thus, we obtain the following criterion for testing a hypothesis H_0 against a complex alternative H_1:

$$\overline{\varphi}^T \Psi^{-1} \overline{\varphi} < b_\alpha \Rightarrow H_0 \text{ is accepted,}$$

$$\overline{\varphi}^T \Psi^{-1} \overline{\varphi} \geq b_\alpha \Rightarrow H_1 \text{ is accepted.} \tag{26}$$

The meaning of this criterion is simple: the hypothesis is accepted if the deviations of the sample values S_n of the CF from its exact values c_n are small in the aggregate.

The power of criterion (26) naturally depends on the specific alternative $\tilde{H}_1$ and can be significantly lower than the power of the most powerful criterion (MPC) for this alternative at small values N.

Let us now consider the case when a certain simple alternative $\tilde{H}_1$ is true, that is, when the exact values of CF in (20) and (21) are d_n. In this case, we represent statistics $\overline{\varphi}$ in the form:

$$\varphi_n = \sqrt{N - n}((S_n - d_n) + (d_n - c_n)) = \mu_n + \Delta_n, \text{ i.e. } \overline{\varphi} = \overline{\mu} + \overline{\Delta},$$

and transform (20) to the form:

$$\overline{\mu}^T G^{-1} \overline{\mu} \leq \overline{\Delta}^T \Psi^{-1} \overline{\Delta} + l_\alpha + 2\overline{\Delta}^T \Psi^{-1} \overline{\mu} + \overline{\mu}^T \Psi^{-1} \overline{\mu}. \tag{27}$$

The value $\overline{\Delta}^T \Psi^{-1} \overline{\Delta}$ infinitely increases with increasing N, and the values $\overline{\mu}$, on average, decrease; therefore, the probability of fulfilling inequality (27) tends to 1 as $N \to \infty$. Thus, for any simple alternative $\tilde{H}_1 \in H_1$ and any level of significance, alternative $\tilde{H}_1$ is accepted with a probability arbitrarily close to 1 at $N \geq N(\tilde{H}_1)$.

Note, however, that there is no reason to say that $N(\tilde{H}_1) \leq N_0$ for everyone $\tilde{H}_1 \in H_1$. Therefore, it is impossible to indicate the sample size N_0 sufficient to ensure the power of criterion (26), not less than the given one, for all alternatives H_1. The existence of such uniform N_0 is possible if H_1 is a class of a certain type alternatives.

Let us now find the threshold b_α in (26) corresponding to a given level of significance. The statistics in (26) has a chi-square distribution with r degrees of freedom for a Gaussian vector $\overline{\varphi}$. In our case, the vector $\overline{\varphi}$ is asymptotically Gaussian, so the critical value of the chi-squared distribution with r degrees of freedom can be taken as a threshold $b_\alpha = \chi^2_{\alpha,r}$. It should be borne in mind that for small values N this threshold may giv5.e an inaccurate value of the significance level due to significant deviations of the distribution of statistics in (26) from the chi-square.

Let us give as an example the application of the presented criterion to test the hypothesis about CF (5). The process with zero mean and covariance function (5) was simulated using an autoregressive model (4) with $\sigma = 1$, $a = 0.8$, $b = 0.8$, $T = 100$ and the set $N_r = N_3 = \{0, T, 2T\}$. Thus, the hypothesis is that the process has CF (5) on the specified set N_3.

The CF estimate was found by (12) at $\mu = 0$ and $N = 400$ that is, realizations of 40,000 samples of this process were used. For this implementation, a value χ^2 was calculated and compared in the decision rule (26) with the threshold $b_{0.05} = \chi^2_{0.05; 3} = 7.815$ corresponding to a significance level $\alpha = 0.05$ with $r = 3$ degrees of freedom.

There have been 10,000 applications of this criterion. It turned out that the correct hypothesis was rejected 512 times, that is, the relative frequency of rejection is 0.0512. This value is in the 99% confidence interval $I_{0.99} = (0.0467; 0.0532)$. Thus, in this experiment, the given level of significance can be considered sustained.

In another experiment, the power P of the test was investigated when testing the same hypothesis $H_0(\sigma = 1, \ a = 0.8, \ b = 0.8, \ T = 100$ and the set $N_r = N_3 = \{0, T, 2T\})$ against simple hypotheses $\tilde{H}_1$ with different values of the parameters σ, a and b. The criterion was applied 10,000 times for each of these sets of values. Figure 14a shows the graph of the power estimated, that is, the relative frequency of an incorrect hypothesis $\tilde{H}_1(\sigma = 1, \ T = 100$, the set $N_r = N_3 = \{0, T, 2T\}$ and different values of $a = b$) rejection. Figure 14b shows the graph of the power estimated, that is, the relative frequency of an incorrect hypothesis $\tilde{H}_1(\ a = 0.8, \ b = 0.8, \ T = 100, \ N_r = N_3 = \{0, T, 2T\}$ and different values of σ) rejection. These data show, that the criterion is quite sensitive to deviations of the process parameters from their assumed values.

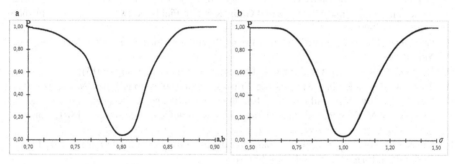

Fig. 14. Dependence of criterion power on parameters of testing image: (a) on $a = b$; (b) on σ.

5 Conclusions

The vast majority of works on image processing deal with images defined on rectangular two-dimensional grids or grids of higher dimension. Sometimes images are set on a cylinder or a circle. Autoregressive models of such images are considered. To represent heterogeneous images with random heterogeneities, doubly stochastic models are used in which one or more images control the parameters of the resulting image. The controlling images affect the properties of resulting image but they are unobserved. Knowledge of this structure is required when developing effective image processing algorithms. So there is the problem of hidden controlling images identification (evaluation). This problem is solved using the pseudo-gradient adaptive algorithms for controlling images parameters evaluation based on the resulting image. A criterion for testing hypotheses about the CF of cylindrical and circular images is proposed. The criterion checks the compliance of several CF estimates with their theoretical values. Examples of applying the proposed criterion showed its high power, that is, sensitivity to deviations of the sample CF from the theoretical one.

Acknowledgment. This study was funded by the RFBR, project number 20–01-00613.

References

1. Soifer, V.A., Popov, S.B., Mysnikov, V.V., Sergeev, V.V.: Computer Image rocessing. Part I: Basic Concepts and Theory. VDM Verlag Dr. Muller (2009)
2. Vizilter, Y.V., Pyt'ev, Y.P., Chulichkov, A.I., Mestetskiy, L.M.: Morphological image analysis for computer vision applications. In: Favorskaya, M.N., Jain, L.C. (eds.) Computer Vision in Control Systems-1. ISRL, vol. 73, pp. 9–58. Springer, Cham (2015). https://doi.org/10.1007/978-3-319-10653-3_2
3. Jain, L.C., Favorskaya, M.N.: Innovative Algorithms in Computer Vision. In: Favorskaya, M.N., Jain, L.C. (eds.) Computer Vision in Control Systems-4. ISRL, vol. 136, pp. 1–9. Springer, Cham (2018). https://doi.org/10.1007/978-3-319-67994-5_1
4. Woods, J.W.: Two-dimensional Kalman Filtering. Topics Appl. Phys. **42**, 11–64 (1981)
5. Habibi, A.: Two-dimensional Bayesian Estimate of Images. Proc. IEEE **60**(7), 878–883 (1972)
6. Gimel'farb, G.L.: Image Textures and Gibbs Random Fields. Kluwer Academic Publishers Dordrecht (1999)
7. Gonzalez, R.C., Woods, R.E.: Digital Image Processing, 4th edn. Pearson Education, New York (2017)
8. Bouman, C.A.: Model Based Imaging Processing. Purdue University (2013)
9. Tincu, A., Ray, A.K.: Image Processing. Principles and Applications. Wiley, New York (2005)
10. Krasheninnikov, V., Vasil'ev, K.: Multidimensional image models and processing. In: Favorskaya, M.N., Jain, L.C. (eds.) Computer Vision in Control Systems-3. ISRL, vol. 135, pp. 11–64. Springer, Cham (2018). https://doi.org/10.1007/978-3-319-67516-9_2
11. Krasheninnikov, V.R.: Correlation analysis and synthesis of random field wave models. Pattern Recognition Image Anal. **25**(1), 41–46 (2015)
12. Dement'iev, V.E., Krasheninnikov, V.R.: Vasil'ev, K.K.: Representation and processing of spatially heterogeneous images and image sequences. In: Favorskaya, M.N., Jain, L.C. (eds.) Computer Vision In Control Systems-5, ISRL, vol. 175, pp. 53–98. Springer, Cham (2015)
13. Vasil'ev, K., Dement'ev, V.E., Andriyanov, N.A.: Doubly stochastic models of images. Pattern Recognition Image Anal. **25**(1), 105–110 (2015)
14. Polyak, B.T., Tsypkin, J.Z.: Optimal pseudogradient adaptation procedure. Autom. Remote Control **8**, 74–84 (1980). (In Russian)
15. Krasheninnikov, V.R., Malenova, O.E., Subbotin, A.U.: The identification of doubly stochastic circular image model. knowledge-based and intelligent information & engineering systems. In: Proceedings of the 24th International Conference KES2020. Procedia Computer Science, vol. 176, 1839–1847 (2020)
16. Krasheninnikov, V.R., Kuvayskova, Yu.E., Subbotin, A.U.: Pseudo-gradient algorithm for identification of doubly stochastic cylindrical image model. In: Knowledge-Based and Intelligent Information & Engineering Systems: Proceedings of the 24th International Conference KES2020. Procedia Computer Science, vol. 176, pp. 1858–1867 (2020)
17. Krasheninnikov, V.R., Gladkikh, E.A.: The criterion for testing hypotheses about the covariance function and spectral density of a random process. Autom. Manage. Processes **1**(35), 24–30 (2014). (In Russian)
18. Anderson, T.W.: The Statistical Analysis of Time Series. Wiley, New York (1971)

One-Class Classification Criterion Robust to Anomalies in Training Dataset

Aleksandr O. Larin⬦, Oleg S. Seredin$^{(\boxtimes)}$ ⬦, and Andrey V. Kopylov⬦

Tula State University, Lenin Ave. 92, Tula 300012, Russia
oseredin@yandex.ru

Abstract. A new version of one-class classification criterion robust to anomalies in the training dataset is proposed based on support vector data description (SVDD). The original formulation of the problem is not geometrically correct, since the value of the penalty for the admissible escape of the training sample objects outside the describing hypersphere is incommensurable with the distance to its center in the optimization problem and the presence of outliers can greatly affect the decision boundary. The proposed criterion is intended to eliminate this inconsistency. The equivalent form of criterion without constraints lets us use a kernel-based approach without transition to the dual form to make a flexible description of the training dataset. The substitution of the non-differentiable objective function by the smooth one allows us to apply an algorithm of sequential optimizations to solve the problem. We apply the Jaccard measure for a quantitative assessment of the robustness of a decision rule to the presence of outliers. A comparative experimental study of existing one-class methods shows the superiority of the proposed criterion in anomaly detection.

Keywords: One-class classification · Outlier detection · Support vector data description

1 Introduction

In the problem of one-class classification [1], the training set is represented only by objects of a single class, and it is necessary to divide the linear space into two non-intersecting regions with a not too "complex" boundary so that the training set is mainly contained in one of them. In this case, the decision rule of one-class recognition determines whether the object of the real world belongs to a given class or not, and the final decision is represented by a two-class index. This work is devoted to the consideration of just this problem.

The task of training on partially labeled data is close to the one-class classification task, in the case when the labeled data belongs to only one class, which is often called positive. This task of learning from positively labeled and unlabeled data is called PU-Learning. A survey of recent methods for solving such a problem can be found in [2]. The unlabeled part of the training sample can also be presented implicitly, in the form of a neural network autoencoder trained on some data, which is used to obtain a feature

© Springer Nature Switzerland AG 2021
A. Del Bimbo et al. (Eds.): ICPR 2020 Workshops, LNCS 12665, pp. 155–165, 2021.
https://doi.org/10.1007/978-3-030-68821-9_15

description of recognition objects [3]. Since these methods are still related to a two-class classification problem, we leave their consideration outside the scope of this paper.

One-class classification is most widely used at the initial stages of solving data mining problems as a tool for searching for anomalies and atypical objects (outliers) in experimental datasets [4], although there are examples of using this tool for solving applied problems, for example, for segmentation of color images [5–7].

Currently, there are many methods for solving the problem of single-class classification [8]. There are usually three groups of them: probabilistic methods, metric methods, and boundary methods.

Probabilistic methods [9] are based on the estimation of the probability density of the training set and choose a threshold value that cuts off objects that do not belong to the target class. The distribution densities, on the one hand, should be flexible enough to describe the data, and on the other hand, the estimation of their parameters should not lead to high demanding computational procedures. The most common types of distributions in practice are the Gaussian mixture model (GMM) [10] and the Parzen distribution [11].

Metric methods exploit various types of pairwise relationships between objects, including relatively simple nearest neighbor or nearest centers methods, as well as more algorithmically complex methods based on minimal spanning trees [12].

Boundary methods, based on the analysis of the training set, construct a boundary that separates objects of the target class from external objects. In general, they can form simpler classifiers than probabilistic ones on smaller data sets. This property of this group of methods is explained by the fact that in the case of a significant limitation of the training set, the solution of a more general problem (probabilistic methods) instead of solving the existing particular one leads to excessive complexity and, possibly, overfitting of the classifier [13]. The most common representative of the methods of this group is the one-class SVM method proposed in [14]. Its essence is in constructing a boundary that provides the maximum gap between the objects of the training set and the zero point of the feature space. Using the kernel methods makes it possible to construct a boundary of a given complexity.

In 1999, D. Tax and R. Duin proposed a method for solving a one-class pattern recognition problem, called the Support Vector Data Description (SVDD) [15], which has an analogy with the V. Vapnik support vector method [13]. The data description model in this method is a hypersphere, which is the closest outer boundary around the target dataset. Although it was shown in [16] that when using the Gaussian Radial Basis Function (RBF), the SVDD and One-class SVM methods are equivalent, SVDD has a more intuitive formulation and geometric interpretation. However, although both methods are used to detect anomalies in data and atypical objects, the presence of such objects can greatly affect the decision boundary. In this paper, we propose a version of the SVDD criterion that eliminates this drawback.

2 Support Vector Data Description

The main idea of the SVDD method [15] is to describe the dataset, represented by n numerical features, $\mathbf{x}_i \in \mathbb{R}^n$, $i = 1, \ldots, N$, by the outer border around the data in the form of a hypersphere. The parameters that define the hypersphere are its center and radius. The hypersphere is selected in such a way that its radius is minimal, but at the same time, most of the objects of the training set do not go beyond its limits (see Fig. 1). Objects that fall outside the border of the hypersphere should be penalized.

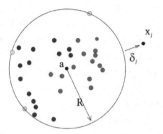

Fig. 1. The spherical model of data description [15]

Thus, it is necessary to minimize the structural error of the model: δ_i

$$
\begin{cases}
R^2 + C \sum_{i=1}^{N} \delta_i \to \min_{R^2, \mathbf{a}, \delta_1, \ldots, \delta_N} , \\
\|\mathbf{x}_i - \mathbf{a}\|^2 \le R^2 + \delta_i, \quad \delta_i \ge 0, \quad i = 1, \ldots, N.
\end{cases}
\tag{1}
$$

The dual problem concerning (1) has the form:

$$
\begin{cases}
\sum_{i=1}^{N} \lambda_i (\mathbf{x}_i \cdot \mathbf{x}_i) - \sum_{i=1}^{N} \sum_{j=1}^{N} \lambda_i \lambda_j (\mathbf{x}_i \cdot \mathbf{x}_j) \to \max_{\lambda_1, \ldots, \lambda_N} , \\
\sum_{i=1}^{N} \lambda_i = 1, \ 0 \le \lambda_i \le C, \quad i = 1, \ldots, N,
\end{cases}
\tag{2}
$$

where $\lambda_1, \ldots, \lambda_N$ are Lagrange multipliers. To describe the entire training set, D. Tax proposes to use only support objects that lie on the border of the hypersphere, i.e. objects for which the Lagrange multipliers $0 \le \lambda_i \le C, i = 1, \ldots, N$. Following Eq. (2), it can be shown that $1/N \le C \le 1$. A new object $\mathbf{z}$ is considered to belong to the class of interest when the distance from it to the center of the hypersphere is less than or equal to its radius. Thus, the one-class decision rule $d\left(\mathbf{z} ; \hat{R}^2, \hat{\lambda}_1, \ldots, \hat{\lambda}_N\right)$ will have the form of an indicator function:

$$
d(\mathbf{z}) = I\left(\|\mathbf{z} - \hat{\mathbf{a}}\|^2 \le \hat{R}^2\right),
\tag{3}
$$

$$
\|\mathbf{z} - \hat{\mathbf{a}}\|^2 = (\mathbf{z} \cdot \mathbf{z}) - 2 \sum_{i=1}^{N_{SV}} \hat{\lambda}_i (\mathbf{z} \cdot \mathbf{x}_i) + \sum_{i=1}^{N_{SV}} \sum_{j=1}^{N_{SV}} \hat{\lambda}_i \hat{\lambda}_j (\mathbf{x}_i \cdot \mathbf{x}_j),
\tag{4}
$$

$$
\hat{R}^2 = (\mathbf{x}_k \cdot \mathbf{x}_k) - 2 \sum_{i=1}^{N_{SV}} \hat{\lambda}_i (\mathbf{x}_k \cdot \mathbf{x}_i) + \sum_{i=1}^{N_{SV}} \sum_{j=1}^{N_{SV}} \hat{\lambda}_i \hat{\lambda}_j (\mathbf{x}_i \cdot \mathbf{x}_j),
\tag{5}
$$

where N_{SV} is the number of support objects, $\mathbf{x}_k$ - an arbitrary support object, $\hat{\mathbf{a}}$, $\hat{R}$ and $\hat{\lambda}_i, i = 1, \ldots, N_{SV}$ - are the optimal values of parameters in (1) and (2).

For describing data in a more "flexible form" than a sphere, D. Tax used the idea of the kernel method, proposed by V. Vapnik, for the transition to the rectifying space of features of higher dimension.

The most commonly used potential functions are polynomial $K(\mathbf{x}_i, \mathbf{x}_j) = (1 + \mathbf{x}_i \cdot \mathbf{x}_j)^p$ and Gaussian radial basis function (RBF) $K(\mathbf{x}_i, \mathbf{x}_j) = \exp(-\gamma ||\mathbf{x}_i - \mathbf{x}_j||^2)$. Thus, in order to obtain an improved model for describing data by the Tax method, it is necessary to replace in (2), (4), and (5) the operation of calculating the inner product of two vectors by the value of the two arguments kernel function.

Kernels functions allow to apply the one-class classification to the problems of featureless pattern recognition [17, 18], in which the vector of features of objects is not available explicitly, but the function of the pair relation between objects is defined.

Later in [19], other formulations were proposed, which differ in the use of penalties for distances from objects located in the outer region of the hypersphere to its boundary:

$$\begin{cases} \bar{R} + C \sum_{i=1}^{N} \delta_i \to \min_{\bar{R},\mathbf{a},\delta_1,\dots,\delta_N}, \\ ||\mathbf{x}_i - \mathbf{a}||^2 \le \bar{R} + \delta_i, \ \delta_i \ge 0, \ i = 1,\dots,N, \end{cases} \quad \text{and} \quad \begin{cases} \bar{R} + C \sum_{i=1}^{N} \delta_i^2 \to \min_{\bar{R},\mathbf{a},\delta_1,\dots,\delta_N}, \\ ||\mathbf{x}_i - \mathbf{a}||^2 \le \bar{R} + \delta_i, \ \delta_i \ge 0, \ i = 1,\dots,N, \end{cases} \tag{6}$$

where $\bar{R} = R^2$. Unfortunately, we did not find ready-made software implementations of optimization procedures for criteria (6).

Another formulation of the problem of one-class classification is the method of one-class SVM (One-class SVM) [14], which aims to construct a boundary that provides the maximum margin between the objects of the training set and the zero point of the feature space. The One-class SVM criterion is as follows:

$$\begin{cases} \frac{1}{2}||\mathbf{w}||^2 + C \sum_{i=1}^{N} \delta_i^2 - b \to \min_{\mathbf{w},b,\delta_1,\dots,\delta_N}, \\ (\mathbf{w} \cdot \Phi(\mathbf{x}_i)) \ge b + \delta_i, \quad \delta_i \ge 0, \quad i = 1,\dots,N, \end{cases} \tag{7}$$

where $\mathbf{w}$ and b are the parameters of the hyperplane that provides the maximum margin between the data of the target class and the origin, $\Phi(\cdot)$ is the mapping of the feature space into the rectifying Hilbert space.

The main problem of the formulations of the one-class classification problem described above is a serious assumption in their mathematical formulation associated with the strategy of outliers penalizing.

The original formulation of the problem is not geometrically correct, since the value of the penalty for the admissible escape of the training sample objects outside the describing hypersphere is incommensurable with the distance to its center in the optimization problem. The experimental studies presented further in the work showed that this does not significantly affect the quality of the method in the absence of anomalies in the training sample and allows to greatly simplify the solution of the original problem, but in the case of the presence of atypical objects in the training set, the quality of the method is greatly deteriorated.

3 Modified One-Class Classification Criterion Robust to the Presence of Outliers

In this paper, in order to solve the problem associated with the presence of outliers in the training set, we propose to modify the statement of the one-class classification problem (1) and its decision rule (3) as follows:

$$
\begin{cases}
R + C \sum_{i=1}^{N} \delta_i \to \min_{R, \mathbf{a}, \delta_1, \ldots, \delta_N}, \\
\rho(\mathbf{x}_i, \mathbf{a}) \le R + \delta_i, \quad \delta_i \ge 0, \quad i = 1, \ldots, N,
\end{cases}
\tag{8}
$$

$$
d(\mathbf{z}) = I(\rho(\mathbf{x}_i, \mathbf{a}) \le R),
\tag{9}
$$

where $\rho(\mathbf{x}_i, \mathbf{a})$ - distance measure between two objects in $\mathbb{R}^n$.

It can be shown that the requirement of non-negativity of R in this setting is redundant and can be omitted.

An attempt to rewrite (8) in a dual form does not lead to a tractable expression. But we can transform criterion (8) to an unconstrained formulation.

Theorem. Criterion (8) is completely equivalent to the following criterion without constraint:

$$
R + C \sum_{i=1}^{N} \max(0, \rho(\mathbf{x}_i, \mathbf{a}) - R) \to \min_{R, \mathbf{a}}.
\tag{10}
$$

Proof. Let problem (8) be solved and $(\hat{R}, \hat{\mathbf{a}}, \hat{\delta}_1, \ldots, \hat{\delta}_N)$ be its solution. In accordance with (8), two cases are possible: if $\rho(\mathbf{x}_i, \mathbf{a}) \le \hat{R}$, then $\hat{\delta}_i = 0$; if $\rho(\mathbf{x}_i, \mathbf{a}) > \hat{R}$, then $\hat{\delta}_i = \rho(\mathbf{x}_i, \mathbf{a}) - \hat{R}$.

Thus, $\hat{\delta}_i = \max\left[0, \left(\rho(\mathbf{x}_i, \mathbf{a}) - \hat{R}\right)\right]$ and these equalities could be considered as an additional constraints in (8):

$$
\delta_i = \max[0, (\rho(\mathbf{x}_i, \mathbf{a}) - R)], \quad i = 1, \ldots, N.
\tag{11}
$$

In such case the problem (8) will have the following form:

$$
\begin{cases}
R + C \sum_{i=1}^{N} \max[0, (\rho(\mathbf{x}_i, \mathbf{a}) - R)] \to \min_{R, \mathbf{a}}, \\
\rho(\mathbf{x}_i, \mathbf{a}) \le R + \max[0, (\rho(\mathbf{x}_i, \mathbf{a}) - R)], \quad i = 1, \ldots, N.
\end{cases}
\tag{12}
$$

Let us show, that inequality constraints are always satisfied under condition (11). Actually, if the constraint $\rho(\mathbf{x}_i, \mathbf{a}) \le R$, $\delta = 0$, then $\max[0, (\rho(\mathbf{x}_i, \mathbf{a}) - R)] = 0$, and the inequality constraint for criterion (12) is always satisfied. If the constrain $\rho(\mathbf{x}_i, \mathbf{a}) > R$, $\delta_i = \rho(\mathbf{x}_i, \mathbf{a}) - R$ is true, then the inequality constrain is equivalent to $\rho(\mathbf{x}_i, \mathbf{a}) \le R + \rho(\mathbf{x}_i, \mathbf{a}) - R$, which in turn is an identity $\underbrace{\rho(\mathbf{x}_i, \mathbf{a}) - \rho(\mathbf{x}_i, \mathbf{a})}_{0} \le \underbrace{R - R}_{0}$.

Thereby the inequality constraint in criterion (12) is redundant and we will have criterion (10), q.e.d.

The rather simple dual form of Tax's original criterion (2) makes it easy to apply the kernel trick by simply replacing the dot product with a kernel function. But in the case of (10) kernel trick is not so straightforward. The idea is to define the center of a circumscribed hypersphere as a linear combination of objects in the training set $\mathbf{a} = \sum_{j=1}^{N} v_j \mathbf{x}_j$.

For Euclidean space the distance function can be defined through kernel as:

$$\rho(\mathbf{x}, \mathbf{a}) = [K(\mathbf{x}, \mathbf{x}) + K(\mathbf{a}, \mathbf{a}) - 2K(\mathbf{x}, \mathbf{a})]^{1/2}. \tag{13}$$

Therefore, the equivalent form of criterion (10) will take the following form:

$$R + C \sum_{k=1}^{N} \max \left[0, \left(K(\mathbf{x}_k, \mathbf{x}_k) - 2 \sum_{i=1}^{N} v_i K(\mathbf{x}_k, \mathbf{x}_i) + \sum_{i=1}^{N} \sum_{j=1}^{N} v_i v_j K(\mathbf{x}_i, \mathbf{x}_j) \right)^{\frac{1}{2}} - R \right] \rightarrow \min_{\substack{R, \\ v_1 \dots v_N}}, \tag{14}$$

$$d(\mathbf{z}) = I \left[\left(K(\mathbf{z}, \mathbf{z}) - 2 \sum_{i=1}^{N} v_i K(\mathbf{z}, \mathbf{x}_i) + \sum_{i=1}^{N} \sum_{j=1}^{N} v_i v_j K(\mathbf{x}_i, \mathbf{x}_j) \right)^{\frac{1}{2}} \leq R \right]. \tag{15}$$

The term $\sum_{i=1}^{N} \sum_{j=1}^{N} v_i v_j K(\mathbf{x}_i, \mathbf{x}_j)$ does not depend from $\mathbf{z}$, and can be calculated in advance.

The criterion (14) is quasi-convex, but not differentiable over the entire domain of definition, and neither the usual gradient methods nor Newton's method can be used to minimize it.

4 The Differentiable Form of Criterion

In this paper, we apply a method for solving this problem, through the use of an algorithm of sequential optimizations that converge to the solution of the original problem based on the proxy-function $P(t, \varepsilon)$ which is a "smoothed" version of the maximum function [20, 21]:

$$P(t, \varepsilon) = \begin{cases} \frac{1}{2} \varepsilon e^{\frac{t}{\varepsilon}}, & t \leq 0, \\ t + \frac{1}{2} \varepsilon e^{-\frac{t}{\varepsilon}}, & t > 0, \end{cases} \quad \frac{\partial}{\partial t} P(t, \varepsilon) = \begin{cases} \frac{1}{2} e^{\frac{t}{\varepsilon}}, & t \leq 0, \\ 1 - \frac{1}{2} e^{-\frac{t}{\varepsilon}}, & t > 0, \end{cases} \tag{16}$$

where ε is a parameter that determines the quality of smoothing, and, therefore, the accuracy of the resulting solution.

Thus, substituting function (13) into the mathematical setting (14), we obtain the following objective function:

$$R + C \sum_{k=1}^{N} P\left(\left[\sqrt{(\mathbf{x}_k \cdot \mathbf{x}_k) - 2 \sum_{i=1}^{N} v_i (\mathbf{x}_i \cdot \mathbf{x}_k) + \sum_{i=1}^{N} \sum_{j=1}^{N} v_i v_j (\mathbf{x}_i \cdot \mathbf{x}_j)} - R \right], \varepsilon \right) \rightarrow \min_{\substack{R, \\ v_1, \dots v_N}}. \tag{17}$$

The problem (17) can be easily solved by the standard Newton method. The average difference between the optimal values of criterion (10), obtained by the brute force method and criterion (17), obtained by Newton method is less than 0.01% in our experiments with parameter $\varepsilon = 0.001$.

The experimental results presented in the next section show the advantage of the proposed formulation (8) and its differentiable version (17) over the standard criterion (1) in the presence of outliers in the training set.

5   Experimental Studies

For experimental studies, two model data sets were generated on the plane (see Fig. 2), which allows us to study the properties of criteria for linear and RBF kernels. The first set is a collection of objects that model the shape of a circle, the second set models a more complex shape in the form of a crescent. In data sets, traditionally used to demonstrate the operation of anomaly detectors, outliers are usually uniformly located around the main population [22], which does not allow us to estimate the bias of the decision rule. In contrast, outliers in our datasets simulate a random bounce in one direction.

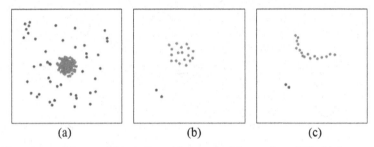

| (a) | (b) | (c) |

Fig. 2. Experimental datasets with outliers: (a) a standard dataset from [21], (b) dataset modeling the shape of a circle, (c) dataset modeling the shape of a crescent

In addition, in real problems, the number of objects in the training set is usually quite small compared to the dimension of the feature space. In this regard, the model data in the Fig. 2 (a) contains an excessive number of objects. The dataset used in this work contain 20 objects, of which two are atypical.

LIBSVM library [23] was used as an implementation of the SVDD method of criterion (1). In addition, studies were carried out for the One-class SVM method (criterion (7)), which is equivalent to (1) when using RBF. Optimization of (17) was done by Sequential Least Squares Programming (SLSQP) method. Experiments with One-class SVM to simulate a linear potential function were carried out at a small parameter value $\gamma = 0.001$ in RBF. The results show that this value is sufficient for an acceptable accuracy of matching the results of training.

For a quantitative assessment of the resistance of classifiers to the presence of outliers in the training set, a method based on the calculation of the Jaccard measure [24] between the areas S_o and S_i, bounded by the decision rule when training with and without outliers (Fig. 3) respectively, is proposed:

$$J(S_o, S_i) = |S_o \cap S_i| / |S_o \cup S_i|. \tag{18}$$

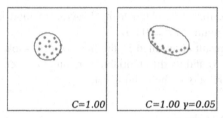

Fig. 3. Decision boundaries for linear (left) and RBF (right) kernels with the penalty parameter $C = 1$ on training datasets without outliers for Jaccard measure evaluation

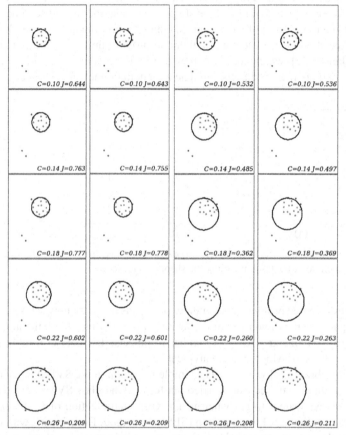

Fig. 4. The results of training one-class classifiers with a linear kernel: first column - the brute-forced criterion (11); second column – the optimized criterion (17), third column – SVDD (1); fourth column - One-class SVM (7)

The higher the value of this measure, the less the influence of the anomalies on the decision rule is. If the value is equal to one, the decision-making areas about the belonging of objects to the target class completely coincide.

The results of the experiments are shown in Fig. 4. The values of the variable parameter "C", which characterizes the penalty for objects going beyond the hypersphere of the minimum radius, and the quantitative assessment of the quality of the classifier "J" in the form (18) are shown in Fig. 4 for each experiment. The learning results for SVDD and One-class SVM show that the influence of atypical objects does not allow the formation of a stable decision rule by selecting the penalty C.

For small values of the parameter, the displacement arising from the requirement to minimize the square of the radius of the hypersphere leaves some of the target objects outside the bounds of a positive decision. With an increase in the parameter C, an excessive increase in the radius of the hypersphere occurs along with a shift of its center towards atypical objects. The solution of the problem based on the proposed criterion (10), on the contrary, demonstrates the stability of the boundary of the target class and the displacement of the center of the hypersphere with an increase in its radius occurs

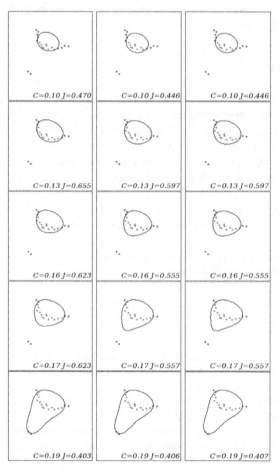

Fig. 5. The results of training one-class classifiers with an RBF kernel: left column - the criterion (17) proposed in this work; center column - SVDD; right column - One-class SVM

at sufficiently large values of C. With the value of the parameter $C = 0.18$ and the use of the formulation (10) proposed in the work as a classifier, the maximum coincidence of the regions in the absence of atypical objects and their presence was obtained; the value of the Jaccard measure in this case was obtained equal to 0.778. The best solution obtained by traditional methods provided the value of this measure at the level of 0.536 ($C = 0.10$). As you can see in Fig. 3, such a solution is unsatisfactory, since a sufficiently large number of objects are outside the zone of making a decision on the target class.

The same behavior can be seen in study of RBF kernel function with parameter value $\gamma = 0.05$ in (Fig. 5).

The maximum of Jaccard measure (value equal to 0.655) was provided by the proposed method with parameter $C = 0.13$ and the best value of Jaccard measure for SVDD and One-Class SVM not exceed 0.6.

In the case of an RBF kernel, the effect of our modification is not so strong as in the case of a linear kernel. In our opinion, the excessive additional complexity of the decision rule leads to lesser robustness to outliers because the accompanying growth of rectified space dimensionality rises the overfitting problem.

6   Conclusion

In this paper, a new formulation of the one-class classification problem is proposed, which makes it possible to eliminate the geometric inconsistencies between penalties for the training sample objects going beyond the boundaries of the enveloping hypersphere and the distance to its center. An optimization criterion and its equivalent form are proposed. Experiments show that it is possible to obtain a more stable decision rule in relation to the presence of outliers than in traditional formulation. For a quantitative assessment of the robustness of classifiers to the presence of outliers in the training set, a method is proposed based on calculating the Jaccard measure between the areas of decision making in favor of the target class in the presence and absence of outliers.

Acknowledgements. The work is supported by the Russian Fund for Basic Research. Grant no: 18-07-00942 and Grant no: 20-07-00441.

References

1. Moya, M.M., Koch, M.W., Hostetler, L.D.: One-class classifier networks for target recognition applications. In: Proceeding WCNN 1993, World Congress on Neural Networks, vol. 3, pp. 797–801 (1993)
2. Bekkerd J., Davis J.: Learning from positive and unlabeled data: a survey. Mach. Learn., **109**(4), 719–760. Springer, US (2020)
3. Xu, D., et al.: Learning deep representations of appearance and motion for anomalous event detection. In: Procedings of the British Machine Vision Conference 2015, pp. 1–12. British Machine Vision Association (2015)
4. Chandola, V., Banerjee, A., Kumar, V.: Anomaly detection: a survey. ACM Comput. Surv. **41**(3), 1–58 (2009)

5. Larin, Aleksandr., et al.: Parametric representation of objects in color space using one-class classifiers. In: Perner, P. (ed.) MLDM 2014. LNCS (LNAI), vol. 8556, pp. 300–314. Springer, Cham (2014). https://doi.org/10.1007/978-3-319-08979-9_23
6. Shi, L.-F.F., et al.: Removing haze particles from single image via exponential inference with support vector data description. IEEE Trans. Multimedia **20**(9), 2503–2512 (2018)
7. Kopylov, A., et al.: Background-invariant robust hand detection based on probabilistic one-class color segmentation and skeleton matching. In: ICPRAM 2018 - Proceedings of the 7th International Conference on Pattern Recognition Applications and Methods. SCITEPRESS - Science and Technology Publications, vol. 2018, pp. 503–510, January (2018)
8. Khan, S.S., Hoey, J.: Review of fall detection techniques: a data availability perspective. Med. Eng. Phys. **39**, 12–22. Elsevier Ltd (2017)
9. Tarassenko, L., et al.: Novelty detection for the identification of masses in mammograms. In: IEE Conference Publication, no. 409, pp. 440–447. IEEE (1995)
10. Duda, R.O., Hart, P.E., Stork, D.G.: Pattern Classification. Wiley, Hoboken (2012)
11. Parzen, E.: On estimation of a probability density function and mode. Ann. Math. Stat. **33**(3), 1065–1076 (1962)
12. Juszczak, P., et al.: Minimum spanning tree based one-class classifier. Neurocomputing **72**(7–9), 1859–1869 (2009)
13. Vapnik, V.N.: Statistical learning theory. In: Haykin, S. (ed.) Interpreting, vol. 2, № 4, p. 736. Wiley, Hoboken (1998)
14. Schölkopf, B., et al.: Estimating the support of a high-dimensional distribution. In: Neural Computation, vol. 13, № 7, pp. 1443–1471. MIT Press, 238 Main St., Suite 500, Cambridge, MA 02142–1046, USA (2001). journals-info@mit.edu
15. Tax, D.M.J.: One-class Classification. Concept-learning in the Absence of Counter-Examples. Delft University of Technology (2001). 202 p.
16. Gornitz, N., et al.: Support vector data descriptions and k-means clustering: one class? IEEE Trans. Neural Netw. Learn. Syst. **29**(9), 3994–4006 (2018)
17. Duin, R.P.W., de Ridder, D., Tax, D.M.J.: Experiments with a featureless approach to pattern recognition. Pattern Recogn. Lett. **18**(11–13), 1159-1166 (1997)
18. Mottl, V., Dvoenko, S., Seredin, O., Kulikowski, C., Muchnik, I.: Featureless pattern recognition in an imaginary hilbert space and its application to protein fold classification. In: Perner, P. (ed.) MLDM 2001. LNCS (LNAI), vol. 2123, pp. 322–336. Springer, Heidelberg (2001). https://doi.org/10.1007/3-540-44596-X_26
19. Chang, W., Lee, C., Lin, C.: A revisit to support vector data description (SVDD), W.Csie.Org, № 1, pp. 1–20 (2013)
20. Nesterov, Y.: Smooth minimization of non-smooth functions. Math. Program. **103**(1), 127–152 (2005). https://doi.org/10.1007/s10107-004-0552-5
21. Liu, B.: On smoothing exact penalty functions for nonlinear constrained optimization problems. J. Appl. Math. Comput. **30**(1–2), 259–270 (2009). https://doi.org/10.1007/s12190-008-0171-z
22. Gramfort, A., Thomas, A.: Comparing anomaly detection algorithms for outlier detection on toy datasets [Электронный ресурс], scikit-learn 0.20.3 documentation, pp. 2–5 (2019). https://scikit-learn.org/stable/auto_examples/miscellaneous/plot_anomaly_comparison.html#sphx-glr-auto-examples-miscellaneous-plot-anomaly-comparison-py. Accessed 20 Oct 2020
23. Chang, C.C., Lin, C.J.: LIBSVM: a library for support vector machines. ACM Trans. Intell. Syst. Technol. **2**(3), 1–27 (2011)
24. Jaccard, P.: Etude comparative de la distribution florale dans une portion des Alpes et des Jura. Bull. Soc. Vaudoise Sci. Nat. **37**, 547–579 (1901)

Recognition of Tomographic Images
in the Diagnosis of Stroke

Kirill Kalmutskiy[1] , Andrey Tulupov[1,2] , and Vladimir Berikov[1,3]([✉])

^{1} Novosibirsk State University, Novosibirsk, Russia
{k.kalmutskii,a.tulupov}@g.nsu.ru, berikov@math.nsc.ru
^{2} International Tomography Center SB RAS, Novosibirsk, Russia
^{3} Sobolev Institute of Mathematics SB RAS, Novosibirsk, Russia

Abstract. In this paper, a method for automatic recognition of acute stroke model using non-contrast computed tomography brain images is presented. The complexity of the task lies in the fact that the dataset consists of a very small number of images. To solve the problem, we used the traditional computer vision methods and a convolutional neural network consisting of a segmentator and classifier. To increase the dataset, augmentations and sub images were used. Experiments with real CT images using validation and test samples showed that even on an extremely small dataset it is possible to train a model that will successfully cope with the classification and segmentation of images. We also proposed a way to increase the interpretability of the model.

Keywords: Acute stroke · Classification · Segmentation · Convolutional neural network · Small dataset

1 Introduction

Today, there are many ways to diagnose an acute cerebrovascular accident or stroke, which are very important for determining further treatment. The most important among them are magnetic resonance imaging (MRI) and computed tomography (CT).

CT consists of a procedure in which an X-ray beam is directed at the organ and rotates around it, generating signals which are automatically processed to obtain a cross-sectional image (slice) of the tissue. Such slices contain much more detailed information about the state of the organs than conventional x-ray images. CT makes it possible to assess the location and size of organs, as well as their structure; identify the presence of additional formations (tumors, cysts, abscesses) and foreign bodies. Another very important advantage of CT is that it can be used for quick early diagnosis of stroke, unlike MRI.

However, the analysis of images obtained by CT is a rather difficult task. Only a very experienced doctor can deal with such an analysis, however, even

The work was partly supported by RFBR grant 19-29-01175.

A. Del Bimbo et al. (Eds.): ICPR 2020 Workshops, LNCS 12665, pp. 166–171, 2021.
https://doi.org/10.1007/978-3-030-68821-9_16

in this case, the probability of error (and making an incorrect diagnosis) is very high and sometimes reaches 10%. Such errors can be associated with a loss of doctor's concentration (since there may be many images of brain slices), or with a lack of qualifications (in cases where it is really difficult to determine the focus of a stroke).

In this regard, the creation of a decision-making assistant system seems to be a promising solution to this problem. As such a system, neural networks can be used. In this case, for each brain slice image, a segmented image with highlighted areas of a stroke can be obtained. Neural network predictions will greatly help in the diagnosis of stroke.

Modern neural network architectures (such as U-Net) are capable of efficiently solving the segmentation problem. However, in order to train them, a large dataset of labeled images is needed. Manual marking of images of brain slices is very expensive, since only a highly qualified specialist is able to do it.

In this paper, we consider related work and propose methods for constructing a decision-making assistant using classical methods of computer vision and neural network approaches in conditions of a small amount of labeled data, provide and analyze the quality and effectiveness of the resulting model.

2   Related Work

Convolutional neural networks (CNN) are actively used for image analysis, including CT images [1]. For example, CNN were used to solve the problems of brain tumor classification [2] and detection of COVID-19 [3]. Article [4] proposes a solution to the problem of ischemic stroke segmentation in contrast CT scans using CNN. However, our task is to make predictions for non-contrast CT scans that provide less information than its contrast counterparts, but are safer for the patient. Article [5] describes the CNN for ischemic and hemorrhagic infarcts using non-contrast CT images.

It should be noted that in all these works, large datasets (consisting of more than 1000 images) were used to train models. It has been experimentally verified that the transfer of training does not improve the quality of segmentation of medical images [6]. The authors of [7] suggest approaches to solve the problem of lack of labeled medical images for training. The main idea is to use the most appropriate augmentations to expand the dataset. Using small sub images for training can greatly improve the quality of segmentation on an extremely small dataset, as noted in [8].

3   Material and Method

A sample of annotated CT images was obtained from International Tomography Center SB RAS. Dataset consists of 34 images of brain slices in DICOM format. In each slice, a radiology specialist performs a manual search and identification of the pathological density area in the substance of the brain. The increased density indicates a hemorrhagic lesion, and the reduced density implies an ischemic lesion. Then, these areas were segmented (precisely circled by a green outline) and the resulting images were converted into JPG format. Thus, for each DICOM image there is a labeled JPG image, see example in Fig. 1. The program code was written in Python on top of PyTorch framework. Also, the OpenCV library was actively used.

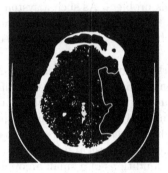

Fig. 1. Example of a labeled image

3.1   Data Expansion

From the very beginning, all images were resized to a single resolution of 512 by 512. To increase the number of objects for training a convolutional neural network, we used two techniques. The first is augmentations: in this case, only horizontal and vertical flips turned out to be useful. Other types of argumentation did not give a gain in quality, and therefore were not used. The second is cutting the image with a uniform grid into sub images. Thus, using a 4×4 grid, 16 images of size 128×128 were obtained from each 512×512 image, see example in Fig. 2. All this made it possible to increase the dataset by 64 times.

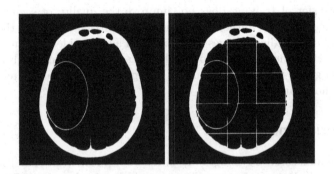

Fig. 2. Example of a cutting the image with a uniform grid

3.2   Convolutional Neural Network Architecture

To improve the accuracy of stroke diagnosis, the model includes two parts: a segmentator and a classifier. Thus, segmentation is performed only if the classifier reveals a stroke in the image.

An architecture including an encoder and a decoder with skip-connections was used as a segmentator. Comparing with the classic U-net, the number of convolutional blocks was reduced and the dilation parameter was increased to obtain the required receptive field. As a classifier, a linear layer (with sigmoid activation) was used at the output of the encoder, which predicted the probability of having a stroke focus in the image.

In this work, we used the loss function, which is the sum of the weighted cross-entropy of the classifier and the weighted cross-entropy of the segmentator. The following code was used, where DoubleConvMaxPool2d is a block from a U-net encoder, DoubleConvUpSample2d is a block from a U-net decoder, logits - classifier predictions, segmented - segmentator predictions:

```
x1 = DoubleConv(1, 16, kernel_size=3)(x)
x2 = DoubleConvMaxPool2d(16, 32, kernel_size=3, dilation=2)(x1)
x3 = DoubleConvMaxPool2d(32, 64, kernel_size=3, dilation=3)(x2)
x4 = DoubleConvMaxPool2d(64, 64, kernel_size=3, dilation=2)

x = DoubleConvUpSample2d(128, 32, kernel_size=3, dilation=2)(x4, x3)
x = DoubleConvUpSample2d(64, 16, kernel_size=3, dilation=3)(x, x2)
x = DoubleConvUpSample2d(32, 16, kernel_size=3, dilation=2)(x, x1)

segmented = Conv2D(16, 1, kernel_size=1)(x)
segmented = Sigmoid()(segmented)

logits = Flatten()(x4)
logits = Linear(16384, 1)(logits)
logits = Sigmoid()(logits)
```

3.3   Model Prediction Processing

To increase the quality of segmentation, the model leaves only the maximum connected component in the resulting segmented image. This approach can be used for the following reason: most often there is only one stroke center in the image, and if there are two of them, the system will inform the doctor about the "suspicious" image and he will manually check the predictions anyway. Additionally, the remaining component can be removed if it is smaller than a certain size, however, setting this threshold is quite difficult and for more labeled images are needed. An example in which this technique can greatly improve the quality of segmentation is presented in Fig. 3.

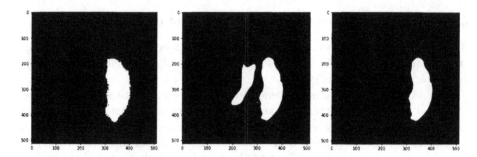

Fig. 3. Left image - ground truth, middle image - all components, right image - only the maximum connected component

4 Results of Experiments

Since there are few labeled images, only 4 images (about 10% of the dataset) were used as a test sample and 8 images as a validation sample. Due to the fact that our convolutional neural network has not so many parameters and the dataset is small, validation took place in 2 stages. This is the so-called incomplete k-fold. In the first stage, 4 images from validation were placed in the training set, the remaining 4 considered the value of quality. In the second stage, the same thing is done, but 4 other images from the validation are added to the training set (those that were not added in the first step).

In this paper, we consider the values of two metrics: the accuracy of the predictions of the classifier and the Intersection over Union (IoU) of the predictions of the segmentator. Predictions are made for sub images obtained after cutting with a uniform grid, which are then collected back into a full image. The results for validation and test samples are presented in Table 1. It may be noticed that the values of the metrics on validation and test do not differ too much, which indicates a lack of overfit. However, the value of the IoU metric turned out to be quite low, due to the small size of the training sample.

Table 1. Validation and test results

Metric	Validation	Test
Accuracy	0.922	0.890
IoU	0.727	0.675

5 Conclusion

In conclusion, it can be said that we managed to build a model for the diagnosis of stroke with good quality. However, due to the limitations of the dataset, the values of the metrics are far from ideal. In the future, it is planned to increase the number and variety of objects (images) in the dataset, as well as to think about increasing the interpretability of the model results. The doctor needs to understand why the model makes this or that decision, but the convolutional neural network is a "black box".

To solve this problem, other machine learning methods, such as decision trees, can be used as classifiers. The most promising option is decision trees based on similarities. This algorithm, making predictions for a new object, tries to find the most similar object from the training set (which consists of labeled images). This approach will be well understood by the doctors for whom our model is intended.

References

1. Yadav, S.S., Jadhav, S.M.: Deep convolutional neural network based medical image classification for disease diagnosis. J. Big Data **6**(1), 1–18 (2019). https://doi.org/10.1186/s40537-019-0276-2
2. Seetha, J., Raja, S.S.: Brain tumor classification using convolutional neural networks. Biomed. Pharmacol. J. **11**(3), 1457–1461 (2018)
3. Polsinelli, M., Cinque, L., Placidi, G.: A light CNN for detecting COVID-19 from CT scans of the chest. arXiv, 2004.12837 (2020)
4. Abulnaga, S.M., Rubin, J.: Ischemic stroke lesion segmentation in CT perfusion scans using pyramid pooling and focal loss. In: Crimi, A., Bakas, S., Kuijf, H., Keyvan, F., Reyes, M., van Walsum, T. (eds.) BrainLes 2018. LNCS, vol. 11383, pp. 352–363. Springer, Cham (2019). https://doi.org/10.1007/978-3-030-11723-8_36
5. Kuang, H., Menon, B.K., Qiu, W.: Segmenting hemorrhagic and ischemic infarct simultaneously from follow-up non-contrast CT images in patients with acute ischemic stroke. IEEE Access **7**, 39842–39851 (2019)
6. Raghu, M., Zhang, M., Kleinberg, J., Bengio, S.: Transfusion: understanding transfer learning for medical imaging. arXiv:1902.07208 (2019)
7. Rizwan, I., Haque, I., Neubert, J.: Deep learning approaches to biomedical image segmentation. Informatics in Medicine Unlocked, ISSN 2352–9148 (2020)
8. Du, H., LaLonde, R., van Mechelen, R., Zhang, S.: Performing Semantic Segmentation on an Extremely Small Dataset, MICS (2016)

Two-Stage Classification Model
for Feather Images Identification

Alina Belko[1]([✉]) [ID], Konstantin Dobratulin[2] [ID], and Andrey Kunznetsov[1] [ID]

[1] Samara National Research University, Samara 443086, Russian Federation
alinabelko@gmail.com
[2] National University of Science and Technology "MISIS",
Moscow 119049, Russian Federation

Abstract. The paper explores the usage of neural networks for bird species identification based on feathers image. The taxonomic identification of birds' feather is widely used in aviation ornithology to analyze collisions with aircraft and develop methods to prevent them. This article presents a novel dataset consisting of 28,272 images of the plumage of 595 bird species. We compare models trained on four subsets from the initial dataset. We propose the method of identifying bird species based on YoloV4 and DenseNet models. The experimental estimation showed that the resulted method makes it possible to identify the bird based on the photograph of the single feather with an accuracy up to 81,03% for precise classification and with accuracy 97,09% for of the first five predictions of the classifier.

Keywords: Pattern recognition · Hierarchical classification ·
Convolutional neural networks

1 Introduction

The classification of bird species by feathers is applied in aviation ornithology for bird identification after a collision with an aircraft and to prevent future collisions. Specialists use DNA analysis and computed tomography scan techniques to meet this challenge, but many airports still use only visual classification. Despite the significant number of unstructured datasets of feather images, this problem has not previously been solved using machine learning methods. At different times, various multimedia guides were created for feather identification, as well as photo collections, systematized by color or size. However, those resources have disadvantages - it requires the user to have some special knowledge about feathers. User needs to search in a large number of variants, which is challenging to use in the field. The classification of images of the plumage of birds is complicated due to large variability between the flight, tail and down feathers of the same bird species, sexual dimorphism of individuals, differences in the color of young and adult individuals, differences in color caused by selection, as well as territorial differences. Plumage can also have different variations due to genetic

© Springer Nature Switzerland AG 2021
A. Del Bimbo et al. (Eds.): ICPR 2020 Workshops, LNCS 12665, pp. 172–181, 2021.
https://doi.org/10.1007/978-3-030-68821-9_17

abnormalities or vitamin deficiencies. One of a substantial part of this work is the creation of a new dataset, that allows performing feather identification using machine learning methods. The resulting dataset is the most extensive plumage images collection published in open access. The first section of this article provides an overview of existing works on similar classification tasks. The second section describes the method of forming the dataset for research. The following sections describe the proposed classification algorithm and its stages. Further, the results of experimental studies of the classification accuracy are given. The last section of work is dedicated to a conclusion.

2 Related Work

Classification of bird species is a standard machine learning task [3,4]. This task relates to the Fine-Grained Visual Classification (FGVC), which it is the subtask of machine vision. FGVC objective is to classify objects of a single global class into subclasses. Common domains for the FGVC task are plant leaves, car models, types of vegetables and others. FGVC is considered to be a challenging task due to the subtle difference between classes. At the same time, intra-class variability may be high due to differences in posture, shooting angles and lighting. In many cases, the same methods can be applied for both FGVC and standard image classification, such as convolutional neural networks. There are several standard methods to improve the accuracy of FCVC. One of the methods to improve the accuracy of classification is to use segmentation of the image parts which are relevant for the classification [8]. This method aims to give equal weight to different details of the image, which may have different sizes but is equally significant for classification [9]. It also better adapts the algorithm to object deformations, because individual parts of the object are less prone to deformation than the object as a whole, especially when classifying live objects with different poses. For example, in the case of birds classification, parts such as the bird's head, tail and wings are labeled [4]. This method can be applied both supervised and unsupervised way. Another systematic approach to improve classification accuracy is foreground segmentation because images with different classes can share almost the same background. Background removal can lead to significant improvement in fine-grained classification accuracy [9]. Foreground segmentation can be done by several algorithms, such as Graph-cut [10] or DPM [11]. Furthermore, for datasets with tree-structured class taxonomies, may be used hierarchic classification methods. This method finds application in botanical and zoological classification since objects of those domains have a strict taxonomic hierarchy. For data with a hierarchical structure, it is possible to perform classification, not on leaf nodes of the graph but parent nodes instead. This method can be applied when there is insufficient confidence to define the class more accurately. Hierarchical classification can be implemented using local classifiers. When applying local classifiers at the node level, a separate classifier is trained for each non-leaf node, which is used to classify only the child classes of this node. The advantage of this method is the high classification accuracy, as well as the simplified addition of new classes to the structure since this requires changing individual, relatively small, local classifiers, and not the entire structure as a whole. The main disadvantage of this method is the need to train a significant number of local classifiers. An alternative method is to apply local classifiers for each level of the tree. Local classifiers of such type classify all units of the tree with the same level. The approach reduces the number of classifiers, but it can lead to a violation of the hierarchical structure due to inconsistencies in the classification at different levels [12].

3   Dataset Construction

As of writing, there was no publicly available dataset with enough images to train machine learning algorithm. Because of that, we had to collect data and create a new dataset. For initial data collection, we selected several data sources. The sources included professional, scientific collections, as well as amateur photographs from various cites and specialized shops. Even though amateur photographs were of lower quality than professional photographs, and often had unrelated objects in the image, the use of amateur photographs added more variety to the data. It made the algorithm more adaptable to photographs with different lighting and background. The use more noisy and diverse photographs can improve the accuracy of the FGVC algorithms [23]. After selecting the sources, the authors were asked for permission to use the photographs. Several sources had on the site a reference of the open license: GNU FDL License, Creative Commons BY 4.0, and Copyleft allowing the use of photographs for research purposes. We received written permissions for the use of photographs from all the authors without the reference of license. After collecting permissions, we started an automated data collection using web scraping technology [14]. The speed of the algorithm was artificially lowered in order to produce less load on sites. The research produced a dataset of 1,565 images, each containing an average of 18 feathers. Each photo contains the feathers of only one bird species. The images were sorted into folders with a four-tier taxonomic organization for Order, Family, Genus and Species. The dataset contains photos of the plumage of 595 bird species. After collection, we labeled the data with bounding boxes in Microsoft VOTT. Each bounding box contains an image of a single feather, sometimes with fragments of next feathers when overlapped on the photo. Some of the feathers have not been labeled unless they are of value to the classification task. These feathers are down and cover feathers, as they look almost identical in different species of birds. As a result, we collected 28,272 labels of feathers in the photograph. After labeling, the coordinates of the rectangles were exported in CSV format. Fragments of images with individual feathers were cut out and saved from the original images at the specified coordinates.

We collected a dataset with 28,272 images of 595 species of birds, where each image contains a single feather. Example of images is presented in Fig. 1. This dataset can be applied to train a classification model. The images are arranged in a hierarchical structure containing data on the Latin name of the order, family and species of bird. The data was published in the GitHub repository.

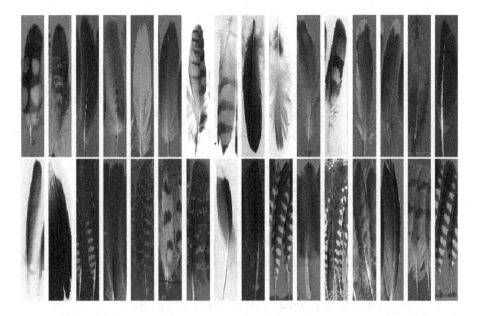

Fig. 1. Dataset images example.

4   Experiment

A two-step sequential classification algorithm has been selected as the solution to this task [15]. The overall diagram of the process of two-stage classification is presented in Fig. 2.

The principle of the method is to conduct a preliminary analysis of the data before the recognition process in order to highlight fragments that potentially contain the information of interest - Regions of Interest (ROI). In this case, we consider each object of "feather" class as an ROI. Then, according to the allocated data, a full analysis is carried out to improve the quality of classification. The small number of analyzed fragments compensates the computational complexity of the analysis produced. This approach can potentially increase the accuracy of object detection, because instead of a small number of objects for each class, the neural network is trained on a large number of objects of the same class, without the need to learn excessive features of differences between classes of feathers. During the localization stage, the entire dataset of feathers, regardless of the class, form the training set for the localization network. After object localization, each image is cut into separate normalized images with a single object on each of them. This method allows getting enough data to train the classifier further and to give more weight, not to the position and number of feathers, but the shape and color of each feather. Then the classification algorithm is used, which learns features for classification.

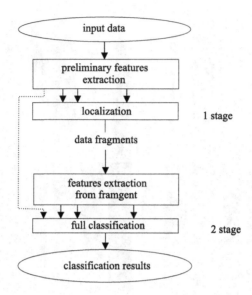

Fig. 2. Sequential two-stage classification scheme.

Hence, it was decided to train two models: the model of the detection of the targets of class "feather" and the model of species classification. In the final form, at the input of the model of object localization are given images with one or more feathers on each image, at the output of the model - normalized images, each containing one feather. The resulting images are at the input to the classification model, which predicts the species of bird to which these feathers belong.

4.1 Localization

The first stage of classification pipeline is a feather localization. We selected the YOLOv4 model as one of the most advanced models of object detection, demonstrating one of the most accurate results at the time of writing. The main feature of this family of architectures compared to others is that most models apply the convolutional neural network (CNA) several times to different regions of the image, while in the YOLO applies once to the entire image at once, which is reflected in the title - You Only Look Once. Network divides the image into the grid, predicts bounding boxes and the probability of object presence in each section. The YOLOv4 model is optimized for training on a single GPU processor; it provides a high-speed algorithm that can be used to work with the video stream. The selected model of the detector was trained using the Google Colaboratory platform. We used transfer learning [18] technique for training, pre-trained on MS COCO dataset [19]. This technique allows for reducing the time of models training. The approximate time of the YOLOv4 model on the feathers dataset was about 40 h for 6,000 epochs.

4.2   Classes Normalization

The main problem for further classification of images is a definite imbalance of classes. The number of images per class can vary between 2 and 620 images, which can lead to overfitting of the model. Several methods have been used to achieve a balance between classes. We created two subsets of the initial dataset: Top-50 and Top-500, which refers to sets with 50 and 100 classes with the highest number of images respectively. This approach was used to remove classes that did not have enough data to perform an accurate classification. As a more complex method of class normalization, it was decided to use a hierarchical data structure and merge species with lack of data. Species have been merged only with other species of the same genus so that they can be classified at the level of the bird genus, forming macro classes. Such classes have the postfix "sp." the name after the genus name. It is a standard term in biology that a taxon has been classified to an accuracy of the genus [20]. Classes that did not have enough data after merging were excluded from subset. Fifty images were selected as the minimum amount of data. The maximum amount of data was also limited to 300 images; excess images were excluded. Hence, one more data subsample was created, which is named "normalized". This approach allows for more class balance while retaining more classes and images. The graph of the distribution of data by class for all four datasets is shown in Fig. 3. The disadvantage of this approach is that part of the data can be only classified to the nearest genus, without providing information about the taxonomic species.

4.3   Classification

For the classification task, it was decided to use convolutional neural networks. We chose three models of the DenseNet group as feature extraction models for classification: DenseNet121, DenseNet169 and DenseNet201 [21]. DenseNet architectures show good results for the fine-grained classification tasks [22]. Each subset was split into training and validation datasets in a proportion of 80 to 20. The number of images in each subset and the number of classes are shown in Table 1. The training was performed on the base of the platform Google Colaboratory using the TensorFlow library. Thus, three models were trained on four datasets.

Table 1. Total number of images and classes for subsets.

Subset	Total classes	Total images
All	595	28272
Top-100	100	14941
Top-50	50	10584
Normalized	213	27582

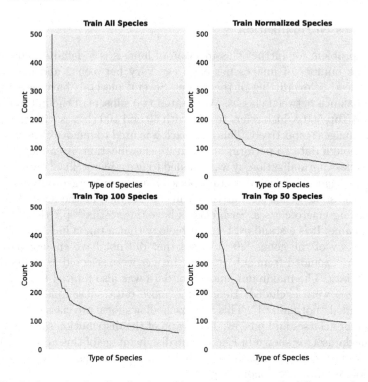

Fig. 3. Quantitative distribution of images per classes in different subsets.

4.4 Results

Accuracy assessment of the developed algorithm We used the mAP metric to measure the accuracy of localization models. The mAP metric uses the average value of the AP metric between all classes. Since there is one class in this task, the AP metric is calculated for one class, and it is not averaged. When measuring the accuracy of the obtained model, the accuracy according to the AP metric was 87,36%, 4620 labels were recognized positively, 490 tags were recognized false positive, and 986 were false negative. Labels were calculated as accurate with Intersection over Union (IoU) > 0,5. IoU is defined as the area of intersection of the true label with the predicted one, divided by the area of combining these labels. The average IoU for the model was 75,22%. During the experiments, 12 results were obtained for three models trained on four datasets. For the comparison of the accuracy of the obtained algorithms, we used Sparse Top-1 Categorical Accuracy and Sparse Top-5 Categorical Accuracy metrics. For the Sparse Top-1 Categorical Accuracy metric, a prediction is considered accurate when the class with the highest prediction confidence level matches the ground truth. For Sparse Top-5 Categorical Accuracy prediction is considered accurate if any of 5 highest probability answers match the ground truth. Results are presented in Table 2. Models trained on full and normalized datasets perform better on average, despite unbalanced data. Therefore, adding rare bird species with few photographs to the dataset has improved the results of the dataset [11].

Table 2. Fine-grained classification results.

Subset	Model	Sparse top 1 categorical accuracy	Sparse top 5 categorical accuracy
Top-50	DenseNet121	0,6394	0,8871
	DenseNet169	0,6684	0,9186
	DenseNet201	0,5700	0,8740
Top-100	DenseNet121	0,7989	0,9709
	DenseNet169	0,7979	0,9695
	DenseNet201	0,7266	0,9491
Normalized	DenseNet121	0,7888	0,9603
	DenseNet169	0,8103	0,9608
	DenseNet201	0,9608	0,9616
All	DenseNet121	0,7642	0,9482
	DenseNet169	0,7181	0,9360
	DenseNet201	0,7978	0,9586

5   Conclusion

Although the DenseNet121 model on the Top-100 dataset has the highest Sparse Top-5 Categorical Accuracy classification results, the DenseNet169 model trained on the normalized dataset performs the best on Sparse Top-1 Categorical Accuracy metric and slightly underperformed on the Sparse Top-5 Categorical Accuracy, which makes DenseNet169 model the most applicable on real data. The obtained model shows a good result of classification for the majority of classes taking into account the complexity of classification and imbalance of data. Due to the hierarchical data structure, the maximum number of images was saved, and the class balance was improved, which led to a more accurate classification.

References

1. Soldatini, C., Georgalas, V., Torricelli, P., Albores-Barajas, Y.V.: An ecological approach to birdstrike risk analysis. Eur. J. Wildlife Res. **56**(4), 623–632 (2010). ISSN 1612–4642
2. Yang, R., Wu, X.B., Yan, P., Li, X.Q.: Using DNA barcodes to identify a bird involved in a birdstrike at a Chinese airport. Mol. Biol. Rep. **37**(7), 3517–3523 (2010). ISSN 0301–4851

3. Berg, T., Liu, J.X., Lee, S.W., Alexander, M.L., Jacobs, D.W., Belhumeur, P.N.: Birdsnap: large-scale fine-grained visual categorization of birds. In: IEEE Conference on Computer Vision and Pattern Recognition (CVPR) 2014, pp. 2019–2026 (2014)
4. Fu, J.L., Zheng, H.L., Mei, T.: Look closer to see better: re-current attention convolutional neural network for fine-grained image recognition. In: 2017 IEEE Conference on Computer Vision and Pattern Recognition (CVPR), pp. 4476–4484 (2017)
5. Araujo, V.M., Britto, A.S., Brun, A.L., Oliveira, L.E.S., Koerich, A.L.: Fine-grained hierarchical classification of plant leaf images using fusion of deep models 2018. In: IEEE 30th International Conference on Tools with Artificial Intelligence (ICTAI) 2018, pp. 4476–4484 (2018)
6. Yang, L.J., Luo, P., Loy, C.C., Tang, X.: A large-scale car dataset for fine-grained categorization and verification. In: 2015 IEEE Conference on Computer Vision and Pattern Recognition (CVPR), pp. 3973–3981 (2015)
7. Hou, S.H., Feng, Y.S., Wang, Z.L.: VegFru: a domain-specific dataset for fine-grained visual categorization. In: 2017 IEEE International Conference on Computer Vision (ICCV), pp. 541–549 (2017)
8. Dai, X.Y., Southall, B., Trinh, N., Matei, B.: Efficient fine-grained classification and part localization using one compact network. In: 2017 IEEE International Conference on Computer Vision Workshops (ICCVW 2017), pp. 996–1004 (2017)
9. Zhao, B., Feng, J.S., Wu, X., Yan, S.C.: A survey on deep learning-based fine-grained object classification and semantic segmentation. Int. J. Autom. Comput. **14**(2), 119–135 (2017)
10. Priyadharshini, P., Thilagavathi, K.: Hyperspectral image classification using MLL and graph cut methods. In: Proceedings of 2016 Online International Conference on Green Engineering and Technologies (ICGET) (2016)
11. Pandey, M., Lazebnik, S.: Scene recognition and weakly supervised object localization with deformable part-based models. In: 2011 IEEE International Conference on Computer Vision (ICCV), pp. 1307–1314 (2011)
12. Silla, C.N., Freitas, A.A.: A survey of hierarchical classification across different application domains. Data Min. Knowl. Discov. **22**(1–2), 31–72 (2011). ISSN 1384-5810
13. Krause, J., et al.: The unreasonable effectiveness of noisy data for fine-grained recognition. In: Leibe, B., Matas, J., Sebe, N., Welling, M. (eds.) ECCV 2016. LNCS, vol. 9907, pp. 301–320. Springer, Cham (2016). https://doi.org/10.1007/978-3-319-46487-9_19
14. Mitchell, R.: Web Scraping with Python: Collecting Data from the Modern Web. O'Reilly Media, Sebastopol (2015)
15. Glumov, N.I., Myasnikov, V.V., Sergeev, V.V.: Detection and Recognition of Objects in Images. Samara University, Samara (2010). in Russian
16. Zhu, Q.F., Zheng, H.F., Wang, Y.B., Cao, Y.G., Guo, S.X.: Study on the evaluation method of sound phase cloud maps based on an improved YOLOv4 algorithm. Sensors **20**(15) (2015). ISSN 1424-8220
17. Redmon, J., Divvala, S., Girshick, R., Farhadi, A.: You only look once: unified, real-time object detection. In: IEEE Conference on Computer Vision and Pattern Recognition (CVPR) 2016, pp. 779–788 (2016)
18. Sarkar, D., Bali, R., Ghosh, T.: Hands-On Transfer Learning with Python. Packt Publishing, Birmingham (2018)

19. Lin, T.Y., et al.: Microsoft COCO: common objects in context. In: Fleet, D., Pajdla, T., Schiele, B., Tuytelaars, T. (eds.) ECCV 2014. LNCS, vol. 8693, pp. 740–755. Springer, Cham (2014). https://doi.org/10.1007/978-3-319-10602-1_48
20. International Code of Zoological Nomenclature. London: I Natural History Museum (1999)
21. Huang, G., Liu, Z., Van Der Maaten, L.: Densely connected convolutional networks. In: 30th IEEE Conference on Computer Vision and Pattern Recognition (CVPR 2017), pp. 2261–2269 (2017)
22. Valev, K., Schumann, A., Sommer, L., Beyerer, J.: A systematic evaluation of recent deep learning architectures for fine-grained vehicle classification. In: Pattern Recognition and Tracking XXIX, vol. 10649 (2018)
23. Everingham, M., Van Gool, L., Williams, C.K.I., Winn, J., Zis-serman, A.: The PASCAL visual object classes (VOC) challenge. Int. J. Comput. Vis. **88**, 303–338 (2017)

An Objective Comparison
of Ridge/Valley Detectors
by Image Filtering

Ghulam-Sakhi Shokouh$^{(\boxtimes)}$, Baptiste Magnier$^{(\boxtimes)}$, Binbin Xu$^{(\boxtimes)}$,
and Philippe Montesinos$^{(\boxtimes)}$

EuroMov Digital Health in Motion, Univ Montpellier, IMT Mines Alès, Alès, France
{ghulam-sakhi.shokouh,baptiste.magnier,binbin.xu,montesin}@mines-ales.fr

Abstract. Ridges and valleys are the principle geometric features for their diverse applications, especially in image analysis problems such as segmentation, object detection, etc. Numerous characterizations have contributed to formalize the ridge and valley theory. The significance of each characterization rely however on its practical usefulness in a particular application. The objective comparison and evaluation of ridgeness/valleyness characterized as thin and complex image structure is thus crucially important, for choosing, which parameter's values correspond to the optimal configuration to obtain accurate results and best performance. This paper presents a supervised and objective comparison of different filtering-based ridge detectors. Moreover, the optimal parameter configuration of each filtering techniques have been objectively investigated.

Keywords: Ridge detection · Valley detection · Image filtering

1 Introduction

The correct detection, localization, and extraction of the salient features in an image, as well as the accurate characterization of its geometric structure are important image processing tasks, related to its wide range of applications. Exhaustive researches have been carried out on the significant image features such as edges, lines, crest lines, blobs, ridges and valley. Ridges and valleys (also called crest lines or roof edges) have stood out to be the most eminent and useful structure for image analysis. Ridges and valleys represent a special type of contours, as shown in Fig. 1. Classical edge detectors are optimized to extract step or ramp edges [1]; however, they fail to detect crest lines. Indeed, a step/ramp edge extractor will return two edges at both sides of the crest line because narrow ridges or valleys on the image surface are composed of two locally parallel step or ramp edges. Roof edges are defined as thin nets in the image, describing for example roads or rivers in satellite images, blood vessels in medical images or plant roots. Hence, finding these dense and thin structures is a significant task in image processing. Meanwhile, there are many inevitable challenges in image processing tasks, such as noise, artifacts, etc. depending on specific applications.

A. Del Bimbo et al. (Eds.): ICPR 2020 Workshops, LNCS 12665, pp. 182–197, 2021.
https://doi.org/10.1007/978-3-030-68821-9_18

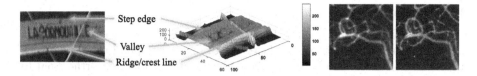

Fig. 1. Illustration of features in images by elevation of the image intensity (left) and ridge detection using LoG filter with $\sigma = 5$, images of size 256×256 (right).

So, the acceptable ridge/valley detection requires cumbersome and manual tuning. Therefore, an extensive evaluation of the different state of the art filtering techniques and approaches in the scope of its most useful application, is indispensable. This paper is dedicated to this objective evaluation and comparison.

2   Ridge Extraction in Images

Originally, a discrete definition for ridges appears in [2], where the underlying function is the image convolved with a Difference Of Low-Pass (DOLP) transform. Indeed, considering two different low-pass filters L_1 and L_2 (i.e., two supports of different widths) both positioned over the center coefficient at the point $(0, 0)$, ridges, valleys and blobs may be extracted efficiently with the DOLP transform: these features are highlighted by applying two different low-pass filters to the same image and then subsequently subtracting these two filtered images. Note that the difference of the filters may be applied before convolving the image with the obtained DOLP filter. Thereafter, crest lines are extracted when the support of the low-pass filter L_1 is smaller than the support of the low-pass filter L_2 and inversely regarding valleys. For the final step of the ridge extraction, the selected pixels correspond to points being local maxima in one of the 4 orientations (modulo 180° in degrees) associated with the 8-neighborhood of the pixels. Even though the results obtained with square shapes are acceptable, the DOLP filter formed by subtracting circularly low-pass filters is preferable. Nevertheless, for their isotropy and circular symmetry properties, the sampled Gaussian filter represents a good achievement. In fact, the Difference of Gaussians (DoG) remains effective in ridge detection and is an approximation of the Laplacian of Gaussian (LoG) when the ratio of the size filters is roughly equal to 1.6 [3]. Usually called Mexican hat or Sombrero filter, the 2D equation of the LoG is given by: $LoG(x, y) = \frac{1}{\pi\sigma^4} \cdot \left(1 - \frac{x^2+y^2}{2\sigma^2}\right) \cdot e^{-(x^2+y^2)/2\sigma^2}$, where (x, y) represents the pixel coordinates and σ is the standard deviation of the Gaussian. A ridge extraction example in Fig. 1 after a non-maxima suppression in the 4 orientations associated with the 8-neighborhood of the pixels. Also, in Haralick's approach [4], the image function is approximated by a cubic polynomial which, sometimes, may distort the detection.

DOLP transform and LoG allow extracting roughly ridges and valleys, but suffer when the desired objects are too thin, thus the detection is disturbed by noise or undesirable artifacts. Additionally, the angle selectivity may be improved by applying other operators, as presented in the following.

2.1 Hessian Matrix

In image filtering, the second order derivative may be used to determine the location of the ridges. Indeed, bright or dark ridges correspond to, respectively, a maximum or minimum of the image intensity in the direction orthogonal to them and a constant image intensity in the direction parallel to them. Considering a grey level image I and its partial derivatives:

- $I_{xx} = \partial^2 I / \partial x^2$, the 2nd image derivative along the x axis,

- $I_{yy} = \partial^2 I / \partial y^2$, the 2nd image derivative along the y axis,

- $I_{xy} = \partial^2 I / \partial x \partial y$, the crossing derivative of I,

the Hessian matrix $\mathcal{H}$ is often computed in image analysis:

$$\mathcal{H}(x,y) = \begin{pmatrix} I_{xx}(x,y) & I_{xy}(x,y) \\ I_{xy}(x,y) & I_{yy}(x,y) \end{pmatrix} = \begin{pmatrix} \mathcal{H}_{11} & \mathcal{H}_{12} \\ \mathcal{H}_{21} & \mathcal{H}_{22} \end{pmatrix}. \tag{1}$$

Image derivatives can be calculated by convolving the image with the $\pm[-1\ 0\ 2\ 0\ -1]$ or the $\pm[-1\ 0\ 1]$ masks in the x and/or y directions.

The matrix $\mathcal{H}$ is symmetric, diagonalizing $\mathcal{H}$ provides the local normal to the ridge or the valley (that is given by the eigenvector related with the highest eigenvalue) and its sharpness (that is related to the values of these eigenvalues) [5,6]. Theoretically, eigenvalues (k_1, k_2) are computed by:

$$\begin{cases} k_1(x,y) & = \frac{1}{2} \cdot (\mathcal{H}_{11} + \mathcal{H}_{22}) - \frac{1}{4}\sqrt{(\mathcal{H}_{11} + \mathcal{H}_{22})^2 + 4 \cdot \mathcal{H}_{12}^2} \\ k_2(x,y) & = \frac{1}{2} \cdot (\mathcal{H}_{11} + \mathcal{H}_{22}) + \frac{1}{4}\sqrt{(\mathcal{H}_{11} + \mathcal{H}_{22})^2 + 4 \cdot \mathcal{H}_{12}^2}, \end{cases} \tag{2}$$

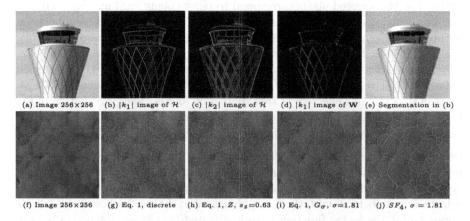

(a) Image 256×256   (b) $|k_1|$ image of $\mathcal{H}$ (c) $|k_2|$ image of $\mathcal{H}$ (d) $|k_1|$ image of $\mathbf{W}$ (e) Segmentation in (b)

(f) Image 256×256   (g) Eq. 1, discrete   (h) Eq. 1, Z, s_z=0.63   (i) Eq. 1, G_σ, σ=1.81   (j) SF_4, $\sigma = 1.81$

Fig. 2. Comparison of valley detection on real images. The image in (f) is obtained using scanning electron microscopy of melt ceramic, where the valleys are detected with 3 different techniques: Hessian matrix $\mathcal{H}$ without and with low pass filter (Z and G_σ) in (g)–(i) and steerable filter of order 4 (SF_4) in (j).

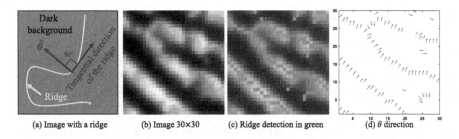

(a) Image with a ridge   (b) Image 30×30   (c) Ridge detection in green   (d) θ direction

Fig. 3. Example of extracted ridges with their tied perpendicular directions.

they are visible in Fig. 2(b), (c). Then, eigenvectors, tied to the direction perpendicular to the ridge/valley, are given by: $\boldsymbol{\theta} = \begin{pmatrix} \mathcal{H}_{12} \\ k_1 - \mathcal{H}_{11} \end{pmatrix}$. The two eigenvalues k_1 and k_2 correspond to the two main curvatures of the local surface. Besides, there exists several functions $D_{i,i \in \{1,2,3,4\}}$ indicating the local image contrast [7]:

- $D_1 = k_1$, corresponding to the main eigenvalue [6],
- $D_2 = \sqrt{k_1^2 + k_2^2}$, see [8],
- $D_3 = (k_1^2 + k_2^2)^2$, see [8],
- $D_4 = |k_1 - k_2| \cdot |k_1 + k_2|$, see [7].

Finally, a pixel is labeled as a ridge/valley pixel if $D_{i,i \in \{1,2,3,4\}}$ is maximum in the $\boldsymbol{\theta}$ direction, it is selected after non-maximum suppression [1], as illustrated in Fig. 3. In practice, regarding real images, due to the luminance variation, acquisition and/or compression noise, the detection of pure ridges/valleys is almost impossible. So, in order to more reliably extract the ridges and illustrated in Fig. 2(f)–(j), the convolution of the image with a low-pass filter is considered, as detailed in Sect. 2.3.

2.2   Weingarten

Weingarten map represents the differential of the Gauss map [9]. This expression can be computed directly from the first (i.e., $I_x = \frac{\partial I}{\partial x}$ and $I_y = \frac{\partial I}{\partial y}$) and second derivatives of the images. The linear invariants of the Weingarten map are the intrinsic curvatures of the surface: the eigenvalues are the principal curvatures, the trace is the mean curvature, and the determinant is the Gaussian curvature:

$$\boldsymbol{W}(x,y) = \frac{1}{(1 + I_x^2 + I_y^2)^{\frac{3}{2}}} \cdot \begin{pmatrix} 1 + I_y^2 & -I_x I_y \\ -I_x I_y & 1 + I_x^2 \end{pmatrix} \cdot \begin{pmatrix} I_{xx} & I_{xy} \\ I_{xy} & I_{yy} \end{pmatrix}. \tag{3}$$

The eigenvalues and eigenvectors of $\boldsymbol{W}$ are extracted with the same procedure as in Eq. 2 and for θ computation, regarding coefficients of the matrix $\boldsymbol{W}$. In [10], ridges or valleys are extracted by smoothing the image with a Gaussian and considering D_1. Note that if $I_x = 0$ and $I_y = 0$, then the ridge extraction technique is equivalent to the hessian matrix diagonalization.

2.3   Low Pass Filters for Ridge Detection

The optimization criteria, based on the Canny theory, are: (i) detection efficiency, (ii) location accuracy of the detected contour and (iii) uniqueness condition of filter response to its output for an input signal [1]. Based on this theory, several low pass filters have been proposed in the literature. In the following, three low-pass filters and their second derivatives are discussed for ridge/valley detection.

Ziou Filter Z. In [11], the author described an optimal line detector allowing an economic temporal complexity. It represents a second order recursive filter. Considering $t \in \mathbb{R}$, the equation of the 1D low pass filter Z is given by:

$$Z(t) = \frac{1}{s_z^2} \cdot (1 + s_z \cdot |t|) \cdot e^{-s_z \cdot |t|}, \tag{4}$$

where s_z represents a positive constant. The second derivative of Z is obtained by derivation as a function of t, two times: $z(t) = (s_z \cdot |t| - 1) \cdot e^{-s_z \cdot |t|}$. Note that the same procedure is available to obtain the 1st derivative of the filter Z, as for the following presented filters.

Gouton Filter R. Gouton *et al.* [12] described a third order recursive filter:

$$R(t) = (K \cdot \sin(s_r \cdot |t|) + D \cdot \cos(s_r \cdot |t|) + E) \cdot e^{-s_r \cdot |t|}, \tag{5}$$

where: $K = \frac{1}{4 \cdot s_r^4}$, $D = \frac{2 s_r^2 \cdot A}{4 \cdot s_r^4}$, $E = \frac{A \cdot s_r + s_r}{s_r^3}$ and $A = \frac{-s_r \cdot (2 s_r^2 - t^2)}{s_r \cdot (2 s_r^2 + t^2)}$. Thus, the second derivative of R is: $r(t) = (\cos(s_r \cdot |t|) - s_r \cdot \sin(s_r \cdot |t|) - (s_r + 1)) \cdot e^{-s_r \cdot |t|}$. The more the s_r decreases, the more r enhances fine ridges/valleys. Furthermore, when s_r decreases, the shape of R is nearly a Gaussian, as shown in Fig. 4.

Gaussian Filter. Gaussian kernels are regularly used for their effectiveness in edge detection [1], the 1D and 2D Gaussian are:

$$G_\sigma(t) = \frac{1}{\sqrt{2\pi}\sigma} \cdot e^{-\frac{t^2}{2\sigma^2}}, \mathbf{G}_\sigma(x,y) = G_\sigma * G_\sigma^\top(x,y) = \frac{1}{2\pi\sigma^2} \cdot e^{-\frac{x^2+y^2}{2\sigma^2}} \tag{6}$$

with σ the standard deviation, "$*$" product of convolution and $\top$ transpose. Using G_σ, the strategy is the same as to compute the second derivative on an image, with G_σ and $g_\sigma^\top$, as an example for an image derivative in y, see Fig. 5(d). The Sect. 2.4 is dedicated to the strategies of the two dimensional filters implementation. Furthermore, these filters in Eq. 4, 5 and 6 are useful for image smoothing extracting edges by computing $\mathcal{H}$ matrix presented in Eq. 1. Additionally, it is also possible to use the Weingarten (cf. Eq. 3) with the Gaussian, as in [10].

Parameters. The three above-mentioned filters are suitable for ridge and valley detection. One can adjust one filter by tuning only one parameter which is the same for the low pass and the derivative filter. Accordingly, s_z, s_r and σ are chosen as a function of the ridge/valley's width. These parameters are thus selected by increasing the filter width as robust as possible in order to extract suitably the feature. Here, the main idea is to compare equivalently the 3 filters z, r and g_σ as a function of the filter width – tuning each filter for a specific width with appropriate s_z, s_r or σ. Thus, in the discrete domain, s_z and s_r are decreasing, and σ is increasing until the filter coefficients cross 0 and the shape filter contains the width of the feature at the same time. Figure 4 illustrates the selected filers computed with different parameters as a function of the width of the feature. In addition, Table in Fig. 4 references the optimum parameters for each filter as a function of the features size from 1 to 15 pixels. Finally, σ of the Gaussian has the same properties regarding oriented filters widths.

2.4   Oriented Filters

One common practice in image processing and computer vision is applying the same filter on different angles in order to detect directional responses as Steerable Filter [13,14], Anisotropic Gaussian Kernel [15] and Logical Linear Filter [16].

Steerable Filter. Gaussian kernels $\mathbf{G}_\sigma$ are very useful for their properties like isotropy, steerability or separability (see Sect. 2.4). Freeman and Adelson proposed an efficient architecture to design oriented filters of arbitrary orientations from linear combinations of basis filters [13]. By applying filter steered in different directions, the filter responses can thus help to detect the orientation for the considered pixel. In ridge/valley detection, the first step is to estimate the orientations with even steered filters. Consequently, the 2nd steerable filter considering the two-dimensional Gaussian $\mathbf{G}_\sigma$ at angle θ is:

$$SF_2^\theta = \cos^2(\theta) \cdot \frac{\partial^2 \mathbf{G}_\sigma}{\partial x^2} + \cos(\theta)\sin(\theta) \cdot \frac{\partial^2 \mathbf{G}_\sigma}{\partial x \partial y} + \sin^2(\theta) \cdot \frac{\partial^2 \mathbf{G}_\sigma}{\partial y^2}. \qquad (7)$$

This allows computing an even filter on any specific orientation, as illustrated in Fig. 5(e). So the ridges or the valleys detection corresponds to a task of finding filter energy in the direction of the maximum response of the template.

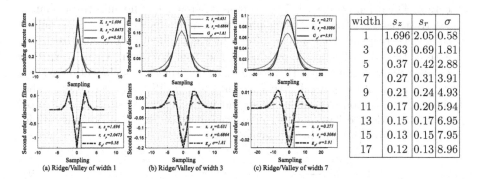

Fig. 4. Visual comparison of tested normalized 1D low-pass filters and 2nd order filters with the ideal parameters tied to the width of the ridge/valley.

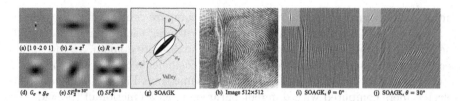

Fig. 5. Representation and visualization of the second derivative an image computed by convolution with the SOAGK with $\sigma_u = 2.88$ and $\sigma_v = 5\sigma_u$.

Jacob and Unser [14] extend the idea of the steerable filter of order 2 (SF_2) with operators having a better orientation selectivity. Indeed, they proposed higher order functions, from higher order Gaussian $\mathbf{G}_\sigma$ derivatives (2nd and 4th: $\mathbf{G}_{yy}$, $\mathbf{G}_{xx}$, $\mathbf{G}_{yyyy}$, $\mathbf{G}_{xxyy}$, $\mathbf{G}_{xxxx}$), resulting in more elongated templates, as shown in Fig. 5(f). Regarding ridge detection, this filter needs to be specified so as to provide the better compromise in terms of signal-to-noise ratio, false detection, and localization (as illustrated in Fig. 2). Thus, the even steerable filter of 4th order (SF_4) is formulated as:

$$SF_4(x,y) = \alpha_1 \cdot \mathbf{G}_{yy} + \alpha_2 \cdot \mathbf{G}_{xx} + \alpha_3 \cdot \mathbf{G}_{yyyy} + \alpha_4 \cdot \mathbf{G}_{xxyy} + \alpha_5 \cdot \mathbf{G}_{xxxx}, \quad (8)$$

with $\alpha_1 = -0.392 \cdot \sigma$, $\alpha_2 = 0.113 \cdot \sigma$, $\alpha_3 = 0.034 \cdot \sigma^3$, $\alpha_4 = -0.184 \cdot \sigma^3$, $\alpha_5 = 0.025 \cdot \sigma^3$ such that the template SF_4 does not produce undesirable oscillations and sidelobes along y (see [14]). This 2D template, presented in Fig. 5(f), can be steered in different orientations θ, as detailed in [14] to extract ridges and valleys.

Anisotropic Gaussian Filter. Though isotropic Gaussian kernels can be successfully applied in some ridge/valley detections, they failed quite often. The main drawback of isotropic Gaussian kernels is the isotropic smoothing property. This makes it difficult to detect crossing lines. And parallel lines could be blurred into one line, especially if the smoothing parameter is too large (i.e., σ parameter in Eq. 6). Kernels based on the derivative of anisotropic Gaussian functions can overcome this problem and have been successfully applied in edge detection. The orientation selectivity is more reliable with the anisotropic Gaussian derivatives. And the anisotropic property is more efficient at level of straight lines. This corresponds to a narrow filter which is applied in different directions to extract the edges when it is steered in the edge direction. Thereafter, it is necessary to filter the image with a set of $360/\Delta\theta$ kernels, as such, leading to the characterization of the partial derivatives in $360/\Delta\theta$ different orientations. The straightforward option to produce single output is thus to retain the result produced by the oriented kernel with the maximum absolute value. An anisotropic 2D Gaussian filter [17] can be defined as:

$$\mathcal{G}_{\sigma_u,\sigma_v,\theta}(x,y) = \frac{1}{2\pi\sigma_u\sigma_v} \cdot e^{-\frac{1}{2}\left(\frac{(x\cos\theta + y\sin\theta)^2}{\sigma_u^2} + \frac{(-x\sin\theta + y\cos\theta)^2}{\sigma_v^2}\right)}. \quad (9)$$

Here, (σ_v, σ_u) represents the standard deviations of the anisotropic Gaussian. When $\sigma_v = \sigma_u$, the kernel $\mathcal{G}$ turned into an isotropic Gaussian kernel. To extract

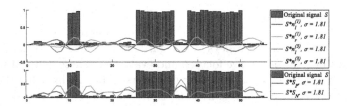

Fig. 6. Convolution of a 1D signal with the n'_l, n'_r, $n_l^{(3)}$ and $n_r^{(3)}$ with $\epsilon = 2$ to compute Positive and Negative contrast lines with $\mathcal{S}_P$ and $\mathcal{S}_N$ respectively.

ridges, the Second-Order Anisotropic Gaussian Kernel (SOAGK) can be applied [15]. Considering the vertical anisotropic Gaussian directed at $\theta = 0$, the second derivative of $\mathcal{G}_{\sigma_u,\sigma_v,\theta=0}$ in the x direction is:

$$\mathcal{G}''_{\sigma_u,\sigma_v,\theta=0}(x,y) = \frac{\partial^2 \mathcal{G}_{\sigma_u,\sigma_v,\theta=0}}{\partial x^2}(x,y) = \frac{x^2 - \sigma_u^3}{2\pi\sigma_u^5\sigma_v} \cdot e^{-\frac{1}{2}\left(\frac{x^2}{\sigma_u^2} + \frac{y^2}{\sigma_v^2}\right)}. \tag{10}$$

The choice of $\sigma_v > \sigma_u$ enables to build a narrow filter smoothing mostly in the y direction while enhancing valleys in the x direction. Now, this 2D kernel can be oriented in different directions to capture valleys (or ridges with the opposite filter) in the image, as illustrated in Fig. 5. To this end, this anisotropic choice produces a smoothing alongside the ridge/valley, which helps to extract easily elongated features, even disturbed by noise. On the contrary, kernels having $\sigma_v/\sigma_u \approx 1$ highlight undesirable features as noise which are interpreted as small, non-elongated ridges [15].

Logical Linear Filter. Similar to the SOAGK, Iverson and Zucker proposed a hybrid filter by combining directional linear filters and a Linear-Logical (L/L) operator which helps to reduce the false positive pixels of ridges/valleys [16]. This technique allows selecting any inflection points within the 1D signal region $[t - \epsilon, t + \epsilon]$, $\epsilon > 0$, see Fig. 6. It depends on the G_σ (see Eq. 6) and its derivatives of the first and third order G'_σ and $G_\sigma^{(3)}$ by computing the four parameters:

$$\begin{cases} n'_l = G'_\sigma(t + \epsilon)/2\epsilon, \ \ n'_r = G'_\sigma(t - \epsilon)/2\epsilon, \\ n_l^{(3)} = G_\sigma^{(3)}(t + \epsilon)/2\epsilon, \ n_r^{(3)} = G_\sigma^{(3)}(t - \epsilon)/2\epsilon, \end{cases} \tag{11}$$

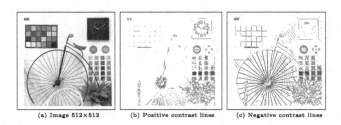

(a) Image 512×512   (b) Positive contrast lines   (c) Negative contrast lines

Fig. 7. Directions of contrast lines obtained by $\mathcal{S}_P$ and $\mathcal{S}_N$ (vectorial images).

thereby, they can be applied to a signal, as shown in Fig. 6.

Concretely, the L/L operator can be utilized on different edge types as ridge P (Positive contrast lines), valleys N (Negative) and Edges E (ramp or step). In this study, only P and N are focused and evaluated. These denoted functions $\mathcal{S}_P$ and $\mathcal{S}_N$ respectively combine linear operators in Eq. 11 by using the logical operator $\mathbb{\wedge}$ such that: $\mathcal{S}_P = \mathrm{n}'_l \mathbb{\wedge} \mathrm{n}'_r \mathbb{\wedge} \mathrm{n}^{(3)}_l \mathbb{\wedge} \mathrm{n}^{(3)}_r$ and $\mathcal{S}_N = -\mathrm{n}'_l \mathbb{\wedge} -\mathrm{n}'_r \mathbb{\wedge} -\mathrm{n}^{(3)}_l \mathbb{\wedge} -\mathrm{n}^{(3)}_r$ where the logical operator $\mathbb{\wedge}$ is represented by, for two hypotheses (a, b):

$$a \mathbb{\wedge} b \triangleq \begin{cases} a + b, & \text{if } a > 0 \wedge b > 0; \quad b, \text{ if } a > 0 \wedge b \leq 0; \\ a + b, & \text{if } a \leq 0 \wedge b \leq 0; \quad a, \text{ if } a \leq 0 \wedge b > 0, \end{cases}$$

In this way, $\mathcal{S}_P$ and $\mathcal{S}_N$ contribute to extract convex and concave points, as shown in Fig. 6.

Next, to extract ridges or valleys and their tied directions, the 2D operator is expressed as the Cartesian product of orthogonal, 1D L/L operators $\mathcal{S}_P$ or $\mathcal{S}_N$ operators and a tangential operator $T(t)$. Moreover, this 2D operator is oriented and uses strategies of the logical operator $\mathbb{\wedge}$ with the tangential operator $T(t)$ to (a) discriminate between locally continuous and discontinuous curves along their tangent direction in the image; and, (b) align the line termination with the line ending (illustrated in Fig. 7, for more details refer to [16]). To sum up, the L/L operator is similar to the SOAGK, with the parameter σ_u tied to the normal operator ($\mathcal{S}_P$ and $\mathcal{S}_N$) and σ_v for the tangential operator T (see Fig. 5(a)).

Implementation and Complexity. Presented filters may be implemented with different strategies. First, separable filters Z, R or G_σ can be written as product of two 1D filters which are equivalent to a typical 2D convolution providing reduction of the computational cost. Secondly, to reduce even more the number of operations per pixel, each 1D Z, R or G_σ filter may be also implemented recursively (also known as Infinite Impulse Response (IIR) filters), representing filters where the output sample is a linear combination of some number of previous inputs and outputs. The recursive implementation strategy is then compared here. Table in Fig. 8 reports the order of these 3 detailed filters.

To reduce the number of operations per pixel, a M-order recursive filter is obtained by calculating its Z transform. Thus, the two-sided sequence of

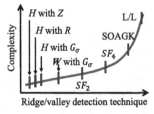

Filter	Z and z	R and r	G_σ and g_σ
Recursive order	2, see [11]	3, see [12]	4, see [18] or 5, see [19]

	Computed basis images	Rotation	Other
LoG	I_{xx} and I_{yy}	-	-
$\mathcal{H}$	I_{xx} , I_{yy} and I_{xy}	-	D_1, D_2, D_3 or D_4
W	I_x, I_y, I_{xx} , I_{yy} and I_{xy}	-	Usually D_1
SF_2	I_{xx} or I_{yy}	yes	max and argmax
SF_4	$I_{xx}, I_{yy}, I_{xxxx}, I_{yyyy}, I_{xxyy}$	yes	max and argmax
SOAGK	I_{xx} or I_{yy}	yes	max and argmax
L/L	I_x, I_{xxx}	yes	$\mathbb{\wedge}$, endline, stabilizer

Fig. 8. *Left*: Complexity schema, depending on the recursive filters order, the number of calculated images and the filter rotation. *Right*: Recursive orders of the filters and image computations as a function of the chosen technique.

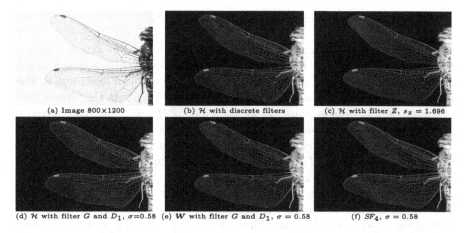

(a) Image 800×1200   (b) $\mathcal{H}$ with discrete filters   (c) $\mathcal{H}$ with filter Z, $s_z = 1.696$

(d) $\mathcal{H}$ with filter G and D_1, $\sigma=0.58$ (e) W with filter G and D_1, $\sigma = 0.58$ (f) SF_4, $\sigma = 0.58$

Fig. 9. Valley detection in green on real image of a dragonfly, with thin, blurred and very close junctions. The original image is inverted for a better visualization.

a filter F is the superposition of a causal filter F_- and anti-causal filter F_+: $F(n) = F_-(n) + F_+(n)$, for $n = \{1, ..., M\}$. To minimize the computational complexity, the authors of [19] proposed to decompose series interconnection into a product of the causal and anti-causal parts, leading to a 3rd-order Gaussian filter, a 4th-order first derivative filter and a 5th-order second derivative filter (many fast approximations have been proposed, some of them are detailed in [20]). Thereafter, table in Fig. 8 specifies the required number of image computations as a function of the segmentation technique (LoG, $\mathcal{H}$, W, SF_2, SF_4, or L/L) and Fig. 8 roughly schematize the complexity. The Hessian Matrix $\mathcal{H}$ needs the second derivatives of the image I_{xx}, I_{yy} and I_{xy}, using Z, R or G filters. Obviously, W is more computationally complex because it needs more image derivatives. Regarding the steerable filters, an operation of filter rotation with an angle θ is necessary (with $360°/\Delta\theta$ total rotations, where $\Delta\theta$ is the angular step); and 5 derivative images are calculated for the steerable filter of order 4 (see Eq. 8). On the other hand, the number of basis filters is large to extract features with the SOAGK, and the basis filters are non-separable, requiring high computational loads. In [17], the anisotropic Gaussian is decomposed into two Gaussian 1D filters by considering $360°/\Delta\theta$ steps of rotation, allowing reducing the operation number per pixel (to approximate the SOAGK, the difference of anisotropic Gaussian with two different standard deviations σ_u in Eq. 9 is calculated [17]). Also, the L/L filter contains several steps of interpolation for the normal operator ($\mathcal{S}_P$ and $\mathcal{S}_N$) and for the tangential operator T which are directed in different directions in the image. Moreover, the L/L uses other strategies such as the endline or the stabilizer to qualify the segmentation; these steps add more filter complexity.

3   Experimental Results and Evaluation

Experiments are carried out on synthetic and real images, showing qualitative and quantitative results. A first result in Fig. 9 illustrates the advantage to use sharp and narrow filters to extract thin and close objects, as filters z and r. The aim here is to extract branches inside the dragonfly wings. As this image does not contain any noticeable noise, the Hessian matrix $\mathcal{H}$ with finite filters like [1 0 -2 0 1] gave interesting results for these thin objects, but created many undesirable edge points around certain valleys (similar segmentation also by SF_4). $\mathcal{H}$ with the Gaussian g_σ and D_1 brings similar but less complete result. Segmentation obtained with $\mathcal{H}$ and D_2, D_3 and D_4 are worse with a lot of missing edge points, as with SF_2. However, the valley extraction using $\mathbf{W}$ is perfectible. On the other hand, the result using $\mathcal{H}$ with z filter is good enough (Fig. 9(c)), this justified the need to use low pass filter. Among all the ridge/valley detectors, exponential (z or r) filters do not delocalize contour points [21], whereas they are sensitive to noise. Techniques using Gaussian filters are less sensitive to noise, but suffer from rounding bends and junctions like the oriented filters SF_2, SF_4 and the SOAGK. The more the 2D filter is elongated, the more the segmentation remains robust against noise. In the following sections, quantitative results are reported.

3.1   Error Quantification and Evaluation Procedure

Evaluations are reported using synthetic images where the true positions of the edges are known. Let G_t be the reference contour map corresponding to the ground truth and D_c the detected contour map of an image I. Comparing pixel by pixel G_t and D_c, a basic evaluation is composed of statistics:

- True Positive (TP), common points of both G_t and D_c;
- False Positive (FP), spurious detected edges of D_c;
- False Negative (FN), missing boundary points of D_c;
- True Negative (TN), common non-edge points.

Thus, as described in [22], the normalized $\mathcal{N}$ edge detection evaluation measure is, for $FN > 0$ or $FP > 0$:

$$\mathcal{N}(G_t, D_c) = \frac{1}{FP+FN} \cdot \left[\frac{FP}{|D_c|} \sum_{p \in D_c} \frac{1}{1+\kappa_{FP} \cdot d_{G_t}^2(p)} + \frac{FN}{|G_t|} \sum_{p \in G_t} \frac{1}{1 + \kappa_{FN} \cdot d_{D_c}^2(p)} \right],$$

(12)

where $(\kappa_{FP}, \kappa_{FN}) \in \,]0, 1]^2$ represent two scale parameters [22], $|\cdot|$ denotes the cardinality of a set, and $d_A(p)$ is the minimal Euclidian distance between a pixel p and a set A [23]. Therefore, the measure $\mathcal{N}$ calculates a standardized dissimilarity score; the closer the evaluation score is to 1, the more the segmentation is qualified as suitable. On the contrary, a score close to 0 corresponds to a poor detection of contours.

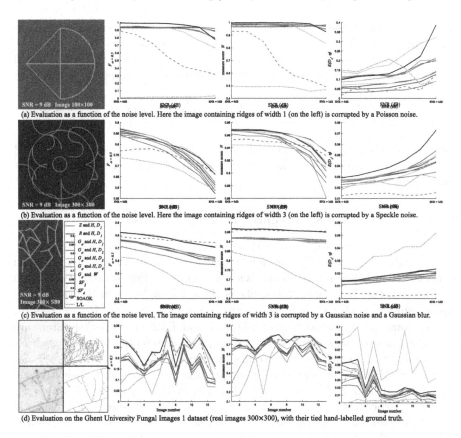

(a) Evaluation as a function of the noise level. Here the image containing ridges of width 1 (on the left) is corrupted by a Poisson noise.

(b) Evaluation as a function of the noise level. Here the image containing ridges of width 3 (on the left) is corrupted by a Speckle noise.

(c) Evaluation as a function of the noise level. The image containing ridges of width 3 is corrupted by a Gaussian noise and a Gaussian blur.

(d) Evaluation on the Ghent University Fungal Images 1 dataset (real images 300×300), with their tied hand-labelled ground truth.

Fig. 10. Evaluation of the different ridge/valley extraction techniques on (a)-(c) synthetic and (d) real images. Legends are in (c)

The objective here is to get the best contour map in a supervised way. For that, the contours are extracted after a suppression of the local non-maxima, then a threshold by hysteresis is applied to obtain a binary segmentation [1]. Theoretically, to be objectively compared, the ideal contour map of a measure must be a D_c at which the supervised evaluation gets the highest score [22,23]. For each better segmentation tied to $\mathcal{N}$, another evaluation measure concerns the angle tied to the ridge/valley, θ. Considering $\mathcal{C}_{D_c}$, the set of contour chains in D_c (i.e., at least 2 pixels per chain), the angle evaluation is computed as follows:

$$E(\mathcal{C}_{D_c}, \theta) = \frac{1}{|\mathcal{C}_{D_c}|} \cdot \sum_{p \in \mathcal{C}_{D_c}} \sum_{d_k \in \omega} \left[1 - \frac{\left| 90° - \left| \overrightarrow{\theta_p} - \overrightarrow{\theta_{d_k}} \right| \right|}{90°} \right] / c_k,$$

where d_k represents a contour pixel belonging to ω, a 3×3 window centered on p, $\overrightarrow{\theta_{d_k}}$ the direction tied to d_k and c_k the number of contour pixels in ω, minus the central pixel. This evaluation linearly ranges from 0 for identical angles of $\overrightarrow{\theta_p}$

and $\overrightarrow{\theta_{d_k}}$ to 1 for angles that differ. Note that when one direction approximates 0 and the other direction 180°, the evaluation remains close to 0.

Also, from proper binary confusion matrix, the precision (P_{rec}) and recall (R_{ec}) evaluations are computed, given the overall quality expressed in terms of:

$$F_\alpha = \frac{P_{rec} \cdot R_{ec}}{\alpha \cdot P_{rec} + (1 - \alpha) \cdot R_{ec}} \text{ with } P_{rec} = \frac{TP}{TP+FP} \text{ and } R_{ec} = \frac{TP}{TP+FN},$$
(13)

note that a values of $\alpha = 0.5$ allows a equal penalization between FN and FP.

These scores are presented in the next section, according to different images and noise types.

3.2   Synthetic Images Corrupted by Poisson Noise

The first image in Fig. 10(a) contains ridges of width 1 pixel and is corrupted by Poisson noise. This noise distribution typically models shot noise in a sensor in which the time between photon arrivals is governed by Poisson statistics. Given λ an integer, the maximum probability is obtained for $t=\lambda$ and the variance of the distribution is also λ ; at a pixel x, the equation is given by: $P_{\lambda_x}(t) = \frac{\lambda^t e^{-\lambda}}{t!}$.

As shown in Fig. 10(a), except SOAGK and L/L, all the other filters are robust to Poisson noise at this scale. SF_2 performed exceptionally well, with F_α almost close to 1. It only started to drop from SNR 5dB. Filters with Z, R, G_σ & SF_4 ranked in the second place, their performances are still sufficiently well (F_α over 0.9). But SF_4 seemed to be less robust to Poisson noise, whose F_α dropped sharply from SNR 6 dB. In comparison, SOAGK showed its relatively poor performance to resist the noise – starting with F_α at 0.85, ending with 0.3 at SNR 3 dB. L/L failed completely in this task. It detected barely any true positive ridges. This poor performance of oriented filters is caused by the small size of these filters where small-scale orientation deforms the kernels. The angular score E is the best for Z and R filters (using $\mathcal{H}$) because they correspond to sharp filters, especially suitable for thin ridges.

3.3   Synthetic Images Corrupted by Speckle Noise

The second image in Fig. 10(b) contains ridges of width 3 pixels and is disturbed by a Speckle noise. This multiplicative noise appears with the image acquisition due to the level of noise in the sensor of a CCD or CMOS camera, increasing in proportion to luminosity [24]. This noise model can be formulated as: $J = I + \sigma \eta I$, where J represents the observed image, I the noise-free image, η is a normalized Gaussian noise distribution centered at 0 of standard deviation σ.

Compared to Poisson noise which is correlated to the original image, Speckle noise adds some independent noise to the images that could corrupt more the image's geometric structure. For filters providing quite good results in previous situation (Fig. 10(a)), they are less efficient in case of Speckle noise. Instead of starting with F_α in the range of [0.83, 0.87], they are now under the threshold of 0.85 corresponding a performance drop of 0.8 at SNR 8dB. And the robustness to noise level decreased much more. This decreasing behavior in the interval [0.85, 0.55] is similar to Speckle noise's granular effect property. Unlike the total failure with Poisson noise, L/L filter worked correctly. However its performance is still the worst compared to other filters. The main reason could be due to the fact that L/L is by definition a 1D filter with additional processing as the endline detection or the stabilizer which are noise sensitive. This makes it be much less robust to structure-correlated noise. As the structure-correlated noise could destroy the 2D visual structures transformed in 1D filter space and cause thus the failure of detection. On the other hand, among the techniques using non-oriented filters, it is noticeable that $\mathcal{H}$ with D_1 and $\mathbf{W}$ with D_1 obtain best scores. Additionally, the extracted ridges are more continuous and less disturbed by undesirable FP pixels. $\mathbf{W}$ with D_1 allows a better quality of detected ridges than with other non-oriented filters (see additional results). Finally, the angular score E obtained by the SOAGK is less penalized because it corresponds to an elongated kernel applied on close-right structures, so the oriented filter is generally the same along these structures (same remark for the Gaussian noise).

3.4   Synthetic Images Corrupted by Gaussian Noise

The last experiment with synthetic images in Fig. 10(c) concerns valleys corrupted by Gaussian blur and Gaussian noise. This type of noise represents additive noise disturbing gray values in images. Gaussian noise blurred more the geometrical structure in images. So, as shown in Fig. 10(c), the general F_α for all filters are decreased compared to those with Poisson and Speckle noises. SOAGK, SF_2, SF_4 filters gave better results ($F_\alpha \sim 0.8$). L/L filter showed always the worst result, even at SNR 9 dB, the F_α is only 0.63. when noise becomes stronger performances decreases. In comparison, $\mathbf{W}$ with D_1 still detects a better quality of ridges than with other non-oriented filters, statistically and visually.

3.5   Evaluation with Real Images

After evaluating the filters on synthetic images with different types of noise, the ridge detection on real-world images is presented. These images are from the Ghent University Fungal Images together with their manually annotated ground-truth ridges [15]. This database is extremely challenging. Here, 13 images with their tied ground truth images are selected randomly for this experiment. The images have very poor contrast and strong noises. Regarding the evaluation of pixel per pixel, due to the hand-labeled ridge points which create inaccurate ground truth (G_t), the overall ridge detection with these filters is around $F_\alpha = 0.2$, and they are image-dependent. In the best situation, F_α can reach 0.3; otherwise, in worst cases, the F_α will drop below 0.5 and are close to 0.06. Oriented filter SF_2, SF_4 and SOAGK performs well, regarding F_α and $\mathcal{N}$, contrary to the L/L and $\mathcal{H}$ with D_4. Regarding $\mathbf{W}$ with D_1, its evaluation is better than other non-oriented filters, even though the angle evaluation E penalizes the directions perpendicular to the detected ridges (however the score remains under 0.1 where it was under 0.2 for Speckle noise).

4   Conclusion

In this paper, the state of art of ridge/valley detection with image-based filtering techniques is explored and compared, involving their mathematical properties, driving parameters and characterizations. The evaluation and comparison of filtering methods have been theoretically and experimentally carried out on both synthetic and real images. Each filtering techniques have been examined on complex images, where different types of noises have been applied. The obtained comparison and evaluation graphs demonstrated which approach is reliable as a function of the width feature. Eventually, this comparative evaluation would serve as ridges/valleys optimal parameter adjustment guide for researchers of this domain. Regarding non-oriented filters, the Z filter performs well when the ridge or the valley are very thin (width of one pixel) and requires the less computational complexity computed the Hessian matrix $\mathcal{H}$. On the other hand, $\mathcal{H}$ associated with the Gaussian G_σ and the highest eigenvalue (D_1) is a good compromise when the feature widths are growing. Yet, the Weingarten $\mathbf{W}$ and its eigenvalue gives suitable and better continuous detected ridges. Steerable filters of order 2 (SF_2) and of order 4 (SF_4) obtain similar results, especially for bended features, contrary to the SOAGK which is well adapted for straight features.

Though computer vision related research is one of the most advanced fields in deep learning, deeper understanding of image structure holds always its role. It could provide finer neural network building and thus improve the performance. This study can further give rise to a tool for the automatic selection of algorithms (and parameters) for the ridge/valley detection and extraction with additional voting steps etc. Future work will consist to investigate multiscale ridge and valley detectors [7,8,10,15] with different scenarios of features even though there exists a difficulty to create real images containing suitable hand-labeled ground truth, as discussed in [23].

References

1. Canny, J.: A computational approach to edge detection. IEEE TPAMI **6**, 679–698 (1986)
2. Crowley, J.L., Parker, A.C.: A representation for shape based on peaks and ridges in the difference of low-pass transform. IEEE TPAMI **2**, 156–170 (1984)
3. Marr, D., Hildreth, E.: Theory of edge detection. Proc. R. Soc. Lond. **207**(1167), 187–217 (1980)
4. Haralick, R.M.: Ridges and valleys on digital images. Comput. Vis. Graph. Image Process. **22**(1), 28–38 (1983)
5. Eberly, D., Gardner, R., Morse, B., Pizer, S., Scharlach, C.: Ridges for image analysis. JMIV **4**(4), 353–373 (1994)
6. Steger, C.: An unbiased detector of curvilinear structures. IEEE TPAMI **20**(2), 113–125 (1998)
7. Tremblais, B., Capelle-Laize, A., Augereau, B.: Algorithms for the extraction of various diameter vessels. Cell. Mol. Biol. **53**(2), 62–74 (2007)
8. Lindeberg, T.: Edge detection and ridge detection with automatic scale selection. Int. J.Comput. Vis. **30**(2), 117–156 (1998)

9. Do Carmo, M.P.: Differential Geometry of Curves and Surfaces: Revised and Updated, 2nd edn. Courier Dover Publications, Mineola (2016)
10. Armande, N., Montesinos, P., Monga, O., Vaysseix, G.: Thin nets extraction using a multi-scale approach. CVIU **73**(2), 248–257 (1999)
11. Ziou, D.: Optimal line detector. In: ICPR, vol. 3, pp. 530–533 (2000)
12. Gouton, P., Laggoune, H., Kouassi, R., Paindavoine, M.: Ridge-line optimal detector. Opt. Eng. **39**(6), 1602–1612 (2000)
13. Freeman, W., Adelson, E.H.: The design and use of steerable filters. IEEE TPAMI **13**(9), 891–906 (1991)
14. Unser, M.: Design of steerable filters for feature detection using canny-like criteria. IEEE PAMI **26**(8), 1007–1019 (2004)
15. Lopez-Molina, C., De Ulzurrun, G., Baetens, J., Van den Bulcke, J., De Baets, B.: Unsupervised ridge detection using second order anisotropic gaussian kernels. Sign. Proc. **116**, 55–67 (2015)
16. Iverson, L., Zucker, S.: Logical/linear operators for image curves. IEEE TPAMI **17**(10), 982–996 (1995)
17. Geusebroek, J.M., Smeulders, A., Van De Weijer, J.: Fast anisotropic gauss filtering. IEEE TIP **12**(8), 938–943 (2003)
18. Deriche, R.: Recursively implementing the Gaussian and its derivatives. In: ICIP, pp. 263–267 (1992)
19. Van Vliet, L., Young, I., Verbeek, P.: Recursive gaussian derivative filters. In: ICPR, vol. 1, pp. 509–514. IEEE (1998)
20. Getreuer, P.: Image demosaicking with contour stencils. Image Process. On Line **2**, 22–34 (2012)
21. Laligant, O., Truchetet, F., Meriaudeau, F.: Regularization preserving localization of close edges. IEEE Sign. Proc. Lett. **14**(3), 185–188 (2007)
22. Magnier, B.: Edge detection evaluation: a new normalized figure of merit. In: IEEE ICASSP, pp. 2407–2411 (2019)
23. Magnier, B., Abdulrahman, H., Montesinos, P.: A review of supervised edge detection evaluation methods and an objective comparison of filtering gradient computations using hysteresis thresholds. J. Imaging **4**(6), 74 (2018)
24. Laligant, O., Truchetet, F., Fauvet, E.: Noise estimation from digital step-model signal. IEEE TIP **22**(12), 5158–5167 (2013)

High-Performance Algorithms Application for Retinal Image Segmentation Based on Texture Features

Nataly Ilyasova[1,2(✉)], Alexandr Shirokanev[1,2], Nikita Demin[1,2], and Andrey Zolotarev[3]

[1] Samara National Research University, Moskovskoye Shosse 34, 443086 Samara, Russia
ilyasova.nata@gmail.com
[2] IPSI RAS – Branch of the FSRC "Crystallography and Photonics" RAS, Molodogvardeyskaya 151, 443001 Samara, Russia
[3] Samara Regional Clinical Ophthalmological Hospital named after T.I. Eroshevsky, Zaporizhzhya str. 26, 443066 Samara, Russia

Abstract. Diabetic retinopathy is a dangerous disease of the eye fundus. If the treatment is untimely or inadequate, people affected by the disease may loose their eyesight for a variety of reasons. Laser photocoagulation is an advanced technique for treating diabetic retinopathy, with an eye surgeon extracting certain retinal areas to be exposed to laser pulses based on his expertise. Laser light parameters and pulse repetition rate are also chosen based on the previous experience of surgical interventions. An automated mapping of a preliminary coagulation pattern enables a number of challenges associated with the surgical procedure on the retina to be addressed. The manual mapping of the coagulation pattern is a highly demanding job that requires high-level concentration. It would be much more convenient if a doctor was able slightly to adjust an automatically mapped preliminary coagulation pattern rather than mapping it themselves. In this way, both the possibility of human error and the preparatory phase the surgical procedure are essentially reduced. Of great interest is an algorithm for extracting a laser coagulation zone, which is based on an algorithm for retinal image segmentation. The algorithm performs segmentation using texture features but takes long to run. Because of this, here, we propose a high-performance algorithm for retinal image segmentation, which enables a consecutive version to be made essentially faster, while outperforming a parallel algorithm.

Keywords: Fundus images · Image processing · Laser coagulation · Image segmentation · Eye retina · Texture features · Diabetic macular edema

1 Introduction

Diabetes mellitus (DM) is one of most essential medical problems of the modern world, which accounts for the largest proportion of endocrinal diseases. The number of cases has been steadily increasing annually, which may be thanks to both earlier diagnosis

© Springer Nature Switzerland AG 2021
A. Del Bimbo et al. (Eds.): ICPR 2020 Workshops, LNCS 12665, pp. 198–210, 2021.
https://doi.org/10.1007/978-3-030-68821-9_19

and a general increase in life expectancy. Currently, there are nearly 400 million people diagnosed with DM, and by the year 2035 the number is expected to reach 592 million people [1–6]. In the Russian Federation, according to the year 2013 State DM Register [7, 8], the number of those seeking help for DM exceeds 3.7 million, with the real number of cases estimated to be over 10 million.

There are a number of problems related to the effectiveness of diabetic macular edema (DME) treatment [9, 10]. At a preparatory stage of the surgical procedure, the surgeon manually inflicts a series of coagulates of a preset power, so that the procedure takes long to perform [11, 12]. Specialists argue that such an approach is far from being perfect due to an irregular arrangement of applied coagulates, resulting in a redundant of insufficient retina coagulation.

Thus, a problem of automated coagulate pattern mapping across the retina is highly relevant because with the currently employed medical equipment, the surgeon has to map the coagulation pattern by hand, which leads to insufficient coagulation and lengthy procedures.

When applying a series of coagulation spots onto the retina, a number of requirements need to be met, such as.

1. The coagulation spot is supposed not to affect the macula area, thick vessels, exudates, and healthy areas;
2. The coagulation zone should cover the maximum exudate area (to rule out under-coagulated areas);
3. The coagulated areas should not overlap to avoid overexposure (to rule out over-coagulated zones).

Requirements 1 and 3 serve to make the laser coagulation procedure safe. Requirement 2 provides the maximum effectiveness of the procedure.

To create an optimal photocoagulation map, a two-stage approach is proposed: at the first stage, a laser exposure zone is extracted [13, 14] (a pathological zone containing a macular edema zone, except for anatomic structures) in accordance with requirement 1 [13]; in the second stage, coagulation spots are mapped in compliance with requirements 2 and 3.

Of great interest is an algorithm for extracting laser exposure zones on the eye fundus. This algorithm contains several steps and has an unacceptably long running time. In this paper, we propose a high-performance algorithm of retinal image segmentation.

2   An Algorithm for Separating a Laser Exposure Zone in the Retinal Image

Extracting a laser exposure area is based on an algorithm for retinal image segmentation. In the best way, this is done using texture features, as these have proven themselves well when processing medical imagery [15–17].

The feature computation stage takes long to run on a CPU [18–20]. For each image pixel, a texture feature vector is computed, meaning that computing features over the entire image may take extremely long. On the average, it takes 55 ms to compute 900 features per pixel using an optimized library version written in C++. Depending on the image size, the total running time may be over an hour. We note that for retinal image segmentation only five features need to be computed. However, an optimized library is intended for computation using a single kernel, allowing a five-feature vector per pixel to be computed for 600 μs. With parallel multi-kernel and/or multi-processor computing, an extra memory needs to be allotted in each kernel. When using a paralellizable algorithm, one pixel will take about 900 μs to process.

However, considering that even with a parallel version, the processor running time will be over 1 min, it is recommended that a CUDA-based high-performance algorithm should be utilized.

3 Development of a High-Performance Segmentation Algorithm Based on the Use of Texture Features

An algorithm for computing texture features is well scalable. Features of different pixels are calculated independently. However, when calculating features, histograms of image neighborhood, adjacency matrix, and gradient fields need to be calculated. Such calculations call for the use of loops and complicated computational procedures, which is normally avoided when developing an algorithm intended for graphics processing units (GPUs).

May there be an image pixel (i, j) and its neighborhood of radius r, denoted as $B_r(i, j)$. May a histogram computed in the pixel neighborhood be given by $H(i, j)$ and an adjacency matrix computed in the pixel neighborhood denoted as $C(i, j)$. Finally, a gradient field in the pixel neighborhood is denoted as $G(i, j)$. In this work, we analyze three major groups of texture features: histogram, Haralick, and gradient texture features. The feature from a particular group is computed based on the corresponding mathematical object; with histogram features computed using a histogram, Haralick texture features – using an adjacency matrix, and gradient features – using a gradient field. Some Haralick features utilize auxiliary objects, e.g. vectors of a sum over the adjacency matrix in the corresponding coordinates. For instance, the horizontal vector of the sum is given by the object $P_x(i) = \sum_j C(i, j)$, whereas the vector of a sum over the difference of coordinates is given by $P_{x-y}(k) = \sum_{k=|i-j|} C(i, j)$. Once the objects have been computed, texture features are computed using standard formulae, which take short to implement.

It takes long to compute objects because here several embedded loops may be utilized. To avoid the ineffective use of memory, the image is fragmented in each iteration of a high-performance algorithm. After the features and the resulting class are computed for each fragment, the latter is recorded into the proper pixel of the resulting image. In each subsequent iteration, the image is fragmented with an offset (*offsetI*, *offsetJ*), so that all pixels of the original image are covered in the course of neighborhood construction. Each fragment is an individual task for the GPU.

3.1 An Algorithm for Histogram Generation

Histogram computation cannot be vectorized because the summation needs to be based on the condition of the correspondence between the histogram index and pixel brightness.

A well-known histogram formula can be written as

$$H(i, j, k) = \frac{\sum\limits_{B_r(i,j)[m,n]=k} 1}{MN} \tag{1}$$

where M, N are the dimensions of the fragment $B_r(i, j)$;

$$0 \leq m < M, 0 \leq n < N.$$

The histogram for specific i and j defining an image fragment is computed and recorded in a cell corresponding to the fragment. Each thread has to perform a double loop in order to run over all fragment pixels. The mathematical thread is numbered by two indices, i and j, realizing task (1).

Concerning the kernel function, the use of local memory is not recommended because this essentially slows down the algorithm. Usually, the use of separable memory is recommended, however for it to be suitable, the tasks need to be separated so that each thread is assigned with an equal task portion. This is impossible to realize because the number of threads is fixed, whereas the window size may not correspond to the number of threads. In this connection, the histogram is computed using only a global memory.

The number of threads is fixed: 32×32. This value is optimal for GPUs utilized for solving the segmentation task. If the number of blocks is $\bar{I} \times \bar{J}$, the total number of virtual threads is $32 \cdot \bar{I} \times 32 \cdot \bar{J}$. However, the number of virtual threads is less than the dimension of the data to be processed. In this connection, a conditional operator is introduced, which checks whether the two-dimensional number of the virtual thread is found to the left of and higher than boundaries defined by the total number of fragments in rows and columns (see Sect. 3.2).

Pre-summation cell zeroing and normalization are implemented using separate kernel functions (see Sect. 3.2). In those functions, the parallelization principle is different because here we know in advance that exactly 256 cells need to be zeroed and normalized. Accordingly, the algorithm is parallelized in 256 threads and several blocks.

3.2 An Algorithm for Adjacency Matrix Generation

The adjacency matrix is computed using a similar principle to computing histogram: a conditional summation. The formula for computing an adjacency matrix relative to fragment (2) reads as

$$C(i, j, k, l) = \frac{\sum\limits_{B_r(i,j)[m,n]=k \wedge B_r(i,j)[m+dy,n+dx]=l} 1}{2\tilde{M}\tilde{N}} \tag{2}$$

where $\tilde{M}, \tilde{N}$ is the number of pixels in rows and columns in the fragment $B_r(i, j)$; $0 \leq m < \tilde{M}, 0 \leq n < \tilde{N}$; dx, dy are the computation parameters of the adjacency matrix.

Similar to computing the histogram, when computing an adjacency matrix, each thread calculates the matrix using (2) for the thread-corresponding fragment. The number of threads is fixed and equal to 32×32, similar to histogram computing. The number of blocks is $\bar{I} \times \bar{J}$, with each thread having to check whether the two-dimensional number of the virtual thread is found to the left of and higher than the boundaries defined by the total number of fragments in rows and columns. The kernel function code is given in Sect. 3.2.

Similar to computing histograms, the zeroing and normalization algorithms are described in separate kernel functions (see Sect. 3.2). The major distinction is that the algorithm is parallelized in 1024 threads, with each thread processing 64 cells. Blocks correspond to fragments. The total number of tasks realized in a single block is 65536, which corresponds to a square matrix of dimension 256, that is, to an adjacency matrix.

3.3 An Algorithm for Computing a Gradient Field

The norm of the gradient field is computed using (3). The algorithm is well vectorized, unlike two previous algorithms.

$$G(i, j, m, n) = \sqrt{\Delta_y B_r(i, j)[m, n]^2 + \Delta_x B_r(i, j)[m, n]^2} \tag{3}$$

where $\Delta_y B_r(i, j)[m, n] = B_r(i, j)[m+1, n] - B_r(i, j)[m+1, n]$;
$\Delta_x B_r(i, j)[m, n] = B_r(i, j)[m, n+1] - B_r(i, j)[m, n-1]$;
M, N is the dimension of the fragment $B_r(i, j)$;

$$0 \leq m < M, 0 \leq n < N.$$

By analogy with the previous algorithms, the number of threads can be fixed at 32×32 and the number of blocks equal to $\bar{I} \times \bar{J}$. Similar to the previous cases, each thread has to check whether the two-dimensional number of the virtual thread is to the left of and higher than the boundaries defined by the total number of fragments in rows and columns. This algorithm version is described in Sect. 3.2.

Let us find the dependence of an image fragment on the original image while taking account of the offset (p, q):

$$B_r^{pq}(i, j)[m, n] = I[2i \cdot r + p + m, 2j \cdot r + q + n].$$

Taking into account this dependence, we derive the dependence of a gradient field computed in a given fragment on the gradient field computed over the entire image:

$$G_r^{pq}(i, j, m, n) = G[2i \cdot r + p + m, 2j \cdot r + q + n] \tag{4}$$

Relationship (4) enables the amount of computations for the gradient field to be essentially reduced. Rather than computing it for each offset value, the gradient field can be computed once for each channel. In this case, the kernel function will not contain functions slowing down the algorithm implementation.

3.4 Algorithms for Computing Sum Vectors

When computing Haralick texture features, four sum vectors are selected, which are deduced from (5)–(8) below. The vectors derived from (5) and (6) can easily be parallelized into 256 threads, with each thread computing the sum for the k-the vector component:

$$P_x(i,j,k) = \sum_{m=0}^{255} C(i,j,m,k) \tag{5}$$

$$P_y(i,j,k) = \sum_{n=0}^{255} C(i,j,k,n) \tag{6}$$

$$P_{x+y}(i,j,k) = \sum_{\substack{m+n=k \\ m=0,255}} C(i,j,m,n) \tag{7}$$

$$P_{x-y}(i,j,k) = \sum_{\substack{|m-n|=k \\ m=0,255}} C(i,j,m,n) \tag{8}$$

Equation (7) can be rearranged to (9) below, which allows computations to be parallelized into 512 threads. Each thread computes the k-the vector component. Unlike the previous formulae, k varies from 0 to 511:

$$P_{x+y}(i,j,k) = \sum_{m=\max(0,k-255)}^{\min(255,k)} C(i,j,k-m,m) \tag{9}$$

Equation (8) can be rearranged to (10) below, allowing computations to be parallelized into 512 threads. Similarly, each thread computes the k-the vector component, with k varying from 0 to 511:

$$P_{x-y}(i,j,k) =_1 (i,j,k,m) +_2 (i,j,k,m) \tag{10}$$

where $C_1(i,j,k) = \sum\limits_{m=0}^{255-k} C(i,j,k+m,m)$;

$$C(i,j,k,m) = \begin{cases} \sum\limits_{m=\max(k,1)}^{255} C(i,j,m-k,m), & \text{if } k > 0 \\ 0, & \text{otherwise} \end{cases}.$$

These algorithms can easily be parallelized, presuppose the use of separable memory, and have a short running time. The implementation of the algorithms is given in Sect. 3.2.

4 Computing Texture Features

The majority of features represent the computation of a sum of certain functions that take values of the vector components of a histogram, an adjacency matrix, a sum vector, or a gradient matrix. In the simplest case, such features are computed through the independent thread-based computation of a particular fragment feature. Another approach to computing such type of features is conducting a thread-based parallel reduction operation, where each term of the sum is computed using a specific formula. For instance, the formula for asymmetry is given b$f(k) = (k + 1 - mean)^3 \cdot h(k)$, where $h(k)$ is the histogram for a particular fragment with number (i, j).

Of special interest is the '*Percentile*' feature, according to which the summation goes on until a stop criterion is fulfilled. Mathematically, the percentile feature is written as:

$$Perc(p) = q : b_1(q, p) \wedge b_2(q, p) \wedge b_3(q, p) \tag{11}$$

where $b_1(q, p) = (temp(q) < p)$;
$b_2(q, p) = (temp(q + 1) \geq p) \wedge (0 \leq q \leq 255)$;
$b_3(q, p) = (0 \leq q \leq 255)$;
$$temp(q) = \sum_{k=0}^{q-1} h(k).$$

In a straightforward way, Eq. (11) is realized using a 'while' cycle, which is an optimal solution for a CPU. However, for a GPU, the while-based solution may prove inefficient.

Let us analyze a different approach and make use of a *sign* function, which returns 1 for a positive argument, -1 – for negative, and 0 – for 0. Equation (11) can be rewritten as

$$Perc(p) = \sum_{i=0}^{255} \left[\frac{sign(p - temp(i)) + 1}{2} \right] \tag{12}$$

where $temp(q)$ denotes the same as in (11); $[\cdot]$ is the operator of down round-off.

The algorithm implementation based on (12) is better suited for CUDA. An algorithm for percentile computing is given in Sect. 3.2.

Haralick texture features are characterized by a different trait, which may be illustrated by an '*Entropy*' feature:

$$E(i, j) = \sum_{m=0}^{255} \sum_{n=0}^{255} C(i, j, m, n) \log_{10} C(i, j, m, n) \tag{13}$$

A simple solution for a two-dimensional case necessitates the use of a conditional operator and double loops. Introducing a correspondence $\tilde{C}(f, l) = C(i, j, m, n)$, the two-dimensional task can be reduced to one-dimensional. Summation needs to be done over all adjacency elements, i.e. 65536 elements. May there be 1024 threads, with each thread processing 64 elements. In this case, a separable memory is utilized to form results for local sums. After recording the result by each thread into the proper matrix cell, the threads need to be clocked and matrix elements summed up. It is usually recommended that summation be done based on tree topology. The kernel function for entropy computing is given in Sect. 3.2.

5   Experimental Study of the High-Performance Algorithm Acceleration

The simplest version of the algorithm for retinal image segmentation with the use of texture features is a consecutive feature vector computation that presupposes the allocation of memory in each iteration. Such a version is parallelized because each iteration is an independent task. The consecutive version can be minimized using a specific construction of the C++ language. For instance, one can utilize stock arrays for the temporal storage of matrices or vectors, as well as allocating the memory only once, rather than doing so each time the features vector is computed.

Table 1 gives the running time for the above-described algorithms for an 740 × 840 image. The study was conducted on an Intel Core i7-9700K processor.

Table 1. Results for running times of algorithms for retinal image segmentation

Algorithm version	Total time, s
Standard consecutive algorithm	548.02
Optimized consecutive algorithm	372.96
Parallel algorithm	121.02

The parallel algorithm turns out to be fastest, although the running time is about 2 min. Meanwhile, for images of this size, it is expected that segmentation should take less than one minute. To comply with this requirement, we utilized a high-performance CUDA-based algorithm.

The study was conducted using a NVidia GeForce RTX 2080 Ti GPU. The first version of algorithms for texture feature computing was realized based on the use of a 'double' type while computing the proper features. The mathematical objects were computed based on a two-dimensional decomposition of tasks. In the second algorithm version, a 'float' type was utilized while computing the proper features. In the third version, a two-dimensional decomposition was replaced by one-dimensional.

Table 2 depicts results for the running times of different versions of the CUDA-based high-performance algorithm.

Table 2. Results for the running times of CUDA-based high-performance versions of the retinal image segmentation algorithm

Algorithm version	Total time, s
2D decomposition, the use of a 'double' type	424.23
2D decomposition, the use of a 'float' type	235.40
1D decomposition, the use of a 'float' type	33.08

The 1D decomposition is based on row-wise unfolding of the mathematical object to form a vector, with each thread processing its own vector fragment, and not an individual fragment of the original image. Thus, parallelization is conducted not only for the fragment but also for objects based on which features are computed. The 1D decomposition is described in Sect. 1, and the algorithm is presented in Sect. 3.2.

Figure 1 depicts results for accelerating a parallel algorithm implemented on a CPU and a high-performance algorithm implemented on a GPU depending on the image dimension.

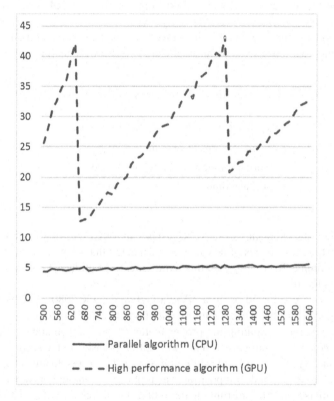

Fig. 1. Acceleration of the parallel and high-performance algorithms versus the segmentation window.

For a 1280-pixel image, the high-performance algorithm reaches 43.3-fold acceleration, whereas the parallel algorithm gives the 5.4-fold acceleration. Meanwhile the parallel algorithm has a linear acceleration, the CUDA-based algorithm provides a saw-tooth acceleration because CUDA extracts from memory a preset-size image, depending on the window size. The acceleration peaks are attained for image sizes multiple to fixed sizes, which are computed by multiplying 32 (the number of threads) by the window size. With every subsequent peak, the acceleration gets higher than the previous one.

Additionally, we studied the dependence of the acceleration of the parallel and high-performance algorithms on the segmentation window. The segmentation was conducted for a standard-size retinal image. Figure 2 depicts results of the study of the acceleration versus the segmentation window.

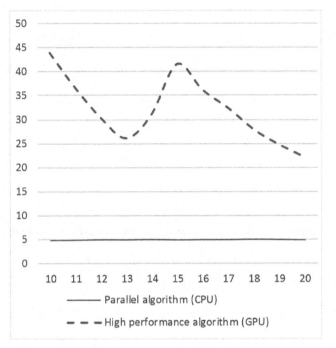

Fig. 2. Acceleration of the parallel and high-performance algorithm versus the segmentation window size.

When using a segmentation window varying from 10 to 20 pixels, the minimal acceleration is 22.1 for the high-performance algorithm compared to 4.8 for the parallel algorithm. A segmentation window with which the accuracy is highest enabled [21] attaining a 30.4-fold acceleration. For a standard 15-pixel window, the acceleration rate is 41.5. Despite a lower accuracy, the standard-size window may be optimal because the total running time essentially reduced.

The acceleration pattern versus the segmentation window size is also sawtooth, but without steep jumps. Figure 3 depicts the running times (ms) for the high-performance algorithm versus the segmentation window size. For a 15-pixel segmentation window, the running time of the high-performance algorithm is about 17 s. It takes an eight-core CPU over 2 min to implement a parallel algorithm. The running time of a consecutive algorithm is unacceptably high, amounting to 12 min.

An optimized step-skip algorithm can process images faster, but with lower accuracy. Figure 4 depicts the dependence of the increase in segmentation error on the number of skipped steps.

However, for the GPU-based segmentation procedure, a step-skip optimization that speeds up the execution at the expense of lower accuracy is not required any more, as the GPU provides adequate accuracy in a shorter time, doing without pixel skipping. The

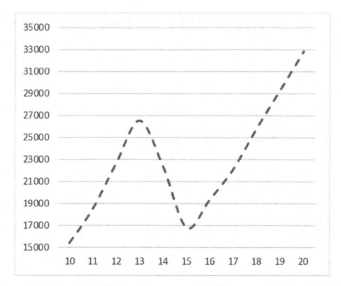

Fig. 3. The running time of the high-performance algorithm versus the segmentation window size.

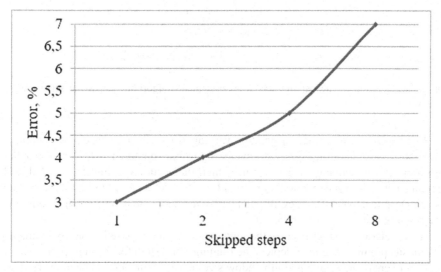

Fig. 4. The dependence of the increase in segmentation error on the number of skipped steps.

extraction of a laser exposure area reduces the image size which undergoes segmentation, further decreasing the running time of the high-performance segmentation.

Thus, the developed CUDA-based algorithm enables the retinal image segmentation to be done in less than a minute. Thanks to the high-performance algorithm, the preparatory phase in eye surgery can be made essentially shorter.

6 Conclusion

Summing up, we have developed a high-performance algorithm for computing texture features and retinal image segmentation, using which a reasonably high acceleration can be attained. Different variants of the use of the high-performance algorithm have been studied and a comparison with consecutive and parallel algorithms has been drawn. The retinal image segmentation procedure has been essentially accelerated by means of CUDA technology. The high-performance algorithm reaches a 40-fold acceleration, which may be even higher at certain parameters. With the high-performance algorithm, the segmentation of standard images can be done in less than a minute. The use of the high-performance algorithm for retinal image segmentation makes unnecessary the use of a consecutive algorithm with step skip, in which the running time is reduced thanks to interpolation but the accuracy is lower.

Acknowledgments. This work was funded by the Russian Foundation for Basic Research under RFBR grants ##19-29-01135, 19-31-90160 and the Ministry of Science and Higher Education of the Russian Federation within a government project of Samara University and FSRC "Crystallography and Photonics" RAS.

References

1. Doga, A.V., Kachalina, G.F., Pedanova, E.K., Buryakov, D.A.: Modern diagnostic and treatment aspects of diabetic macular edema. Ophthalmol. Diab. **4**, 51–59 (2014)
2. Bratko, G.V., Chernykh, V.V., Sazonova, O.V.: On early diagnostics and the occurence rate of diabetic macular edema and identification of diabetes risk groups. Siberian Sci. Med. J. **35**(1), 33–36 (2015)
3. Zamytskiy, E.: Analysis of the coagulates intensity in laser treatment of diabetic macular edema in a Navilas robotic laser system. Saratov J. Med. Sci. Res. **13**(2), 375–378 (2017)
4. Amirov, A.N., Abdulaeva, E.A., Minkhuzina, E.L.: Diabetic macular edema: epidemiology, pathogenesis, diagnosis, clinical presentation, and treatment. Kazan Med. J. **96**(1), 70–74 (2015)
5. Iskhakova, A.G.: Results of clinical & economic analysis of diabetic macular edema treatment. Povolzhye Postgraduate-Study Herald **1**, 96–98 (2014)
6. Umanets, N.N., Prozanova, Z.A., Makher, A.: Intravitreal injection of ranobizumab in the cystic diabetic macular edema treatment. Ophthalmol. J. **2**, 56–60 (2013)
7. Whiting, D.R.: IDF diabetes atlas: global estimates of the prevalence of diabetes for 2011 and 2030. Diabetes Res. Clin. Pract. **94**(3), 311–321 (2011)
8. Acharya, U.R., Ng, E.Y., Tan, J.H., Sree, S.V., Ng, K.H.: An integrated index for the identification of diabetic retinopathy stages using texture parameters. J. Med. Syst. **36**(3), 2011–2020 (2012)
9. Astakhov, Y.S., Shadrichev, F.E., Krasavira, M.I., Grigotyeva, N.N.: Modern approaches to the treatment of diabetic macular edema. Ophthalmol. Sheets **4**, 59–69 (2009)
10. Tan, G.S., Cheung, N., Simo, R.: Diabetic macular oedema. Lancet Diab. Endocrinol. **5**, 143–155 (2017)
11. Kernt, M., Cheuteu, R., Liegl, R.: Navigated focal retinal laser therapy using the NAVILAS® sys-tem for diabetic macula edema. Ophthalmologe **109**, 692–700 (2012)

12. Ober, M.D.: Time required for navigated macular laser photo coagulation treatment with the Navilas®. Graefes Arch. Clin. Exp. Ophthalmol. **251**(4), 1049–1053 (2013)
13. Ilyasova, N., Paringer, R., Kupriyanov, A.: Regions of interest in a fundus image selection technique using the discriminative analysis methods. In: Chmielewski, L.J., Datta, A., Kozera, R., Wojciechowski, K. (eds.) ICCVG 2016. LNCS, vol. 9972, pp. 408–417. Springer, Cham (2016). https://doi.org/10.1007/978-3-319-46418-3_36
14. Ilyasova, N.Yu., Kupriyanov, A.V., Paringer, R.A.: The discriminant analysis application to refine the diagnostic features of blood vessels images. Opt. Mem. Neural Netw. (Inf. Opt.) **24**(4), 309–313 (2015)
15. HeiShun, Yu., et al.: Using texture analyses of contrast enhanced CT to assess hepatic fibrosis. Eur. J. Radiol. **85**(3), 511–517 (2016)
16. Gentillon, H., Stefańczyk, L., Strzelecki, M., Respondek Liberska, M.: Parameter set for computer-assisted texture analysis of fetal brain. BMC Res. Notes **9**, 496 (2016)
17. Hajek, M., Dezortova, M., Materka, A., Lerski, R.: Texture Analysis for Magnetic Resonance Imaging, p. 234. Med4publishing (2006)
18. Strzelecki, M., Szczypinski, P., Materka, A., Klepaczko, A.: A software tool for automatic classification and segmentation of 2D/3D medical images. Nucl. Instrum. Methods Phys. Res. **702**, 137–140 (2013)
19. Szczypiński, M., Strzelecki, M., Materka, A., Klepaczko, A.: MaZda – a software package for image texture analysis. Comput. Methods Programs Biomed. **94**(1), 66–76 (2009)
20. Fukunaga, K.: Introduction to Statistical Pattern Recognition, p. 369. Academic Press, New York and London (1972)
21. Ilyasova, N., Shirokanev, A.S., Kupriyanov, A.V., Paringer, R.A.: Technology of intellectual feature selection for a system of automatic formation of a coagulate plan on retina. Comput. Opt. **43**(2), 304–315 (2019)

Learning Topology: Bridging Computational Topology and Machine Learning

Davide Moroni◉ and Maria Antonietta Pascali$^{(\boxtimes)}$◉

Institute of Information Science and Technologies, National Research
Council of Italy, Via Moruzzi, 1, 56124 Pisa, Italy
{davide.moroni,maria.antonietta.pascali}@isti.cnr.it
http://www.isti.cnr.it

Abstract. Topology is a classical branch of mathematics, born essentially from Euler's studies in the XVII century, which deals with the abstract notion of shape and geometry. Last decades were characterised by a renewed interest in topology and topology-based tools, due to the birth of computational topology and Topological Data Analysis (TDA). A large and novel family of methods and algorithms computing topological features and descriptors (e.g. persistent homology) have proved to be effective tools for the analysis of graphs, 3d objects, 2D images, and even heterogeneous datasets. This survey is intended to be a concise but complete compendium that, offering the essential basic references, allows you to orient yourself among the recent advances in TDA and its applications, with an eye to those related to machine learning and deep learning.

Keywords: Computational topology · Persistent homology · Machine learning · Deep learning · Image and shape analysis · Data analysis

1 Introduction

Topology is a branch of mathematics dealing with shape and geometry. Complexity and size of current collections of natural or synthetic dataset (2D, 3D, and multidimensional) is rapidly increasing. Hence, the ability to look at the shape of data and to discover patterns in any dimension is gaining great importance. Recently, successful applications of computational topology [27] to data analysis boosted a renewed interest in that field, and Topological Data Analisys (TDA) [10] has earned a prominent place in contemporary research, as a rich family of algorithms and methods from computational topology (e.g. Morse theory or persistent homology) to analyse and visualize data.

Focusing on image analysis, in low dimensions (typically 2 or 3), techniques from TDA are used to extract and classify geometric features, e.g. level sets or integral lines in [50]. For what regards Persistent Homology (PH), in [59] the authors describe how to define the Morse complex of a two or three-dimensional grayscale digital image, which is simpler than the cubical complex originally used

© Springer Nature Switzerland AG 2021
A. Del Bimbo et al. (Eds.): ICPR 2020 Workshops, LNCS 12665, pp. 211–226, 2021.
https://doi.org/10.1007/978-3-030-68821-9_20

to represent the image and to compute persistent homology. Also, [46] show that *persistence diagrams* built from functions defined on objects are compact and informative descriptors and, for example, can be used for retrieval of images and shapes. Also, the topological representation of data could provide tools for hierarchical image segmentation, as in [67].

Looking at higher dimensions, e.g. to multidimensional datasets, techniques from TDA have been adapted to develop novel algorithms of data clustering: in 2008 Carlsson, with Singh and Sexton, contributed to founding Ayasdi (www.ayasdi.com), maybe the first machine intelligence platform with a TDA core able to compute groupings and similarity across large and high dimensional data sets, and to generate network maps visually supporting analysts in understanding data clusters (for example showing high dimensional patterns and trends) and which variables are relevant.

Several works have shown that TDA can be beneficial in a diverse range of problems, even very distant from each other, such as: studying the manifold of natural image patches [9]; analyzing activity patterns of the visual cortex [60]; in the classification of 3D surface meshes [46,57]; complex networks [41,56]; clustering [20,55]; recognition of 2D object shapes [63]; protein folding [7,42,66]; viral evolution [18].

In this survey, we focus specifically on persistent homology (PH), because we found this technique the most interesting with respect to the interplay with machine and deep learning.

Outline. The following section is devoted to providing the reader basic notions and a historical overview of the main results in the theory of persistence in computational topology, starting from early works by P. Frosini, V. Robins and H. Edelsbrunner, which established independently the very first definitions and theorems. Section 3 deals with the computability of the most used PH descriptors, together with a summary of the software developed to compute PH. Section 4 explains the versatility of such methods, applied in several domains: one of the main factors of the recent interest around PH. Section 5 gives the reader a tour in the most promising applications of TDA in machine and deep learning, showing the great potential of embedding topological tools in the learning pipeline along with implementations of *topological layers*. These recent efforts have given rise to the novel field of Topological Machine Learning. The last section concludes the paper, and it is devoted to emerging studies focused on the interplay of topological data analysis and deep learning theory: e.g. concerning how to exploit tools from topological analysis to enhance explainability and interpretability of artificial intelligence methods.

2 Persistence Homology: History and Basic Notions

Algebraic topology is a branch of mathematics using tools from abstract algebra to study and characterise topological spaces (see [38] for an introductory textbook). The basic aim is to find algebraic invariant able to classify topological spaces up to homeomorphism. Persistent Homology bridges algebraic topology with the Morse theory core idea: exploring topological attributes of an object in an evolutionary context. The concept of *persistence* was introduced independently in 1990 by P. Frosini, M. Ferri and collaborators in Bologna (Italy), by V. Robins in 2000 in her PhD thesis devoted to multi-scale topology applied to fractals and dynamics, and by the group of Edelsbrunner at Duke (North Carolina).

2.1   Basics

In order to understand the core idea of PH, it is necessary to be familiar with the basics of algebraic topology. A simplicial complex is the standard algebraic object used to represent shapes of any dimension; simplices are its building blocks.

Definition 1. *A k-simplex is the k-dimensional convex hull of $k + 1$ vertices. The convex hull of any nonempty subset of the $k + 1$ vertices is called a* face *of the simplex*

A simplicial complex K is a set built from 0-dimensional simplices (0-simplices or points), 1-dimensional simplices (line segments), 2-simplices (triangles), 3-simplices (tetrahedra) and so on. The dimension of K is defined as the largest dimension of any simplex in it. Actually, to be a simplicial complex, K should satisfy the following conditions.

Definition 2. *A simplicial complex K is a set of simplices such that:*

- *every face of a simplex is also a simplex of K;*
- *the intersection of any two simplices σ_1 and σ_2 in K is either a face of both σ_1 and σ_2, or the empty set.*

Fig. 1. a. An example of a simplex for each dimension from 0 to 3. b. An example of a 3-dimensional simplicial complex.

These conditions allow defining the *boundary* operator, which is fundamental to define the homology, an algebraic object computable (via linear algebra) for K that accounts for the number of connected components, holes, voids, etc. The *boundary* of a k-simplex $\partial(\sigma_j)$ is the formal sum of the $(k-1)$-dimensional faces of σ_j. For example, the boundary of a triangle $\{a, b, c\}$ of vertices a, b and c is given by the sum of the edges $\{b, c\} + \{a, c\} + \{a, b\}$. More formally,

$$\partial(\{v_0, \ldots, v_k\}) = \sum_{i=0}^{k} (-1)^i \{v_0, \ldots, \hat{v}_i, \ldots, v_k\}$$

It's straightforward that a boundary has no boundary: $\partial \circ \partial = \partial^2 = 0$. Let K be a k-simplicial complex, and F a field; in PH the most used F is the two-element field $\mathbb{F}_2 = \mathbb{Z}/2\mathbb{Z}$. Let $\{\sigma_1, \ldots, \sigma_n\}$ be the set of p-simplices of K, where $p \in \{0, 1, \ldots, k\}$. $C_p(K)$ denotes the vector space generated over F by the p-dimensional simplices of K; hence, $C_p(K)$ is made of all p-chains, which are the formal sums over the p-simplex $c = \sum_{j=1}^{n} a_j \sigma_j$ where $a_j \in F$ and σ_j is a p-simplex in K. Hence, the boundary operator defined above is a linear operator between chain vector spaces: $\partial_p : C_p(K) \rightarrow C_{p-1}(K)$; also, now we define p-cycles $Z_p(K)$ and k-boundaries $B_p(K)$

$$Z_p(K) := \mathrm{Ker}(\partial : C_p \rightarrow C_{p-1}) \text{ and } B_p(K) := \mathrm{Im}(\partial : C_{p+1} \rightarrow C_p).$$

And it yields that: $B_p(K) \subset Z_p(K) \subset C_p(K)$. Finally, the p-th homology group $H_p(K)$ is defined as the quotient space Z_p/B_p: two cycles c_1 and c_2 are *homologous* if they are in the same homology class: $\exists b \in B_p(K)$ such that $c_2 - c_1 = b$. In algebraic topology, the homology group of a complex is one of the most studied and used. Also, the homology group is linked to the Betti numbers β_p, very important topological invariants: $\beta_p(K) = \dim(H_p(K))$. The p-th Betti number, informally, counts the number of p-dimensional holes on a topological surface; for example, a two-dimensional torus has $\beta_0 = 1$ (it is connected), $\beta_1 = 2$ (it shows two independent loops on its surface), and $\beta_2 = 1$ (only one cavity). Back to the case of a simplicial complex K, the 0-dim Betti number is the number of connected components and 2-dim Betti number is the number of voids of K.

The homology group and the Betti numbers are able to encode the global topological properties of a shape, represented by a simplicial complex.

Persistence needs a core ingredient: filtrations. A filtration of a simplicial complex K is a sequence of nested sub-complexes:

$$\emptyset = K^0 \subset K^1 \subset \cdots \subset K^m = K$$

In a few words, think of a filtration as a way to build the given complex iteratively by adding simplices, starting from vertices, step by step. Of course, given a complex, there are many ways to define a filtration. Depending on the data, different filtered simplicial complexes are considered, and the definition of most of them is based on the distance induced by the metric of the ambient space of data. At each filtration step t_j consider the simplicial complex K^j, sub-complex of K, and compute the rank of each p-th homology group (i.e. β_p) for each $p \in \{0, 1, \ldots, k\}$: the variation of the β_0 (or β_1) will account for the birth or death of connected components (or loops). Increasing p, the variation of Betti numbers will account for p-dimensional *topological features*, whose evolution is able to encode precious information about the global structure of the growing complex looking at the lifespan (death - birth) of each topological feature.

2.2   History

Frosini, Ferri and collaborators [30–32,65] in a family of papers published in between 1990 and 1993, introduced the size functions, which are equivalent to the

0-dimensional persistent homology. The size functions are defined as functions from the real plane to the natural numbers which describe the *shape of the objects* (seen as sub-manifolds of a Euclidean space). Also, different techniques of computation of size functions are provided, together with the definition of a deformation distance between manifolds measuring the *difference in shape* of two manifolds, and applications to shape analysis.

Edelsbrunner et al. in 2002 [28] formalize the notion of persistence within the framework of a filtration, which is the history of a growing complex. They introduced the classification of a topological event occurring during growth as either a *feature* or *noise*, depending on its lifespan within the filtration. The algorithm provided in this paper for computation yields only for sub-complexes of spheres and only with coefficients in $\mathbb{F}_2$.

Zomorodian and Carlsson in 2005 [68] show that the persistent homology of a filtered d-dimensional simplicial complex is simply the standard homology of a particular graded module over arbitrary field coefficients. In the same paper, authors provide an algorithm for computing individual persistent homology groups over an arbitrary principal ideal domain in any dimension. They also introduced *barcodes*, a combinatorial invariant; a complete introduction to persistence homology and its application from the perspective of barcodes is provided by Ghrist in [35].

From now on, the research community becomes more and more interested not only in the theoretical advances in persistence, but also in how to implement the persistence algorithms, in order to exploit the existence of computable topological descriptors in shape analysis, and, more generally, in data analysis. In 2010 Plex, the first software for computing persistence is released (see also Sect. 3.1).

2.3 Persistence Diagrams

The first descriptors derived from PH are persistence diagrams. Such descriptors provide a (visual) summary of births and deaths of topological events. e.g. they track when a loop appears and disappears while the complex is growing (i.e.while the filtration parameter increases). From another viewpoint, they can be seen as a parametrized version of the Betti numbers.

More in detail, a persistence diagram is a collection of points in R^2: any topological feature has a birth b and a death d, and is represented in diagrams as a point of coordinates (b, d). Two persistence diagrams may be compared efficiently using proper distances such as the p-Wasserstein distance, or the bottleneck distance which is the limit over p of the p-Wasserstein distance with p going to infinity. The Bottleneck (or matching) distance d_B between two subsets X and Y of a metric space (M, d) is:

$$d_B(X, Y) := \inf_{\phi} \sup_{x \in X} d(x, \phi(x))$$

where ϕ runs over all bijections between X and Y.

Bottleneck distance is used to compare persistence diagrams and to derive their stability. Indeed, despite the way these descriptors are built, they show robustness with respect to noise, as stated in the stability theorem [6,21]: persistence diagrams are stable with respect to perturbations of the data, and such a stability yields also for multidimensional persistent homology, as shown in [16].

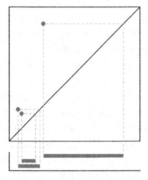

Fig. 2. Diagrams and barcodes are equivalent representations of topological persistence, and the correspondence is visually proved in this picture. (credits: Matthew L. Wright, 2014 http://www.mrwright.org)

An alternative way to represent topological persistence is given by *barcodes*, which are equivalent to diagrams, and their equivalence is shown in Fig. 2. Topological features, in barcodes, are represented as line segments of length $(d - b)$ where b is its birth, and d is its death; hence, a barcode is a collection of horizontal bars in a plane: the horizontal axis corresponds to the filtration parameter growing the complex, while the vertical axis represents an (arbitrary) ordering of homology generators. Barcodes have been introduced in [68] along with an algorithm to compute them, via linear algebra on the boundary matrix. The runtime of that algorithm is $O(n^3)$, where n is the number of simplices.

In Fig. 3 the first row shows a growing complex associated to a set of points sampled on a torus. The filtration is defined using the Euclidean metric (Rips complex). In the second row, there are its barcodes of dimension 0, 1, and 2. The length of each bar is the *lifespan* of the corresponding generator: long bars are interpreted as relevant features, while short bars as noise. Equivalently in diagrams, as can be seen from Fig. 2, dots near the diagonal represent noise.

Unfortunately, persistence diagrams and barcodes exhibit a complex structure, and are difficult to integrate into today's machine learning workflows. This is why the community currently works to define novel topological descriptors derived from the topological ones, or defining novel differentiation rules applicable to known topological descriptors.

In the following section, a list of the most successful PH-based descriptors is provided and discussed, together with the current algorithms and software used (and developed) by the research community to compute them.

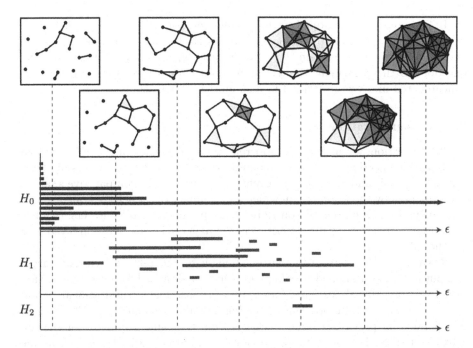

Fig. 3. The rank of the homology groups of dimension 0, 1, and 2 associated with a sequence of nested sub-complexes. Look at the longest feature in H_0: it represents that along the sequence only one connected component survives. This figure is by R. Ghrist [35].

3   PH-Based Descriptors and Implementations

After persistence diagrams, other PH-based descriptors were defined, implemented, and used: persistence silhouette, persistence landscape, and persistence images.

The birth of them was motivated by the need for stronger properties of stability and for easy and fast algorithms to compute and compare them, in order to increase their usage and efficacy in data analysis.

In 2015 Bubenik [8] developed the notion of a *persistence landscape*, a stable functional representation of a persistence diagram that lies in a Banach space (Hilbert, for $p = 2$), where statistical learning methods can be directly applied. The persistence landscape is a collection of continuous, piecewise linear functions $\lambda_p : \mathbb{N} \times \mathbb{R} \to \mathbb{N}$ that summarizes a persistence diagram. For $1 \leq p \leq \infty$ the p-landscape distance between two landscapes λ_1 and λ_2 is defined as $\|\lambda_1 - \lambda_2\|_p$; the ∞-landscape distance is stable with respect to the bottleneck distance, and the p-landscape distance is continuous with respect to the p-Wasserstein distance on persistence diagrams. Statistical properties of landscapes and similar descriptors (average landscape, silhouette) are investigated in [19], resulting in establishing useful stability properties.

In [1] barcodes are mapped to the so-called persistence surfaces. This is done by computing a weighted sum of normalized (isotropic) Gaussians, evaluated at each point in the diagram. Upon discretization of this persistence surface, one obtains the persistence image, stable and computable, that can then be concatenated in a vector and fed to a support vector machine.

3.1 Implementations

In this subsection, we present the most relevant implementations of PH. The goal is to provide effective tools for the computation of barcodes as well as methods for their analysis and comparison. A reference paper for the comparative analysis is represented by the work [54], in which a benchmark of the selected open-source implementations is carried out on 12 reference public-available datasets. In addition, other software tools not described in the paper [54] are briefly surveyed here for the sake of completeness.

Javaplex [2] implements persistent homology and related techniques from computational and applied topology, in a library designed for ease of use, ease of access from Matlab and java-based applications. The Computational Topology workgroup at Stanford University has mainly developed JavaPlex, which is grounded on previous similar packages from the same group. Among them, **Plex** is the first known software providing computation of PH, as well as the first proposing the use of zigzag persistence [11].

Dionysus [51], and its new version **Dionysus 2**, are C++ libraries for the computation of persistent homology. Dionysus has been the first software package to implement the dual algorithm [23], but it is also known since it contains advanced tools for the construction of vineyards (i.e. continuous families of persistence diagrams) [22], for the determination of homology generators and for the computation of Wasserstein and bottleneck distances.

Another interesting C++ software package is **Perseus** [53] which computes the persistent homology leveraging Morse-theoretic reduction. Since the standard algorithm for computing persistence intervals relies on Smith normal form and is therefore of super-cubical complexity in the total number of cells, reducing the number of cells might result in relevant savings both in memory and time. Perseus achieves a drastic reduction of the number of cells in the original filtration in linear time via discrete Morse theory without altering its persistent homology [49]. In addition, being based on general discrete Morse theory, this preprocessing step does not rely on peculiarities of a particular type of complex structure, but it can be applied straightforwardly to simplicial complexes, cubic complexes and Vietoris-Rips complexes to name a few.

More recently, **PHAT** [5] (and its spin-off **DIPHA** [4] devoted to distributed calculus) proposed a C++ implementation focused on the efficient and fast computation of PH based on matrix reduction. The authors aimed at a generic design that decouples algorithms from data structures; several different reduction strategies as well as data types to store and manipulate the boundary matrix are provided. **GUDHI** [47] is a C++ library with a Python interface implementing an efficient data structure for general simplicial complexes (*simplex tree*) as well as the possibility to compute simultaneously persistence diagrams with coefficients over multiple finite fields $\mathbb{F}_p$.

The **R package TDA** [29] provides an R interface for the efficient algorithms of the C++ libraries GUDHI, Dionysus and PHAT, including the PH of Rips filtrations and of sublevel sets of arbitrary functions evaluated over a grid of points.

SIMBA [24] implements a new algorithm, leveraging on a batch collapse strategy as well as a new sparse Rips-like filtration, that enables the approximation the persistent homology of Rips filtrations with quality guarantees. A software, developed in C++, is made available upon request and, in practical application, is an order of magnitude faster than existing methods.

The **Topology ToolKit (TTK)** [48] is an open-source library for TDA which implements, in a generic and efficient way, a substantial collection of reference algorithms, including those for the computation of persistence diagrams. The main merit of TTK is having made such algorithms accessible to a wider community by proving a library integrated with state-of-the-art libraries for scientific visualization (VTK) and image analysis (ITK) and with a graphical front-end, i.e. Paraview.

4   A Plethora of Applications

PH, as concern data analysis, is a versatile method: there is no restriction to apply to any particular kind of data (such as images, sensor measurements, time-series, graphs, etc.). When we want to analyse an image, a shape or a dataset, generally we choose a representation for the input data, e.g. the vertices of a triangulation for a shape or an n-dimensional point cloud for a dataset, along with a (natural) notion of distance, or similarity, between them. This distance is generally induced by the metric in the ambient space (e.g. the Euclidean metric) or may come as an intrinsic metric defined by a pairwise distance matrix. It is important to notice that the choice of the metric may be critical to reveal interesting topological and geometric features of the data. To exploit PH methods, depending on the data, different filtered simplicial complexes may be used, e.g. Vietoris-Rips complex, Čech complex, Alpha complex, Witness complex, Morse complex, cubical complex, clique (or flag) complex, or CW complex.

In general, the TDA pipeline consists of the following three steps: 1. Give to input data a multi-scale topological structure, i.e. a complex along with a filtration; 2. Compute multi-scale topological signature (as PH-based descriptors); 3. Take advantage of the signature to perform pattern analysis tasks, exploiting machine learning methods (i.e. looking at statistical aspects and representations of topological persistence).

In the following, there is a focus on applications of PH to image and signal analysis.

Image and Shape Analysis. Results in [9] provide an example of how unexpected could be the findings of topological enquire of imaging: the authors showed that the space of 3×3 high-contrast patches from digital images has the topology of a Klein bottle, and suggested to use this fact to implement a novel compression method of 2D images.

First applications of PH were in 2D and 3D shape analysis, and specifically in diverse tasks, i.e. classification, segmentation, retrieval, and many others. We list here just a few examples: in 2006 [17] the original size functions were used to generate 25 measuring functions for automatic retrieval of trademark images, outperforming existing whole-image matching techniques; In 2010 [61] a persistence based clustering and the Heat Kernel Signature function are combined to achieve a multi-scale isometry invariant segmentation of deformable shapes; in [63], Turner and colleagues demonstrated how PH may be used to represent shapes and execute operations such as computing distances between shapes or classifying and modeling shapes and surfaces. Persistence descriptors have been used also statistical shape analysis, as in [34].

Signal Processing and Time Series Analysis. Even if PH originates in the context of image and shape analysis, due to its versatility it was successfully and largely applied in signal processing and analysis. Indeed PH provides efficient tools to denoise and analyse both homogeneous and heterogeneous time series, and many researchers exploited topological features.

Perea and Harer [55] used a sliding window approach to obtain a point cloud from a time series; the point cloud is then analysed looking at periodicity as the repetition of patterns, quantifying this recurrence as the degree of circularity/roundness in the generated point-cloud. This approach has been applied data from gene expression and physiology, astronomical data, and weather.

Y. Umeda, in [64], proposed a novel approach for the classification of volatile time series: TDA is used to extract the structure of attractors, resulting efficient for both chaotic and non-chaotic time series, achieving performances improved of 18.5% compared to conventional approaches.

In [3] the occupancy of specific areas or rooms in a smart building is monitored, using a method based on the analysis of a set of topological features extracted from the data acquired in a room for a week by three different low-cost sensors.

The set of signals to which TDA can be applied is today quite rich; it includes, for example, physiological signals such as EEG or ECG (as in [26]), and financial time series such as stock market indices. The analysis of market crashes in [36] is quite interesting, because was the first application of TDA to this kind of data, providing a new type of econometric analysis, which complements the standard statistical measures, to perform a reliable early detection of early warning signals of imminent market crashes.

5   New Trends: PH into ML

The idea of allowing neural networks to learn topological information has been explored most frequently by feature engineering, looking at some predefined standard features conveying topological information. Only very recently, researchers devoted such an effort in building topological layers to be used in deep learning. Unfortunately, even if persistence diagrams and barcodes found a large number of applications, the space of persistence diagrams lacks structure, e.g. dierent persistence diagrams may have a dierent number of points, and several basic operations are not well-dened, such as addition and scalar multiplication: the (metric) space of persistence diagrams is not a Hilbert space. In addition, the cost of computing the bottleneck or Wasserstein distance grows quickly as the number of off-diagonal points in the diagrams increases [25].

To tackle this issue, a lot of effort has been devoted to vectorization and kernel methods. Vectorizations of persistence diagrams is based on the construction of either nite-dimensional embeddings [1,14,19], i.e., embeddings turning persistence diagrams into vectors in Euclidean space $\mathbb{R}^d$. We already met some of them in Sect. 3: landscapes and images are the most referred and used.

Persistence kernels are generalized scalar products that implicitly turn persistence diagrams into elements of innite-dimensional Hilbert spaces. As for vectorization, the construction of kernels for persistence diagrams, preserving their stability properties has attracted some attention. Most kernels have been obtained by considering diagrams as discrete measures in $\mathbb{R}^2$. Convolving a symmetrized (with respect to the diagonal) version of persistence diagrams with a 2D Gaussian distribution, Reininghaus et al. [57] introduce a multi-scale kernel to perform shape classification and texture recognition. Considering Wasserstein distance between projections of persistence diagrams on lines, Carriere and Oudot [13] build another kernel and test its performance on several benchmarks. Other kernels, still obtained by considering persistence diagrams as measures, have also been proposed by Kusano et al. [44] and Le et al. [45].

Refer to [40] for further details about vectorization and kernel approaches to represent barcodes.

Even though vectorization and kernel methods improved the use of persistence diagrams in machine learning tremendously, several issues remain. For instance, most of them only have a few trainable parameters; therefore, it may be very dicult to determine which vectorization is going to work best for a given task. On the contrary, kernel methods are generally ecient, but require large memory resources to compute and store the kernel evaluations (whose computations have at least linear complexity) for each pair of persistence diagrams. Hence, such methods are very costly with respect to memory usage and running time on large datasets.

In general, a framework using topological signatures in a neural network could suffer from some limitations: *(i)* it may rely on a particular filtration, *(ii)* it may lack stability results, and *(iii)* the differentiability of persistent homology generally is not guaranteed with respect to the layer's input. Hence, such a *topological* layer cannot be placed in the middle of a deep network. In the following a list of most used and successful topological layers, most of them published with code, is provided.

5.1   Topological Layers

In these last five years, many research groups defined and implemented topological layers to exploit topological features in deep learning pipeline.

Hofer et al. [39] first developed a technique to input persistence diagrams into neural networks by introducing their own topological layer, able to learn a task-optimal representation during training.

In [33] the authors propose a differentiable **Topology Layer** that computes persistent homology, based on level set filtrations and edge-based filtrations. It is publicly available and its implementation is based on PyTorch. A note: this layer may be placed at the beginning of a deep network and, using the fact that our input layer is differentiable, it can be used to perform adversarial attacks (gradient attack), i.e. cause a trained neural network to misclassify input.

PersLay [15] is one of the first neural network layers, designed to handle persistence diagrams. It is based on a general framework for diagram vectorization: maybe the simplest way to generate a permutation-invariant and differentiable feature map is to turn each point of the persistence diagram into a vector, and then sum over all such vectors to eventually get a single vector. This is the core idea of Perslay: depending on the way the diagram points are turned into vectors and on the permutation-invariant operation that is being used, one can show that one can compute persistence images, persistence landscapes, persistence silhouettes as particular instances of Perslay.

Very recently, in [43] the authors propose **PLLAY**, a layer based on the weighted persistence landscapes. They show a tight stability bound that does not depend on the input complexity; therefore PLLAY is less prone to extreme topological distortions. Importantly, they provide guarantees of the differentiability of PLLAY with respect to the layer's input: hence, such a layer may be placed anywhere in the network.

In [62] it is demonstrated how to fuse persistence image computation in supervised deep learning architectures: **PI-Net** is maybe the first framework using deep learning for computing topological features directly from data. Authors tested such framework on two applications: human activity recognition using tri-axial accelerometer sensor data and image classification. Also, the authors speeded up the extraction of persistence images form data of several orders of magnitude, paving the way to new real-time applications for TDA.

6   Conclusions

The present paper provides an overview of TDA and PH, enabling the reader to appreciate the remarkable steps to the spread and great popularity of such methods: *(i)* from persistence theory to computable topological descriptors, *(ii)* from algorithms to fast computation, enabling people to compute topological features and explore their efficacy (e.g. classification or clustering) in several application domains; *(iii)* from the computation of PH-descriptors to the development of topological layers for deep learning.

Moreover, PH gave rise to novel techniques for improving or even understanding CNN. For example, Guss and Salakhutdinov [37], Rieck et al. [58] proposed a complexity measure for neural network architectures based on topological data analysis; Carlsson and Gabrielsson [12] applied topological approaches to deep convolutional networks to understand and improve the computations of the network; and Naitzat et al. [52] provide insights in how shallow and deep nets behave with respect to the topology of input data.

In this perspective, we have foreseen that the interplay of PH with machine learning and deep learning techniques will continue to be successful, for example, in machine learning explainability, using the topological lens to look into the black-box.

References

1. Adams, H., et al.: Persistence images: a stable vector representation of persistent homology. J. Mach. Learn. Res. **18**(1), 218–252 (2017)
2. Adams, H., Tausz, A., Vejdemo-Johansson, M.: javaPlex: a research software package for persistent (co)homology. In: Hong, H., Yap, C. (eds.) ICMS 2014. LNCS, vol. 8592, pp. 129–136. Springer, Heidelberg (2014). https://doi.org/10.1007/978-3-662-44199-2_23
3. Barsocchi, P., Cassará, P., Giorgi, D., Moroni, D., Pascali, M.: Computational topology to monitor human occupancy. In: Multidisciplinary Digital Publishing Institute Proceedings, vol. 2, p. 99 (2018)
4. Bauer, U., Kerber, M., Reininghaus, J.: Dipha (a distributed persistent homology algorithm). Software available at (2014). https://github.com/DIPHA/dipha
5. Bauer, U., Kerber, M., Reininghaus, J., Wagner, H.: Phat-persistent homology algorithms toolbox. J. Symbol. Comput. **78**, 76–90 (2017)
6. Biasotti, S., Cerri, A., Frosini, P., Giorgi, D., Landi, C.: Multidimensional size functions for shape comparison. J. Math. Imag. Vis. **32**(2) 161 (2008)
7. Bowman, G., et al.: Structural insight into RNA hairpin folding intermediates. J. Am. Chem. Soc. **130**(30), 9676–9678 (2008)
8. Bubenik, P.: Statistical topological data analysis using persistence landscapes. J. Mach. Learn. Res. **16**(3), 77–102 (2015)
9. Carlsson, G., Ishkhanov, T., de Silva, V., Zomorodian, A.: On the local behavior of spaces of natural images. Int. J. Comput. Vision **76**, 1–12 (2008)
10. Carlsson, G.: Topology and data. Bull. Amer. Math. Soc. **46**, 255–308 (2009)
11. Carlsson, G., De Silva, V.: Zigzag persistence. Found. Comput. Math. **10**(4), 367–405 (2010)
12. Carlsson, G., Gabrielsson, R.B.: Topological approaches to deep learning. In: Baas, N.A., Carlsson, G.E., Quick, G., Szymik, M., Thaule, M. (eds.) Topological Data Analysis, pp. 119–146. Springer International Publishing, Cham (2020)
13. Carrière, M., Cuturi, M., Oudot, S.: Sliced wasserstein kernel for persistence diagrams. In: Proceedings of the 34th International Conference on Machine Learning, vol. 70. p. 664–673. ICML 2017, JMLR.org (2017)
14. Carriére, M., Oudot, S.Y., Ovsjanikov, M.: Stable topological signatures for points on 3d shapes. Comput. Graph. Forum **34**(5), 1–12 (2015)
15. Carrière, M., Chazal, F., Ike, Y., Lacombe, T., Royer, M., Umeda, Y.: Perslay: A neural network layer for persistence diagrams and new graph topological signatures (2020)

16. Cerri, A., Fabio, B., Ferri, M., Frosini, P., Landi, C.: Betti numbers in multidimensional persistent homology are stable functions. Math. Methods Appl. Sci. **36**, 1543–1557 (2013)
17. Cerri, A., Ferri, M., Giorgi, D.: Retrieval of trademark images by means of size functions. Graph. Models **68**(5), 451–471 (2006)
18. Chan, J.M., Carlsson, G., Rabadan, R.: Topology of viral evolution. Proc. Natl. Acad. Sci. **110**(46), 18566–18571 (2013)
19. Chazal, F., Fasy, B.T., Lecci, F., Rinaldo, A., Wasserman, L.: Stochastic convergence of persistence landscapes and silhouettes. In: Proceedings of the Thirtieth Annual Symposium on Computational Geometry, p. 474–483. SOCG 2014, Association for Computing Machinery, New York, USA (2014)
20. Chazal, F., Guibas, L.J., Oudot, S.Y., Skraba, P.: Persistence-based clustering in riemannian manifolds. J. ACM, **60**(6) (2013)
21. Cohen-Steiner, D., Edelsbrunner, H., Harer, J.: Stability of persistence diagrams. Discr. Comput. Geom. **37**, 103–120 (2007)
22. Cohen-Steiner, D., Edelsbrunner, H., Morozov, D.: Vines and vineyards by updating persistence in linear time. In: Proceedings of the Twenty-second Annual Symposium On Computational Geometry, pp. 119–126 (2006)
23. De Silva, V., Morozov, D., Vejdemo-Johansson, M.: Dualities in persistent (co) homology. Inverse Prob. **27**(12), 124003 (2011)
24. Dey, T.K., Shi, D., Wang, Y.: SimBa: an efficient tool for approximating Rips-filtration persistence via simplicial batch collapse. J. Exp. Algorithmics **24**(1), 1–6 (2019)
25. Di Fabio, B., Ferri, M.: Comparing persistence diagrams through complex vectors. In: Murino, V., Puppo, E. (eds.) ICIAP 2015. LNCS, vol. 9279, pp. 294–305. Springer, Cham (2015). https://doi.org/10.1007/978-3-319-23231-7_27
26. Dindin, M., Umeda, Y., Chazal, F.: Topological data analysis for arrhythmia detection through modular neural networks. In: Goutte, C., Zhu, X. (eds.) Canadian AI 2020. LNCS (LNAI), vol. 12109, pp. 177–188. Springer, Cham (2020). https://doi.org/10.1007/978-3-030-47358-7_17
27. Edelsbrunner, H., Harer, J.: Computational Topology: An Introduction. American Mathematical Society (2010)
28. Edelsbrunner, H., Letscher, D., Zomorodian, A.: Topological persistence and simplification. Discr. Comput. Geom. **28**, 511–533 (2002)
29. Fasy, B.T., Kim, J., Lecci, F., Maria, C.: Introduction to the r package tda. arXiv preprint arXiv:1411.1830 (2014)
30. Frosini, P.: A distance for similarity classes of submanifolds of a euclidean space. Bull. Australian Math. Soc. **42**(3), 407–416 (1990)
31. Frosini, P.: Discrete computation of size functions. J. Comb. Inf. Syst. Sci. **17**(3–4), 232–250 (1992)
32. Frosini, P.: Measuring shapes by size functions. In: Casasent, D.P. (ed.) Intelligent Robots and Computer Vision X: Algorithms and Techniques, vol. 1607, pp. 122–133. International Society for Optics and Photonics, SPIE (1992)
33. Gabrielsson, R.B., Nelson, B.J., Dwaraknath, A., Skraba, P.: A topology layer for machine learning. In: Chiappa, S., Calandra, R. (eds.) Proceedings of the Twenty Third International Conference on Artificial Intelligence and Statistics. Proceedings of Machine Learning Research, vol. 108, pp. 1553–1563. PMLR (2020)
34. Gamble, J., Heo, G.: Exploring uses of persistent homology for statistical analysis of landmark-based shape data. J. Multi. Anal. **101**(9), 2184–2199 (2010)
35. Ghrist, R.: Barcodes: the persistent topology of data. Bull. Am. Math. Soc. **45**(1), 61–75 (2008)

36. Gidea, M., Katz, Y.: Topological data analysis of financial time series: landscapes of crashes. Phys. A **491**, 820–834 (2018)
37. Guss, W.H., Salakhutdinov, R.: On characterizing the capacity of neural networks using algebraic topology. CoRR abs/1802.04443 (2018)
38. Hatcher, A.: Algebraic topology. Cambridge University Press, Cambridge (2000)
39. Hofer, C., Kwitt, R., Niethammer, M., Uhl, A.: Deep learning with topological signatures. In: Proceedings of the 31st International Conference on Neural Information Processing Systems, p. 1633–1643. NIPS 2017, Curran Associates Inc., Red Hook, NY, USA (2017)
40. Hofer, C.D., Kwitt, R., Niethammer, M.: Learning representations of persistence barcodes. J. Mach. Learn. Res. **20**(126), 1–45 (2019). http://jmlr.org/papers/v20/18-358.html
41. Horak, D., Maletić, S., Rajković, M.: Persistent homology of complex networks. J. Stat. Mech: Theory Exp. **2009**(03), P03034 (2009)
42. Ichinomiya, T., Obayashi, I., Hiraoka, Y.: Protein-folding analysis using features obtained by persistent homology. Biophys. J. **118**(12), 2926–2937 (2020)
43. Kim, K., Kim, J., Zaheer, M., Kim, J.S., Chazal, F., Wasserman, L.: Pllay: Efficient topological layer based on persistence landscapes (2020)
44. Kusano, G., Fukumizu, K., Hiraoka, Y.: Persistence weighted gaussian kernel for topological data analysis. In: Proceedings of the 33rd International Conference on International Conference on Machine Learning. vol. 48, pp. 2004–2013. ICML 2016, JMLR.org (2016)
45. Le, T., Yamada, M.: Persistence fisher kernel: A riemannian manifold kernel for persistence diagrams. In: Proceedings of the 32nd International Conference on Neural Information Processing Systems, pp. 10028–10039. NIPS 2018, Curran Associates Inc., Red Hook, NY, USA (2018)
46. Li, C., Ovsjanikov, M., Chazal, F.: Persistence-based structural recognition. In: 2014 IEEE Conference on Computer Vision and Pattern Recognition, pp. 2003–2010 (2014)
47. Maria, C., Boissonnat, J.-D., Glisse, M., Yvinec, M.: The Gudhi Library: Simplicial Complexes and Persistent Homology. In: Hong, H., Yap, C. (eds.) ICMS 2014. LNCS, vol. 8592, pp. 167–174. Springer, Heidelberg (2014). https://doi.org/10.1007/978-3-662-44199-2_28
48. Masood, T.B., et al.: An overview of the topology toolkit. In: TopoInVis 2019- Topological Methods in Data Analysis and Visualization (2019)
49. Mischaikow, K., Nanda, V.: Morse theory for filtrations and efficient computation of persistent homology. Discr. Comput. Geom. **50**(2), 330–353 (2013)
50. Monasse, P., Guichard, F.: Fast computation of a contrast-invariant image representation. IEEE Trans. Image Process. **9**(5), 860–872 (2000)
51. Morozov, D.: Dionysus, a c++ library for computing persistent homology. https://www.mrzv.org/software/dionysus/ (2007)
52. Naitzat, G., Zhitnikov, A., Lim, L.H.: Topology of deep neural networks. J. Mach. Learn. Res. **21**(184), 1–40 (2020)
53. Nanda, V.: Perseus: the persistent homology software. Software available at http://www.sas.upenn.edu/vnanda/perseus (2012)
54. Otter, N., Porter, M.A., Tillmann, U., Grindrod, P., Harrington, H.A.: A roadmap for the computation of persistent homology. EPJ Data Sci. **6**(1), 17 (2017)
55. Pereira, C.M., de Mello, R.F.: Persistent homology for time series and spatial data clustering. Expert Syst. Appl. **42**(15), 6026–6038 (2015)
56. Petri, G., Scolamiero, M., Donato, I., Vaccarino, F.: Topological strata of weighted complex networks. PLoS ONE **8**(6), 1–8 (2013)

57. Reininghaus, J., Huber, S., Bauer, U., Kwitt, R.: A stable multi-scale kernel for topological machine learning. In: IEEE Conference on Computer Vision and Pattern Recognition (CVPR), pp. 4741–4748 (2015)
58. Rieck, B., et al.: Neural persistence: a complexity measure for deep neural networks using algebraic topology. In: International Conference on Learning Representations (ICLR) (2019)
59. Robins, V., Wood, P., Sheppard, A.: Theory and algorithms for constructing discrete morse complexes from grayscale digital images. IEEE Trans. Pattern Anal. Mach. Intell. **33**(8), 1646–1658 (2011)
60. Singh, G., Memoli, F., Ishkhanov, T., Sapiro, G., Carlsson, G., Ringach, D.: Topological analysis of population activity in visual cortex. J. Vis. **8**(8), 1–18 (2008)
61. Skraba, P., Ovsjanikov, M., Chazal, F., Guibas, L.: Persistence-based segmentation of deformable shapes. In: 2010 IEEE Computer Society Conference on Computer Vision and Pattern Recognition - Workshops, pp. 45–52 (2010)
62. Som, A., Choi, H., Ramamurthy, K.N., Buman, M.P., Turaga, P.: Pi-net: a deep learning approach to extract topological persistence images. In: Proceedings of the IEEE/CVF Conference on Computer Vision and Pattern Recognition (CVPR) Workshops (2020)
63. Turner, K., Mukherjee, S., Boyer, D.: Persistent homology transform for modeling shapes and surfaces. Inf. Inf. A J. IMA **3**(4), 310–344 (2014)
64. Umeda, Y.: Time series classification via topological data analysis. Trans. Japanese Soc. Artif. Intell. **32**(3), D-G72$_1$- -12 (2017)
65. Verri, A., Uras, C., Frosini, P., Ferri, M.: On the use of size functions for shape analysis. Biol. Cybern. **70**, 99–107 (1993)
66. Xia, K., Wei, G.: Persistent homology analysis of protein structure, flexibility, and folding. Int. J. Numer. Method Biomed. Eng. **30**(8), 814–844 (2014)
67. Xu, Y., Carlinet, E., Géraud, T., Najman, L.: Hierarchical segmentation using tree-based shape spaces. IEEE Trans. Pattern Anal. Mach. Intell. **39**(3), 457–469 (2017)
68. Zomorodian, A., Carlsson, G.: Computing persistent homology. Discr. Comput. Geom. **3**, 249–274 (2005)

Library of Sample Image Instances
for the Cutting Path Problem

Alexander Petunin[1,2]($\boxtimes$) (iD), Alexander Khalyavka[1], Michael Khachay[1,2] (iD),
Andrei Kudriavtsev[1,2] (iD), Pavel Chentsov[1,2], Efim Polishchuk[1],
and Stanislav Ukolov[1] (iD)

[1] Ural Federal University, Yekaterinburg, Russia
a.a.petunin@urfu.ru
[2] N.N. Krasovskii Institute of Mathematics and Mechanics, UB RAS, Yekaterinburg, Russia

Abstract. The Cutting Path Problem (CPP) is a complex continuous and combinatorial optimization problem that is about finding an optimal tool path for CNC
technologies equipment. The problem has many valuable industrial applications
arising from the Industry 4.0 strategy, such as those, related to tool path routing for
the sheet metal cutting machines. The CPP is strongly NP-hard enclosing variants
of the well-known Traveling Salesman Problem (TSP) as sub-problems. In this
paper, we for the first time propose an open access library of sample instances
(CPPLib) for the CPP to facilitate the benchmarking of optimization algorithms,
most of them are heuristics or metaheuristics. Each instance is obtained as an
image of a finite set of mutually nested industrial parts on a metal sheet and is
presented in the DXF vector format that is induced by a solution result of the
well-known 2D nesting problem. For the first time we propose geometric and
quantitative principles for constructing different groups (classes) of such image
instances. Along with continuous CPP settings, the library contains their discrete
counterparts presented in the form of instances of the Precedence Constraints Generalized Traveling Salesman Problem (PCGTSP), since the solution processes for
the CPP mostly based on discretizing boundary contours of parts. In addition, the
paper presents examples of testing some optimization algorithms for solving the
cutting path problem on test instances from the developed CPPLib library.

Keywords: Cutting path problem · Library of test image instances · Precedence
constraints · Continuous Cutting Problem · GTSP

1 Introduction

The Cutting Path Problem (CPP) is a complex continuous and combinatorial optimization
problem, where it is required to find an optimal tool path for the CNC technologies equipment. The problem has many valuable industrial applications arising from the Industry 4.0 strategy, including the tool path optimization for sheet metal cutting machines
[1, 2]. The CPP is strongly NP-hard as it is enclosing several variants of the well-known
Traveling Salesman Problem (TSP). An instance of the CPP is given by an image of
finite set of mutually nested parts located on a sheet obtained as a result of solving an

A. Del Bimbo et al. (Eds.): ICPR 2020 Workshops, LNCS 12665, pp. 227–233, 2021.
https://doi.org/10.1007/978-3-030-68821-9_21

appropriate instance of the well-known 2D nesting problem [3]. Result of CPP solving (the cutting path) is trajectory of the cutting tool during cutting process of nested parts. Figure 1 (a) illustrates an example of a nesting map image for 15 parts (21 boundary contours) and a tool path with minimum of total idle path (nonproductive air motion) should be cut out entirely by one movement of the tool, but cutting can start at any point (and completed at the same point). This is a special case of the CPP problem or so-called the Continuous Cutting Problem, CCP). In this case, each closed contour (that bounds a part). To solve the cutting path problem, an approach based on reducing the problem to a Generalized Traveling Salesman Problem (GTSP) with additional constraints is mainly used. For some special types of precedence constraints polynomial time exact algorithms are known. In particular, for Balas type constraints such algorithms were proposed in [4, 5], whilst, for the constraints inducing generalized pyramidal optimum solutions, efficient parameterized algorithms were introduced in [6, 7].

GTSP is an extension of the Traveling Salesman Problem, where the node set is partitioned into clusters, and the objective is to find the shortest cycle that visits exactly (or, in some variations) at least) one node in each cluster. For case CCP number of clusters is equal number of boundary contours. This approach uses a discretization of parts contours: cutting process can start only at one of the predefined points on the contour and the contour must be cut entirely. On Fig. 1 (b) the optimal cutting path for CCP reduced o GTSP is shown. Currently, optimal solutions for GTSP can only be guaranteed for dimensions less than 30 contours [8].

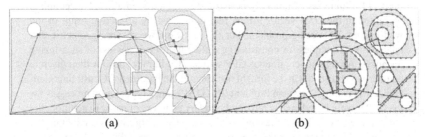

(a)   (b)

Fig. 1. An example of a nesting map image for 15 nested parts (21 boundary contours) and a tool (cutting) path with minimum of the total idle path for CCP (a) and for GTSP (b)

There are no any open access libraries of the test instances for the cutting path problem and also for CCP, especially presented in the form of vector images. Since solving of the cutting path problem is mainly based on reducing the problem to GTSP, it would seem possible to use TSPLIB and GTSPLIB. TSPLIB is a library of sample instances for the TSP (and related problems) from various sources and of various types. TSPLIB is created by Gerhard Reinelt [9]. GTSP Instances Library (GTSPLIB) is created and maintained in particular by Daniel Karapetyan [10]. Other new Library (PCGTSPLIB) [11] is developed by R. Salman, F. Ekstedt and P. Damaschke, but TSPLIB and GTSPLIB don't contain any instances with precedence constraints at all. PCGTSPLIB contains the instances with precedence constraints, but does not contain the samples in terms of the cutting path problem (geometric constraints) and geometrical information about image of nested parts as well. This type of constraint will be described in the next paragraph. But this constraint is a fundamental requirement when developing tool routing optimization algorithms for CNC sheet cutting machines. Thus, the aforementioned libraries of sample instances cannot be used to test the efficiency of optimization algorithms; moreover, they are not intended to test algorithms for solving the CCP problem.

It means for testing the optimization algorithms for CPP we should have a special Library for CCP (continuous version) as set of geometric 2D images and for GTSP and PCGTSP (discrete version).

2 General Definition and Statements

As we noted above, the initial information for the CPP is a cutting map, which is uniquely determined by a finite set of boundary contours of the nested parts. Let $C_0, C_1 \ldots C_n \subset R^2$ is finite set of these boundary contours.

The tool (cutting) path always contains the following common main components, regardless of the cutting technology, features of equipment and material for cutting (see, in particular, [12]):

- pierce points (piercings) of sheet material by tool;
- points of switching the tool off;
- tool trajectory from piercing up to point of switching the tool off (the cutting segment);
- Airtime motions/ idling tool path (linear movement from tool switching off point up to the next piercing).

Geometrically, the cutting segment is a curve defined on the Euclidean plane. We will assume that all segments match the boundary contours. This means that all pierce points belong to the boundary contours and coincide with the points of switching the tool off. So the problem under consideration is equivalent to CCP. Then the problem will be define as follows.

It is necessary to find the piercing points $M_i \in C_i$, $i \in \overline{1, n}$ and the order of bypassing the contours (permutation $I = (i_1, i_2, \ldots i_n)$), which will ensure the minimum of total idling tool path

$$L_{off} = \sum_{j=0}^{n} M_{i_j} M_{i_{j+1}} \vee \to min, \tag{1}$$

where $M0$ - some starting point and $M0 = Mn+1$.

In this case, the precedence conditions must be met, due to the technological features of cutting sheet materials on CNC machines. In general, the precedence constraints for CPP can be formulated as follows.

When choosing a sequence of segments (contours), you should adhere to the following rules.

Rule 1. If the external contour has one or more internal contour, the external contour must be cut after the cutting of all internal contours.

Rule 2. If the internal contour of part contains the external contour/contours of another part, then this part should be cut first according to Rule 1.

Thus, the test case library should contain various cases of precedence conditions. It should be emphasized that the library will allow testing optimization algorithms for other objective functions (1) and for other CPP classes (not only for the Cutting Continuous Problem).

3 Formation Principles for Specific Groups (Classes) of Image Instances in the Library

Each image instance in the Library [14] encapsulates information about parts allocated on sheet material (2D nesting result).

We offer 9 (nine) main classes of image instances in Library:

- Instances with precedence constraints (maximum depth of precedence constraints for nesting contours from 1 to 7);
- Instances without precedence constraints;
- Instances with used special cutting technique CPP ("chained" cutting, common edge, etc. [13]).

Library subclasses are determined by the quantitative and geometric characteristics of the parts used in the concrete sample instance. Examples of subclasses:

- Instances with small quantity of parts contours (or clusters for discrete version) in instance (15–30) for testing exact algorithms
- Instances with middle quantity of parts contours (or clusters) in instance (30–100) for testing heuristic algorithms
- Instances with big quantity of parts contours (or clusters) in instance (100–250) for testing heuristic algorithms

Types of parts by size criterion:

- large (both sizes are larger than 500 mm);
- medium (both sizes are more than 200 mm but less than 500);
- small (both dimensions are less than 350 mm);
- long (one overall size is 5 or more times larger than the other). (For an example see Fig. 2).

It should be especially noted that the existing libraries of examples for testing discrete optimization algorithms are based on the use of a random number generator, i.e. are mainly created artificially. The CPPLib contains images of cutting maps obtained in real production. The geometry of the parts corresponds to the nomenclature of parts manufactured at a number of Russian machine-building enterprises.

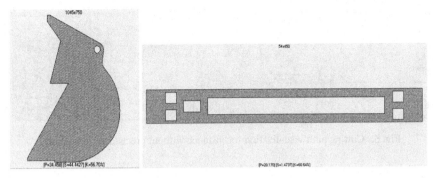

Fig. 2. The samples of big and long parts

4 Computing Experiments

As an illustration, we present below the results of constructing the cutting path for three test problems from the CPPLib library (see Fig. 3, Fig. 4, Fig. 5). Calculations have been performed using algorithms developed by the authors.

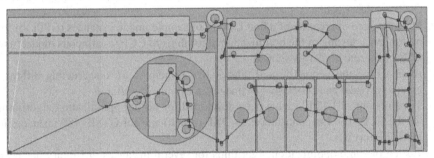

Fig. 3. Cutting path visualization for image instance with precedence constraints (maximum depth of precedence constraints is 3) and with long parts (continuous version of samples instances for CCP).

For solving this instance is used CCP-Relax algorithm [15].

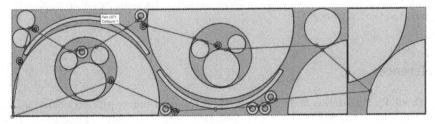

Fig. 4. Cutting path visualization for instance with precedence constraints (maximum depth of precedence constraints is 3) and with big parts (discrete version of samples instances for GTSP)

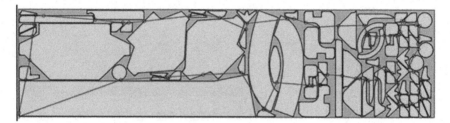

Fig. 5. Cutting path visualization for instance without precedence constraints

Recently developed heuristic solver for the Precedence Constrained Generalized Traveling Salesman Problem [16] incorporating the well-known Adaptive Large Neighborhood Search strategy and reinforcement learning has been successfully employed for numerical evaluation of two classes of instances.

5   Conclusion

1. Cutting path problem (CPP) and one of its class (the Continuous Cutting Problem, CCP) are described.
2. The relevance of creating of a first Library of sample image instances (CPPLib) for performance testing of the optimization algorithms of CCP (continuous model) and GTSP (discrete model) is shown.
3. At first time the geometric and quantitative principles for constructing different groups (classes) and subclasses of images in Library are offered.
4. Two versions of CPPLib have been developed for testing optimization algorithms for the CCP (168 image instances in DXF format) and for GTSP (189 instances in PCGTSP format).
5. Testing of some optimization algorithms for several instances of Library has been performed.
6. The library is prepared for open access and is preliminary hosted on Google Drive.

Acknowledgements. This research was performed as part of research conducted in the Ural Mathematical Center and funded by the Russian Foundation for Basic Research, grants no. 19-01-00573 and no. 20-08-00873.

References

1. Dewil, R., Vansteenwegen, P., Cattrysse, D.: A review of cutting path algorithms for laser cutters. Int. J. Adv. Manuf. Technol. **87**(5–8), 1865–1884 (2016). https://doi.org/10.1007/s00 170-016-8609-1
2. Petunin, A.: General Model of Tool Path Problem for the CNC Sheet Cutting Machines. IFAC-PapersOnLine **52**(13), 2662–2667 (2019). https://doi.org/10.1016/j.ifacol.2019.11.609

3. Oliveira J.F.C., Ferreira J.A.S.: Algorithms for nesting problems. In: Vidal R.V.V. (eds) Applied Simulated Annealing. Lecture Notes in Economics and Mathematical Systems, vol 396. Springer, Berlin, Heidelberg (1993). https://doi.org/https://doi.org/10.1007/978-3-642-46787-5_13

4. Chentsov, A.G., Khachai, M.Yu., Khachai, D.M.: An exact algorithm with linear complexity for a problem of visiting megalopolises. Proc. Steklov Inst. Math. **295**(1), 38–46 (2016). https://doi.org/10.1134/S0081543816090054

5. Chentsov, A.G., Khachay, M.Yu., Khachay, D.M.: Linear time algorithm for precedence constrained asymmetric Generalized Traveling Salesman Problem. IFAC-PapersOnLine **49**(12), 651–655 (2016). https://doi.org/https://doi.org/10.1016/j.ifacol.2016.07.767. 8th IFAC Conference on Manufacturing Modelling, Management and Control MIM 2016

6. Eremeev, A., Khachay, M., Kochetov, Y., Pardalos, P. (eds.): OPTA 2018. CCIS, vol. 871. Springer, Cham (2018). https://doi.org/10.1007/978-3-319-93800-4

7. Khachay, M., Neznakhina, K.: Complexity and approximability of the Euclidean generalized traveling salesman problem in grid clusters. Ann. Math. Artif. Intell. **88**(1–3), 53–69 (2019). https://doi.org/10.1007/s10472-019-09626-w

8. Chentsov, A.G., Chentsov, P.A., Petunin, A.A., Sesekin, A.N.: Model of megalopolises in the tool path optimisation for CNC plate cutting machines. Int. J. Prod. Res. **56**(14), 4819–4830 (2018)

9. TSPLIB Homepage. https://elib.zib.de/pub/mp-testdata/tsp/tsplib/tsplib.html. Accessed 01 Nov 2020

10. GTSPLIB Homepage. https://www.cs.nott.ac.uk/~pszdk/gtsp.html. Accessed 01 Nov 2020

11. PCGTSPLIB Homepage. https://www.fcc.chalmers.se/external/PCGTSPLIB/. Accessed 01 Nov 2020

12. Petunin, A.A.: Modeling of tool path for the CNC sheet cutting machines. In: Pasheva, B., Popivanov, N., Venkov, G. (eds.) 41st International Conference "Applications of Mathematics in Engineering and Economics", AMEE 2015, 1690. [060002] (AIP Conference Proceedings; 1690. American Institute of Physics Publising LLC (2015). https://doi.org/10.1063/1.4936740

13. Tavaeva, A.F., Petunin, A.A., Polishchuk, E.G.: Methods of Cutting Cost Minimizing in Problem of Tool Route Optimization for CNC Laser Machines. In: Radionov, A.A., Kravchenko, O.A., Guzeev, V.I., Rozhdestvenskiy, Y.V. (eds.) ICIE 2019. LNME, pp. 447–455. Springer, Cham (2020). https://doi.org/10.1007/978-3-030-22063-1_48

14. CCPLIB Homepage, https://drive.google.com/drive/folders/1e95DUVXq0XAX7UI15wUa NpAY0exbXc8T?usp=sharing. Accessed 01 Nov 2020

15. Petunin, A.A., Polishchuk, E.G., Ukolov, S.S.: On the new Algorithm for Solving Continuous Cutting Problem. IFAC-PapersOnLine **52**(13), 2320–2325 (2019). https://doi.org/10.1016/j.ifacol.2019.11.552

16. Khachay, M., Kudriavtsev, A., Petunin, A.: PCGLNS: A Heuristic Solver for the Precedence Constrained Generalized Traveling Salesman Problem. In: Olenev, N., Evtushenko, Y., Khachay, M., Malkova, V. (eds.) OPTIMA 2020. LNCS, vol. 12422, pp. 196–208. Springer, Cham (2020). https://doi.org/10.1007/978-3-030-62867-3_15

Interest Points Detection Based on Sign Representations of Digital Images

Alexander Karkishchenko[✉] and Valeriy Mnukhin

Southern Federal University,
105/42, Bolshaya Sadovaya, 344006 Rostov-na-Donu, Russia
karkishalex@gmail.com, mnukhin.valeriy@mail.ru

Abstract. In this work, we present a method for detecting interest points in digital images that is robust under a certain class of brightness transformations. Importance of such method is due to the fact that current video surveillance systems perform well under controlled environments but tend to suffer when variations in illumination are present.

Novelty of the method is based on the use of so-called sign representation of images. In contrast to representation of a digital image by its brightness function, sign representation associates with an image a graph of brightness increasing relation on pixels. As a result, the sign representation determines not a single image but a class of images, whose brightness functions are differ by monotonic transforms.

Other feature of the method is in interpretation of interest points. This concept in image processing theory is not rigorously defined; in general, a point of interest can be characterized by increased "complexity" of image structure in its vicinity. Since the sign representation associates with an image a directed graph, we consider interest points as "concentrators" of paths from/to vertices of the graph.

The results of experiments confirm the efficiency of the method.

Keywords: Digital image · Image processing on graphs · Sign representations · Interest points · Brightness function · Monotonous transformations

1 Introduction

Recent progress of graph signal processing (GSP) has initiated intensive studies of signals defined naturally on irregular data structures described by graphs (e.g., social networks, wireless sensor networks). As noticed in [1], "...though a digital image contains pixels that reside on a regularly sampled 2D grid, if one can design an appropriate underlying graph that reflects the image structure, then one can interpret the image as a signal on a graph". In this article, we use such approach to associate with images weighted digraphs related with so-called

This research has been supported by the Russian Foundation for Basic Research grant no. 19-07-00873.

A. Del Bimbo et al. (Eds.): ICPR 2020 Workshops, LNCS 12665, pp. 234–242, 2021.
https://doi.org/10.1007/978-3-030-68821-9_22

sign representations introduced previously in [2–6]. As it has been noted in [7], sign representations are closely related with the morphology of Pyt'ev [8].

The important feature of sign representations is their invariance under group of strictly monotonous transformations of brightness [9]. We introduce a modification of sign representations called *reduced sign representations* that share the same property of invariance. Such invariance occurs to be an important tool to construct interest points in images.

Indeed, the notion of an *interest point* (also known as a *feature point*, a *salient point* or a *key point*) is one of basic notions in image processing and computer vision [10]. This concept is not rigorously defined; in general it is a point in the image which can be characterized as follows [11,12]:

- it has a clear mathematical definition,
- it has a well-defined position in image space,
- the local image structure around the interest point is rich in terms of local information contents, such that the use of interest points simplify further processing in the vision system,
- it is stable under such image transformations as illumination/brightness variations, rotations, shifts and scaling.

In this work, we present a method for fast and efficient detection of interest points in digital images that is robust under strictly monotonous brightness transformations and stable under rotations. The method is based on interpretation of images as digraphs of binary relations that correspond to reduced sign representations.

To formulate the previous notions formally in the next sections, we need some notations and definitions. Note that our use of graph theory terminology follows the book [13], while in matrix theory we follow [14].

2   Reduced Sign Representations and Their Graphs

For a natural M we denote the interval $\{1, \ldots, M\} \subset \mathbb{N}$ by I_M. For any $M, N \in \mathbb{N}$ let $\Omega = I_M \times I_N \subset \mathbb{N}^2$ be the $M \times N$-grid. Let $f \colon \Omega \to [0,1]$ be a function of range $[0,1]$ defined on Ω.

A *digital image* of size $M \times N$ is a pair $\langle f, \Omega \rangle$ where f is called the *brightness function* of the image. For brevity, when the size of image is fixed, it is convenient to identify image with the function f. The pair $\mathbf{x} = (x_1, x_2) \in \Omega$, ($x_1 \in I_M$, $x_2 \in I_N$), is a *pixel* or a *point* of the image, while $f(\mathbf{x})$ is the *brightness* of pixel $\mathbf{x}$. Let $K = MN = |\Omega|$ be the total number of pixels in f and let $\mathcal{F}$ be the set of all images of a fixed size $M \times N$.

We associate with f an oriented weighted graph $G_f = \langle \Omega, E_f, w \rangle$ on the set Ω of pixels as follows. The set E_f of arcs (i.e. directed edges) of G_f is

$$E_f = \left\{ \langle \mathbf{x}, \mathbf{y} \rangle \ : \ \mathbf{x}, \mathbf{y} \in \Omega, f(\mathbf{x}) > f(\mathbf{y}) \right\} \subseteq \Omega^2$$

and the weight function $w \colon E_f \to [0,1]$ assigns to an arc $e = e_{\mathbf{xy}} = \langle \mathbf{x}, \mathbf{y} \rangle \in E_f$ the weight $w(e_{\mathbf{xy}}) = f(\mathbf{x}) - f(\mathbf{y})$. In other words, every two pixels of different brightness are connected by a directed edge that starts at the brighter pixel and ends at the dim one, while the weight of edge is the brightness difference. Evidently, $|E_f| \leqslant K(K-1)/2$.

Since number of arcs in G_f can be quite large, it is convenient to reduce it as follows. Fix a real number $r > 0$ and call it a *radius*. Let

$$E_f^{(r)} = \left\{ \langle \mathbf{x}, \mathbf{y} \rangle \in E_f \ : \ \|\mathbf{x} - \mathbf{y}\| \leqslant r \right\} \subseteq E_f,$$

where $\|\mathbf{x} - \mathbf{y}\|$ stands for a distance between $\mathbf{x} = (x_1, x_2)$ and $\mathbf{y} = (y_1, y_2)$. As a rule, the Manhattan distance

$$\|\mathbf{x} - \mathbf{y}\| = |x_1 - x_2| + |y_1 - y_2|$$

will be used further, though the Euclidean metric

$$\|\mathbf{x} - \mathbf{y}\| = \sqrt{|x_1 - x_2|^2 + |y_1 - y_2|^2}$$

may be useful in some cases.

Evidently, the weighted digraph $G_f^{(r)} = \langle \Omega, E_f^{(r)}, w \rangle$ is a spanning subgraph of G_f with the same weight function w. In contrast with G_f, two pixels can be connected by an arc in $G_f^{(r)}$ only if the distance between them does not exceed r. Thus, only pixels in r-neighbourhood of a pixel $\mathbf{x}$ can be adjacent with $\mathbf{x}$, see Fig. 1. The next proposition is evident.

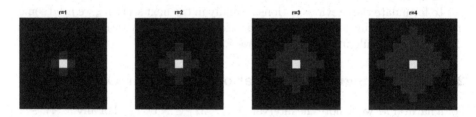

Fig. 1. Neighbourhoods of radius r in Manhattan metric for $r = 1, 2, 3, 4$.

Proposition 1. *Digraphs $G_f^{(r)}$ possess the following properties:*

1. *If there is a path $\mathbf{x_1} \to \mathbf{x_2} \to \cdots \to \mathbf{x_k}$ of length $k \leq r$ in $G_f^{(r)}$, then also $\mathbf{x_1} \to \mathbf{x_k}$ is an arc in $E_f^{(r)}$.*
2. *There are no cycles in $G_f^{(r)}$. In other words, the digraph $G_f^{(r)}$ is acyclic.*

It is natural idea to associate with digraphs $G_f^{(r)}$ binary relations $\gamma^{(r)}$ which are irreflexive, asymmetric and transitive and so are strict partial orders. In fact, such relations are very similar to sign representations of images.

Definition 1. *A binary relation* $\tau \subseteq \Omega \times \Omega$ *is called* sign representation *of an image* f *if the following conditions hold:*

1. $(\mathbf{x}, \mathbf{y}) \in \tau$, *if* $f(\mathbf{x}) \leqslant f(\mathbf{y})$;
2. $(\mathbf{x}, \mathbf{y}) \in \tau$, $(\mathbf{y}, \mathbf{x}) \notin \tau$, *if* $f(\mathbf{x}) < f(\mathbf{y})$.

Sign representations are reflexive and not antisymmetric in general; nevertheless, $\gamma^{(r)} \subset \tau$. In view of this, the next definition seems to be natural.

Definition 2. *Binary relations* $\gamma^{(r)}$ *are called* reduced sign representations *of images.*

Note that different images can share the same sign representation. Indeed, for any brightness function f and for any $\varphi \colon [0, 1] \rightarrow [0, 1]$, the function $\varphi(f)$ also defines an image. Thus, such φ can be considered as a transformation $\varphi \colon \mathcal{F} \rightarrow \mathcal{F}$. We say that the sign representation τ is *invariant under* the brightness transformation φ if for every $f \in \mathcal{F}$ holds $\tau(f) = \tau(\varphi(f))$.

Let $\Phi = \{\varphi\}$ be the set of all strictly monotonous functions $\varphi \colon [0, 1] \rightarrow [0, 1]$ such that $\varphi(0) = 0$ and $\varphi(1) = 1$. Evidently, the set Φ may be considered as a group under compositions and with the identity transformation as unity. The next result has been proven in [6].

Theorem 1. *Sign representations are invariant under the group of transformations* Φ.

The same is also true for reduced sigh representations and so for graphs $G_f^{(r)}$.

3   Interest Points as Concentrators of Paths

In this section we consider an interpretation of interest points in images. This is not a rigorously defined concept; in general, a point of interest can be characterized by increased "complexity" of image structure in its vicinity. Since reduced sign representations associate with an image f digraphs $G_f^{(r)}$, our idea is to consider interest points as "concentrators" of paths from/to vertices of the graph. Let us formulate it formally.

Let

$$\mathbf{x_i} = \mathbf{x}_{\alpha_1} \rightarrow \mathbf{x}_{\alpha_2} \rightarrow \cdots \rightarrow \mathbf{x}_{\alpha_{k+1}} = \mathbf{x_j}$$

be a directed path of length $k \leq r$ from a vertex $\mathbf{x_i}$ to a vertex $\mathbf{x_j}$ in $G_f^{(r)}$. Let the *weight* $w_{ij}^{(k)}$ *of the path* be the product of weights of all its arcs:

$$w_{ij}^{(k)} = \prod_{s=1}^{k} w\left(\mathbf{x}_{\alpha_s} \rightarrow \mathbf{x}_{\alpha_{s+1}}\right) = \prod_{s=1}^{k} \left(f(\mathbf{x}_{\alpha_s}) - f(\mathbf{x}_{\alpha_{s+1}})\right) > 0.$$

Evidently, $w_{ij} = w_{ij}^{(1)}$ is either the weight of arc $\mathbf{x_i} \rightarrow \mathbf{x_j}$, or 0 if such arc does not exist in $G_f^{(r)}$.

Definition 3. *For a fixed radius $r > 1$, the* input *r-complexity (or just* input complexity*) $c_r^-(\mathbf{x})$ of a vertex $\mathbf{x}$ is the total sum of weights of all paths in the graph $G_f^{(r)}$ that start at $\mathbf{x}$. Similarly,* output *complexity $c_r^+(\mathbf{x})$ is the sum of weights of all paths that terminate at $\mathbf{x}$.*

We will use the notion of complexity as a measure of pixel "interest". First, we will show that complexities c_r^+ and c_r^- can be efficiently evaluated.

Let $A_r = (w_{ij})$, $(i, j = 1, \ldots, K)$, be the adjacency matrix of digraph $G_f^{(r)}$ with weights of arcs as its elements. Previously it has been noticed that digraphs $G_f^{(r)}$ are acyclic. The next results follow immediately.

Lemma 1. *1. It is possible to enumerate vertices of $G_f^{(r)}$ in such a way that the matrix A_r will be upper triangular with zero diagonal elements.*
2. The matrix A_r is nilpotent of degree $k < K$, i.e.,

$$A_r^k = \mathbf{0} \quad \text{for some natural } k < K.$$

3. The next equality holds:

$$\sum_{k=0}^{\infty} A_r^k = E + A_r + A_r^2 + A_r^3 + \cdots = \left(E - A_r\right)^{-1},$$

where $E = \mathrm{diag}(1, 1, \ldots, 1)$ is the identity matrix of size $K \times K$.

Let

$$C_r^- = \left(c_r^-(\mathbf{x_1}), \ldots, c_r^-(\mathbf{x_K})\right)^\top \quad \text{and} \quad C_r^+ = \left(c_r^+(\mathbf{x_1}), \ldots, c_r^+(\mathbf{x_K})\right)^\top$$

be the column vectors of output and input complexities of vertices in $G_f^{(r)}$ respectively, and let $I = (1, 1, \ldots, 1)^\top$ be the column vector of length K. The next result easily follows from the properties of adjacent matrices of digraphs [13] and from the previous Lemma.

Proposition 2. *For the vectors C_r^- and C_r^+ hold*

$$C_r^- = \left(\left(E - A_r\right)^{-1} - E\right) I \quad \text{and} \quad C_r^+ = \left(\left(E - A_r\right)^{-1} - E\right)^\top I.$$

To introduce the notion of *interest point* in an image f we consider sets

$$X_r^-(f) = \arg \max_{\mathbf{x} \in \Omega} \{c_r^-(\mathbf{x})\} \subseteq \Omega \quad \text{and} \quad X_r^+(f) = \arg \max_{\mathbf{x} \in \Omega} \{c_r^+(\mathbf{x})\} \subseteq \Omega$$

of pixels with maximal (input or output) complexity . It is easy to note that

$$X_r^-(f) = X_r^+(1 - f).$$

Example 1. Let all but one pixels of an image f are black, while the only white pixel $\mathbf{x}$ with $f(\mathbf{x}) = 1$ is located at the center of the image. It is easy to note that $c_r^-(\mathbf{x}) = 2r(r+1)$ and $X_r^-(f) = \{\mathbf{x}\}$. At the same time, $X_r^+(f)$ coincides with the r-neighbourhood of $\mathbf{x}$ (see Fig. 1), and all pixels in $X_r^+(f)$ are of the same input complexity 1. Nevertheless note that the "central" pixel in $X_r^+(f)$ is again $\mathbf{x}$.

The previous example shows that it is reasonable to average sets $X_r^-(f)$ and $X_r^+(f)$ as follows. Let $X_r^+(f)$ consists of S pixels,

$$X_r^+(f) = \{\mathbf{x}_{\alpha_k} = (a_{\alpha_k}, b_{\alpha_k}) \in \Omega : k = 1, 2, \ldots, S\},$$

and let $\overline{X_r^+}$ be the "mean" pixel

$$\overline{X_r^+} = \left[\frac{1}{S} \sum_{k=1}^{S} \mathbf{x}_{\alpha_k} \right] \in \Omega,$$

where $[\ ]$ stands for the integer part of expression in brackets. The pixel $\overline{X_r^-}$ can be introduced in exactly the same way. Finally, for any real number $\beta \in [0,1] \subset \mathbb{R}$ let

$$P_r^{(\beta)}(f) = \left[\beta\overline{X_r^+} + (1-\beta)\overline{X_r^-} \right], \qquad (0 \le \beta \le 1),$$

be the weighted average of X_r^- and X_r^+, so that $P_r^{(0)} = X_r^-$ and $P_r^{(1)} = X_r^+$. Then the point $P_r^{(\beta)}(f)$ is unique and is completely defined by the parameters r and β.

Definition 4. *We call $P_r^{(\beta)}$ the interest point in an image f.*

4   Results of Computer Experiments

To construct interest points in real-world images the method of sliding window has been used. Analysed images were partitioned into small rectangular regions (windows) and then the interest point $P_r^{(\beta)}$ was evaluated in each window. In the most cases square windows of size between 8 and 24 have been used.

Some of results are shown in Fig. 2. The original image f of size 650×650 is in top left part of the figure. The top right part demonstrates (in red) the set of 4036 interest points $P_6^{(0.5)}$ in 13×13-windows shifting through f with step 6.

The bottom left part of Fig. 2 shows the same image f after a strictly monotonous brightness transformation

$$\varphi(z) = \begin{cases} \frac{1-(1-2z)^\alpha}{2} & \text{when } 0 \le z \le 0.5, \\ \frac{1+(2z-1)^\alpha}{2} & \text{when } 0.5 < z \le 1, \end{cases}$$

where $\alpha = 1.72$. The 4174 interest points constructed by the proposed algorithm are shown in red on the right hand side of the figure; as it is easy to note, the

Fig. 2. Interest points in the original and the transformed images. (Color figure online)

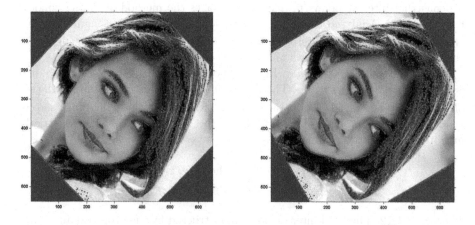

Fig. 3. Interest points in the image rotated by 45° and by 60°.

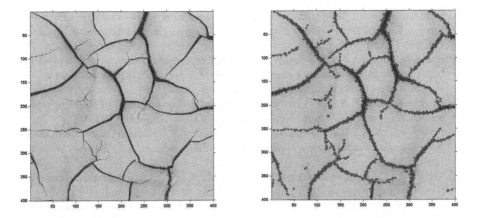

Fig. 4. Interest points in an image of cracks on clay.

points were mostly not affected by the transformation. Next Fig. 3 demonstrates stability of the algorithm under rotations.

Finally, it is worth to mention that the proposed algorithm occurs to be especially effective when applied to images of thin elongated objects such as, for example, cracks on different surfaces. A result of such application is in Fig. 4, where 1527 interest points $P_6^{(0.5)}$ in 13×13-windows sliding with step 6 through 400×400-image of cracked clay are shown.

5   Conclusion

This paper proposes a method for interest points detection in digital images, based on interpretation of such points as "concentrators" of paths in digraphs of reduced sign representations. Since such representations are invariant under strictly monotonous transformations of brightness functions, the proposed algorithm is robust under such transformations. The results of experiments confirm the efficiency of method and also demonstrate its stability under transformations of rotations and shifts. The method is especially effective for images of such thin elongated objects as cracks on different surfaces. However, apart from this work, there remain issues such as the detailed study of properties of the introduced notions, the study of possibilities of its generalizations, as well as the details of practical application. Authors hope to return to the study of these issues in the future.

References

1. Cheung, G., Magli, E., Tanaka, Y., Ng, M.: Graph spectral image processing. Proc. IEEE **106**(5), 907–930 (2018)
2. Goncharov, A.V., Karkishchenko, A.N.: Effects of illumination and quality of frontal faces recognition. SFedU Proc. Eng. Sci. **81**(4), 82–92 (2008)

3. Goncharov, A.V.: Investigation of properties of sign representations in pattern recognition problems. SFedU Proceedings in Engineering Sciences (Special Issue) 178–188 (2009)
4. Karkishchenko, A.N., Goncharov, A.V.: Sign reprsentations geometry applied for noise stability investigations. In: 8th International Conference on Intellectualization of Images Processing (IIP-8), pp. 335–339 (2010)
5. Karkishchenko, A.N., Goncharov, A.V.: Stability investigation of the sign representation of images. Autom. Remote Control **71**(9), 1793–1803 (2010)
6. Bronevich, A.G., Karkishchenko, A.N., Lepskiy, A.E.: Uncertainty Analysis of Informational Features Selection and Images Representations. Fizmatlit, Moscow (2013)
7. Myasnikov, V.V.: Description of images based on configurational equivalence relation. Computer Optics **42**(6), 998–1007 (2018)
8. Pyt'ev, YuP, Chulichkov, A.I.: Methods for Morphological Analysis of Images. Fizmatlit, Moscow (2010)
9. Karkishchenko, A.N., Mnukhin, V.B.: On the metric on images invariant with respect to the monotonic brightness transformation. Pattern Recogn. Image Anal. **30**(3), 359–371 (2020)
10. Schmid, C., Mohr, R., Bauckhage, C.: Evaluation of interest point detectors. Int. J. Comput. Vis. **37**(2), 151–172 (2000)
11. Lindeberg, T.: Scale selection properties of generalized scale-space interest point detectors. J. Math. Imaging Vis. **46**(2), 177–210 (2013)
12. Lindeberg, T.: Image matching using generalized scale-space interest points. J. Math. Imaging Vis. **52**(1), 3–36 (2015)
13. Cvetković, D.M., Doob, M., Sachs, H.: Spectra of Graphs – Theory and Application. Berlin (1980)
14. Horn, R.A., Johnson, C.R.: Matrix Analysis. Cambridge University Press, Cambridge (1985)

Memory Consumption and Computation Efficiency Improvements of Viola-Jones Object Detection Method for UAVs

Sergey A. Usilin[1,2,3](✉) iD, Oleg A. Slavin[1,2,3] iD, and Vladimir V. Arlazarov[1,2,3] iD

[1] Federal Research Center "Computer Science and Control" of the Russian Academy of Sciences, Vavilova st. 44 bld. 2, 119333 Moscow, Russia
[2] Smart Engines Service LLC, Nobelya st. 7, 121205 Moscow, Russia
usilin@smartengines.com
[3] Moscow Institute of Physics and Technology, Institutskiy per. 9, Dolgoprudny 141701 Moscow, Russia

Abstract. In this paper, we consider object classification and detection problems for autonomous UAVs. We propose an algorithm that is effective from the point of view of computational complexity and memory consumption. The proposed algorithm can be successfully used as a basic tool for building an autonomous UAV control system. The algorithm is based on the Viola-Jones method. It is shown in the paper, that the Viola-Jones method is the most preferable approach to detect objects on-board UAVs because it needs the least amount of memory and the number of computational operations to solve the object detection problem. To ensure sufficient accuracy, we use a modified feature: rectangular Haar-like features, calculated over the magnitude of the image gradient. To increase computational efficiency, the L1 norm was used to calculate the magnitude of the image gradient. The PSN-10 inflatable life raft (an example of an object that is detected during rescue operations using UAVs) and oil tank storage (such kind of objects are usually detected during the inspection of industrial infrastructure) are considered as target objects in this work. The performance of the trained detectors was estimated on real data (including data obtained during the real rescue operation of the trawler "Dalniy Vostok" in 2015).

Keywords: Machine learning · Object detection · Viola-jones · Classification · UAVs · Edge computing · Memory consumption · Computational efficiency

1 Introduction

Nowadays various types of unmanned aerial vehicles (UAVs) have been used for quite a long time [1–4]. They are used in a variety of tasks such as surveillance, inspection, land surveying, rescue operations, package delivery services, industrial inspection, and others.

In general, UAVs are mainly equipped with optoelectronic or thermal imaging detection equipment [3]. The technical vision systems can serve as irreplaceable sources of

© Springer Nature Switzerland AG 2021
A. Del Bimbo et al. (Eds.): ICPR 2020 Workshops, LNCS 12665, pp. 243–252, 2021.
https://doi.org/10.1007/978-3-030-68821-9_23

information for automatic recognition, navigation, guidance, and information support for search and rescue operations. Different computer vision algorithms can significantly improve the autonomous of UAVs [4]. But at the same time, the most part of such algorithms need a huge power consumption [6, 7]. The purpose of this paper is to suggest an object detection algorithm that is suitable to use onboard UAVs.

In the paper [5] there is a comparison of modern convolutional neural network architectures with the Viola and Jones object detection method concerning memory consumption and computation efficiency on the problem of face detection on FDDB dataset [8]. The results are presented in Table 1.

Table 1.

Detector	Time, GFLOPS	Memory consumption, GB
Viola-Jones	0.6	0.1
HeadHunter DPM	5.0	2.0
SSD	45.8	0.7
Faster R-CNN	223.9	2.1
R-FCN 50	132.1	2.4
R-FCN 101	186.6	3.1
PVANET	40.1	2.6
Local RCNN	1206.8	2.1
Yolo 9000	34.90	2.1

Table 1 shows that the Viola-Jones method in the inference mode is almost 10 times faster than the fastest neural network architecture (HeadHunter DPM) and almost 60 times faster than the Yolo 9000 universal neural network architecture. The Viola-Jones method also shows the best performance.

To summarize the results shown in Table 1 we can conclude that the Viola-Jones method is the most preferable approach to detect objects on-board UAVs because it needs the least amount of memory and the number of computational operations to solve the object detection problem. Unfortunately, the Viola-Jones method "from the box" does not provide enough detection quality for most types of objects. That is why the Viola-Jones method should be modified before using the method in real practice applications.

In the paper, we describe a modified Viola-Jones method and consider the training of Viola-Jones detectors for two kinds of objects: a life raft PSN-10 [9, 10] and an oil storage tank [11]. The typical image of these kinds of objects obtained from UAV is shown in Fig. 1. These objects illustrate the application of the proposed approach to common practice problems.

A PSN-10 [9, 10] life raft is a typical object which is usually detected by UAVs during any rescue operation. The oil storage tank is an example of a typical man-made building, the condition of which can be periodically monitored with UAVs.

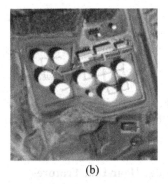

(a)   (b)

Fig. 1. Sample aerial images of subject objects: (a) life raft PSN-10, (b) an oil storage tank

This paper is structured as follows: in the next section, we give an overview of the Viola-Jones object detection method and describe the significant modification which allows building an effective and resistant to different luminance object detector. In Sect. 3 we apply the described method to train detectors for both objects (a PSN-10 life raft and an oil storage tank) and show results.

2 Viola-Jones Object Detection Method

The Viola-Jones object detection method was developed for real-time face detection in images [12, 13]. This method reduces the detection task to the task of binary classification at each image point, that is, for each rectangular image area taken with all kinds of shifts and scales, the hypothesis of the presence of the target object in the area is checked using a pre-trained classifier.

The Viola-Jones method uses rectangular Haar-like features [14], the value of which is calculated as the difference between the sums of the pixel's intensity of the image areas inside the adjacent rectangles. For efficient calculation of the value of Haar-like features, an integral image is used. The integral image is also known in the literature under the term "summed-area table" [15] which for a grayscale image $f(y, x)$ with dimensions $M \times N$ is determined as follows:

$$I_f(y, x) = \sum_{i \le y, j \le x} f(i, j) \tag{1}$$

With each feature, the Viola-Jones method associates a binary "weak" classifier $h(x) : X \to \{+1, -1\}$, usually presented as a decision tree with one branch:

$$h(x) = \begin{cases} +1 & if \, p \cdot f(x) < p \cdot \theta \\ -1 & otherwise \end{cases} \tag{2}$$

where θ and p are the threshold value of the feature and the parity of the classifier, respectively. Using the AdaBoost machine learning method, a "strong" classifier is constructed as a linear superposition of the above "weak" classifiers:

$$S(x) = \text{sign}\left(\sum_{t=1}^{T} (\alpha_t \cdot h_t(x))\right). \tag{3}$$

The high speed of the Viola-Jones method operation is ensured through the use of a cascade of "strong" classifiers, which allows localizing "empty" (object-free) image areas in a small number of calculations:

$$Cascade(x) = \prod_{i=1}^{N} [S_i(x) > 0], \tag{4}$$

where $[\cdot]$ is an indicator function. The object detection in the image is performed using the constructed binary cascade classifier using the sliding window method [12, 13].

2.1 Edge Haar-Like Features

To build an effective and resistant to different luminance object detector, one uses a different kind of edge features. In our work, we use the original feature space described in the papers [10, 16, 17]. These features are rectangular Haar-like features, calculated over the magnitude of the image gradient.

Unlike the classical Haar-like features, such edge features are effective in generalizing objects containing a huge number of edges and robust to different luminance conditions. To increase computational efficiency, the L1 norm was used to calculate the magnitude of the image gradient.

Fig. 2 demonstrates a sample of PSN-10 life raft image: both the source grayscale image and the magnitude of the image gradient computed using the L1 norm.

(a)   (b)

Fig. 2. A sample of PSN-10 image: (a) the of the image gradient. source grayscale image, (b) the magnitude

3   Experiments

As we mentioned above, we applied the proposed approach to train object detector for two kinds of object: a life raft PSN 10 and an oil storage tank. The first kind of object is a typical object which is usually detected by UAVs during any rescue operation. The second type of object is an example of a typical man-made building, the condition of which can be periodically monitored with UAVs.

3.1 An Inflatable Life Raft PSN-10

Training Dataset. It is quite difficult to find enough training data for such kinds of objects as a life raft because this can be collected only during real rescue operations. Fortunately, rescue operations in our world do not take place very often. As a result, it is not possible to collect enough real training samples.

However, it is known that Viola-Jones algorithm allows to train an efficient detector based on synthetic data [10, 21].

To obtain 2D images, it is necessary to simulate the PSN-10 raft, simulate the water surface, place all objects on the scene, and create animation for the objects. To build a correct 3D model, we found enough information about the life raft characteristics and a set of images. In Fig. 3(a) there is one sample photo of the real PSN-10 life raft.

Based on the found photos, a 3D model of the raft was built (see Fig. 3 (b)). To simplify the modeling process, it was decided to divide the raft into the following components: sides, awning, rope, bottom, small pillow.

 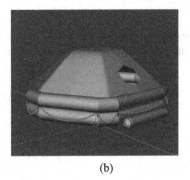

(a)   (b)

Fig. 3. The life raft PSN-10: (a) the source image of the raft, (b) the 3D model of PSN-10 be visually noticeable, but this approach allows us to draw the object in the final image quicker

After modeling, textures (images that reproduce the visual properties of any surfaces or objects) and shaders (programs for the graphics card processor that are used in 3D graphics to determine the final parameters of an object or image) must be applied to all parts of the raft.

The stage of modeling the scene consists of placing objects, setting up animation, lights, camera movement, etc. Since the task is to detect a drifting raft, the PSN-10 model will move along the wave due to the movement of water. In Fig. 4 there are some samples of the modeled scenes.

So, following the described above technique we prepared 3003 synthetic images. This dataset was separated into two parts: the first one contained 600 images and was used to train the life raft detector while the remaining part (2403 images) was used to evaluate the quality of the trained detector.

The training dataset was used for the generation of both positive and negative samples. The negative samples are produced by cutting "empty" sub-windows (image regions without life rafts) from the source images.

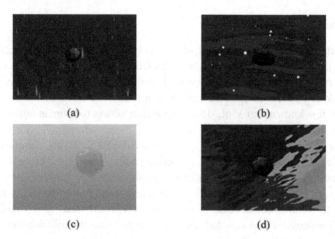

(a)

Fig. 4. Different weather conditions of modeled scenes: (a) rain, (b) snow, (c) frog, and (d) fair-weather function allows you to keep the raft in focus.

Structure. The cascade classifier was trained. it consisted of 11 levels and contained 55 features. The structure of the trained cascade classifier is presented in Table 2.

Table 2. The structure of the trained cascade classifier of the life raft PSN-10

Level No	1	2	3	4	5	6	7	8	9	10	11
Weak Classifier Count	2	2	3	5	4	6	7	5	5	9	7

Inference. Using the rest part of the synthetic dataset the following measures were calculated: True positive (actual positives that are correctly identified), False positive (actual negatives are classified as positives), and false negative (actual positives but not detected with the trained detector). Based on specified statistical measures precision (positive predictive value), recall (true positive rate), and f-measure were calculated. all values are presented in Table 3.

Table 3. The quality of trained life raft detector evaluated on the synthetic data

True Positive	False Positive	False Negative	Precision	Recall	F-measure
2374	69	29	0.972	0.988	0.980

To estimate the applicability of the trained detector for real cases we have found a few images from the real rescue operation. The Russian-flagged fishing trawler Dalniy Vostok sank on 1 April 2015, off Russia's Kamchatka Okhotsk. Half of the crew was rescued thanks to the fact that they successfully evacuated on time on inflatable life rafts PSN-10. There is a set of videos of this rescue operation on the Internet in free access.

So, based on the video we have prepared a small dataset contained 161 images. Clearly, such a small dataset cannot be used to fully-featured evaluation of the detector but can be useful to estimate the applicability of the trained detector to real data. Table 4 shows the quality of the trained detector on the real data.

Table 4. The quality of trained life raft detector evaluated on the real data (rescue operation of the Russian-flagged fishing trawler Dalniy Vostok in 2015).

True Positive	False Positive	False Negative	Precision	Recall	F-measure
143	48	18	0.749	0.888	0.813

In general, the quality on the real data is less than the quality on the synthetic data. This fact can be explained by significantly different weather conditions. In the real dataset, the excitement of the water is big enough while in our synthetic data it did not exceed 2 points.

In Fig. 5 one can see the demonstration of how the trained detector works on real data.

Fig. 5. Evaluation of the trained life raft detector on the real data (rescue operation of the Russian-flagged fishing trawler Dalniy Vostok in 2015)

3.2 An Oil Storage Tank

Training Dataset. A training dataset consisting of 20 × 20 px 70 oil storage tank images, as well as 22 full-size remote probing images without oil tanks, was prepared to train the oil storage tank detector. Since the initial number of the training dataset was small, we used augmentation [17–20].

Structure. Following the proposed algorithm we trained a cascade classifier. it consisted of 4 levels and contained 41 features. Trained classifier features are mainly concentrated around the object perimeter. The full structure of the trained cascade classifier is presented in Table 5.

Table 5. The structure of the trained cascade classifier of the oil storage tank

Level No	1	2	3	4
Weak Classifier Count	3	7	20	11

Inference. The trained cascade was applied to test images to assess the cascade classifier's quality. The test dataset contained 73 target objects. Table 6 shows the result of applying the cascade to the test dataset.

Table 6. The quality of trained oil tank storage detector

True Positive	False Positive	False Negative	Precision	Recall	F-measure
72	3	1	0.960	0.986	0.973

The visualization of applying the trained cascade is shown in Fig. 6. One can see that all oil tank storages (both small and large ones) are detected correctly.

Fig. 6. An example of oil storage localization with a trained cascade

The average number of determined features in the image is 3.1908. Concerning the trained classifier structure (with three features at the first cascade level), this means that, in the case of the majority of analyzed image sections, at the first cascade level, the trained classifier presented a confident answer that the specified region does not belong to the target object.

4 Conclusion

This paper considers object classification and detection problems for autonomous UAVs. We proposed effective from the point of view of computational complexity and memory consumption algorithm that can be successfully used to build an autonomous UAV control system. The algorithm is based on the Viola-Jones method. As a feature space, edge Haar-like features were used, which allowed training the detector that is resistant to various lighting conditions. To increase computational efficiency, the L1 norm was used to calculate the magnitude of the image gradient.

We applied the proposed algorithm to two types of objects: a PSN-10 inflatable life raft and an oil tank storage. The PSN-10 inflatable life raft is a good example of an object that is detected during rescue operations using UAVs while the oil tank storage is a kind of object that is usually detected during the inspection of industrial infrastructure. The performance of the proposed algorithm was estimated on real data (including data obtained during the rescue operation of the trawler "Dalniy Vostok").

Acknowledgments. This work is partially supported by the Russian Foundation for Basic Research (projects 18–29-26022 and 18–29-2602).

References

1. Yu, H., Li, G., Zhang, W., Huang, Q., Du, D., Tian, Q., Sebe, N.: The unmanned aerial vehicle benchmark: Object detection, tracking and baseline. Int. J. Comput. Vis. **128**(5), 1141–1159 (2020)
2. Leira, F.S., Johansen, T.A., Fossen, T.I.: Automatic detection, classification and tracking of objects in the ocean surface from UAVs using a thermal camera. In: 2015 IEEE Aerospace Conference, p. 10. IEEE (2015)
3. Du, D., et al.: The Unmanned aerial vehicle benchmark: object detection and tracking. In: Ferrari, V., Hebert, M., Sminchisescu, C., Weiss, Y. (eds.) ECCV 2018. LNCS, vol. 11214, pp. 375–391. Springer, Cham (2018). https://doi.org/10.1007/978-3-030-01249-6_23
4. Muraviev, V.S., Smirnov, S.A., Strotov, V.V.: Aerial vehicles detection and recognition for UAV vision system. Comput. Opt. **41**(4), 545 (2017)
5. Granger, E., Kiran, M., Blais-Morin, L.A.: A comparison of CNN-based face and head detectors for real-time video surveillance applications. In: 2017 Seventh International Conference on Image Processing Theory, Tools and Applications (IPTA), pp. 1–7. IEEE (2017)
6. Hulens, D., Goedemé, T., Verbeke, J.: How to choose the best embedded processing platform for on-board UAV image processing? In: The Proceedings VISAPP 2015, pp. 1–10 (2015)
7. Bertran, E., Sànchez-Cerdà, A.: On the tradeoff between electrical power consumption and flight performance in fixed-wing UAV autopilots. IEEE Trans. Veh. Technol. **65**(11), 8832–8840 (2016)
8. Jain, V., Learned-Miller, E.: Fddb: A benchmark for face detection in unconstrained settings. Technical report, University of Massachusetts, Amherst (2010)
9. Afanasyev, I.I., Laptev, V.N., Pirogov, V.P.: Analysis of the rescue assets range of the Russian navy. Sci. Bull. Volsk Mil. Inst. Mater. Support: Mil. Sci. J. **2**, 150–154 (2015)

10. Usilin, S.A., Arlazarov, V.V., Rokhlin, N. S., Rudyka, S.A., Matveev, S.A., Zatsarinny A.A.: Training Viola-Jones detectors For 3D objects based on fully synthetic data for use in rescue missions with UAV. In: Bulletin of the South Ural State University. Ser. Mathematical Modelling, Programming and Computer Software (Bulletin SUSU MMCS), vol. 13(4), pp. 96–108 (2020). https://doi.org/10.14529/mmp200408
11. Cho, J., Lim, G., Biobaku, T., Kim, S., Parsaei, H.: Safety and security management with unmanned aerial vehicle (UAV) in oil and gas industry. Procedia Manuf. 3, 1343–1349 (2015)
12. Viola, P., Jones, M.: Rapid object detection using a boosted cascade of simple features. In: Proceedings of the 2001 IEEE Computer Society Conference on Computer Vision and Pattern Recognition (CVPR 2001), vol. 1, pp. 511–518. IEEE (2001)
13. Viola, P., Jones, M.: Robust real-time object detection. Proc. Int. J. Comput. Vis. 4, 34–47 (2001)
14. Papageorgiou, C.P., Oren, M., Poggio, T.: A general framework for object detection. In: Proceedings of the Sixth International Conference Computer Vision IEEE Cat No. 98CH36271, vol. 6, pp. 555–562, January 1998
15. Lewis, J.P.: Fast template matching. In: Proceedings of the Vision Interface, pp. 120–123 (1995)
16. Kotov, A.A., Usilin, S.A., Gladilin, S.A., Nikolaev, D.P.: Construction of robust features for detection and classification of objects without characteristic brightness contrasts. J. Inf. Technol. Comput. Syst. 1, 53–60 (2014)
17. Matalov, D.P., Usilin, S.A., Arlazarov, V.V.: Modification of the Viola-Jones approach for the detection of the government seal stamp of the Russian Federation. In: the Proceedings of Eleventh International Conference on Machine Vision (ICMV 2018): International Society for Optics and Photonics, p. 11041 (2019). https://doi.org/10.1117/12.2522793
18. Gayer, A.V., Chernyshova, Y.S., Sheshkus, A.V.: Effective real-time augmentation of training dataset for the neural networks learning. In: Proceedings of the Eleventh International Conference on Machine Vision (2019). https://doi.org/10.1117/12.2522969
19. Usilin, S.A., Bezmaternykh, P.V., Arlazarov, V.V.: Fast approach for QR code localization on images using Viola-Jones method. In: Proceedings of the Twelfth International Conference on Machine Vision (2020). https://doi.org/10.1117/12.2559386
20. Lv, J.J., Shao, X.H., Huang, J.S., Zhou, X.D., Zhou, X.: Data augmentation for face recognition. Neurocomputing 230, 184–196 (2017)
21. Akimov, A.V., Sirota, A.A.: Synthetic data generation models and algorithms for training image recognition algorithms using the Viola-Jones framework. Comput. Opt. 40(6), 911–918 (2016)

Automation of the Detection of Pathological Changes in the Morphometric Characteristics of the Human Eye Fundus Based on the Data of Optical Coherence Tomography Angiography

Igor Gurevich[1] , Maria Budzinskaya[2] , Vera Yashina[1]([✉]) , Adil Tleubaev[1] ,
Vladislav Pavlov[2] , and Denis Petrachkov[2]

[1] Federal Research Center "Computer Science and Control" of the Russian Academy of
Sciences, 44/2, Vavilov Street, Moscow 119333, Russian Federation
igourevi@ccas.ru, werayashina@gmail.com,
adil.tleubayev.3.14159@gmail.com
[2] Scientific Research Institute of Eye Disease, 11A, Rossolimo Street, Moscow 119021,
Russian Federation
m_budzinskaya@mail.ru, pavlovoculis@yandex.ru,
petrachkov@doctor.com

Abstract. This paper presents the results of the joint work of image analysis specialists and ophthalmologists on the task of analyzing images obtained by the method of optical coherence tomography angiography. A method was developed to automate the detection of pathological changes in the morphometric characteristics of the fundus. The solution of the image recognition problem assumes the presence of certain image representations, the presence of effective recognition algorithms, and the compliance of the used image representations with the requirements of the recognition algorithms for the source data. To reduce images to a form that is easy to recognize we considered sets of features that met all the necessary requirements of specialists. Chosen feature model was implemented to the problem of classification of images of patients with and without pathologies. The developed method makes it possible to classify pathological changes in the vascular bed of the human eye with high accuracy.

Keywords: Image analysis · Mathematical morphology · Automation of scientific research · Biomedical images · Ophthalmology · Angiogram · Vascular detection · Extraction of ischemia zones · Segmentation

1 Introduction

At present, the development of image processing and analysis has reached a high level that allows us to apply these developments in various tasks that were previously either

This work was supported in part by the Russian Foundation for Basic Research (Project no. 20-57-00025).

practically unsolvable or too resource-intensive. The use of image processing tools for medical purposes, as a means of presenting the results of biological and clinical research in the main sections of medical science and practical medicine, makes it possible to more accurately and quickly diagnose various pathologies, or the beginning of the development of these pathologies. Vessels are one of the main objects of analysis on ophthalmic images. The human visual system evaluates well the qualitative characteristics of objects, but the quantitative description of the same objects in most cases is quite subjective. Automation of object characterization (counting and measuring their parameters) allows not only to increase the accuracy of object estimation, but also allows you to save images and the results of their processing in a large-capacity database, therefore, to use large volumes of training, control and test data in diagnostics, which, along with unification of measurements, allows to carry out diagnostics fairly objectively (Gurevich et al. 2018).

The presence of a large number of diverse and multifaceted tasks requires an individual approach to their solution, while the use of tools for extracting information from images will make it possible to advance in solving problems by automating scientific research. For many years, the authors of the article have been developing and experimentally investigating new methods for automating image analysis for processing, analyzing and interpreting the results of biomedical research (Gurevich et al. 2006, 2015, 2017a, b, 2018; Nedzved et al. 2017).

The analysis of ophthalmic images is a long and laborious process that requires the involvement of several specialists. Since for some kind of tasks the subjective opinion of one specialist turns out to be insufficient. For adequate analysis and ophthalmological images, for assessing the prevalence of the pathological process, it is necessary to develop and implement in practice the appropriate software for digital image analysis. Automated tools for processing and analysis of biomedical images can reduce the time and material costs for morphological studies, and are also used in the analysis of ophthalmic images (Gurevich et al. 2018).

2   Problem Statement

An early assessment of pathological changes in the vessels of the microvasculature due to diabetic retinopathy will allow timely and high-quality screening and monitoring of diabetic retinopathy, start therapy in the early stages of the disease, which will lead to a decrease in severe, proliferative forms of the disease, and the number of complications.

Diabetic retinopathy (DR) is a chronic progressive disease affecting retinal micro vessels in patients with diabetes mellitus (DM). DR is the main cause of vision loss among working-age population (Cheung et al. 2010).

Diabetes mellitus is considered a pandemic in developed countries since 21st century. Prevalence is 3–4% across the population that increases with age. Approximately one in 10 individuals suffers from type 1 diabetes. In addition, it's considered that half of the cases of type 2 diabetes remain undiscovered due to asymptomatic course. The proportion of DR in patients with diabetes is about 30% after 10–20 years from the onset of the disease, and this ratio is gradually increasing. At the same time, proliferative diabetic retinopathy (PDR), leading to blindness, develops in 10% of patients, and non-proliferative DR - in 90% (Dedov et al. 2017).

A serious problem in the treatment of DR is its asymptomatic progression. Patients often remain unaware of the gradual development of retinal vascular dysfunction. The manifestations of DR usually occur in the later stages or when clinically significant macular edema (CSME) occurs.

Treatment of DR, started in the early stages of the disease, is more effective compared to its effect at the stage of PDR and in CSME. That is why early detection of DR is relevant for the appointment of timely treatment and minimization of its complications, leading to blindness and low vision in the working population (Fong et al. 2001; Sinclair and Delvecchio 2004; Vujosevic et al. 2020).

Since pathogenesis of DR is based changes in micro circulation, thus techniques that help visualize these changes can reveal valuable biomarkers of DR. Optical coherence tomography angiography (OCT-A), allows a high resolution to study the vascular plexus of the retina in layers (Hirano et al. 2020, Gildea et al. 2019) is such technique. An important advantage of this technique is that the most frequent retinal changes in DR (microaneurysms, neovascularization and ischemia) can be qualitatively and quantitatively assessed using OCT-A (Hirano et al. 2019).

Optical coherence tomography angiography (OCT-A) is a new, non-invasive imaging technique for retinal and choroidal blood vessels that is used to study changes in blood vessels in patients with diabetes mellitus (Spaide et al. 2018).

Spaide RF in his article emphasized that time being, OCT-A faces two main challenges: smoothing the depth information within a given layer, which causes the loss of vascular relationships within the layer and the need for segmentation. In many eyes with pathological changes, accurate segmentation is not possible, as the layers cannot be accurately identified (Spaide 2015). OCT-A shows the fundus vascular anatomy by detecting the contrast of movement between repeated OCT B-scans at the same location. Since the only moving objects in the fundus are erythrocytes, the images obtained are a blood flow map (Spaide 2015).

Currently, based on the image (Fig. 1.) obtained with the Spectralis HRA + OCT device with the OCT Angiography module "Heidelberg Engineering", the researcher subjectively evaluates the condition of the retinal vascular plexuses and their qualitative characteristics, for example, the presence of ischemic zones and the density of the vascular pattern. The availability of software that allows evaluating the indicated parameters of the images obtained will make it possible to obtain an objective assessment of the state of the choroid plexuses of the retina and track its changes with time. In particular, the assessment of vascular density is of greatest interest. The presence of software capabilities for detecting changes in this indicator will make it possible to objectively assess the development of neovascularization processes and the degree of retinal ischemia.

The parameters that the software must meet are as follows:

- Determination of the localization of the foveolar avascular zone (FAZ) on the OCT-angiograms loaded into the program.
- Based on the data on the localization of the FAZ, carry out image processing in order to obtain a quantitative estimate of the parameter of the area of the FAZ. The parameter of the area of the FAZ with its dynamic assessment allows one to judge the development of ischemia of the macular zone of the retina.

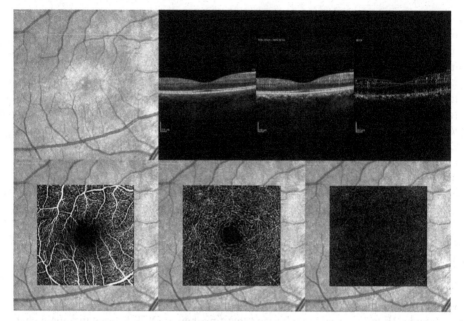

Fig. 1. OCT-A image.

- Carrying out the processing of the OCT-angiogram in order to visualize the complex of vessels that make up the vascular plexuses of the retina.
- Based on the data obtained during image processing, conduct a quantitative assessment of the vascular density parameter (by determining the ratio of the area of the vascular complex to the area of the image). The vascular density parameter is integrative in reflecting the processes of neovascularization and the severity of retinal ischemia.
- Processing OCT-angiogram in order to visualize the components of the "vascular framework" (areas in which there are vessels that make up the vascular plexus of the retina)
- Based on the data obtained during image processing, quantify the vascular tortuosity parameter.

Approaches to solution of the problem of vessel allocation on images of the human fundus were studied. In (João et al. 2006), pixels are classified into "vessels" and "non-vessels". The authors of this article use two-dimensional Morlet wavelets as features, and Bayesian classifiers as a classifier. In (Vermeer 2004) the method of "tracking along the line" is used: from the starting point belonging to the vessels, there is movement along the neighboring pixels, if they belong to the vessels. In (Zhang et al. 2010), the authors use the "matched filters" method to highlight the vessels in the image. The extended matched filter with the first derivative of the Gaussian filter allows you to highlight the boundaries of the vessels. (Chu 2016) uses a quantitative analysis of OCT-A, they present a five-index quantitative analysis to detect and evaluate vascular anomalies from different points of view. Indices include vascular area density, vascular skeletal density, vascular diameter index, vascular perimeter index, and vascular complexity index.

The images were provided by the Federal State Budgetary Scientific Institution "Research Institute of Eye Diseases", they are color images of the retinal tissue, broken into several layers. The spectralis HRA + OCT with OCT Angiography module (Heidelberg Engineering's) provides high resolution OCTA images with a side-to-side resolution of 5.7 μm/pixel. Machine with TruTrack Active Eye Tracking accuracy, the OCTA module allows fine visualization of fine capillary networks. Axial resolution of 3.9 μm/pixel allows to segmentate all four histologically confirmed retinal choroid plexuses. Via built-in software, the device selects 3 layers of the retina for which it shows the corresponding vascular patterns. Internal Limiting Membrane (ILM) to Inner Plexiform Layer (IPL) constitutes superficial capillary plexus (SCP), IPL to Outer Plexiform Layer (OPL) constitutes deep capillary plexus (DCP), and OPL to Bruch Membrane (BM) constitutes avascular zone (AZ).

The foveolar avascular zone (FAZ) can normally differ - it has a different diameter and shape, but it always tends to take a rounded shape. The vascular pattern may also vary, but its density and brightness depends on the presence or absence of pathological changes, in particular the presence of angioretinopathy. Reduced vascular pattern means impairment of blood supply to the retina (ischemia). An increase in the vascular pattern and an increase in its brightness may be a manifestation of the formation of newly formed pathological vessels that pass fluid through their walls.

The main problem solved in this work is the automatic calculation of morphometric characteristics, based on which it is possible to assess pathological changes in blood vessels.

The database of images consists of two parts. The first part represents images of the eyes of completely healthy people, without disturbances in the vascular bed, etc. The second group contains images of the eyes of people with a confirmed diagnosis of diabetes; the same group is subdivided into 3 subgroups:

1. Images of eyes with a healthy vascular bed, with characteristics very close to healthy ones (Fig. 2a).

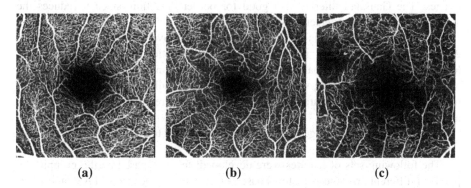

     (a)   **(b)**   **(c)**

Fig. 2. (a, b, C) The state of the vascular network of various groups.

2. Images of eyes with incipient pathological changes, an increase in FAZ, a decrease in vascular density, the so-called "borderline" case (Fig. 2b).
3. Images of eyes with obvious pathologies (Fig. 2c).

3   A Method for Automating the Detection of Pathological Changes in the Morphometric Characteristics of the Fundus

The first stage of the method is image preprocessing in order to improve image quality, filter, and reduce the impact of various noise and artifacts that occur during image capture on the further calculation of morphological features.

The source images are colored with three color channels, and the areas of interest in the images are monochrome. From the full image, three images with a dimension of 512×512 pixels are selected, representing three different layers of the retina of the eye (Fig. 3).

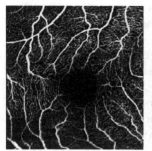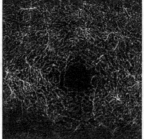

Fig. 3. Three layers of the retina.

To reduce noise, a Gaussian filter (Sauvola 2000) is applied to each of the three images. The Gaussian filter is also good for border detection, since it reduces the sensitivity of the border detector to noise.

To the obtained images is applied binarization of Sauvola (Shapiro and Stockman 2001). Some of the images are not uniform in illumination, due to the difficulty of long-term fixed gaze of the patient, so adaptive binarization is used.

After binarization, along with the vessels, noise (small components) due to inhomogeneity of illumination are also released, which are removed from the image by area.

Based on the binary image, images of the vessel skeleton and pixels on the border (perimeter) are obtained) (Fig. 4).

The following sets of features were developed: features based on the grouping of pixels of different brightness, features based on the ratio of the area of FAZs and zones of ischemia, and features based on quantitative analysis.

Based on expert opinion, pixels were classified into three classes based on their brightness (João et al. 2006): "bright vessels", "dull vessels" and "non-vessels". To do this, a combination of the source and binary images was used. Optimal thresholds were

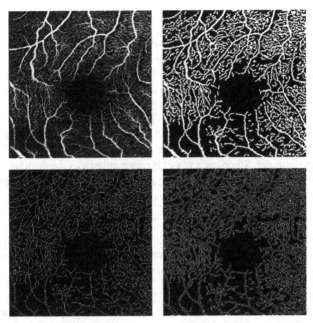

Fig. 4. The top row contains the original and binarized images. In the bottom row there are images of the skeleton and the perimeter.

selected for dividing pixels into three groups. All the black pixels in the binary image once belonged to the group of "non-vessels"; all the white pixels in the binary image were analyzed for source: if the brightness was less than the first threshold, then the pixel also belonged to the class of "non-vessels"; if the brightness was above the first threshold but below a second, then the pixel belonged to the class of "dull vessels"; if the brightness of the pixel is above the second threshold, then this pixel was considered "bright vessels". The percentage ratio of three pixel classes to the entire image was calculated.

Features based on the area of FAZ and ischemia zones were calculated by searching for large areas of "black" pixels in the binary image. The search for zones was carried out taking into account the fact that their size in cases of healthy patients can not be less than a certain size. And in the case of diabetics, FAZ tends to expand. A dilation operation (image expansion) was applied to the binary image, a negative was taken from the resulting image, and an image was obtained with FAZ and possible zones of ischemia, which were additionally filtered by area.

Chu et al. 2016 uses five index quantitative analysis to detect and evaluate vascular abnormalities from different angles.

We introduce the following notation: $\sum_{i=1,j=1}^{n} A(i,j)$ the sum of white pixels in a binarized image; $\sum_{i=1,j=1}^{n} X(i,j)$ the sum of the total number of pixels in the image; $\sum_{i=1,j=1}^{n} S(i,j)$ the sum of white pixels in the skeleton image; $\sum_{i=1,j=1}^{n} P(i,j)$ the sum of white pixels in the perimeter image.

These five features will be computed using the following calculations.

Vessel area density (VAD): $VAD = \frac{\sum_{i=1,j=1}^{n} A(i,j)}{\sum_{i=1,j=1}^{n} X(i,j)}$

VAD provides an estimate of the actual density of the choroid plexus, since it takes into account both the length and the diameter of the vessels. However, problems can arise when there is a simultaneous decrease in the vascular bed and vasodilation, which can lead to false negative results in relation to vascular pathology.

Vessel skeleton density (VSD): $VSD = \frac{\sum_{i=1,j=1}^{n} S(i,j)}{\sum_{i=1,j=1}^{n} X(i,j)}$,

VSD provides an estimate of the density of the choroid plexus, taking into account only the very existence of the vessel, since only the length of the vessel is estimated, regardless of its diameter. Since each vessel is represented as a single pixel line, large and capillary vessels contribute equally to the quantification of VSD. Therefore, compared to VAD, VSD is more sensitive in reducing the vascular bed.

Vessel diameter index (VDI): $VDI = \frac{\sum_{i=1,j=1}^{n} A(i,j)}{\sum_{i=1,j=1}^{n} S(i,j)}$,

VDI allows you to calculate the average diameter of the vessels in the image, but it does not display the change in vessel density. The index is sensitive to changes in vascular dilation, but does not take into account its length in any way.

Vessel perimeter index (VPI): $VPI = \frac{\sum_{i=1,j=1}^{n} P(i,j)}{\sum_{i=1,j=1}^{n} X(i,j)}$,

VPI provides an estimate of the density of the choroid plexus, in contrast to VSD, the perimeter of the vessels is taken into account, which makes it possible to take into account both the length and the diameter of the vessels, similar to VAD.

Vessel complexity index (VCI): $VCI = \frac{\left(\sum_{i=1,j=1}^{n} A(i,j)\right)^2}{4\pi \sum_{i=1,j=1}^{n} X(i,j)}$ (pixels),

VCI provides an estimate of the complexity of the choroid plexus, a decrease in the vascular bed leads to a decrease in complexity.

As a result, the following set of features is collected for each vascular layer: the area of the dark zone (FAZ and ischemia), the occupied area by "bright vessels", "dull vessels", "not vessels", VAD, VSD, VDI, VPI, VCI. And since for each eye image we have images of three layers, in the end we collect 27 features, on the basis of which we carried out further experiments.

4   Experimental Investigation of the Proposed Method

The base of images was provided for the work: 70 images of eyes of healthy people and 370 images of eyes of people with a confirmed diagnosis of diabetes. In turn, the patient base was divided into three more subgroups: 100 images close to normal, 150 images with pathology, and 120 with the so-called "borderline" case.

Several experiments were carried out with these groups in the form of two class and three class classification.

First of all, we analyzed the features we used. Table 1 and 2 shows the mean values of features and standard deviations for different groups and layers. After analyzing the obtained values, we can conclude that the groups are mostly distinguishable from each other, and that the features fully correspond to the properties with which they were declared.

Table 1. Statistical values of features for different groups and layers. (In the first line, the average value, in the second, the standard deviation) (pixel/pixel)

	Dark zone	Bright vessels	Dull vessels	Not vessels
Healthy 1layer	0.0457	0.2122	0.1413	0.6462
	0.018	0.0353	0.0097	0.0394
Healthy 2layer	0.0207	0.1406	0.1749	0.6845
	0.0121	0.034	0.0127	0.0423
Healthy 3layer	0.2709	0.0039	0.0518	0.9443
	0.0904	0.0016	0.0164	0.0177
Normal 1layer	0.0521	0.1983	0.1375	0.6642
	0.0202	0.0367	0.0141	0.0439
Normal 2layer	0.0257	0.1303	0.1704	0.6993
	0.0143	0.037	0.0156	0.0482
Normal 3layer	0.2915	0.0034	0.0491	0.9474
	0.1031	0.0015	0.0177	0.019
Borderline 1layer	0.0582	0.1789	0.1272	0.6939
	0.0223	0.0424	0.0151	0.053
Borderline 2layer	0.0286	0.1216	0.1606	0.7177
	0.0163	0.0418	0.022	0.0604
Borderline 3layer	0.3013	0.0039	0.0514	0.9447
	0.1411	0.0027	0.0234	0.0255
Pathology 1layer	0.1058	0.1567	0.1045	0.7389
	0.0898	0.0533	0.0239	0.0732
Pathology 2layer	0.0751	0.1036	0.1296	0.7667
	0.1173	0.0415	0.0365	0.0735
Pathology 3layer	0.3716	0.0053	0.0446	0.9502
	0.1507	0.023	0.0215	0.0401

We also analyzed the relationship of various features based on the Pearson correlation coefficient, which characterizes the measure of intensity and direction of the linear relationship between two variables. Features that belong to the same layer show a high positive or negative correlation between each other, which follows from the fact that all features are based on different ratios of light and dark pixels. There is also a certain correlation of features belonging to different layers, which indicates that the changes in different layers are connected.

The high correlation of features in this problem is not a disadvantage, since all the features are based on the same data, but they operate in different ways, which allows you to create groups of signs of different sensitivity to pathological changes.

In the first experiment, a two-class approach was chosen, images of healthy people, patients close to normal and with pathology were used for training. The groups were divided into two classes: conditionally healthy and pathological. The sample was divided into two parts, training and test, with equal shares of each class.

Table 2. Statistical values of features for different groups and layers. (In the first line, the average value, in the second, the standard deviation)

	VAD	VSD	VDI	VPI	VCI
	Pixel/pixel				Pixel^2/pixel
Healthy 1layer	0.4471 0.0296	0.1099 0.009	4.0754 0.1021	0.1977 0.0121	1824 113.9
Healthy 2layer	0.4598 0.0323	0.1198 0.0099	3.8413 0.0617	0.2291 0.0136	2178 123.8
Healthy 3layer	0.1599 0.0371	0.0435 0.0102	3.6775 0.0706	0.089 0.0196	1034 215.1
Normal 1layer	0.4384 0.0351	0.1036 0.0104	4.1452 0.1225	0.189 0.0145	1739 134.3
Normal 2layer	0.4413 0.0416	0.1134 0.0129	3.901 0.0998	0.2096 0.018	2078 166.5
Normal 3layer	0.1512 0.041	0.041 0.0115	3.7029 0.1459	0.0842 0.022	979 247.9
Borderline 1layer	0.3997 0.0454	0.0949 0.013	4.2272 0.1379	0.1756 0.0189	1610 171.5
Borderline 2layer	0.4212 0.0553	0.1069 0.0162	3.955 0.1108	0.1994 0.0237	1969 213.7
Borderline 3layer	0.1534 0.0521	0.0415 0.0144	3.7093 0.1397	0.0848 0.0277	978 308.8
Pathology 1layer	0.3403 0.0745	0.0784 0.0193	4.3779 0.1949	0.1465 0.0313	1316 281.3
Pathology 2layer	0.356 0.0885	0.0869 0.0241	4.142 0.1841	0.1656 0.0411	1607 400.9
Pathology 3layer	0.1337 0.0554	0.0357 0.0149	3.7632 0.1729	0.073 0.0274	832 290.8

The random forest algorithm was used as a classifier. As a result of training on a test sample, it was possible to achieve a classification result of 92%. From the obtained result, it follows that on the basis of the features we use, it is possible to achieve separability of the two classes with high accuracy. Applying the trained classifier to the images from the "borderline" case group, it was found that 58% of the images are classified as conditionally healthy, the rest are patients. Which proves the statement that these images are at the "borderline" stage, when pathological changes have already begun, but they are still difficult to determine.

Table 3 shows the matrix of answers for two class classifiers, although the overall classification accuracy is 92%, it is still clear that the error in the classification of healthy people is lower, which means that we have a type II error (incorrect acceptance of the patient as healthy). Hence, it can be assumed that a reduction in the type II error will allow for a more accurate classification of borderline cases.

Table 3. Confusion matrix for two class classifiers.

	Answer: pathology	Answer: normal
Pathology	89%	11%
Healthy/Normal	6%	94%
Borderline	42%	58%

In the second experiment, all three classes were selected for training: conditionally healthy, borderline, and sick. The sample was also split into two parts, with equal shares for each class.

In this experiment, the classification algorithm showed an accuracy of 71%. With a more accurate analysis of the results, it was found that individual accuracy by class gave the following results: classification accuracy of conditionally healthy 81%, classification accuracy of patients 78%, classification accuracy of borderline cases 40%. Compared to the results of the two-class algorithm, the classification accuracy of sick and healthy decreased, but not to a critical level. The accuracy of borderline cases turned out to be rather low, of the incorrectly classified images, 38% were classified as healthy, the remaining 22% as sick. The results are shown in Table 4, from the results obtained it follows that the "borderline" case is really very close to both healthy and sick, as this class itself is almost evenly distributed among all three classes, and in the case of the other two, errors are mainly made towards border class. So far, based on our features, it has not been possible to classify images with a border case at a high level.

Table 4. Confusion matrix for three class classifiers

	Answer: pathology	Answer: normal	Answer: borderline
Pathology	78.5%	8%	13.5%
Healthy/Normal	4.5%	81%	14.5%
Borderline	22%	38%	40%

5 Conclusions

We used the methods of image processing and analysis in the task of image analysis of OCT-angiograms. A feature space has been developed that can be used to identify pathological changes in the structure of the vascular plexuses of the human retina.

It was possible to achieve high accuracy of classification of images of healthy and with the presence of eye pathology. So far, low results have been achieved in the classification of borderline cases.

In the future, work will be carried out to expand the feature space, improve the algorithms and obtain more detailed markup of images of patients with a confirmed diagnosis of diabetes.

A number of factors, such as: uneven numbers of patients during screening for diabetic retinopathy and the need to review a tomogram by an experienced ophthalmologist-retinologist, under borderline conditions, the need to convene a consultation, physician overload, all this makes it extremely relevant to create an automated system for determining pathological changes on tomograms. Replacing one retinologist with a diagnostic system will help liberate time of medical ophthalmologists through prompt consultative assistance, reducing the psychological burden on both patients and physicians. Visual tomogram analysis cannot always help to accurately assess patient's condition, therefore, methods and algorithms are needed to intelligently support the image review and the final diagnosis.

Nowadays, a large number of works are underway to create automated systems for analyzing color images of the eye fundus in patients with diabetes (Olvera-Barrios et al. 2020). However, OCT angiography is the one and only method to assess all three choroid plexuses of the eye fundus. Alteration of retinal hemodynamics in diabetes patients presents itself in the deep vascular plexus. In our study, a program that has been created allows, with high accuracy, in an autonomous mode, to carry out differential diagnosis of the normal state of the vessels from the pathological one, which increases its diagnostic value. In the future, more detailed work is planned with "borderline" conditions, which constitute the main problem in screening patients with diabetes.

References

Cheung, N., Mitchell, P., Wong, T.Y.: Diabetic retinopathy. Lancet **376**, 124–146 (2010). https://doi.org/10.1016/S0140-6736(09)62124-3

Chu, Z., et al.: Quantitative assessment of the retinal microvasculature using optical coherence tomography angiography. J. Biomed. Opt. **21**(6), 066008 (2016)

Dedov, I., Shestakova, M., Vikulova, O.: Epidemiology of diabetes mellitus in Russian Federation: clinical and statistical report according to the federal diabetes registry. Diabetes Mellitus **20**(1), 13–41 (2017)

Fong, D.S., Gottlieb, J., Ferris, F.L., Iii, Klein, R.: Understanding the value of diabetic retinopathy screening. Arch. Ophthalmol. **119**(5), 758–760 (2001). https://doi.org/10.1001/archopht.15.758

Gildea, D.: The diagnostic value of optical coherence tomography angiography indiabetic retinopathy: a systematic review. Int. Ophthalmol. **39**(10), 2413–2433 (2019). https://doi.org/10.1007/s10792-018-1034-8

Gurevich, I.B., Yashina, V.V., Ablameyko, S.V., et al.: Development and experimental investigation of mathematical methods for automating the diagnostics and analysis of ophthalmological images. Pattern Recognit. Image Anal. **28**, 612–636 (2018)

Gurevich, I.B., Harazishvili, D.V., Salvetti, O., Trykova, A.A., Vorob'ev, I.A.: Elements of the information technology of cytological specimens analysis: taxonomy and factor analysis. Pattern Recognit. Image Anal. Adv. Math. Theory Appl. MAIK Nauka/Interperiodica **16**(1), 114–116 (2006)

Gurevich, I.B., Yashina, V.V., Fedorov, A.A., Nedzved, A.M., Ospanov, A.M.: Development, investigation, and software implementation of a new mathematical method for automated identification of the lipid layer state by the images of eyelid intermarginal space. Pattern Recognit. Image Anal. Adv. Math. Theory Appl. **27**(3), 53–549 (2017a)

Gurevich, I.B., Yashina, V.V., Fedorov, A.A., Nedzved, A.M.. Tleubaev. A.T.: Development, investigation, and software implementation of a new mathematical method for automatizing analysis of corneal endothelium images. Pattern Recognit. Image Anal. Adv. Math. Theory Appl. **27**(3), 550–559 (2017b)

Gurevich, I.B., Zhuravlev, Yu.I., Myagkov, A.A., Trusova, Yu.O., Yashina, V.V.: On basic problems of image recognition in neurosciences and heuristic methods for their solution. Pattern Recognit. Image Anal. Adv. Math. Theory Appl. **25**(1), 132–160 (2015)

Hirano, T., et al.: Vitreoretinal interface slab in OCT angiography for detecting diabetic retinal neovascularization. Ophthalmol. Retina **pii**, S2468-6530(20)30017-8 (2020). https://doi.org/10.1016/j.oret.2020.01.004

Hirano, T., Kitahara, J., Toriyama, Y., et al.: Quantifying vascular density and morphology using different swept-source optical coherence tomography angiographic scan patterns in diabetic retinopathy. Br. J. Ophthalmol. **103**, 216–221 (2019). https://doi.org/10.1136/bjophthalmol-2018-311942

João, V.B., et al.: Retinal vessel segmentation using the 2-D Morlet wavelet and supervised classification. IEEE Trans. Med. Imag. **25**(9), 1214–1222 (2006)

Nedzved, A., Nedzved, O., Glinsky, A., Karapetian, G., Gurevich, I.B., Yashina, V.V.: Detection of dynamical properties of flow in an eye vessels by video sequences analysis. In: Proceedings of the International Conference on Information and Digital Technologies, Zilina, Slovakia, 5–7 July, pp. 280–285. The Institute of Electrical and Electronics Engineers, Inc. (2017)

Olvera-Barrios, A., Heeren, T.F., Balaskas, K., et al.: Diagnostic accuracy of diabetic retinopathy grading by an artificial intelligence-enabled algorithm compared with a human standard for wide-field true-colour confocal scanning and standard digital retinal images. Br. J. Ophthalmol. (2020). https://doi.org/10.1136/bjophthalmol-2019-315394

Sauvola, J., Pietikainen, M.: Adaptive document image binarization. Pattern Recognit. **33**(2), 225–236 (2000)

Sinclair, S.H., Delvecchio, C.: The internist's role in managing diabetic retinopathy: screening for early detection. Cleve. Clin. J. Med. **71**(2), 151–159 (2004). https://doi.org/10.3949/ccjm.71.2.151

Shapiro, L.G., Stockman, G.C.: Computer Vision, pp. 137, 150. Prentice Hall, Englewood (2001)

Spaide, R.F., Fujimoto, J.G., Waheed, N.K., Sadda, S.R., Staurenghi, G.: Optical coherence tomography angiography. Prog Retin Eye Res. **64**, 1–55 (2018)

Spaide, R.F.: Volume-rendered optical coherence tomography of diabetic retinopathy pilot study. Am. J. Ophthalmol. **160**, 1200–1210 (2015)

Vermeer, K.A., Vos, F.M., Lemij, H.G., Vossepoel, A.M.: A model based method for retinal blood vessel detection. Comput. Biol. Med. **34**, 209–219 (2004)

Vujosevic, S., et al.: Screening for diabetic retinopathy: new perspectives and challenges. Lancet Diabetes Endocrinol. **8**(4), 337–347 (2020). https://doi.org/10.1016/S2213-8587(19)30411-5

Zhang, B., Zhang, L., Zhang, L., Karray, F.: Retinal vessel extraction by matched filter with first-order derivative of Gaussian. Comput. Biol. Med. **40**(4), 438–445 (2010)

MobileEmotiFace: Efficient Facial Image Representations in Video-Based Emotion Recognition on Mobile Devices

Polina Demochkina[✉] and Andrey V. Savchenko[ID]

HSE University, Nizhny Novgorod, Russia
pvdemochkina@edu.hse.ru, avsavchenko@hse.ru

Abstract. In this paper, we address the emotion classification problem in videos using a two-stage approach. At the first stage, deep features are extracted from facial regions detected in each video frame using a MobileNet-based image model. This network has been preliminarily trained to identify the age, gender, and identity of a person, and further fine-tuned on the AffectNet dataset to classify emotions in static images. At the second stage, the features of each frame are aggregated using multiple statistical functions (mean, standard deviation, min, max) into a single MobileEmotiFace descriptor of the whole video. The proposed approach is experimentally studied on the AFEW dataset from the EmotiW 2019 challenge. It was shown that our image mining technique leads to more accurate and much faster decision-making in video-based emotion recognition when compared to conventional feature extractors.

Keywords: Emotion recognition · Facial analysis · Face classification · Deep features · Convolutional neural networks (CNN) · Mobile device

1 Introduction

Nowadays there is a high demand for facial image models, representations, and features that can be used to improve the speed and accuracy of emotion recognition tasks. Existing methods for recognizing facial expressions in videos include temporal classification using Dynamic Bayesian Networks [1], spatial classification using Support Vector Machines (SVM) [2, 3], multiple kernel learning [4], and others. Nowadays it is typical to use deep neural networks in emotion recognition [5], as well as frame-attention networks [6] and a combination of recurrent networks and 3D convolutional networks [7].

It is known that image models trained using the above-mentioned techniques have performed well on the conventional Acted Facial Expressions in the Wild (AFEW) dataset [8] from EmotiW 2019 (Emotion Recognition in the Wild) challenge [9]. However, many of these approaches are ensemble methods that consider other modalities besides videos. Unfortunately, the speech of the person being recognized may be either completely unavailable or too complicated for reliable processing due to the presence

© Springer Nature Switzerland AG 2021
A. Del Bimbo et al. (Eds.): ICPR 2020 Workshops, LNCS 12665, pp. 266–274, 2021.
https://doi.org/10.1007/978-3-030-68821-9_25

of noise or voices of other subjects. Moreover, the run-time and space complexities of the best image models are too high for many practical applications. One of the main challenges here is the limited run-time complexity of the devices that would be used on-premises to perform inference of the learned models on real-world data.

Thus, in this paper, we propose a lightweight approach that we called MobileEmotiFace. We examine the possibility to develop a representation of a facial image suitable for emotion recognition in videos. In particular, we automatically analyze large, detailed databases of static facial images, e.g., AffectNet [10], and extract useful information about emotional faces. Our main contribution consists of, firstly, the MobileNet-based feature extractor model that was pre-trained to identify the age, gender, and identity of a person [10, 11] and then additionally fine-tuned on the AffectNet dataset [10]. Secondly, we propose the novel representation of a set of video frames with the same face that is calculated by concatenating statistical functions, e.g., mean, min, max, standard deviation (std) of MobileNet features extracted from each frame of the given video. It was experimentally shown that the usage of simple linear SVM for such MobileEmotiFace video descriptor leads to rather accurate and very fast decision-making.

The remaining part of the paper is structured as follows. Section 2 consists of a detailed description of the proposed approach. Section 3 contains experimental results for the AFEW dataset [8] and a comparison of our technique to the conventional solutions by accuracy and time. Concluding comments are given in Sect. 4.

2 Proposed Approach

The task of the paper can be formulated as follows: it is necessary to assign an emotion (class) label $c_n \in \{1,...,C\}$ to an input sequence of video frames $\{X(t)\}, t = 1, 2,..., T$. Here t is the number of the frame, T is the total number of frames in the video sample., and C is the total number of emotional classes. For simplicity, we assume that every video clip contains a single person in each frame.

The proposed pipeline is presented in Fig. 1. Since the key information about an emotion is encoded in the facial expression of the observed person, it is necessary to detect a facial region in each frame of a given video with e.g., MTCNN [12]. In the case when a face is not found on a frame, the entire frame is passed to the network. If multiple faces are detected, the face with the maximal detection score is used.

Then deep facial features are extracted from every detected facial region, which is used in RGB format. While it is common to use facial descriptors from pre-trained networks, such as VGGFace (VGG-16) [13], VGGFace2 (ResNet-50) [14], ResFace, CenterFace, etc., the above-mentioned models are characterized by considerable computational time and complexity. To speed up this step, we decided to borrow the lightweight multi-output extension [11] of the MobileNet v1 model that was pre-trained for identity prediction on VGGFace2 dataset. It is impossible to use identity features for emotion recognition because the facial features of the same person with different emotions should be approximately identical in order to achieve accurate face recognition. Hence, we fine-tuned this model to classify seven basic human emotions (Anger, Disgust, Fear, Happiness, Neutral, Sadness, and Surprise) from the large emotional dataset AffectNet [10]. Since AffectNet is highly imbalanced, the softmax loss function with class weights was used during fine-tuning. We use the output from the penultimate layer of this network is used to extract 1024-dimensional feature vectors for every video frame.

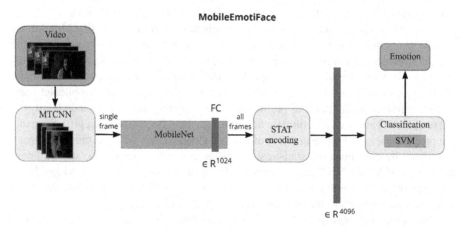

Fig. 1. Proposed MobileEmotiFace pipeline

For feature-level frame aggregation, we use a statistical (STAT) encoding module that was proposed by Bargal et al. [3]. We concatenate the mean, variance, minimum, and maximum of the features over all frames, which produces a single feature vector quadrupled in size that represents the entire video. After that, we apply L2 normalization globally to the resulting video descriptor. Finally, the classification module consists of training a linear SVM for classification using the resulting feature vectors.

The proposed pipeline was implemented in a mobile emotion recognition demo application[1], which can predict the emotion of each person in a given input image or video. A sample screenshot from the application demonstrates the emotion recognition results for a sample input image (Fig. 2).

Fig. 2. An example of emotion recognition in the demo application.

---

[1] https://github.com/HSE-asavchenko/MADE-mobile-image-processing/tree/master/lesson6/src/FacialProcessing.

3   Experimental Results

In the experimental study, we used the AFEW dataset [8] from EmotiW 2019 [9], which consists of short video clips extracted from movies. The train set contains 773 video files, and the validation set contains 383 videos. Every sample belongs to one of the $C = 7$ categories presented in the dataset, namely, Neutral class (207 training examples) and 6 basic emotions: Anger, Disgust, Fear, Happiness, Sadness, and Surprise with 197, 114, 127, 212, 179 and 120 examples, respectively. Keras 2.2 framework with TensorFlow 1.15 backend was used in all experiments.

The first experiment was conducted to choose the best facial detector (Table 1). We examined the proposed MobileEmotiFace method (Fig. 1) and considered 2 different detectors: MTCNN [12] and the facial detector from Dlib. Here, firstly, the detector from the Dlib library had a higher false positive rate than the MTCNN detector. Secondly, the usage of MTCNN in our MobileEmotiFace made it possible to increase the overall accuracy by 3.92% in comparison to the results obtained using the Dlib detector that was used in many emotion recognition methods [2].

Table 1. Dependence of emotion recognition accuracy on face detector.

Facial detector	Accuracy (%)
MTCNN	54.05
Dlib	50.13

In the next experiment, we examined different pre-processing techniques and their combinations to see how they affect the accuracy of the trained model. We considered applying L2 normalization, rootSIFT normalization, and global standardization to the deep facial features extracted in the MobileEmotiFace pipeline (Fig. 1). In addition, we tried to remove the max statistics from the STAT encoding as proposed in [2]. The top-6 combinations that gave the best results on the validation set are presented in Table 2.

Table 2. Preprocessing/postprocessing for the MobileEmotiFace facial features

Max features?	L2 norm	rootSIFT	Standardization	Accuracy (%)
+	+	−	−	**54.05**
+	−	+	−	53.26
−	+	−	−	53.26
+	−	+	+	52.48
−	−	+	−	52.22
−	−	+	+	51.96

Here the best results were achieved when applying just L2 normalization to the feature vectors causing the Euclidean distance between normalized features to be equivalent to the cosine similarity. Removing the max features from the STAT encoding appeared to have a negative effect on the accuracy in all cases.

In the next experiment, we compared our approach with existing emotion recognition methods (Table 3). Here one can notice that the proposed technique is 15.25% more accurate than the baseline of the EmotiW 2019 sub-challenge and on par with the best performing single neural models that only use the video modality. Another model that we looked at is an LSTM model that utilizes our MobileEmotiFace facial features as an input. However, this combination of feature extractor and classification model based on LSTM did not prove to be effective for the AFEW 8.0 dataset.

Table 3. Validation accuracy of known techniques for AFEW 8.0 dataset

Method	Details	Modality	Accuracy (%)
Hu et al. [15]	Ensemble	Audio, video	59.01
Kaya et al. [16]	Ensemble	Audio, video	57.02
VGG13 + VGG16 + ResNet [3]	Ensemble	Video	59.42
Four face recognition networks [2]	Ensemble	Video	55.17
Noisy student with iterative training [17]	Single model	Video	55.17
Noisy student w/o iterative training [17]	Single model	Video	52.49
DenseNet-161 [18]	Single model	Video	51.44
FAN [6]	Single model	Video	51.18
VGG-Face [19]	Single model	Video	49.00
VGG-Face + LSTM [20]	Single model	Video	48.60
DSN-HoloNet [15]	Single model	Video	46.47
LBP-TOP (baseline) [9]	Single model	Video	38.90
Our MobileNet + LSTM	Single model	Video	48.85
Proposed MobileEmotiFace (SVM)	Single model	Video	**54.05**

It is known [2] that the usage of facial descriptors pre-trained on face identification, e.g., VGG-Face, VGGFace2, ResFace, etc. may be used to increase the accuracy of emotion classifiers [21, 22]. However, we decided to test the hypothesis that models pre-trained to identify facial attributes (such as age and gender) before being fine-tuned on external datasets, extract better quality features than those models that skip the pre-training step. Therefore, we compare the validation accuracy of our MobileEmotiFace network that was pre-trained to identify the age, gender, and identity of a person before the fine-tuning step, to other networks, namely VGGFace, VGGFace2, MobileNet v1, Inception v3, and EfficientNet v3, that were not trained beforehand to identify facial attributes. These models were fine-tuned on AffectNet [10], used as feature extractors in the proposed pipeline to train a linear SVM (Fig. 1), and evaluated on the AFEW

8.0 dataset. In this setup, Inception v3 and EfficientNet v3 models reached the best accuracy when using all functions from the STAT encoding module (mean, std, min, max), while the best result for MobileNet v1 was achieved with only 1 statistical function (mean). The remaining two networks performed better with 3 statistics: mean/std/min for VGGFace with and mean/min/max for VGGFace2. For VGGFace we used the 4096-dimensional outputs from the fc6 layer as face embeddings, while for the VGGFace2 network we used the 2048-dimensional feature vectors obtained from the layer before the last one. We applied L2 normalization to these feature vectors, put them through the STAT encoding module, and trained a linear SVM. All the results are summarized in Table 4. The proposed MobileEmotiFace (Fig. 1) outperformed all other models that skipped either pre-training on face recognition or emotion classification. Thus, this result proves our hypothesis that only fine-tuning models on an external large dataset for the face recognition task is not enough: preliminary training of networks for the recognition of facial attributes significantly boosts the performance on the emotion recognition task. Moreover, existing facial descriptors (VGGFace and VGGFace2) that were not fine-tuned on external datasets did not perform well.

Table 4. Validation accuracy of linear SVM for features extracted by various models

Neural model	Pre-training	Fine-tuning	Accuracy (%)
Proposed MobileEmotiFace	VGGFace2	AffectNet	**54.05**
EfficientNet v3	ImageNet	AffectNet	50.65
ResNet-50 (VGGFace2)	VGGFace2	AffectNet	50.13
Inception v3	ImageNet	AffectNet	49.35
MobileNet v1	ImageNet	AffectNet	46.74
VGG-16 (VGGFace)	VGGFace	AffectNet	43.86
ResNet-50 (VGGFace2)	VGGFace2	–	40.47
VGG-16 (VGGFace)	VGGFace	–	39.94

Additionally, we studied the size and inference time (Table 5) of several models using the proposed pipeline (Fig. 1). Unfortunately, most of the known methods do not provide the inference time, so we took it upon ourselves to calculate it for the most frequently used facial descriptors in combination with an SVM, namely, VGGFace (VGG-16) and VGGFace2 (ResNet-50). We decided to compute the feature extraction time and the time it takes to complete the postprocessing and classification step since the feature should be extracted from each frame depends on the number of frames in a given video, while the latter step runs for the descriptor of the whole video. Therefore, the feature extraction (inference) time is measured in milliseconds per face by using either CPU (12 core AMD Ryzen Threadripper) or GPU (Nvidia GTX1080TI) on a special server. The classification time (average number of milliseconds per input video) is measure on CPU only because simple linear SVM is used and this time depends only on the dimensionality of video descriptor. As can be seen from Table 5, our feature extractor is faster than the widely used VGGFace and VGGFace2 models of facial images, which results in improved total inference time, allowing our approach to be used on mobile devices and other gadgets with limited run-time complexities.

Table 5. Performance of emotion recognition models

Method	Feature extraction time, ms		Classification time, ms	Model size, Mb
	CPU	GPU	CPU	
MobileEmotiFace	20.6	4.8	0.38	13.5
VGGFace2 (pre-trained)	56.2	10.1	0.68	90.3
VGGFace (pre-trained)	103.6	7.6	1.13	448.0

4 Conclusion

The specificity, complexity, and difficulties of emotional image analysis for real-time video analytics on mobile devices stem from the necessity to achieve some balance between such highly contradictory factors as appropriate classification accuracy, fast decision-making, and small size of the neural model. In this paper, we proposed a novel efficient MobileEmotiFace approach (Fig. 1) for the emotion recognition task in videos. Our main idea is a two-step training procedure. At first, the face recognition model is trained on a very large dataset, e.g., VGGFace2 [14]. Secondly, this model is fine-tuned on a large dataset with emotional labels, e.g., AffectNet [10]. It was experimentally shown that such approach leads to higher accuracy when compared to either the conventional VGGFace/VGGFace-2 facial descriptors or fine-tuning of neural networks on AffectNet if these networks were pre-trained on ImageNet-1000 (Table 4). Moreover, our method is one of the most accurate techniques with single neural networks, though deeper models are sometimes slightly more accurate (Table 3). Finally, the proposed pipeline is very efficient (Table 5) and can be implemented in mobile applications (Fig. 2). In the future, it is necessary to study the possibility to use audio modality to further improve the accuracy of our model. Moreover, our current model simply treats the whole video as a set of frames. Indeed, the first attempts to use LSTMs were not successful (Table 3). However, it is important to train the state-of-the-art networks, e.g., attention models [6], to further improve emotion recognition accuracy.

Acknowledgements. The work is supported by RSF (Russian Science Foundation) grant 20–71–10010.

References

1. Walecki, R., Rudovic, O., Pavlovic, V., Pantic, M.: Variable-state latent conditional random fields for facial expression recognition and action unit detection. In: 2015 11th IEEE International Conference and Workshops on Automatic Face and Gesture Recognition (FG), vol. 1, pp. 1–8. IEEE (2015)
2. Knyazev, B., Shvetsov, R., Efremova, N., Kuharenko, A.: Convolutional neural networks pretrained on large face recognition datasets for emotion classification from video. arXiv preprint arXiv:1711.04598 (2017)
3. Bargal, S.A., Barsoum, E., Ferrer, C.C., Zhang, C.: Emotion recognition in the wild from videos using images. In: Proceedings of the 18th ACM International Conference on Multimodal Interaction, pp. 433–436 (2016)
4. Sikka, K., Dykstra, K., Sathyanarayana, S., Littlewort, G., Bartlett, M.: Multiple kernel learning for emotion recognition in the wild. In: Proceedings of the 15th ACM on International conference on multimodal interaction, pp. 517–524 (2013)
5. Khorrami, P., Le Paine, T., Brady, K., Dagli, C., Huang, T.S.: How deep neural networks can improve emotion recognition on video data. In: 2016 IEEE international conference on image processing (ICIP), pp. 619–623. IEEE (2016)
6. Meng, D., Peng, X., Wang, K., Qiao, Y.: Frame attention networks for facial expression recognition in videos. In: 2019 IEEE International Conference on Image Processing (ICIP), pp. 3866–3870. IEEE (2019)
7. Fan, Y., Lu, X., Li, D., Liu, Y.: Video-based emotion recognition using CNN-RNN and c3d hybrid networks. In: Proceedings of the 18th ACM International Conference on Multimodal Interaction, pp. 445–450 (2016)
8. Dhall, A., Goecke, R., Lucey, S., Gedeon, T.: Collecting large, richly annotated facial-expression databases from movies. IEEE multimedia, 3, 34–41. IEEE (2012)
9. Dhall, A.: EmotiW 2019: Automatic emotion, engagement and cohesion prediction tasks. In: 2019 International Conference on Multimodal Interaction, pp. 546–550 (2019)
10. Mollahosseini, A., Hasani, B., Mahoor, M.H.: AffectNet: A database for facial expression, valence, and arousal computing in the wild. IEEE Transactions on Affective Computing 10(1), 18–31 (2017)
11. Savchenko, A.V.: Efficient facial representations for age, gender and identity recognition in organizing photo albums using multi-output ConvNet. PeerJ Computer Science 5, e197 (2019)
12. Zhang, K., Zhang, Z., Li, Z., Qiao, Y.: Joint face detection and alignment using multitask cascaded convolutional networks. IEEE Signal Processing 23(10), 1499–1503 (2016)
13. Parkhi, O.M., Vedaldi, A., Zisserman, A.: Deep face recognition. British Machine Vision Association (2015)
14. Cao, Q., Shen, L., Xie, W., Parkhi, O.M., Zisserman, A.: Vggface2: A dataset for recognising faces across pose and age. In: 2018 13th IEEE International Conference on Automatic Face & Gesture Recognition (FG 2018), pp. 67–74. IEEE (2018)
15. Hu, P., Cai, D., Wang, S., Yao, A., Chen, Y.: Learning supervised scoring ensemble for emotion recognition in the wild. In: Proceedings of the 19th ACM international conference on multimodal interaction, pp. 553–560 (2017)
16. Kaya, H., Gürpınar, F., Salah, A.A.: Video-based emotion recognition in the wild using deep transfer learning and score fusion. Image Vis. Comput. 65, 66–75 (2017)
17. Kumar, V., Rao, S., Yu, L.: Noisy Student Training using Body Language Dataset Improves Facial Expression Recognition. arXiv preprint arXiv:2008.02655 (2020)
18. Liu, C., Tang, T., Lv, K., Wang, M.: Multi-feature based emotion recognition for video clips. In: Proceedings of the 20th ACM International Conference on Multimodal Interaction, pp. 630–634 (2018)

19. Aminbeidokhti, M., Pedersoli, M., Cardinal, P., Granger, E.: Emotion recognition with spatial attention and temporal softmax pooling. In: Karray, F., Campilho, A., Yu, A. (eds.) ICIAR 2019. LNCS, vol. 11662, pp. 323–331. Springer, Cham (2019). https://doi.org/10.1007/978-3-030-27202-9_29

20. Vielzeuf, V., Pateux, S., Jurie, F.: Temporal multimodal fusion for video emotion classification in the wild. In: Proceedings of the 19th ACM International Conference on Multimodal Interaction, pp. 569–576 (2017)

21. Kaya, H., G̈urpınar, F., Salah, A.A.: Video-based emotion recognition in the wild using deep transfer learning and score fusion. Image Vision Comput., **65**, 66–75 (2017)

22. Rassadin, A., Gruzdev, A., Savchenko, A.: Group-level emotion recognition using transfer learning from face identification. In: Proceedings of the 19th ACM International Conference on Multimodal Interaction, pp. 544–548 (2017)

Basic Models of Descriptive Image Analysis

Igor Gurevich$^{(\boxtimes)}$ ⓘ and Vera Yashina ⓘ

Federal Research Center "Computer Science and Control" of the Russian Academy of Sciences,
44/2, Vavilov Street, Moscow 119333, Russian Federation
igourevi@ccas.ru, werayashina@gmail.com

Abstract. This paper is devoted to the basic models of descriptive image analysis, which is the leading branch of the modern mathematical theory of image analysis and recognition.

Descriptive analysis provides for the implementation of image analysis processes in the image formalization space, the elements of which are various forms (states, phases) of the image representation that is transformed from the original form into a form that is convenient for recognition (i.e., into a model), and models for converting data representations. Image analysis processes are considered as sequences of transformations that are implemented in the phase space and provide the construction of phase states of the image, which form a phase trajectory of the image translation from the original view to the model.

Two types of image analysis models are considered: 1) models that reflect the general properties of the process of image recognition and analysis – the setting of the task, the mathematical and heuristic methods used, and the algorithmic content of the process: a) a model based on a reverse algebraic closure; b) a model based on the equivalence property of images; c) a model based on multiple image models and multiple classifiers; 2) models that characterize the architecture and structure of the recognition process: a) a multilevel model for combining algorithms and source data in image recognition; b) an information structure for generating descriptive algorithmic schemes for image recognition.

A brief description, a comparative analysis of the relationships and specifics of these models are given. Directions for further research are discussed.

Keywords: Descriptive image analysis · Image analysis models · Image recognition · Image analysis · Image mining · Image models · Models of image transformations processes · Modeling · Descriptive algorithmic schemes

1 Introduction

This paper is devoted to basic models of descriptive image analysis (DA), which is the leading branch of the modern mathematical theory of image analysis and recognition. Its rationale and the process of formation are described in the article [1]; the main publications on DA are also given there.

This work was supported in part by the Russian Foundation for Basic Research (Project No. 20-07-01031).

© Springer Nature Switzerland AG 2021
A. Del Bimbo et al. (Eds.): ICPR 2020 Workshops, LNCS 12665, pp. 275–288, 2021.
https://doi.org/10.1007/978-3-030-68821-9_26

The theoretical basis of DA is a Descriptive approach to the analysis and understanding of images, proposed by I. B. Gurevich and developed by his students [2, 3].

Common methods of standardization in applied mathematics and computer science are the construction and use of mathematical and simulation models of objects under study and procedures used for their transformation. Due to the extremely complex informational nature and technical features involved in the digital representation of an image, it is impossible to construct a classical mathematical model of an image as an information object.

When working with images, the correct result is achieved if the analysis is based on the use of some formalized description of the image that properly represents it, as much as possible corresponds to a priori knowledge and context, and is compatible with the problem being solved. In this sense, the synthesis of a formalized image description is an optimization problem, and its solution must be stable, meet the time and other resource constraints determined by the nature of the applied problem, and, if possible, have a certain generality, i.e., allow use in solving new problems.

When recognizing (i.e., when formalizing an image as an object of recognition), the" content " of an image is characterized by four types of information: a) identifiable objects with a well-defined structure; b) identifiable objects with a poorly defined structure; C) unidentifiable objects; d) background, i.e., in general, everything else.

The standard form of representing images as feature vectors is not the best in all problems, since such a representation loses a large amount of information that the image contains or "represents". On the other hand, the specifics of pattern recognition problems are such that not all information about a new recognition object is necessary for its successful classification. Applied problems use representations of images as a matrix (raster), as a set of features, as chains of transformation of one image to another, and many others. When using a model image representation, it is not always possible to reconstruct the source image, but it is possible to successfully classify it.

In order to achieve correspondence between the algebraic representation of algorithms and unformalized information specified in the form of images, it is proposed to formalize the types of image representations to which they are brought. To do this, DA classes of image models were selected [4].

DA provides the ability to solve both problems related to the construction of formal descriptions of images as recognition objects, and problems of synthesis of recognition and image understanding procedures. The operational approach to image characterization provides that in general, the processes of analyzing and evaluating information presented in the form of images-the trajectory of problem solving-can be considered as a certain sequence/combination of transformations and calculating a certain set of intermediate and final (decision-making) estimates.

Consider the set of acceptable representations of images [5] as a set of "phase states" of the image ("source image", "image realization", intermediate states of the image, "parametric image model", "procedural image model", "generating image model").

Let also the set of admissible algorithmic schemes for image transformation form a set of "phase states" - a set of descriptive algorithmic schemes (DAS). DAS is a certain transformation system applied to the source image, which implements mathematical methods for image processing, analysis, and recognition and provides: a) construction of a model or representation of an image that allows the use of classical or "spatial" recognition algorithms by means of sequential transformation of the "states "of the processed image corresponding to the degree of its current" formalization; b) solving the problem of image recognition by applying recognition algorithms to the image model/representation constructed in accordance with paragraph "a" of this definition.

Image Formalization Scheme (IFS) [5] includes states (phases of formal description/representation) of an image and many "states" of image transformation schemes. In this sense, the IFS is a phase space. The topology of this space can be defined by some algebraic system, namely descriptive image algebras (DIA) [6], defining operations on image elements, their values, and the image "states" representations constructed as a result of applying these operations.

The IFS consists of image models and data transformation models.

DA provides for the implementation of image analysis processes in IFS, the elements of which are various forms (states, phases) of the image representation that is converted from the original form to a form that is convenient for recognition (i.e., to a model), and models for converting data representations. Image analysis processes are considered as sequences of transformations that are implemented in the phase space and provide the structure of the phase States of the image, which together form the phase trajectory of the image translation from the original view to the model. The study of IFS leads to the formalization of the concepts of image representation/model, as well as to the construction of models of image recognition and analysis processes and the formulation of mathematical statements of problems of image recognition and analysis.

The paper provides a brief description of the models. A comparative analysis of the relationships and specifics of the models is carried out. Directions for further research are discussed.

2   Descriptive Image Models and Representations in Image Analysis

The structure of relations between the considered descriptive models and image representations in image analysis is shown in Fig. 1.

Figure 1 shows two types of descriptive image models and representations: a) block «Models and Representations of Data» (up arrow); b) block «Models of Image Recognition and Analysis Processes» (down arrow).

The solution of the image recognition problem assumes the presence of certain image representations, the presence of effective recognition algorithms, and the compliance of the used image representations with the requirements of the recognition algorithms for the source data [6].

Let us consider the source data and its representation in the process of solving the image recognition and analysis problem in more detail. [7]. There are two fundamentally different types of image representation (block «Models and Representations of Data»):

1. using a system of objects and relationships that are selected in the image (in Fig. 1 - «Descriptive Image Models» [8]);

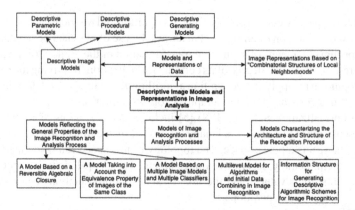

Fig. 1. Descriptive image models and representations in image analysis

2. using representations of the "combinatorial structures of local neighborhoods" type)- the spatial information itself (for example, image fragments-pixels or pixel aggregates that form a local neighborhood of some order on the image) (in Fig. 1, this type of representation is specified in the block "Image Representations based on Combinatorial Structures of Local Neighborhoods").

Semantic information presented in the image or associated with the reproduced scene allows you to use a variety of contextual information for analysis and recognition (forbidden and impossible order relations, partial order relations, and other conditions and restrictions that reflect the physical and logical organization of the real world). To apply the recognition algorithm, it is necessary to use procedures to bring the source data to a form that is convenient for recognition.

In the first case, the procedures for converting the source data to a form that is convenient for recognition should ensure the construction of a mathematical model of the image. In DA, descriptive image models are selected as formalized models: parametric, procedural, and generative models (see the corresponding blocks in Fig. 1).

In the second case, the recognition algorithm must accept the source data, which is the image itself or its fragments (block «Image Representations based on Combinatorial Structures of Local Neighborhoods»). For recognition, "spatial" algorithms are used (algorithms that allow spatial information as the source), and the procedures for bringing the source data to a form that is convenient for recognition are generally reduced to image segmentation, choosing the shape of fragments that are used to compare the recognized and standard objects, splitting the image into fragments, and so on.

The recognition algorithms used to process each of the two types of image representation differ.

Let us consider the block "Models of Image Recognition and Analysis Processes" in more detail. During the development of DA, two types of models were built, which are reflected in the corresponding blocks in Fig. 1:

1. block «Models Reflecting the General Properties of the Image Recognition and Analysis Process» ;
2. block «Models Characterizing the Architecture and Structure of the Recognition Process» .

Models of image recognition and analysis processes reflect the problem statement, mathematical and heuristic methods used, and the algorithmic content of the process. These models include: a model based on a reverse algebraic closure [9]; a model based on the equivalence property of images of the same class [10]; a model based on multiple image models and multiple classiferis [8] (see the corresponding blocks in Fig. 1).

The model of image recognition and analysis based on reverse algebraic closure provides a multi-level and multi-aspect structure of the recognition process. All transformations are implemented by the method of reverse algebraic closure.

The model that takes into account image equivalence is based on the following assumptions: a) the image is a partial representation of some (scene); b) on a set of images, you can determine the equivalence relation corresponding to the image belonging to the same scene. This model leads to 2 new formulations of the image recognition problem.

A model based on multiple models and algorithms implements the principles of multi-algorithmicity and multi-modelness and uses the merging of results obtained for individual algorithms and models. The model provides: a) parallel application of several different algorithms for processing the same model and several different models of the same source data; b) combining the results to increase the exact solution.

Models that characterize the architecture and structure of the recognition process include: a multi-level model for combining algorithms and source data in image recognition (MMCAI) [11]; information structure for generating DAS for image recognition (ISG DAS) [12] (see the corresponding blocks in Fig. 1).

MMCAI is based on the joint use of methods for combining algorithms and methods for combining fragmentary source data-partial descriptions of the object of analysis and recognition - images. The architecture, functionality, limitations, and characteristics of this class of models are justified and defined.

ISG DAS is a tool for representing and implementing information processing while solving an image recognition problem for arbitrary formulations, scenarios, models, and solution methods; it can also emulate any descriptive algorithmic scheme and combinations thereof, which are used and generated when solving an image recognition problem.

3   Models Reflecting the General Properties of the Image Recognition and Analysis Process

3.1   A Model Based on a Reversible Algebraic Closure

DA defines the standard organization of information processing and presentation procedures for solving recognition problems. The structure of the recognition process is multilevel and multiaspect. When considering each level/aspect, the features used to build an image model corresponding to this level/aspect are selected, searched for, or calculated. The following features are used: statistical, topological, geometric, structural and spectral characteristics of the image and its local fragments (neighborhoods), generalized features-objects selected in the image, procedures-features that establish the admissibility of defining standard transformation systems in the image, features that characterize the results of applying standard transformation systems to the image and its local neighborhoods (spans, mid-axes). When selecting features, we use knowledge about the subject area and logical and physical constraints inherent in the scene presented in the image. The model is synthesized within each aspect/level by the method of reverse algebraic closure. Moving from a lower-level model ("initial sketch") to models of higher levels and, ultimately, to the desired description that serves as a solution to the recognition problem, it is carried out using transformations that are also included in the structure of the reverse algebraic closure. The organization of the recognition process is structured both horizontally (when building an image model) and vertically (when actually "recognizing") in the sense that each iteration is implemented as a reverse algebraic closure.

The model based on the reverse algebraic closure of images is described in more detail in [9] and presented in Fig. 2.

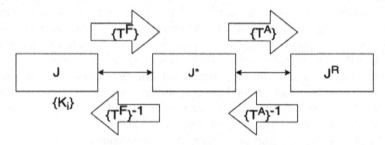

Fig. 2. A model based on a reversible algebraic closure of images.

In Fig. 2: $\{J\}$ is a set of ideal images; $\{J^*\}$ is a set of the observed images; $\{J^R\}$ is a set of images - results of solving the recognition problem; $\{T^F\}$ is a set of acceptable transformations that lead to image formation; $\{T^A\}$ is a set of acceptable transformations that lead to image recognition; $\{K_i\}$, $i = 1, \ldots, m$ are equivalence classes.

Let J is some true image of the object being studied. The process of obtaining, forming, sampling, etc. (all the procedures necessary to work with the image) can be considered as the transmission of a true image over a channel with interference. As a result, the subject of analysis is not a true image, but a real (observed) image J^*. In the process of analysis, the latter must be classified, i.e. the prototype must be defined in the true equivalence class, or the regularity (regularity) of the given type J^R should be detected on the image J^*.

This way it can be defined the sets $\{J\}$, $\{J^*\}$ and $\{J^R\}$ and transformations of image generations (T^F) and image recognition (T^A):

$$T^F : J \rightarrow J^* \tag{1}$$

$$T^A : J^* \rightarrow J^R \tag{2}$$

Image recognition is reduced to determining algebraic transformation systems $\{T^F\}$ и $\{T^A\}$ on the equivalence classes of the set $\{J\}$ and applying them to the observed images J^* for:

a) analysis of "back" - separation images in accordance with the nature of regularity (the restoration of true images, i.e. an indication of the equivalence classes to which they belong);

b) analysis of "forward" - search on the image of J^* regularities of the definite type J^R and their localization.

This formulation of the analysis problem allows us to define a class of image processing procedures characterized by a fixed structure of the analysis process, and the interpretation (specific implementation) depends on the goals and type of analysis.

The introduction of a descriptive model based on a reversible algebraic closure of images leads to the introduction of special mathematical formulations of the problem of image analysis and recognition.

3.2   A Model Taking into Account the Equivalence Property of Images of the Same Class

One of the main ideas of the proposed approach to image recognition is the idea that a particular image is not the only possible visual representation of objects, but only one of the possibilities. This means that the same objects can correspond to other images that differ in scale, viewing angle, lighting, and so on. Thus, the problems of image recognition from the point of view of this approach are as follows: a) the image is a partial representation of some entity (object, scene), which can only be used as such partial descriptions; b) on a set of images, you can determine the equivalence relation corresponding to the image belonging to the same entity; c) images from the same class must have the same belonging vectors; d) the transition from images to features is not set in advance, so in real problems, you can vary the features.

The equivalence relation on a set of images can be entered in different ways [10]. Recall that the equivalence relation must be reflexive, symmetric, and transitive, and it splits the entire set of images into disjoint classes – image equivalence classes.

$Z(I_0,S_1,...,S_q,P_1,...,P_l)$ is a recognition problem where I_0 is acceptable initial information, $S_1,...,S_q$ are acceptable objects described by feature vectors, $K_1,...,K_l$ are recognition classes, $P_1,...,P_l$ are predicates on acceptable objects, $P_i = P_i(S)$, $i = 1,2,...,l$. Problem Z is to find the values of $P_1 ...,P_l$.

The problem statement is as follows. A set of K objects is given for which classification is performed. It is known that the set K is representable as a sum of subsets $K_1, \ldots, K_l$, called classes: $K = \bigcup_{j=1}^{l} K_j$. Some information about classes is set $I_0(K_1, \ldots, K_l)$.

In accordance with the approach described above, images are visual representations of some entity S (object, scene), and each scene s corresponds to a set of images that differ in mass, viewing angle, lighting, and etc. In other words, these images are equivalent (in the sense of one of the definitions given in [10]). Consider a situation where each of the images is represented by a vector of invariant features.

The main task is to use information about classes $I_0(K_1, \ldots, K_l)$ and image description $I \ D(I) = (a_1, a_2, \ldots, a_n)$ to calculate predicate values $P_j(I) - I \in K_j, j = 1, 2, \ldots, l$.

Let A is a recognition algorithm that translates the training information $I_0(K_1, \ldots, K_l) = I_0(l)$ and the image description $D(I) = (a_1, a_2, \ldots, a_n)$ into the information vector $\left\{\alpha_j^A\right\}_{1 \times l}$ where $\alpha_j^A = 1$ if the image I belongs to class K_j, $\alpha_j^A = 0$ if the image I doesn't belong class K_j, $\alpha_j^A = \Delta$ if the algorithm didn't determine whether or not the image I belongs to class $K_j, j = 1, \ldots, l$. It can be written:

$$A(I_0(l), D(I)) = \left\{\alpha_j^A\right\}_{1 \times l}.$$

Since when solving real image recognition problems, we are not dealing with objects, but only with their images, we will assume that the entire set of images is somehow divided into equivalence classes. At the same time, we assume that there is a correspondence between the image equivalence classes and objects, but in the future we will not mention objects in the statement of the recognition problem. Taking into account the introduced concept of image equivalence [10], the problem of image recognition can be formulated as follows.

$$Z^1(\left\{I_i^{j_i}\right\}_{i=1,2,\ldots,q}^{j_i=1,2,\ldots,p_i}, \{M_i\}_{i=1,2,\ldots,q}, \{K_t\}_{t=1,2,\ldots,l}, \left\{P_t^{ij_i}\right\}_{t=1,2,\ldots,l}^{i=1,2,\ldots,q;j_i=1,2,\ldots,p_i}) \quad \text{is}$$

a recognition problem Z^1 where $\left\{I_i^{j_i}\right\}$ are images, $i = 1, 2, \ldots, q$, j_i is an image number inside the i-th equivalence class, p_i – is a number of images in the i-th equivalence class, $j_i = 1, 2, \ldots, p_i$; $M_i = \left\{I_{i_1}, I_{i_2}, \ldots, I_{i_{pi}}\right\}$, $i = 1, 2, \ldots, q$, are equivalence classes on the set $\left\{I_i^{j_i}\right\}$; $K_1, K_2, \ldots, K_l$ are classes in the problem of image recognition; $P^{ij_i} : I_i^{j_i} \in K_t, t = 1, 2, \ldots, l, i = 1, 2, \ldots, q, j_i = 1, 2, \ldots, p_i$ are predicates. The problem Z^1 is to find the values of the predicates $P_t^{ij_i}$.

The difference between Z^2 and problem Z^1 is that each equivalence class is replaced by a single image – a representative of the class – with the number n_i, $1 \leq n_i \leq p_i$, where i is the number of equivalence class.

$Z^2(\{I_i^{n_i}\}_{i=1,2,\ldots,q}^{1 \leq n_i \leq p_i}, \{K_t\}_{t=1,2,\ldots,l}, \{P_t^i\}_{t=1,2,\ldots,l}^{i=1,2,\ldots,q})$ is a recognition problem Z^2 where $I_i^{n_i}$, $i = 1, 2, \ldots, q$ are images, $I_i^{n_i} \in M_i$; $K_1, K_2, \ldots, K_l$ are classes in the problem of image recognition; $P_t^i : I_i^{n_i} \in K_t, t = 1, 2, \ldots, l, i = 1, 2, \ldots, q$ are predicates. The problem Z^2 is to find the values of the predicates P_t^i.

3.3 A Model Based on Multiple Image Models and Multiple Classifiers

This model is characterized by a tendency to multiplicity (multi-algorithm and multi-model) and merging of results – i.e., to parallel use of several different algorithms for processing the same model and several different models of the same source data when solving a problem, followed by combining the results to obtain the most accurate solution (see Fig. 3). Common means of implementing these multiplicities and merges are multiple classifiers (MAC) [13, 14] and multimodal and multiaspect representations of images. Note that the first and fundamental results in this direction were obtained by Yu. I. Zhuravlev in the 1970s [15].

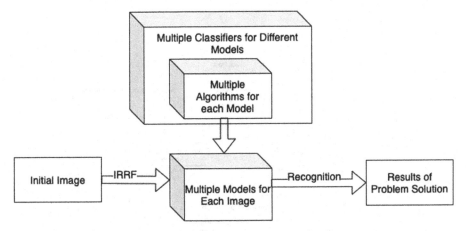

Fig. 3. A model based on multiple image models and multiple classifiers.

DA provides for significant use of combining algorithms within multialgorithmic schemes and extensive use of multimodel and multi-aspect representations of images in recognition problems. The central problem is reducing images to a form that is easy to recognize (recognizable form) (RIRF).

4   Models Characterizing the Architecture and Structure of the Recognition Process

4.1   Multilevel Model for Algorithms and Initial Data Combining in Image Recognition

In the paper [11] a new class of models for the image analysis and recognition process and its constituent procedures is introduced and described – a multilevel model of image analysis and recognition procedures (MMCAI) – which is based on the joint use of methods of combining algorithms and methods of combining fragmentary initial data – partial descriptions of the object of analysis and recognition – an image. The architecture, functionality, limitations, and characteristics of the MMCAI are justified and defined.

The main properties of the MMCAI class are as follows: (a) combining the fragments of the initial data and their representations and combining algorithms at all levels of image analysis and recognition processes; (b) the use of multialgorithmic schemes in the image analysis and recognition process; and (c) the use of dual representations of images as input data for the analysis and recognition algorithms. The problems arising in the development of the MMCAI are closely related to the development of the following areas of the modern mathematical theory of image analysis: (a) algebraization of image analysis [16]; (b) image recognition algorithms accepting spatial information as input data [17]; (c) multiple classifiers (MACs) [13, 14].

A new class of models for image analysis is introduced in order to provide the following possibilities: (a) standardization, modeling, and optimization of DAS that form the brainware of the MMCAI and processing heterogeneous ill-structured information

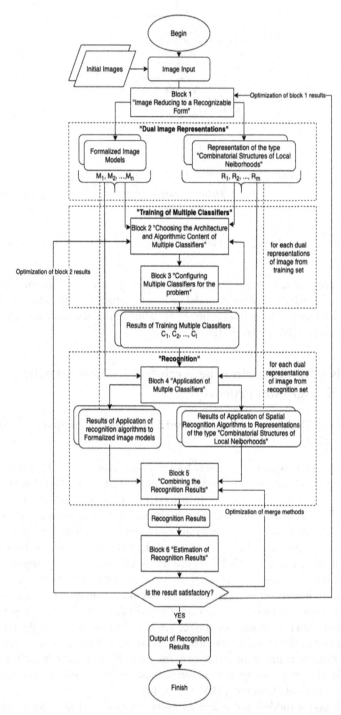

Fig. 4. Block scheme of the model MMCAI based on combined use of MAC and dual representations of initial data.

– dual representations – spatial, symbolic, and numerical representations of the Initial data; (b) comparative analysis, standardization, modeling, and optimization of different algorithms for the analysis and recognition of spatial information.

The introduction of the MMCAI as a standard structure for representing algorithms for the analysis and recognition of two-dimensional information and dual representations of images allow one to generalize and substantiate well-known heuristic recognition algorithms and assess their mathematical properties and applied utility.

The main features of the MMCAI architecture are as follows:

1. the joint use of MACs and dual representations of initial data;
2. combination of data and algorithms at three levels of processing, analysis, and recognition of the initial data, including images.

The implementation of the mechanism for the joint use of MACs and the dual representations of the initial data of the CSLN/formalized model type is represented by the block diagram shown in Fig. 4. In [11] we gave a description of the model of the image analysis implemented in accordance with the block diagram within the MMCAI model.

4.2 Information Structure for Generating Descriptive Algorithmic Schemes for Image Recognition

This study [12] is devoted to regularizing the generation of descriptive algorithmic image analysis and recognition schemes. The main result is the definition of a new mathematical structure with the following functional capabilities: 1) solution of an image recognition problem in a given formulation, with given initial data and a scenario that determines the sequence of application of information processing procedures and their iterative loops; 2) construction of descriptive algorithmic schemes for solving a problem with given initial data in the absence of a given scenario; in the case of a successful solution, the fixation of the sequence of procedures and information processing loops that yielded its solution governs the corresponding descriptive algorithmic schemes and scenarios that can be further used to solve the corresponding class of image recognition problems; 3) comparative analysis and optimization of methods for solving image recognition problems via their realization as descriptive algorithmic schemes and scenarios allowed by the structure.

The introduced structure is a tool for representing and implementing information processing while solving an image recognition problem for arbitrary formulations, scenarios, models, and solution methods; it can also emulate any DAS and combinations thereof, which are used and generated when solving an image recognition problem.

The introduced structure is interpreted as a fundamental model for generating and emulating image recognition procedures.

A type characteristic of the introduced information structure for generating descriptive algorithmic schemes is as follows: 1) the set of structure elements consists of two subsets: a) a subset of functional blocks that perform mathematical operations of information processing necessary to implement the used of processing, analysis, and image recognition methods; b) a subset of control blocks for information processing procedures, which verify the logical conditions for branching of processing procedures, whether the

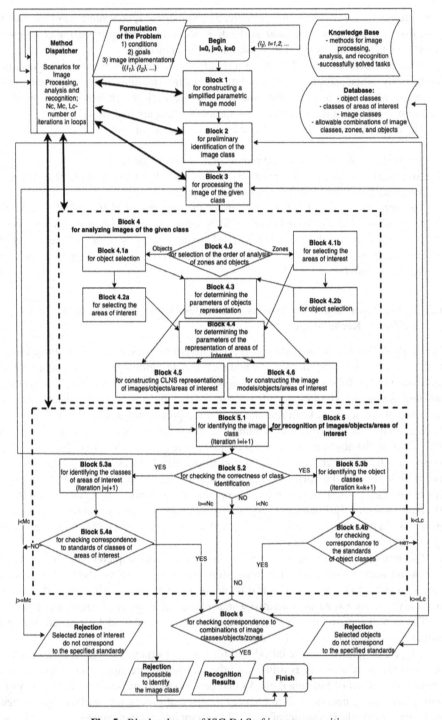

Fig. 5. Block scheme of ISG DAS of image recognition.

rules for stopping information processing are met, etc.; 2) relations given over the elements of the set of the structure, mainly, the partial ordering relations that determine the sequence of execution and methods for combining the functional and control blocks of the structure; 3) these relations, by definition, must satisfy the axioms of the Descriptive Approach to Image Analysis and Understanding.

Since this structure is interpreted in this context as a mathematical model of information processing processes in solving problems of image recognition and emulation of sequences and combinations of transformations that ensure the implementation of these processes, we will call the introduced structure the information structure for generating DAS (ISG DAS).

The paper [12] presents the basic definitions associated with the introduction of a new information structure and describes the information processing procedures implemented therein, as well as the main blocks and loops. Block diagrams of the information structure is given in Fig. 5. Detailed description of blocks is in [12].

5 Conclusion

The fundamental task of the research is to automate the extraction of information from images that is necessary for making intelligent decisions.

The fundamental importance of these studies for the development of the mathematical theory of image analysis and their scientific novelty are associated with the objectives and development of methods of modeling of processes of automation of image analysis when used as input poorly formalized representations of the images comprising actual spatial data – images and their fragments, image models, not a fully formalized representations and subsets of combinations of these representations.

Further research in this area is expected to be devoted to the definition, construction, and research of a generalized information structure that provides modeling capabilities for both the recognition methodology used, including the mathematical apparatus, and the structural properties of recognition processes – multilevel, multi-algorithmic, and multi-model. The strategic goal is to use it as a standard information structure for presenting algorithms for analyzing and recognizing 2-dimensional information and presenting procedures for constructing dual representations of images in the form of DAS. Automating and regularizing the generation of such DAS will allow you to generalize and justify well-known heuristic recognition algorithms, conduct their comparative analysis, and evaluate their mathematical properties and applied utility.

References

1. Gurevich, I.B., Yashina, V.V.: Descriptive image analysis. genesis and current trends. Pattern Recogn. Image Anal.: Adv. Math. Theory Appl. **27**(4), 653–674 (2017)
2. Gurevitch, I.B.: The descriptive framework for an image recognition problem. In: 6th Scandinavian Conference on Image Analysis, vol. 1, pp. 220–227 (1989). Pattern Recognition Society of Finland

3. Gurevich, I.: The descriptive approach to image analysis. current state and prospects. In: Kalviainen, J., Parkkinen, A.K. (eds.) 14th Scandinavian Conference on Image Analysis, LNCS, vol. 3540, pp. 214–223. Springer, Heidelberg (2005). https://doi.org/10.1007/114991 45_24

4. Gurevich, I.B., Yashina, V.V.: Descriptive approach to image analysis: image models. Pattern Recog. Image Anal. Adv. Math. Theory Appl. **18**(4), 518–541 (2008)

5. Gurevich, I.B., Yashina, V.V.: Descriptive approach to image analysis: image formalization space. Pattern Recognition and Image Analysis: Advances in Mathematical Theory and Applications **22**(4), 495–518 (2012)

6. Gurevich, I.B., Yashina, V.V.: Descriptive image analysis. foundations and descriptive image algebras. Int. J. Pattern Recogn. Artif. Intell. **33**(12), 1940018-1–1940018-25 (2019)

7. Gurevich, I.B., Yashina, V.V.: Descriptive image analysis: III. multilevel model for algorithms and initial data combining in pattern recognition. Pattern Recogn. Image Anal. **30**(3), 328–341 (2020)

8. Gurevich, I.B., Yashina, V.V.: Descriptive image analysis: part II. descriptive image models. Pattern Recogn. Image Anal. **29**(4), 598–612 (2019). https://doi.org/10.1134/S10546618190 40035

9. Gurevitch, I.B.: Image analysis on the base of reversing algebraic closure technique. In: The Problems of Artificial Intelligence and Pattern Recognition, Scientific Conference with Participation of Scientists from Socialistic Countries (Kiev, May 13–18 1984), pp. 41—43. V.M. Glushkov Institute of Cybernetics of the Academy of Sciences of the Ukrainian SSR (1984). [in Russian]

10. Gurevich, I.B., Yashina, V.V.: Computer-aided image analysis based on the concepts of invariance and equivalence. Pattern Recogn. Image Anal. Adv. Math. Theory Appl. **16**(4), 564–589 (2006)

11. Gurevich, I.B., Yashina, V.V.: Descriptive image analysis: iii. multilevel model for algorithms and initial data combining in pattern recognition. Pattern Recogn. Image Anal.: Adv. Math. Theory Appl. **30**(3), 328–341 (2020)

12. Gurevich, I.B., Yashina, V.V.: Dscriptive image analysis: part iv. information structure for generating descriptive algorithmic schemes for image recognition. Pattern Recogn. Image Anal. Adv. Math. Theory Appl. **30**(4), 649–665 (2020)

13. Kittler, J., Hatef, M., Duin, R., Matas, J.: On combining classifiers. IEEE Trans. Pattern Anal. Machine Intell. **20**(3), 226–239 (1998)

14. Suen, C.Y., Lam, L.: Multiple classifier combination methodologies for different output levels. In: Kittler, J., Roli, F. (eds.) MCS 2000. LNCS, vol. 1857, pp. 52–66. Springer, Heidelberg (2000). https://doi.org/10.1007/3-540-45014-9_5

15. Zhuravlev, Y.I.: An algebraic approach to recognition and classification problems. Pattern Recogn. Image Anal. Adv. Math. Theory Appl. **8**, 59–100 (1998)

16. Gurevich, I.B. Yashina V.V.: Descriptive image analysis. genesis and current trends. In: Pattern Recognition and Image Analysis: Advances in Mathematical Theory and Applications, Pleiades Publishing, Ltd. **27**(4), 653–674 (2017)

17. Gurevich, I.B., Nefyodov, A.V.: Block diagram representation of a 2d-aec algorithm with rectangular support sets. Pattern Recogn. Image Anal. Adv. Math. Theory Appl. **15**(1), 187–191 (2005)

Evaluation of Spectral Similarity Measures and Dimensionality Reduction Techniques for Hyperspectral Images

Evgeny Myasnikov$^{(\boxtimes)}$ (iD)

Samara University, Moskovskoe Shosse 34A, 443086 Samara, Russia
mevg@geosamara.ru

Abstract. Hyperspectral data is becoming more and more in demand these days. However, its effective use is hindered by significant redundancy. In this paper, we analyze the effectiveness of using common dimensionality reduction methods together with known measures of spectral similarity. In particular, we use Euclidean distance, spectral angle mapper, and spectral divergence to measure dissimilarity in hyperspectral space. For the mapping to lower-dimensional space, we use nonlinear methods, namely, Nonlinear Mapping, Isomap, Locally Linear Embedding, Laplacian Eigenmaps, and UMAP. Quality assessment is performed using known hyperspectral scenes based on the results provided by the nearest neighbor classifier and support vector machine.

Keywords: Hyperspectral image · Dimensionality reduction · PCA · Nonlinear mapping · Isomap · Locally linear embedding · Laplacian eigenmaps · UMAP

1 Introduction

Hyperspectral images differ from full-color images primarily by their high spectral resolution and spectral range. These differences determine not only their discriminatory properties but also significant redundancy, which entails additional costs for their processing and storage.

Redundancy elimination can be performed using compression methods. However, compressed data cannot be directly used for solving applied problems, since preliminary decompression is required.

In the case when the target indicators of applied problems are known, feature selection techniques based on the optimization of such indicators are effective means of redundancy elimination. But in this case, significant efforts are required to generate the labeled training data.

In connection with the above, unsupervised dimensionality reduction techniques have become increasingly popular. In this paper, we use nonlinear methods, namely, Isomap [1], Locally Linear Embedding (LLE) [2], Laplacian Eigenmaps [3], Nonlinear Mapping (NLM) [4], and Uniform Manifold Approximation

© Springer Nature Switzerland AG 2021
A. Del Bimbo et al. (Eds.): ICPR 2020 Workshops, LNCS 12665, pp. 289–300, 2021.
https://doi.org/10.1007/978-3-030-68821-9_27

and Projection (UMAP) [5] as well as the linear Principal Component Analysis (PCA) [6] technique to tackle the problem of redundancy elimination.

The nonlinear dimensionality reduction techniques listed above have already been used earlier for the analysis of hyperspectral images, but this was done, as a rule, in combination with Euclidean distances. There are only a few works in which particular dimensionality reduction methods are used with alternative dissimilarity measures (see [7–11] for examples).

In this paper, we combine these general-purpose dimensionality reduction methods with three dissimilarity measures often used in hyperspectral image analysis, namely, Euclidean distance, Spectral Angle Mapper (SAM) [12] and Spectral Information Divergence (SID) [13]. Particularly, we use these measures to evaluate the dissimilarity between image pixels in hyperspectral space and apply nonlinear dimensionality reduction techniques to embed high-dimensional data into lower-dimensional reduced space. Then we utilize the Nearest Neighbor (NN) and Support Vector Machine (SVM) classifiers to assess the quality of the embeddings. The analysis is done using several known hyperspectral scenes available online.

The paper has the following structure. Section 2 is devoted to the brief description of dimensionality reduction techniques used in the paper. Section 3 describes the results of the experiments. The paper ends up with the conclusion and the list of references.

2   Methods

2.1   Dimensionality Reduction Techniques Used in the Study

In this study, we use both linear PCA and nonlinear dimensionality reduction methods. A brief description of the used techniques is given below.

In this section, we assume that the hyperspectral dataset X consists of N vectors (data points) $x_i, i = 1..N$ in the multidimensional hyperspectral space R^M. The result Y of a particular dimensionality reduction technique consists of corresponding vectors $y_i, i = 1..N$ in the lower-dimensional space R^m.

Principal Component Analysis. The Principal Component Analysis technique [6] is the most well-known linear dimensionality reduction technique, which is used in a wide range of applications. This method searches for a linear projection into the subspace of a smaller dimensionality that maximizes the variance of data. The general idea of PCA consists in solving the eigenvalue problem:

$$C = W^T \Lambda W, \tag{1}$$

where C is the covariance matrix $C = X^T X$, W is the matrix of eigenvectors, Λ is the diagonal matrix of eigenvalues λ_k of the covariance matrix. After the subsequent sorting of eigenvalues in the descending order and the corresponding rearrangement of columns in the matrix W of eigenvectors, the linear projection of the dataset X can be obtained using truncation of the matrix W:

$$Y = XW_m,\qquad(2)$$

where W_m is a truncated M x m matrix of principal components.

Nonlinear Mapping. The Nonlinear Mapping (NLM) method is based on the principle of preserving the pairwise distances between data points. While the basics of this method were developed in the 1960-s in works by J. B. Kruskal [14] and J. W. Sammon [4], here we use a different version of the method [10], which differs from the base method in PCA-based initialization and stochastic gradient descent.

The considered method is a gradient descent based technique, which minimizes the following data mapping error:

$$\varepsilon_{ED} = \mu \cdot \sum_{i,j=1,i<j}^{N} \rho_{ij}(d(x_i, x_j) - d(y_i, y_j))^2,\qquad(3)$$

where $d()$ is a distance function, which is usually the Euclidean distance, μ and ρ_{ij} are constants, which define a specific error function. In this paper, we used

$$\mu = \left(\sum_{i<j} d^2(x_i, x_j)\right)^{-1}, \rho_{i,j} = 1.\qquad(4)$$

The implemented method consists of the following steps:

1. Initialization of low-dimensional coordinates $y_i(t_0), i = 1..N$ using PCA.
2. Iterative refinement of the embedding coordinates of points:

$$y_i(t+1) = y_i(t) + 2\alpha\mu \cdot \sum_{j=1}^{L} \frac{d(x_i, x_{r_j}) - d(y_i, y_{r_j})}{d(y_i, y_{r_j})} \cdot (y_i(t) - y_{r_j}(t)).\qquad(5)$$

Here t is the number of an iteration, r is a random subsample used to approximate the gradient at the iteration t of the optimization process, r_j is the j-th element of this subsample, L is the cardinality of subset r, α is the coefficient of the gradient descent (step size).

ISOMAP. Isomap method was introduced by J. B. Tenenbaum in papers [1,15]. The main idea of this method consists in the use of geodesic distances instead of Euclidean distances in classical metric multidimensional scaling (MDS).

This method can be briefly described as the following:

1. Given the set $X = \{x_i\}, i = 1..N$ of data points in a high dimensional space R^M, find neighbor points $\mathcal{N}_i$ of each data point $x_i, i = 1..N$.
2. Construct the neighborhood graph $G = <V, E>$, which vertices $V = \{v_i\}, i = 1..N$ correspond to the data points x_i. Edges $E = \{(v_i, v_j)\}, v_i \in V, v_j \in \mathcal{N}_i$ connect only neighbor data points, and the weights of edges are defined by Euclidean distances between corresponding data points:

$$w_{i,j} = \sqrt{(x_i - x_j)^T (x_i - x_j)}. \tag{6}$$

3. Compute the shortest path distances $W = \{W_{i,j}\}, i, j = 1..N$ between all pairs of data points using the Floyd-Warshall (or Dijkstra) algorithm.
4. Perform multidimensional scaling to compute low-dimensional coordinates $Y = \{y_i\} i = 1..N$ of data points.

Locally Linear Embedding. The Locally Linear Embedding (LLE) technique was introduced by S. T. Roweis and L. K. Saul in the paper [2]. This technique is based on the idea that each particular data point and its neighbors lie close to a locally linear patch of the nonlinear manifold, and can be reconstructed as a linear combination of its neighbors in both high-dimensional and embedding spaces.

This technique consists of the following three steps:

1. Given the set $X = \{x_i\}, i = 1..N$ of data points in a high-dimensional space R^M, find neighbor points $\mathcal{N}_i$ of each data point $x_i, i = 1..N$.
2. Find reconstruction weights $W_{i,j}$ by minimizing the reconstruction error

$$\varepsilon(W) = \sum_i \left(x_i - \sum_j (W_{i,j} x_j) \right)^2 \tag{7}$$

with constraints:

$$\sum_j W_{i,j} = 1, i = 1..N, \textbf{ and } W_{i,j} = 0, i = 1..N, j \notin \mathcal{N}_i. \tag{8}$$

3. Map data points $\{x_i\}, i = 1..N$ to their low-dimensional representations $\{y_i\}, i = 1..N$ by minimizing

$$\Phi(Y) = \sum_i \left(y_i - \sum_j (W_{i,j} y_j) \right)^2. \tag{9}$$

Laplacian Eigenmaps. The Laplacian Eigenmaps technique was introduced by M. Belkin and P. Niyogi in the paper [3]. This technique is based on the eigenvalue decomposition of the graph Laplacian matrix. It consists of the following three steps:

1. Given the set $X = \{x_i\}, i = 1..N$ of data points in a high dimensional space R^M, find neighbor points $\mathcal{N}_i$ of each data point $x_i, i = 1..N$.
2. Construct the neighborhood graph $G = < V, E >$, which vertices $V = \{v_i\}, i = 1..N$ correspond to the data points x_i. Edges $E = \{(v_i, v_j)\}, v_i \in V, v_j \in \mathcal{N}_i$ connect only neighbor data points, and the weights of edges are equal to 1 (first option) or defined by the Heat kernel (second option):

$$W_{i,j} = exp(-||x_i - x_j||^2/t). \tag{10}$$

3. Construct a diagonal weight matrix D:

$$D_{i,i} = \sum_j W_{i,j} \tag{11}$$

and the Laplacian matrix $L = W - D$. Then solve the eigenvector problem:

$$LY = \lambda DY \tag{12}$$

The solution Y_m in the embedding space R^m is given by the first m vectors $y_1..y_m$ in the matrix Y after rearranging vectors $y_i, i = 1..M$ according to their eigenvalues.

Uniform Manifold Approximation and Projection. The Uniform manifold approximation and projection technique (UMAP) was introduced by L. McInnes, J. Healy, and J. Melville and later described in the paper [5].

This technique consists in constructing a weighted graph, followed by force-directed placement of the graph into low-dimensional space. The main steps of the method are described below:

1. Given the set $X = \{x_i\}, i = 1..N$ of data points in a high dimensional space R^M, find the sets η_i consisting of k neighbor points for each data point $x_i, i = 1..N$.
2. For each i-th data point, find its nearest neighbor and the distance

$$\rho_i = min(d(x_i, x_j)|x_j \in \eta_i, d(x_i, x_j) > 0) \tag{13}$$

as well as the value σ_i so that

$$\sum_{x_j \in \eta_i} exp\left(\frac{-max(0, d(x_i, x_j) - \rho_i)}{\sigma_i}\right) = log_2 k. \tag{14}$$

3. Construct the UMAP graph G as an undirected weighted graph with an adjacency matrix

$$B = A + A^t - A \circ A^t, \tag{15}$$

where the elements of A are given by weights in the corresponding directed graph:

$$w(x_i, x_j) = exp\left(\frac{-max(0, d(x_i, x_j) - \rho_i)}{\sigma_i}\right). \tag{16}$$

4. The coordinates $y_i, i = 1..N$ of the data points in low dimensional space are defined by the force-directed placement of the graph using the following attractive F^a and repulsive F^r forces between vertices i and j (a, b, ϵ are constant parameters):

$$F_{i,j}^a = \frac{-2ab\|y_i - y_j\|_2^{2(b-1)}}{1 + \|y_i - y_j\|_2^2} w(x_i, x_j)(y_i - y_j), \tag{17}$$

$$F_{i,j}^r = \frac{b}{(\epsilon + \|y_i - y_j\|_2^2)(1 + \|y_i - y_j\|_2^2)}(1 - w(x_i, x_j))(y_i - y_j). \tag{18}$$

Integration of Spectral Similarity Measures in Nonlinear Dimensionality Reduction Techniques. In all the nonlinear techniques described above, it is assumed that the Euclidean distance is used as a dissimilarity measure. As we said in the Introduction, in this paper, we also use the SAM and SID measures.

The SAM measure is defined as the following [12]:

$$\theta(x_i, x_j) = arccos\left(\frac{x_i \cdot x_j}{\|x_i\|\|x_j\|}\right). \tag{19}$$

The SID measure is given by the expression [13]:

$$SID(x_i, x_j) = D(x_i\|x_j) + D(x_j\|x_i), \tag{20}$$

$$D(x_i\|x_j) = \sum_{k=1}^{M} p_k(x_i)log(p_k(x_i)/p_k(x_j)), \tag{21}$$

$$p_k(x_i) = \frac{x_{ik}}{\sum_{l=1}^{M} x_{il}}. \tag{22}$$

In this paper, we use quite a straightforward approach to use the above measures with the described nonlinear techniques. In particular, for the Nonlinear Mapping technique, we replace the calculation of Euclidean distances in hyperspectral space with the calculation of a given measure in the data mapping error (3). According to [10], this replacement does not lead to any changes in the recurrence Eq. (5) other than the replacement of the corresponding Euclidean distances $d(x_i, x_{r_j})$ with the given measures. In fact here we try to approximate the SAM or SID measures by Euclidean distances in the reduced space.

In the ISOMAP technique, we use the given measures to find neighbor points at step 1 and to define the weights of edges (see Eq. (6)) at step 2.

In the Locally linear embedding method, we use given measures only to find neighbor points at step 1.

In the Laplacian Eigenmaps technique, we use given measures to find neighbor points at step 1 and to define the Heat kernel (see Eq. (10)) at step 2.

In the UMAP technique, the given measures are used at steps 1–3. In particular, we use the measures to form the sets of neighbor points in step 1. Then, in step 2, we use the given measures to find the nearest points, the distances ρ_i, and the parameters σ_i. Later, the measures affect the graph construction in step 3 as they are involved in weights' calculation.

3   Experiments

Experimental Setup. For the reported study, we used several well-known hyperspectral image scenes [16], which were supplied with ground-truth segmentation. A brief description of the used images is given in the Table 1 below.

Table 1. Test hyperspectral image scenes.

Scene	Sensor	Height	Width	Number of bands
Indian pines	AVIRIS	145	145	220(200)
Salinas	AVIRIS	512	217	224(204)
Botswana	Hyperion	1476	256	145
Kennedy space center	AVIRIS	512	614	176

As almost all the presented image scenes contain more than 100000 pixels, and it was necessary to perform a lot of runs of nonlinear dimensionality reduction techniques, in some cases we used regularly sampled test images, which could optionally be masked with ground-truth masks for the experiments.

To perform the experiments, we used PCA implementation provided with Matlab, C++ implementation of Nonlinear Mapping method, and for LLE, Laplacian Eigenmaps, and Isomap, we used Matlab Toolbox for Dimensionality Reduction [17]. We used the UMAP implementation installed by PyPI.

As was said in the introduction, we used the Nearest Neighbor (NN) and Support Vector Machine (SVM) classifiers to estimate the embeddings generated by dimensionality reduction techniques. Besides, we selected the overall classification accuracy (*Acc*), defined as the proportion of correctly classified pixels of the test set, as a quality indicator. To obtain train and test subsets, we split the set of ground truth pixels with a 60:40 proportion.

Experimental Results. In our first experiment, we evaluated different dimensionality reduction techniques in normal mode, i.e. when the Euclidean distance serves as a similarity measure. To perform the experiment, we varied the output dimensionality from 2 to 20, performed dimensionality reduction, split the sample, trained two classifiers on the training subset and estimated the classification accuracy on the test subset.

The results of the experimental study are shown in Fig. 1. As it can be seen in the figure, in almost all the considered cases, UMAP outperforms other techniques in low-dimensional embeddings for $Dim \leq 3$. With the growth of the output dimensionality, the advantages of UMAP disappear, and NLM and PCA techniques take leadership for $Dim = 10..20$. Here NLM seems to be more appropriate choice for the NN classifier. For the SVM classifier, we cannot choose between them, except KSC image.

It is worth noting that KSC image was the most tricky for the linear PCA technique. The accuracy was about 40% for $Dim = 2, 3$ and even for $Dim = 20$, PCA results stayed below any other nonlinear technique. UMAP and NLM provided the best results here, nevertheless.

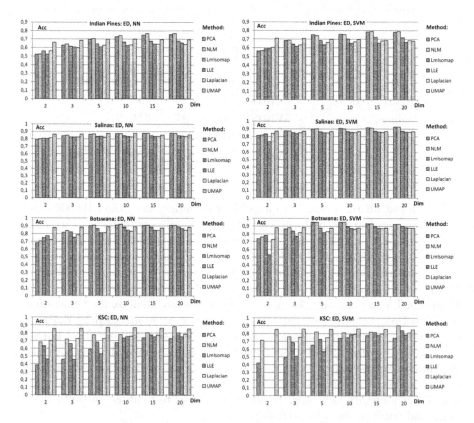

Fig. 1. Classification accuracy Acc for the evaluated dimensionality reduction techniques based on the Euclidean distance (ED) for NN classifier (left column) and SVM classifier (right column).

In our second experiment, we studied the performance of the dimensionality reduction techniques with the SAM as a similarity measure. The results of this experiment are shown in Fig. 2. As can be seen, we can make similar conclusions here: in most cases, UMAP provided the best results for $Dim \leq 3$. In many other cases, NLM seems to be a good choice for the NN classifier, and PCA is slightly better for SVM (except KSC).

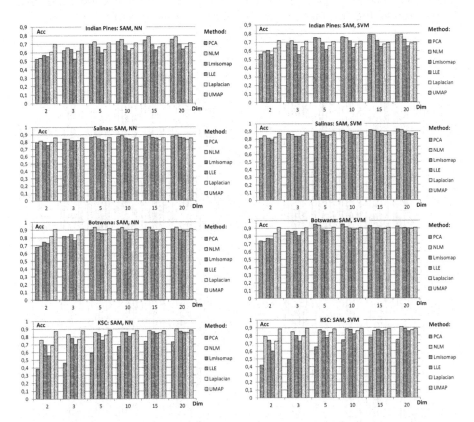

Fig. 2. Classification accuracy Acc for the evaluated dimensionality reduction techniques based on the Spectral angle mapper (SAM) for NN classifier (left column) and SVM classifier (right column).

Our third experiment included the study of the SID measure. Figure 3 presents the results of this experiment. In this case, we observed that UMAP was the first for $Dim \leq 5$ for the NN classifier and for $Dim \leq 3$ for SVM. Besides, it outperformed all the other techniques for the KSC image. For other images and for $Dim \geq 5$ (for SVM), the best results were provided by linear PCA.

Surprisingly, NLM was the weakest technique in almost all cases when the SID measure is used. It seems that the generated embeddings poorly approximate source SID values by Euclidean distances. It is worth noting, however, that there is a specialization of the nonlinear mapping technique for the SID measure, namely, Spectral Divergence Preserving Mapping (SDPM) described in [11]. SDPM provided much higher accuracy when working with SID measures. For example, it provided 80.7% accuracy for $Dim = 10$ at the Indian Pines scene, which is more than 7% higher than the PCA (best) approach. Nevertheless, we do not provide a comparison to SDPM here as this technique cannot be considered as a general-purpose, and the utilization of SDPM embeddings assumes that corresponding classifiers based on the SID measure are used.

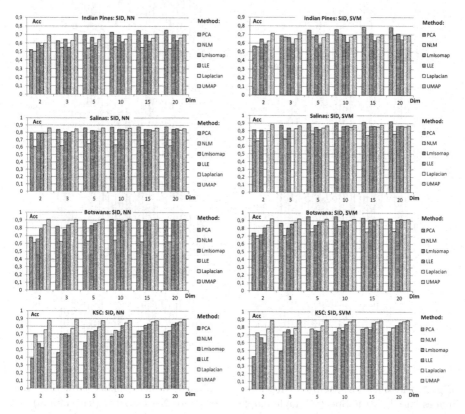

Fig. 3. Classification accuracy Acc for the evaluated dimensionality reduction techniques based on the Spectral information divergence (SID) for NN classifier (left column) and SVM classifier (right column).

Finally, to show the best result for all the images and dimensionalities, we present Table 2.

As it can be seen in the table, for low dimensionalities $Dim = 2, 3$, the UMAP technique can be used with SAM or SID measures. For higher dimensionalities $Dim = 10..20$, NLM with SAM measure seems to be a preferable choice for the

Table 2. Best combinations of measures and techniques.

NN classifier						
Dim	2	3	5	10	15	20
IPc	UMAP,SAM	UMAP,SID	NLM,SAM	NLM,SAM	NLM,SAM	NLM,SAM
SLc	UMAP,ED	UMAP,ED	UMAP,ED	NLM,SAM	NLM,SAM	NLM,SAM
BO	UMAP,SAM	UMAP,SAM	NLM,SAM	NLM,SAM	NLM,SAM	NLM,SAM
KSC	UMAP,SID	UMAP,SID	UMAP,SID	UMAP,SID	UMAP,SID	NLM,SAM
SVM classifier						
Dim	2	3	5	10	15	20
IPc	UMAP,SAM	NLM,SAM	PCA	PCA	NLM,ED	NLM,ED
SLc	UMAP,SID	UMAP,SAM	NLM,ED	PCA	PCA	PCA
BO	UMAP,SID	UMAP,SID	PCA	NLM,ED	NLM,ED	NLM,ED
KSC	UMAP,SAM	UMAP,SAM	UMAP,SAM	UMAP,SAM	UMAP,SAM	NLM,SAM

NN classifier. For the SVM classifier and higher dimensionalities, the choice is not obvious, as NLM with ED shares the place with PCA.

4   Conclusion

In this paper, we analyzed the effectiveness of common dimensionality reduction methods together with known measures of spectral similarity. In particular, we studied linear PCA as well as Nonlinear Mapping, Isomap, LLE, Laplacian eigenmaps, and UMAP dimensionality reduction techniques. Besides, we considered Euclidean distance, SAM, and SID as similarity measures.

To evaluate the quality of the embeddings produced by the considered techniques in combination with the above measures, we estimated the classification accuracy of the NN and SVM classifiers using four known hyperspectral scenes.

The experiments showed that for low output dimensionalities (2,3), the best results are provided by the UMAP technique with SAM or SID measures. For higher dimensionalities (10..20), NLM with SAM seems to be a preferable choice for the NN classifier. For the SVM classifier and higher dimensionalities, the NLM or PCA can be used.

It is worth noting that for hyperspectral scenes containing noisy data or substantial nonlinear effects, the traditional PCA can be a bad choice, and nonlinear techniques should be considered.

Acknowledgment. The reported study was funded by RFBR according to the research project no. 18-07-01312-a.

References

1. Tenenbaum, J.B., de Silva, V., Langford, J.C.: A global geometric framework for nonlinear dimensionality reduction. Science **290**, 2319–2323 (2000)
2. Roweis, S.T., Saul, L.K.: Nonlinear dimensionality reduction by locally linear embedding. Science **290**, 2323–2326 (2000)

3. Belkin, M., Niyogi, P.: Laplacian eigenmaps and spectral techniques for embedding and clustering. Adv. Neural Inf. Process. Syst. **14**, 585–591 (2001)
4. Sammon, J.W.: A nonlinear mapping for data structure analysis. Trans. Comput. **18**, 401–409 (1969)
5. McInnes, L., Healy, J., Melville, J.: Umap: uniform manifold approximation and projection for dimension reduction. arXiv:1802.03426 (2018)
6. Fukunaga, K.: Introduction to Statistical Pattern Recognition, 2nd edn. Academic Press, London (2003)
7. Bachmann, C.M., Ainsworth, L., Fusina, R.A.: Exploiting manifold geometry in hyperspectral imagery. IEEE Trans. Geosci. Remote Sens. **43**(3), 441–454 (2005)
8. Ding, L., Tang, P., Li, H.: Dimensionality reduction and classification for hyperspectral remote sensing data using ISOMAP. Infrared Laser Eng. **6**(10), 2707–2711 (2013)
9. Du, P., Wang, X., Tan, K., Xia, J.: Dimensionality reduction and feature extraction from hyperspectral remote sensing imagery based on manifold learning. Geomatics Inf. Sci. Wuhan Univ. **36**(2), 148–152 (2011)
10. Myasnikov, E.: Nonlinear mapping based on spectral angle preserving principle for hyperspectral image analysis. In: Felsberg, M., Heyden, A., Krüger, N. (eds.) CAIP 2017. LNCS, vol. 10425, pp. 416–427. Springer, Cham (2017). https://doi.org/10.1007/978-3-319-64698-5_35
11. Myasnikov, E.: Nonlinear dimensionality reduction of hyperspectral data based on spectral information divergence preserving principle. J. Phys. Conf. Ser. **1368**, 032030 (2019)
12. Kruse, F.A., et al.: The Spectral Image Processing System (SIPS) - interactive visualization and analysis of imaging spectrometer data. Remote Sens. Environ. **44**, 145–163 (1993)
13. Chang, C.-I.: Hyperspectral Data Processing: Algorithm Design and Analysis. Wiley, Hoboken (2013)
14. Kruskal, J.B.: Multidimensional scaling by optimizing goodness of fit to a nonmetric hypothesis. Psychometrika **29**, 1–27 (1964)
15. Tenenbaum, J.: Mapping a manifold of perceptual observations. In: Jordan, M., Kearns, M., Solla, S. (eds.) Advances in Neural Information Processing, vol. 10, pp. 682–688. MIT Press, Cambridge (1998)
16. Hyperspectral Remote Sensing Scenes. http://www.ehu.eus/ccwintco/index.php?title=Hyperspectral_Remote_Sensing_Scenes
17. Van der Maaten, L.J.P., Postma, E.O., van den Herik, H.J.: Dimensionality Reduction: A Comparative Review. Tilburg University Technical Report, TiCC-TR 2009-005 (2009)

Maximum Similarity Method for Image Mining

Viacheslav Antsiperov$^{(\boxtimes)}$

Kotelnikov Institute of Radioengineering and Electronics of RAS, Mokhovaya 11-7,
Moscow, Russian Federation
antciperov@cplire.ru

Abstract. The paper discusses a new Image Mining approach to extracting and
exploring relations in the image repositories. The proposed approach, called Maximum Similarity Method, is based on the identification of characteristic fragments
in images by a set of predefined patterns. Such an identification is basically carried
out as a comparison of the fragment intensity shape with the shapes of already
registered patterns - precedents. Mathematically (statistically) such a comparison
implies a selection of some measure of similarity and optimization (maximization) of that measure on a set of precedents. In the paper, basing on the principles
of machine learning, a special type of similarity measure is proposed, and its
reliability is discussed. In fact, this measure represents conditional probability
distribution of the registered data - counts of a fragment tested when analogous
data for the patterns are given. So, the search for the optimal precedent pattern
that maximized the chosen similarity measure constitutes the proposed method.

Keywords: Big data · Image metadata · Precedent–based identification · Naive
bayes model · Instance-based learning · Nearest neighbor classification

1 Introduction

Over the past few decades, almost all areas of human activity have meet with an avalanche
growth of digital technologies. First of all, the miscellaneous services of the World Wide
Web should be noted here. The number of the Web services is increasing now thick and
fast before our eyes and, in turn, motivating the development of new directions in the
digital data applications. That motivation is primarily due to the parallel growth of the
new data produced by WWW. Now this phenomenon is referred to as the Big Data
problem and it is the main challenge for modern information, communication, control,
management, and other technologies [1].

The problem of Big Data is obviously multidimensional – it is not measured by the
only characteristic – the mammoth amount of produced digital data. In fact there is a
full spectrum of Big Data characteristics that needs careful consideration.

Basing on the experience accumulated, the following three most important characteristics could be noted (3V's characteristics) - Volume, Velocity and Variety [2]. The
importance of the first two V's is obvious – it is the size of the memory required to store
Big Data – for example, the content of the WWW estimated now at several zettabytes ~
10^{21}–10^{22} bytes, and the rate of new Big Data production - for example, Google alone

© Springer Nature Switzerland AG 2021
A. Del Bimbo et al. (Eds.): ICPR 2020 Workshops, LNCS 12665, pp. 301–313, 2021.
https://doi.org/10.1007/978-3-030-68821-9_28

returns to the WWW every day tens of petabytes - 10^{16}–10^{17} bytes. It is clear that, given the huge values of these characteristics, working with Big Data is an exceedingly difficult technical problem. However, the really difficult problem is related to the third V - Variety.

Variety makes Big Data really big given its complexity. Big Data comes from a great variety of sources such as text docs, sensor data, audio, photo, video, click streams, emails, log files etc. Generally each of these entities is one of three types: structured, semi-structured or unstructured data. Structured data depend on the existence of a data model, determining how data can be stored, processed and accessed. Common examples of structured data are Excel files or SQL databases. Unstructured data represent the information that either does not have a predefined data model or is not organized in a pre-defined manner. Common examples of unstructured data include audio, video files or No-SQL databases. Semi-structured data are some form of structured data that do not conform to the formal structure of the data model, but nonetheless contain tags or other markers to separate semantic elements. Examples of semi-structured data include JSON and XML. In a sense, it could be said that semi-structured data, without having a rigid model, nevertheless have a soft model that describes them at the semantic level.

Up to 80% of the world's global data is unstructured (uncertain) today [2]. Extracting information from them is, as a rule, a laborious and low effective process (compared to queries to relational SQL databases). This is due to the lack of homogeneity, consistency, and the common attributes in the variety of unstructured data, which makes it difficult to create universal, systematic approaches to process them. As a result, meaningful and unique information, which is rich in Big Data, often remains unvalued by interested users. Unfortunately, images also fall into an unstructured data category. Considering the WWW to be the largest global repository of images, one can fancy how much valuable information surrounds us, which we cannot use. Every day an extremely large number of medical, geophysical, historical, astronomical images, digital photos, scanned docs and books, business graphics, etc. are created on the Internet, but we use only a tiny part of the information they contain.

In connection with the Big Data problem outlined, today a large amount of research is carried out around the world to find methods for effective management of unstructured data, images in particular. As a result, a relative understanding of possible ways of solving this problem was achieved. In particular, a new concept was elaborated: a paradigm of transforming unstructured data into semi-structured by expanding them with metadata – "data about data". In simple cases, such as E-mail messages, some header describing the letter is simply added before the message body. In more complex cases, such as converting plain text documents to XML (HTML) web pages, tags are added directly into the text, transforming it in the structure of well-defined XML elements. As for images, semantic elements such as points of interest, graphic primitives, patterns and their relationships, hierarchies, etc. can be utilized as metadata added to the original low-level (pixel) representation. The set of such elements for some image sometimes is called "the bag of features" (BoF or rarely BoW – Bag of Words) [3]. Formally, BoF is a visual description of images in terms of features similar to those from feature dictionary, which were previously generated from a set of training images. The features are usually associated with the local image areas (fragments), that are like the key words located in the text. It is normal for feature dictionaries (codebooks) to be created from millions (or billions) of local functions selected from training images.

The purpose of this article is to propose a novel original approach to metadata extracting from unstructured images in order to transform them into available semi-structured data. Namely, it is proposed to represent images by given size sets of random samples (counts) from probability distributions that follow the shape of the image intensity (pixel values). On the basis of these count representations, considered as metadata, the measure (function) of image similarity is established and the Maximum Similarity Method for searching relations (identification) of tested images with predefined examples (precedents) is substantiated. To substantiate the proposed approach, the problems mentioned in the introduction are interpreted below in terms and concepts of Image (Data) Mining. This allows to introduce an appropriate mathematical tool for the problem under consideration and revise it as a special optimization problem. Then it is shown how computer algorithms for the similarity estimation and for finding the maximum similarity of image fragments could be synthesized on this mathematical basis with the use of standard statistical modeling technique.

2 Characterization of the Identification Problem in the Context of Image Mining

The main task of Image Mining (IM), as noted in [4], is to extract knowledge, relations, and patterns (metadata) that are not clearly present in raw images represented by pixels (data) at low level. At the same time, unlike traditional methods of image processing, IM does not aim at understanding the structure or extracting certain knowledge for any single image. It is focused on discovering common patterns, metadata in large sets of images. In a sense, IM is the border zone between Data Mining (DM), Machine Learning (ML), and Artificial Intelligence (AI). At the same time, IM, due to the specifics of its subject area, is not a special section of any of the fields listed. For example, unlike most DM problems, where the text data are given in an already specified (vocabulary) representation, in the case of IM, there is no a priori predetermined images representation and the problem of choosing an adequate representation usually requires significant efforts [5]. Nevertheless, the image mining largely borrows the existing approaches, methods and concepts from neighboring fields, adapting them for its own needs. In particular, IM uses many approaches and concepts of ML [6] and DM [7]. In this regard, for a more accurate formulation of the main problems considered further in the work, it is useful to use the general concepts of these disciplines.

The main problem considered in the work refers to the general problem of data classification - one of the most widely studied issues in both ML and DM. However, due to the fact that classification is a rather diverse topic, including a wide range of problem areas, data processing scenarios and methods used, it is not enough to note that the problem under consideration belongs to the classification problem, for more certainty, it is necessary to more accurate define its specifics, in particular its method.

Most classification methods consist of two phases - a training stage, at which a data model is built using training examples, and a testing stage, at which, in accordance with the constructed model, each new data example is classified. These methods are commonly referred to as greedy learning, as they strive to build the final data model from existing examples without waiting for new ones. There is, however, another less common but popular approach called lazy learning [7]. Within the framework of this approach, there is no training stage, and the classification is performed directly on the basis of establishing relations between the training and the test examples. Apart from the term lazy learning method, the term instance-based learning is often used [7]. The simplest example of an instance-based learning is the nearest neighbor classification method. It is important to note that although there is clearly no training stage in instance-based methods, however, to ensure efficiency at the testing stage, some preprocessing of data examples in order to retrieve some of their features, metadata is still necessary [8].

In the light of the above interpretation, the problem of image fragments identification considered in the work and the Maximum Similarity Method proposed for its solution belong to instance-based methods for Image Mining. This characterization presupposes that the problem has a number of other important characteristics. In particular, since any classification problem suggests the segmentation of data examples into groups (classes), problem under consideration is also a segmentation problem. But the peculiarity of this segmentation is not in assigning labels to classes (encoding knowledge about the structure of classes), as it is usual in traditional two-phase classification methods. The segmentation related to the identification problem is aimed at establishing similarities between the tested examples and representatives of classes (without deep understanding of the structure of the classes). The latter leads to the fact that if traditional methods have, as a rule, the nature of supervised learning, the instance-based methods, to which the investigated problem belongs, are often implemented as unsupervised learning, allowing, in particular, more possibilities for classification automating.

Another characteristic, following from the previous one, is the local character of related classification. Since the use of similarity between the tested examples and the class representatives is based on the optimization of a certain measure of similarity, classification will be carried out mainly using the closest in this measure examples, i.e. locally in relation to the test one. Local classifiers are generally more reliable because of the simplified distribution of classes within a test example location, although in practice significant deviations from global segmentation carried out by traditional methods can be found.

Further the general features and specific details of instance-based methods implementation can be found, respectively, in [7] and [8]. Here, we note only that among the three main components, which make up the basis of instance-based methods - Similarity or Distance Function, Classification Function and Concept Description Updater [7], the most critical for the algorithmic implementation of the method and, accordingly, for its efficiency, stability, accuracy, etc. is the first of them. In [9], it is emphasized that the successful choice of Similarity Function (Similarity Measure [8]) is extremely important for many computer vision tasks, image classification tasks and content-based image search (CBIR). Accumulated experience shows that the quality of search in CBIR systems is "highly dependent on the criterion used to define similarity between images and has motivated significant research in learning good distance metrics from training data" [9]. Actually, the choice of the similarity measure practically, up to the choice of the computational optimization method, determines the criterion, the method for establishing the similarity. On the other hand, the choice of the similarity measure itself strongly depends on the type of data presentation, on the choice of metadata used to establish similarity, identification. Since this article proposes some new, not widely known choice of metadata it is worth discussing it in detail.

3 Image Representation by a Random Counts Set

To substantiate our proposed method for representing images with random counts a small review should be done first related to the radiation detection by photosensitive detectors and to the so-called semiclassical mechanism of photodetection [10]. The semiclassical treatment of photodetection has the benefit of being comparatively simple in terms of the mathematical background required and it gives a clear concept of an ideal image.

The registration of radiation (light) by material photosensitive detector, for example a semiconductor with p–n junction, results in the electric current (at the output of the detector), that consists of released electrons, called photocounts. In the semiclassical approximation, the number of registered photocounts K is random and described by a simple Poisson probability distribution [10]:

$$P(K) = \frac{1}{K!}(\alpha W)^K \exp\{-\alpha W\},\tag{1}$$

where $W = I_0 A T$ is the integrated intensity of the incident radiation, I_0 is its intensity, A is the area of the sensitive surface of the detector, T is the registration time. Integrated intensity W can be also expressed in terms of a number N of incident photons as $W = Nh\bar{v}$, where h is the Planck's constant, $\bar{v}$ is the average frequency of the incident radiation. The parameter α in (1) is related to the dimensionless detector quantum efficiency parameter η as $\alpha = \eta/h\bar{v}$. Parameter η has a sense of the ratio of the average photocounts number $\bar{K} = \alpha W$ to the number of incident photons N.

Note that in (1) it is assumed that the intensity I_0 is uniform over the area A and is constant over time T. For smoothly varying intensities I_0, (1) is valid only approximately. This approximation is more accurate, when the area A becomes smaller and/or the exposure time T is shorter. Note that in this extreme case (in the case of the "point detector" $A \to 0$) the average number of photocounts $\bar{K} = \alpha W$ also tends to zero and it leads to practically binary mode $K \in \{0, 1\}$ of the detector operation. In this case, only one $K = 1$ photocount can be registered (or not registered for $K = 0$), so, (1) is simplified to Bernoulli distribution:

$$P_{\vec{x}}(K) = \begin{cases} 1 - \alpha W(\vec{x}), & K = 0; \\ \alpha W(\vec{x}), & K = 1; \end{cases} \quad W(\vec{x}) = I(\vec{x})AT,\tag{2}$$

where the dependence of the intensity of the incident radiation $I(\vec{x})$ on the coordinates $\vec{x}$ of the point detector allocation (coordinates of its photocount) is clearly indicated.

Based on the above description of the registration mechanism (1) and its idealization (2), the ideal image model [11] can be defined as follows. An ideal image is the result of registration by an ideal imaging device on its sensitive surface Ω, during not a long exposure time T of incident radiation of intensity $I(\vec{x}), \vec{x} \in \Omega$. An ideal imaging device, in turn, is a spatial array, a matrix of a large number of identical point detectors (with the same, in particular, A and η), located close to each other in the Ω surface. The result of the registration is an ideal image X, thus, the set of coordinates $X = \{\vec{x}_i\}$ of the point detectors that actually registered photocounts ($K_{\vec{x} \in X} = 1, K_{\vec{x} \notin X} = 0$). In what follows, for brevity, $X = \{\vec{x}_i\}$ will be called the full set of counts of an ideal image, or simply all counts of the image.

Note, that in the cited work [11], the authors admit the possibility of registering more than one photocount by point detector. This is due to the fact that at the time of its writing (1991), the technological implementation of point detectors was considered a matter of the future. A contemporary discussion of ideal imaging devices and ideal images can be found in [12]. It is noted in the paper, that one way to build binary detectors is to modify standard memory chip technology, where each memory bit cell is designed to be sensitive to light. With current CMOS technology, the level of integration of such cells can exceed 10^9–10^{10} (i.e., 1 to 10 giga) items per chip. In this case, the corresponding cell sizes would be ~50 nm (detailed technological characteristics regarding the possibilities of radiation detection with modern (2017) visual devices can be found in [13]). From this short overview we can draw conclusions about the adequacy of the above described ideal image counts model to the capabilities of modern technologies. It is easy to see that an ideal image resembles a digital photographic film, where every exposed silver grain is a binary bit, and the spatial density of grains encodes the intensity distribution $I(\vec{x}), \vec{x} \in \Omega$.

Taking into account, that for a given intensity distribution $I(\vec{x}), \vec{x} \in \Omega$ the counts of different point detectors are independent, taking into account (2), we can deduce by standard methods [14], that the joint probability distribution of the N – the number of counts and a set of their coordinates $\{\vec{x}_1, \ldots, \vec{x}_N\}$ satisfies the multivariate Poisson distribution:

$$\rho(N, \vec{x}_1, \ldots, \vec{x}_N | \alpha W(\vec{x})) = \frac{1}{N!} \prod_{i=1}^{N} \alpha W(\vec{x}_i) \times \exp\left\{ -\int_{\Omega} \alpha W(\vec{x}) d\vec{x} \right\}, \quad (3)$$

in other words, the counts of ideal image are the realization of point Poisson processes (PPP) on Ω with the intensity function $\lambda(\vec{x}) = \alpha W(\vec{x}) = \alpha A T I(\vec{x})$ [15].

Note, that the model stated is not new, (3) was successfully used for special areas of image processing in which low intensities of radiation $I(\vec{x})$ are registered. Traditional areas of its application are fluorescence microscopy, positron emission tomography (PET), single photon emission computerized tomography (SPECT), optical and infrared astronomy, etc. [16]. This is explained by the simple fact that in these special areas the approximation $\alpha W \to 0$ (2) is initially valid, which, however, is achieved not due to $A \to 0$, but because $I(\vec{x}) \to 0$.

While the registration model (3) is similar for the cases of low and usual intensities, there is one fundamental difference between these cases. It consists in the fact, that the average number of counts $\bar{N} = \int_{\Omega} \alpha W(\vec{x}) d\vec{x}$ for the low-intensity case can be, albeit large, but amenable to accounting; for the case of usual intensities this number is huge (gigabits, see above short overview). Therefore, real work with the ideal image model $X = \{\vec{x}_i\}$ for common intensities seems to be exceedingly difficult. We propose to solve this problem by representing an ideal image $X = \{\vec{x}_1, \ldots, \vec{x}_N\}$ not by the full set of counts, but by some of its subset of an acceptable given size $n \ll \bar{N} \colon X_n = \{\vec{x}_1, \ldots, \vec{x}_n\}$. To obtain the marginal distribution of $\{\vec{x}_1, \ldots, \vec{x}_n\}$, it is necessary to sum (integrate) (3) over all additional counts $\{\vec{x}_{n+1}, \ldots, \vec{x}_N\}$ within Ω and then sum the result over all $N \geq n$. The final result is the following:

$$
\begin{aligned}
\rho_n(\vec{x}_1, \ldots, \vec{x}_n | \alpha W(\vec{x})) &= \prod_{i=1}^{n} \rho(\vec{x}_i | I(\vec{x})) \\
\rho(\vec{x} | I(\vec{x})) &= \frac{I(\vec{x})}{\int_{\Omega} I(\vec{x}) d\vec{x}}
\end{aligned}
\tag{4}
$$

The probabilistic model (4) of random counts image representation $X_n = \{\vec{x}_1, \ldots, \vec{x}_n\}$ was discussed earlier in [15]. It was noted there, that distribution (4) reflects the well-known property of PPP consisting in the decomposition of the conditional joint distribution of the counts with given n into a product of identical distributions $\rho(\vec{x} | I(\vec{x}))$ of each of them [14]. In other words, for a given n, the counts $\{\vec{x}_1, \ldots, \vec{x}_n\}$ are a set of independent, identically distributed (iid) random vectors. Such a decomposition is the initial assumption for most statistical approaches, for example, naive Bayesian one [17], and this makes representation of images by random counts extremely attractive. Moreover, the distribution of counts $\vec{x}_i$ is determined only by the shape of the intensity $I(\vec{x})$ – its normalized version $\rho(\vec{x})$, therefore, it does not depend on the detector quantum efficiency η, or on the average radiation frequency $\bar{v}$, or on the area A of the detector, or on the exposure time T. In view of these remarkable properties the random counts image representation $X_n = \{\vec{x}_1, \ldots, \vec{x}_n\}$ has a universal character and for this reason is proposed as a statistical basis for the proposed approach.

Another important topic related to the proposed representation of images in the form of a set of counts concerns the issues of its formation. According (4), if the value of number of counts n is specified, the formation of counts coordinates $= \{\vec{x}_1, \ldots, \vec{x}_n\}$ is carried out as the generation of n samples of iid random vectors distributed according $\rho(\vec{x} | I(\vec{x}))$, which coincides with the normalized on the Ω intensity $I(\vec{x})$. If the original image is specified by pixels values P_{ij}, given at the (i, j) nodes of the covering Ω integer grid, then by interpolating these values on the Ω between the nodes, we obtain piecewise constant approximation of $I(\vec{x})$ up to the quantization gain. By normalizing this approximation, we obtain a piecewise constant approximation of the required distribution $\rho(\vec{x} | I(\vec{x}))$, and this approximation also does not depend on the quantization gain. After that, it remains to perform the sampling procedure from the resulting distribution approximation in order to form a representation.

In the field of Machine Learning there is a large discipline under the general name of Monte-Carlo methods [18], devoted to sampling procedures from various probability distributions. It includes such well-known techniques as Importance sampling, Accept-Reject scheme, Metropolis-Hastings algorithm, Gibbs sampling, etc. The adaptation of these methods to the image counts formation is not a problem. Let us give, for example, the adaptation of the Accept-Reject scheme to generate n samples $X_n = \{\vec{x}_1, \ldots, \vec{x}_n\}$ from $\rho(\vec{x} | I(\vec{x}))$. Let us take as a proposal density uniform distribution $q(\vec{x}) = 1/\Omega$. Then the procedure for generating samples will be reduced to sequential generation of uniformly distributed (according $q(\vec{x})$) vectors $\vec{x}$ on Ω and accepting as counts those of them for which the accompanying auxiliary random variable u, uniformly distributed on $[0, \rho_{max})$ turns out to be less than $\rho(\vec{x} | I(\vec{x}))$, where ρ_{max} is the maximum value $\rho(\vec{x} | I(\vec{x}))$ on Ω. While this short example is probably the most inefficient in Monte-Carlo methods, it clearly shows how powerful Machine Learning methods can be adapted to imaging problems.

The last short remark regarding the proposed representation of images concerns its association with the stochastic screening or FM screening – a halftone representation of images by pseudo-random distribution of halftone dots [19]. An interesting connection between Monte Carlo methods – Importance sampling and the popular Floyd-Steinberg FM grayscale algorithm [21] was noted in [20]. In this regard, another interpretation of the proposed representation of images as a random FM distribution of counts arises. Apparently, this remark can be quite fruitful.

4 Maximum Similarity Method

The Maximum Similarity Method assumes that there is some image repository, where the images can be equipped by the metadata in a form of proposed random counts representations $X_n = \{\vec{x}_1, \ldots, \vec{x}_n\}$. The number n of counts in representation can be arbitrary. The method of X_n formation is not specified. For the Maximum Similarity Method presented below, only the statistical description of representation X_n is essential.

From the statistical point of view, it is assumed that each count $\vec{x}_i$ is random and the process of its registration is described by some parametric probability distribution with density $\rho(\vec{x} \mid \vec{\theta})$, $\vec{\theta} \in \Theta \subset \mathbb{R}^p$ (parametric model). It is assumed, following the Bayesian point of view, that the parameters $\vec{\theta}$ are also random variables with a certain prior distribution density $\mathcal{P}(\vec{\theta})$, the exact form of which, however, is not essential. Both assumptions made, allow us to speak about the counts $\vec{x}$ and parameters $\vec{\theta}$ joint distribution density $\rho(\vec{x}; \vec{\theta}) = \rho(\vec{x}|\vec{\theta})\mathcal{P}(\vec{\theta})$.

The presented parametric model belongs to the class of the so-called generative models [22], which imply a correspondence of certain values of the parameters $\vec{\theta}_1, \vec{\theta}_2, \ldots, \vec{\theta}_k, \cdots \in \Theta$ to the some images (by means, for example, of an exact sequence of mappings $\Theta \to I(\vec{x}; \vec{\theta}) \to X_n = \{\vec{x}_1, \ldots, \vec{x}_n\}$, see (4)). However, the problem with generative models is that the exact values of the parameters corresponding to the image are unknown, only their statistical estimates, based on the available representations (metadata) $X_n = \{\vec{x}_1, \ldots, \vec{x}_n\}$ are available.

In particular, the maximum likelihood estimates $\vec{\theta}_{ML}$ [23], determined from the R. Fisher's ML equations, can be used as such estimates:

$$\vec{\theta}_{ML} = \underset{\vec{\theta} \in \Theta}{\mathrm{argmax}}\, \varrho\left(X_n | \vec{\theta}\right). \tag{5}$$

As follows from (5), to find maximum likelihood estimates, it is necessary for each n, as well as for $n = 1$, to determine its parametric n–model of the set of counts X_n – the corresponding probability distribution density $\varrho\left(\vec{x}_1, \ldots, \vec{x}_n | \vec{\theta}\right)$ (these models for different n should be consistent in accordance with the Kolmogorov theorem, see [24]). However, it is possible to significantly simplify the problem of determining n –models by using conditional (for a given $\vec{\theta}$) independence of individual counts of the representations (see (4)):

$$\varrho\left(X_n | \vec{\theta}\right) = \prod_{i=1}^{n} \rho\left(\vec{x}_i | \vec{\theta}\right). \tag{6}$$

Note that factorization (6) is actively used in Machine Learning problems, for example, within the framework of the naive Bayesian method [17], which is one of the ten most popular modern algorithms [25].

The problem of identification, relation of some test images with one of the previously registered training examples (hereinafter called precedents) is formalized now in the context of the presented parametric model as the problem of maximizing some measure of similarity of the test image representation $X_n = \{\vec{x}_1, \ldots, \vec{x}_n\}$ with the data set of representations $X_{n_1}^{(1)}, X_{n_2}^{(2)}, \ldots, X_{n_k}^{(k)}, \ldots$, obtained earlier for the precedents. Since no additional knowledge about the image and precedents except for metadata $X_n, X_{n_1}^{(1)}, X_{n_2}^{(2)}, \ldots, X_{n_k}^{(k)}, \ldots$ is assumed (including the values of the characteristic parameters $\vec{\theta}_1, \vec{\theta}_2, \ldots, \vec{\theta}_k, \cdots \in \Theta$, characteristics of $\mathcal{P}\left(\vec{\theta}\right)$, etc.), it is highly desirable that the corresponding similarity measure $\mu\left(X_n, X_{n_k}^{(k)}\right)$ could be expressed in terms of this and only this data.

A natural quantitative characteristic of the consistency of representation X_n and an arbitrary representation X_k as the sets of counts is the probability density of their joint distribution $p\left(X_n, X_{n_k}^{(k)}\right)$. Taking into account the basic assumption about the considered models (6) (as well as the conditions for independence of the sets X_n and $X_{n_k}^{(k)}$), the density $p\left(X_n, X_{n_k}^{(k)}\right)$ can be written in the following form:

$$\begin{aligned}
p\left(X_n, X_{n_k}^{(k)}\right) &= \int p\left(X_n, X_{n_k}^{(k)} | \vec{\theta}\right) \mathcal{P}\left(\vec{\theta}\right) d\vec{\theta} \\
&= \int \varrho\left(X_n | \vec{\theta}\right) \varrho\left(X_{n_k}^{(k)} | \vec{\theta}\right) \mathcal{P}\left(\vec{\theta}\right) d\vec{\theta} \\
&= \int \prod_1^n \rho\left(\vec{x}_i | \vec{\theta}\right) \prod_1^{n_k} \rho\left(\vec{x}_j | \vec{\theta}\right) \mathcal{P}\left(\vec{\theta}\right) d\vec{\theta} \\
&= \int \varrho\left(X_n \cup X_{n_k}^{(k)} | \vec{\theta}\right) \mathcal{P}\left(\vec{\theta}\right) d\vec{\theta}
\end{aligned} \tag{7}$$

where $\{\vec{x}_j\}$ is a set of n_k counts of $X_{n_k}^{(k)}$, $X_n \cup X_{n_k}^{(k)}$ is a set of $n + n_k$ counts obtained by uniting X_n and $X_{n_k}^{(k)}$. In other words, $p\left(X_n, X_{n_k}^{(k)}\right)$ (7) is the type (6) distribution density of the united set of counts $\{\vec{x}_j\} \cup \{\vec{x}_i\}$.

Considering the above interpretation, it is clear that $p\left(X_n, X_{n_k}^{(k)}\right)$ in some sense reflects the degree of consistency between X_n and $X_{n_k}^{(k)}$. Indeed, if all $X_{n_1}^{(1)}, X_{n_2}^{(2)}, \ldots, X_{n_k}^{(k)}, \ldots$ would be of the same size $n_1 = n_2 = \cdots = n_k = m$, then all the sets $\{X_n, X_{n_k}^{(k)}\}$ would be random samples within the same parametric $(n+m)$–model $\varrho\left(X | \vec{\theta}\right)$ (6). In this case, the degree of consistency $X_n \sim X_{n_k}^{(k)}$ would be determined by the probability of their joint counts $X_n \cup X_{n_k}^{(k)}$, i.e. $p\left(X_n, X_{n_k}^{(k)}\right)$, indeed, could be considered as a similarity measure. The problem, however, is that, due to the arbitrary value of n_k, the sets $\{X_n \cup X_{n_k}^{(k)}\}$ belong to different models and, therefore, the comparison of $p\left(X_n, X_{n_k}^{(k)}\right)$ values for different $X_{n_k}^{(k)}$ should be corrected for this circumstance.

In the proposed Maximum Similarity Method, the corresponding correction is specified by normalizing the values $p\left(X_n, X_{n_k}^{(k)}\right)$ (7) to the probabilities $p\left(X_{n_k}^{(k)}\right)$:

$$\mu\left(X_n, X_{n_k}^{(k)}\right) = \frac{p\left(X_n, X_{n_k}^{(k)}\right)}{p\left(X_{n_k}^{(k)}\right)} = p\left(X_n | X_{n_k}^{(k)}\right), \tag{8}$$

i.e. the similarity measure $\mu\left(X_n, X_{n_k}^{(k)}\right)$ is chosen as the ratio of the probability of the $X_n \cup X_{n_k}^{(k)}$ counts to the probability of the only X_k counts. In this case, the maximum similarity method consists in choosing the precedent for which the expansion of its counts $X_{n_k}^{(k)}$ by the X_n leads to the greatest increase in probability ratio.

As follows from (8), the chosen probability ratio formally coincides with the conditional probability of the set X_n with the given precedent counts $X_{n_k}^{(k)}$. The latter leads to an alternative interpretation of the proposed method: the tested image is identified with that precedent, the representation $X_{n_k}^{(k)}$ of which leads to the maximum conditional probability of a tested representation X_n.

Using the selected measure of similarity $\mu\left(X_n, X_{n_k}^{(k)}\right)$ (8), the Maximum Similarity Method can be formalized as a solution to the following maximum similarity (MS) equation:

$$k_{MS} = \underset{k}{argmax}\,\mu\left(X_n, X_{n_k}^{(k)}\right) = \underset{k}{argmax}\; p\left(X_n | X_{n_k}^{(k)}\right). \tag{9}$$

To substantiate the proposed method, namely, the choice of the similarity measure in the form (8), it is convenient to turn to the asymptotic case of large counts of precedents $n_k \gg 1$. Note that, in addition to questions of convenience, this case quite adequately reflects the specifics of the process of representations preparation.

In the general (not necessarily asymptotic) case, within the framework of the Bayesian approach, the conditional probability $p\left(X_n | X_{n_k}^{(k)}\right)$ in terms of the parametric model (7) can be written as:

$$p\left(X_n | X_{n_k}^{(k)}\right) = \frac{p\left(X_n, X_{n_k}^{(k)}\right)}{p\left(X_{n_k}^{(k)}\right)} = \frac{\int \varrho\left(X_n | \vec{\theta}\right) \varrho\left(X_{n_k}^{(k)} | \vec{\theta}\right) \mathcal{P}\left(\vec{\theta}\right) d\vec{\theta}}{\int \varrho\left(X_{n_k}^{(k)} | \vec{\theta}\right) \mathcal{P}\left(\vec{\theta}\right) d\vec{\theta}}. \tag{10}$$

In the case $n_k \gg 1$ for $\varrho\left(X_{n_k}^{(k)} | \vec{\theta}\right)$ in neighbourhood of its likelihood estimate $\vec{\theta}_{ML}^{(k)}$ (1) the well-known asymptotic approximation (with regard to $\vec{\theta}$) holds [26]:

$$\varrho\left(X_{n_k}^{(k)} | \vec{\theta}\right) \cong \varrho\left(X_{n_k}^{(k)} | \vec{\theta}_{ML}^{(k)}\right)$$
$$\times \exp\left[-\frac{n_k}{2}\left(\vec{\theta} - \vec{\theta}_{ML}^{(k)}\right)^T I\left(\vec{\theta}_{ML}^{(k)}\right)\left(\vec{\theta} - \vec{\theta}_{ML}^{(k)}\right)\right], \tag{11}$$

where T is the transposition operation, $I\left(\vec{\theta}_{ML}^{(k)}\right)$ is the Fisher's information matrix for the distribution $\rho\left(\vec{x}|\vec{\theta}\right)$ – one of the most important characteristics of the adopted parametric model:

$$I_{ij}\left(\vec{\theta}\right) = -\int \rho\left(\vec{x}|\vec{\theta}\right)\left[\partial^2 \ln\rho\left(\vec{x}|\vec{\theta}\right)/\partial\theta_i\partial\theta_j\right]d\vec{x}. \tag{12}$$

Considering the sharpness of the peak of asymptotic (11) in the vicinity of $\vec{\theta}_{ML}^{(k)}$, the numerator (10) can be approximated by:

$$\begin{aligned}&\int \varrho\left(X|\vec{\theta}\right)\varrho\left(X_k|\vec{\theta}\right)\mathcal{P}\left(\vec{\theta}\right)d\vec{\theta}\\ &\approx \varrho\left(X|\vec{\theta}_k^{(ML)}\right)\int \varrho\left(X_k|\vec{\theta}\right)\mathcal{P}\left(\vec{\theta}\right)d\vec{\theta}\end{aligned}. \tag{13}$$

As a result, $p\left(X_n, X_{n_k}^{(k)}\right)$ (7) is simplified to $\varrho(X_n|\vec{\theta}_{ML}^{(k)})$, and the similarity measure $\mu\left(X_n, X_{n_k}^{(k)}\right)$ (8) takes the following simple form:

$$\mu\left(X_n, X_{n_k}^{(k)}\right) \cong \varrho\left(X_n|\vec{\theta}_{ML}^{(k)}\right). \tag{14}$$

In other words, in the case of large sizes of precedent sets of counts $X_{n_1}^{(1)}, X_{n_2}^{(2)}, \ldots, X_{n_k}^{(k)}, \ldots, n_k \gg 1$ (the number of observations n of a set X_n of an identified image does not have to be large), the naive Bayesian distribution density $\varrho\left(X_n|\vec{\theta}\right)$ (6) for the values of the parameter $\vec{\theta} = \vec{\theta}_{ML}^{(k)}$ can be used as a similarity measure $\mu\left(X_n, X_{n_k}^{(k)}\right)$. The latter means that for arbitrary precedents (arbitrary n_k), the similarity measures $\mu\left(X_n, X_{n_k}^{(k)}\right)$ (14) are determined within the same n–model, so the comparison of their values is quite justified.

From an applied point of view, expression (14) for the similarity measure $\mu\left(X_n, X_{n_k}^{(k)}\right)$ seems even more attractive than (8). The corresponding formulation of the Maximum Similarity Method, which is the asymptotic limit of the general formulation (9), takes on a form like the maximum likelihood method (1)

$$k_{MS} = \arg\max_k \varrho\left(X|\vec{\theta}_k^{(ML)}\right) = \arg\max_{\vec{\theta}\in\{\vec{\theta}_k^{(ML)}\}} \varrho\left(X|\vec{\theta}\right). \tag{15}$$

with the only exception that maximization is performed not over all $\vec{\theta} \in \Theta$, but only over a finite set of estimates $\vec{\theta}_{ML}^{(1)}, \vec{\theta}_{ML}^{(2)}, \ldots, \vec{\theta}_{ML}^{(k)}, \cdots \in \Theta$. Note that, from a practical point of view, in this case, there is also no need to store the full sets of counts of precedents $X_{n_1}^{(1)}, X_{n_2}^{(2)}, \ldots, X_{n_k}^{(k)}, \ldots$, it is enough to save only the parameter estimates (statistics) $\left\{\vec{\theta}_{ML}^{(k)}\right\}$, which can be considered as metadata.

5 Conclusions

The Maximum Similarity Method proposed in paper, the simplicity of its interpretation and explicit schemes of its realization as optimization problems (9), (15) makes it very attractive both in theoretical and practical terms, especially in the context of modern, oriented to Machine Learning and Data Mining approaches. In a sense, for Machine Learning problems, the proposed method is an adaptation of the Maximum Likelihood method widely used in traditional statistics. The fruitful use of the latter, as is known, has led to a huge number of important statistical results. In this regard, it is hoped that the proposed Maximum Similarity Method will also be useful in solving a wide range of modern problems in the field of Image Mining.

Acknowledgements. The author is grateful to the Russian Foundation for Basic Research (RFBR), grant N 18–07-01295 A for the financial support of the work.

References

1. Brady, H.E.: The Challenge of Big Data and Data Science. Ann. Rev. Polit. Sci. **22**, 297–323 (2019)
2. Hariri, R.H., Fredericks, E.M., Bowers, K.M.: Uncertainty in big data analytics: survey, opportunities, and challenges. J. Big Data **6**(1), 1–16 (2019). https://doi.org/10.1186/s40537-019-0206-3
3. O'Hara, S., Draper, B.: Introduction to the bag of features paradigm for image classification and retrieval. arXiv:1101.3354, Cornell University (2011)
4. Burl, M.C., Fowlkes, C., Rowden, J.: Mining for image content. In: SCI-ISAS99 Proceedings, Orlando, FL (1999)
5. Zhang, J., Hsu, W., Lee, M.L.: Image mining: issues, frameworks, and techniques. In: 2nd International Workshop Proceedings on MDM/KDD, pp. 13–20 (2001)
6. Mitchell, T.: Machine Learning. McGraw Hill, New York (1997)
7. Aggarwal, C.C.: Data Classification: Algorithms and Applications. CRC Press, Boca Raton (2014)
8. Garcia, S., Luengo, J., Herrera F.: Data Preprocessing in Data Mining. Springer, Cham (2015). https://doi.org/10.1007/978-3-319-10247-4
9. Yang, L., Jin, R.: Distance metric learning: a comprehensive survey. Technical report, Department of Computer Science and Engineering, Michigan State University (2007)
10. Goodman, J.W.: Statistical Optics, 2nd edn. Wiley, New York (2015)
11. Pal, N.R., Pal, S.K.: Image model, poisson distribution and object extraction. J. Pattern Recogn. Artif. Intell. **5**(3), 459–483 (1991)
12. Yang, F., Lu, Y.M., Sbaiz, L., Vetterli, M.: Bits from photons: oversampled image acquisition using binary poisson statistics. IEEE Trans. Image Process. **21**(4), 1421–1436 (2012)
13. Fossum, E.R., Teranishi, N., Theuwissen, A., Stoppa, D., Charbon, E. (eds.) Photon–Counting Image Sensors. MDPI Books under CC BY–NC–ND license (2017)
14. Streit, R.L.: Poisson Point Processes. Imaging, Tracking and Sensing. Springer, New York (2010). https://doi.org/10.1007/978-3-319-05852-8_4
15. Antsiperov, V.: Machine learning approach to the synthesis of identification procedures for modern photon-counting sensors. In: 8th International Conference on Pattern Recognition Applications and Methods ICPRAM Proceedings, Prague, vol. 1, pp. 19–21 (2019)
16. Bertero, M., Boccacci, P., Desidera, G., Vicidomini, G.: Topical review: image deblurring with poisson data: from cells to galaxies. Inverse Prob. **25**, 123006 (2009)
17. Barber, D.: Bayesian Reasoning and Machine Learning. Cambridge Univ. Press, Cambridge (2012)

18. MacKay, D.J.C.: Information Theory, Inference, and Learning Algorithms. Cambridge University Press, Cambridge (2003)
19. Gooran, S., Yang, L.: Basics of Tone Reproduction. In: Handbook of Digital Imaging, Kriss, M. (ed.) (2015).
20. Szirmay-Kalos, L., Szecsi, L., Penzov A.A.: Importance sampling with floyd-steinberg halftoning. In: Eurographics Short Papers, pp. 69–72 (2009)
21. Floyd, R., Steinberg, L.: An adaptive algorithm for spatial gray scale. Proc. Soc. Inf. Display **17**(2), 75–77 (1976)
22. Jebara, T.: Machine Learning: Discriminative and Generative. Kluwer, Dordrecht (2004)
23. Efron, B.: Maximum likelihood and decision theory. Ann. Statist. **10**, 340–356 (1982)
24. Billingsley, P.: Probability and Measure, 2nd edn. Wiley, New York (1986)
25. Wu, X., et al.: Top 10 algorithms in data mining. Knowl. Inf. Syst. **14**(1), 1–37 (2007)
26. Wasserman, L.: All of Statistics: A Concise Course in Statistical Inference. Springer, New York (2004)

First Step Towards Creating a Software Package for Detecting the Dangerous States During Driver Eye Monitoring

Nikita Andriyanov[✉]

Financial University under the Government of the Russian Federation, Leningradsky av., h. 49, 125167 Moscow, Russia
nikita-and-nov@mail.ru

Abstract. The problem of detecting human fatigue by the state of the eyes is considered. A program for detecting the state of open/closed eyes has been developed. The Haar cascades were used to search for faces. Then the eyes were detected on the video from simple web-camera, which allowed us to accumulate a sufficient dataset. Training took place using convolutional neural networks, and due to different lighting conditions, different accuracy characteristics were obtained for the left and right eyes. Using Python programming language with the Jupyter Notebook functionality and the OpenCV library, a software package has been developed that allows us to highlight closed eyes when testing for a learning subject (certain person from whose images the model was trained) with an accuracy of about 90% on a camera with a low resolution (640 by 480 pixels). The proposed solution can be used in the tasks of monitoring driver's state because one of the most frequent reasons of road accidents is driver fatigue.

Keywords: Eye detection · Face detection · Haar cascades · OpenCV · Convolutional neural networks · Human Condition Monitoring · Pattern recognition

1 Introduction

The task of monitoring the condition of drivers is relevant for taxi ordering services [1, 2], which are trying to control the safety of customers, drivers and vehicles. Also, this problem arises in the case of monitoring long-distance drivers working at night and in the morning [3]. However, nowadays, methods are often used that do not allow accurate assessment of the driver's condition in real time. For example, there may be restrictions on the duration of the shift and blocking the driver from taking orders for a certain period of time.

© Springer Nature Switzerland AG 2021
A. Del Bimbo et al. (Eds.): ICPR 2020 Workshops, LNCS 12665, pp. 314–322, 2021.
https://doi.org/10.1007/978-3-030-68821-9_29

Today, computer vision technologies are developing quite quickly. And a lot of the problems of object detection and recognition are successfully solved using convolutional neural networks (CNN) [4–6]. However, CNNs are usually used in areas where the error is less critical than in the problem under consideration. In addition, research in this area is underway for images taken in good lighting conditions, and the processing of complex night images is not well understood. At the same time, the set goal aimed at solving the problem of recognizing the driver's sleepy state in various conditions is extremely relevant, especially in the evening or at night, for which the risk of falling asleep on the road is much higher than during the day. Thus, in this article, we will consider the first step towards the development of such a system, namely, training and implementation of a model that makes it possible to identify the states of open and closed human eyes, including recognition in bad light conditions.

2   Algorithms for Eye Detection and Systems for Driver Monitoring

An analysis of the literature in the field of eye detection and recognition of their state has shown that modern technologies use algorithms based on the Viola-Jones methods and Haar cascades to solve this problem [7]. Moreover, such problems are usually considered in good lighting conditions [8]. In addition, the characteristics of the camera or other recording device are often neglected.

Based on the results of the analysis, the following conclusions can be drawn. Firstly, it is widespread to reduce this problem to solutions based on libraries in the Python programming language. At the same time, there are a number of datasets for which images containing eyes have already been selected. For example, the MRL Eyes dataset [9] consists of the number of images with marked eyes. Nevertheless, from the condition of our task it follows that the system should be adaptable. It means that ideally it should be adjusted for each specific driver.

Considering the above, it is necessary to implement in the software system a special module for collecting information for training the model. The analysis showed that the simplest way to collect images of a particular person's eyes is to use the Open CV library tools based on cascades (trained models). However, the addition of eyes is required in bad lighting conditions, which these models do not yet allow to do in full.

Among the existing analogues, it is possible to single out the driver monitoring system (DMS) produce by JSC SOVA, Russian Federation, and provides the functionality of the driver control system using artificial intelligence. However the complex solutions of such system are characterized by high cost, which does not allow ordinary motorists to apply these solutions [10]. In addition, there is the Toyota Driver Monitoring System (the manufacturer is a public company Toyota), within the framework of which the driver's eyes are tracked. However, the question arises about the quality of operation of this system at night or for drivers wearing sunglasses [11].

Finally, other existing driver state analysis systems process the features other than eye or face analysis based on computer vision. In particular, other existing systems, e.g. Ford Driver Alert, Mercedes Attention Assist, Volvo Driver Alert Control, Bosch Driver Drowsiness Detection from the respective manufacturers of cars to a greater extent reveal the abnormal state of the driver by assessing the trajectories of the vehicle [11]. They analyze the steering angle, the position of the car on the road and etc. Such a system, in conjunction with smart solutions based on artificial intelligence, will also make it possible to detect the state of drunkenness of the driver.

3   Hardware Analysis for Driver's Eyes Monitoring System

With the future implementation of the solution in the transport industry, it is planned that images will be obtained from a conventional IP camera that has the ability to transmit video (with a priority of wireless transmission). These cameras can be easily found on the market today at prices ranging from $10 to $100. At the same time, it is important to be able to shoot at night, for example, using special IR LEDs. Usually the video resolution in such cameras complies with the HD (1280 × 720 pixels) or Full HD (1920 × 1080 pixels) standards, which, taking into account the installation of the camera directly next to the driver's face, will be sufficient. However, the developed algorithm can be retrained using the data obtained from cameras with the worst characteristics, and the article discusses its application in such conditions. The dimensions of modern mini cameras vary from 20 × 20 × 20 mm (Mini HD camera SQ) to 60 × 105 × 60 mm (IP Digma Division). The IP Digma Division camera provides illumination at a distance of up to 10 m when shooting at night. In most cases such cameras have ports with a universal serial bus, e.g. miniUSB, microUSB, USB2.0. For greater reliability, two cameras can be used (on the left side and on the right side of the driver's face). Since the work of the video processing program will be performed on the basis of the studied model, it is not required to install a powerful computing device in the car, which allows significant savings on the final product. For example, nVidia Jetson microcomputers used in neural network tasks cost between $200 and $1000. Rasberry Pi microcomputers (cost is about $25– $35) can be used as processors, which have the necessary interfaces and work in the Linux OS, as well as technical means oriented to artificial intelligence systems, such as the Intel Neural Computer Stick (approximate cost is 90$). Moreover, for Intel-based solutions, it is possible to significantly speed up real-time video processing, even with mediocre processor performance. For this, Open VINO can be used and the assembly of the finished model for it [12].

As noted earlier, existing driver monitoring systems such as Ford Driver Alert, Mercedes Attention Assist, Volvo Driver Alert Control, Bosch Driver Drowsiness Detection are based on mechanical data of the vehicle condition associated with the assessment of steering movements, vehicle movements on the highway. However, the Toyota Driver Monitoring System monitors the direction of the driver's gaze and detects when attention is lost. There is also a SOWA's DMS that solves similar driver monitoring tasks. However, the algorithms on which the operation of this system is based are not known, and the total cost of design solutions can reach $600. It should also be noted that the solutions offered by SOWA are focused more on large vehicles and long-distance transportation and such solutions usually use a number of cameras that provides good recognition characteristics.

In contrast to such systems, an adaptable model (for a specific driver) will have a number of advantages. Firstly, the low cost, achieved through the implementation of the training process for a specific driver in the software package. The model will not be universal, but it will can to recognize open/close eyes for the specific user.

4   Collecting and Preparing Data for Training

Since it was decided to collect data taking into account the individual characteristics of a person's face, the data collection module was prepared in the Jupyter Notebook environment. To collect images, a conventional camera integrated into a laptop with a resolution of 640 × 480 pixels was used. To obtain images from the camera, the Open CV library for Python was used. The shooting took place in various lighting conditions. At the same time, to determine the eyes in the image, Haar cascades were used, which made it possible to find a face. Then, relative to the coordinates of the face for the eyes, a search was performed as a percentage of the length and height of the rectangle bounding the face. For example, the eyes were searched for in the range of height from 0.25 h to 0.5 h, where h is the height of the rectangle bounding the face. And the width was chosen depending on the eye: for the right eye, the width range was chosen from 0.2 w to 0.45 w, and for the left one - from 0.55 w to 0.8 w, where w is the width of the rectangle bounding the face. Thus, the eyes were cut out even under conditions bad enough to be detected directly by the cascade.

It should be noted that 2 models were implemented for the left and right eyes, respectively. Moreover, there were only 2 states for each eye: an open eye or a closed eye. 5000 images were obtained for each eye and each condition. Moreover, they were all made for the same person. This allows to avoid the additional data augmentation. However, the images were taken in different lighting conditions for different eyes in different proportions.

Figure 1 shows the examples of images of an open right eye and Fig. 2 shows the images with closed left eye.

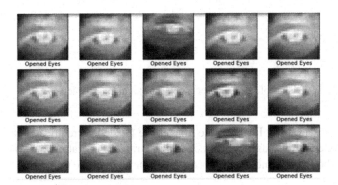

Fig. 1. Open right eye

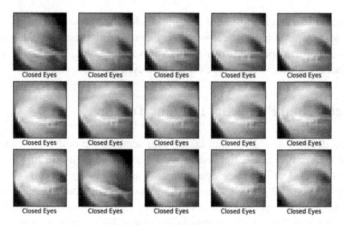

Fig. 2. Closed left eye

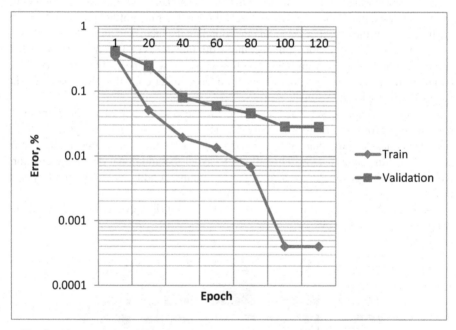

Fig. 3. Characteristics of learning process on the example of the left eye state recognition

As can be seen from Fig. 2, these images are labeled correctly and can be used to train the model. In this case, two models will be trained separately: one that recognizes the state of the left eye and one that recognizes the state of the right eye.

Figure 3 shows the learning process based on the simplest gradient descent (SGD) algorithm for 120 training epochs (training and validation samples are divided in a ratio of 90% by 10%).

The analysis of the presented curves shows that a sharp relative drop in the value of erroneous recognitions occurs for the training sample after the 80th epoch. Until then, it can be assumed that the overfitting effect is not significant. It should be noted that the graph is presented on a logarithmic scale, and instead of accuracy, the Y-axis represents the proportion of erroneous recognitions, the X-axis represents number of training epoch.

5   Results of the Software Implementation

The trained model was tested in real time mode. At the same time, the possibility of determining closed eyes with some error was revealed. It should be noted that the distance from the camera within the permissible values practically did not affect the recognition accuracy. However, with sufficient removal, the system errors increased significantly. For example, for a distance of more than 1 m, the work results are greatly degraded. Figure 4 shows the values of the average accuracy at different distances of the face from the camera.

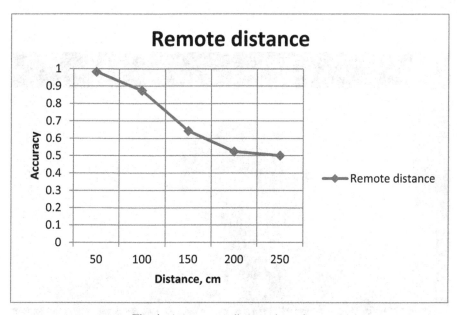

Fig. 4. Accuracy on distance dependence

Figure 5, 6 and 7 show examples of the work of the developed software in Python using Jupyter Notebook and OpenCV. Moreover, Fig. 5 corresponds to the state with open eyes, Fig. 6 - with one eye closed, Fig. 7 - with both eyes closed.

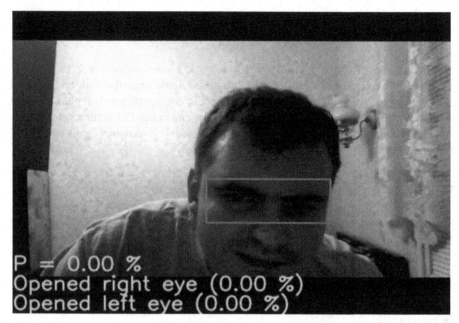

Fig. 5. Open eyes recognition: the percents indicate model's estimated probability of closed eye statement

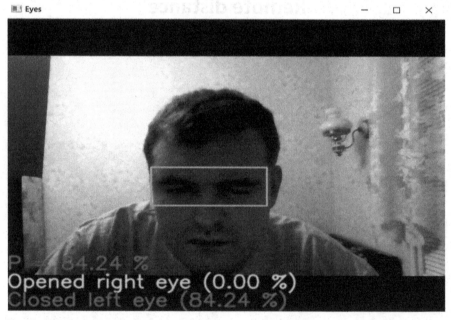

Fig. 6. Closed eye (only one eye) recognition: the percents indicate model's estimated probability of closed eye statement

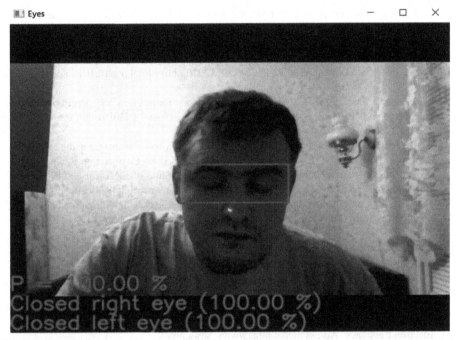

Fig. 7. Closed eyes (both eyes) recognition: the percents indicate model's estimated probability of closed eye statement

It should be noted that as a percentage, the neural network displays the probability that a particular eye is closed, even if an open eye is detected.

In addition, it should be noted that the shooting was made in average lighting conditions in dim light (not dark, not light), and the result of the program is positive.

6   Conclusion

The article considered the task of analyzing the state of the driver. One of the elements of such an analysis can be an analysis of the state of the eyes, which makes it possible to identify drowsy drivers. The developed closed-eye recognition algorithms provide, on average, the accuracy of such a system over 90% with a camera with a low resolution and medium lighting conditions. In the future, it is planned to refine the system for images obtained using cameras with IR illumination.

Acknowledgement. The reported study was funded by RFBR, Project number 19-29-09048.

References

1. Lim, S.M., Chia, S.E.: The prevalence of fatigue and associated health and safety risk factors among taxi drivers in Singapore. Singapore Med. J. **56**(2), 92–97 (2015). https://doi.org/10. 11622/smedj.2014169

2. Andriyanov, N.A.: Development of prediction methods for taxi order service on the basis of intellectual data analysis. Adv. Intell. Syst. Comput. **1230**, 652–664 (2020). https://doi.org/10.1007/978-3-030-52243-8_49
3. Filina-Dawidowicz, L., et al.: Information support of cargo ferry transport: case study of Latvia. Procedia Comput. Sci. **176**, 2192–2201 (2020). https://doi.org/10.1016/j.procs.2020.09.256
4. Gurevich, I., Yashina, V.: Descriptive image analysis. foundations and descriptive image algebras. Int. J. Pattern Recogn. Artif. Intell. **33**(11), 1940018 (2019). https://doi.org/10.1142/s0218001419400184
5. Andriyanov, N.A., Andriyanov, D.A.: pattern recognition on radar images using augmentation. In: Proceedings - 2020 Ural Symposium on Biomedical Engineering, Radioelectronics and Information Technology, USBEREIT 2020. Institute of Electrical and Electronics Engineers Inc., pp. 289–291 (2020). https://doi.org/10.1109/usbereit48449.2020.9117669
6. Jiang, Y., Li, C.: Convolutional neural networks for image-based high-throughput plant phenotyping: a review. Plant Phenomics **24**, 415–426 (2020). https://doi.org/10.34133/2020/4152816
7. Pimplaskar, D., Nagmode, M., Borkar, A.: Real time eye blinking detection and tracking using openCV. Comput. Sci. **3**, 1780–1787 (2013)
8. Panwar, N.: Real time face and eyes detection using Open CV. Electronic resource. Access mode: https://medium.com/@nitinpanwar98/real-time-face-and-eyes-detection-using-open-cv-1e477ee17d46
9. Electronic resource. Access mode: http://mrl.cs.vsb.cz/eyedataset
10. Electronic resource. Access mode: https://www.sowa.pro/
11. Kozlovsky, A.I., Porvatov, I.N., Podolsky, M.S.: Review of automotive systems for operational monitoring of the driver's condition. Results of own research. Science of Science 6, 1–12 (2013)
12. Andriyanov, N.A.: Analysis of the acceleration of neural networks inference on intel processors based on openVINO toolkit. In: 2020 Systems of Signal Synchronization, Generating and Processing in Telecommunications, SYNCHROINFO 2020. Institute of Electrical and Electronics Engineers Inc., pp. 1–5 (2020). https://doi.org/10.1109/synchroinfo49631.2020.9166067

IUC 2020 - The 1st International Workshop on Human and Vehicle Analysis for Intelligent Urban Computing

Workshop on Human and Vehicle Analysis for Intelligent Urban Computing (IUC)

Workshop Description

The rapid proliferation of urbanization has modernized people's lives and at the same time engendered critical challenges, such as traffic congestion, energy consumption, public security, and environmental pollution. Today, multiple multimedia sensing technologies and large-scale computing infrastructures are producing at a rapid velocity a wide variety of big multi-modality data in urban spaces, which provide rich knowledge about a city to help tackle these challenges. Consequently, intelligent urban computing has been attracting increasing attention from academia and industry. Among them, human analysis and vehicle analysis constitute the most important foundation for intelligent urban computing. These applications are becoming pervasive in the field of urban planning, transportation systems, environmental conservation, energy consumption, economy, and public security. The goal of this workshop is to: 1) bring together the state of the art research on human and vehicle analysis for intelligent urban computing; 2) call for a coordinated effort to understand the opportunities and challenges emerging in human and vehicle analysis; 3) identify key tasks and evaluate the state-of-the-art methods; 4) showcase innovative methodologies and ideas; 5) introduce interesting real-world intelligent urban computing systems or applications; and 6) propose new real-world datasets and discuss future directions. We solicit original contributions in all fields of human and vehicle analysis that explore the big data in big cities to help us understand the nature of urban phenomena and even predict the future of cities. We believe the workshop will offer a timely collection of research updates to benefit the researchers and practitioners working in the broad computer vision, multimedia, and pattern recognition communities.

The first edition of the International Workshop on Human and Vehicle Analysis for Intelligent Urban Computing (IUC 2020) was held in Milan, Italy. For the first time, this workshop was organized in conjunction with the 25th International Conference on Pattern Recognition. The format of the workshop included a keynote followed by technical presentations.

This year we received 14 submissions for reviews, from authors belonging to 4 distinct countries. Each paper was reviewed by at least three reviewers. After an accurate and thorough peer-review process, we selected 7 papers for presentation at the workshop. The review process focused on the quality of the papers, their scientific novelty and applicability to existing intelligent urban computing problems and frameworks. The acceptance of the papers was the result of the reviewers' discussion and agreement. All the high quality papers were accepted, and the acceptance rate was 50%. The accepted articles represent an interesting mix of techniques to solve recurrent as well as new problems in intelligent urban computing, such as facial landmark detection, multi-camera tracking, 3D action recognition, arithmetic evaluation system, city-scale vehicle detection, vehicle re-identification, and taxi pick-up area recommendation.

We also invited three keynote-speak: 1) "Challenges in Face Recognition and Solutions" given by Prof. Stan Z. Li from Westlake University, China; 2) "Deploy Robotaxi at Scale in China", given by Dr. Tony Han from WeRide.ai, California, USA; 3) "Human Object Interaction Detection and Segmentation", given by Si Liu from Beihang University, China.

Last but not least, we would like to thank the IUC 2020 Program Committee, whose members made the workshop possible with their rigorous and timely review process. We would also like to thank ICPR 2020 for hosting the workshop and our emerging community, and the ICPR 2020 workshop chairs for the valuable help and support.

Organization

Organization Chairs

Wu Liu	JD AI Research, Beijing, China
Hailin Shi	JD AI Research, Beijing, China
Yunchao Wei	University of Technology Sydney, Australia
Dan Zeng	Shanghai University, China
Jiebo Luo	University of Rochester, USA

Program Committee

Bowen Cheng	University of Illinois Urbana-Champaign, USA
Cheng Zhang	The Ohio State University, USA
Chenyu Li	Institute of Information Engineering, Chinese Academy of Sciences, China
Chuangchuang Tan	Beijing Jiaotong University, China
Dawei Du	Kitware, Inc., USA
Fan Ma	University of Technology Sydney, Australia
Feng Zhu	University of Technology Sydney, Australia
Guangrui Li	University of Technology Sydney, Australia
Hang Du	Shanghai University, China
Kangkai Zhang	Chinese Academy of Sciences, China
Kecheng Zheng	University of Science and Technology of China, China
Kun Liu	Beijing University of Posts and Telecommunications, China
Lingxiao He	AI Research of JD.com, China
Lingyang Chu	Simon Fraser University, Canada
Peike Li	University of Technology Sydney, Australia
Qi Wang	Hasselt universty, Belgium
Qian Bao	AI Research of JD.com, China
Shan An	JD.COM, China
Shikun Li	Chinese Academy of Sciences, China
Shiyin Zhang	Beijing Jiaotong University, China
Ting Liu	Beijing Jiaotong University, China
Weijian Ruan	Wuhan University, China
Xiao Wang	Wuhan University, China
Xiaopeng Yang	Huawei Technologies, Canada
Xinchen Liu	AI Research of JD.com, China
Xindi Gao	Chinese Academy of Sciences, China

Unbalanced Optimal Transport
in Multi-camera Tracking Applications

Quoc Cuong Le[1], Donatello Conte[1(✉)], and Moncef Hidane[2]

[1] Université de Tours Laboratoire d'Informatique Fondamentale et Appliquée
de Tours, EA - 6300, Tours, France
`quoccuong.le@etu.univ-tours.fr`, `donatello.conte@univ-tours.fr`
[2] INSA Centre Val de Loire Laboratoire d'Informatique Fondamentale et Appliquée
de Tours, EA - 6300, Tours, France
`moncef.hidane@insa-cvl.fr`

Abstract. Multi-view multi-object tracking algorithms are expected to resolve multi-object tracking persistent issues within a single camera. However, the inconsistency of camera videos in most of the surveillance systems obstructs the ability of re-identifying and jointly tracking targets through different views. As a crucial task in multi-camera tracking, assigning targets from one view to another is considered as an assignment problem. This paper is presenting an alternative approach based on Unbalanced Optimal Transport for the unbalanced assignment problem. On each view, targets' position and appearance are projected on a learned metric space, and then an Unbalanced Optimal Transport algorithm is applied to find the optimal assignment of targets between pairs of views. The experiments on common multi-camera databases show the superiority of our proposal to the heuristic approach on MOT metrics.

Keywords: Multi-object tracking · Multi-view tracking · Unbalanced optimal transport

1 Introduction

Multiple Object Tracking (MOT) is still one of the most challenging and vital problems in computer vision. Therein, the goal is to determine the position and identity of a variable number of targets throughout video frames. In the past recent years, the rise of deep learning approaches [17] has led to an increase in the performance, robustness and reliability of *Single* Object Tracking (SOT) algorithms. Implementing these SOT trackers to track multiple objects simultaneously, however, appears challenging for many typical reasons, such as initialization step at every frame, interactions between targets causing frequent mutual occlusions and identity switches.

A popular approach to track multiple objects is to adopt the *tracking-by-detections* paradigm [1,40], relying on detections at every frame. This approach has been reinforced in the recent years since many powerful object detection algorithms [16,23,29], e.g., Faster R-CNN, Mask R-CNN, YOLO, SSD, have

© Springer Nature Switzerland AG 2021
A. Del Bimbo et al. (Eds.): ICPR 2020 Workshops, LNCS 12665, pp. 327–343, 2021.
https://doi.org/10.1007/978-3-030-68821-9_30

emerged and even outperformed humans in the past recent years. In principle, the detection-based MOT methods directly link together detections which belong to targets, on the entire videos, in order to form their final trajectories. *Tracking-by-detection* MOT methods lead to *data association algorithms*, often formulated as a global optimization problems in which a graph-based representation of detections with edges weighted by a distance (or similarity) is adopted. The distance between detections mostly includes Euclidean distance, time delay, and appearance affinity [2,32,35,40]. The online/offline distinguishes between methods that solely use results from previous detections, and the ones that consider the whole (or batch) time-sequence in order to compute data associations.

Both SOT-based and *online* association-based methods require an efficient way to control the state of targets in order to prevent missing tracks, occlusions, and identity switches. For SOT-based methods, Markov Decision Processes (MDP) were adopted in the papers [38,42] to tackle this issue. This approach has been extended to an overlapping multiple camera setting in [21] and has shown capability in allowing the individual cameras to recapture/re-identify their lost targets.

Within multiple camera systems, Multi-Camera Multi-Object Tracking (MCMOT) or Multi-Target Multi-Camera Tracking (MTMCT) problem is frequently formulated as an assignment problem or, in many cases, the re-identification/ recognition problems as the object of interest is mainly human or transport vehicle. Since data association approaches are extendable in multi-camera cases, most of MCMOT algorithms of the state-of-the-art are mainly derived from single-camera association-based MOT approaches. Indeed, the role of multi-camera tracking is to link detections or tracklets *across* cameras in the network. Generally, associating targets between two views is formulated as assignment problem, or bi-graph matching problem, which is originally resolved by Hungarian or Munkres algorithms. This is not the case of MOT because of the varying target number. As a solution to this issue, the modified version of the Munkres algorithm is used with virtual targets.

In our case study, we address the target association problem between different views within an overlapping camera system for online multi-camera applications. The target matching is well defined by the unbalanced assignment problem, in which the number of targets in one view is not equal to those in another view. In this paper, we propose a novel assignment approach formulated as an unbalanced optimal transport problem for multi-view tracking applications. Our second contribution is to develop a deep distance learning framework for Optimal Transport. Our third contribution is to adopt the target association between two cameras within multiple camera systems. Our multi-camera tracking framework is functional with mere pairs of cameras, which is called as "dual-camera" approach in the multi-camera tracking problem (Fig. 1). Our approach helps elevate the all-camera condition, renders it more flexible to any number of cameras inside the camera system, and essentially adapts well with our proposed assignment problem at the early of this paper.

The structure of this paper is as follows: we first mention the works related to ours; secondly, we describe the formulation of our dual-camera target association problem as unbalanced optimal transport; then introduce our proposed distance learning method of Optimal Transport based on a deep neural network; and finally, we present our experimental results showing the advantage of our method.

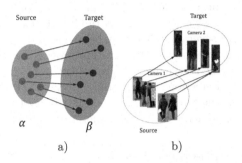

Fig. 1. (a) Assignment between two distributions as Optimal Transport problem (b) Target assignment across cameras in multiple cameras tracking application

2   Related Works

2.1   Single View Multi-object Tracking

Since handling multiple different targets is the main work of MOT algorithms, the tracking-by-detection paradigm has evolved as their major approach. This is especially true as the result of the advent of high-performing category detectors. Tracking-by-detection approaches can be sorted into the following two groups.

Offline Approaches. Following the tracking-by-detection paradigm [2,40], graph optimization problems are formulated to create links between detections of targets, in successive frames, then the chain of detections through frames determines the full trajectory of a target. These methods have become popular because they simplified the classic issues mentioned above, such as trackers management, interaction, initialization, and update. The data association problem is formulated via a graph whose nodes represent the detections/features and whose edges are weighted by the distance (or similarity) between detections. Association methods usually collect all detections/features over the video, the current position of a target (a node of the graph) being thus determined by adjacent nodes that represent past and future detections. The goal of data association methods is to optimize the cost made by the edges of the graph. There are various methods using global and flow network optimization algorithms [41], and relying on criteria such as Graph Clique [36,40], Graph Multicut [18,31], Network Flow [2,7,27,41], Maximum Weight Independent Set [5,8,20].

Online Approaches. To fulfill the need for immediate tracking results in many applications, numerous papers proposed online tracking methods [1,11,27,32, 42]. Within the tracking-by-detection paradigm, only detections in the current and previous frames are used to form targets' trajectories. One of the most popular approaches to associate detections is the bipartite matching formulation [28,32,42], usually solved by using the Hungarian algorithm or heuristic approaches. Some offline methods, which can perform online when their optimization process only uses detections from the first to current frames of videos (i.e., causal system), or several methods can be considered as "near-online" methods such as [8,31], as their offline optimization process applies on a window of frames at the time in videos, which causes the delay on tracking results. Alternatively, the tracking-by-detection strategy and multiple SOT algorithms are combined to benefit from the SOT trackers, and the ability to recover lost targets of data association approaches in [38,42], classified as SOT-based approaches.

2.2 Multi-view Multi-object Tracking

MOT approaches based on a single camera have recently been extended to multiple cameras. These approaches have been proposed in an attempt to cover the observation of the objects fully. Multiple-camera tracking can solve the problem of occlusion, where the interesting targets are frequently occluded by the environment or by other targets. First attempts in using multiple (non-overlapping) cameras dealt with the re-identification problem, in order to track objects between cameras [37]. Following this approach, many researchers studied the problem of collaboratively using overlapping cameras for tracking. Almost all authors made the hypothesis that the exact position of each camera is already known, and camera calibration has been done before applying the tracking process. In the tracking phase, the trackers implemented on different cameras usually pool their results with 3-D coordination via projection from the image plane to ground plane in the real world [24,26,33]. This allows combining the different results, and in particular, reconnecting detections/tracklets to missing targets. Meanwhile, K-shortest path (KSP) [15] only uses detections from all cameras to first detect targets' positions on the ground via a POM (Probabilistic Occupancy Map), then perform tracking later.

Besides of the above generic multi-camera tracking approaches, the methods based on the tracking-by-detection arises as an alternative. These methods inherit from most of the global optimization methods of MOT in single view such as graph multicuts [18,31,35], graph cliques [10,40], network flow [7,27,41]. Meanwhile, the other data association methods including bipartite matching [1,32] and independent set [5,20] do not address multi-camera tracking problem, because the tracklets are formed through the detections in consecutive frames (i.e., a short time window) of a single view, whereas tracking with multiple cameras is to connect trajectories of targets at different times. Some other approaches [19,36] generalize multi-camera tracking into two main steps: MOT on every single view, then linking the trajectories across cameras. Unfortunately, none of those mentioned methods perform online. Recently, Le et al. [21]

introduced an online multi-camera tracking based on data association on each processing frame. In the next section, we introduce our dual-camera tracking approach in a multi-camera setting based on unbalanced optimal transport to handle hard occlusions and prevents identity switches. Our strategy is to assign targets from one to another view with the help of Deep Neural Nets. In literature, there are several approaches that have the same initiative to combine deep neural nets and optimization methods on which gradients are backpropagated such as [4,39]. However, to the best of our knowledge, our paper is the first one applying this strategy in MOT with the multiple overlapping cameras.

3   Proposed Method

3.1   Targets Association Across Cameras as an Unbalanced Optimal Transport Problem

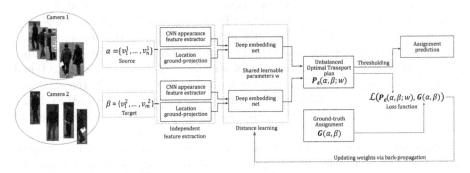

Fig. 2. The pipeline of our distance learning framework. The red arrow indicates the direction during training process, meanwhile the blue lines for testing. (Color figure online)

This section describes in detail our approach to solving target association across cameras via optimal transport. Within a frame-synchronized, overlapping camera network, associating targets between different cameras emerges as the main issue for collaborative tracking.

Let us start by considering the case of a network consisting of two cameras C_1 and C_2. At a given *frame index* F, we have $\{v^1_{1,F}, \ldots, v^1_{n,F}\}$ targets detected in Camera C_1 and $\{v^2_{1,F}, \ldots, v^2_{m,F}\}$ targets detected in Camera C_2. In order to simplify our notations, we drop the F subscript in sequel. In general, $n \neq m$, since some targets can be seen by only one camera. This can happen either because a given target occupies a position that does not belong the common field of view or, more crucially, because of occlusion.

Each detection v^k_i, $k \in \{1, 2\}$ is characterized by an *feature vector* generally consisting of an *appearance vector*, extracted from the bounding box provided by the detector, and the target's position. The current practice leverages the capability of recent deep convolutional neural networks to extract useful appearance features from the bounding boxes provided by the detectors, e.g. by using VGG [34] or ResNet [17] as a 'backbone'. For the target's position, it is necessary to define a common coordinate system, where the position of targets can be converted into the same measure unit. For pedestrian tracking, this issue is usually resolved by projecting the target's feet point on the image into the ground plane via the homography matrix of the camera. This is the solution we retain in our current setting.

These feature vectors allow to define a cost matrix $\mathbf{C} \in \mathbb{R}^{n \times m}$, whose entry $\mathbf{C}_{i,j}$ defines the cost of associating target v_i^1 to target v_j^2. The matrix C allows, in turn, to formulate the problem of target association between Cameras C_1 and C_2, at frame index F, as a, possibly unbalanced, *assignment problem*. These problems amount to solving integer linear programs, using either combinatorial algorithms such as the Hungarian or the auction algorithm, or, ignoring the integer constraints, continuous linear programming.

For associating targets across *different* cameras, the definition of an appropriate cost matrix poses two serious problems. The first one is related to the definition of appearance features. These features should incorporate some kind of invariance with respect to the different cameras, that is, the appearance feature of the same target computed through two different cameras should be close. This invariance is not necessarily enforced when using popular convolutional networks such as VGG or ResNet. The second issue is related to the combination of the appearance features and the position, the appearance features being generally in the range $[0, 1]$, while the position extending to the whole field of view.

In order to solve the issues raised by the two previous problems, we propose to adopt a learning-based approach, where *the appearance features and their combination with the target's position* are learned from a set of examples. The training data in this case are generated from the training sequences of the datasets we consider. More precisely, we extract from each training video frame the provided bounding boxes and the corresponding ground-truth assignments. With this training set at hand, we aim at *end-to-end gradient-based learning*, that is, the empirical loss that we minimize for learning should be related to the assignment task we consider, and implemented by (automatically computed) gradient descent.

Using combinatorial algorithms such as the Hungarian or auction algorithms rules out the possibility of using automatic differentiation engines for performing gradient descent. Furthermore, even when ignoring integer constraints, linear programming solvers can hardly be differentiated, since their solutions are not unique. To deal with this problem, we follow a recent line of works [9] by considering the natural relaxation of the assignment, namely the optimal transport problem and its entropic regularization [25].

In our formulation of assignment problem of targets in two views via Optimal Transport, the sets of targets $v_i^{1^n}$ in one view is being matched with those $v_i^{2^m}$ in other view. Those two sets represents two empirical distributions: one *Source* and one *Target*, supported on a feature space $\mathcal{X}$.

$$\alpha := \sum_{i=1}^{n} \mathbf{a}_i \delta_{x_i}, \quad \beta := \sum_{j=1}^{m} \mathbf{b}_j \delta_{y_j}, \tag{1}$$

where δ_x is the Dirac at $x \in \mathcal{X}$ and $\mathbf{a}_i$ and $\mathbf{b}_j$ are the corresponding weights. In our setting, we will consider uniform discrete measures, which is, all the components of a weight vector are equal.

The optimal transport between *source* ans *target* is represented by an *optimal transport plan* $\mathbf{P}$, which minimizes the following transportation cost:

$$\mathbf{L_C}(\mathbf{a},\mathbf{b}) := \min_{\mathbf{P} \in \mathbf{U}(\mathbf{a},\mathbf{b})} \langle \mathbf{C}, \mathbf{P} \rangle = \min_{\mathbf{P} \in \mathbf{U}(\mathbf{a},\mathbf{b})} \sum_{i,j} \mathbf{C}_{ij} \mathbf{P}_{ij}, \tag{2}$$

where $\mathbf{C}$ is the ground cost matrix, whose elements $\mathbf{C}_{ij}$ are the pairwise distance between the Dirac δ_{x_i} of the source measure α and those δ_{y_j} of the target measure β, and $\mathbf{U}(\mathbf{a},\mathbf{b})$ is a coupling from the *source* $\mathbf{a}$ to the *target* $\mathbf{b}$. The feasible couplings are defined by a set of coupling matrices $\{\mathbf{P} \in \mathbb{R}_+^{n \times m}\}$, where $\mathbf{P}_{ij}$ depicts the amount of mass flowing from x_i toward y_j, under the mass preservation constraint.

$$\mathbf{U}(\mathbf{a},\mathbf{b}) = \{\mathbf{P} \in \mathbb{R}_+^{n \times m} : \mathbf{P}\mathbb{1}_m = \mathbf{a} \text{ and } \mathbf{P}^T \mathbb{1}_n = \mathbf{b}\}. \tag{3}$$

The Optimal Transport (OT) problem with entropic regularization has a dual form following [13]:

$$\min_{\mathbf{P}>0} \max_{(\mathbf{f},\mathbf{g}) \in \mathbb{R}^n \times \mathbb{R}^m} \langle \mathbf{C}, \mathbf{P} \rangle - \varepsilon \mathbf{H}(\mathbf{P}) + \langle \mathbf{a} - \mathbf{P}\mathbb{1}_m, \mathbf{f} \rangle + \langle \mathbf{b} - \mathbf{P}^T \mathbb{1}_n, \mathbf{g} \rangle \tag{4}$$

where the set of admissible dual variables (called *potentials*) $(\mathbf{f} \in \mathbb{R}^n, \mathbf{g} \in \mathbb{R}^m)$. The optimal transport plan solved via the dual problem (4) has a closed-form [13]:

$$\mathbf{P}^{\star} = \pi = \exp\left(\frac{1}{\varepsilon}(\mathbf{f} \oplus \mathbf{g} - \mathbf{C})\right) \cdot (\alpha \otimes \beta), \tag{5}$$

where $\mathbf{f} \oplus \mathbf{g}$ is denoted as a sum matrix of 2 vectors f and g whose cell $\{\mathbf{f} \oplus \mathbf{g}\}_{ij}$ is equal to $\mathbf{f}_i + \mathbf{g}_j$, in the same manner, $\alpha \otimes \beta$ is also denoted as a product matrix of 2 vectors α and β whose cell $\{\alpha \otimes \beta\}_{ij}$ is equal to $\alpha_i \beta_j$.

3.2 Ground Cost Learning for UOT-Based Targets Association Across Cameras

This section describes our proposed deep distance learning framework, which helps to compute an appropriate distance for the Optimal Transport problem between targets of one camera and those of another. More concretely, on each camera, the appearance feature of each target is extracted from its image patch via a deep convolutional neural network, e.g. VGG [34], ResNet [17]. Meanwhile, its position x is determined by projecting the target's feet point on the image into the ground plane via the homography matrix of the camera. Both the appearance and location feature vectors are the input of a deep neural network whose output is an embedding in a feature space $\mathcal{X}$. The collection of all points mapped from all targets of a camera via the deep neural net generates a distribution. As discussed in the previous section, given two distributions originated from the targets of a pair of cameras, target association in a pair of two cameras is an Unbalanced Optimal Transport from a distribution, called *source*, to the other one, called *target*. Therefore, the Optimal Transport plan is followed by a thresholding step, to obtain a binary matrix as the association matrix of targets between the two cameras. Figure 2 displays the pipeline of our distance learning framework, which aims to learn ground cost between targets across cameras so that the optimal transport plan approximates the ground-truth assignment.

Because our deep-learning-based method is a supervised learning approach, it is required a training data with labels. Our training data are directly generated from the training sequences of a dataset. Precisely, for each frame of videos, every pair of cameras gives a single assignment as the label of a sample, while the data of the sample is extracted from the ground-truth bounding boxes via the deep extracting feature net. In the case of N cameras in the network, the combination of camera possible pairs is $N(N-1)/2$, which is also the number of samples generated in each frame instant.

In our formulation, for each target i, given $\Phi_i \in \mathbb{R}^{2048}$ (i.e., output of ResNet50 backbone [17]) and $x_i \in \mathbb{R}^2$ (i.e., target coordinate on ground), the embedding function f_w, via our deep neural network (see Fig. 3), projects the appearance feature and location of target i into the feature space $\mathcal{X}$,

$$f_w : (\Phi, x) \to \mathcal{X},$$

where w is the parameters of the deep neural net. As a result of unbalanced optimal transport, the transport plan shows the mass flows from point i of *source* to point j of *target*. Based on the properties of optimal transport [25], any pair of close points distributions *source* and *target* results in a significant mass flow on its transport plan compared with others. Figure 4 (a) is an optimal transport plan in which i^{th} row represents the mass of the ith *source* point being transferred to all *target*. Since only consistent mass transfers from one point on *source* to a unique point in *target* is sought, the optimal transport plan between *source* and *target* is expected to be well "sparse", which means that the matching can be deduced straightforwardly (see Fig. 4 (b)) by thresholding the optimal transport plan. We then can obtain the assignment from *source* to *target*.

In terms of optimization, the dissimilarity between the optimal transport plan $\mathbf{P}_\varepsilon(\alpha, \beta)$ and the ground-truth assignment $\mathbf{G}(\alpha, \beta)$ is measured by a loss function $\mathcal{L}$. The learnable parameters w of our neural net is then determined via a minimization problem:

$$w = \arg\min_w \mathcal{L}\left(\mathbf{P}_\varepsilon\left(.; w\right), \mathbf{G}(.)\right) \tag{6}$$

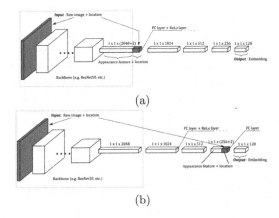

(a)

(b)

Fig. 3. Proposed distance learning neural net. The neural net consists of a CNN backbone (e.g. ResNet50 in our case), which extract appearance features from raw image, and a series of Fully Connected (FC) layers with ReLU layers as activations. Model (a) with locations at the bottom of the deep distance network, meanwhile, model (b) with locations at the second last FC layer.

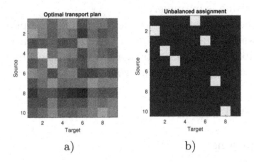

a)   b)

Fig. 4. Comparison between optimal transport plan (a) and assignment matrix (b)

The loss functions in our framework are formulated as following. Given two sets of targets $\left\{v_i^{k_1}\right\}_n$ and $\left\{v_j^{k_2}\right\}_m$, each belongs to a single camera, the assignment task is to find the correspondence of common targets in the pair of cameras k_1 and k_2 while excluding the targets which can be seen in only one view. Given $\mathbf{P}_\varepsilon \in \mathbb{R}_+^{n \times m}$ the transport plan and $\mathbf{G} \in \{0,1\}^{n \times m}$ the ground-truth assignment, we propose our loss which is delivered from the dual problem of regularized optimal transport problem (4). Therefore, the first order condition to reach the optimal solution [25] yields to:

$$\log(\mathbf{P}_{ij}) = \frac{\mathbf{f}_i + \mathbf{g}_j - \mathbf{C}_{ij}}{\varepsilon} \tag{7}$$

In the training phase of our experiments, by default, both total masses of the measure α and β are equal 1. The constraint of mass conservation in the

Balanced Optimal Transport problem leads to the sum of all elements of the optimal transport plan $\mathbf{P}$ smaller or equal 1. The equality happens in the case of the balanced optimal transport, and the inequality for the Unbalanced Optimal Transport case. As a result, the ground-truth assignment $\mathbf{G}$ needs to be normalized to keep the assignment matrix and optimal transport plan comparable. Hence, from the expression of the transport plan (7), our loss is formulated as follows:

$$\mathcal{L}\left(\mathbf{P}_\varepsilon, \mathbf{G}\right) = \sum_{i,j} \left| \log(\mathbf{G}'_{ij}) - \max\left(\frac{\mathbf{f}_i + \mathbf{g}_j - \mathbf{C}_{ij}}{\varepsilon}, \log \sigma\right)\right| \tag{8}$$

where the normalized assignment coupling $\mathbf{G}_{i,j}$ is defined as

$$\mathbf{G}'_{ij} = \frac{\mathbf{G}_{ij}}{\sum_{i,j} \mathbf{G}_{ij} + \gamma} + \sigma \geq \sigma \tag{9}$$

with σ is a tiny threshold value, and γ is a normalization constant. This threshold value is added to avoid the logarithm of zero value in the loss function (8) and to set a margin for any near-zero transport, which does not contribute to the distance loss if its value is extremely low.

Additionally, the parameters of our neural net w are updated iteratively via minimizing the loss $\mathcal{L}$. The derivation of the loss function to the net parameters $\partial \mathcal{L}/\partial w$ is computed via back-propagation, which occurs after every optimal transport of a *source-target* pair from two cameras.

4   Experimental Results

4.1   Implementations

In our implementations, we build two versions of distance learning neural nets in order to compute the source-target distance in the Optimal Transport:

(a) The appearance feature of targets obtained from the backbone of ResNet50, in addition to their location, is considered as the inputs of our distance learning network. Our deep network is a series of Full Connected Layers with ReLU layer on the top of each. The outputs of FC layers are respectively 1024, 512, 256 and 128 (see Fig. 3 (a)).
(b) The second model is modified from the original one, but instead of using locations in the first layer, it is concatenated with the second last output layer. The intuition behind is to emphasize the location feature of targets, because, in tracking applications, positions of targets are crucial to the performance of tracking algorithm (see Fig. 3 (b)).

In the deployment phase, numerous experiments with different configurations are conducted within the framework of multiple camera tracking of the paper [21]. Therefore, the target assignment or matching is applied on only two cameras, collaborative tracking in our multiple camera approach occurs on pairs of cameras, but one camera can reach all others through the whole tracking process. Precisely, at each frame, each camera consecutively pairs with all other cameras, then within each pair of cameras, an optimal transport plan $\mathbf{C}$ is computed in order to link targets from one camera to the other in the pair. As mentioned in the Sect. 3.1, the value of each cell C_{ij} of the optimal transport plan implies how likely element i of *source* set is matched to element j of *target* set based on the amount of mass being transferred, named *OT value*. Therefore, each missing target on one view is associated with its corresponding target on each other view by an OT value obtained from its optimal transport plan. Hence, the tracking result of the missing target is replaced by the "tracked" target with the *highest* value among its correspondences on all other cameras.

The Optimal Transport algorithm we used in this paper is a public Optimal Transport library [14] on Python with GPU parallelization support, named KeOps-GeomLoss[1]. The parameters of the unbalanced optimal transport problem (4) are set as follows:$p = 2$; "blur" $= 0.5 \to \varepsilon = blur^p$; "reach" $= 0.1 \to \tau_1 = \tau_2 = \tau = reach^p$; $D_\varphi = KL$: soft Kullback–Leibler divergence.

Meanwhile, the other parameters in the expression (9) are adjusted for $\sigma = 10^{-8}$ and $\gamma = 10^{-4}$. The value of threshold to convert transport plan to assignment matrix is set equal to 10^{-3}, which is greater than σ in order to reduce the sensibility during testing phrase. The detailed implementation of our deep distance learning method will be available publicly on our project page.

4.2 Benchmarking Performance

This section shows our experimental results verifying the efficiency of the multi-camera MOT algorithm with various appearance features. As a performance evaluation for MOT algorithms, the benchmark MotChallenge [22] has been released with two datasets (MOT15 and MOT16), which contain many single-view video sequences recorded by static or dynamic cameras, and the evaluation metrics of CLEAR MOT [3] and ID measure [30] are used. Additionally, the MotChallenge also provides multiple video sequences, but most of them are not from multiple camera aspect, which requires overlapping zones, synchronization, calibration. Therefore, these datasets, unfortunately, unfit to this case study that focuses on using multiple overlapping views to tackle the targets missing by occlusions. As the multi-camera method aims to improve identity robustness in single views, we will emphasize ID scores in the sequel.

Datasets. In our experiments we used the well-known PETS2009 [12] and EPFL Multi-camera Pedestrian Videos [2] datasets. Among all sequences of PETS2009, the most relevant and suitable for our multiple-camera tracking system is "PETS09-S2L1" with 7 views from 7 synchronized and calibrated cameras. For our experiment, only one main view (from the camera 1) and 4 close-up views (from the cameras 5, 6, 7, and 8) are used. Besides of the sequence "PETS09-S2L1" with 7 cameras, the sequence "PETS09-S2L2" is also available with only

---

[1] https://www.kernel-operations.io/geomloss/.

3 cameras. The scenario of surveillance is to track an influx of people moving on the roads with different speed, and this makes it far more crowded that "PETS09-S2L1". Since the lack of cameras in this sequence, we set up dual-camera tracking experiments on View 1 and View 2. View 3 is excluded, due to its small impact on the sequence and the absence of ground-truth data as well. On the other hand, the EPFL dataset provides multiple indoor and outdoor video sequences, recording pedestrians by 4 different cameras. Due to the similarity between sequence scenarios, only the sequence "Terrace1" is selected for the experiments. In terms of camera topology, only about 15–20% of the observable zones are covered by all cameras in our tracking sequences.

Detection. In all tracking-by-detection approaches, the detector plays an important role in tracking performance. Detections in video frames are generated by the public high-accuracy detectors such as OpenPose [6] and R-CNN [16].

Evaluation Metric. To validate the efficiency of our various settings on the multi-camera MOT approach, we adopt the CLEAR MOT metrics and ID measures and in particular the following scores: MOTA (multiple-object tracking accuracy), MOTP (multiple-object tracking precision), IDs (identity switches), IDF1 (ID F1-score), IDP (ID precision), IDR (ID Recall), False Positive (FP) and False Negative (FN). For further details on the metric, we recommend the MOTChallenge website[1]. In comparison between MOT scores and ID-measures, all multiple camera approaches slightly improves both MOTA and MOTP scores, regarding to ID-measures. Because the CLEAR MOT metric does not focus on re-identification ability of tracking algorithms [30], while ID-measure scores does. In other words, the significant improvement can be seen on IDF1 and IDP score. As another important indicator for tracking performance in CLEAR MOT metric, IDs score (i.e. identity switches) relates more to ID preservation, which is essential in multiple camera tracking. Therefore, in the following analysis, we measure the impact of methods based on IDF1, IDP and IDs scores rather than MOTA and MOTP.

4.3   Performance Analysis

The results shown in the following tables are the average values of all views. Concretely, the overall tracking results of the PETS sequence can be seen in the Table 1, Table 2 and Table 3. Each score column has either a ↑ or a ↓ indicating whether better corresponds to higher or lower, respectively. The red color indicates the best score and the blue for the second best .

Primarily, our multi-camera tracking method aims to address hard occlusion problems. It leads to an important reduction of identity switches and a significant improvement of ID measures in comparison with the single-camera method. In the sequence "PETS09-S2L1", the targets have their complex movements and mutual interactions inside the overlapped area of the tracking scene. All the methods using the target trajectory as the features of the affinity measure show the better scores in all categories, in comparison with the approaches, which do not consider historical position record of targets (i.e., trajectories), but only

Table 1. Scores on "PETS09-S2L1" multi-camera sequence.

Method + Feature	IDF1↑	IDP ↑	IDs↓	MOTA↑	MOTP↑
Single cam [38]+∅	57.49	62.24	333	68.44	68.83
All cam [21]+path	72.8	78.53	98	73.26	70.69
KSP [15]+∅	21.51	18.16	812	−29.63	64.27
Dual-cam [21]+path	67.96	72.72	126	73.4	70.65
Dual-cam UOT+DL (a)	68.15	73.41	153	73.16	70.81
Dual-cam UOT+DL (b)	66.71	71.73	174	72.19	70.65
Dual-cam UOT+pos	66.04	70.66	163	72.76	70.60

the instant measure including image patch and position of targets. In detail, the method with full camera collaboration (All-cam) [21] shows off its superiority. Meanwhile, our Unbalanced Optimal Transport approach (UOT) is less robust, but still significantly improves tracking scores compared to single-camera approach. Notwithstanding, in the tests with the sequence "EPFL/terrace1", the tracking scene composes 8 identities moving mainly around a relatively small area covered by a smaller camera number, which makes the scene more crowded and targets hardly seen by all cameras. Consequently, the original approach [21] failed to improve tracking results, because, with a smaller camera amount, it is obviously less probable that there are more than 2 or 3 cameras observed the same target at the same time. The results in Table 2 show that all other approaches with dual-camera mode perform significantly better than the original ones. The next remark is that in the scenario where there are only short trajectories that can be seen, the trajectory feature is less reliable. In other words, shorter trajectories, less effective the original approach is. Hence, in Table 2, our distance learning method based on Optimal Transport outweighs the conventional approaches which only use position or trajectory of target as input feature for affinity measure.

Table 2. Scores on "terrace1" multi-camera sequence.

Method + Feature	IDF1↑	IDP ↑	IDs↓	MOTA↑	MOTP↑
Single cam [38]+∅	21.88	25.66	388	55.98	72.53
All cam [21]+path	21.32	25.05	461	54.14	72.47
KSP [15]+∅	25.85	23.51	695	19.57	62.26
Dual-cam [21]+path	23.23	26.72	382	56.71	72.43
Dual-cam UOT+DL (a)	24.36	31.40	305	46.86	72.91
Dual-cam UOT+DL (b)	25.15	28.88	385	56.93	72.63
Dual-cam UOT+pos	22.00	25.32	381	56.40	72.48

Secondly, the KSP method performs poorly on the sequence PETS09-S2L1, but gives a greater score on EPFL/terrace1. We can explain that KSP method was developed on the EPFL Multiple View Pedestrian Dataset. In fact, they assume that the targets being observed by cameras system does not leave the scene during their presence. In other words, the targets have to finish their complete trajectories before leaving the scene. The out/in positions of targets is also fixed on the scene, so we can see the actors walking in and out at the same place. Under these conditions, they came up with the K-shortest path problem where K, which is the number of targets in the tracking videos. On EPFL/terrace1, the algorithm has found 8 paths, which exactly corresponds to 8 targets in the video that help them get the highest IDF1 score. Back to the sequence PETS09, the algorithm cannot deal with the targets that usually went out of and returned to the scene. It only found the longest paths and ignored the targets which appeared in a short period of time and regularly got confused by other targets at the boundary. Moreover, in this database, there is no constrain on where people will appear and disappear on the scene. Apparently, this leads to a negative score on MOTA. It indicates that the KSP algorithm cannot handle the enter/exit of targets. Another problem with KSP is that the tracking process occurs on a grid, called Probabilistic Occupancy Map (POM), the discrete unit size directly affects the accuracy of the tracker. Unfortunately, increasing the size of POM required more iterations to make sure the occupancy map converged correctly.

Table 3. Scores on "PETS09-S2L2" dual-camera sequence.

Method + Feature	IDF1↑	IDP ↑	IDs↓	MOTA↑	MOTP↑
Single cam [38]+∅	53.46	55.53	321	63.66	75.14
Dual-cam [21]+path	55.63	57.67	327	63.79	75.16
Dual-cam UOT+DL (a)	53.16	55.76	310	62.62	75.16
Dual-cam UOT+DL (b)	53.75	55.83	329	63.51	75.16
Dual-cam UOT+pos	57.30	59.38	312	63.74	74.98

Finally, on the tests with dual-camera sequence "PETS09-S2L2", we excluded the methods which require more than 2 cameras to be operational, including all camera [21] and KSP [2]. As single object trackers can generate long trajectories for targets, trajectories are still an important feature to distinguish targets that we can see in Table 3. The approach [21] with dual-camera only using trajectory as target features archived the second-best result on ID-measures and the best on MOT-scores. Meanwhile, our UOT dual-cam approach based on position only obtained the best scores on ID-measures and the second-best on MOT-scores. Unfortunately, two of our UOT methods using distance learning could not outperform others in this sequence.

5   Conclusion

In this paper, we proposed a novel unbalanced assignment method based on optimal transport to address the target assignment problem between two cameras in an online multi-camera tracking application. A deep metric learning method is introduced with an efficient metric loss function. Our experiments showed the effectiveness of our approach to the multiple camera tracking systems.

References

1. Andriluka, M., Roth, S., Schiele, B.: People-tracking-by-detection and people-detection-by-tracking. In: 2008 IEEE Conference on CVPR, pp. 1–8. IEEE (2008)
2. Berclaz, J., Fleuret, F., Turetken, E., Fua, P.: Multiple object tracking using k-shortest paths optimization. IEEE Trans. on PAMI **33**(9), 1806–1819 (2011)
3. Bernardin, K., Stiefelhagen, R.: Evaluating multiple object tracking performance: the clear mot metrics. J. Image Video Process. **2008**, 1 (2008)
4. Brachmann, E., Rother, C.: Neural-guided ransac: learning where to sample model hypotheses. In: ICCV, pp. 4322–4331 (2019)
5. Brendel, W., Amer, M., Todorovic, S.: Multiobject tracking as maximum weight independent set. In: CVPR 2011, pp. 1273–1280. IEEE (2011)
6. Cao, Z., Simon, T., Wei, S.E., Sheikh, Y.: Realtime multi-person 2d pose estimation using part affinity fields. In: CVPR (2017)
7. Chari, V., Lacoste-Julien, S., Laptev, I., Sivic, J.: On pairwise costs for network flow multi-object tracking. In: CVPR, pp. 5537–5545 (2015)
8. Choi, W.: Near-online multi-target tracking with aggregated local flow descriptor. In: ICCV, pp. 3029–3037 (2015)
9. Cuturi, M., Teboul, O., Vert, J.P.: Differentiable ranks and sorting using optimal transport. arXiv preprint arXiv:1905.11885 (2019)
10. Dehghan, A., Modiri Assari, S., Shah, M.: Gmmcp tracker: Globally optimal generalized maximum multi clique problem for multiple object tracking. In: CVPR, pp. 4091–4099 (2015)
11. Fagot-Bouquet, L., Audigier, R., Dhome, Y., Lerasle, F.: Improving multi-frame data association with sparse representations for robust near-online multi-object tracking. In: Leibe, B., Matas, J., Sebe, N., Welling, M. (eds.) ECCV 2016. LNCS, vol. 9912, pp. 774–790. Springer, Cham (2016). https://doi.org/10.1007/978-3-319-46484-8_47
12. Ferryman, J., Shahrokni, A.: Pets 2009: Dataset and challenge. In: PETS-Winter, pp. 1–6. IEEE (2009)
13. Feydy, J., Séjourné, T., Vialard, F.X., Amari, S.I., Trouvé, A., Peyré, G.: Interpolating between optimal transport and mmd using sinkhorn divergences. arXiv preprint arXiv:1810.08278 (2018)
14. Feydy, J., Séjourné, T., Vialard, F.X., Amari, S.i., Trouve, A., Peyré, G.: Interpolating between optimal transport and mmd using sinkhorn divergences. In: The 22nd International Conference on Artificial Intelligence and Statistics, pp. 2681–2690 (2019)
15. Fleuret, F., Berclaz, J., Lengagne, R., Fua, P.: Multicamera people tracking with a probabilistic occupancy map. IEEE Trans. on PAMI **30**(2), 267–282 (2008)
16. He, K., Gkioxari, G., Dollár, P., Girshick, R.: Mask r-cnn. In: Proceeding of the IEEE International Conference on Computer Vision, pp. 2961–2969 (2017)

17. He, K., Zhang, X., Ren, S., Sun, J.: Deep residual learning for image recognition. In: CVPR, pp. 770–778 (2016)
18. Keuper, M., Tang, S., Zhongjie, Y., Andres, B., Brox, T., Schiele, B.: A multi-cut formulation for joint segmentation and tracking of multiple objects. arXiv preprint arXiv:1607.06317 (2016)
19. Khan, S., Shah, M.: Consistent labeling of tracked objects in multiple cameras with overlapping fields of view. IEEE Trans. on PAMI **25**(10), 1355–1360 (2003)
20. Kim, C., Li, F., Ciptadi, A., Rehg, J.M.: Multiple hypothesis tracking revisited. In: ICCV, pp. 4696–4704 (2015)
21. Le, Q.C., Conte, D., Hidane, M.: Online multiple view tracking: Targets association across cameras. In: 6th Workshop on AMMDS (2018)
22. Leal-Taixé, L., Milan, A., Reid, I., Roth, S., Schindler, K.: MOTChallenge 2015: Towards a benchmark for multi-target tracking. arXiv:1504.01942 [cs] (2015)
23. Liu, W., et al.: SSd: single shot multibox detector. In: Leibe, B., Matas, J., Sebe, N., Welling, M. (eds.) ECCV 2016. LNCS, vol. 9905, pp. 21–37. Springer, Cham (2016). https://doi.org/10.1007/978-3-319-46448-0_2
24. Mikic, I., Santini, S., Jain, R.: Video processing and integration from multiple cameras. In: Proceedings of the 1998 Image Understanding Workshop. vol. 6 (1998)
25. Peyré, G., Cuturi, M., et al.: Computational optimal transport. Foundations and Trends® in Machine Learning **11**(5–6), 355–607 (2019)
26. Pflugfelder, R., Bischof, H.: Localization and trajectory reconstruction in surveillance cameras with nonoverlapping views. IEEE Trans. Pattern Anal. Mach. Intell. **32**(4), 709–721 (2010)
27. Pirsiavash, H., Ramanan, D., Fowlkes, C.C.: Globally-optimal greedy algorithms for tracking a variable number of objects. In: CVPR, pp. 1201–1208 (2011)
28. Reilly, V., Idrees, H., Shah, M.: Detection and tracking of large number of targets in wide area surveillance. In: Daniilidis, K., Maragos, P., Paragios, N. (eds.) ECCV 2010. LNCS, vol. 6313, pp. 186–199. Springer, Heidelberg (2010). https://doi.org/10.1007/978-3-642-15558-1_14
29. Ren, S., He, K., Girshick, R., Sun, J.: Faster r-cnn: Towards real-time object detection with region proposal networks. In: Advances in Neural Information Processing Systems, pp. 91–99 (2015)
30. Ristani, E., Solera, F., Zou, R., Cucchiara, R., Tomasi, C.: Performance measures and a data set for multi-target, multi-camera tracking. In: Hua, G., Jégou, H. (eds.) ECCV 2016. LNCS, vol. 9914, pp. 17–35. Springer, Cham (2016). https://doi.org/10.1007/978-3-319-48881-3_2
31. Ristani, E., Tomasi, C.: Tracking multiple people online and in real time. In: Cremers, D., Reid, I., Saito, H., Yang, M.-H. (eds.) ACCV 2014. LNCS, vol. 9007, pp. 444–459. Springer, Cham (2015). https://doi.org/10.1007/978-3-319-16814-2_29
32. Sadeghian, A., Alahi, A., Savarese, S.: Tracking the untrackable: Learning to track multiple cues with long-term dependencies. arXiv:1701.01909 **4**(5), 6 (2017)
33. Sankaranarayanan, A.C., Veeraraghavan, A., Chellappa, R.: Object detection, tracking and recognition for multiple smart cameras. Proc. IEEE **96**(10), 1606–1624 (2008)
34. Simonyan, K., Zisserman, A.: Very deep convolutional networks for large-scale image recognition. arXiv preprint arXiv:1409.1556 (2014)
35. Tang, S., Andres, B., Andriluka, M., Schiele, B.: Subgraph decomposition for multi-target tracking. In: Proceedings of the IEEE Conference on Computer Vision and Pattern Recognition, pp. 5033–5041 (2015)

36. Tesfaye, Y.T., Zemene, E., Prati, A., Pelillo, M., Shah, M.: Multi-target tracking in multiple non-overlapping cameras using constrained dominant sets. arXiv preprint arXiv:1706.06196 (2017)
37. Wang, X.: Intelligent multi-camera video surveillance: a review. Pattern Recogn. Lett. **34**(1), 3–19 (2013)
38. Xiang, Y., Alahi, A., Savarese, S.: Learning to track: Online multi-object tracking by decision making. In: 2015 IEEE International Conference on Computer Vision (ICCV). pp. 4705–4713. No. Epfl-conf-230283, IEEE (2015)
39. Xu, Y., Osep, A., Ban, Y., Horaud, R., Leal-Taixé, L., Alameda-Pineda, X.: How to train your deep multi-object tracker. In: Proceedings of the IEEE/CVF Conference on Computer Vision and Pattern Recognition, pp. 6787–6796 (2020)
40. Zamir, A.R., Dehghan, A., Shah, M.: Gmcp-tracker: Global multi-object tracking using generalized minimum clique graphs. ECCV **2012**, 343–356 (2012)
41. Zhang, L., Li, Y., Nevatia, R.: Global data association for multi-object tracking using network flows. CVPR **2008**, 1–8 (2008)
42. Zhu, J., Yang, H., Liu, N., Kim, M., Zhang, W., Yang, M.H.: Online multi-object tracking with dual matching attention networks. In: Proceedings of the European Conference on Computer Vision (ECCV), pp. 366–382 (2018)

Arithmetic Evaluation System Based on MixNet-YOLOv3 and CRNN Neural Networks

Tianliang Liu[1]([✉])[iD], Congcong Liang[1][iD], Xiubin Dai[1][iD], and Jiebo Luo[2][iD]

[1] College of Telecommunications and Information Engineering, Nanjing University of Posts and Telecommunications, Nanjing 210003, China
{liutl,liangcc,daixb}@njupt.edu.cn
[2] Department of Computer Science, University of Rochester, NY 14627, USA
jluo@cs.rochester.edu

Abstract. In the traditional teaching procedure, the repetitive labor of correcting arithmetic exercise brings huge human costs. To reduce these costs and improve the given teaching efficiency, we propose a novel intelligent arithmetic evaluation system, which can automatically identify the meaning of each arithmetic question and make a reasonable judgment or decision. The designed evaluation system can be divided into two modules with detection and identification. In the detection module, due to the intensive distribution and various formats of arithmetic questions in the test papers, we adopt the MixNet-YOLOv3 network with scale balance and lightweight to achieve speed-accuracy trade-off with the mAP being up to 0.989; In the recognition module, considering the formats of each arithmetic problem are mostly fixed, we employ the CRNN network based on the CTC decoding mechanism to achieve an accuracy being up to 0.971. By the incorporation of two networks, the proposed system is capable of intelligently evaluating arithmetic exercise in mobile devices.

Keywords: Arithmetic evaluation · YOLOv3 · MixNet · CRNN

1 Introduction

With the advancement of society and the transformation of the education industry, the teachers now should pay more attention to the students' learning methods and their abilities, but correcting the assignments every day takes up most of the teacher's time and affects the quality and efficiency of teaching to a certain extent in school. Taking primary school teachers as an example, correcting arithmetic problems is a laborious and repetitive task.

T. Liu, C. Liang, X. Dai are also with Jiangsu Provincial Key Laboratory of Image Processing and Image Communication, Key Laboratory of Broadband Wireless Communication and Sensor Network Technology, Ministry of Education, and also with Jiangsu Provincial Engineering Research Center for High Performance Computing and Intelligent Processing.

A. Del Bimbo et al. (Eds.): ICPR 2020 Workshops, LNCS 12665, pp. 344–355, 2021.
https://doi.org/10.1007/978-3-030-68821-9_31

In this paper, we propose an intelligent arithmetic evaluation system which can automatically correct arithmetic problems to solve the issues mentioned above. Given a test paper, this evaluation system firstly extracts all arithmetic problems by detection technique, then obtains their semantic information by recognition method, and finally evaluates their correctness by arithmetic logic. As shown in Fig. 1, automatic correction needs only 1 s while manual review takes a few minutes. This greatly improves the efficiency of review and reduces the related labor costs.

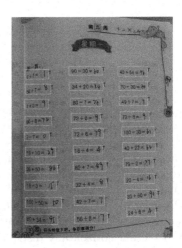

Fig. 1. Performance of arithmetic evaluation system. Left: input image. Right: our result in which every arithmetic question is detected, identified and discriminated.

Nowadays, most of arithmetic problems are composed of print and handwriting. Their formats are complicated due to different publishers and students. Thus, traditional Optical Character Recognition (OCR) algorithms [1–3] can not meet the requirements of detection in complex scenes based on image processing and machine learning techniques. In order to solve this issue, we propose an end-to-end arithmetic evaluation system. The proposed evaluation system mainly covers the detection and identification with two branches. First, the YOLOv3 algorithm [4] is applied to detect the boundary of the regions with respect to each question, and improving the weight distribution makes the network easier to learn the horizontal boundary. Further, we replace the feature extraction network with more lightweight MixNet network [5] without losing accuracy; while in the recognition part, we utilize CRNN [6] network that combines accuracy and efficiency. Through the fusion of CNN [7] and LSTM [8] networks, the fused networks can accurately learn the semantics of the arithmetic problems, and finally judge whether the given arithmetic logic is right or not.

The rest of this manuscript is organised as follows. Section 2 discusses the related work in the fields of text detection and recognition. Section 3 gives the demonstration of our proposed arithmetic evaluation system and relevant details of the given model. Some experimental results can be seen in Sect. 4. Finally, Sect. 5 draws the conclusions and the prospects of future work for this paper.

2   Related Work

The arithmetic evaluation system essentially belongs to the field of optical character recognition, which majorly consists of two branches such as text detection and text recognition. In this part, we briefly introduce related work and algorithms.

Traditional text detection methods are based on manually extracting the visual features, and some of the given features are classically SWT [1], MSER [2], HOG [3] and so on. With the rapid development of deep learning in recent years, great achievements have emerged in various industries including wireless communications [9,10], safety monitoring [11] and intelligent making system [12]. Especially, text detection algorithms based on deep learning have gradually matured and gone beyond past methods, roughly dividing into candidate box-based [13,14], segmentation-based [15,16] and other effective methods [17,18].

For the candidate box-based methods, the basic idea is to utilize several anchors to generate a large number of candidate text boxes, and then to obtain the final detection result through non-maximum suppression (NMS) technique. The CTPN network [13] inherits the idea of RPN network in Faster RCNN [19], and introduces vertical anchor box and bidirectional LSTM to achieve better results in detecting horizontally distributed text; TextBoxes [14] is inspired by SSD [20] and combines feature maps of different scales for joint text detection. The aspect ratio of the anchor is suitable for the detection of text lines.

For text detection based on segmentation, the basic idea is to perform pixel-level semantic segmentation by segmenting the network structure, and construct text lines based on the segmentation results. MaskTextSpotter [15] follows the network structure of Mask RCNN [21] and modifies the output of the mask branch to include global text instance segmentation and character segmentation; PSENet [16] uses a feature pyramid network structure (FPN) to achieve detection of text lines in the nature scene through feature fusion and progressive scale expansion.

For other methods, the implementation theories are quite different. EAST [17] combines the features of DenseBox and Unet networks to detect text in different directions and sizes; ITN [18] uses the method of in-network transformation embedding to learn geometric perception coding to achieve one-pass text detection.

Recently, text recognition algorithms based on deep learning are majorly based on CTC and Attention [22]. CRNN firstly apply CNN and bidirectional LSTM to extract the sequence features of the text, and then the semantic information of the text is recognized by CTC decoding; Aster [23] uses the SeqSeq model with attention mechanism to realize the recognition of irregular text based on the STN affine transformation.

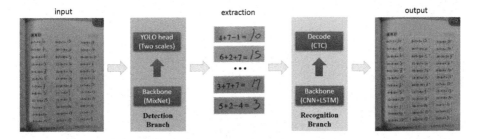

Fig. 2. Architecture of the arithmetic evaluation system. The system inputs the test paper to the detection branch, locates each arithmetic question and sends it to the recognition branch separately to obtain the final semantic information.

3   Overall Architecture

The arithmetic evaluation system we propose is shown in Fig. 2, which consists of two branches of text detection and recognition. The detection branch attempts to replace the original backbone of the YOLOv3 algorithm with the MixNet network to reduce the model parameters and speed up the inference speed; the identification branch applies the CRNN algorithm which uses the bidirectional LSTM to obtain its sequence characteristics.

3.1   Detection Branch

Existing detection algorithms based on deep learning are roughly divided into one-stage and two-stage algorithms. Faster RCNN on behalf of the two-stage algorithm utilizes RPN to generate candidate regions, and then classifies and regressions on this basis. One-stage algorithms majorly include SSD, YOLOv3, et al. Considering about performance and efficiency, we finally design the detection module of the system based on YOLOv3.

Compressed-YOLOv3. The YOLOv3 algorithm draws on the idea of FPN and obtains information of different scales through the fusion of shallow and deep features for multi-scale training. The low-level classification network uses Darknet-53 to extract features. After each convolution layer, BN regularization and Leaky-ReLU activation are connected to accelerate convergence and avoid overfitting. In addition, the structure of the residual network is combined to enhance the learning ability of the network. For the prediction of the bounding box, YOLOv3 first clusters 9 prior boxes divided into three scales by K-means algorithm. Each time the relative position of the bounding box is predicted, it is converted to an absolute position and probability by the following Eq. (1)–(6). Then the best prior boxes can be applied to prediction through Intersection over Union(IoU) between prediction boxes and prior boxes.

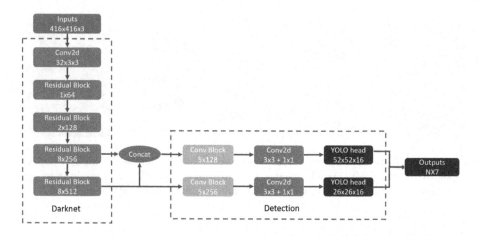

Fig. 3. Architecture of compressed YOLOv3

$$b_x = \sigma(t_x) + c_x \tag{1}$$
$$b_y = \sigma(t_y) + c_y \tag{2}$$
$$b_w = p_w \exp(t_w) \tag{3}$$
$$b_h = p_h \exp(t_h) \tag{4}$$
$$b_c = \sigma(t_c) \tag{5}$$
$$b_o = \sigma(t_o) \tag{6}$$

where the symbols t_x, t_y, t_w, t_h are the relative predicted coordinates and b_x, b_y, b_w, b_h are the ground truth coordinates. t_c, t_o denote the relative predicted probability while b_c, b_o represent the absolute probability.

In the detection branch, there are existing several common problems. (1) the distribution of arithmetic questions is relatively dense; (2) the bounding boxes of arithmetic questions are fairly similar; (3) the format of texts is diverse. Therefore, we attempt to compress the original YOLOv3 framework to prevent the scale of the maximum receptive field from interfering with the detection task. In particular, the initial three scales are reduced to two scales, and the compressed network structure is shown in Fig. 3.

In addition, since the width and height coordinates change more than the center coordinate when regressing the arithmetic problem border, it is more difficult to converge. Then, we modify its loss function to give the border width and height greater weight to accelerate the convergence of the border coordinates, and the modified expression is as Eq. (7):

$$Loss = \lambda_{center} \sum_{i=0}^{S^2} \sum_{j=0}^{B} l_{ij}^{obj} [(x_i - \hat{x}_i)^2 + (y_i - \hat{y}_i)^2]$$

$$+ \lambda_{coord} \sum_{i=0}^{S^2} \sum_{j=0}^{B} l_{ij}^{obj} [(w_i - \hat{w}_i)^2 + (h_i - \hat{h}_i)^2]$$

$$- \sum_{i=0}^{S^2} \sum_{j=0}^{B} l_{ij}^{obj} [\hat{C}_i \log C_i + (1 - \hat{C}_i) \log(1 - C_i)]$$

$$- \lambda_{noobj} \sum_{i=0}^{S^2} \sum_{j=0}^{B} l_{ij}^{noobj} [\hat{C}_i \log C_i + (1 - \hat{C}_i) \log(1 - C_i)]$$

$$- \sum_{i=0}^{S^2} l_i^{obj} \sum_{c \in cls} [\hat{p}_i(c) \log p_i(c) + (1 - \hat{p}_i(c)) \log(1 - p_i(c))] \qquad (7)$$

where S^2 is the number of grids, B is the number of predicted borders, and l_{ij}^{obj} represents whether the j_{th} box of the i_{th} grid is responsible for detecting this object.

The first two items denote the coordinate loss using mean square error function. λ_{center} and λ_{coord} are applied to control the weights of center regression and width-height regression (generally set to 1, 2); the third and fourth terms denote the loss of confidence using the cross-entropy function. Considering about the proportion of borders that are not responsible for detection is high, so the convergence of confidence is accelerated by setting $\lambda_{noobj} = 2$; the last term denotes the category loss using cross-entropy function. Each grid responsible for the detection calculates the category probability.

MixNet-YOLOv3. Though the original YOLOv3 model is compressed from three scales to two scales, the whole model architecture is hard to meet real-time needs. For this reason, we attempt to replace the darknet backend with a lightweight network.

At present, lightweight networks are widely applied in embedded and mobile devices. MobileNetV2 [24] uses deep separable convolution with higher efficiency. MixNet fuses different convolution kernel sizes into a single convolution operation. EfficientNet [25] obtains the optimal composite coefficients through neural structure search technology. GhostNet [26] splits the original feature map into partial feature maps and its linear operation.

Finally, we select MixNet to replace original darknet backend, as shown in the Fig. 4. Compared with darknet-YOLOv3, grouped convolutions under different convolution kernel sizes can fuse feature information of different receptive fields to extract more complex features, which is helpful for the deployment of the system in edge devices.

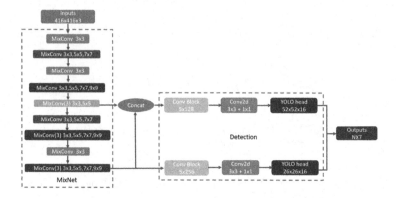

Fig. 4. Architecture of MixNet-YOLOv3

3.2 Recognition Branch

The existing recognition algorithms based on deep learning consist of two categories based on CTC and attention. Taking into account of comprehensive accuracy and efficiency, the system finally selects the most representative CRNN algorithm in the former as the recognition branch.

The CRNN model is majorly used for end-to-end variable-length text sequence recognition. Instead of segmenting a single text first, it converts text recognition into a time-dependent sequence learning problem. Given the input grayscale image, the network first extracts the features through CNN to get the feature map, then converts it into a sequence which is sent to the bidirectional LSTM to obtain the sequence features, and finally transcribe the final label sequence through CTC.

The whole network architecture is shown in Fig. 5. It is noticeable that the last two pooling layers in CNN are changed from 2×2 to 1×2. This is because most of the text output of the detection module is long and narrow, so using a 1×2 pooling window can ensure that information in the width direction is saved.

When we translate the sequence output by the LSTM into the final recognition result, inevitably there will be a lot of redundant information, such as a character is recognized twice in succession. In such case we need to use the blank mechanism to solve redundancy of output Information. By inserting "-" (representing blank) between repeated characters and merging the same characters (except those separated by blank characters), the problem of repeated characters can be solved.

For the output probability distribution matrix $x = (x^1, x^2, ..., x^T)$ of LSTM, where T is the sequence length, the probability of mapping to the label text l is calculated as follows:

$$p(l|x) = \sum_{\pi \in (B^{-1}(l))} p(\pi|x) \tag{8}$$

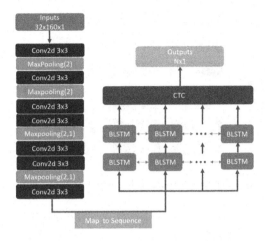

Fig. 5. Architecture of CRNN

where $B^{-1}(l)$ is the set of all paths which sequence-to-sequence mapping function B transform into l, and π is one of the paths. In particular, the probability of each path is the product of corresponding character distribution probability in each time step.

We maximize this probability value by training the network, and the loss function is defined as the negative maximum likelihood function of the probability. In the test stage, only the characters with the highest probability of each time step need to be spliced, and then according to the above blank mechanism, the final semantic information can be obtained.

4 Experiments

4.1 Dataset

Since there is no public available dataset for arithmetic exercises, we collect a large number of arithmetic exercises in several primary schools and mark the corresponding bounding boxes by LabelImg software to build our dataset of the detection module of the arithmetic evaluation system. The self-built dataset for detection consists of 2000 images for training and 200 images for testing with 10–100 exercises in each image. Different backgrounds, angles, fonts and characters (e.g., 1, 9, +, x) make the arithmetic exercises complex and diverse.

When the detection model outputs the bounding boxes of each arithmetic problem, we extract each problem as a separate image and label its semantic information to build our dataset for recognition, as is shown in Fig. 6. The recognition dataset is divided into traning set and test set by 9:1 which each picture has only one arithmetic problem.

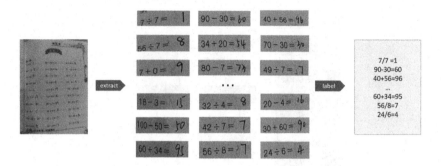

Fig. 6. The extracted and labeled arithmetic problems build our dataset for recognition.

4.2 Evaluation

Experimental platform is based on Ubuntu 16.04, PyTorch 1.5.0 with cuda 9.0. The training process can be divided into two stages: detection and recognition.

Detection Performance. In the detection stage, we resize all input images to 416 * 416 for the training of Darknet-YOLOv3 network which sets three anchors according to K-means clustering in the training data and adopt the Adam optimizer which learning rate is set to 1e−4. Besides, data augmentation (such as translation, scaling, and rotation) is used to increase the variability of the input images, so that the detection model has higher robustness to the images obtained from different environments. After obtaining fine performance, we choose multiple lightweight backbones for the same training and test the results in the testing set.

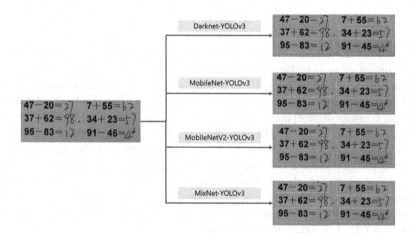

Fig. 7. Visualization of detection results in four backbones.

Figure 7 visualizes the detection results in four backbones. We find that detected boundary boxes by Darknet-YOLOv3 deviate from realistic locations. This may be due to the semantic information of deep level interfering with the location information of shallow level. MobileNet-YOLOv3 and MobileNetV2-YOLOv3 compress the original network by reducing scale but smaller backbone lowers the ability of feature extraction so that the boxes are still indistinctive. Therefore, MixNet-YOLOv3 can make up for the shortcomings of the above two networks and adopt grouped convolutions under different convolution kernel sizes to fuse location and semantic information to extract more complex features. And the boxes are relatively accurate compared with other three networks.

The detection performance in terms of Params and mAP (mean Average Precision) is shown in Table 1. As we can see, MobileNet-YOLOv3 and MobileNetV2-YOLOv3 have a certain loss of mAP compared with Darknet-YOLOv3 with reducing the model params. However, MixNet-YOLOv3 could increase the mAP from 0.983 to 0.989 and realize a great reduction of params of 0.94. The experimental results indicate that MixNet-YOLOv3 has great advantages of the balance of accuracy and speed as the detection network of our arithmetic evaluation system.

Table 1. Performance of the detection module

Detection model	Params	FLOPs	Recall	Precision	mAP
Darknet-YOLOv3	20.18 M	26.50 G	0.993	0.967	0.985
MobileNet-YOLOv3	6.92 M	7.96 G	0.997	0.953	0.982
MobileNetV2-YOLOv3	0.72 M	0.91 G	0.998	0.943	0.983
MixNet-YOLOv3	1.14 M	1.12 G	0.998	0.975	0.989

Recognition Performance. In the recognition stage, we extract the output image of the detection module and send it to the CRNN network for training. The Adam optimizer is used for optimization which the learning rate is initialized to 1e–4 and halved every 60 epochs. In order to compress the model , we introduce a simple parameter α called width multiplier. The role of the width multiplier α is to thin a network uniformly at each layer. For a given layer and width multiplier α, the number of input channels M becomes αM and the number of output channels N becomes αN.

Table 2. Performance of the recognition module

Recognition model	Params	FLOPs	Accuracy
CRNN($\alpha = 1.00$)	8.32 M	1.01 G	0.971
CRNN($\alpha = 0.75$)	4.68 M	0.57 G	0.967
CRNN($\alpha = 0.50$)	2.08 M	0.25 G	0.956

Table 2 shows the results of the recognition module. The recognition accuracy rate of original CRNN network can reach 0.971. When the width multiplier $\alpha < 1$, there is a little decline in the accuracy. Considering about precision and efficiency, the model with $\alpha = 0.75$ is applied to the recognition of the system. Finally, semantic information by the recognition module is combined with arithmetic logic to judge every arithmetic problem true or false.

5   Conclusion

In this paper, we propose a novel arithmetic evaluation system based on MixNet-YOLOv3 and CRNN networks. With a more lightweight network structure and higher accuracy, the presented evaluation system is expected to be deployed on the mobile devices, greatly reducing labor costs and improving teaching quality. For the future work, more efforts will be applied to expand diverse types of arithmetic operations and achieve more higher accuracy.

Acknowledgments. This work was supported in part by the National Natural Science Foundation of China (61001152, 61071091, 31671006, 61572503, 61772286, 61872199, 61872424 and 6193000388), China Scholarship Council.

References

1. Epshtein, B., Ofek, E., Wexler, Y.: Detecting text in natural scenes with stroke width transform. In: IEEE Computer Society Conference on Computer Vision and Pattern Recognition, pp. 2963–2970 (2010)
2. Huang, W., Qiao, Y., Tang, X.: Robust scene text detection with convolutional neural networks induced mser trees. Eur. Conf. Comput. Vis. **1**(2), 3 (2014)
3. Tian, S., Pan, Y., Huang, C., Lu, S., Yu, K., Tan, C.L.: Text flow: a unified text detection system in natural scene images. In: IEEE International Conference on Computer Vision, pp. 4651–4659 (2015)
4. Redmon, J., Farhadi, A.: Yolov3: An incremental improvement, arXiv preprint arXiv:1804.02767 (2018)
5. Tan, M., Le, Q.V.: Mixconv: Mixed depthwise convolutional kernels, arXiv preprint arXiv:1907.09595 (2019)
6. Shi, B., Bai, X., Yao, C.: An end-to-end trainable neural network for image-based sequence recognition and its application to scene text recognition. IEEE Trans. Pattern Anal. Mach. Intell. **39**(11), 2298–2304 (2016)
7. Krizhevsky, A., Sutskever, I., Hinton, G.E.: Imagenet classification with deep convolutional neural networks. In: Advances in Neural Information Processing Systems, pp. 1097–1105 (2012)
8. Watter, M., Springenberg, J., Boedecker, J., Riedmiller, M.: Embed to control: a locally linear latent dynamics model for control from raw images. In: Advances in Neural Information Processing Systems, pp. 2746–2754 (2015)
9. Liu, M., Yang, J., Song, T., Hu, J., Gui, G.: Deep learning-inspired message passing algorithm for efficient resource allocation in cognitive radio networks. IEEE Trans. Veh. Technol. **69**(1), 641–653 (2019)

10. Wang, Y., Liu, M., Yang, J., Gui, G.: Data-driven deep learning for automatic modulation recognition in cognitive radios. IEEE Trans. Veh. Technol. **68**(4), 4074–4077 (2019)

11. Zhao, Y., Chen, Q., Cao, W., Yang, J., Xiong, J., Gui, G.: Deep learning for risk detection and trajectory tracking at construction sites. IEEE Access **7**, 30905–30912 (2019)

12. Shao, L., Li, M., Yuan, L., Gui, G.: InMAS: deep learning for designing intelligent making system. IEEE Access **7**, 51104–51111 (2019)

13. Tian, Z., Huang, W., He, T., He, P., Qiao, Yu.: Detecting text in natural image with connectionist text proposal network. In: Leibe, B., Matas, J., Sebe, N., Welling, M. (eds.) ECCV 2016. LNCS, vol. 9912, pp. 56–72. Springer, Cham (2016). https://doi.org/10.1007/978-3-319-46484-8_4

14. Liao, M., Shi, B., Bai, X., Wang, X., Liu, W.: Textboxes: a fast text detector with a single deep neural network. In: Thirty-First AAAI Conference on Artificial Intelligence (2017)

15. Lyu, P., Liao, M., Yao, C., Wu, W., Bai, X.: Mask textspotter: an end-to-end trainable neural network for spotting text with arbitrary shapes. In: European Conference on Computer Vision (ECCV), pp. 67–83 (2018)

16. Wang, W., et al.: Shape robust text detection with progressive scale expansion network. In: IEEE Conference on Computer Vision and Pattern Recognition, pp. 9336–9345 (2019)

17. Zhou, X., et al.: East: an efficient and accurate scene text detector. In: IEEE Conference on Computer Vision and Pattern Recognition, pp. 5551–5560 (2017)

18. Pusateri, E., Ambati, B.R., Brooks, E., Platek, O., McAllaster, D., Nagesha, V.: A mostly data-driven approach to inverse text normalization. In: INTERSPEECH, pp. 2784–2788 (2017)

19. Ren, S., He, K., Girshick, R., Sun, J.: Faster r-cnn: towards real-time object detection with region proposal networks. In: Advances in Neural Information Processing Systems, pp. 91–99 (2015)

20. Liu, W., et al.: SSD: Single shot multibox detector. In: Leibe, B., Matas, J., Sebe, N., Welling, M. (eds.) ECCV 2016. LNCS, vol. 9905, pp. 21–37. Springer, Cham (2016). https://doi.org/10.1007/978-3-319-46448-0_2

21. He, K., Gkioxari, G., Dollár, P., Girshick, R.: Mask r-cnn: In: IEEE International Conference on Computer Vision, pp. 2961–2969 (2017)

22. Vaswani, A., et al.: Attention is all you need. In: Advances in Neural Information Processing Systems, pp. 5998–6008 (2017)

23. Shi, B., Yang, M., Wang, X., Lyu, P., Yao, C., Bai, X.: Aster: an attentional scene text recognizer with flexible rectification. IEEE Trans. Pattern Anal. Mach. Intell. **41**(9), 2035–2048 (2018)

24. Sandler, M., Howard, A., Zhu, M., Zhmoginov, A., Chen, L.-C.: Mobilenetv2: inverted residuals and linear bottlenecks. In: IEEE Conference on Computer Vision and Pattern Recognition, pp. 4510–4520 (2018)

25. Tan, M., Le, Q.V.: Efficientnet: Rethinking model scaling for convolutional neural networks, arXiv preprint arXiv:1905.11946 (2019)

26. Han, K., Wang, Y., Tian, Q., Guo, J., Xu, C., Xu, C.: Ghostnet: more features from cheap operations. In: IEEE Conference on Computer Vision and Pattern Recognition, pp. 1580–1589 (2020)

HSS-GCN: A Hierarchical Spatial Structural Graph Convolutional Network for Vehicle Re-identification

Zheming Xu[1], Lili Wei[1], Congyan Lang[1(✉)], Songhe Feng[1], Tao Wang[1], and Adrian G. Bors[2]

[1] Beijing Jiaotong University, Beijing, China
{18120433,20112014,cylang,shfeng,twang}@bjtu.edu.cn
[2] University of York, York, UK
adrian.bors@york.ac.uk

Abstract. Vehicle re-identification (Re-ID) is the task aiming to identify the same vehicle from images captured by different cameras. Recent years have seen various appearance-based approaches focusing only on global features or exploring local features to obtain more subtle details which can alleviate the subtle inter-instance problem. However, few emphasize the spatial geometrical structure relationship among local regions or between the global region and local regions. To explore abovementioned spatial structure relationship, this paper proposes a hierarchical spatial structural graph convolutional network (HSS-GCN) for vehicle Re-ID, in which we firstly construct a hierarchical spatial structural graph with the global region and local regions as nodes and a two-hierarchy relationship as edges, and later learning discriminative structure features with a GCN module under the constraints of metric learning. To augment the performance of our proposed network, we jointly combine the classification loss with metric learning loss. Extensive experiments conducted on the public VehicleID and VeRi-776 datasets validate the effectiveness of our approach in comparison with recent works.

Keywords: Vehicle re-identification · Graph convolution network · Deep learning

1 Introduction

Vehicle re-identification (vehicle Re-ID) which aims to identify the same vehicle from cross-cameras, has attracted much attention in the computer vision community. Vehicle Re-ID has been widely applied in urban surveillance scenarios such as traffic management and security. Despite recent progress, this task still remains challenging since different vehicles present similar appearances when captured with similar angles and illumination conditions, *i.e.*, subtle inter-instance variance.

Early research studies [1,7,19] mainly utilized different deep convolutional networks to extract global features and then proposed different loss functions for the

© Springer Nature Switzerland AG 2021
A. Del Bimbo et al. (Eds.): ICPR 2020 Workshops, LNCS 12665, pp. 356–364, 2021.
https://doi.org/10.1007/978-3-030-68821-9_32

network. Considering that global feature lacks detailed information (*e.g.*, light and brand details), more approaches [4,8,16] focus on extracting local features as a supplement for global features in order to alleviate the subtle inter-instance challenge. Liu *et al.* [8] used global and local branches to perform classification tasks respectively. In the local branch, the feature map is divided into three overlapping local feature maps for later extraction. He *et al.* [4] utilized object detection algorithms to detect local areas like vehicle lights and windows and then extracted local features for classification tasks. Recent works turn to aggregate local and global features. For example, Wang *et al.* [16] obtained viewpoint representation by fusing weighted local features of key points via linear operations.

However, most existing works either pay attention to discriminative feature learning including global and local feature or metric learning to learn an embedding. Few emphasize the intrinsic structure of the vehicle to assist distinguishing inter-class subtleties, especially the spatial relationship among local parts. Viewing that vehicle as essentially a rigid object, such structure information can be modelled as a graph. Meanwhile, inspired by the powerful graph convolutional network (GCN), we propose a hierarchical spatial structural graph convolutional network (HSS-GCN) for vehicle Re-ID. Specifically, we first construct a graph with one global node and five local nodes. Edges are assigned in a two-hierarchy manner, one denotes the relationship between the global node and local nodes and the other one indicates the relationship between pairs of local nodes. Then we feed the constructed graph into the GCN module to learn a more discriminative structure representation while incorporating global and local features. To further boost the performance, we also utilize a combination of classification loss and metric learning loss to adapt to our framework.

The main contributions of this paper can be summarized as:

- We propose a hierarchical spatial structural graph to contain the structural information among local regions and that between local regions and global image.
- We utilize a GCN module to incorporate the geometrical structural information so as to extract structural features from the proposed hierarchical spatial structural graph.
- Extensive comparison experiments and ablation studies on the benchmark datasets demonstrate the promising performance of our model over other approaches.

2   Related Work

2.1   Vehicle Re-ID

Most of the existing work rely on extracting robust features. Liu *et al.* [9] used hand-crafted descriptors to extract local texture and colour features of the vehicle. Liao *et al.* [6] proposed LOMO descriptor to learn a more stable feature. He *et al.* [4] proposed a part-regularized method and considered local part such as vehicle windows, brands and lights to learn more discriminate global features.

Liu *et al.* [8] proposed RAM by dividing the network into four branches including the conv branch, BN branch, regional branch, and attribute branch to learn global, local and attribute features. Zhou [21] proposed a VAMI model consisting of an attention model and a GAN architecture to predict multi-viewpoint features from single-view input, and improve the model's robustness to multiple view problem in vehicle Re-ID task. Wang *et al.* [16] mined the vehicle viewpoint information by extracting invariant orientation features.

2.2 GCN and GCN in Vehicle Re-ID

Graph convolutional network (GCN) is a network that can extract the spatial features of the graph structure. In recent years, GCN has been used in multiple computer vision tasks, such as skeleton-based action recognition [17] and social relation recognition [11]. Recent Re-ID approaches also utilize GCN in person Re-ID field [14,18]. Shen *et al.* [14] proposed SGGNN to learn the relation between probe images and gallery images by building a pairwise relation graph. Yang *et al.* [18] focused on video-based tasks and proposed an STGCN to learn temporal relations from different frames and spatial relations within a frame. However, these works all focus on person re-identification task. Liu *et al.* [12] proposed a Parsing-guided Cross-part Reasoning Network (PCRNet) to extract part-level features and then adopted a GCN to explore the relations between different parts. However, this work requires to train an image segmentation model on the established Multi-grained Vehicle Parsing (MVP) dataset in advance.

3 Methodology

To tackle the problem of vehicle re-identification, we propose a hierarchical spatial structural graph convolution network (HSS-GCN) to learn the structure information in a hierarchical manner, aiming to aggregate the global and local features. In particular, we formulate the structure information as a graph with one global node and five local nodes, which represents the overall image and five uniformly-cropped regions of the image. Edges are assigned to those pairs of local nodes with spatial adjacency relationship and pair of the global node and local nodes. The overall framework takes triplets as input and jointly utilize the classification loss and metric learning to enhance the expressive power of the proposed network. Notice that our framework consists of two branches for extracting global representation and structure feature via a global module and GCN module, respectively.

3.1 Global Module

The global module is designed to extract global representation of the input for classification tasks. In the module, we adopt ResNet-50 to implement the feature extraction. Meanwhile, we retain the global feature maps and then feed them into the local branch in Sect. 3.2 to further explore the structural information between the global image and local regions.

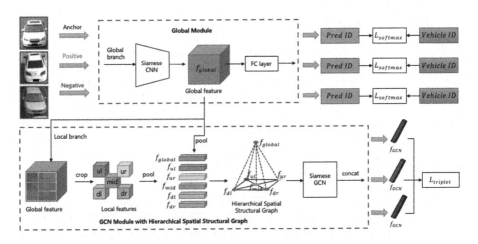

Fig. 1. The overall framework of the proposed HSS-GCN method.

3.2 GCN Module with Hierarchical Spatial Graph

The GCN module aims to learn structural feature from a graph representing the relationship between global and local regions.

The graph is constructed with six nodes including five local nodes and one global node. In general, the middle part of the image contains rich local details because the vehicle is cropped to the middle by the object detection algorithms. Meanwhile, the vehicle is a rigid object and the information of the key points representing the shape of the vehicle usually fall in the four corners of the image. Therefore, we represent the four corners and the middle region of the image as the local nodes because those area contain different discriminative local features. As shown in the GCN module in Fig. 1, to represent the five local nodes in the graph, we uniformly crop the global feature maps into five regions including the upper-left, upper-right, middle, down-left, and down-right of the feature. In order to ensure the robustness of the information contained in each region to the perspective projection effect in the image, we set the length of the region to two-thirds of the length of the image and allow overlap between the local regions. We further introduce the whole image as the global node. After pooling layers, the features of the six nodes in the HSS graph are represented as f_{global}, f_{ul}, f_{ur}, f_{mid}, f_{dl} and f_{dr}, respectively.

The edges in the graph are assigned in a two-hierarchy manner, as illustrated in Fig. 1, the dotted lines indicate the relationships between the global image and local regions. The solid lines denote the relationships between pairs of local regions.

Following Kipf [5], a two-layer GCN module is utilized to extract the structural features from the proposed graph. The output features of the six nodes are then concatenated as f_{GCN} to implement metric learning.

3.3   Joint Optimization of Multiple Losses

As illustrated in Fig. 1, we use the triplet loss $\mathcal{L}_{triplet}$ and softmax loss $\mathcal{L}_{softmax}$ respectively after the GCN module and the global module to do metric learning and classification task. In this work, the triplet loss and the softmax loss are jointly learned. Thus the final loss function is represented as,

$$\mathcal{L}_{total} = \mathcal{L}_{triplet} + \mathcal{L}_{softmax} \tag{1}$$

4   Experiments

In this paper, we evaluate our HSS-GCN on two common datasets VehicleID [7] and VeRi-776 [10] with Cumulative Matching Characteristic (CMC) and mean Average Precision (mAP), which are two common evaluation metrics used for the Vehicle ID tasks. CMC@K is often used to represent the hit accuracy of the top K retrieval results. mAP calculates the mean average precision for all query images.

4.1   Experiment Settings

In this work, ResNet is used for extracting basic features of input images and is pre-trained on ImageNet [2]. The resolution of the input images is resized to 256×256. The batch size is set as 32 for VehicleID, in which the number of the IDs per batch is 8 while the number of images per ID is 4. For VeRi, the batch size is set as 16 with 4 IDs per batch. In each mini-batch, Adam optimizer is adopted to train the network with the weight decay of 0.0005 and the initial learning rate of 0.00005. Learning rate starts decaying exponentially at epoch 200 for VehicleID while at epoch 1300 for VeRi-776. Our model is implemented by PyTorch, a popular deep learning framework. The network is trained and tested on 4 paralleling 12G NVIDIA TITAN XP GPUs.

4.2   Experimental Results and Analysis

Results on VehicleID Dataset. In Table 1, we compare our proposed method with some state-of-the-art methods. It can be observed that our method achieves the best performance compared with others, obtaining 0.727 Rank-1 accuracy and 0.773 mAP on VehicleID-800. C2F-Rank [3] proposed four levels of losses to learn multi-grained structured feature. As can be seen from Table 1, our method outperforms C2F-Rank by 13.1% in mAP and by 11% in Rank-1 accuracy on VehicleID-2400. Compared with VAMI [21] that focuses on using GANs to create fake images with different views and learn multi-view features, our method has 15.1% improvements on Rank-1 accuracy on VehicleID-2400. Such significant improvements demonstrate that the structural feature learned by our method is more useful and effective.

Table 1. Performance comparison on the VehicleID.

Method	VehicleID-800			VehicleID-1600			VehicleID-2400		
	Rank-1	Rank-5	mAP	Rank-1	Rank-5	mAP	Rank-1	Rank-5	mAP
LOMO [6]	0.198	0.320	–	0.189	0.292	–	0.153	0.253	–
CCL [7]	0.436	0.642	0.492	0.370	0.571	0.448	0.329	0.533	0.386
Mixed Diff + CCL [7]	0.490	0.735	0.546	0.428	0.668	0.481	0.382	0.616	0.455
XVGAN [20]	0.529	0.808	–	0.496	0.714	–	0.449	0.667	–
C2F-Rank [3]	0.611	0.817	0.635	0.562	0.762	0.600	0.514	0.722	0.530
VAMI [21]	0.631	0.833	–	0.529	0.751	-	0.473	0.703	–
FDA-Net [13]	–	–	–	0.598	0.771	0.653	0.555	0.747	0.618
HSS-GCN (Ours)	**0.727**	**0.918**	**0.773**	**0.679**	**0.878**	**0.724**	**0.624**	**0.843**	**0.661**

Results on VeRi-776 Dataset. Table 2 illustrates the performance of different approaches on VeRi-776. Our proposed HSS-GCN yields 64.4% mAP which outperforms methods focusing on multi-viewpoint learning [6,20]. Compared with the approach [10] which uses the license plate and spatial-temporal information as auxiliary information, our method achieves 17.1% mAP improvement which demonstrates the effectiveness of our proposed HSS-GCN.

Table 2. Performance comparison on the VeRi-776.

Method	VeRi-776		
	Rank-1	Rank-5	mAP
LOMO [6]	0.253	0.465	0.096–
FACT [9]	0.510	0.735	0.185
FACT + Plate-SNN + STR [10]	0.614	0.788	0.277
XVGAN [20]	0.602	0.770	0.247
Siamese visual [15]	0.411	0.603	0.295
HSS-GCN (Ours)	**0.644**	**0.861**	**0.448**

4.3 Ablation Study

In this section, we conduct several ablation studies to analyze the contributions of the proposed GCN module with hierarchical spatial graph and explore the effectiveness of the joint learning in our framework on VehicleID and VeRi-776 datasets, as shown in Table 3. The $ResNet50 + Triplet_{global}$ refers to a baseline using the global features for learning the metric representation, while the $ResNet50+Triplet_{GCN}$ and $HSS-GCN : ResNet50+Triplet_{GCN}+Softmax$ refer to our GCN module and the whole model, respectively. As shown in Table 3, $ResNet50 + Triplet_{GCN}$ do improve the result compared with $ResNet50 + Triplet_{global}$. The joint learning method boosts performance when only adopting metric learning. The numerical results demonstrate the improvement achieved by our GCN module and the joint learning strategy.

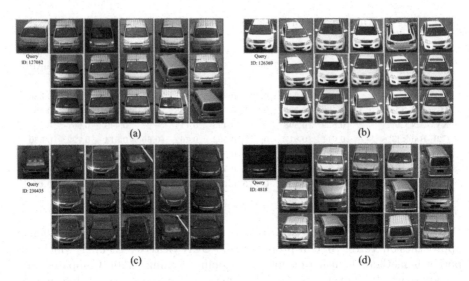

Fig. 2. Examples of Rank-5 retrieval results on VehicleID in single-gallery-shot condition.

In particular, to visualize the effectiveness of our model, the Rank-5 retrieval results of four example query images from VehicleID are shown in Fig. 2. In each subgraph, the first, second and third row show top five images returned by $ResNet50 + Triplet_{global}$, our $ResNet50 + Triplet_{GCN}$ and HSS-GCN respectively. Images with light blue box denote queries while the images with green boxes and red boxes are correct and incorrect retrieve results, respectively. Except for Fig. 2(d), our HSS-GCN has successfully retrieved the correct sample at the 1st position. Although the HSS-GCN does not get the best results on Rank-1, it performs the best within the three methods while $ResNet50+Triplet_{GCN}$ we proposed ranks second, which demonstrate the effectiveness of our model.

To conclude, the ablation experiments validate the effectiveness of our approach as the statistic and visualization results show that our GCN module with hierarchical spatial graph and the joint learning strategy both play important roles in the effectiveness of the Re-ID model.

Table 3. Ablation study.

Method	VehicleID-800		VehicleID-1600		VehicleID-2400		VeRi-776	
	Rank-1	mAP	Rank-1	mAP	Rank-1	mAP	Rank-1	mAP
ResNet50 + Triplet$_{global}$	0.623	0.662	0.561	0.602	0.496	0.525	0.540	0.304
ResNet50 + Triplet$_{GCN}$	0.701	0.736	0.626	0.677	0.570	0.611	0.560	0.323
HSS-GCN:ResNet50 + Triplet$_{GCN}$+Softmax	**0.727**	**0.773**	**0.679**	**0.724**	**0.624**	**0.661**	**0.644**	**0.448**

5 Conclusion

In this paper, we propose a hierarchical spatial structural graph convolutional network (HSS-GCN) for vehicle Re-ID. The HSS-GCN model first constructs a spatial structural graph with one global node and five local nodes in a hierarchical manner. Then the GCN module is used to learn a more discriminative structural representation among local regions and between global images and local regions. To boost the performance of our framework, metric learning is combined with the classification metric. Experimental results demonstrate that the proposed methodology achieves promising performances on the VehicleID and VeRi-776 datasets.

Acknowledgement. This work was supported by the Fundamental Research Funds for the Central Universities (No. 2020JBM403), the Beijing Natural Science Foundation (Grants No. 4202057, No. 4202058, 4202060), National Natural Science Foundation of China (No. 62072027, 61872032), and the Ministry of Education - China Mobile Communications Corporation Foundation (No. MCM20170201).

References

1. Bai, Y., Lou, Y., Gao, F., Wang, S., Wu, Y., Duan, L.Y.: Group-sensitive triplet embedding for vehicle reidentification. IEEE Trans. Multimed. **20**(9), 2385–2399 (2018)
2. Deng, J., Dong, W., Socher, R., Li, L.J., Li, K., Fei-Fei, L.: Imagenet: a large-scale hierarchical image database. In: 2009 IEEE Conference on Computer Vision and Pattern Recognition, pp. 248–255. IEEE (2009)
3. Guo, H., Zhao, C., Liu, Z., Wang, J., Lu, H.: Learning coarse-to-fine structured feature embedding for vehicle re-identification. In: Thirty-Second AAAI Conference on Artificial Intelligence (2018)
4. He, B., Li, J., Zhao, Y., Tian, Y.: Part-regularized near-duplicate vehicle re-identification. In: Proceedings of the IEEE Conference on Computer Vision and Pattern Recognition, pp. 3997–4005 (2019)
5. Kipf, T.N., Welling, M.: Semi-supervised classification with graph convolutional networks. arXiv preprint arXiv:1609.02907 (2016)

6. Liao, S., Hu, Y., Zhu, X., Li, S.Z.: Person re-identification by local maximal occurrence representation and metric learning. In: Proceedings of the IEEE Conference on Computer Vision and Pattern Recognition, pp. 2197–2206 (2015)
7. Liu, H., Tian, Y., Yang, Y., Pang, L., Huang, T.: Deep relative distance learning: Tell the difference between similar vehicles. In: Proceedings of the IEEE Conference on Computer Vision and Pattern Recognition, pp. 2167–2175 (2016)
8. Liu, X., Zhang, S., Huang, Q., Gao, W.: Ram: a region-aware deep model for vehicle re-identification. In: 2018 IEEE International Conference on Multimedia and Expo (ICME), pp. 1–6. IEEE (2018)
9. Liu, X., Liu, W., Ma, H., Fu, H.: Large-scale vehicle re-identification in urban surveillance videos. In: 2016 IEEE International Conference on Multimedia and Expo (ICME), pp. 1–6. IEEE (2016)
10. Liu, X., Liu, W., Mei, T., Ma, H.: A deep learning-based approach to progressive vehicle re-identification for urban surveillance. In: Leibe, B., Matas, J., Sebe, N., Welling, M. (eds.) ECCV 2016. LNCS, vol. 9906, pp. 869–884. Springer, Cham (2016). https://doi.org/10.1007/978-3-319-46475-6_53
11. Liu, X., et al.: Social relation recognition from videos via multi-scale spatial-temporal reasoning. In: Proceedings of the IEEE Conference on Computer Vision and Pattern Recognition, pp. 3566–3574 (2019)
12. Liu, X., Liu, W., Zheng, J., Yan, C., Mei, T.: Beyond the parts: Learning multi-view cross-part correlation for vehicle re-identification. In: Proceedings of the 28th ACM International Conference on Multimedia, pp. 907–915 (2020)
13. Lou, Y., Bai, Y., Liu, J., Wang, S., Duan, L.: Veri-wild: A large dataset and a new method for vehicle re-identification in the wild. In: Proceedings of the IEEE Conference on Computer Vision and Pattern Recognition, pp. 3235–3243 (2019)
14. Shen, Y., Li, H., Yi, S., Chen, D., Wang, X.: Person re-identification with deep similarity-guided graph neural network. In: Proceedings of the European Conference on Computer Vision (ECCV), pp. 486–504 (2018)
15. Shen, Y., Xiao, T., Li, H., Yi, S., Wang, X.: Learning deep neural networks for vehicle re-id with visual-spatio-temporal path proposals. In: Proceedings of the IEEE International Conference on Computer Vision, pp. 1900–1909 (2017)
16. Wang, Z., et al.: Orientation invariant feature embedding and spatial temporal regularization for vehicle re-identification. In: Proceedings of the IEEE International Conference on Computer Vision, pp. 379–387 (2017)
17. Yan, S., Xiong, Y., Lin, D.: Spatial temporal graph convolutional networks for skeleton-based action recognition. arXiv preprint arXiv:1801.07455 (2018)
18. Yang, J., Zheng, W.S., Yang, Q., Chen, Y.C., Tian, Q.: Spatial-temporal graph convolutional network for video-based person re-identification. In: Proceedings of the IEEE/CVF Conference on Computer Vision and Pattern Recognition, pp. 3289–3299 (2020)
19. Zhang, Y., Liu, D., Zha, Z.J.: Improving triplet-wise training of convolutional neural network for vehicle re-identification. In: 2017 IEEE International Conference on Multimedia and Expo (ICME), pp. 1386–1391. IEEE (2017)
20. Zhou, Y., Shao, L.: Cross-view gan based vehicle generation for re-identification. BMVC. 1, 1–12 (2017)
21. Zhouy, Y., Shao, L.: Viewpoint-aware attentive multi-view inference for vehicle re-identification. In: 2018 IEEE/CVF Conference on Computer Vision and Pattern Recognition, pp. 6489–6498 (2018)

A Novel Multi-feature Skeleton Representation for 3D Action Recognition

Lian Chen[1], Ke Lu[1,2], Pengcheng Gao[1], Jian Xue[1(✉)] (ID), and Jinbao Wang[3]

[1] University of Chinese Academy of Sciences, Beijing, China
{chenlian17,gaopengcheng15}@mails.ucas.ac.cn
{luk,xuejian}@ucas.ac.cn
[2] Peng Cheng Laboratory, Vanke Cloud City Phase I Building 8, Xili Street,
Nanshan District, Shenzhen, China
[3] Southern University of Science and Technology, Shenzhen, China
linkingring@163.com

Abstract. Deep-learning-based methods have been used for 3D action recognition in recent years. Methods based on recurrent neural networks (RNNs) have the advantage of modeling long-term context, but they focus mainly on temporal information and ignore the spatial relationships in each skeleton frame. In addition, it is difficult to handle a very long skeleton sequence using an RNN. Compared with an RNN, a convolutional neural network (CNN) is better able to extract spatial information. To model the temporal information of skeleton sequences and incorporate the spatial relationship in each frame efficiently using a CNN, this paper proposes a multi-feature skeleton representation for encoding features from original skeleton sequences. The relative distances between joints in each skeleton frame are computed from the original skeleton sequence, and several relative angles between the skeleton structures are computed. This useful information from the original skeleton sequence is encoded as pixels in grayscale images. To preserve more spatial relationships between input skeleton joints in these images, the skeleton joints are divided into five groups: one for the trunk and one for each arm and each leg. Relationships between joints in the same group are more relevant than those between joints in different groups. By rearranging pixels in encoded images, the joints that are mutually related in the spatial structure are adjacent in the images. The skeleton representations, composed of several grayscale images, are input to CNNs for action recognition. Experimental results demonstrate the effectiveness of the proposed method on three public 3D skeleton-based action datasets.

Keywords: 3D action recognition · Convolutional neural network · Deep learning · Skeleton representation

This work is supported by the National Key R&D Program of China (2017YFB1002-203), National Natural Science Foundation of China (62032022, 61671426, 61972375, 61871258, 61929104), Beijing Municipal Natural Science Foundation (4182071), the Fundamental Research Funds for the Central Universities (Y95401YXX2) and Scientific Research Program of Beijing Municipal Education Commission (KZ201911417048).

© Springer Nature Switzerland AG 2021
A. Del Bimbo et al. (Eds.): ICPR 2020 Workshops, LNCS 12665, pp. 365–379, 2021.
https://doi.org/10.1007/978-3-030-68821-9_33

1   Introduction

In recent years, human action recognition has been applied to many fields, such as video surveillance, medical monitoring, security, intelligent houses, and content-based video retrieval [8,10]. With the development of deep learning, action recognition has proved to be highly effective in these application areas. The modalities of input data usually include RGB videos, depth maps, and three-dimensional (3D) skeleton data. RGB is widely used in action recognition, but it can easily be affected by illumination changes and appearance of texture, resulting in ambiguity. Since the appearance of 3D cameras, such as the Microsoft Kinect, the use of skeleton data has become increasingly popular. Skeleton data are robust to variations in illumination, camera viewpoint changes, and texture variation in comparison with RGB and depth data. In this paper, we focus on 3D skeleton-based action recognition.

A skeleton data sequence consists of a series of 3D coordinates of body joints. In each skeleton sequence, the temporal information of the whole sequence describes the dynamics of action, and the spatial information in each skeleton frame describes the relationship between joints. It is of great importance to extract features from the original skeleton sequence and retain temporal and spatial information, as much as possible, for further classification. The recurrent neural network (RNN) and its extended version with long short-term memory (LSTM) [7] have been used for skeleton-based action recognition and have been shown to be effective [6,20,22,24,25,28,30]. They are mainly used to model the long-term context information along the temporal dimension by representing motion-based dynamics [19]. However, the RNN and LSTM lack the ability to model the entire information of a very long sequence. In addition, they focus mainly on the temporal relationship between skeleton frames, paying less attention to spatial structure in a single frame. However, the structure of joints in each skeleton frame is very important for discrimination between action categories. Not only in the field of action recognition, but also in other fields such as person re-identification, the importance of capturing and understanding information about various parts of the human body is raised. In [12], human body semantic analysis is used to extract local visual clues. In [36], the structure of the human body is used to enhance the recognition capability. [29] also proposed the importance of accurately locating each part of pedestrian and consider the continuity of information transition between each part. The convolutional neural network (CNN) [15] performs well in representation learning and has been proved effective in skeleton-based action recognition [1,2,4,5,13,34]. Compared with an LSTM, a CNN has the advantage of learning spatial structure information. In the CNN-based method for action recognition, the manner in which the spatial relationship is extracted and the method of modeling the long-term sequence are of crucial importance.

In this paper, we propose a CNN-based method for extracting useful features from an original skeleton sequence and encoding them into grayscale images. The association between skeleton frames reflects the temporal information of the action, whereas the relationship between skeleton joints in each frame reflects the spatial information of the action. Qiuhong Ke et al. [13] proposed an effective encoding method that models the temporal dynamics of the original skeleton sequence as a single image. By selecting several key joints in a single frame and calculating the relative distance between other joints and the key joints, each image reveals the connection information of the skeleton structure, and all images incorporate the spatial information of the whole sequence. In addition, the arrangement of data in the encoded image reflects the spatial connection between the joints in each skeleton frame. In this paper, we propose a new method that divides the skeleton structure into five parts and rearranges the skeleton joints. In this manner, the encoded images can better represent the relationships in the original skeleton structure. In addition, we define several important angles in a single skeleton frame. These data are encoded into an image, to incorporate more useful information and better describe the spatial features. In this manner, each original skeleton sequence can be encoded into six grayscale images: five images corresponding to five key joints and one image corresponding to the angles. These images are then input to six identical CNNs, which are trained simultaneously. Finally, we conduct score fusion to obtain the final action classification.

The main contributions of our work are as follows:

- A multi-feature skeleton representation, based on spatio-temporal information processing, is proposed.
- A useful method for space division and encoding, which corresponds to the human skeleton structure, is proposed. This can efficiently incorporate information about the relationships between adjacent joints in human movement.
- Several important joint angles, for the human skeleton structure, are defined and calculated to reflect the changes of movement and incorporate spatial motion information.

Experiments were conducted on three 3D skeleton-based action recognition datasets (NTU RGB+D [27], NTU RGB+D 120 [17] and UTKinect-Action3D Dataset [33]) with standard evaluation protocols. The results demonstrate the effectiveness of the proposed method for 3D skeleton-based action recognition.

In this paper, we introduce related work in Sect. 2. The process of selecting features from the original skeleton data and encoding them into grayscale images for CNN classification is described in Sect. 3. In Sect. 4, the implementation details of the experiments are explained, and the ablation study and experimental results are presented and compared with other related methods. Finally, Sect. 5 presents our conclusions.

2   Related Work

In this section, we introduce some related work on skeleton-based action recognition.

An end-to-end hierarchical RNN was proposed in [6]. The skeleton is divided according to the human body structure into five parts, which are input to five networks for classification. In [5], the joint coordinates of a skeleton sequence are concatenated as a matrix, which is then quantified into an image for further classification, such that each image corresponds to a skeleton sequence. In [13], each skeleton sequence is used to generate four images, each of which incorporates the temporal information of the entire sequence and the spatial relationship in each frame. The four images incorporate different aspects of the spatial information of the whole sequence. To focus more attention on the most informative joints in skeleton frames, [22] proposed the global context-aware attention LSTM (GCA-LSTM). A two-stream RNN was proposed in [30] to handle the temporal and spatial information of a skeleton sequence. For temporal dynamics, a stacked RNN and a hierarchical RNN were proposed. For spatial information, a method of converting a spatial graph into a series of joints was proposed. In [19], a gating mechanism was used in an LSTM module to process the noise in a skeleton sequence. A method for multi-modal feature fusion using an LSTM was also proposed. Zhengyuan Yang et al. [34] proposed the idea of applying depth-first tree traversal in a skeleton representation, in the tree structure skeleton image (TSSI) method. Carlos Caetano et al. [1] combined the ideas of [13] and TSSI [34] to propose a new skeleton representation called the tree structure reference joints image (TSRJI). In the method of [24], features are separately extracted from the pose coordinate system and the trajectory coordinate system, which are the result of conversion from the original coordinate system of skeleton joints. These two types of features are then input to two LSTM networks and concatenated, for further classification.

3   The Proposed Method

This section introduces our method for generating the skeleton representation from original skeleton sequences. The skeleton sequences are trajectories of 3D coordinates of skeleton joints. The skeleton sequence is converted into several grayscale images, which incorporate both the dynamics and spatial information of the original skeleton structure. The method of calculating the relative distance between joints and important angles in the skeleton structure is explained.

Fig. 1. 3D skeleton joints structure. Joints 1, 4, 8, 12, 16 are key joints defined in [13]. Relative distance calculated by each key joint with other skeleton joints are preserved in an array according to the sequential order from 0 to 24.

The method of rearranging the pixels in the encoded images, depending on the spatial relationship between skeleton joints, can preserve much of the motion information. CNNs are then employed to extract features from these images for classification.

3.1   Encoding Process

In a skeleton sequence, each frame consists of several skeleton joints. The relative position of any two joints describes the motion migration. In previous work, the movement information of each frame has often been encoded to a single image; however, a long sequence contains too many images for this to be practical. According to [13], it is hard to learn temporal dynamics, and therefore each image will be very sparse. A new method for encoding the dynamics of skeleton sequences was proposed by [13] to overcome these weaknesses. In this paper, we propose an improved method using the skeleton representation of [13].

In the method of [13], the temporal dynamics of a skeleton sequence are encoded in an image, and the spatial information of the skeleton joints is incorporated into multiple images. It selects four key joints, which are considered to be stable throughout the action. But in our method, five key joints (the middle of the spine, left shoulder, right shoulder, left hip, and right hip) are chosen for use, as shown in Fig. 1. The relative distance between each key joint and other joints can then be computed. The skeleton joints in each skeleton frame are all numbered and arranged from 0 to 24. For each key joint, there is a corresponding array C with a size of $N \times T$ (N is the number of skeleton joints in each frame and T is the number of frames in each sequence). Each value in the array is scaled to 0–255 by a linear transformation.

In the above encoding process for skeleton data, the arrangement of skeleton joints (i.e., the distance between a key joint and other joints in the calculated array) is in order of serial number, from 0 to 24, as shown in Fig. 1. However, in this order, the adjacent joints in each array lose some spatial relationships that are present in the original skeleton structures. For example, joint number 1 is the middle of the spine and joint number 20 is also the spine. They are adjacent in the original skeleton structure, but the direct adjacency relationship is lost after the encoding process. Conversely, joint number 11 is the right hand and joint number 12 is the left hip. Their numbers are consecutive, and so they are encoded adjacent to each other in the grayscale image, but they have no spatial relationship in the original skeleton structure. If this problem is not solved, the generated grayscale images are likely to lose many of the direct, or highly relevant, spatial relationships between the skeleton joints.

In this study, we propose a new method in which the skeleton joints are divided into groups according to the limb relationships. The positions of pixels in encoded images are changed according to that division, to enhance the spatial information preserved in encoded grayscale images. The original skeleton structure consists of 25 joints, which we divide into five groups according to the human body structure, as shown in Fig. 2. The five parts of the body are the

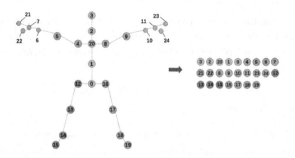

Fig. 2. Skeleton structure is divided into five parts: the trunk (3, 2, 20, 1, 0), the left hand (4, 5, 6, 7, 21, 22), the right hand (8, 9, 10, 11, 23, 24), the left leg (12, 13, 14, 15) and the right leg (16, 17, 18, 19). The new array is concatenated by the five groups as (3, 2, 20, 1, 0, 4, 5, 6, 7, 21, 22, 8, 9, 10, 11, 23, 24, 12, 13, 14, 15, 16, 17, 18, 19).

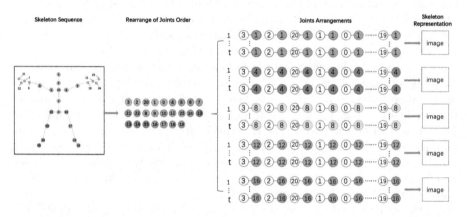

Fig. 3. The process of encoding skeleton representation from original skeleton sequence. For each input skeleton sequence, the order of the serial number of joints is first rearranged by our proposed method. Then the relative distance between key joint and other joints are calculated respectively. Each key joint corresponds to an encoded grayscale image and five images revealing the relative distance are generated.

trunk (3, 2, 20, 1, 0), left hand (4, 5, 6, 7, 21, 22), right hand (8, 9, 10, 11, 23, 24), left leg (12, 13, 14, 15), and right leg (16, 17, 18, 19). These five groups of joints are concatenated together to obtain a new array (3, 2, 20, 1, 0, 4, 5, 6, 7, 21, 22, 8, 9, 10, 11, 23, 24, 12, 13, 14, 15, 16, 17, 18, 19), as shown in Fig. 2. The five arrays, corresponding to the five key joints of a sequence, are used to generate five grayscale images. In this manner, the joints that are directly related in each part of the original skeleton structure are adjacent in the encoded images. The whole process of feature encoding is depicted in Fig. 3. The experiments in Sect. 4 indicate the effectiveness of our method of rearranging the order of joints according to the body joint relationships.

3.2 Important Angles Between Joints

Changes in the relative distance between joints in the skeleton structure can characterize action movements, so we encode five skeleton grayscale images, related to the five key joints from a skeleton sequence. Similarly, every pair of joints in a single skeleton frame can be treated as a vector, and the angle between two vectors can reveal the action gesture. In each skeleton sequence, a change of these angles provides motion information. In this paper, nine important angles are defined and calculated, as shown in Fig. 4. Each angle is defined by the following equation:

$$\theta = \cos^{-1}(\frac{\vec{a} \cdot \vec{b}}{|\vec{a}| \cdot |\vec{b}|}) \tag{1}$$

where $\vec{a}$ and $\vec{b}$ are vectors that include the same joint vertex and θ is the angle between the two vectors. For example, as shown in Fig. 4, θ_4 is the angle between the arm and the trunk. To calculate θ_4, three joints (4, 5, and 12) are selected, to form two 3D vectors using the joints' coordinates. θ_4 is calculated according to Eq. (1) and these vectors. For a skeleton sequence, we calculate the nine defined angles of each skeleton frame and arrange the values of each frame in a row. The values are quantified as an integer in [0, 255], corresponding to the gray scale. The generation of the grayscale image for angle is similar to that of the grayscale image for relative distance, as shown in Fig. 4. However, in this section, the nine angle values are copied three times, to fill a row of the image, to enhance the effect of changes in angles. The effectiveness of this technique has been proved in our experiments. Thus, from each sequence, we generate a grayscale image that incorporates angle displacement information.

In summary, from each sequence, we generate five images by calculating the relative positions of joints and one image by computing important angles. These six grayscale images are then input to CNN for feature extraction and action classification. The integral pipeline is shown in Fig. 5.

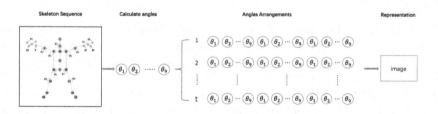

Fig. 4. Nine angels labeled from θ_1 to θ_9 are defiened in the left of the figure. These angles are calculated and quantified as an integer in [0, 255], then the nine angle values are copied three times to fill each row of the image.

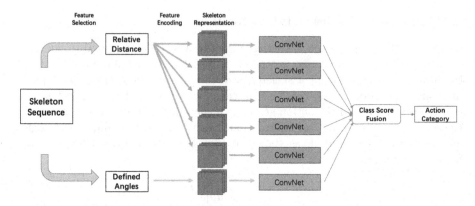

Fig. 5. The architecture of the recognition process. For each skeleton sequence, the relative distance corresponding to five key joints are computed to generate five skeleton images, and the defined angles are calculated to generate one skeleton image. The six grayscale images are fed into six identical CNNs for feature extraction simultaneously. At last, the class scores of different networks are fused to yield final classification results.

4 Experiments and Analysis

In this section, we evaluate the performance of our proposed multi-feature skeleton representation for 3D skeleton-based action recognition. The experiments were conducted on three 3D skeleton datasets: NTU RGB+D [27], NTU RGB+D 120 [17], and UTKinect-Action3D [33]. In particular, ablation experiments were conducted on the NTU RGB+D dataset, to assess the effectiveness of each component of our proposed model. We then compare our results with other methods on the three datasets, with standard evaluation protocols. The neural network architecture and implementation details are also explained.

4.1 Datasets

NTU RGB+D Dataset [27]. This is a large dataset for action recognition with more than 56,000 video samples and 4 million frames, performed by 40 distinct subjects. It contains 60 action classes, including 40 daily actions (e.g., standing up, reading, and making a phone call), nine health-related actions (e.g., staggering and falling down), and 11 mutual actions (e.g., pushing, hugging, and shaking hands). All the data were collected by three Microsoft Kinect v2 cameras from different viewpoints simultaneously. This dataset provides four major data modalities: depth maps, RGB frames, IR sequences, and 3D skeleton sequences, consisting of 3D coordinates of 25 human body joints. Because of the large quantity and wide variety of views and classes, it is a challenging dataset.

NTU RGB+D 120 Dataset [17]. This is the latest large-scale dataset for 3D skeleton-based human action recognition. It contains 120 action classes and more than 114,000 video clips, performed by 106 distinct subjects. It extends the NTU

RGB+D dataset [27] by adding more action classes and samples. It also provides daily, mutual, and health-related activities and several data modalities: depth maps, RGB frames, IR sequences, and 3D skeleton sequences. This dataset is very challenging because of its distinct action categories, varied human subjects, and diverse environmental conditions.

UTKinect-Action3D Dataset [33]. This dataset contains 10 categories of action classes: walk, sit down, stand up, pick up, carry, throw, push, pull, wave, and clap hands. These actions are performed by 10 subjects, each performing every action twice. There are 200 action clips and 6220 frames in total. The dataset is challenging because of its intra-class variation.

4.2 Implementation Details

The neural network architecture employed in our method is derived from temporal segment networks, which were proposed by [31], choosing Inception with batch normalization (BN-Inception) [11] as building block. Besides, the mean and variance paramenter of Batch Normalization layers are frozen except the first one, and a dropout layer is added after the global pooling layer to reduce over-fitting. Each grayscale image is generated with the size of 340 × 256, the number of segments in the network is set to six, corresponding to our six generated grayscale images, which are input to six identical CNNs. The class scores of each image are fused by an function to obtain a consensus of class hypothesis among them, then the Softmax function is used to predict the action class based on the consensus, as [31] did.

In experiments on the NTU RGB+D and NTU RGB+D 120 datasets, we exploited models pretrained on the ImageNet [3] dataset, to initialize the network weights, and we use stochastic gradient descent to learn network parameters, as [31] did. We set the initial learning rate to 0.001, which is reduced by a factor of 10 after 10,000, 18,000, and 26,000 iterations. The maximum number of iterations was 36,000 and the batch size was set to 16. In experiments on the UTKinect-Action3D dataset, the model trained on the NTU RGB+D dataset by our method was used as the pretrained model, because of the small size of the UTKinect-Action3D dataset. The initial learning rate was 0.001, the stepsize was 1500, and the maximum number of iterations was 3500. The number of units in the fully connected layer was the same as the number of action categories in each dataset.

4.3 Experimental Evaluation

In this section, we show the results of the ablation evaluation on the NTU RGB+D dataset. We then present the recognition results on the three 3D skeleton-based datasets and make comparisons with other methods, to demonstrate the effectiveness of the proposed multi-feature skeleton representation.

NTU RGB+D Dataset [27]. The author of the dataset provided two protocols for training and testing. Cross-subject evaluation splits the dataset into

40,320 samples performed by 20 subjects for training, and 16,560 samples by the remaining 20 subjects for testing. Cross-view evaluation picks 37,920 samples from cameras 2 and 3 for training and 18,960 samples from camera 1 for testing. We followed the two protocols and report the experimental results from each.

Table 1. Ablation study and recognition performance compared with other methods on NTU RGB+D dataset. Accuracy on standard cross-subject and cross-view protocols are reported.

Method	Cross-subject	Cross-view
Dynamic skeletons [9]	60.23%	65.22%
Deep LSTM [27]	60.69%	67.29%
Part-aware LSTM [27]	62.93%	70.27%
ST-LASTM [20]	69.2%	77.7%
Two-stream RNN [30]	71.3%	79.5%
STA-LSTM [28]	73.4%	81.2%
TSRJI (late fusion) [1]	73.3%	80.3%
5 Key Joints	74.93%	79.11%
5 Key Joints + Angles	75.59%	80.56%
5 Key Joints + Rearrangement	76.03%	81.21%
5 Key Joints + Rearrangement + Angles	**77.33%**	**82.48%**

First, we examine the contributions of each component of our proposed representation, as shown in Table 1. The method of generating the skeleton representation named '5 Key Joints' is based on the idea of [13], but the neural network architecture and implementation details are replaced. By reclassifying the skeletal structure and rearranging the pixels in the generated grayscale images according to the joints' relevance, we can observe that '5 Key Joints + Rearrangement' outperformed '5 Key Joints' by 1.1% and 2.1% on the cross-subject and cross-view protocols, respectively. The results demonstrate the effectiveness of the proposed method of rearranging the order of joints according to the five body parts in the encoding process. It also indicates that two adjacent joints (connected by an edge) in the original skeleton structure incorporate more spatial information than two joints that are not adjacent. Our method allows the encoded images to preserve more spatial structure information of the skeleton joints that are adjacent to each other in space. Another component is the nine defined angles between joints in the skeleton structure; the calculated angles were added to '5 Key Joints'. '5 Key Joints + Angles' achieved an accuracy of 75.59% and 80.56% on the cross-subject and cross-view protocols, respectively, outperforming '5 Key Joints' on both protocols. This indicates that these angles play an important role in skeleton movements, so that the change of the angles reflects the action. This proves the effectiveness of the selected angles for action recognition. Finally, we combined the two methods (Rearrangement and Angles) together. '5 Key Joints + Rearrangement + Angles' achieved the best result, with 77.33% and 82.48% on the cross-subject and cross-view protocols, respectively. In particular, this result was obtained by using the strategy of copying the values of the angles three times as much as before, in the encoded grayscale image. We also conducted the experiments with no copying operation; the accuracy was 81.27% on the cross-view protocol and 76.17% on the cross-subject protocol, which is a worse result than that obtained with the copying operation. This indicates the effectiveness of the proposed strategy. Based on these results, we used this combined representation, '5 KeyJoints + Rearrangement + Angles', in the following experiments for comparison with other methods.

We compared the proposed method with other methods using the NTU TGB+D dataset, as shown in Table 1. Our method achieved better results than others, on both the cross-subject and cross-view evaluation protocols. The best accuracy on the cross-view protocol was 82.48%, which is 2.18% higher than the best CNN-based method TSRJI (Late Fusion) [1], and higher than the best RNN-based method STA-LSTM [28] by 1.28%. On the cross-subject protocol, the proposed method achieved an accuracy of 77.33%. In comparison with the previous best method STA-LSTM [28], tested on the cross-subject protocol, the accuracy has been improved by 3.93%.

Table 2. Evaluation results on NTU RGB+D 120 Dataset. We list the accuracy on standard cross-subject and cross-setup protocols. Results of other methods for comparison are from [17].

Method	Cross-subject	Cross-setup
Dynamic skeletons [9]	50.8%	54.7%
Spatio-temporal LSTM [20]	55.7%	57.9%
Internal feature fusion [19]	58.2%	60.9%
GCA-LSTM [22]	58.3%	59.2%
Multi-task learning network [13]	58.4%	57.9%
FSNet [18]	59.9%	62.4%
Skeleton visualization (single stream) [23]	60.3%	63.2%
Two-stream attention LSTM [21]	61.2%	63.3%
Multi-task CNN with RotClips [14]	62.2%	61.8%
Magnitude-orientation (TSA) [2]	62.9%	63.0%
TSRJI (late fusion) [1]	**65.5%**	59.7%
5 key joints + rearrangement + angles	65.44%	**65.15%**

NTU RGB+D 120 Dataset [17]. This dataset is more challenging than the NTU RGB+D dataset, because it has many more action categories, performers, and skeleton sequences. There are two standard evaluation protocols for testing on this dataset. Cross-subject evaluation splits the 106 human subjects into training and testing sets by the subjects' identifiers. Cross-setup evaluation selects samples with even setup identifiers for training and odd identifiers for testing.

According to the experimental results shown in Table 1, the proposed method '5 Key Joints + Rearrangement + Angles' achieved the best performance on the NTU RGB+D dataset, so we tested this method on the NTU RGB+D 120 dataset. As shown in Table 2, the proposed method outperformed all other methods on the cross-setup protocol, with an accuracy of 65.15%. On the cross-subject protocol, the best result was achieved by [1] with an accuracy of 65.5%. However, our method still achieved a competitive result, with an accuracy of 65.44%.

UTKinect-Action3D Dataset [33]. In the evaluation on the UTKinect dataset, we used the cross-subject evaluation protocol, as [26] did. Half of the subjects in the dataset were used for training and the remaining subjects were used for testing. The evaluation result of our method is shown in Table 3. The results of the other methods in Table 3 were all evaluated with the same cross-subject protocol. Compared with other methods, our method achieved the highest accuracy, 97.0%.

Table 3. Experimental results on UTKinect-Action3D Dataset.

Method	Accuracy
JL-d [35]	95.96%
Lie group representation [26]	96.68%
Ensemble TS-LSTM v2 [16]	96.97%
HST-RNN [32]	96.97%
5 key joints + rearrangement + angles	**97.0%**

5   Conclusions

In this paper, we proposed a method of extracting features from an original skeleton sequence as a multi-feature skeleton representation, which is then input to CNNs for further action classification. To enable the pixels in the generated grayscale images to preserve more of the spatial information of the original skeleton structure, we proposed the strategy of dividing the skeleton joints into several groups in which joints are related to each other, and rearranging the positions of pixels according to the relationships. This method proved effective for improving the recognition accuracy. In addition, a set of important angles in the skeleton structure was calculated, to form a multi-feature representation and utilize more spatial information. The proposed method was evaluated with standard evaluation protocols on three 3D skeleton-based action datasets: NTU RGB+D [27], NTU RGB+D 120 [17], and UTKinect-Action3D Dataset [33]. The experimental results indicated the effectiveness of our method of using a novel spatio-temporal skeleton representation for 3D skeleton-based action recognition.

Acknowledgment. The research in this paper used the NTU RGB+D and NTU RGB+D 120 Action Recognition Dataset made available by the ROSE Lab at the Nanyang Technological University, Singapore.

References

1. Caetano, C., Brémond, F., Schwartz, W.R.: Skeleton image representation for 3D action recognition based on tree structure and reference joints. In: 2019 32nd SIB-GRAPI Conference on Graphics, Patterns and Images (SIBGRAPI), pp. 16–23. IEEE (2019)
2. Caetano, C., Sena, J., Brémond, F., Dos Santos, J.A., Schwartz, W.R.: Skelemotion: a new representation of skeleton joint sequences based on motion information for 3D action recognition. In: 2019 16th IEEE International Conference on Advanced Video and Signal Based Surveillance (AVSS), pp. 1–8. IEEE (2019)
3. Deng, J., Dong, W., Socher, R., Li, L.J., Li, K., Fei-Fei, L.: Imagenet: a large-scale hierarchical image database. In: 2009 IEEE Conference on Computer Vision and Pattern Recognition, pp. 248–255. IEEE (2009)
4. Ding, Z., Wang, P., Ogunbona, P.O., Li, W.: Investigation of different skeleton features for CNN-based 3D action recognition. In: 2017 IEEE International Conference on Multimedia & Expo Workshops (ICMEW), pp. 617–622. IEEE (2017)
5. Du, Y., Fu, Y., Wang, L.: Skeleton based action recognition with convolutional neural network. In: 2015 3rd IAPR Asian Conference on Pattern Recognition (ACPR), pp. 579–583. IEEE (2015)
6. Du, Y., Wang, W., Wang, L.: Hierarchical recurrent neural network for skeleton based action recognition. In: Proceedings of the IEEE Conference on Computer Vision and Pattern Recognition, pp. 1110–1118 (2015)
7. Graves, A.: Supervised sequence labelling. In: Graves, A. (ed.) Supervised Sequence Labelling with Recurrent Neural Networks, pp. 5–13. Springer, Heidelberg (2012). https://doi.org/10.1007/978-3-642-24797-2_2
8. Hbali, Y., Hbali, S., Ballihi, L., Sadgal, M.: Skeleton-based human activity recognition for elderly monitoring systems. IET Comput. Vision **12**(1), 16–26 (2017)
9. Hu, J.F., Zheng, W.S., Lai, J., Zhang, J.: Jointly learning heterogeneous features for RGB-D activity recognition. In: Proceedings of the IEEE Conference on Computer Vision and Pattern Recognition, pp. 5344–5352 (2015)
10. Huang, C.D., Wang, C.Y., Wang, J.C.: Human action recognition system for elderly and children care using three stream convnet. In: 2015 International Conference on Orange Technologies (ICOT), pp. 5–9. IEEE (2015)
11. Ioffe, S., Szegedy, C.: Batch normalization: accelerating deep network training by reducing internal covariate shift. arXiv preprint arXiv:1502.03167 (2015)
12. Kalayeh, M.M., Basaran, E., Gökmen, M., Kamasak, M.E., Shah, M.: Human semantic parsing for person re-identification. In: Proceedings of the IEEE Conference on Computer Vision and Pattern Recognition, pp. 1062–1071 (2018)
13. Ke, Q., Bennamoun, M., An, S., Sohel, F., Boussaid, F.: A new representation of skeleton sequences for 3D action recognition. In: Proceedings of the IEEE Conference on Computer Vision and Pattern Recognition, pp. 3288–3297 (2017)
14. Ke, Q., Bennamoun, M., An, S., Sohel, F., Boussaid, F.: Learning clip representations for skeleton-based 3D action recognition. IEEE Trans. Image Process. **27**(6), 2842–2855 (2018)
15. LeCun, Y., Bengio, Y., et al.: Convolutional networks for images, speech, and time series. Handb. Brain Theory Neural Netw. **3361**(10), 1995 (1995)

16. Lee, I., Kim, D., Kang, S., Lee, S.: Ensemble deep learning for skeleton-based action recognition using temporal sliding LSTM networks. In: Proceedings of the IEEE International Conference on Computer Vision, pp. 1012–1020 (2017)

17. Liu, J., Shahroudy, A., Perez, M.L., Wang, G., Duan, L.Y., Chichung, A.K.: NTU RGB+D 120: a large-scale benchmark for 3D human activity understanding. IEEE Trans. Pattern Anal. Mach. Intell. **42**(10), 2684–2701 (2019)

18. Liu, J., Shahroudy, A., Wang, G., Duan, L.Y., Chichung, A.K.: Skeleton-based online action prediction using scale selection network. IEEE Trans. Pattern Anal. Mach. Intell. **42**(6), 1453–1467 (2019)

19. Liu, J., Shahroudy, A., Xu, D., Kot, A.C., Wang, G.: Skeleton-based action recognition using spatio-temporal LSTM network with trust gates. IEEE Trans. Pattern Anal. Mach. Intell. **40**(12), 3007–3021 (2017)

20. Liu, J., Shahroudy, A., Xu, D., Wang, G.: Spatio-temporal LSTM with trust gates for 3D human action recognition. In: Leibe, B., Matas, J., Sebe, N., Welling, M. (eds.) ECCV 2016. LNCS, vol. 9907, pp. 816–833. Springer, Cham (2016). https://doi.org/10.1007/978-3-319-46487-9_50

21. Liu, J., Wang, G., Duan, L.Y., Abdiyeva, K., Kot, A.C.: Skeleton-based human action recognition with global context-aware attention LSTM networks. IEEE Trans. Image Process. **27**(4), 1586–1599 (2017)

22. Liu, J., Wang, G., Hu, P., Duan, L.Y., Kot, A.C.: Global context-aware attention LSTM networks for 3D action recognition. In: Proceedings of the IEEE Conference on Computer Vision and Pattern Recognition, pp. 1647–1656 (2017)

23. Liu, M., Liu, H., Chen, C.: Enhanced skeleton visualization for view invariant human action recognition. Pattern Recogn. **68**, 346–362 (2017)

24. Pan, G., Song, Y., Wei, S.: Combining pose and trajectory for skeleton based action recognition using two-stream RNN. In: 2019 Chinese Automation Congress (CAC), pp. 4375–4380. IEEE (2019)

25. Pan, H., Chen, Y.: Multilevel LSTM for action recognition based on skeleton sequence. In: 2019 IEEE 21st International Conference on High Performance Computing and Communications; IEEE 17th International Conference on Smart City; IEEE 5th International Conference on Data Science and Systems (HPCC/SmartCity/DSS), pp. 2218–2223. IEEE (2019)

26. Rhif, M., Wannous, H., Farah, I.R.: Action recognition from 3D skeleton sequences using deep networks on lie group features. In: 2018 24th International Conference on Pattern Recognition (ICPR), pp. 3427–3432. IEEE (2018)

27. Shahroudy, A., Liu, J., Ng, T.T., Wang, G.: NTU RGB+D: a large scale dataset for 3D human activity analysis. In: Proceedings of the IEEE Conference on Computer Vision and Pattern Recognition, pp. 1010–1019 (2016)

28. Song, S., Lan, C., Xing, J., Zeng, W., Liu, J.: Spatio-temporal attention-based LSTM networks for 3D action recognition and detection. IEEE Trans. Image Process. **27**(7), 3459–3471 (2018)

29. Sun, Y., Zheng, L., Yang, Y., Tian, Q., Wang, S.: Beyond part models: person retrieval with refined part pooling. In: ECCV (2018)

30. Wang, H., Wang, L.: Modeling temporal dynamics and spatial configurations of actions using two-stream recurrent neural networks. In: Proceedings of the IEEE Conference on Computer Vision and Pattern Recognition, pp. 499–508 (2017)

31. Wang, L., et al.: Temporal segment networks: towards good practices for deep action recognition. In: Leibe, B., Matas, J., Sebe, N., Welling, M. (eds.) ECCV 2016. LNCS, vol. 9912, pp. 20–36. Springer, Cham (2016). https://doi.org/10.1007/978-3-319-46484-8_2

32. Wei, S., Song, Y., Zhang, Y.: Human skeleton tree recurrent neural network with joint relative motion feature for skeleton based action recognition. In: 2017 IEEE International Conference on Image Processing (ICIP), pp. 91–95. IEEE (2017)
33. Xia, L., Chen, C., Aggarwal, J.: View invariant human action recognition using histograms of 3D joints. In: 2012 IEEE Computer Society Conference on Computer Vision and Pattern Recognition Workshops (CVPRW), pp. 20–27. IEEE (2012)
34. Yang, Z., Li, Y., Yang, J., Luo, J.: Action recognition with spatio-temporal visual attention on skeleton image sequences. IEEE Trans. Circuits Syst. Video Technol. **29**(8), 2405–2415 (2018)
35. Zhang, S., Liu, X., Xiao, J.: On geometric features for skeleton-based action recognition using multilayer LSTM networks. In: 2017 IEEE Winter Conference on Applications of Computer Vision (WACV), pp. 148–157. IEEE (2017)
36. Zheng, Z., Zheng, L., Yang, Y.: Pedestrian alignment network for large-scale person re-identification. IEEE Trans. Circuits Syst. Video Technol. **29**(10), 3037–3045 (2018)

R2SN: Refined Semantic Segmentation Network of City Remote Sensing Image

Chenglong Wang[1], Dong Wu[2], Jie Nie[1(✉)], and Lei Huang[1]

[1] Ocean University of China, Qingdao, China
niejie@ouc.edu.cn
[2] JD.com, Beijing, China
wudong99@gmail.com

Abstract. Semantic segmentation is always a key problem in remote sensing image analysis. Especially, it is very useful for city-scale vehicle detection. However, multi-object and imbalanced data classes of remote sensing images bring a huge challenge, which leads that many traditional segmentation approaches were often unsatisfactory. In this paper, we propose a novel Refined Semantic Segmentation Network (R2SN), which apply the classic encoder-to-decoder framework to handle segmentation problem. However, we add the convolution layers in encoder and decoder to make the network can achieve more local information in the training step. The design is more suitable for high-resolution remote sensing image. More specially, the classic Focal loss is introduced in this network, which can guide the model focus on the difficult objects in remote sensing images and effectively handle multi-object segmentation problem. Meanwhile, the classic Hinge loss is also utilized to increase the distinction between classes, which can guarantee the more refined segmentation results. We validate our approach on the International Society for Photogrammetry and Remote Sensing (ISPRS) semantic segmentation benchmark dataset. The evaluation and comparison results show that our method exceeds the state-of-the-art remote sensing image segmentation methods in terms of mean intersection over union (MIoU), pixel accuracy, and F1-score.

Keywords: Semantic segmentation · Focal loss · Remote sensing

1 Introduction

With the development of satellite space technology and the progress of image acquisition technology, remote sensing images have been widely applied in road extraction [27], building detection [25], plant classification [1], semantic segmentation [18] and other aspects with their extensive perceptual coverage and consistent image scale. However, due to the explosive growth of data and the periodicity of image collection, reasonable and efficient analysis and utilization of these data have become an urgent problem to be solved. Therefore, it is an

© Springer Nature Switzerland AG 2021
A. Del Bimbo et al. (Eds.): ICPR 2020 Workshops, LNCS 12665, pp. 380–396, 2021.
https://doi.org/10.1007/978-3-030-68821-9_34

important means to infer the object category of each pixel from the high spatial resolution remote sensing image.

As one of the most important image analysis technologies [14, 15], image semantic segmentation has been extensively studied in recent years and made great progress, especially after the fully convolutional network (FCN) [17] model was proposed. Semantic segmentation using the convolutional neural network has become a trend and generated many segmentation architectures. FCN can input images of any size and output segmentation maps of the same size, which is the first to realize an end-to-end segmentation network. Other network structures include, for example, a U-net network [23] that adapts to multi-scale, large size image segmentation and concatenating features at the channel latitude. SegNet network [2] that improves memory utilization and model segmentation rate, and Pyramid Scene Parsing Network (PSPNet) [31], which is proposed for better use of global scene information Network, a DeepLabv3 network [4] that uses atrous convolution [29] to expand the receptive field and solve the problem of multi-scale image segmentation.

1.1 Motivation

Although these networks have achieved excellent results in the segmentation of natural images, there are often two problems in the segmentation process of remote sensing images. First, the distribution of pixel categories in the remote sensing dataset is imbalanced. Second, during image segmentation, the distance between different classes of pixels is not obvious, and the accuracy needs to be further improved. The unbalanced distribution of remote sensing images and the scale change of different objects are mainly reflected in two aspects. First, the scale of objects in different categories is significantly different [20]. For instance, in the same remote sensing image, the object scales of the two categories of houses and vehicles are very different. The distribution of houses is dense and continuous, and the distribution of vehicles is sparse. Therefore, it is difficult to take into account small targets while segmenting large objects. Second, there are significant differences in the proportion of objects of the same category. For example, the distribution of buildings in cities is dense and continuous, the size of different buildings varies greatly, the distribution of buildings in rural areas is sparse, and the size of different buildings is small. This makes it difficult to capture the invariance of objects and affects the accuracy of the network. Because the boundary category of image segmentation is not clear, and the interval between different classes is too small, it often results in misclassification in the boundary area, which affects our image segmentation effect and accuracy. Such as the area that should have been classified as a road is classified as a house or vegetation, or the original two houses are separated by a result and the effect is a whole house together. In practical applications, it often affects our judgment of real things.

In this paper, a new loss function is proposed to solve the problem of unbalanced classification in remote sensing image segmentation and the problem that the boundary between classes of image segmentation results is not obvious.

We introduce the Focal Loss (FL) [12] to resolve the imbalance of remote sensing image categories. Focal Loss was proposed to solve the problem of an unbalanced distribution of positive and negative samples in object detection [22]. This Loss function reduces the weight of simple samples in training while increasing the weight of difficult samples. In this paper, Focal loss is used to reduce the weight of easily classified samples and focus on the difficult samples. At the same time, the loss function designed by Nie et al. [19] has a great inspiration for our method. In order to solve the problem that the distance between samples of different categories is not obvious, we introduce Hinge Loss, which is a loss function that maximizes the interval between different types of samples. Hinge Loss is a loss function often used in maximum interval classification in machine learning. It is usually used in support vector machine (SVM) to make the score of correct classification higher than the score of incorrect classification by a threshold, and the distance between different classes of samples becomes larger. In summary, the loss function we introduced is to change the weights of different categories of samples to reduce the weight of easy-to-learn categories, increase the weight of difficult-to-learn categories, and control the boundaries of different categories of samples, making the segmentation of difficult learning samples more accurate. The boundary between samples of different categories becomes larger. We use the SegNet network as the backend, using its efficient use of memory, faster segmentation speed can quickly achieve the target segmentation.

1.2   Contributions

The main contributions of this paper are as follows:

- We proposes a novel loss function to solve the category imbalance and at the same time to increase the sample spacing of different categories, to achieve a more accurate segmentation boundary and more accurate segmentation effect;
- The popular remote sensing image dataset are utilized to demonstrate the performance of the proposed method. Several classic methods are used for comparison. The final experiment also demonstrates the superiority of our approach.

The overall structure design of our paper is as follows: First, in Sect. 2, we introduce the design of semantic segmentation network models for various scenes, as well as some classic improvement methods to improve segmentation performance from different angles. Then, in Sect. 3, we introduced the network we designed and the improvement of the loss function. The Sect. 4 introduces the comparative experiments of different loss functions, as well as the parameter ablation experiments and the comparison with the state-of-the-art methods. The Sect. 5 summarizes our work and introduces the advantages of the method proposed in this paper.

2   Related Work

The research of pixel-wise semantic segmentation of images is a hot research area in computer vision [13,24]. Before deep network is applied to image segmentation, the best performing method is to rely on manually designed features to classify pixels independently. Usually, a block is fed into a classifier, such as random forest [3], to predict the probability of a central pixel. The classifier then smoothed the prediction of each pixel with the conditional random field (CRF) [8]. With the emergence of FCNs, deep learning has officially entered the field of image semantic segmentation. FCNs replaced the fully connected network with a convolutional network and proposed a fully convolutional network, which allows the network to accept pictures of any size and output segmented pictures of the same size as the original picture. It uses a skips structure to improve the accuracy and robustness of the segmentation results and uses a deconvolution [30] layer to map the feature to the original picture size. The U-net network proposed to deal with the segmentation of large-scale medical images is a typical encoding and decoding paradigm. It concatenates features at the channel dimension to form thicker features, which is suitable for the segmentation of large-scale datasets with a small amount of data but requires a large amount of computing power. Another encoding and decoding paradigm is the SegNet network designed to solve the semantic segmentation of autonomous driving scenes, which can realize faster segmentation and efficient utilization of computing power. It differs from U-net networks in that the latter is a feature extracted [26] during the downsampling process and then connected in the upsampling process, while SegNet is using the transferred pool indices from its encoder. In order to solve the problem that the FCN-based model lacks the ability to use global scene information, the PSPNet network appears. It uses a pyramid pooling module to aggregate context information of different regions, thereby improving the ability to obtain global information. The use of the Deeplab V3 model is to solve the problem of the multi-scale segmentation of objects. Multi-scale context information is captured by a multi-scale atrous ratio through cascading or parallel atrous convolution. In addition to the above segmentation models, there is still some work to segment images from the perspective of multi-scale fusion [11], and some are segmentation models designed from the perspective of considering intra-class and inter-class changes [21].

Semantic segmentation is not only widely used in the field of computer vision [5,10,28], but also meaningful in the field of medical images and remote sensing images. At present, more and more semantic segmentation networks based on deep learning are applied to the semantic segmentation of remote sensing images. Remote sensing images are different from natural images in terms of scale changes, color distribution, and angle transformation, so remote sensing images cannot be directly applied to these segmentation models. In order to enable high-resolution, large-scale remote sensing images to be trained normally in neural networks, Liu et al. [16] proposed a method for patch-wise training of large-scale remote sensing images. Firstly, the image is crop to a suitable size, and then the image is preprocessed with color adjustment, multi-scale transformation and deformation, etc. Finally, the image is entered into the patchwise convolutional neural network. Foivos et al. [6] proposed ResUNet-a, a new network model for remote sensing image segmentation, by using the U-net network as the backbone and integrating many advanced technologies such as residual block [7], atrous convolution, and pyramid pooling. Li et al. [9] designed a new remote sensing image segmentation network, SCAttNet, which combines the two attention mechanisms of the channel attention module and the spatial attention module, which significantly improves the segmentation accuracy. Due to the wide-scale range of remote sensing images and large changes in object size, there is a clear category imbalance in remote sensing data. At the same time, remote sensing image segmentation may have pixel classification errors in practical applications, and the interval between different types of pixels may be small. In order to solve the above problems, this paper first performs image cropping, rotation transformation, filtering, flipping and other preprocessing on remote sensing data, and proposes an optimized loss function combining Focal Loss and Hinge Loss.

3   Our Approach

3.1   Structure

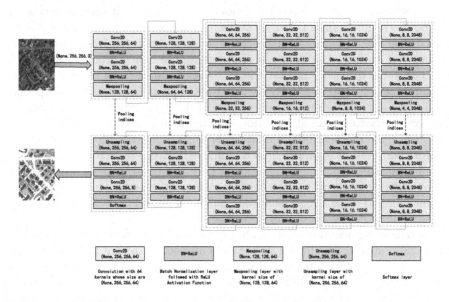

Fig. 1. The overall architecture of the proposed method. The training data is preprocessed and fed into the SegNet network,and the parameters are updated by backpropagation after calculating the loss. Finally,the best parameters are used to predict the result.

The proposed method is shown in Fig. 1. The segmentation network is modified from SegNet, which applies the classic encoder-to-decoder architecture. In this paper, we modified the structures of SegNet and add the Focal loss and Hinge loss according to the characteristic of remote sensing image. We will details the network in the next subsections.

3.2 Architecture of Network

The detail of the architecture of the network is shown in Fig. 1. According to the high-resolution of remote sensing images, we hope the segmentation network can focus on more local information in the training and provide more accurate segmentation results. Thus, we apply two methods to handle this problem. 1) The up-samples operation on remote sensing image: the operation can show more local information in the training step. However, the operation will add the complexity of the approach and require more memory. To handle this problem, we change the size of the epoch and batch size. 2) We add the convolution layers in the encoder and decoder. The reason is that the traditional SegNet does not get the local information because of the high-resolution remote sensing image, which forces us to add the convolution layers and make the network can touch more local information for more accurate segmentation results.

3.3 Focal Loss

The sample categories of the dataset are unevenly distributed, the number of negative samples is too large and most of them are easy to classify, which often results in invalid learning during the training process. Focal loss (FL) is proposed to deal with the extreme imbalance between the foreground and background in the object detection scene. Focal loss is improved based on cross entropy loss. Compared with cross entropy, it has a modulating factor:

$$FL(p_t) = -\sum_{t=1}^{M} (1 - p_t)^\gamma \log(p_t). \tag{1}$$

In this formula, $\gamma \geq 0$ is an tunable hyperparameter. $(1 - p_t)^\gamma$ is the modulating factor. For the sample that is easy to learn, its p_t value is close to 1, and then the modulation factor tends to 0. For the sample that is difficult to learn or misclassified, p_t is small, and its modulation factor will increase accordingly. Therefore, the loss value of the difficult samples is retained, and the loss value of the simple samples is reduced, and the training of the difficult samples is emphasized during the training process. Focal loss is also applicable to the pixel-wise classification problem. In order to adapt to multi-category segmentation, the formula is adjusted as follows:

$$FL(p_t) = -\sum_{t=1}^{M} (\lambda - p_t)^\gamma \log(p_t). \tag{2}$$

In the above formula, λ represents the hyperparameter. In the experiment, using Focal Loss as a loss function, we found that when $\lambda = 1$, using Focal Loss as a loss function is not as effective as using cross entropy loss directly. After analysis, we believe that Focal Loss is designed for the imbalance of the two categories of foreground and background, and our pixel-wise semantic classification has multiple categories, so there are two categories or multiple categories with similar probability. When λ equal to 1, these probabilities are similar, and they cannot highlight the difficult sample classes. Therefore, we change the probability distribution of the classes by changing λ , that is, the rate of change of loss.

3.4   Hinge Loss

Hinge Loss (HL) is commonly used in the maximum interval classification task in SVM to achieve the maximum boundary. In the case of binary classifications, its formula is as follows:

$$Hinge = \max(0, 1 - y * y_{pre}). \tag{3}$$

In this formula, y is the real label, with a value of 1 or -1. y_{pre} is the prediction. When $|y_{pre}| \geq 1$, the distance between the sample and the dividing line is greater than 1, there is no reward, because it only requires a sample to be properly classified. This makes the classifier more focused on the overall classification error. Hinge Loss in case of multiple classifications is:

$$Hinge = \max(0, 1 + \max w_{wrong} - w_{correct}). \tag{4}$$

where w_{wrong} is a misclassified sample, and $w_{correct}$ is a correctly classified sample.

In order to solve the imbalance of categories while increasing the sample interval of different categories and improving the accuracy of segmentation, we propose a method that combines Focal loss and Hinge loss to optimize our loss function. The specific formula is as follows:

$$FH = -\sum_{t=1}^{M} (\lambda - p_t)^\gamma \log(p_t) + \beta \max(0, 1 + \max w_{wrong} - w_{correct}). \tag{5}$$

The β is a hyperparameter to control the ratio of hinge loss. In the final analysis, the semantic segmentation of images is a problem of pixel-wise classification. In order to make the classification result more accurate, it is necessary to maximize the spacing of different kinds of pixels and make the same kind of pixels more aggregated. So the core idea of the loss function we proposed is to make the sample distances of the same class smaller and the sample of different classes larger.

Our loss function consists of two parts. The first part is the Focal loss term. Considering that Focal loss adds a modulating factor to the cross entropy loss, in addition to solving the problem of uneven distribution of sample categories. The focal loss also reduces the distance between samples of the same category. The second part is realized by the hinge loss which makes the distance between different types of samples larger. Through experiments, we found that the introduction of Hinge loss on the basis of Focal loss not only improves our segmentation accuracy to a certain extent but also significantly improves the value of MIoU.

4   Experiments

4.1   Implementation Details

We validate our approach with experiments on the Vaihingen data set of the ISPRS 2D semantic labeling contest. Vaihingen dataset, which includes 33 true ortho photo(TOP) of different sizes, as well as the corresponding digital surface models(DSM), we use only 16 of these labeled images. The TOP are 8 bit TIFF files with three bands; the three RGB bands of the TIFF files correspond to the near infrared, red, and green bands delivered by the camera. This dataset defines six categories, including Impervious surfaces, Building, and Low vegetation, Tree, Clutter/background. The resolution of each image is 9 cm. We selected 12 images[1] from the 16 labeled images as the training set, and the remaining 4 images[2] as the test set.

As a deep neural network is a data-driven method, it is difficult to accurately segment the sparse dataset, so it is necessary to preprocess the data to expand the dataset. The image is smoothed by Gaussian blur and bilateral filtering to achieve the purpose of preserving the edge and removing noise. The variation of target rotation also affects the segmentation of remote sensing images. Due to the shooting angle of aerial images, the targets on the ground will have many different directions, which hinders the network segmentation and extraction of common features. Normal images are unaffected by the rotation problem. To solve the problem of changing the object rotation, we rotated the images in the dataset by 3 angles (90,180,270). At the same time, we flip the image up, down, left, and right. In this experiment, we randomly crop 12 training set images into 100,000 image blocks of 256 * 256 size after the above enhancement operation. In the network model, we use SegNet as the backbone to verify the proposed method. And our training epoch is 16, considering the limitation of memory, batch-size adopts 16. All our experiments are implemented on the Tensorflow platform, using NVIDIA Tesla P100 GPU.

In order to evaluate our method, this article uses three metrics to evaluate our segmentation performance: F1-score(F_1), MIoU, and pixel accuracy [7].

4.2   Ablation Experiment

In order to verify the efficiency of our proposed method, we use SegNet as the network backbone and compare our performance under different loss functions. In this section, we conducted four main experiments. The experiment using

---

[1] image ID: 1, 3, 11, 13, 15, 17, 21, 26, 28, 32, 34, 37.

[2] image ID: 5,7,23,30.

the cross entropy loss (CE) function is used as our baseline. The other three experiments include the tuning experiment of Focal loss function, the experiment of using cross entropy loss and Hinge loss together, and our tuning experiment of FH as a loss function. First, we train our model with cross-entropy loss. Next, we used FL as a loss function to perform tuning experiments under different parameters. Compares the effect of γ at four values of 0, 0.5, 1, and 2 when λ is 1 or 2. The experimental results are shown in Table 1.

In Table 1, when γ is equal to 0, FL is equivalent to the cross entropy loss. Therefore, we can find that when λ is equal to 1, the performance of FL is worse than the performance of cross entropy loss. And with the increase of γ, the values of various metrics are gradually decreasing.

Table 1. When FL is a loss function and $\lambda = 1$ or 2, the performance comparison of γ at different values

λ	γ	Pixel Acc	F_1	MIoU
$\lambda = 1$	$\gamma = 0$	0.9426	0.9428	0.7595
	$\gamma = 0.5$	0.9360	0.9361	0.7425
	$\gamma = 1$	0.9336	0.9333	0.7366
	$\gamma = 2$	0.9166	0.9150	0.6940
$\lambda = 2$	$\gamma = 0$	—	—	—
	$\gamma = 0.5$	0.9461	0.9462	0.7766
	$\gamma = 1$	0.9428	0.9428	0.7649
	$\gamma = 2$	**0.9482**	**0.9482**	**0.8181**

After analysis, we believe that the application of Focal loss is to classify the two categories with very different foreground and background. However, in the application scenario of remote sensing image semantic segmentation, there are six categories, and two or more of them have similar probability. When $\lambda = 1$, the change rate of these categories could not be significantly changed. So similar classes are not easy to distinguish, and in training we need to focus on the difficult classes. Therefore, in order to solve this situation, we should change the rate of the modulation factor, so that the weight of the difficult sample is increased and the weight of the simple sample is reduced, the value of λ is equal to 2. When $\lambda = 2$, the change rate of the modulation factor becomes faster with the increase of γ.

It can be seen from Table 1 that when $\lambda = 2$, the value of MIoU has a better improvement than $\lambda = 1$, and it also improves slightly in pixel accuracy and F_1, so the use of FL has significantly improved our segmentation performance. We can find that among the parameters we compare, the best segmentation results are obtained when $\lambda = 2$ and $\gamma = 2$.

We select the best segmentation parameters for the following experiments to verify the impact of our proposed loss function on the segmentation results.

We compared the situation of different β when combining FL with HL. The experiment results are shown in Table 2. Table 2 shows that with the increase of β in the range of 0 to 1, the three values of pixel accuracy, F1 score, and MIoU will increase. These three values become smaller as β increases between 1 and 2. Among the parameters in our experiments, $\beta = 1$ is the best performance.

Table 2. When FH is the loss function, the performance comparison of β at different values

β	pixel acc	F_1	MIoU
0	0.9482	0.9482	0.8181
0.2	0.9559	0.9559	0.8641
0.5	0.9571	0.9570	0.8736
1.0	**0.9597**	**0.9596**	**0.8803**
1.5	0.9577	0.9576	0.8750
2.0	0.9549	0.9548	0.8685

4.3 Comparison with Different Loss Functions

We select the segmentation performance comparison of the best parameters of the four losses of CE, FL, CE+HL, and FH, and the results are shown in Table 3. Among them, CE represents cross entropy loss, FL is Focal loss, CE + HL represents cross entropy loss used in conjunction with Hinge loss, FH is our proposed loss function. Through experiments, we found that using Hinge loss as a loss function alone is not suitable for our image segmentation scene. However, when Hinge loss is used in combination with Focal loss, the segmentation effect is significantly improved. The parameters for the best FL results are $\lambda = 2$ and $\gamma = 2$, respectively. The best performance parameter for FH is $\beta = 1$. Experimental results show that under the same conditions, using FL as a loss function increases the MIoU value by about 5% compared to CE. Using our proposed FH loss, the MIoU value is increased by about 12% over CE and about 6% over FL. We compare the effect of image segmentation under different loss functions, as shown in Fig. 2. This image shows the segmentation results of the two photos in the test set under the three loss functions of CE, FL, and FH.

Table 3. Performance comparison of different loss functions

Loss Function	pixel acc	F_1	MIoU
CE	0.9426	0.9428	0.7595
FL	0.9539	0.9538	0.8247
CE+HL	0.9554	0.9555	0.8499
FH(our)	**0.9597**	**0.9596**	**0.8803**

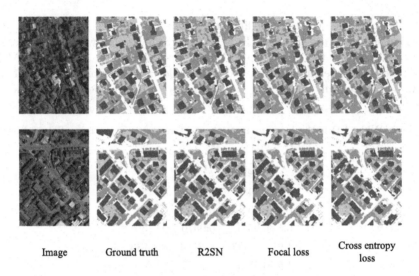

| Image | Ground truth | R2SN | Focal loss | Cross entropy loss |

Fig. 2. Comparison of segmentation graphs under different loss functions

To verify the adaptability of our proposed loss function, we downsampled the Vinhingen dataset twice and then retrained our model with different loss functions. The specific implementation details are as follows: After first downsampling, the original image and label twice in the dataset, and after the same data preprocessing process, we generate $100,000$ images of 256×256 size, use the generated images to train a model on the four loss functions of CE, FL, CE+HL, and FH, respectively, and observe whether our proposed loss function can also improve the segmentation performance on this dataset. The segmentation effect under different loss functions is shown in Fig. 3.

The segmentation results after twice the downsampling of the data set are shown in Table 4. The values of λ, β and γ are the same as those in Table 3. From Table 4, we can prove that our proposed loss function also has the best performance compared to CE and FL on different datasets. Comparing with CE, our loss function is improved by about 11% in MIoU. At the same time, this new loss is about 3% higher than FL. As with the process of downsampling the dataset twice, we downsample the dataset four times and then train our model. The experimental results of the four loss functions are shown in Table 5. The segmentation effect is shown in Fig. 4. Finally, we compare the experimental results of three different sampling datasets and compare the overall accuracy, F1 score and MIoU changes in three cases. The results are shown in Fig. 5, 6, and 7.

4.4   Comparison with State-of-the-Art Methods

In this paper, our method can be seen as the modified SegNet. Our approach focuses on the local information and provides more accurate segmentation results than SegNet. In order to demonstrate the conclusion, some classic semantic segmentation methods, such as FCN, U-Net, U-Net++, are utilized as the

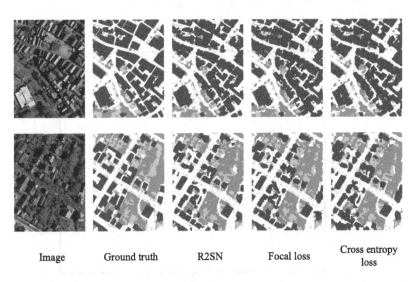

| Image | Ground truth | R2SN | Focal loss | Cross entropy loss |

Fig. 3. Comparison of segmentation graphs under different loss functions after twice downsampling of the dataset

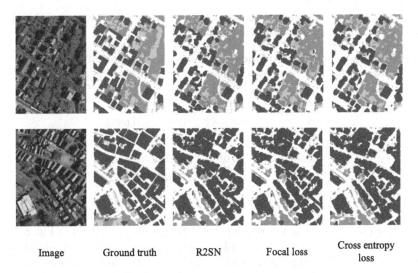

| Image | Ground truth | R2SN | Focal loss | Cross entropy loss |

Fig. 4. Comparison of segmentation graphs under different loss functions after twice downsampling of the dataset

Table 4. Comparison of segmentation performance under different loss functions after double downsampling of Vaihingen dataset

Loss Function	pixel acc	F_1	MIoU
CE	0.9280	0.9282	0.7294
FL	0.9456	0.9456	0.8129
CE+HL	0.9339	0.9339	0.7605
FH(our)	**0.9513**	**0.9511**	**0.8414**

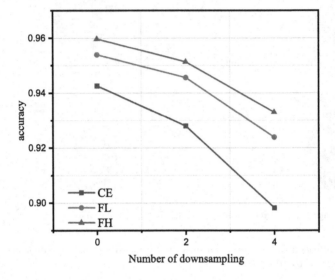

Fig. 5. Comparison of segmentation accuracy on the original dataset, double downsampling and quadruple downsampling datasets

Table 5. Comparison of segmentation performance under different loss functions after four downsampling of the Vaihingin dataset

Loss Function	pixel acc	F_1	MIoU
CE	0.8982	0.8982	0.6854
FL	0.9239	0.9236	0.7683
CE+HL	0.9185	0.9185	0.6860
FH(our)	**0.9330**	**0.9327**	**0.7820**

comparison methods. The related experimental results are shown in Fig. 8. From this segmentation results, we can find that our approach achieves more accurate segmentation results, which also demonstrates the rationality and validity of our approach.

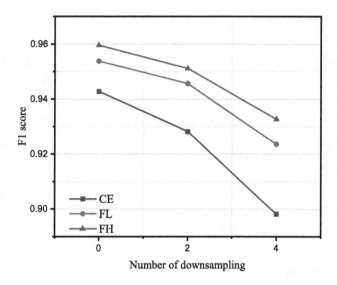

Fig. 6. Comparison of F1 score on the original dataset, double downsampling and quadruple downsampling datasets

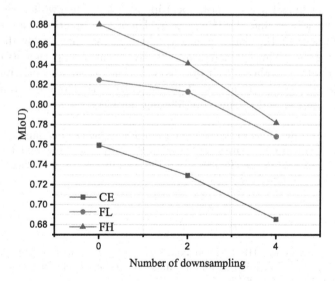

Fig. 7. Comparison of MIoU on the original dataset, double downsampling and quadruple downsampling datasets

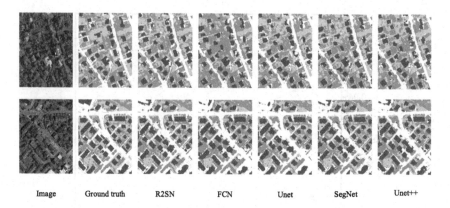

| Image | Ground truth | R2SN | FCN | Unet | SegNet | Unet++ |

Fig. 8. Comparison with state-of-the-art methods

5   Conclusion

In this paper, we proposed a novel Refined Semantic Segmentation Network (R2SN) for city remote sensing image to handle city-scale vehicle detection. In this work, we modified the classic SegNet to make the new network is suitable for remote sensing image to save more local information. Meanwhile, we introduce the classic Focal loss and the Hinge Loss. These loss functions can reduce the sample distances of the same category and increase the sample distances of different categories. Through the comprehensive ablation experiments on remote sensing data sets, it is shown that our loss function can significantly improve the effect of image segmentation, and it is also proved that our loss function has good generalization performance on different datasets.

Acknowledgement. This work was supported in part by the Fundamental Research Funds for the Central Universities (202042008), the Major Scientific and Technological Innovation Project (2019JZZY020705), and the National Natural Science Foundation of China (61702471, 62072418).

References

1. Ahmed, O.S., et al.: Hierarchical land cover and vegetation classification using multispectral data acquired from an unmanned aerial vehicle. Int. J. Remote Sens. **38**(8–10), 2037–2052 (2017)
2. Badrinarayanan, V., Kendall, A., Cipolla, R.: Segnet: a deep convolutional encoder-decoder architecture for image segmentation. IEEE Trans. Pattern Anal. Mach. Intell. **39**(12), 2481–2495 (2017)
3. Breiman, L.: Random forests. Mach. Learn. **45**(1), 5–32 (2001)
4. Chen, L.C., Papandreou, G., Schroff, F., Adam, H.: Rethinking Atrous convolution for semantic image segmentation. arXiv preprint arXiv:1706.05587 (2017)

5. Chen, L.-C., Zhu, Y., Papandreou, G., Schroff, F., Adam, H.: Encoder-decoder with Atrous separable convolution for semantic image segmentation. In: Ferrari, V., Hebert, M., Sminchisescu, C., Weiss, Y. (eds.) ECCV 2018. LNCS, vol. 11211, pp. 833–851. Springer, Cham (2018). https://doi.org/10.1007/978-3-030-01234-2_49

6. Diakogiannis, F.I., Waldner, F., Caccetta, P., Wu, C.: Resunet-a: a deep learning framework for semantic segmentation of remotely sensed data. ISPRS J. Photogrammetry Remote Sens. **162**, 94–114 (2020)

7. He, K., Zhang, X., Ren, S., Sun, J.: Deep residual learning for image recognition. In: Proceedings of the IEEE Conference on Computer Vision and Pattern Recognition, pp. 770–778 (2016)

8. Lafferty, J., McCallum, A., Pereira, F.C.: Conditional random fields: probabilistic models for segmenting and labeling sequence data (2001)

9. Li, H., Qiu, K., Chen, L., Mei, X., Hong, L., Tao, C.: Scattnet: semantic segmentation network with spatial and channel attention mechanism for high-resolution remote sensing images. IEEE Geosci. Remote Sens. Lett. **14**, 1–5 (2020)

10. Li, H., Xiong, P., Fan, H., Sun, J.: DfaNet: deep feature aggregation for real-time semantic segmentation. In: Proceedings of the IEEE Conference on Computer Vision and Pattern Recognition, pp. 9522–9531 (2019)

11. Lin, G., Milan, A., Shen, C., Reid, I.: RefineNet: Multi-path refinement networks for high-resolution semantic segmentation. In: Proceedings of the IEEE Conference on Computer Vision and Pattern Recognition, pp. 1925–1934 (2017)

12. Lin, T.Y., Goyal, P., Girshick, R., He, K., Dollár, P.: Focal loss for dense object detection. In: Proceedings of the IEEE International Conference on Computer Vision, pp. 2980–2988 (2017)

13. Liu, W., Liu, X., Ma, H., Cheng, P.: Beyond human-level license plate super-resolution with progressive vehicle search and domain priori GAN. In: Proceedings of the 25th ACM International Conference on Multimedia. MM 2017, Association for Computing Machinery, New York, NY, USA, pp. 1618–1626 (2017). https://doi.org/10.1145/3123266.3123422

14. Liu, X., Liu, W., Mei, T., Ma, H.: PROVID: progressive and multimodal vehicle reidentification for large-scale urban surveillance. IEEE Trans. Multimedia **20**(3), 645–658 (2018). https://doi.org/10.1109/TMM.2017.2751966

15. Liu, X., Zhang, M., Liu, W., Song, J., Mei, T.: BraidNet: braiding semantics and details for accurate human parsing, October 2019. https://doi.org/10.1145/3343031.3350857

16. Liu, Y., Ren, Q., Geng, J., Ding, M., Li, J.: Efficient patch-wise semantic segmentation for large-scale remote sensing images. Sensors **18**(10), 3232 (2018)

17. Long, J., Shelhamer, E., Darrell, T.: Fully convolutional networks for semantic segmentation. In: Proceedings of the IEEE Conference on Computer Vision and Pattern Recognition, pp. 3431–3440 (2015)

18. Marmanis, D., Wegner, J.D., Galliani, S., Schindler, K., Datcu, M., Stilla, U.: Semantic segmentation of aerial images with an ensemble of CNSs. ISPRS Ann. Photogram. Remote Sens. Spatial Inf. Sci. **3**, 473–480 (2016)

19. Nie, W.Z., Liu, A.A., Zhao, S., Gao, Y.: Deep correlated joint network for 2-d image-based 3-d model retrieval. IEEE Trans. Cybernet. (2020)

20. Nie, W., Jia, W., Li, W., Liu, A., Zhao, S.: 3d pose estimation based on reinforce learning for 2d image-based 3d model retrieval. IEEE Trans. Multimedia (2020)

21. Peng, C., Zhang, X., Yu, G., Luo, G., Sun, J.: Large kernel matters-improve semantic segmentation by global convolutional network. In: Proceedings of the IEEE Conference on Computer Vision and Pattern Recognition, pp. 4353–4361 (2017)

22. Ren, S., He, K., Girshick, R., Sun, J.: Faster R-CNN: towards real-time object detection with region proposal networks. In: Advances in Neural Information Processing Systems, pp. 91–99 (2015)
23. Ronneberger, O., Fischer, P., Brox, T.: U-Net: convolutional networks for biomedical image segmentation. In: Navab, N., Hornegger, J., Wells, W.M., Frangi, A.F. (eds.) MICCAI 2015. LNCS, vol. 9351, pp. 234–241. Springer, Cham (2015). https://doi.org/10.1007/978-3-319-24574-4_28
24. Sun, Y., et al.: Synthetic training for monocular human mesh recovery, October 2020
25. Vakalopoulou, M., Karantzalos, K., Komodakis, N., Paragios, N.: Building detection in very high resolution multispectral data with deep learning features. In: 2015 IEEE International Geoscience and Remote Sensing Symposium (IGARSS), pp. 1873–1876. IEEE (2015)
26. Wang, Q., Liu, X., Liu, W., Liu, A., Liu, W., Mei, T.: Metasearch: incremental product search via deep meta-learning. IEEE Trans. Image Process. **29**, 7549–7564 (2020). https://doi.org/10.1109/TIP.2020.3004249
27. Wang, W., Yang, N., Zhang, Y., Wang, F., Cao, T., Eklund, P.: A review of road extraction from remote sensing images. J. Traff. Transp. Eng. (Eng. Ed.) **3**(3), 271–282 (2016)
28. Yu, C., Wang, J., Peng, C., Gao, C., Yu, G., Sang, N.: Learning a discriminative feature network for semantic segmentation. In: Proceedings of the IEEE Conference on Computer Vision and Pattern Recognition, pp. 1857–1866 (2018)
29. Yu, F., Koltun, V.: Multi-scale context aggregation by dilated convolutions. arXiv preprint arXiv:1511.07122 (2015)
30. Zeiler, M.D., Krishnan, D., Taylor, G.W., Fergus, R.: Deconvolutional networks. In: 2010 IEEE Computer Society Conference on Computer Vision and Pattern Recognition, pp. 2528–2535. IEEE (2010)
31. Zhao, H., Shi, J., Qi, X., Wang, X., Jia, J.: Pyramid scene parsing network. In: Proceedings of the IEEE Conference on Computer Vision and Pattern Recognition, pp. 2881–2890 (2017)

Light-Weight Distilled HRNet for Facial Landmark Detection

Ziye Tong[1,2] , Shenqi Lai[1(✉)] , and Zhenhua Chai[1]

[1] Vision Intelligence Center of Meituan, Beijing, China
{tongziye,laishenqi,chaizhenhua}@meituan.com
[2] Xi'an Jiaotong University, Xi'an, China

Abstract. A light-weight facial landmark detection model is proposed in this paper (we named it "LDHRNet"), which can be trained in an end-to-end fashion and could perform precise facial landmark detection in various conditions including those with large pose, exaggerated expression, non-uniform lighting and occlusions. Firstly, in order to deal with these challenging cases above, a light-weight HRNet (LHRNet) structure is proposed as the backbone while the bottleneck block is used to replace the standard residual block in the original HRNet and the group convolution is used to replace the standard convolution in the original HRNet. Then in order to prevent the accuracy loss by the coordinates quantization, we use function named dual soft argmax (DSA) to map the heatmap response to final coordinates. And then we proposed Similarity-FeatureMap knowledge distillation model which guides the training of a student network such that input pairs that produce similar (dissimilar) feature maps in the pre-trained teacher network produce similar (dissimilar) feature maps in the student network. Finally, we combine the distillation loss and NME loss to train our model. The best result 79.10% for AUC is achieved on the validation set.

Keywords: Light-weight HRNet · Similarity-FeatureMap knowledge distillation · Facial landmark detection

1 Introduction

Facial landmark detection is a very crucial step in numerous face related applications, such as face alignment for recognition, facial pose estimation, face image synthesis, etc. Liu et al. [6] introduced a series of excellent methods. This paper attempts to give a promising solution to Grand Challenge of 106-p Facial Landmark Localization which is held in ICPR 2020. This challenge provides a large scale unconstrained facial landmark detection dataset, which contains 20,386 images for training and 2,000 images for validation with 106 landmark annotations. So far as we know, this is the first large scale dataset with more 100 landmarks open to public. In the past decades, a large number of methods related to the facial landmark detection have been studied and can obtain good

A. Del Bimbo et al. (Eds.): ICPR 2020 Workshops, LNCS 12665, pp. 397–406, 2021.
https://doi.org/10.1007/978-3-030-68821-9_35

results in some relatively controlled environments. However, a more challenging dataset was provided in this competition. All the images are captured under unconstrained environment, which are full with large variations in identity, pose, expression, lighting conditions and occlusion. Besides, a strict limit of model weights is employed for computational efficiency (the upper bound of computational complexity is 1 GFLOPs, and the upper bound of model size is 20 MB).

Thanks to the development of deep learning and establishing of large scale public available databases [3,7], deep neural networks could be a good solution to this task. Tweaked CNNs (TCNN) [15] add an unsupervised clustering after the network output, in this way the problem can be divided according to some semantic attributes (e.g. the head pose or facial attribute). The specific parameters to each pose are further finetuned in each sub problem. Most existing methods recover high-resolution representations from low-resolution representations produced by a high-to-low resolution network. Instead, HRNet [11] maintains high-resolution representations through the whole process. The accuracy has been signicantly improved by these novel but large capacity networks mentioned above, However, real world tasks often aim at obtaining best accuracy under a limited computational budget, given by target platform (e.g., hardware) and application scenarios (e.g., auto driving requires low latency, and some realtime cases). Most of the methods mentioned above is too slow to be acceptable in some realtime cases, or can meet real-time scenarios (e.g. in 3000fps [10]) but at the cost of reduced accuracy. This motivates us to design a fast and accurate light-weight network.

Heatmap prediction is prevalent in some more recent solutions to this problem. However, heatmap prediction uses argmax and other post-process operation to get final coordinates, which may cause the quantization errors. In order to overcome this problem, soft argmax is proposed and plays an important role in both 2d [8] and 3d pose estimation [12], but it still has some drawbacks. For pixels at different positions in heatmap, they have different gradients of weight during BP. The dual soft argmax (DSA) [5] was proposed to solve this problem, which could map heatmap into numerical coordinate and make all pixels get equal weights.

Knowledge distillation is a widely applicable technique for training a student neural network under the guidance of a trained teacher network. Similarity-preserving knowledge distillation model [14] guides the training of a student network such that input pairs that produce similar (dissimilar) activations in the pre-trained teacher network produce similar (dissimilar) activations in the student network. Inspired by [14], we proposed Similarity-FeatureMap knowledge distillation model which guides the training of a student network such that input pairs that produce similar (dissimilar) feature maps in the pre-trained teacher network produce similar (dissimilar) feature maps in the student network, and we derive similarity matrices from the feature maps, and compute a distillation loss on the matrices produced by the student and the teacher.

The contributions of the proposed method can be summarized as follows: Firstly, a fast and accurate light-weight network is proposed; Secondly, a Similarity-FeatureMap knowledge distillation model is proposed; Finally, dual soft argmax is used to further improve the performance.

2   Proposed Method

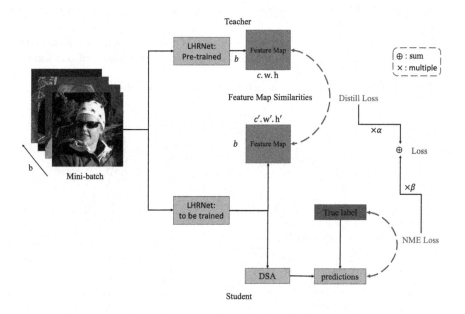

Fig. 1. The framework of our proposed method.

A robust facial landmark detection framework is proposed in this paper, which can be trained in an end-to-end fashion and could perform precise facial landmark localization in various conditions including those with large pose, exaggerated expression, non-uniform lighting and occlusions. The framework of our proposed method can be seen as Fig. 1.

2.1   Light-Weight HRNet

HRNet has achieved high accuracy, but its computational complexity is too high and its model size is too big, so we proposed a light-weight HRNet (LHRNet) sructure which made the following improvements to hrnet:

– Taking into account the HRNet's problem mentioned above, we have optimized the model structure which has lower computational complexity and smaller model size

- The bottleneck block [1] is used to replace the standard residual block in the original HRNet, which allows our model to maintain a basically consistent accuracy while greatly reducing the model size
- The group convolution [13] is used to replace the standard convolution in the original HRNet, which can greatly reduce the GFLops required by the model while our method keeps the network structure unchanged and maintains a small decrease in accuracy
- We replace the "Relu" activation function with the "HardSwish" [2] activation function, which improves the accuracy of the model at a small computational cost
- We use function named dual soft argmax (DSA) [5] to map the heatmap response to final coordinates, which increase the performance of our model

The details of our model structure can be found in Table 1.

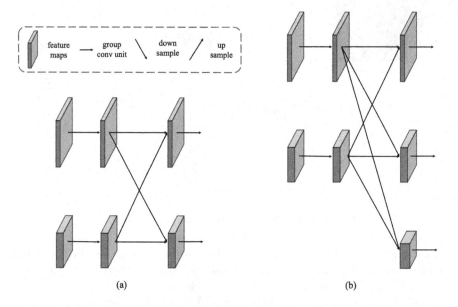

Fig. 2. (a) Fusion 2 layer. (b) 2 branch - 3 branch.

2.2 Dual Soft Argmax

In order to prevent the accuracy loss by the coordinates quantization, we use function named dual soft argmax (DSA) [5] to map the heatmap response to final coordinates, which increases the performance of our model and is shown in Eq. 1 and 2.

$$x = \frac{\langle Z, X \rangle_F + W - \langle Z, flip_x(X) \rangle_F}{2} \tag{1}$$

Table 1. Light-weight HRNet. Fusion $n(n = 2)$ layer can be seen as Fig. 2 (a). $n(n = 2)$ branch - $m(m = n + 1)$ branch can be seen as Fig. 2 (b).

Depth	Numbers	Type	Filters	Size	Group	Stride	Output
1	1	Conv	9	3 * 3	1	2	112 * 112
2	1	Conv	18	3 * 3	1	2	56 * 56
3	3	Conv	36	1 * 1	1	1	-
		Conv	36	3 * 3	9	1	-
		Conv	36	1 * 1	1	1	-
		Residual	-	-	-	-	56 * 56
4-1	1	Conv	36	1 * 1	1	1	-
		Conv	36	3 * 3	9	1	-
		Conv	36	1 * 1	1	1	-
		Residual	-	-	-	-	56 * 56
4-2	1	Conv	72	1 * 1	1	1	-
		Conv	72	3 * 3	9	2	-
		Conv	72	1 * 1	1	1	-
		Residual	-	-	-	2	28 * 28
5	1	Fusion 2 Layer					56 * 56
							28 * 28
6	1	2 branch - 3 branch					56 * 56
							28 * 28
							14 * 14
7	3	Fusion 3 Layer					56 * 56
							28 * 28
							14 * 14
8	1	3 branch - 4 branch					56 * 56
							28 * 28
							14 * 14
							7 * 7
9	2	Fusion 4 Layer					56 * 56
							28 * 28
							14 * 14
							7 * 7
10	1	Fusion 4 Layer					56 * 56
11	1	Conv	106	3 * 3	1	1	56 * 56

$$y = \frac{\langle Z, Y \rangle_F + H - \langle Z, flip_y(Y) \rangle_F}{2} \qquad (2)$$

$flip_x$ means flip matrix horizontally, and $flip_y$ means flip matrix vertically.

2.3   Similarity-FeatureMap Knowledge Distillation

Similarity-preserving knowledge distillation model [14] guides the training of a student network such that input pairs that produce similar (dissimilar) activations in the pre-trained teacher network produce similar (dissimilar) activations in the student network. Inspired by [14], we proposed Similarity-FeatureMap knowledge distillation model which guides the training of a student network such that input pairs that produce similar (dissimilar) feature maps in the pre-trained teacher network produce similar (dissimilar) feature maps in the student network, and we derive similarity matrices from the feature maps, and compute a distillation loss on the matrices produced by the student and the teacher. The Similarity-FeatureMap knowledge distillation model can be seen as Fig. 3.

We use Distance-wise distillation loss [9] to compute the similarity of feature maps. Given a pair of training examples, distance-wise potential function ψ_D measures the Euclidean distance between the two examples in the output representation space:

$$\psi_D(t_i, t_j) = \frac{1}{\mu} \|t_i - t_j\|_2 \qquad (3)$$

where μ is a normalization factor for distance. To focus on relative distances among other pairs, we set μ to be the average distance between pairs from $\mathcal{X}^2$ in the mini-batch:

$$\mu = \frac{1}{|\mathcal{X}^2|} \sum_{(x_i, x_j) \in \mathcal{X}^2} \|t_i - t_j\|_2 \qquad (4)$$

Since distillation attempts to match the distance-wise potentials between the teacher and the student, this mini-batch distance normalization is useful particularly when there is a significant difference in scales between teacher distances $\|t_i - t_j\|_2$ and student distances $\|s_i - s_j\|_2$, e.g., due to the difference in output dimensions. In our experiments, we observed that the normalization provides more stable and faster convergence in training.

Using the distance-wise potential function measured in both the teacher and the student, a distance-wise distillation loss is defined as:

$$\mathcal{L}_{RKD-D}(\psi_{DT}, \psi_{DS}) = \sum_{(x_i, x_j) \in \mathcal{X}^2} l_\delta(\psi_D(t_i, t_j), \psi_D(s_i, s_j)) \qquad (5)$$

where l_δ is Huber loss, which is defined as:

$$l_\delta(x, y) = \begin{cases} \frac{1}{2}(x-y)^2 & \text{for } |x-y| \leq 1 \\ |x-y| - \frac{1}{2}, & \text{otherwise} \end{cases} \qquad (6)$$

The distance-wise distillation loss transfers the relationship of examples by penalizing distance differences between their output representation spaces.

We use Normalized Mean Error (NME) Loss [4] to compute loss of predictions, which is one of the most popular evaluation metrics in facial landmark detection benchmark. The equation is shown as (Eq. 7):

$$\mathcal{L}_{NME}(\Delta x, \Delta y) = \frac{1}{N}\sum_{i=1}^{N}\sqrt{\Delta x_i^2 + \Delta y_i^2}, \tag{7}$$

where d denotes the normalized term and N is the number of facial landmarks. Δx_i and Δy_i are deviations between the i_{th} predicted landmark and ground truth in x-axis and y-axis.

Finally, we define the total loss for training the student network as:

$$\mathcal{L} = \alpha\mathcal{L}_{\text{NME}}(\Delta x, \Delta y) + \beta\mathcal{L}_{\text{RKD-D}}(\psi_{\text{DT}}, \psi_{\text{DS}}) \tag{8}$$

where α and β are two hyperparameters.

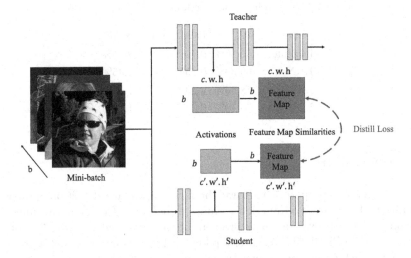

Fig. 3. Similarity-FeatureMap knowledge distillation guides the training of a student network such that input pairs that produce similar (dissimilar) feature maps in the pre-trained teacher network produce similar (dissimilar) feature maps in the student network. Given an input mini-batch of b images, we derive similarity matrices from the feature maps, and compute a distillation loss on the matrices produced by the student and the teacher.

3   Experiment and Results

All the experiments are implemented by Pytorch v1.2.0. During training, both weight decay and momentum are set to 0 while the batch size is set to 60. The learning rate is initialized to 1e−3, and will be divided by 10 at epoch 80 and

180 separately. The total number of epochs is set to 200. The validation set consist of 2000 cropped images, in this way there will not be too much context information. Area Under Curve (AUC), Failure Rate and Normalized Mean Error (NME) will be used to evaluate the performance of all methods, and only AUC value determines the final ranking. α and β is 0.2 and 0.8, respectively.

The AUC value of the baseline is 65.10%, and it is easy to get a better result (69.34%) by only using a single HRNet structure (when GFLops < 1.0). We optimize the model structure while the bottleneck block is used to replace the standard residual block in the original HRNet and the group convolution is used to replace the standard convolution in the original HRNet, the AUC can be greatly improved. Then, the dual soft argmax (DSA) is applied to the optimized model, the AUC can be further improved. Finally, we use Similarity-FeatureMap knowledge distillation model for self-distillation, the best result 79.10% for AUC is achieved on the validation set. Part localization results on the validation set have been shown in Fig. 4 (Table 2).

Table 2. The results of our method on the validation set.

Name	AUC	Failure Rate	NME
baseline	65.10%	0.40%	2.80%
HRNet	69.34%	0.05%	2.45%
LHRNet	78.99%	0.00%	1.68%
LDHRNet	79.10%	0.00%	1.67%

4 Conclusion

In this paper, we propose a light-weight facial landmark detection framework and use dual soft argmax function to map probability of heatmap to numerical coordinates, which overcome the problem of weight imbalance problem of soft argmax (SA). A Similarity-FeatureMap knowledge distillation model is proposed and applied, which derives similarity matrices from the feature maps, and compute a distillation loss on the matrices produced by the student and the teacher. Finally, we combine the distillation loss and NME loss to train our model. The computational complexity and the model size is respectively 0.996 GFLops and 3.757 MB. Replacing NME with ENME [4] or using a larger teacher model can further improve performance of our model. Besides, boundary aware face alignment method may also bring some help.

A Part Localization Results

Part localization results on the validation set have been shown in Fig. 4.

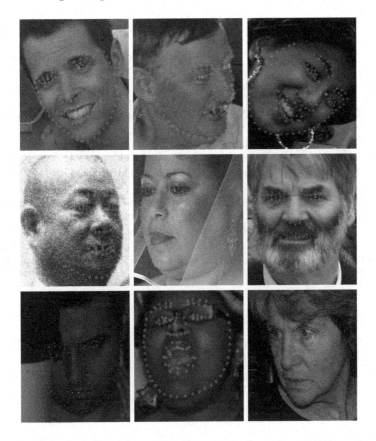

Fig. 4. Part localization results of out method on the validation set.

References

1. He, K., Zhang, X., Ren, S., Sun, J.: Deep residual learning for image recognition. In: CVPR (2016)
2. Howard, A., et al.: Searching for mobilenetv3. In: ICCV (2019)
3. Köstinger, M., Wohlhart, P., Roth, P.M., Bischof, H.: Annotated facial landmarks in the wild: a large-scale, real-world database for facial landmark localization. In: ICCVW (2011)
4. Lai, S., Chai, Z., Li, S., Meng, H., Yang, M., Wei, X.: Enhanced normalized mean error loss for robust facial landmark detection. In: BMVC (2019)
5. Lai, S., Chai, Z., Wei, X.: Improved hourglass structure for high performance facial landmark detection. In: ICMEW (2019)
6. Liu, Y., et al.: Grand challenge of 106-point facial landmark localization. In: ICMEW (2019)
7. Masi, I., Tran, A.T., Hassner, T., Leksut, J.T., Medioni, G.: Do we really need to collect millions of faces for effective face recognition? In: Leibe, B., Matas, J., Sebe, N., Welling, M. (eds.) ECCV 2016. LNCS, vol. 9909, pp. 579–596. Springer, Cham (2016). https://doi.org/10.1007/978-3-319-46454-1_35

8. Nibali, A., He, Z., Morgan, S., Prendergast, L.: Numerical coordinate regression with convolutional neural networks. CoRR (2018)
9. Park, W., Kim, D., Lu, Y., Cho, M.: Relational knowledge distillation. In: CVPR (2019)
10. Ren, S., Cao, X., Wei, Y., Sun, J.: Face alignment at 3000 FPS via regressing local binary features. In: CVPR (2014)
11. Sun, K., Xiao, B., Liu, D., Wang, J.: Deep high-resolution representation learning for human pose estimation. In: CVPR (2019)
12. Sun, X., Xiao, B., Wei, F., Liang, S., Wei, Y.: Integral human pose regression. In: Ferrari, V., Hebert, M., Sminchisescu, C., Weiss, Y. (eds.) ECCV 2018. LNCS, vol. 11210, pp. 536–553. Springer, Cham (2018). https://doi.org/10.1007/978-3-030-01231-1_33
13. Ting, Z., Guo-Jun, Q., Bin, X., Jingdong, W.: Interleaved group convolutions for deep neural networks. In: ICCV (2017)
14. Tung, F., Mori, G.: Similarity-preserving knowledge distillation. In: ICCV (2019)
15. Wu, Y., Hassner, T., Kim, K., Medioni, G.G., Natarajan, P.: Facial landmark detection with tweaked convolutional neural networks. IEEE TPAMI 40(12), 3067–3074 (2018)

DeepFM-Based Taxi Pick-Up Area Recommendation

Xuesong Wang[1,2], Yizhi Liu[1,2(✉)], Zhuhua Liao[1,2], and Yijiang Zhao[1,2]

[1] School of Computer Science and Engineering, Hunan University of Science and Technology,
Xiangtan 411201, China
yizhi_liu@sina.cn
[2] Key Laboratory of Knowledge Processing and Networked Manufacturing in Hunan Province,
Xiangtan 411201, China

Abstract. Recommending accurately pick-up area with sparse GPS data is valuable and still challenging to increase taxi drivers' profits and reduce fuel consumption. In recent years, the recommendation approach based on matrix factorization has been proposed to deal with sparsity. However, it is not accurate enough due to the regardless of the interaction effect between features. Therefore, this paper proposes DeepFM-based taxi pick-up area recommendation. Firstly, the research area is divided into grid area of equal size, the pick-up point information is extracted from the original GPS trajectory data, the pick-up point information and POI data are mapped to the grid area, the corresponding grid attributes are calculated and the grid feature matrix is constructed; Then, DeepFM is used to mine the combined relationship between the grid features, combining spatial information to recommend the most suitable grid area for drivers; Finally, the performance evaluation is carried out using DiDi's public data. The experimental results show that this method can significantly improve the quality of the recommended results and is superior to some existing recommended methods.

Keywords: Trajectory mining · Location-based service · Taxi pick-up area recommendation · DeepFM · Feature interaction

1 Introduction

Online ride-sharing platforms, such as DiDi and UBER, not only provide online booking services for drivers, but also record the information of taxi drivers' trajectories. Mining these data to understand the service strategy of taxi drivers and provide better recommendation service for drivers [1]. Pick-up area recommendation is benefit to improve the efficiency of seeking passengers and then to reduce fuel consumption and exhaust emissions.

Compared with the traditional recommendation services, pick-up area recommendation faces new challenges. First, the continuous growth of taxi trajectory data takes up a lot of storage resources, and the excessive historical trajectory data may contain too much noise. Noise data causes trouble in data processing and reduces recommendation

© Springer Nature Switzerland AG 2021
A. Del Bimbo et al. (Eds.): ICPR 2020 Workshops, LNCS 12665, pp. 407–421, 2021.
https://doi.org/10.1007/978-3-030-68821-9_36

performance. Therefore, some researchers [2, 3] focused on pick-up area recommendation with sparse GPS data in a short time. However, because taxis have limited access to the area in the short term, data sparseness problems arise. In recent years, the recommendation approach based on matrix factorization has been proposed [2, 4, 5], which is resistant to sparsity, but the interaction effect between features has not been considered. There are many evaluation features of taxi pick-up area, such as spatial features, the number of historical pick-up points, and so on. Considering extracting multidimensional feature attributes and mining the interaction effect between features [6] can improve the accuracy of recommendation services. Then, the geographic information that exists in the real geographic environment, such as the amount and type of POI (Point of Interest), is also a driver's concern. On the way of taxi cruising, the driver's preference changes with the change of geographical information, and the passenger demand information and driver's preference in the area around the driver also changed with the change of geographical location.

The Deep Factorization Machine (DeepFM) has contributed to many fields, such as intrusion detection [7], web service recommendation [6], stock market forecasting [8]. DeepFM consists of two parts: FM (Factorization Machines) and Deep (deep neural networks), which can effectively extract and classify features by combining the advantages of FM in processing low-level features and deep neural network in processing high-order features. since the FM introduces hidden vectors, it has some anti-thinning, DeepFM can process high-dimensional data in the sparse data environment.

This paper proposes DeepFM-based taxi pick-up area recommendation. Firstly, the area pick-up features in the original trajectory data are extracted, and the multidimensional attribute features are constructed. Then, DeepFM is used to realize low-order and high-order feature interactions [9]. Finally, according to the driver's current spatial information and the output information of DeepFM, the best pick-up area is recommended to the driver. The main contributions of this paper are:

- In this paper, we propose a feature gain method of pick-up area based on DeepFM, further improves the accuracy of the description of the characteristics of the pick-up area. This method extracts the potential pick-up information implicit in the taxi GPS trajectory and combines the POI data with the relevant geographical information.
- The real data set is used for experimental evaluation. The experimental results show that this method is superior to the latest recommended methods.

2 Related Work

In the past, passenger discovery strategies have been extensively studied to improve the accuracy of taxi service recommendation selection and discovery. Most papers focus on recommending hot spots to no-load taxi drivers. The literature [10] indicated that taxis would stay in place to wait or cruise longer to find new passengers, and then use L1-Norm support vector machines to determine whether taxi drivers should wait or cruise according to their current time and location. Mu et al. [11] proposed a new recommendation model for taxi pick-up hot spots based on the improved DBSCAN algorithm. Huang et al. [12] recommend hot spots to drivers through an efficient passenger search recommendation framework with multi-task deep learning.

Some studies focus on providing taxi drivers with a range of hotspots to maximize the possibility of carrying passengers at shorter cruise distances. Liu et al. [13] obtained candidate pick-up points by proposing a different spatiotemporal analysis method. And they used project-based collaborative filtering with a probabilistic optimization model to create a series of personalized hot spots. Verma et al. [14] developed a system based on reinforcement learning (RL), which can be learned from the driver's real track log to provide the driver with the correct location advice to find passengers who can bring high income to the driver. Zou et al. [15] proposed a dynamic probability model to recommend cruise routes with high pick-up probability to no-load taxis. Jain et al. [16] used spatial scanning statistics to represent the spatiotemporal analysis of taxi hotspots and search for potential areas with high reservation demand distribution, thus recommending hot spots for no-load taxis.

In recent years, some researchers had divided the original data within its spatial range, and then replaced the original data with the spatial grid formed by the division, and then processed these grids accordingly, recommended hot spots to taxi drivers. The area recommendation method also has a good processing ability to noise data and can find the overall distribution of data well. Liao et al. [2] proposed a hidden factor model that integrates geographic information, recommended pick-up hot area to taxis. Hwang et al. [17] proposed a graph model of the OFF-ON model to obtain the relationship between the current passenger drop-off location and the next passenger get-on location. And they also used switches ON-OFF estimated the expected fare for orders starting from the recommended location. Zhang et al. [18] proposed an improved density-based DBSCAN clustering algorithm that combines partitioning methods and kd-tree structures to discover demand hotspots. Kong et al. [3] used the Gaussian process regression and statistical method to predict the passenger distribution in each grid and recommended area with densely distributed passengers for drivers. Tang et al. [19] used the DBSCAN algorithm to cluster extracted pick-up and drop-off records, identified some travel hotspots, and then uses Huff models to describe the attractiveness of the pick-up area.

These methods improve the accuracy of the taxi recommendation service to some extent. However, these methods do not consider the learning of high-order feature interaction, which can improve the accuracy of service recommendation. Combined with previous achievements and our previous research [2, 13], our work takes into account the distribution of historical pick-up points and the driver's pick-up preference to provide regional recommendations for taxi drivers.

3 Framework

In the course of taxi operation, it is the first task to find the next passenger quickly and reduce the cruise time when the taxi is in a no-load state. Taxi is more inclined to look for passengers in hot areas. Based on the balance between supply and demand between taxi and passenger, there are some drawbacks in the method of recommending hot location only for taxis, which leads to the phenomenon of multiple taxis snatching passengers. In this paper, we analyze the taxi GPS trajectory, POI data, consider the geographical information location, and provide a potential candidate area for the taxi according to the time and location of the taxi, thus increasing the taxi driver's income.

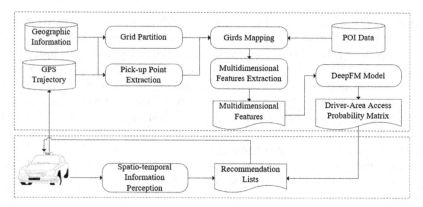

Fig. 1. The proposed method framework

To improve the efficiency of processing GPS trajectory big data, we use the method of map gridding [20] to provide recommended services to taxi drivers. Figure 1 shows the method framework of this paper. Taxi pick-up recommendation has two parts: offline mining and online recommending, corresponding to the upper and lower parts of Fig. 1. Divide the study area into non-overlapping square grids through latitude and longitude, and one grid represents a candidate recommendation area. By traversing the GPS trajectory data, we obtain the pick-up point [3] in the taxi trajectory and map both the POI and the pick-up point to the corresponding grid.

Then the attribute features of each grid area are calculated in grid units: the number of historical pick-up points, the number of POI points, the driving distance and time after carrying passengers, and the distribution of various POI types in the area.

Multidimensional features are the combination of various features in the area with any actual valuable feature vector. The DeepFM model predicts the scores of all candidate areas and constructs a driver-area access probability matrix, the values in the matrix are the predicted driver-to-area access probabilities. According to the matrix and the driver's current geographic information, the top-N result area will be recommended to the taxi driver.

4   Method

4.1   Score Prediction Based on DeepFM

DeepFM is the model proposed by Guo et al. [9] in 2017. As shown in Fig. 2, the DeepFM consists of the deep neural network and factorization machine, which share the input vector. The DeepFM output formula is as follows:

$$\hat{y} = sigmoid(y_{FM} + y_{DNN}) \tag{1}$$

The $\hat{y}$ is the prediction result, and the score of the regional recommendation. y_{FM} is the output result of the factorization machine part. y_{DNN} is the output result of the deep neural network part.

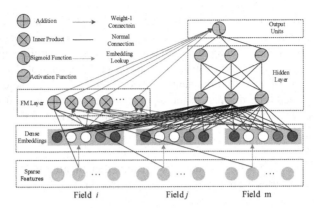

Fig. 2. Framework of DeepFM [9]

FM is a machine learning algorithm based on matrix factorization proposed by Rendle in 2010 [21]. Besides linear interactions among features, FM models pairwise (order-2) feature interactions as the inner product of respective feature latent vectors. When the data is sparse, FM can obtain the interaction between the features more effectively. FM of 2-order is defined as follows:

$$\hat{y}_{FM} = w_0 + \sum_{i=1}^{n} w_i x_i + \sum_{i=1}^{n} \sum_{j=i+1}^{n} \langle v_i, v_j \rangle x_i x_j \tag{2}$$

n represents the length or number of features, w_0 indicates the global bias. w_i models the importance of the i-th feature, $x_i x_j$ refers to interaction feature which indicates the training instance has both feature value x_i and x_j, $\langle v_i, v_j \rangle$ represents that factorization machine models the interaction between x_i and x_j. x represents the input vector of the dataset, $\hat{y}_{FM}$ is the target vector.

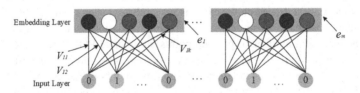

Fig. 3. The structure of embedding layer

Figure 3 shows the subnet structure from the input layer to the embedding layer. This network structure has two characteristics: 1) Although the length of the input vectors can be different, their embedding size (k) is the same; 2) The latent feature vectors (V) in FM as network weights and used to compress the input field vector to embedding vectors [9].

Conventional FM models are limited to computational complexity in practical applications, and generally only considers the 2-order interaction feature. DeepFM can extract both low-order and high-order features between data, DeepFM in addition to including FM components, another component is the deep neural network component. The deep neural network component is a feedforward neural network for learning high-order feature interactions. The input data usually contains a large amount of discrete data, so it can't be directly inputted into the neural network, which leads to the decline of the learning effect. Therefore, this part of the input is also a low-dimensional dense vector processed by the embedded layer, expressed by the following formula:

$$a^{(0)} = [e^1, e^2, \ldots, e^m] \tag{3}$$

where the $e^1, e^2, \ldots, e^m$ is the output of the i feature domain after the embedding layer processing, and then uses the $a^{(0)}$ as the input of the neural network to extract the feature, as follows:

$$a^{(l+1)} = \sigma(W^{(l)}a^{(l)} + b^{(l)}) \tag{4}$$

where the σ represents the activation function of the hidden layer of the neural network, $a^{(l)}$, $W^{(l)}$, $b^{(l)}$ represents the output, weight, deviation parameters of the l hidden layer, respectively, and then the output of the last layer is used as the output of the deep neural network part.

$$y_{DNN} = \sigma(W^{|H|+1}a^{|H|} + b^{|H|+1}) \tag{5}$$

H is the hidden layer. FM model and deep neural networks share the same feature embedding, which allows the model to learn low-order and high-order feature interactions from raw data.

4.2 Important Attribute of Area

In this paper, we use the method of map grid division to divide the research area. Through the grid size in the reference [22], we divide the research area into 300 m × 300 m and other size grids.

The selection of grid attributes has a vital impact on the accuracy of the taxi pick-up area recommendation. Based on the existing research [2, 13] and analysis, we find some area attributes that have an impact on the recommendation accuracy. Area attributes include the historical number of pick-up points, number of POI, type of area, the geometric center position of the area, the average driving time and distance after carrying passengers of the area. After obtaining the pick-up points in the car rental trajectory, both the POI and the pick-up points are mapped to the corresponding grid and the grid attribute characteristics are calculated. The grid features we selected are as follows.

Time Slots and Geographical Locations. Time slots and geographical locations are crucial time and space factors in taxi services. As we all know, taxi drivers may find more passengers in hot areas than in urban fringe areas in terms of taxi demand. Also, the high demand for taxis usually occurs around department stores or business districts during the day and near bars at night. Therefore, geographical location and time slots are important area attributes. In this paper, we divide a day into 24 time slots of equal length (time slot length is one hour) and select the geometric center distance of the area to represent the geographical location of the grid.

The Historical Number of Pick-Up Points. For taxi drivers, the historical number of taxi pick-up points is an important factor in the strategy of finding passengers. The distribution of the number of historical pick-up points in different areas is very different, which can reflect the influence of spatial factors on the number of carrying passengers. Areas with large historical pick-up points numbers are more likely to encounter potential ride users. Its quantity can often represent the pick-up needs of the area.

The Average Driving Time and Distance After Carrying Passengers of the Area. The income for taxi travel is affected by many factors, including driving time and distance.

By analyzing historical GPS data, we obtain the average driving time after carrying passengers of each area. The driving time after carrying passengers in the area is obtained by dividing the total driving time after picking up passengers by the number of carrying passengers in the area. The average driving time after carrying passengers is an important factor that affects the taxi driver's decision to go to the next pick-up location. The specific calculation formula for the average driving time after carrying passengers is as follows:

$$T_{i-on} = \frac{1}{Num} \sum_{j=1}^{Num} (t_{j(on)} - t_{j(off)})(psegment_{i-on}) \tag{6}$$

T_{i-on} represents the average driving time after carrying passengers in the area G_i. $psegment$ represents the set of track segments of all taxis in the on-load state in the trajectory history, $psegment_{i-on}$ represents the trajectory segment of passengers carried in area G_i, Num is the number of these trajectory segments, $t_{j(on)}$ represents the start time of the j-th trajectory segment, $t_{j(off)}$ represents the end time of the j-th trajectory segment.

By analyzing historical GPS data, we obtain the average driving distance after carrying passengers of each area. The driving distance after carrying passengers in the area is obtained by dividing the total driving distance after picking up passengers by the number of carrying passengers in the area. The average driving distance after carrying passengers is an important factor that affects the taxi driver's decision to go to the next pick-up location. The specific calculation formula for the average driving distance after carrying passengers is as follows:

$$D_{i-on} = \frac{1}{Num} \sum_{j=1}^{Num} distance_j(psegment_{i-on}) \tag{7}$$

D_{i-on} represents the average driving distance after carrying passenger in the area G_i, $distance_j$ is the actual distance of the j-th trajectory segment.

POI type distribution. By the number of regional various types of POI, we can obtain the type and judge the hot POI type distribution. POI type distribution is mainly determined by the number distribution of different type's POI in the grid (Part 5 of this paper describes POI types). This paper takes the grid area as the unit and uses the ratio of the number POI each subclass to the total number of POI as the value of the corresponding POI type attribute of the area. Calculation of the ratio POI for each sub-type is shown below:

$$type_{g(j)} = |POI_{type_j}| \left/ \left| \sum_{i=1}^{n} POI_{type_i} \right| \right. \tag{8}$$

g represents as a grid area, $|POI_{type_j}|$ represents the number of POIs of type j.

4.3 Feature Extracting in DeepFM

This section describes how to extract the valuable features implied in the original dataset and convert them to the input format of the DeepFM model.

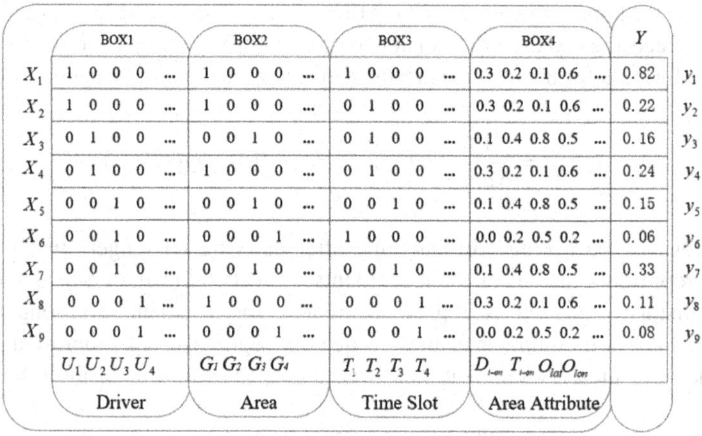

	BOX1	BOX2	BOX3	BOX4	Y	
X_1	1 0 0 0 ...	1 0 0 0 ...	1 0 0 0 ...	0.3 0.2 0.1 0.6 ...	0.82	y_1
X_2	1 0 0 0 ...	1 0 0 0 ...	0 1 0 0 ...	0.3 0.2 0.1 0.6 ...	0.22	y_2
X_3	0 1 0 0 ...	0 0 1 0 ...	0 1 0 0 ...	0.1 0.4 0.8 0.5 ...	0.16	y_3
X_4	0 1 0 0 ...	1 0 0 0 ...	0 1 0 0 ...	0.3 0.2 0.1 0.6 ...	0.24	y_4
X_5	0 0 1 0 ...	0 0 1 0 ...	0 0 1 0 ...	0.1 0.4 0.8 0.5 ...	0.15	y_5
X_6	0 0 1 0 ...	0 0 0 1 ...	1 0 0 0 ...	0.0 0.2 0.5 0.2 ...	0.06	y_6
X_7	0 0 1 0 ...	0 0 1 0 ...	0 0 1 0 ...	0.1 0.4 0.8 0.5 ...	0.33	y_7
X_8	0 0 0 1 ...	1 0 0 0 ...	0 0 0 1 ...	0.3 0.2 0.1 0.6 ...	0.11	y_8
X_9	0 0 0 1 ...	0 0 0 1 ...	0 0 0 1 ...	0.0 0.2 0.5 0.2 ...	0.08	y_9
	$U_1 U_2 U_3 U_4$	$G_1 G_2 G_3 G_4$	$T_1 T_2 T_3 T_4$	$D_{i-an} T_{i-an} O_{lat} O_{lon}$		
	Driver	Area	Time Slot	Area Attribute		

Fig. 4 The input data of DeepFM

Figure 4 is an example of DeepFM data format. We extract multiple features from the original dataset and construct feature vectors O and target scores Y. They are divided into four parts. Among them:

BOX1: We assume that U represent driver, $O_U = \{O_{U1}, O_{U2}, O_{U3}, \ldots, O_{UN}\}$ is the one-hot code of each driver ID. The dimension of O_{U1} is N, for example, the one-hot code of the first user ID is $O_{U1} = [1, 0, 0, \ldots, 0]_{1 \times N}$.

BOX2: We define that the grid area is represented as G, the one-hot code of each area ID as $O_G = \{O_{G1}, O_{G2}, O_{G3}, \ldots, O_{GN}\}$.

BOX3: We define that the time slot is represented as T, the time slot one-hot code of the driver's access to the area as $O_T = \{O_{T1}, O_{T2}, O_{T3}, \ldots, O_{T24}\}$. A day is divided into 24 time slots.

BOX4: For this part, we define the attributes of the area as A. Area attributes that include: historical number of pick-up points, number of POI, the average driving time and distance after carrying passengers, distribution of 12 POI types, the geometric center position of the area (The center point of each area is set to O, O_{lat} and O_{lon} indicate the

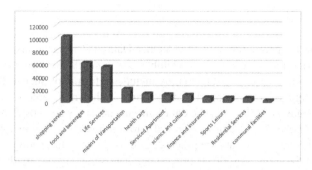

Fig. 5 POI type distribution diagram

latitude and longitude of the point), These attribute have different effects on the accuracy of taxi pick-up area recommendation, the data of this part are normalized.

Target Y: Y obtained by normalizing the number of carrying passengers in the corresponding area within the driver's slot. DeepFM output is the recommended score for the pick-up area.

4.4 Taxi Pick-Up Recommendation

DeepFM can predict the pick-up probability of all candidate area for a driver, and based on predicting the area recommendation probability, we can recommend high-quality service to the driver. Algorithm 1 is an in-depth and complete description of the taxi pick-up recommendation considering spatial information (TPR_SI). In the following algorithm, $dist$ (G_i, G_j) refers to the distance between the grid areas, because the taxi pick-up area is generally not far from its current position, so this paper uses the Euclidean distance between the geometric center points of the two grids.

Algorithm 1 TPR_SI

Input: Trajectory $t_1, t_2, \ldots, t_n$; grid side length l; POIset $p_1, p_2, \ldots, p_n$; the current position grid g
    of driver u;
Output: Driver-area access probability matrix C, $gridset$
  1. $GridSet\ G = GridDivide\ (l)$
  2. $U = Driverset(Trajectory)$
  3. $A = AreaAttribute(G, Trajectory, POIset)$
  4. $O = multidimensionalmatrix(G, A, T, U\ )$
  5. $C = DeepFM(O)$
  6. $gridset = Top\ (Sort\ (C_{u*}))$ // $Sort()$ sorts from high to low.
  7. return $Sort(gridset, dist[g,\ gridset[grid]]\ )$ // The $Sort()$ function sorts according to the
    distance between the driver and the candidate area from near to far

---

5 Experiment

GPS data of this paper are from Didi GAIA Open Dataset. The data is taxi trajectory data in the second ring area of Chengdu in October 2016, and the data points are collected at intervals of 2–4 s. Each track data mainly includes information such as taxi ID, order ID, latitude, longitude, timestamp. The data format is shown in Table 1. Since the GPS trajectory data may be affected by the data sampling accuracy and position offset, it has a certain impact on the data analysis. In order to improve the recommended accuracy, the original GPS trajectory data are preprocessed. Including eliminating redundant and noise points in the data, map offset processing. The study area is divided into 300 m × 300 m square mesh areas through latitude and longitude during the experiment. GPS data are divided into working days and weekends in order to observe the attributes of taxi demand reasonably.

Table 1. Format of dataset

Name	Annotation
Driver ID	Taxi sign
Order ID	Order ID
Timestamp	yymmddhhmmss
Longitude	ddd.ddddddd
Latitude	ddd.ddddddd

About 340,000 POI data in this paper are crawled from Amap. Each piece of data includes POI name, latitude and longitude information for POI, and POI type information, etc. POI classification information is derived from Amap, POI specific types are: food and beverages, tourist attraction, communal facilities, means of transportation, science and culture, finance and insurance, shopping service, serviced apartment, life services, sports leisure, health care, residential services. POI type distribution diagram is shown below.

This paper uses Mean Absolute Error (MAE) and Root Mean Square Error (RMSE) as performance evaluation indicators. MAE is the average of the absolute error between the actual value and the predicted value. RMSE is the square root of the ratio of the square of the deviation between the predicted value and the true value to the number of observations n. The larger the MAE and RMSE value, the worse the accuracy of prediction recommendation, and the smaller the MAE and RMSE value, the higher the accuracy. The calculation formulas for MAE and RMSE are as follows.

$$MAE = \frac{1}{|N|} \sum_{u,i} |y_{u,i} - \hat{y}_{u,i}| \quad RMSE = \sqrt{\frac{1}{|N|} \sum_{u,i} (y_{u,i} - \hat{y}_{u,i})^2} \quad (9)$$

Among them, $y_{u,i}$ is the actual access probability of user u on the grid i, and $\hat{y}_{u,i}$ is the predicted access probability value. $|N|$ is the number of test sets.

To demonstrate the effectiveness of the proposed method, we compare with several competitive approaches which are related to our work: (1) User-based collaborative filtering (UBCF) [23]: The idea is to calculate the similarity between the driver U and other users, and then use the prediction value of other users in the grid area similar to the driver U to predict the access value of the target grid area for the driver U. (2) A two-layer approach (Abbreviated as ATLA) [19]: ATLA used DBSCAN to cluster the carrier points into fewer clusters, and analyze the driver's choice behavior by Huff Model. In this way, the number of pick-up points in the target area and the product of driving overhead together constitute the basis for the selection of pick-up areas. (3) Recommendation based on time-location-relationship (TLR) [3]: TLR used the Gaussian process Regression and the statistical method to obtain the passenger volume, the average travel distance and the average travel time of each period, and recommends the grid area with many passengers, close distance and short time-consuming for different drivers. (4) Fusing geographic information into latent factor model (GeoLFM) [2]: The recommendation method of taxi pick-up area is based on the latent factor model and integrating geographic information. The model combines the objective geographical environment information of taxi drivers into the process of matrix factorization of driver-grid access matrix, to make up for the deficiency of data sparsity.

Experiment 1. We select four feature matrices of driver U, area G, time slot T, and area attribute A as input data. To better judge the characteristic matrix and the influence of their interaction on the experimental results, the four feature matrices are combined and sorted, and the data after feature combination are input into the model to determine the effect of feature combination on the experimental results. Because this paper is to recommend the pick-up area, each feature combination contains area G. In this experiment, the target variables change with the transformation of the data set because of the different contents of the input data set. When the input data is $\{U, A, T, G\}$ or $\{U, T, G\}$, the target variable is the number of times the driver carrying passengers in the corresponding grid area. When the input data is $\{T, G, A\}$ or $\{T, G\}$, the target variable is the number of historical carrying passengers in the grid area on the corresponding time slot. when the input data is $\{U, G, A\}$ or $\{U, G\}$, the target variable is the number of times the driver carrying passengers in the corresponding grid area. When the input data is $\{G, A\}$, the target variable is the number of historical pick-up points of the area. For this experiment, the explained variance score is added as the rating index: This score is used to measure the ability of our model to interpret data set fluctuations. If the score is 1.0, then it shows that our model is perfect and *Var* is variance. The experimental results after the feature combination are shown in Table 2.

$$explaine\_variance(y, \hat{y}) = 1 - \frac{Var\{y - \hat{y}\}}{Var\{y\}} \tag{10}$$

Observed through the table that experimental results with the set $\{U, A, T, G\}$ has the best effect, indicating that the combination of drivers U, grid G, time slot T, area attribute features A promotes accuracy of the experiment. It shows that the interaction between features can improve experimental performance. The addition of A in $\{U, G\}$, $\{T, G\}$ leads to an increase of about 10% in RMSE, and the MAE also increased, it is biggest performance increases, this is because the attribute feature of the area contained in A can

Table 2. Experimental results of feature combinations

	$\{U, G\}$	$\{T, G\}$	$\{G, A\}$	$\{U, T, G\}$	$\{U, G, A\}$	$\{T, G, A\}$	$\{U, A, T, G\}$
RMSE	29.42%	18.33%	10.31%	15.223%	19.15%	9.95%	9.57%
MAE	7.73%	3.95%	2.64%	3.74%	5.00%	2.65%	2.56%
explained_variance	69.82%	90.67%	96.94%	93.02%	88.47%	97.49%	97.71%

directly reflect the area carrying efficiency. Adding U to $\{G, A\}$, and $\{T, G\}$ respectively leads to better performance of the former and lower performance of the latter, indicating that the interaction between $\{U, T, G\}$ features can improve the performance of the experiment, $\{U, G, A\}$ reduces the performance. U is added to the experiment to provide personalized service to the driver. Adding T to $\{U, G\}$, and $\{G, A\}$ respectively, the experimental performance is improved.

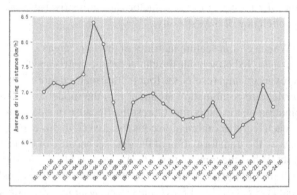

Fig. 6. Average driving distance after carrying passenger of taxis per period

The driving time and distance after carrying passengers of the area are important indicators to evaluate the impact of the area on rental income. Figure 6 shows the average driving distance after carrying passengers of each taxi at various times. As shown in Fig. 6, the average driving distance after carrying passengers of taxis in each period is different, so adding T, to different feature combinations can improve the performance of the experiment. During the period from 00:00 to 06:00, the average driving distance after carrying passengers is significantly higher than that of other periods, during which other means of transport other than taxis have ceased to operate. Except for a few office workers, most of the people that taxis face are people who have night entertainment in entertainment venues. So the distance of carrying the passengers is longer, which also reflects that the function area with a large demand for a taxi in the early morning is the entertainment place.

Experiment 2. The (a) and (b) in Fig. 7 represent the values of the five methods on the test set during the working day and weekend, respectively. It can be seen from

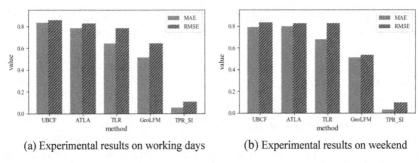

(a) Experimental results on working days   (b) Experimental results on weekend

Fig. 7. Comparison of experimental results

the figure that the method in this paper has the best effect regardless of MAE and RMSE. The situation is roughly the same on weekends and weekdays. In the case of experimental results in working days, comparing with UBCF, ATLA, TLR, GeoLFM, we can observe that the MAE of TPR_SI, decreased by 78.13%, 72.99%, 58.98%, 46.23%, respectively. Meanwhile, RMSE decreased by 75.01%, 71.92%, and 67.58%, and 53.51%, respectively. Because of the sparsity of data, the utilization rate of TLR, UBCF, ATLA method to data is not high, which leads to its low performance. GeoLFM is based on matrix decomposition methods, which has a certain degree of anti-sparseness and improves the utilization of data to a certain extent. TPR_SI is the recommendation of taxi pick-up area based on depth factor decomposer, can realize low-order and high-order feature interactions, and construct multi-dimensional input data for taxi recommendation high-profit taxi pick-up area. Features such as the number of historical pick-up points can be used to find areas where drivers often carry passengers in the real world. Compared with other methods, it can recommend the best area results. This paper carries on the model training through a large amount of data, the recommendation accuracy is high, but the training time is longer.

6 Summary

DeepFM-based taxi pick-up area recommendation is proposed in this paper. Firstly, the research area is divided into grid areas of equal size, and the pick-up point information is obtained from the trajectory data, pick-up points and the POI data are mapped into the area to obtain the grid attributes. The multidimensional matrix is input into the DeepFM to realize end-to-end low-order and high-order feature interactive learning, which greatly promotes high-quality area recommendation. Finally, a comparative experiment is carried out on the actual data set. The experimental results show that our method greatly improves the performance of the pick-up area recommendation. In future work, we will focus on the improvement of recommendation performance and recommend taxi pick-up areas to drivers at a faster speed.

Acknowledgments. This project was funded by the National Natural Science Foundation of China (41871320), Provincial and Municipal Joint Fund of Hunan Provincial Natural Science Foundation of China (2018JJ4052), Hunan Provincial Natural Science Foundation of China

(2017JJ2081), the Key Project of Hunan Provincial Education Department (17A070, 19A172, 19A174), the Scientific Research Project of Hunan Education Department (19C0755).

References

1. Zhang, D., Sun, L., Li, B., et al.: Understanding taxi service strategies from taxi GPS traces. IEEE Trans. Intell. Transp. Syst. **16**(1), 123–135 (2015)
2. Liao, Z., Zhang, J., Liu, Y., Xiao, H., Zhao, Y.: Fusing geographic information into latent factor model for pick-up region recommendation. In: 2019 IEEE International Conference on Multimedia & Expo Workshops (ICMEW), Shanghai, pp. 330–335 (2019)
3. Kong, X., Xia, F., Wang, J.: Time-location-relationship combined service recommendation based on taxi trajectory data. IEEE Trans. Ind. Inf. **13**(3), 1202–1212 (2017)
4. Lian, D., Zhao, C., Xie, X.: GeoMF: joint geographical modeling and matrix factorization for point-of-interest recommendation. In: Proceedings of the 20th ACM SIGKDD International Conference on Knowledge Discovery and Data Mining, New York, NY, USA, pp. 831–840 (2014)
5. Ling, C., Xu, J., Liu, J.: Integrating spatial and temporal contexts into a factorization model for POI recommendation. Int. J. Geograph. Inf. Sci. **32**, 524–546 (2018)
6. Zhang, X., Liu, J., Cao, B., et al.: Web service recommendation via combining Doc2Vec-based functionality clustering and DeepFM-based score prediction. In: 2018 IEEE SmartWorld, Ubiquitous Intelligence & Computing, Advanced & Trusted Computing, Scalable Computing & Communications, Cloud & Big Data Computing, Internet of People and Smart City Innovation, Australia, pp. 509–516 (2018)
7. Ji, Y., Li, X.: An efficient intrusion detection model based on DeepFM. In: 2020 IEEE 4th Information Technology, Networking, Electronic and Automation Control Conference (ITNEC), pp. 778–783 (2020)
8. Huang, J., Zhang, X., Fang, B.: CoStock: a DeepFM model for stock market prediction with attentional embeddings. In: 2019 IEEE International Conference on Big Data (Big Data), pp. 778–783 (2020)
9. Guo, H., Tang, R., Ye, Y., et al.: DeepFM: a factorization-machine based neural network for CTR prediction. In: 2017 International Joint Conference on Artificial Intelligence, pp. 1725–1731 (2017)
10. Li, B., Zhang, D., Sun, L., et al.: Hunting or waiting? Discovering passenger-finding strategies from a large-scale real-world taxi dataset. In: 2011 IEEE International Conference on Managing Ubiquitous Communications and Service (MUCS), Seattle, United States, pp. 63–68 (2011)
11. Mu, B., Dai, M.: Recommend taxi pick-up hotspots based on density-based clustering. In: 2019 IEEE 2nd International Conference on Computer and Communication Engineering Technology (CCET), Beijing, China, pp. 176–181 (2019)
12. Huang, Z., Tang, J., Shan, G., et al.: An efficient passenger-hunting recommendation framework with multi-task deep learning. IEEE Internet Things J. **6**(5), 7713–7721 (2019)
13. Liu, Y., Liu, J., Liao, Z., et al.: Recommending a personalized sequence of pick-up points. J. Comput. Sci. **28**, 382–388 (2018)
14. Verma, T., Varakantham, P., Kraus, S., et al.: Augmenting decisions of taxi drivers through reinforcement learning for improving revenues. In: International Conference on Automated Planning & Scheduling (ICAPS), pp. 409–417 (2017)
15. Zou, Q., Xue, G., Luo, Y., Yu, J., Zhu, H.: A novel taxi dispatch system for smart city. In: Streitz, N., Stephanidis, C. (eds.) DAPI 2013. LNCS, vol. 8028, pp. 326–335. Springer, Heidelberg (2013). https://doi.org/10.1007/978-3-642-39351-8_36

16. Jain, R., Garg, S., Gangal, S., et al.: TaxiScan: a scan statistics approach for detecting taxi demand hotspots. In: 2019 Twelfth International Conference on Contemporary Computing (IC3), Noida, India, pp. 1–6 (2019)

17. Hwang, R., Hsueh, Y., Chen, Y.: An effective taxi recommender system based on a spatiotemporal factor analysis model. Inf. Sci. **314**, 28–40 (2015)

18. Zhang, L., Chen, C., Wang, Y., et al.: Exploiting taxi demand hotspots based on vehicular big data analytics. In: 2016 IEEE 84th Vehicular Technology Conference (VTC-Fall), Montreal, QC, pp. 1–5 (2016)

19. Tang, J., Jiang, H., Li, Z., et al.: A two-layer model for taxi customer searching behaviors using GPS trajectory data. IEEE Trans. Intell. Transp. Syst. **17**(11), 3318–3324 (2016)

20. Liu, L., et al.: Research on taxi drivers' passenger hotspot selecting patterns based on GPS data: a case study in Wuhan. In: 2017 4th International Conference on Transportation Information and Safety (ICTIS), pp. 432–441 (2017)

21. Rendle, S.: Factorization machines. In: 2010 IEEE International Conference on Data Mining, Sydney, NSW, pp. 995–1000 (2010)

22. Huang, Z., Shan, G., Cheng, J., et al.: TRec: an efficient recommendation system for hunting passengers with deep neural networks. Neural Comput. Appl. **31**(1), 209–222 (2018). https://doi.org/10.1007/s00521-018-3728-2

23. Wang, C., Zhu, Z., Zhang, Y., Su, F.: Recommendation efficiency and personalized improvement of user-based collaborative filtering algorithm. Mini-Micro Syst. **37**(03), 428–432 (2016). (in Chinese)

IWBDAF 2020 - International Workshop on Biometric Data Analysis and Forensics

International Workshop on Biometric Data Analysis and Forensics (IWBDA)

Law Enforcement Agencies (LEA) all around the world are increasingly using biometric technologies for crime scene analysis. Face identification from footage of security cameras around the scene, fingerprint discovery and study, the examination of the voices captured by smart devices are only a few examples of the situation that involves biometric technologies in the analysis of a crime scene.

In this scenario, a new actor appeared: the IoT devices that are increasingly present in our home and smart cities and collecting a considerable quantity of data continuously. Finding evidence in such a big mass of digital data can be frustrating, if not impossible, without techniques of data analysis specifically designed for this goal.

In other fields of Digital Forensics, techniques to manage big data and extract pieces of forensics evidence from them are already frequently used, is this the case e.g. of Digital Video Forensics.

The goal of the workshop is to propose new techniques and methodologies for the study of biometric evidence on the crime scenes, taking particular care of the data coming from IoT devices, eventually adopting them form other well-studied fields of Digital Forensics.

The first edition of the workshop was held on 11 January, 2021, in conjunction with the 25th International Conference on Pattern Recognition (ICPR2020), that will be held from 10 to 15 January 2021 in Milan, Italy. The workshop was held in online form due the COVID 19 pandemic situation. The format of the workshop included a keynote followed by technical presentations.

This year we received 14 submissions for reviews, from authors belonging to 6 distinct countries. After an accurate and thorough double blind peer-review process, we selected 8 papers for presentation at the workshop. The review process focused on the quality of the papers, their scientific novelty and applicability to existing Biometric and Data Forensics problems. The acceptance of the papers was the result of the reviewers' discussion and agreement. All the high quality papers were accepted, and the acceptance rate was 57%. The accepted articles represent an interesting mix of techniques to solve recurrent as well as new problems in Biometry and Data Forensics fields.

Last but not least, we would like to thank the IWBDAF 2020 Program Committee, whose members made the workshop possible with their rigorous and timely review process. We would also like to thank ICPR2020 for hosting the workshop and our emerging community, and the ICPR2020 workshop chairs for the valuable help and support.

November 2020

Organization

General Chairs

Andrea Francesco Abate   Università degli Studi di Salerno
Giuseppe Cattaneo   Università degli Studi di Salerno
Andrea Bruno   Università degli Studi di Salerno

Program Committee

Fabio Narducci   Università degli Studi di Salerno
Silvio Barra   Università di Napoli Federico II
Aniello Castiglione   Università degli Studi di Napoli "Parthenope"
David Freire-Obregón   Universidad de Las Palmas de Gran Canaria
Chiara Galdi   EURECOM
Umberto Ferraro Petrillo   Università degli Studi di Roma "La Sapienza"
Paola Barra   Università degli Studi di Salerno
Chiara Pero   Università degli Studi di Salerno
Paola Capasso   Università degli Studi di Salerno
Eslam Farsimadan   Università degli Studi di Salerno
Zahra Ebadi Ansaroudi   Università degli Studi di Salerno
Carmen Bisogni   Università degli Studi di Salerno
Lucia Cascone   Università degli Studi di Salerno
Lucia Cimmino   Università degli Studi di Salerno
Andrea Casanova   Università degli Studi di Cagliari

Blockchain-Based Iris Authentication in Order to Secure IoT Access and Digital Money Spending

Gerardo Iovane[1] , Antonio Rapuano[1](✉) , and Patrizia Di Gironimo[2]

[1] Dipartimento di Informatica, University of Salerno, Fisciano, Italy
{giovane,arapuano}@unisa.it
[2] Dipartimento di Matematica, University of Salerno, Fisciano, Italy
pdgironimo@unisa.it

Abstract. In this work we use two approaches to prevent double spending and secure IoT transaction through Blockchain and information fusion techniques: the first method is based on Smart Contracts; while the second method is implemented by a novel Blockchain system. Both methods use a hybrid RSA and biometric codes fusion in order to have an encrypted, taking account of the privacy, identity of the spender. In Blockchain a contract between the parties is stipulated and the biometric fused code are kept. The used coin pack is tagged, so a future double spending or any illegal action on the IoT network or Smart city becomes forbidden and prosecutable legally. The second part of the work will present a novel Blockchain where a transaction can be signed only if the user is successfully authenticated though his biometric fused key.

Keywords: Blockchain · IoT · Authentication · Smart contracts · Biometrics · Information fusion

1 Introduction

Cities and industries are starting to adopt Internet-of-Things (IoT) technology to automate the management processes through the data provided by the sensors and to remotely monitor and control digital devices. The key functional elements of IoT include sensing, computation, communication, and control or actuation. These functionalities are realized through a combination of embedded devices, wireless communication technologies, sensors, and actuators. A careful configuration and distribution of hardware, software and networking components are essential to delivering the application goals. "Connected things" layer consists of sensors, actuators, embedded devices, mobile phones, and smart appliances capable of collecting data from their operational environment or actuation of electronic appliances including digital door lock, lamps, garage doors, among other things. To develop meaningful applications or services using the "connected things", it is essential to deliver the data to the desired application end-points. Depending on the application requirement, the data from the end devices flow

© Springer Nature Switzerland AG 2021
A. Del Bimbo et al. (Eds.): ICPR 2020 Workshops, LNCS 12665, pp. 427–441, 2021.
https://doi.org/10.1007/978-3-030-68821-9_37

either to the edge layer or cloud layer, or in some cases, the edge layer aggregates the data and reports it to the cloud layer for further processing, analytics, and visualization. The communication layer enables the devices to transmit to and receive from other devices in the application stack. IoT application developers build visualization, analytics, and other applications on cloud infrastructure or mobile devices and servers. Machine learning and AI algorithms can use the environmental sensor data to better understand the climate change or correlate the environmental data with the traffic sensor data to study the patterns and recommend routes that have less pollution. All these types of applications require data from a large collection of sensors from wide geographical neighbourhood. But, the deployment of sensors and the necessary communication infrastructure at cityscale require significant financial resource while introducing high management and maintenance complexity. In the Internet of Things field, typically, the devices are limited in compute, storage, and network capacity, and they are more vulnerable to attacks with respect some devices as smartphones, tablets, or computers. In [2,3] and [4], the authors describe some issues of the IoT devices and the relative solutions. In particular in these works, emerges that the Blockchain is the best technology which can secure the IoT security issues. Also the Blockchain has some vulnerabilities which we will present in the following sections. In this work, we use the information fusion iris algorithm provided in the work [1]. This work is divided in the following sections: In the Sect. 2, there will be presented an introduction to the Blockchain technology background and the attacks to it; in the Sect. 3 there will be presented the state of the art related work; in the Sect. 4, for better understanding the proposed method, the IIF method [1] is described; in the Sect. 5, the Smart Contract approach is described both strategically and technically; in the Sect. 6, the novel Blockchain approach is described; in the Sect. 7 there is a recall of the analysis of the used hybrid key and of the proposed method from a privacy point of view; finally, in the Sect. 8 there is an overview on the work and on our future work on this field.

2   Blockchain

Since 2008, the digital coin double spending has been a critical problem. In cash money the problem of double spending is not present: if A gives to B a coin or currency, they can not be spended anymore by A. In electronic cash, to prevent the double spending, a trusted third part should be present to define if a transaction is valid or not. In peer to peer digital currencies transaction, the double spending was a big problem: A can send an electronic coin to B, copy and spend again it. The first solution at this problem was Bitcoin [5]. In order to prevent the copy of money and create a digital currency without a centralized trusted third party, Nakamoto gives an incentive to users to do a proof of work. Since Nakamoto's white paper in 2008, different type of digital coin have been proposed, but none of these completely solved the double spending problem. The 51% attack continues to be a real threat for the Blockchain. Most Blockchain platforms rely on the elliptic curve public-key cryptography (ECDSA) or the large integer factorization problem (RSA) to generate a digital signature. One of the technologies on which Bitcoin is based is the SHA-256, a cryptographic hashing function which turns arbitrary input data into a 256 bit string (the "hash"). This is a one-way function, so that it is easy to find the hash from an input but not the other way around. The security of these algorithms is based on the assumption of computational complexity of certain mathematical problems [6]. However, the value of Bitcoin comes from the difficulty of finding such solutions, which gives it "proof of work". This paper proposes a novel approach for transacting digital coins basing on information fusion between biometrics and cryptographic keys in order to prevent the double spending in a Blockchain context.

2.1 Transaction Validation

The mostly used consensus algorithm is the proof of work. In the proof of work, miners validate the transaction by founding blocks in Blockchain doing repeated computations. In Bitcoin, in order to find a block, we have to find an hash of the block plus a nonce, which is an iterator, with a target value of 0:

$$SHA256(Block(Nonce)),$$

where the block usually contains the variable nonce, the transactions and other fields. In order to found a valid block, the miner have to try each combination of nonce in the block. In Fig. 1 we have a proof of work with a target of 4 zeros. The target value is continually readjusted such that the average time between blocks is 10 min.

Obviously, two nonce could produce two different valid blocks with the same target, in this case, what is called *soft fork* is produced (Fig. 2). After a soft fork, the miners will mine only the longest chain and the mined orphan blocks will not be valid anymore. After the Bitcoin whitepaper, more and more consensus algorithms and proof of works were developed. The most important goal of proof of work algorithms is to reach a full decentralization being ASIC-resistant [7–10]. In this way it is more difficult for miners to reach the 51% of computational power. ASICs are dedicated circuits for proof of work, we analyze the proof of work evolution in the next paragraph. ASICs cetralize the mining market to big mining industries. A depth analisys on more consensus and mining algorithms could be found in [11].

The proof of work is too expensive in terms of electric power: the only hardware required, in the beginning, was a simple computer. Things have changed a lot in less than 10 years. In 2009 the first Bitcoin miners used standard multicore CPUs to produce BTC at a rate of 50 per block. The difficulty of mining (amount of computing power necessary) was so low. In October 2010 the code for mining bitcoin with GPUs was released to the general public. As mining difficulty increased so did the need for better and more dedicated hardware. GPUs were up to the task. By June 2011 field-programmable gate arrays (FPGAs) were becoming widespread. Mining began to scale once FPGAs were modified for the purpose. The biggest draw to this hardware was the fact that it used three times less power than simple GPU setups to effectively accomplish the same task.

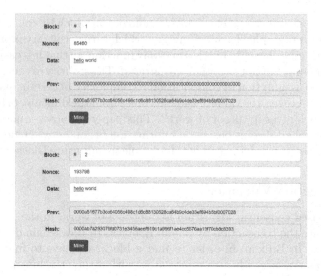

Fig. 1. In this example, the genesis (which is the first block ever mined) block has a nonce of 85460 to be a valid block. The second block is bounded to the first by the previous hash of the block and the first valid nonce is 193798.

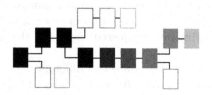

Fig. 2. Example of a soft fork.

FPGAs soon gave way to application-specific integrated circuit (ASIC) systems, and Bitcoin went from hobby to industry. Stoll et al. [12] in their research estimated that the Bitcoin yearly mining energy power is of 45.8 TWh and the Co2 yearly emission is between 22 and 22.9 MtCO2 during the 2018. In order to prevent the waste of electric power, the proof of stake has been provided. In the proof of stake, the block creator will be selecteded basing on the fidelity of the user. The miner will freeze the coins in order to be selected as block creator. The more coin will be freezed, the more it is probable for the miner to be selected. The proof of stake is more green than the proof of work, but today is an unripe technology. The proof of stake suffers of attacks like nothing at stake problem and other attacks [14,15].

2.2   Blockchain Attacks

The double spending attack is the biggest problem in Blockchain finalized to digital coins area. There are some different approaches to perform a double spending attack. Satoshi Nakamoto, who designed Bitcoin, analyzed the possibility of a double-spending attack on the Bitcoin system using the gamblers ruin problem. Here, let Qz denote the probability that an attacker would catch up with the normal chain from behind z blocks:

$$Qz = \begin{cases} 1 & \text{if } p \leq q \\ (\frac{q}{z})^z & \text{otherwise,} \end{cases}$$

where p is the probability that a honest node finds the next block, q is the probability that the attacker finds the next block, and p + q = 1. This equation indicates that if the attacker's hash power is less than that of a honest miner, the probability decreases exponentially as z increases. Otherwise, the attack may succeed by 100%. We will describe some of those attacks in the next paragraphs.

51% Attack. The 51% attack is the most famous and most dangerous attack in digital coins field. In the proof of work oriented Blockchain, if two miners found a block in the same time, there will be a fork (Fig. 3). After, the longest chain will be the main chain. This thing can be exploited for the 51% attack. The 51% attack is performed when a single entity has the 51% of computational power in Blockchain. This miner can mine blocks faster than other miners in the network, so he can mine blocks locally on a longer chain, spend the coin on the main Blockchain, broadcast mined blocks and spend the digital coin a second time because the first transaction is on a shorter chain and will be deleted.

Fig. 3. An example of malicious mining with 51% of computational power. The private chain is malicious as the miner could spend his coins on the public one and then nullify the transaction publishing his private longest chain.

Alternate History Attack. This attack has a chance to work even if the merchant waits for some confirmations, but requires relatively high hashrate and risk of significant expense in wasted electricity to the attacking miner. The attacker submits a transaction which pays the merchant, while privately mining an alternative Blockchain fork in which a fraudulent double-spending transaction is included. After waiting for N confirmations, the merchant sends the product. If the attacker finds more than N blocks at this point, he releases his fork and regains his coins; otherwise, he can try to continue extending his fork with the

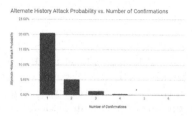

Fig. 4. The probability of alternate history attack with an hashrate of 10%.

hope of being able to catch up with the network. If he never manages to do this, the attack fails and the attacker wasted a significant amount of electricity and the payment to the merchant will be confirmed. The probability of success depends by the attacker's hashrate (as a proportion of the total network hashrate) and the number of confirmations the merchant waits for. For example, if the attacker controls the 10% of the network hashrate but the merchant waits for 6 confirmations, the success probability is on the order of 0.1% [31]. Other attacks like this, race attack, Finney attack and so on, relay on the merchant's oversight.

2.3   Blockchain and IoT

From the born of both IoT and Blockchain, this last has ever been a key technology and has been applied to the IoT several times. The IoT networks are decentralized networks as the Blockchain. Moreover, the IoT networks benefits the Blockchain as it is reliable, fault tollerant, immutable and gives innegable financial benefits to the users. The most famous example, even if it is based on tangles, which are an evolution of Blockchains is [18]. An example of application of the Blockchain to the IoT is the supply chain. With a Blockchain, each step of a supply chain is certified and this increases the value of the provided supply. This is the best example in order to let understand the potential of the Blockchain applied to IoT networks, but the applications are potentially infinite. In this work, our aim is to secure the IoT transactions and avoid the potential double spending in a Blockchain transaction through an hybrid iris and prime numbers signing which can control the identity of the eventual attacker keeping security and privacy.

3   Related Work

In the IoT field, several proposals have been proposed in literature in order to secure the devices and the exchange of information. The IoT devices are more vulnerable to attacks than classical ones such as computers, smartphones or tablets. Kortesniemi et al. [19] and Thwin [21] propose a decentralized approach in order to improve the privacy in IoT networking. Kavianpour [20] made a literature review from a general point of view in the IoT authentication context while Ferrag et al. [17] made an overview on the IoT authentication based on biometrics. In the last part of their work, the authors encourage the research trend of a Blockchain oriented authentication with a particular attention to the Blockchain vulnerabilities. From the first release of Bitcoin, the double spending problem has been a relevant focus in literature. In Blockchain technology it is important to wait more confirmation before accepting an incoming transaction, but if a miner have the 51% mining power in hands, it could perform a double spending transaction indipendently of confirmations. The most used approach to prevent the double spending, is the lowering of the probability of reaching the 51% computational power. Eyal et al. provide a solution in order to do not reach the 51% computational power in mining pools [26] and Bastiaan provide an analysis of this two phase proof of work [27]. The work in [28] provides an analisys of Blockchain security in the cloud computing area. In [32], Bae et al. proposed a random mining group selection in order to reduce the probability of successful double-spending attacks. The analysis results of the paper demonstrate that if the number of groups is greater than or equal to two, the probability that the attacker will find the next block is less than 50%. Lee et al. provide a recipient oriented transaction [30]. Shreshta et al. investigate how to design the regional blockchain, while achieving a low 51% attack success probability. They derive a condition which guarantees a low 51% attack success probability in terms of the numbers of good nodes and malicious nodes, the message delivery time, and the puzzle computation time. The condition can provide a useful guideline for selecting several control parameters guaranteeing the stable operation of the Blockchain [33]. Horizen proposes a modify of the Satoshi consensus protocol introducing a delayed block submission penalty mechanism [34]: the proposed penalty system increase the attacking cost extensively so that the potential advantage cannot be achieved towards exploitation. A penalty is applied considering the amount of time a block is hidden from the blockchain network. The time is calculated basing on the interval duration between blocks. This security protection technique notifies the entire network about the continuous fork, and during that period, the participants, miners, and exchanges are restricted from performing fraudulent transactions until the delay is lifted. The delay is calculated as follows:

$$DelayBlock = \frac{\sum_{i=1}^{n} n(n+1)}{2}$$

where n is defined as:

$$lastAttackerBlock - firstAttackerBlock$$

The PirlGuard protocol [35] is mainly built for Ethash. When an attacker starts peering with the network by confirming their privately built blocks, PirlGuard leaves the peer instantly by penalization to mine x number of blocks. The number of penalized blocks is determined by the number of blocks the adversary manages to mine in secret. PirlGuard also introduces notary contracts, which are controlled by the master nodes. The main task of the master nodes includes notarizing the Blockchain and penalizing the malicious actors by retrieving the legit consensus on the Pirl Blockchain. The notary contracts are implemented on the Pirl and Ethereum Blockchain. ChainLocks results from the implementation of long living masternode quorums (LLMQs) to mitigate the 51% attack [36]. ChainLocks executes a network-wide vote process which uses a first-seen policy. For each particular block, a long living masternode quorum (LLMQ) of a large number of master nodes is approved. It requires each participant to sign the noticed block so that the active chain can be extended. The majority of the participants, 60% or more, verify the distinct block and generate a peer to peer message (CLSIG) to broadcast the event in the network. The CLSIG message cannot be generated unless enough members comply with it. The message involves a valid signature for authenticity and verifiable by all the nodes within the network. In this security protection technique, the transaction gets confirmed after the first confirmation. This security feature lifts the six confirmation aspects and enhances a secure transaction after just one confirmation, resisting each attack based on confirmations, selfish mining and 51% attack.

4   Information Fusion of Prime Numbers and Biometrics for Encrypting Coding

This work uses a key building procedure which employs a biometric component to guarantee the user identity so, in this work, hypotetical Blockchains are not completely anonymous. These characteristics are obtained by fusing an asymmetric cryptography algorithm (RSA) and Biometrics. In particular, the original work [1] uses the iris biometrics. The algorithm coinsists in the following steps (Fig. 5):

- Iris acquisition;
- iris preprocessing: the image is prepared for the features extraction; it is segmented, filtered, etc;
- iris features extraction;
- the features are converted in a numerical vector through the IIF algorithm;
- RSA keys calculation;
- square matrix production which is composed by biometric component and the RSA private key;

The result of the computation is a key which have a NIST [37] value for 100 iris on which all P-values are greater than 0.01. A greater P-value than 0.01 certify that a sequence of bit is random. In this work, we developed an application which is composed by two components:

- the client, that is a mobile application which does the iris acquisition, the RSA key generation, the information fusion and the Smart Contract/Blockchain signing;
- the backend, that is a Smart Contract/Blockchain decentralized backend and manage deposits and signatures.

In the following section, we are going to describe the two Blockchain approaches developed in this work.

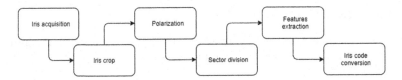

Fig. 5. The acquired iris (b), the polar visualization (c) and the sector division of the polar representation (d)

5 A Smart Contract in Order to Prevent Double Spending

In this work, we use the iris and prime numbers method [1]. Thanks to this method, when a transaction is made, the application will create a Smart Contract between the parts, and the sender will sign this Smart Contract with his IIF code. This approach is divided in the following steps:

- the client will instantiate the RSA key;
- the client will do the iris acquisition, calculate the IIF code and will store the product of two prime numbers and the RSA key with AES encryption and will instantiate the contract;
- the client will create the Smart Contract, keep the AES key and both parts will sign the contract with their IIF code;
- the Smart Contract goes into the Blockchain to its execution phase;
- the buyer will deposit the digital coins in the Contract account;
- both parts will accept the transaction;
- when the parts will accept the transaction, the funds are transferred from the contract to the seller.

The AES key is stored offchain and can be accessed only if the double spending is prooved and the miners agree on the release of the key. In order to enforce this approach, a third Smart City or not legal enthity could be involved.

As the used coin pack is tagged, a future double spending of the same coins becomes forbidden and legally prosecutable, since into the system are recognized who you are, thanks to the biometric data, which can be calculated. In case of double spending, for getting back the AES key in order to get the double spender biometrics there will be a voting phase in where the miners will vote for have back the AES key and the encrypted data to the owner of the contract. The IIF is implemented into the Blockchain, through an accessory of Smart Contract which gives the opportunity to the users to give a biometric certificate of transactions, the legal responsibility, and it forbid frauds. Consequently, the double spending problem is solved via IIF by using a IIF tagging of coins pack. From a computational point of view this required just the client component into the device of owners, IIF component, to sign the Smart Contract with IIF personal code, which has got into itself biometric data, numeric data (via prime numbers and RSA), and the scheme of IIF fusion as described previously.

5.1   The Smart Contract

The Ethereum Smart Contract is created by the application when a transaction is executed. The Smart Contract is builded as follows:

- when a transaction is started, the buyer encrypted IIF is stored in the contract thorugh the constructor;
- the contract have a payable[1] function where the buyer, after being identified, deposits the founds in the contract (i.e. the escrow account.). This function can be accessed only to the buyer.
- after that, the seller have to register his IIF and address on the contract through the register() function.
- at this point, the buyer have to accept the transaction through the accept() function and the funds are unlocked and transferred to the seller. This function could attend for N confirmations before unlocking funds in order to highly secure the transaction;
- the parts can also destroy the contract through the cancel() function, and the funds are returned to the buyer;

In this way, the parts signed the contract and the funds are frozen in the Smart Contract account until the parts will accept the transaction. Consequently, the seller is protected by the Smart Contract and if the buyer will do any illegal operation, it can be legally persecuted thanks to its biometric information and the consensus on the AES key releasing. In Fig. 6 we show how the client is built. When the sender deposits the funds, the contract will be created and signed with the sender IIF. Subsequently, the sender deposits the funds on the contract through the deposit() function, which is a contract function. On the other hand, the sender deposit is notified to the recipient, who is recognized. When the recipient accepts the funds registering itself on the Smart Contract through the register() function, it is notified to the sender. Finally, the sender accepts the transfer as well, is recognized and the funds are unlocked and transfered to the recipient.

6   IIF Approach with a Novel or a Generalized Blockchain

In the second part of this work we create a novel Blockchain which uses the IIF coding. But the method is general so, any Blockchain could be used as backend. This Blockchain will prevent the double spending thanks to the IIF codes as well as the Smart Contract approach.

---

[1] A payable function it is a function where an account can send funds in order to deposit it in a contract.

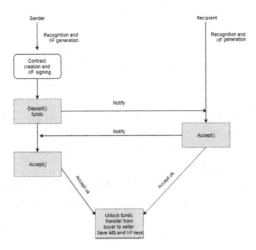

Fig. 6. The scheme of the transaction cycle. The client creates the Smart Contract and calls his functions; the blue diagrams represent the Smart Contract functions. 1)The sender creates the Smart Contract and sign it with IIF. 2)The sender deposits funds. 3)The recipient accepts the transaction. 4)The sender accepts the transaction. 5)The funds are unlocked and the IIF and AES key of the sender are saved in order to prevent the double spending. (Color figure online)

6.1 Blockchain Enrollment and Wallet Creation

As first step, the user have to register on the Blockchain with the client providing the biometric component. When the user will provide the biometric component, an RSA key will be generated, after that, the RSA key and the biometric key will be fused and the IIF code will be enrolled in the Blockchain. At first, when the wallet is created, the AES encrypted IIF code is associated to the wallet and stored on a support permissioned Blockchain. Indeed, the enrollment process includes the following steps:

- encode the sender biometric data;
- generate the IIF starting from biometric data and RSA private key;
- sign the transaction with RSA key;
- save the IIF code on the blockchain;
- store the biometric key in the permissioned support Blockchain.

6.2 Permissioned Support Blockchain

In order to keep the users privacy, the biometric key and the public keys are stored in a permissioned private Blockchain. This Blockchain can be accessed only by a trusted part and if and only if a double spending is prooved. If a double spending is prooved, the biometric key become public and the attacker can be legally prosecuted. In order to guarantee the biometric and IIF key, the public key is stored as well and it can be used to verify the attacker signs.

Enrollment

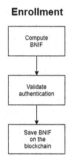

Transaction

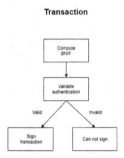

Fig. 7. The enrollment process.

Fig. 8. How the transactions are structured in the iif protocol.

6.3 Authentication

A user can sign a transaction with his private key if and only if the user has been successfully authenticated with the IIF key. As the biometric key and the private key are only possessed by the wallet owner, those information will be computed with the IIF algorithm which is not invertible without both biometric and private keys. The transaction method has the following steps:

- encode the withdrew biometric data;
- generate the IIF starting from biometric data and RSA private key;
- other miners validate the authentication;
- if the authentication data corresponds with the enrolled data, the user can sign the transaction with his RSA private key;
- the IIF key is stored in the public Blockchain;
- the biometric and the public key are stored in the private Blockchain.

7   Analysis

7.1   Security of the Hybrid Key

The result which determines the randomness of a sequence is the P-value, which is a value oscillating between 0 and 1. According to this value, a sequence is considered as random when P-value is bigger than 0.01. In this test, Iovane et al. used 1024 as bit as dimension of the private key of RSA, the Hybrid Iris Codes generated present all a dimension of 2048 bits. Figure 9 shows the results of the P-value regarding the sequence generated by IIF System on 100 iris. The P-value results are all bigger than 0,01, and this means that the sequences with a dimension of 2048 bit can be considered a random sequence. The randomness makes it more suitable to be used in security systems.

Test NIST	*P-value*
Frequency	0,574873
Block Frequency	0,794211
Cumulative Sums1	0,483279
Cumulative Sums2	0,412537
Runs	0,293751
Longest Run	0,426564

Fig. 9. P-value test NIST.

IIF, presents a general philosophy completely independent from the biometric and is completely reversible, but only if the biometric component and the private key generated by the algorithm of public-key cryptography are available.

7.2 Privacy

In both methods, the IIF hybrid code will be on the Ethereum blockchain. Thanks to the relative P-value, we can say that the hybrid code is pratically a random number. On the Blockchain there will be saved the IIF and the biometric and public key are stored on a private Blockchain these can be owned by the enthity which keep the network if and only if the miners vote for this process. In this way, the users privacy is guaranteed as long as the user will no double spend his money and if the nodes will vote for the IIF reverse process.

8   Conclusions and Future Work

We proposed two methods in order to prevent the double spending problem in Blockchains. The first method can be used for prevent the double spending in the Ethereum Blockchain, this method has been developed with a client and a Smart Contract. The client acquires the biometric key, computes the IIF key and create the contract. Then, the Smart Contract, works like an escrow, and the funds will be transferred as soon as both sender and recipient will accept the transaction. In the second part of the work, we developed a novel Blockchain where a transaction can be executed only if the user will be successfully authenticated with his/her IIF key, using a more secure key than the public key and the biometric key is saved on a private Blockchain. In this way, the double spending problem is solved since a future double spending becomes forbidden and prosecutable legally and the identity of the double spender is known thanks to the biometric key. In the near future, we will organize a simulated Smart City with a trusted party which will execute and keep the private Blockchain. We will test the system with real people since this was impossible due to the Covid19 emergency during the drafting of this work.

References

1. Iovane, G., Nappi, M., Chinnici, M., Petrosino, A., Castiglione, A., Barra, S.: A novel blockchain scheme combining prime numbers and iris for encrypting coding. In: 2019 IEEE International Conference on Dependable, Autonomic and Secure Computing, International Conference on Pervasive Intelligence and Computing, International Conference on Cloud and Big Data Computing, International Conference on Cyber Science and Technology Congress (DASC/PiCom/CBDCom/CyberSciTech), Fukuoka, Japan, 2019, pp. 609–618. https://doi.org/10.1109/DASC/PiCom/CBDCom/CyberSciTech.2019.00117
2. Salah, K., Khan, M.: IoT security: review, blockchain solutions, and open challenges. Future Generation Comput. Syst. (2017). https://doi.org/10.1016/j.future.2017.11.022
3. Xu, Z., Liu, W., Huang, J., Yang, C., Lu, J., Tan, H.: Artificial Intelligence for Securing IoT Services in Edge Computing: A Survey, Security and Communication Networks, vol. 2020, Article ID 8872586, 13 pages (2020)
4. Jesus, E.F., Chicarino, V.R.L., de Albuquerque, C.V.N., de A. Rocha, A.A.: A Survey of How to Use Blockchain to Secure Internet of Things and the Stalker Attack, Security and Communication Networks, vol. 2018, Article ID 9675050, 27 pages (2018)
5. Nakamoto, S.: Bitcoin: A Peer-to-Peer Electronic Cash System (2008)
6. Schneier, B.: Applied Cryptography. Wiley, New York (1996)
7. Percival, C.: Stronger key derivation via sequential memory-hard functions (2011)
8. Black, T., Weight, J.: X16R ASIC Resistant by Design (2018)
9. Dryja, T.: Hashimoto: I/O bound proof of work (2014)
10. Georghiades, Y., Flolid, S., Vishwanath, S.: HashCore: Proof-of-Work Functions for General Purpose Processors (2019)
11. Wang, W., et al.: Survey on Consensus Mechanisms and Mining Strategy Management in Blockchain Networks (2019)
12. Stoll, C., Klaaßen, L., Gallersd orfer, U.: The Carbon Footprint of Bitcoin (2019)
13. Brown-Cohen, J., Narayanan, A., Psomas, C., Weinberg, S.M.: Formal Barriers to Longest-Chain Proof-of-Stake Protocols (2018)
14. Buterin, V.: On Stake (2014)
15. Poelstra, A.: On Stake and Consensus (2015)
16. Ozisik, A.P., Levine, B.N.: An Explanation of Nakamoto's Analysis of Double-spend Attacks (2013)
17. Ferrag, M.A., Maglaras, L., Derhab, A.: Authentication and Authorization for Mobile IoT Devices Using Biofeatures: Recent Advances and Future Trends, Security and Communication Networks, vol. 2019, Article ID 5452870, 20 pages (2019)
18. The Tangle Whitepaper, Serguei Popov, April 30 2018 (2018)
19. Yki, K., Dmitrij, L., Tommi, E., Nikos, F.: Improving the privacy of IoT with decentralised identifiers (DIDs). J. Comput. Netw. Commun. **2019**, Article ID 8706760, 10 pages (2019)
20. Kavianpour, S., et al.: A systematic literature review of authentication in internet of things for heterogeneous devices. J. Comput. Netw. Commun. **2019**, Article ID 5747136, 14 pages (2019)
21. Thwin, T.T., Vasupongayya, S.: Blockchain-Based Access Control Model to Preserve Privacy for Personal Health Record Systems, Security and Communication Networks, vol. 2019, Article ID 8315614, 15 pages (2019)

22. Cui, Z., et al.: A hybrid blockchain-based identity authentication scheme for multi-WSN. In: IEEE Transactions on Services Computing, vol. 13, no. 2, pp. 241–251, 1 March–April 2020, https://doi.org/10.1109/TSC.2020.2964537
23. Li, D., Peng, W., Deng, W., Gai, F.: A blockchain-based authentication and security mechanism for IoT. In: 2018 27th International Conference on Computer Communication and Networks (ICCCN), Hangzhou, 2018, pp. 1–6, https://doi.org/10.1109/ICCCN.2018.8487449
24. Almadhoun, R., Kadadha, M., Alhemeiri, M., Alshehhi, M., Salah, K.: A user authentication scheme of IoT devices using blockchain-enabled fog nodes. In: 2018 IEEE/ACS 15th International Conference on Computer Systems and Applications (AICCSA), Aqaba, 2018, pp. 1–8 (2018). https://doi.org/10.1109/AICCSA.2018.8612856
25. Hammi, M.T., Hammi, B., Bellot, P., Serhrouchni, A.: Bubbles of trust: a decentralized blockchain-based authentication system for IoT, Comput. Secur. **78** (2018)
26. Eyal, I., Sirer, E.G.: How to disincentivize large bitcoin mining pools (2014)
27. Bastiaan, M.: Preventing the 51% Attack: a Stochastic Analysis of Two Phase Proof of Work in Bitcoin (2015)
28. Ho Park, J., Hy. Park, J.: Blockchain Security in Cloud Computing: Use Cases, Challenges, and Solutions (2017)
29. Crosby, M., Nachiappan Pattanayak, P., Verma, S., Kalyanaraman, V.: Blockchain technology: beyond bitcoin. Appl. Innov. Rev. **2**, 6–19 (2016)
30. Lee, H., Shin, M., Kim, K.S., Kang, Y., Kim, J.: Recipient-Oriented Transaction for Preventing Double Spending Attacks in Private Blockchain (2018)
31. Rosenfeld, M.: Analysis of hashrate-based double-spending (2012)
32. Bae, J., Lim, H.: Random Mining Group Selection to Prevent 51% Attacks on Bitcoin (2018)
33. Rakesh, S., Yeob, N.S.: Regional Blockchain for Vehicular Networks to Prevent 51% Attacks. IEEE Access, p. 1 (2019) https://doi.org/10.1109/ACCESS.2019.2928753
34. Garoffolo, A., Stabilini, P., Viglione, R., Stav, U.: A Penalty System for Delayed Block Submission (2018)
35. Fawkes, PirlGuard Innovative Solution against 51% Attacks (2018)
36. Block, A.: Mitigating 51% Attacks with LLMQ-based ChainLocks (2018)
37. Iovane, G., Amorosia, A., Benedetto, E., Lamponi, G.: An information fusion approach based on prime numbers coming from RSA algorithm and fractals for secure coding. J. Discrete Math. Sci. Cryptography **18**(5), 455–479 (2015)

DeepFakes Evolution: Analysis of Facial Regions and Fake Detection Performance

Ruben Tolosana[✉], Sergio Romero-Tapiador, Julian Fierrez,
and Ruben Vera-Rodriguez

Biometrics and Data Pattern Analytics,
Universidad Autonoma de Madrid, Madrid, Spain
{ruben.tolosana,julian.fierrez,ruben.vera}@uam.es,
sergio.romerot@estudiante.uam.es

Abstract. Media forensics has attracted a lot of attention in the last years in part due to the increasing concerns around DeepFakes. Since the initial DeepFake databases from the 1st generation such as UADFV and FaceForensics++ up to the latest databases of the 2nd generation such as Celeb-DF and DFDC, many visual improvements have been carried out, making fake videos almost indistinguishable to the human eye. This study provides an exhaustive analysis of both 1st and 2nd DeepFake generations in terms of facial regions and fake detection performance. Two different methods are considered in our experimental framework: *i)* the traditional one followed in the literature and based on selecting the entire face as input to the fake detection system, and *ii)* a novel approach based on the selection of specific facial regions as input to the fake detection system.

Among all the findings resulting from our experiments, we highlight the poor fake detection results achieved even by the strongest state-of-the-art fake detectors in the latest DeepFake databases of the 2nd generation, with Equal Error Rate results ranging from 15% to 30%. These results remark the necessity of further research to develop more sophisticated fake detectors.

Keywords: Fake news · DeepFakes · Media forensics · Face manipulation · Fake detection · Benchmark

1 Introduction

Fake images and videos including facial information generated by digital manipulations, in particular with DeepFake methods [25, 26], have become a great public concern recently [4, 6]. The very popular term "DeepFake" is referred to a deep learning based technique able to create fake videos by swapping the face of a person by the face of another person. Open software and mobile applications such as ZAO[1] allow nowadays to automatically generate fake videos by anyone, without a

---

[1] https://apps.apple.com/cn/app/id1465199127.

© Springer Nature Switzerland AG 2021
A. Del Bimbo et al. (Eds.): ICPR 2020 Workshops, LNCS 12665, pp. 442–456, 2021.
https://doi.org/10.1007/978-3-030-68821-9_38

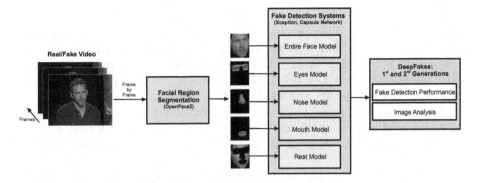

Fig. 1. Architecture of our evaluation framework to analyse both facial regions and fake detection performance in DeepFake video databases of the 1ˢᵗ and 2ⁿᵈ generations. Two different approaches are studied: *i)* selecting the entire face as input to the fake detection system, and *ii)* selecting specific facial regions.

prior knowledge of the task. But, how real are these fake videos compared with the authentic ones[2]?

Digital manipulations based on face swapping are known in the literature as Identity Swap, and they are usually based on computer graphics and deep learning techniques [25]. Since the initial publicly available fake databases, such as the UADFV database [14], up to the recent Celeb-DF and Deepfake Detection Challenge (DFDC) databases [9,16], many visual improvements have been carried out, increasing the realism of fake videos. As a result, Identity Swap databases can be divided into two different generations.

In general, fake videos of the 1ˢᵗ generation are characterised by: *i)* low-quality synthesised faces, *ii)* different colour contrast among the synthesised fake mask and the skin of the original face, *iii)* visible boundaries of the fake mask, *iv)* visible facial elements from the original video, *v)* low pose variations, and *vi)* strange artifacts among sequential frames. Also, they usually consider controlled scenarios in terms of camera position and light conditions. Many of these aspects have been successfully improved in databases of the 2ⁿᵈ generation. For example, the recent DFDC database considers different acquisition scenarios (i.e., indoors and outdoors), light conditions (i.e., day, night, etc.), distances from the person to the camera, and pose variations, among others. So, the question is, how easy is for a machine to automatically detect these kind of fakes?

Different fake detectors have been proposed based on the visual features existed in the 1ˢᵗ generation of fake videos. Yang *et al.* performed in [27] a study based on the differences existed between head poses using a full set of facial landmarks (68 extracted from DLib [12]) and those in the central face regions to differentiate fake from real videos. Once these features were extracted, Support Vector Machines (SVM) were considered for the final classification, achieving an Area Under the Curve (AUC) of 89.0% for the UADFV database [14].

---

[2] https://www.youtube.com/watch?v=UlvoEW7l5rs.

The same authors proposed in [15] another approach based on the detection of face warping artifacts. They proposed a detection system based on Convolutional Neural Networks (CNN) in order to detect the presence of such artifacts from the face and the surrounding areas. Their proposed detection approach was tested using the UADFV and DeepfakeTIMIT databases [13,14], outperforming the state of the art with 97.4% and 99.9% AUCs, respectively.

Agarwal et al. proposed in [2] a detection technique based on facial expressions and head movements. Their proposed approach achieved a final AUC of 96.3% over their own database, being robust against new manipulation techniques.

Finally, Sabir et al. proposed in [22] to detect fake videos through the temporal discrepancies across frames. They considered a Recurrent Convolutional Network similar to [10], trained end-to-end instead of using a pre-trained model. Their proposed detection approach was tested using FaceForensics++ database [21], achieving AUC results of 96.9% and 96.3% for the DeepFake and FaceSwap methods, respectively.

Therefore, very good fake detection results are already achieved on databases of the 1st generation, being an almost solved problem. But, what is the performance achieved on current Identity Swap databases of the 2nd generation?

The present study provides an exhaustive analysis of both 1st and 2nd Deep-Fake generations using state-of-the-art fake detectors. Two different approaches are considered to detect fake videos: i) the traditional one followed in the literature and based on selecting the entire face as input to the fake detection system [25], and ii) a novel approach based on the selection of specific facial regions as input to the fake detection system. The main contributions of this study are as follow:

- An in-depth comparison in terms of performance among Identity Swap databases of the 1st and 2nd generation. In particular, two different state-of-the-art fake detectors are considered: i) Xception, and ii) Capsule Network.
- An analysis of the discriminative power of the different facial regions between the 1st and 2nd generations, and also between fake detectors.

The analysis carried out in this study will benefit the research community for many different reasons: i) insights for the proposal of more robust fake detectors, e.g., through the fusion of different facial regions depending on the scenario: light conditions, pose variations, and distance from the camera; and ii) the improvement of the next generation of DeepFakes, focusing on the artifacts existing in specific facial regions.

The remainder of the paper is organised as follows. Section 2 describes our proposed evaluation framework. Section 3 summarises all databases considered in the experimental framework of this study. Section 4 and 5 describe the experimental protocol and results achieved, respectively. Finally, Sect. 6 draws the final conclusions and points out future research lines.

2   Proposed Evaluation Framework

Figure 1 graphically summarises our evaluation framework. It comprises two main modules: *i)* facial region segmentation, described in Sect. 2.1, and *ii)* fake detection systems, described in Sect. 2.2.

2.1   Facial Region Segmentation

Two different approaches are studied: *i)* segmenting the entire face as input to the fake detection system, and *ii)* segmenting only specific facial regions.

Regarding the second approach, 4 different facial regions are selected: eyes, nose, mouth, and rest (i.e., the part of the face obtained after removing the eyes, nose, and mouth from the entire face). For the segmentation of each region, we consider the open-source toolbox OpenFace2 [3]. This toolbox extracts 68 total landmarks for each face. Figure 2 shows an example of the 68 landmarks (blue circles) extracted by OpenFace2 over a frame of the Celeb-DF database. It is important to highlight that OpenFace2 is robust against pose variations, distance from the camera, and light conditions, extracting reliable landmarks even for challenging databases such as the DFDC database [9]. The specific key landmarks considered to extract each facial region are as follow:

- *Eyes*: using landmark points from 18 to 27 (top of the mask), and using landmarks 1, 2, 16, and 17 (bottom of the mask).
- *Nose*: using landmark points 22, 23 (top of the mask), from 28 to 36 (line and bottom of the nose), and 40, 43 (width of the middle-part of the nose).
- *Mouth*: using landmark points 49, 51–53, 55, and 57–59 to build a circular/elliptical mask.
- *Rest*: extracted after removing eyes, nose, and mouth masks from the entire face.

Each facial region is highlighted by yellow lines in Fig. 2. Once each facial region is segmented, the remaining part of the face is discarded (black background as depicted in Fig. 1). Also, for each facial region, we keep the same image size and resolution as the original face image to perform a fair evaluation among facial regions and the entire face, avoiding therefore the influence of other pre-processing aspects such as interpolation.

2.2   Fake Detection Systems

Two different state-of-the-art fake detection approaches are considered in our evaluation framework:

- *Xception* [5]: this network has achieved very good fake detection results in recent studies [7,9,18,21]. Xception is a CNN architecture inspired by Inception [24], where Inception modules have been replaced with depthwise separable convolutions. In our evaluation framework, we follow the same training

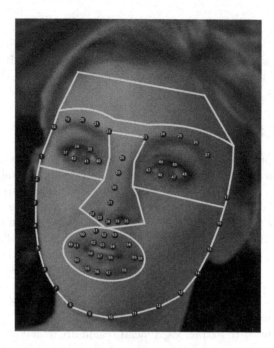

Fig. 2. Example of the different facial regions (i.e., *Eyes, Nose, Mouth*, and *Rest*) extracted using the 68 facial landmarks provided by OpenFace2 [3]. (Color figure online)

approach considered in [21]: *i)* we first consider the Xception model pre-trained with ImageNet [8], *ii)* we change the last fully-connected layer of the ImageNet model by a new one (two classes, real or fake), *iii)* we fix all weights up to the final fully-connected layer and re-train the network for few epochs, and finally *iv)* we train the whole network for 20 more epochs and choose the best performing model based on validation accuracy.

- *Capsule Network* [19]: we consider the same detection approach proposed by Nguyen *et al.*, which is publicly available in GitHub[3]. It is based on the combination of traditional CNN and recent Capsule Networks, which require fewer parameters to train compared with traditional CNN [11]. In particular, the authors proposed to use part of the VGG19 model pre-trained with ImageNet database for the feature extractor (from the first layer to the third max-pooling layer). The output of this pre-trained part is concatenated with 10 primary capsules and finally 2 output capsules (real and fake). In our evaluation framework, we train only the capsules following the procedure described in [19].

Finally, as shown in Fig. 1, it is important to highlight that we train a specific fake detector per database and facial region.

---

[3] https://github.com/nii-yamagishilab/Capsule-Forensics-v2.

Table 1. Identity swap publicly available databases of the 1st and 2nd generations considered in our experimental framework.

1st Generation		
Database	*Real videos*	*Fake videos*
UADFV (2018) [14]	49 (Youtube)	49 (FakeApp)
FaceForensics++ (2019) [21]	1,000 (Youtube)	1,000 (FaceSwap)
2nd Generation		
Database	*Real videos*	*Fake videos*
Celeb-DF (2019) [16]	408 (Youtube)	795 (DeepFake)
DFDC Preview (2019) [9]	1,131 (Actors)	4,119 (Unknown)

3   Databases

Four different public databases are considered in the experimental framework of this study. In particular, two databases of the 1st generation (UADFV and FaceForensics++) and two recent databases of the 2nd generation (Celeb-DF and DFDC). Table 1 summarises their main features.

3.1   UADFV

The UADFV database [14] comprises 49 real videos downloaded from Youtube, which were used to create 49 fake videos through the FakeApp mobile application[4], swapping in all of them the original face with the face of the actor Nicolas Cage. Therefore, only one identity is considered in all fake videos. Each video represents one individual, with a typical resolution of 294×500 pixels, and 11.14 s on average.

3.2   FaceForensics++

The FaceForensics++ database [21] was introduced in 2019 as an extension of the original FaceForensics [20], which was focused only on Expression Swap manipulations. FaceForensics++ contains 1,000 real videos extracted from Youtube. Fake videos were generated using both computer graphics and deep learning approaches (1,000 fake videos for each approach). In this study we focus on the computer graphics approach where fake videos were created using the publicly available FaceSwap algorithm[5]. This algorithm consists of face alignment, Gauss Newton optimization and image blending to swap the face of the source person to the target person.

---

[4] https://fakeapp.softonic.com/.
[5] https://github.com/MarekKowalski/FaceSwap.

3.3   Celeb-DF

The aim of the Celeb-DF database [16] was to generate fake videos of better visual quality compared with their original UADFV database. This database consists of 408 real videos extracted from Youtube, corresponding to interviews of 59 celebrities with a diverse distribution in terms of gender, age, and ethnic group. In addition, these videos exhibit a large range of variations in aspects such as the face sizes (in pixels), orientations, lighting conditions, and backgrounds. Regarding fake videos, a total of 795 videos were created using DeepFake technology, swapping faces for each pair of the 59 subjects. The final videos are in MPEG4.0 format.

3.4   DFDC

The DFDC database [9] is one of the latest public databases, released by Facebook in collaboration with other companies and academic institutions such as Microsoft, Amazon, and the MIT. In the present study we consider the DFDC preview dataset consisting of 1,131 real videos from 66 paid actors, ensuring realistic variability in gender, skin tone, and age. It is important to remark that no publicly available data or data from social media sites were used to create this dataset, unlike other popular databases. Regarding fake videos, a total of 4,119 videos were created using two different unknown approaches for fakes generation. Fake videos were generated by swapping subjects with similar appearances, i.e., similar facial attributes such as skin tone, facial hair, glasses, etc. After a given pairwise model was trained on two identities, they swapped each identity onto the other's videos.

It is important to highlight that the DFDC database considers different acquisition scenarios (i.e., indoors and outdoors), light conditions (i.e., day, night, etc.), distances from the person to the camera, and pose variations, among others.

4   Experimental Protocol

All databases have been divided into non-overlapping datasets, development ($\simeq$80% of the identities) and evaluation ($\simeq$20% of the identities). It is important to remark that each dataset comprises videos from different identities (both real and fake), unlike some previous studies. This aspect is very important in order to perform a fair evaluation and predict the generalisation ability of the fake detection systems against unseen identities. For example, for the UADFV database, all real and fake videos related to the identity of Donald Trump were considered only for the final evaluation of the models. For the FaceForensics++ database, we consider 860 development videos and 140 evaluation videos per class (real/fake) as proposed in [21], selecting different identities in each dataset (one fake video is provided for each identity). For the DFDC Preview database, we follow the same experimental protocol proposed in [9] as the authors already considered this concern. Finally, for the Celeb-DF database, we consider real/fake videos of 40 and 19 different identities for the development and evaluation datasets, respectively.

5   Experimental Results

Two experiments are considered: *i)* Sect. 5.1 considers the traditional scenario of feeding the fake detectors with the entire face, and *ii)* Sect. 5.2 analyses the discriminative power of each facial region. Finally, we compare in Sect. 5.3 the results achieved in this study with the state of the art.

5.1   Entire Face Analysis

Table 2 shows the fake detection performance results achieved in terms of Equal Error Rate (EER) and AUC over the final evaluation datasets of both 1st and 2nd generations of fake videos. The results achieved using the entire face are indicated as *Face*. For each database and fake detection approach, we remark in **bold** the best performance results achieved.

Analysing the fake videos of the 1st generation, AUC values close to 100% are achieved, proving how easy it is for both systems to detect fake videos of the 1st generation. In terms of EER, higher fake detection errors are achieved when using the FaceForensics++ database (around 3% EER), proving to be more challenging than the UADFV database.

Regarding the DeepFake databases of the 2nd generation, a high performance degradation is observed in both fake detectors when using Celeb-DF and DFDC databases. In particular, an average 23.05% EER is achieved for Xception whereas for Capsule Network, the average EER is 22.84%. As a result, an average absolute worsening of around 20% EER is produced for both fake detectors compared with the databases of the 1st generation. This degradation is specially substantial for the Celeb-DF database, with EER values of 28.55% and 24.29% for Xception and Capsule Network fake detectors, respectively. These results prove the higher realism achieved in the 2nd in comparison with the 1st DeepFake generation.

Finally, we would like to highlight the importance of selecting different identities (not only videos) for the development and final evaluation of the fake detectors, as we have done in our experimental framework. As an example of how relevant this aspect is, Table 3 shows the detection performance results achieved using Xception for the *Same* and *Different* identities between development and evaluation of Celeb-DF. As can be seen, much better results are obtained for the scenario of considering the *Same* identities, up to 5 times better compared with the *Different* identities scenario. The *Same* identities scenario generates a misleading result because the network is learning intrinsic features from the identities, not the key features to distinguish among real and fake videos. Therefore, poor results are expected to be achieved when testing with other identities. This is a key aspect not considered in the experimental protocol of many previous studies.

Table 2. Fake detection performance results in terms of EER (%) and AUC (%) over the final evaluation datasets. Two approaches are considered as input to the fake detection systems: *i)* selecting the entire face (*Face*), and *ii)* selecting specific facial regions (*Eyes, Nose, Mouth, Rest*). 1st generation databases: UADFV and FaceForensic++. 2nd generation databases: Celeb-DF and DFDC. For each database, we remark in **bold** the best fake detection results, and in blue and orange the facial regions that provide the best and worst results, respectively.

Xception	Face		Eyes		Nose		Mouth		Rest	
	EER (%)	AUC (%)	EER (%)	AUC (%)	EER (%)	AUC (%)	EER (%)	AUC (%)	EER (%)	AUC (%)
UADFV (2018) [14]	1.00	100	2.20	99.70	13.50	94.70	12.50	95.40	7.90	97.30
FaceForensics++ (2019) [21]	3.31	99.40	14.23	92.70	21.97	86.30	13.77	93.90	22.37	85.50
Celeb-DF (2019) [16]	28.55	83.60	29.40	77.30	38.46	64.90	39.37	65.10	43.55	60.10
DFDC Preview (2019) [9]	17.55	91.17	23.82	83.90	26.80	81.50	27.59	79.50	29.94	76.50

Capsule Network	Face		Eyes		Nose		Mouth		Rest	
	EER (%)	AUC (%)	EER (%)	AUC (%)	EER (%)	AUC (%)	EER (%)	AUC (%)	EER (%)	AUC (%)
UADFV (2018) [14]	2.00	99.90	0.28	100	3.92	99.30	3.20	99.56	12.30	94.83
FaceForensics++ (2019) [21]	2.75	99.52	10.29	95.32	17.51	90.09	9.66	96.18	21.58	86.61
Celeb-DF (2019) [16]	24.29	82.46	30.58	76.64	37.39	66.24	35.36	67.75	36.64	68.56
DFDC Preview (2019) [9]	21.39	87.45	25.06	83.12	26.53	81.50	27.92	78.14	32.56	72.42

Table 3. Fake detection results in terms of EER (%) using Xception over the final evaluation dataset of Celeb-DF. Two scenarios are analysed regarding whether the same identities are used for the development and final evaluation of the detectors or not. In both scenarios, different videos (real and fake) are considered in each dataset.

	Face	Eyes	Nose	Mouth	Rest
Same identities	**5.66**	12.06	23.44	17.81	21.58
Different identities	**28.55**	29.40	38.46	39.37	43.55

5.2 Facial Regions Analysis

Table 2 also includes the results achieved for each specific facial region: *Eyes, Nose, Mouth,* and *Rest*. For each database and fake detection approach, we remark in blue and orange the facial regions that provide the best and worst results, respectively. It is important to remark that a separate fake detection model is trained for each facial region and database. In addition, we also visualise in Fig. 3 which part of the image is more important for the final decision, for both real and fake examples. We consider the popular heatmap visualisation technique Grad-CAM [23]. Similar Grad-CAM results are obtained for both Xception and Capsule Network.

In general, as shown in Table 2, the facial region *Eyes* provides the best results whereas the *Rest* (i.e., the remaining part of the face after removing eyes, nose, and mouth) provides the worst results.

For the UADFV database, the *Eyes* provides EER values close to the results achieved using the entire *Face*. It is important to highlight the results achieved by the Capsule Network as in this case the fake detector based only on the *Eyes* has outperformed the case of feeding the detector with the entire *Face* (2.00% vs. 0.28% EER). The discriminative power of the *Eyes* facial region was preliminary studied by Matern *et al.* in [17], proposing features based on the missing reflection details of the eyes. Also, in this particular database, Xception achieves good results using the *Rest* of the face, 7.90% EER. This is produced due to the different colour contrast among the synthesised fake mask and real skin, and also to the visible boundaries of the fake mask. These aspects can be noticed in the examples included in Fig. 3.

Regarding the FaceForensics++ database, the *Mouth* is the facial region that achieves the best result for both Xception and Capsule Network with EER values of 13.77% and 9.66%. This is produced due to the lack of details in the teeth (blurred) and also the lip inconsistencies among the original face and the synthesised. Similar results are obtained when using the *Eyes*. It is interesting to see in Fig. 3 how the decision of the fake detection systems is mostly based on a single eye (the same happens in other databases such as UADFV). Finally, the fake detection system based on the *Rest* of the face provides the worst result, EER values of 22.37% and 21.58% for Xception and Capsule Network, respectively. This may happen because both colour contrast and visible boundaries were further improved in FaceForensics++ compared with the UADFV database.

It is also interesting to analyse the ability of each approach for the detection of fake videos of the 1st generation. In general, much better results are obtained using Capsule Networks compared with Xception. For example, regarding the UADFV database, EER absolute improvements of 1.92%, 9.58%, and 9.30% are obtained for the *Eyes*, *Nose*, and *Mouth*, respectively.

Analysing the Celeb-DF database of the 2nd generation, the best results for local regions are achieved when using the *Eyes* of the face, with EER values around 30%, similar to using the entire *Face* for Xception. It is important to remark that this EER is over 13 times higher than the original 2.20% and 0.28% EERs achieved by Xception and Capsule Network on the UADFV. Similar poor detection results, around 40% EER, are obtained when using other facial regions, being one of the most challenging databases nowadays. Figure 3 depicts some fake examples of Celeb-DF, showing very realistic features such as the colour contrast, boundaries of the mask, quality of the eyes, teeth, nose, etc.

Regarding the DFDC database, better detection results are obtained compared with the Celeb-DF database. In particular, the facial region *Eyes* also provides the best results with EER values of 23.82% and 25.06%, an absolute improvement of 5.58% and 5.52% EER compared with the *Eyes* facial region of Celeb-DF. Despite this performance improvement, the EER is still much worse compared with the databases of the 1st generation.

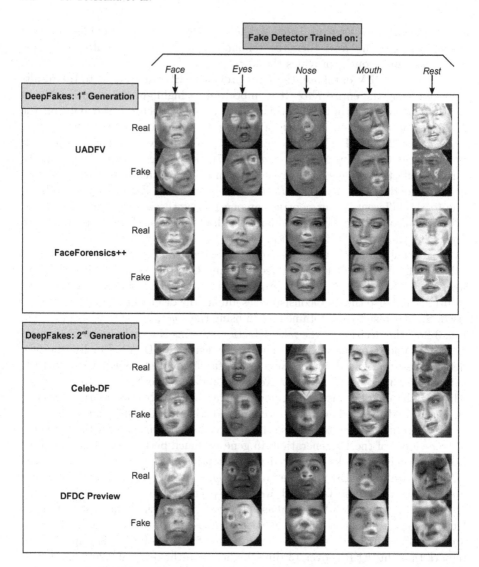

Fig. 3. Real and fake image examples of the DeepFake video databases evaluated in the present paper with their corresponding Grad-CAM heatmaps, representing the facial features most useful for each fake detector (i.e., *Face*, *Eyes*, *Nose*, *Mouth*, and *Rest*).

Table 4. Comparison in terms of AUC (%) of different state-of-the-art fake detectors with the present study. The best results achieved for each database are remarked in **bold**. Results in *italics* indicate that the evaluated database was not used for training [16].

Study	Method	Classifiers	AUC results (%)			
			UADFV [14]	FF++ [21]	Celeb-DF [16]	DFDC [9]
Yang *et al.* [27]	Head Pose Features	SVM	89.0	*47.3*	*54.6*	*55.9*
Li *et al.* [16]	Face Warping Features	CNN	97.7	*93.0*	*64.6*	*75.5*
Afchar *et al.* [1]	Mesoscopic Features	CNN	*84.3*	84.7	*54.8*	*75.3*
Sabir *et al.* [22]	Image + Temporal Features	CNN + RNN	–	96.3	–	–
Dang *et al.* [7]	Deep Learning Features	CNN + Attention Mechanism	98.4	–	*71.2*	–
Present Study	Deep Learning Features	Xception [5]	**100**	99.4	**83.6**	**91.1**
		Capsule Network [19]	**100**	**99.5**	82.4	87.4

To summarise this section, we have observed significant improvements in the realism of DeepFakes of the 2nd in comparison with the 1st generation for some specific facial regions. In particular, for the *Nose, Mouth,* and the edge of the face (*Rest*). This realism provokes a lot of fake detection errors even for the advanced detectors explored in the present paper, which result in EER values between 24% and 44% depending on the database. The quality of the *Eyes* has also been improved, but it is still the facial region most useful to detect fake images, as depicted in Fig. 3.

5.3   Comparison with the State of the Art

Finally, we compare in Table 4 the AUC results achieved in the present study with the state of the art. Different methods are considered to detect fake videos: head pose variations [27], face warping artifacts [16], mesoscopic features [1], image and temporal features [22], and pure deep learning features in combination with attention mechanisms [7]. The best results achieved for each database are remarked in **bold**. Results in *italics* indicate that the evaluated database was not used for training. These results are extracted from [16].

Note that the comparison in Table 4 is not always under the same datasets and protocols, therefore it must be interpreted with care. Despite of that, it is patent that both Xception and Capsule Network fake detectors have achieved state-of-the-art results in all databases. In particular, for Celeb-DF and DFDC, Xception obtains the best results whereas for FaceForensics++, Capsule Network is the best. The same good results are obtained by both detectors on UADFV.

6   Conclusions

In this study we have performed an exhaustive analysis of the DeepFakes evolution, focusing on facial regions and fake detection performance. Popular databases such as UADFV and FaceForensics++ of the 1st generation, as well as the latest databases such as Celeb-DF and DFDC of the 2nd generation, are considered in the analysis.

Two different approaches have been followed in our evaluation framework to detect fake videos: *i)* selecting the entire face as input to the fake detection system, and *ii)* selecting specific facial regions such as the eyes or nose, among others, as input to the fake detection system.

Regarding the fake detection performance, we highlight the very poor results achieved in the latest DeepFake video databases of the 2nd generation with EER values around 20–30%, compared with the EER values of the 1st generation ranging from 1% to 3%. In addition, we remark the significant improvements in the realism achieved at image level in some facial regions such as the nose, mouth, and edge of the face in DeepFakes of the 2nd generation, resulting in fake detection results between 24% and 44% EERs.

The analysis carried out in this study provides useful insights for the community, e.g.: *i)* for the proposal of more robust fake detectors, e.g., through the fusion of different facial regions depending on the scenario: light conditions, pose variations, and distance from the camera; and *ii)* the improvement of the next generation of DeepFakes, focusing on the artifacts existing in specific regions.

Acknowledgments. This work has been supported by projects: PRIMA (H2020-MS CA-ITN-2019-860315), TRESPASS-ETN (H2020-MSCA-ITN-2019-860813), BIBECA (MINECO FEDER RTI2018-101248-B-I00), and Accenture. R. T. is supported by Comunidad de Madrid y Fondo Social Europeo.

References

1. Afchar, D., Nozick, V., Yamagishi, J., Echizen, I.: MesoNet: a compact facial video forgery detection network. In: Proceedings of International Workshop on Information Forensics and Security (2018)
2. Agarwal, S., Farid, H., Gu, Y., He, M., Nagano, K., Li, H.: Protecting world leaders against deep fakes. In: Proceedings of Conference on Computer Vision and Pattern Recognition Workshops (2019)
3. Baltrusaitis, T., Zadeh, A., Lim, Y.C., Morency, L.P.: OpenFace 2.0: facial behavior analysis toolkit. In: Proceedings of IEEE International Conference on Automatic Face & Gesture Recognition (2018)
4. Cellan-Jones, R.: Deepfake Videos Double in Nine Months (2019). https://www.bbc.com/news/technology-49961089
5. Chollet, F.: Xception: deep learning with Depthwise separable convolutions. In: Proceedings of IEEE/CVF Conference on Computer Vision and Pattern Recognition (2017)
6. Citron, D.: How DeepFake Undermine Truth and Threaten Democracy (2019). https://www.ted.com

7. Dang, H., Liu, F., Stehouwer, J., Liu, X., Jain, A.: On the detection of digital face manipulation. In: Proceedings of IEEE/CVF Conference on Computer Vision and Pattern Recognition (2020)

8. Deng, J., Dong, W., Socher, R., Li, L., Li, K., Fei-Fei, L.: Imagenet: a large-scale hierarchical image database. In: Proceedings of IEEE/CVF Conference on Computer Vision and Pattern Recognition (2009)

9. Dolhansky, B., Howes, R., Pflaum, B., Baram, N., Ferrer, C.C.: The Deepfake Detection Challenge (DFDC) Preview Dataset. arXiv preprint arXiv:1910.08854 (2019)

10. Güera, D., Delp, E.: Deepfake video detection using recurrent neural networks. In: Proceedings of IEEE International Conference on Advanced Video and Signal Based Surveillance (2018)

11. Hinton, G., Sabour, S., Frosst, N.: Matrix capsules with EM routing. In: Proceedings of International Conference on Learning Representations Workshop (2018)

12. King, D.: DLib-ML: a machine learning toolkit. J. Mach. Learn. Res. 10, 1755–1758 (2009)

13. Korshunov, P., Marcel, S.: Deepfakes: a New Threat to Face Recognition? Assessment and Detection. arXiv preprint arXiv:1812.08685 (2018)

14. Li, Y., Chang, M., Lyu, S.. In Ictu oculi: exposing AI generated fake face videos by detecting eye blinking. In: Proceedings of IEEE International Workshop on Information Forensics and Security (2018)

15. Li, Y., Lyu, S.: Exposing DeepFake videos by detecting face warping artifacts. In: Proceedings of IEEE/CVF Conference on Computer Vision and Pattern Recognition Workshops (2019)

16. Li, Y., Yang, X., Sun, P., Qi, H., Lyu, S.: Celeb-DF: a large-scale challenging dataset for DeepFake forensics. In: Proceedings of IEEE/CVF Conference on Computer Vision and Pattern Recognition (2020)

17. Matern, F., Riess, C., Stamminger, M.: Exploiting visual artifacts to expose Deep-Fakes and face manipulations. In: Proceedings of IEEE Winter Applications of Computer Vision Workshops (2019)

18. Neves, J.C., Tolosana, R., Vera-Rodriguez, R., Lopes, V., Proença, H., Fierrez, J.: GANprintR: improved fakes and evaluation of the state-of-the-art in face manipulation detection. IEEE J. Sel. Top. Signal Process. 14, 1038–1048 (2020)

19. Nguyen, H., Yamagishi, J., Echizen, I.: Use of a Capsule Network to Detect Fake Images and Videos. arXiv preprint arXiv:1910.12467 (2019)

20. Rössler, A., Cozzolino, D., Verdoliva, L., Riess, C., Thies, J., Nießner, M.: Face-Forensics: A Large-Scale Video Dataset for Forgery Detection in Human Faces. arXiv preprint arXiv:1803.09179 (2018)

21. Rössler, A., Cozzolino, D., Verdoliva, L., Riess, C., Thies, J., Nießner, M.: Face-Forensics++: learning to detect manipulated facial images. In: Proceedings of IEEE/CVF International Conference on Computer Vision (2019)

22. Sabir, E., Cheng, J., Jaiswal, A., AbdAlmageed, W., Masi, I., Natarajan, P.: Recurrent convolutional strategies for face manipulation detection in videos. In: Proceedings of Conference on Computer Vision and Pattern Recognition Workshops (2019)

23. Selvaraju, R., Cogswell, M., Das, A., Vedantam, R., Parikh, D., Batra, D.: Grad-CAM: visual explanations from deep networks via gradient-based localization. In: Proceedings of IEEE International Conference on Computer Vision (2017)

24. Szegedy, C., et al.: Going deeper with convolutions. In: Proceedings of IEEE/CVF Conference on Computer Vision and Pattern Recognition (2015)

25. Tolosana, R., Vera-Rodriguez, R., Fierrez, J., Morales, A., Ortega-Garcia, J.: Deep-Fakes and beyond: a survey of face manipulation and fake detection. Inf. Fusion **64**, 131–148 (2020)
26. Verdoliva, L.: Media forensics and DeepFakes: an overview. IEEE J. Sel. Top. Signal Process. **14**, 910–932 (2020)
27. Yang, X., Li, Y., Lyu, S.: Exposing deep fakes using inconsistent head poses. In: Proceedings of IEEE International Conference on Acoustics, Speech and Signal Processing (2019)

Large Scale Graph Based Network Forensics Analysis

Lorenzo Di Rocco, Umberto Ferraro Petrillo[✉], and Francesco Palini

Dipartimento di Scienze Statistiche, Università di Roma "La Sapienza", Roma, Italy
{umberto.ferraro,francesco.palini}@uniroma1.it

Abstract. In this paper we tackle the problem of performing graph based network forensics analysis at a large scale. To this end, we propose a novel distributed version of a popular network forensics analysis algorithm, the one by Wang and Daniels [18].

Our version of the Wang and Daniels algorithm has been formulated according to the MapReduce paradigm and implemented using the Apache Spark framework. The resulting code is able to analyze in a scalable way graphs of arbitrary size thanks to its distributed nature. We also present the results of an experimental study where we assessed both the time performance and the scalability of our algorithm when run on a distributed system of increasing size.

1 Introduction

Nowadays, the menace of cyber-security attacks is becoming increasingly pervasive. It has been estimated that these are the fastest growing crimes and they are predicted to cost to the world about $6 trillion annually by 2021 [6]. Actually, complex attacks may involve the participation of even millions of devices, of the most disparate types, spread on a worldwide scale and coordinated to perform a multi-stage attack that may target a single device as well as an entire organization.

Indeed, there are several tools and data sources that an investigator can use to discover traces of an ongoing attack as well as determining the origin and/or the evolution of an attack that has already been carried out. Think, for example, to the log files collected on the different devices of an organization under analysis and to the precious information that could be gathered by intrusion detection systems (IDSs). Indeed, the challenge here is to put together a representation of these information that is meaningful and easy to analyze. A simple but effective approach is to model all the devices that may be involved in a cyber attack as the nodes of a graph, and the communications occurring between these devices as edges of the same graph. This approach, usually referred to as *Graph Based Network Forensics Analysis,* has one important advantage: it is possible to discover patterns or properties that may denote a malicious activity on a network of devices by examining the structure of the corresponding graph. There is, however, one important shortcoming. What happens if the network of devices under

© Springer Nature Switzerland AG 2021
A. Del Bimbo et al. (Eds.): ICPR 2020 Workshops, LNCS 12665, pp. 457–469, 2021.
https://doi.org/10.1007/978-3-030-68821-9_39

analysis is very large? Processing the corresponding graph on a single workstation may be not possible at all, for huge graphs and, anyway, it could be very time-consuming. Indeed, there would be need of a workstation equipped with a very fast CPU and very large amount of memory, this would be a very expensive option. As an alternative, it could be possible to process huge graphs anyway by resorting to solutions like external memory algorithms, but at the expense of much longer execution times.

In this paper we explore a different possibility, by proposing an algorithm for performing graph based network forensics analysis leveraging the capabilities of a distributed system. The algorithm we propose, based on the original sequential algorithm by Wang and Daniels [18], has been developed using the MapReduce paradigm and implemented by means of the Apache Spark framework.

1.1 Organization of the Paper

In Sect. 2, we review some of the main contributions in the field of graph based network forensics algorithms. In Sect. 3, we describe in details the algorithm by Wang and Daniels. In Sect. 4, we introduce our distributed algorithm. In Sect. 5, we present and discuss the results of an experimental study considering our distributed algorithm. Finally, in Sect. 6, we give some concluding remarks.

2   Related Work

Since their initial development, almost all Internet services have been provided with the ability of generating and collecting log files describing their status as well as error conditions or warning messages. Along the same line, also Internet connected devices are usually provided with the ability of logging their connectivity status as well as monitoring, at different level of details, incoming and outcoming connection activities. In addition, there are plenty of software and/or hardware solutions that are able to sit on top of a network connection and sniff and parse all the ongoing traffic, at different protocol levels.

Indeed, the analysis of all these data sources, usually referred to as *Network Forensics* (see [5]), may provide valuable information to diagnose an ongoing cyber attack or to find traces of a past attack. However, analyzing each data source separately may be very time-consuming and may cause an investigator to miss the big picture.

Starting from these considerations, a new approach has been introduced with the aim of reasoning at a more abstract level. The idea was to develop the ability to see all the devices belonging to a network involved in a cyber attack not as separate entities but as a part of a whole plan where interactions occur in order to carry on a coordinated attack. The pioneering work in this area is the one presented by Wang and Daniels in [18]. They propose to model the network of devices involved in an attack as nodes of an *evidence graph*, where directed edges connecting these nodes were used to model assessed forensics evidences. Then, their idea is to analyze the structure and the properties of this graph. The final goal is to derive important information about the possible role played by each device in carrying on a cyber attack.

The approach by Wang and Daniels has been followed and improved by several other authors, as witnessed by the many publications in this field (see, e.g., [1,13,14,17]). Of these publications, we cite the work by Liu *et al.* ([14]), where it has been faced the problem of integrating multiple evidence graphs in one, as needed when investigating about different attacks targeting the same network. We also cite the work by [13], where the authors propose a refinement of the algorithm by Wang and Daniels, essentially based on the ability of integrating evidence data from multiple sources as well as including the usage of support vector machines in order to better filter suspicious data.

3   The Algorithm by Wang and Daniels

Wang and Daniels proposed in [18] an integrated network forensics analysis system. The core of their approach is an evidence graph model that facilitates evidence presentation and automated reasoning. These two activities are carried out in their proposal by two modules named *evidence graph manipulation module* and *attack reasoning module*. The first is in charge of producing the *evidence graph* starting from a repository of evidences previously collected, filtered and normalized as well as from a knowledge base describing the inventory of network devices under analysis and a standardized description of network attacks. The second implements an hierarchical reasoning framework operating at two levels:

- *local-reasoning level*. Its purpose is to infer the functional state of a graph node starting from the information available for that node as well as for its immediate neighborhood;
- *global-reasoning level*. Its purpose is to determine a set of highly correlated graph nodes that are likely to be part of a coordinated attack. Such inferring is done by analyzing the global graph structure.

Indeed, the global reasoning level is the most challenging part, from a computational viewpoint, of this algorithm as it requires the ability to analyze the whole structure of the evidence graph. So, in the rest of this paper, we will focus on the development of a distributed version of this part of the Wang and Daniels algorithm.

3.1   Global Reasoning

The global reasoning task implemented by the Wang and Daniels analysis system is formulated as a *group detection* problem. It works in two steps:

- **Step 1: Seed Generation.** In this step, the goal is to identify nodes of the graph that are important both in functional and structural terms. From the functional viewpoint, we refer to the classification outcoming from the local reasoning step to identify those nodes that have been classified to be relevant either because they are supposed to be the nodes originating an attack or the nodes being targeted by an attack. From the structural viewpoint, we take into account graph centrality metrics to filter those nodes that are relevant because of their position in the evidence graph. Nodes that are relevant from both viewpoints are named *seed nodes* and are used, as input, to run step 2.

– **Step 2: Group Expansion.** In this step, we derive the *attack group* by iteratively considering all those nodes that are strongly correlated with initial seed nodes. The correlation applies to nodes that are adjacent to those under analysis and so that the connecting edges are labeled with information denoting a strong attack correlation.

4   Our Algorithm

In this section we briefly introduce the MapReduce paradigm and its implementation provided by the Apache Spark Framework. Then, we introduce and discuss our implementation of the algorithm by Wang and Daniel based on this paradigm.

4.1   The MapReduce Paradigm

The MapReduce paradigm [8] is a programming model conceived for simplifying the development of algorithms in order to process very large amount of data. Assuming the availability of an input dataset organized as a collection of key-value pairs, it is based on the execution of a sequence of two types of functions:

– *map functions.* They take as input a key-value pair returning, as output, a (possibly empty) set of key-value pairs.
– *reduce functions.* They take as input a collection of key-value pairs sharing a same key, so to produce, as output, a (possibly empty) set of key-value pairs.

Computations with varying degree of complexity can be modeled in MapReduce by defining pipelines of map and reduce functions, so that the output of each function is the input for the next one.

4.2   Apache Spark

Apache Spark [2] is a framework supporting the MapReduce paradigm, used mainly to develop programs with in-memory computing and acyclic data-flow model to be executed on a distributed computing architecture. In simple and intuitive terms, this latter can be described as a set of computing nodes that cooperate in order to solve a problem via local computing and by exchange of "messages" [15]. On that type of architecture, Spark can be used for applications that reuse a working set of data across multiple parallel operations (e.g., iterative algorithms) and it allows the combination of streaming and batch processing.

Spark is becoming the de-facto standard framework for the implementation of MapReduce algorithms and it is used in several application domains (see, e.g., [4, 10, 11]). One of the key factors motivating its success is the availability of a high-level programming API which support multiple languages and is made of two fundamental logic blocks: a programming model that creates a task dependency graph, and an optimized runtime system which exploits this graph to deploy code and data and schedule work units on the distributed system nodes. At the core of the Spark programming model is the *Resilient Distributed Dataset* (RDD) abstraction, a fault-tolerant, distributed data structure that can be created and manipulated using a rich set of operators: programmers start by defining one or more RDDs that are instantiated by fetching data that originally resides on stable storage or other RDDs. Then, a typical Spark application goes on by processing the content of a RDD by means of distributed operations called *actions* and *transformations*. Once the processing has finished, one may retrieve the results of a computation by collecting the content of the outcoming RDDs. Spark offers also an alternative type of distributed data structure called *DataFrame*, that provides a more abstract and high-level representation than the one available with RDDs.

GraphX. The MapReduce paradigm is powerful enough to model different type of problems, however modeling graph-based tasks can be tricky. In order to model this kind of problems as graph objects, Spark makes available an official library called GraphX [19]. The library allows to analyze the graph by applying functions directly on the nodes and the edges of the graph, however, under the hood, the computation is always performed on the elements of a Spark RDD.

Pregel. Pregel [16] is a computation model based on the updating of the nodes properties and on a multi-iteration procedure. In each iteration, the adjacent nodes share and modify their attributes according to a user-provided function. The GraphX API provides a framework to elaborate a Pregel schema in a Spark cluster, where the messages sent between nodes are processed in parallel.

GraphFrames. GraphFrames is a third-party library [7] which allows to efficiently perform SQL-like queries on the graph and exposes a set of useful high-level graph functions, not available in GraphX.

4.3 Our MapReduce Version of the Algorithm by Wang and Daniels

The MapReduce algorithm we propose operates in two steps. In the first step, an appropriate starting point on the network is found. It will be defined as the *seed node*. Then, in the second step, the global reasoning algorithm is iteratively executed starting from the seed node. More details about these two steps are provided in the following.

Step 1: Seed Generation. In this step, a starting point on the network has to be chosen in order to run the algorithm. Among all the possible choice criteria, the selected approach consists on selecting the node with largest value of the eigenvectors centrality from the set of those with an highly activated attacker state (see Sect. 3). The attacker state is a fuzzy parameter estimated through the local reasoning process. Nodes with this parameter greater than 0.6 are highly suspected to be a source of attack.

The computation of the eigenvectors centrality is done using the *GraphX Pregel API* (see Sect. 4.2) to implement the power iteration and find the eigenvector associated with the largest eigenvalue, where the i-th element corresponds to the centrality measure x_i of the i-th node.

In our algorithm, we assume to take as input an evidence graph, $G = (N, E)$, initially encoded as a GraphFrames distributed data structure and instantiated over a Spark cluster. When needed, this graph will be converted to its corresponding GraphX representation. This will occur for those functions existing in GraphX but not in GraphFrames. When using the GraphX representation, the attributes of the nodes and the properties of the edges are grouped in two different RDDs. Instead, when using the GraphFrames representation, these data structures will be maintained using two Spark DataFrames.

The Pregel-based algorithm we introduce for computing the eigenvectors takes, for each node, the value $\frac{1}{|N|}$ as initial guess of the centrality index. Then, it iterates the process where, through each edge, the values x_k of the source nodes are sent to the respective destination ones by means of messages. In each node, all the received messages are summed and normalized with respect to the square root of the sum of their squares, obtaining the update of the eigenvector components.

Step 2: Group Expansion. The global reasoning algorithm adds gradually new members to the local list *attack_group* that, at the beginning, contains only the seed node. First of all, a map function initializes, for each edge in the graph, two *boolean* attributes. The first tells if the source node belongs or not to an attack group. The same happens for the second attribute, but for the destination node. This allows to easily track the expansion of the attack group, achieved through the iteration of two functions. The *findCandidates* function applies a filter and a map transformation to extract nodes that do not belong to the attack group but have a direct connection with one of the attackers. More precisely, only the edges with just one boolean attribute set to true are kept. Then, for each of them, only the endpoint not belonging to the attack group is extracted. The output of the function is a new RDD containing elements potentially related to the attack. The *groupExpansion* function finds the nodes to merge to the attack group. This is done by using the Dijkstra algorithm [9] to compute the shortest paths between all the elements in the attack group and the other nodes in the *correlation graph*. The correlation graph is the undirected version of the evidence graph, where the weights are inversely proportional to the correlation of two nodes. Consequently, the more two nodes are correlated, the closer they are in the correlation graph.

Algorithm 1: Global Reasoning

---

input: graph G, seed node n_s, threshold T, step size k

$attack\_group \leftarrow \{n_s\}$
$candidates \leftarrow \emptyset$
$delta\_group \leftarrow \{n_s\}$

while $delta\_group$ *is not empty* **do**
$\quad | \quad candidates \leftarrow candidates \cup findCandidates(G)$
$\quad | \quad delta\_group \leftarrow groupExpansion(G, attack\_group, candidates, T, k)$
$\quad | \quad attack\_group \leftarrow attack\_group \cup delta\_group$
end

---

return $attack\_group$

The Dijkstra implementation we use is implemented according to the GraphX Pregel paradigm. It works by associating to each node n of the graph an array x, where the i-th entry represents the shortest path to the i-th element of the local *attack_group* list. In details, the array associated to a generic node n is initialized as follows:

$$x[i] = \begin{cases} 0 & \text{if } n = attack\_group[i], \\ \infty & \text{otherwise} \end{cases}$$

In each iteration, the nodes update their attributes according to the message received from one of the linked neighbors:

$$x[i] = \begin{cases} x[i] & \text{if } x[i] < x_{src}[i] + w, \\ x_{src}[i] + w & \text{otherwise} \end{cases}$$

where $x_{src}[i]$ is the i-th entry of the array sent by the source node and w is the weight that connects the current pair of nodes. Regarding only those nodes belonging to the *candidates* set, the minimum value of the respective array is found with the final goal of evaluating the distance of the shortest path for reaching any element of the *attack_group*. Then, only the candidates with a distance smaller than T are considered. Among these, only the k closer ones are added to attack group. The step size parameter k defines the growth rate of the group in each iteration. At the end of each iteration, the boolean parameters of each edge are updated with a map transformation that takes into account the attackers derived during the last iteration.

5   Experimental Evaluation

We conducted an experimental analysis with the goal of assessing the scalability of our distributed algorithm and its sensitivity to the variation of computing units employed. For each experiment, we took into account the overall execution time, measured by collecting the job execution elapsed time returned by the

Spark web interface. In the following, we provide details about the dataset used for our experiments, describe our reference hardware platform used for running these experiments and, finally, we introduce the layout of these experiments and comment their results.

5.1 Dataset

In our experiments we considered the CTU-13 dataset [12], which contains botnet traffic captured in the CTU University. It consists of 13 scenarios with different botnet samples (see Table 1) and a large amount of data traffic, for this reason it is well suited for our study.

The algorithm by Wang and Daniels builds the evidence graph by considering the alerts generated by an intrusion detection system (IDS). The mapping between the two data sources is established only when attack is identified. Since this type of information is not natively available in the CTU-13 dataset, we simulated the existence of an IDS. This has been done by labeling entries of the CTU-13 dataset with randomly generated information describing the occurrence of attacks. Namely, the simulated IDS generates an alert when the flow comes from the botnet, with confidence and severity chosen uniformly at random in the interval $[0.5, 1]$. A user-defined percentage of the non-malicious traffic is identified as an attack, as false positives, with confidence and severity chosen uniformly at random in the interval $[0, 0.5)$.

Table 1. Characteristics of the 13 botnet scenarios in CTU-13. CF: ClickFraud, PS: Port Scan, FF: FastFlux, US: Compiled and checked by the creators of the dataset.

ID	IRC	SPAM	CF	PS	DDoS	FF	P2P	US	HTTP	Note
1	X	X	X							
2	X	X	X							
3	X			X			X			
4	X			X			X			UDP and ICMP DDoS
5		X		X				X		Scan web proxies
6				X						Proprietary C& C. RDP
7								X		Chinese hosts
8				X						Proprietary C& C. Net-BIOS, STUN
9	X	X	X	X						
10	X			X			X			UDP DDoS
11	X			X			X			ICMP DDoS
12						X				Synchronization
13		X		X				X		Captcha. Web mail

The resulting *evidence graph* will be used as input to the global reasoning algorithm introduced in Sect. 3. Among the node (host) properties defined for the evidence graph, we consider the following:

- **ID:** host identity.
- **Attacker:** a fuzzy value that indicates the belief that the current node is a source of attack. Attacker $\in [0, 1]$.
- **Value:** asset value of the host. Value $\in [0, 1]$.

Table 2. Structural information of the evidence graph generated from each scenario, belonging to the CTU-13 dataset, associating an alert to each flow recorded.

ID	# Nodes	# Edges	Size (MB)
1	607,565	2,824,636	369
2	442,471	1,808,122	236
3	434,988	4,710,638	611
4	186,244	1,121,076	147
5	41,658	129,832	17
6	107,341	558,919	74
7	38,204	114,077	15
8	383,788	2,954,230	386
9	367,263	2,087,508	273
10	197,824	1,309,791	171
11	41,931	107,251	14
12	94,434	325,471	43
13	315,769	1,925,149	251

We consider a subset of the edge (action) properties defined for the *evidence graph*. The properties are the following:

- **Weight:** a fuzzy value denoting the seriousness of the action. Weight $\in [0, 1]$.
- **Relevancy:** the belief that the action, represented by the edge, would successfully achieve its expected impact. Relevancy can have three values: 0 (false/non-relevant positive), 0.5 (unverifiable) or 1 (relevant true positive).
- **Host Importance:** defined as $\max(Value_{src}, Value_{dst})$.

A summary of the statistics about the evidence graphs generated starting from the CTU-13 dataset is available in Table 2.

5.2 Hardware

The experiments have been performed on a 48 nodes Linux-based cluster, with one node acting as *resource manager* and the remaining nodes being used as workers. The cluster is installed with Hadoop 3.1.3 and the Spark 2.3.3 software distributions. Each node of this cluster is equipped with one 8-core Intel Xeon E3-12@2.40 GHz processor and 32 GB of RAM. Moreover, each node has a 200 GB virtual disk reserved to HDFS, for an overall capacity of about 6 TB.

5.3   Results

In this section, we report the experimental results obtained executing the distributed implementation of the global reasoning algorithm on the CTU-13 dataset. We recall that the input of the algorithm is the evidence graph, built using the traffic related to one or more of the 13 scenarios.

In order to test the scalability of our distributed algorithm, we have considered the scenario with the largest traffic data, i.e., Scenario 3. In Table 2 is shown the size of each scenario belonging to the dataset and the number of nodes and edges of the corresponding evidence graph.

In Fig. 1 it is reported the execution time measured running the algorithm on the traffic data recorded in Scenario 3. The computing units of the underlying Spark installation vary from 48 to 288, doubling the units in each test. In order to maximize the input size and stress the distributed implementation of the algorithm, we assumed an alert associated to each flow, i.e., each record in Scenario 3 is represented as an edge of the evidence graph. The algorithm has been executed with threshold $T = 1$ and step size $k = 50$.

The results show that the proposed algorithm succeeds in exploiting the availability of more computing units, as its overall execution time decreases as the size of the underlying distributed framework increases. However, we notice that, at the beginning, the algorithm scales pretty well. When a certain number of computing units is reached, adding more units does not bring a significant performance advancement.

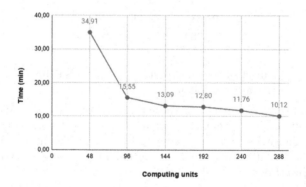

Fig. 1. Execution time of our MapReduce algorithm on Scenario 3, as a function of the computing units.

To investigate this issue, we performed a second experiment where we profiled the time spent by the MapReduce algorithm during the computation, using Scenario 3 as input using, respectively, 144 computing units and 288 computing units. In Table 3 we report the execution time of the Spark transformations, aggregated according to the algorithm function being executed. Of these transformations, the ones about *evidenceGraph* and *correlationGraph* are executed only once during the lifespan of the algorithm and their computational cost is pretty small. As for the others, we recall that the *seedGeneration* function, described in Sect. 4.3, computes the eigenvector centrality performing many iterations until the convergence is reached. In this particular setting, the algorithm performs 12 iterations lasting about 40 s each.

The *findCandidates* and *groupExpansion* functions are chained by Spark in the same execution stage. Both of them are executed iteratively, as shown in the pseudocode of the Algorithm 1. In this setting, the algorithm performs 2 iterations lasting about 30 s each. As it can be seen, the algorithm achieves a 0.5x speed-up when doubling the number of computing units. This behavior is not relegated to one single function but it is consistent across all the considered functions, thus calling for the need of a further investigation on this matter.

Table 3. Execution time, in minutes, of the Spark transformations required by our distributed algorithm, aggregated according to the algorithm function being executed, when executed using, respectively, 144 computing units and 288 computing units.

Task	144 computing units	288 computing units
evidenceGraph	2.50	1.97
correlationGraph	1.64	1.13
seedGeneration	9.92	7.53
findCandidates groupExpansion	1.27	0.97

6   Conclusions

In this paper we presented a novel distributed algorithm for graph-based network forensics analysis. Our algorithm is a revisited version of a popular sequential algorithm for solving this problem, developed according to the MapReduce paradigm for distributed computing. The algorithm we proposed is able to process very large networks in a scalable way, thus delivering execution time performance that are inversely proportional to the amount of computing resources. As a further research, we plan to conduct more experiments to investigate other application scenarios. We are also interested in the development of more graph-based network forensics analysis algorithms according to a distributed approach.

Acknowledgements. All authors would like to thank the Department of Statistical Sciences of University of Rome - La Sapienza for computing time on the TeraStat [3] cluster and for other computing resources, and the GARR Consortium for having made available a cutting edge OpenStack Virtual Datacenter for this research.

References

1. Alabdulsalam, S.K., Duong, T.Q., Choo, K.-K.R., Le-Khac, N.-A.: evidence identification and acquisition based on network link in an internet of things environment. In: Herrero, Á., Cambra, C., Urda, D., Sedano, J., Quintián, H., Corchado, E. (eds.) CISIS 2019. AISC, vol. 1267, pp. 163–173. Springer, Cham (2021). https://doi.org/10.1007/978-3-030-57805-3_16
2. Apache Software Foundation: Apache Spark (2016). http://spark.apache.org
3. Bompiani, E., Ferraro Petrillo, U., Jona Lasinio, G., Palini, F.: High-performance computing with TeraStat. In: Proceedings of the 2020 IEEE International Conference on Dependable, Autonomic and Secure Computing, October 2020. https://doi.org/10.1109/DASC-PICom-CBDCom-CyberSciTech49142.2020.00088
4. Cattaneo, G., Ferraro Petrillo, U., Nappi, M., Narducci, F., Roscigno, G.: An efficient implementation of the algorithm by Lukáš et al. on Hadoop. In: Au, M.H.A., Castiglione, A., Choo, K.-K.R., Palmieri, F., Li, K.-C. (eds.) GPC 2017. LNCS, vol. 10232, pp. 475–489. Springer, Cham (2017). https://doi.org/10.1007/978-3-319-57186-7_35
5. Corey, V., Peterman, C., Shearin, S., Greenberg, M.S., Van Bokkelen, J.: Network forensics analysis. IEEE Internet Comput. 6(6), 60–66 (2002)
6. Cybercrime Magazine: Global Cybercrime Damages Predicted To Reach $6 Trillion Annually By 2021 (2018). cybersecurityventures.com/cybercrime-damages-6-trillion-by-2021
7. Dave, A., Jindal, A., Li, L.E., Xin, R., Gonzalez, J., Zaharia, M.: GraphFrames: an integrated API for mixing graph and relational queries. In: Proceedings of the Fourth International Workshop on Graph Data Management Experiences and Systems, pp. 1–8 (2016)
8. Dean, J., Ghemawat, S.: MapReduce: simplified data processing on large clusters. Commun. ACM 51, 107–113 (2008)
9. Dijkstra, E.W., et al.: A note on two problems in connexion with graphs. Numerische mathematik 1(1), 269–271 (1959)
10. Ferraro Petrillo, U., Roscigno, G., Cattaneo, G., Giancarlo, R.: Informational and linguistic analysis of large genomic sequence collections via efficient Hadoop cluster algorithms. Bioinformatics 34(11), 1826–1833 (2018)
11. Ferraro Petrillo, U., Sorella, M., Cattaneo, G., Giancarlo, R., Rombo, S.E.: Analyzing big datasets of genomic sequences: fast and scalable collection of k-mer statistics. BMC Bioinform. 20(4), 1–14 (2019)
12. Garcia, S., Grill, M., Stiborek, J., Zunino, A.: An empirical comparison of botnet detection methods. Comput. Secur. 45, 100–123 (2014)
13. He, J., Chang, C., He, P., Pathan, M.S.: Network forensics method based on evidence graph and vulnerability reasoning. Future Internet 8(4), 54 (2016)
14. Liu, C., Singhal, A., Wijesekera, D.: Creating integrated evidence graphs for network forensics. In: Peterson, G., Shenoi, S. (eds.) DigitalForensics 2013. IAICT, vol. 410, pp. 227–241. Springer, Heidelberg (2013). https://doi.org/10.1007/978-3-642-41148-9_16
15. Lynch, N.A.: Distributed Algorithms. Morgan Kaufmann, San Francisco (1996)
16. Malewicz, G., et al.: Pregel: a system for large-scale graph processing. In: Proceedings of the 2010 ACM SIGMOD International Conference on Management of Data, pp. 135–146 (2010)
17. Pelaez, J.C., Fernandez, E.B.: VoIP network forensic patterns. In: 2009 Fourth International Multi-Conference on Computing in the Global Information Technology, pp. 175–180. IEEE (2009)

18. Wang, W., Daniels, T.E.: A graph based approach toward network forensics analysis. ACM Trans. Inf. Syst. Secur. **12**(1), October 2008. https://doi.org/10.1145/1410234.1410238
19. Xin, R.S., Gonzalez, J.E., Franklin, M.J., Stoica, I.: GraphX: a resilient distributed graph system on spark. In: First International Workshop on Graph Data Management Experiences and Systems, pp. 1–6 (2013)

Deep Iris Compression

Ehsaneddin Jalilian$^{(\boxtimes)}$, Heinz Hofbauer, and Andreas Uhl

Department of Computer Science, University of Salzburg,
Jakob-haringer-straße 2, 5020 Salzburg, Austria
{ejalilian,hhofbaue,uhl}@cs.sbg.ac.at

Abstract. Lossy image compression can reduce the space and bandwidth required for image storage and transmission, which is increasinly in demand by the iris recognition systems developers. Deep learning techniques (*i.e.* CNN, and GAN networks) are quickly becoming a tool of choice for general image compression tasks. But some key quality criteria, such as high perceptual quality and the spatial precision of the images, need to be satisfied when applying such modules for iris images compression tasks. We investigate and evaluate the expediency of a deep learning based compression model for iris data compression. In particular, we relate rate-distortion performance as measured in PSNR, and Multi-scale Structural Similarity Index (MS-SSIM) to the recognition scores as obtained by a concrete recognition system. We further compare the model performance against a state-of-the-art deep learning base image compression technique as well as some lossy compression algorithms currently used for iris compression (namely: the current ISO standard JPEG2000, JPEG, H.265 derivate BPG, and WEBP), to figure out the most suited compression algorithm which can be used for this purpose. The experimental results show superior compression, and promising recognition performance of the model over all other techniques on different iris data.

Keywords: Deep learning · Iris compression · Iris recognition

1 Introduction

Efficient storage and rapid transmission of iris biometric records is a driving implementation factor in iris recognition systems (especially on low-powered mobile sensors and for portable devices). The International Organization for Standardization (ISO) specifies that iris biometric data should be recorded and stored in (raw) image form (ISO/IEC FDIS 19794-6), rather than in extracted templates (e.g. iris-codes). Such deployments can directly benefit from future improvements which can be easily incorporated, thus enabling more interoperability and vendor neutrality [5]. Image compression techniques can be generally divided into lossless and lossy compression. Lossless techniques compress an image by removing statistical redundancy while lossy compression algorithms typically use inexact approximations, and partial data discarding, to represent

© Springer Nature Switzerland AG 2021
A. Del Bimbo et al. (Eds.): ICPR 2020 Workshops, LNCS 12665, pp. 470–485, 2021.
https://doi.org/10.1007/978-3-030-68821-9_40

the content, exploiting the fact that the human eye is insensitive to certain visual features. Rapid development of deep learning theory and neural networks has introduced a new image compression paradigm to the lossy compression technology. Deep learning based methods mostly use convolutional neural networks (CNNs) to design image codecs. Benefiting from the strong learning ability of neural networks, these models can learn image characteristics through back propagation and conduct the compression of image information without too much prior knowledge. Recently, it was shown that deep learning can even synthesize a image using only a semantic segmentation map as input, thanks to the generative adversarial networks (GAN) technology [6]. This advocates the possibility of developing efficient image compression modules employing deep learning networks and the associated image synthesis. The major draw back of applying the GAN networks is their lack of spatial precision, which results in structural distortions in the reconstructed images. This could cripple the functionality of the key iris recognition modules such as the segmentation (which e.g. is based on circular features) and/or the feature extraction algorithms. Thus, the ability of the compression module to preserve the unique iris features in the reconstructed images, with high the spatial precision and perceptual quality, is required when it comes to iris image compression.

In this work we investigate the expediency of a deep semantic segmentation-based layered image compression (DSSLIC) model [3] for iris compression within a biometric recognition framework. The model leverages the power of GAN networks to encode the key iris features with high precision in the compressed images, while preserving the spatial precision and perceptual quality of the reconstructed iris images. The GAN network takes the segmentation map as the input and tries to learn the missing detail information of the up-sampled version of a compacted input image to minimize the distortion of the synthesized images. The segmentation map of the iris (raw) image is losslessly encoded as the base layer of the bit-stream. At the same time, the input image and the segmentation map are used by a deep network to obtain a low-dimensional compact representation of the input, which is encoded into the bit-stream as the first enhancement layer. The compact image and the segmentation map are then used to obtain a coarse reconstruction of the image. The residual between the input and the coarse reconstruction is encoded as the second enhancement layer in the bit-stream.

We use this model along with four other commonly used compression algorithms (BPG, JPEG2000, JPEG, WEBP) as well as a state-of-the-art deep learning based model to compress iris images in five well-known datasets. The visual quality of the compression in each cases is measured and compared against each other in terms of Peak Signal to Noise Ratio (PSNR), and Multi-scale Structural Similarity Index (MS-SSIM). Then the biometric recognition performance is evaluated, in terms of Equal Error Rate (EER), by using the compressed iris images in a regular iris biometric system. At the end, the compression and the corresponding recognition results are compared and carefully investigated to figure out a well suited compression algorithms to be employed in iris recognition systems.

2   Related Work

Classic Iris Image Compression: Numerous studies are conducted on iris image compression and recognition during the past decades (*e.g.* [5,9]). Grother [7] explored existing approaches and compared JPEG and JPEG2000 to provide a quantitative support to the revision of the ISO/IEC IS 19794-6, including a cropped format (IREX K3), masked and cropped image format (IREX K7), and an unsegmented polar format (IREX K16). Matschitsch *et al.* [15] investigated the impact of using different lossy compression algorithms on the matching accuracy of iris recognition systems, relating rate-distortion performance to the matching scores. They concluded that JPEG2000, SPIHT and PRVQ are almost equally well suited for iris compression. Korvath *et al.* [8] investigated the impact of dedicated lossless image codecs (lossless JPEG, JPEG-LS, PNG, and GIF), lossless variants of lossy codecs (JPEG2000, JPEG XR, and SPIHT), and some general purpose file compression schemes on the iris images.

Deep Image Compression: In recent years, number of learning based image compression methods have been proposed as well. Toderici *et al.* [24] proposed recurrent neural networks based on convolution and deconvolution long short-term memory (LSTM) to extract binary representations, which are then compressed with entropy coding. In [4], a model that involved a generalized divisive normalization (GDN)-based nonlinear analysis transform, a 2-uniform quantizer, and a nonlinear synthesis transform were proposed. Johnston *et al.* [12] used the structural similarity (SSIM) quality measure and spatially adaptive bit allocation to further improve the performance. Theis *et al.* [23] proposed an auto-encoder where they used smooth approximation instead of quantization to get different rates. Agustsson *et al.* [1], introduced a soft-to-hard vector quantization model along with a unified formulation for both the compression of deep learning models and image compression. The authors in [25] proposed a compression bit allocation algorithm to allow the recurrent neural network (RNN)-based compression network to hierarchically compress the images according to semantic importance maps. Li *et al.* [13] proposed a model based on image content weighting. They used the edge feature map, extracted by the convolution neural network, as the importance map of the original image. In [11], a compact convolutional neural network (ComCNN) and a reconstruction convolutional neural network (RecCNN), were used to encode and decode the original image, respectively. An innovative algorithm solves the non-differentiated calculation in the quantization rounding function to achieve a backward propagation gradient in the standard image algorithm. In [14] the authors combined image compression and classification to reconstruct the images and generate corresponding semantic representations at the same time. Mantzer *et al.* [16] proposed a conditional probability models for deep image compression (CPDIC), focusing on improving the entropy rate of the latent image representation using a context model (a 3D-CNN which learns a conditional probability model of the latent distribution of the auto-encoder). During training the auto-encoder makes use of the context model to estimate the entropy of its representation, and the context model

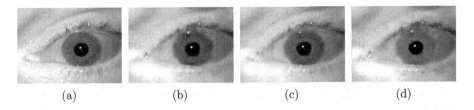

Fig. 1. An iris image (a) and its corresponding output using a GAN based model (b), along with their difference image (c), and the overlaid ground-truth (d)

is concurrently updated to learn the dependencies between the symbols in the latent representation.

Some recent works used generative adversarial networks (GAN) in their learning-based image compression schemes. Santurkar *et al.* [21], used a discriminator to help training an decoder. They used perceptual loss based on the feature map of an, ImageNet-pretrained, AlexNet, although only low-resolution image coding results were reported. Ripple *et al.* [20] embedded an auto-encoder in a GAN framework in which the feature extraction adopted a pyramid of inter-scale alignments. They considered the target and its reconstruction jointly as a single example and, instead of producing an output for classification at the last layers of the pipeline, accumulated scalar outputs along branches constructed at different depths. An average of these scalars was used as the final value provided to a sigmoid function. The discriminator also extracted outputs from different layers, similar to the pyramid feature generation. Augustesson *et al.* [2] proposed a segmentation map-based image synthesis model based on the GAN networks operating at extremely low bitrates. The framework combines an encoder, decoder/generator and a multi-scale discriminator, which are trained jointly for a generative learned compression objective. The main draw back of these models (which operate directly on the input image) is that they generate outputs which have some structural distortions and lack the sufficient spatial precision. In fact, as already mentioned, such distortions will change the iris structure and can cause the different system modules to fail. Figure 1 shows a sample iris image (Fig. 1a) (from the Notredame iris dataset, as used in this work), and its compressed version (Fig. 1b), using the last GAN based model, along with their difference image (Fig. 1c), and the overlaid ground-truth mask (Fig. 1d). Gray regions in the difference image show where the two images have the same intensities, and magenta and green regions show where the intensities are different. Also the overlaid ground-truth mask shows how the actual iris outer and inner boundaries (as specified by the mask) are distorted in the compressed (reconstructed) image.

3   Deep Compression Model

Figure 2 illustrates the overall scheme of the model used in this work, which is derived from the model already proposed in [3]. As a key distinction to the current GAN based models, the embedded GAN network in this model does not operate directly on the input the iris image. Instead it takes the segmentation map as the input and tries to learn the missing detail information of the up-sampled version of the compacted input image to minimize the distortion of the synthesized images. This is made practical due to the recent advancement in deep learning techniques which have made it easy to access such segmentations with very high accuracy and in a timely manner (*i.e.* [10]). In fact here we didn't use a segmentation network in our model, and fed the manually segmented labels directly to the model instead. Doing so we helped to improve the models performance by introducing more accurate labeling data to the model. The encoder includes two deep learning networks: CompNet and FiNet (GAN-based network). An input iris image is fed into the ComNet, while the segmentation map is encoded to serve as side information to this network for generating a low-dimensional version of the original image. Both the segmentation map and compact version are losslessly encoded using the FLIF codec [22], which is a state-of-the-art lossless image codec. Given the segmentation map and up-sampled compact image, the FiNet tries to obtain a high-quality reconstruction of the input image. Note that although GAN-based synthesized images from segmentation maps are visually appealing their details can be quite different from the original images. To minimize the distortion of the synthesized images the up-sampled version of the compact image, as an additional input, is added to it. In this way the FiNet is trained to learn the missing detail information of the up-sampled version of a compact image with respect to the input image, which in turn controls the output of the GAN network. After adding the up-sampled version of the compact image and the FiNet's output we get a better estimate of the input. The residual difference between the input and the estimate is then obtained and encoded by a lossy codec (H.265/HEVC intra coding-based BPG). In order to deal with negative values, the residual image is re-scaled to [0, 255] with a min-max normalization before encoding. The min and max values are also sent to decoder for inverse scaling. In this scheme the segmentation map serves as the base layer and the compact image and the residual are the first and second enhancement layers respectively. At the decoder side the segmentation map and the compact representation are decoded to be used by the FiNet to get an estimate of the input image. The output of FiNet is then added to the decoded residual image to get the reconstructed image as output.

4   Experimental Framework

Datasets: We used five different iris datasets in our experiments: The Notredame dataset (including 835 iris images of 30 different subjects)[1]. The Casia4i dataset (containing 2640 iris images of 249 subjects)[2]. The IITD dataset

---

[1] https://sites.google.com/a/nd.edu/public-cvrl/data-sets.
[2] http://biometrics.idealtest.org.

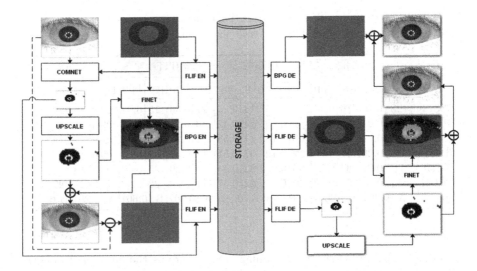

Fig. 2. The deep learning based iris compression model

(containing 2240 iris images of 224 subjects)[3]. The Casia5a dataset (including 1880 images of both eyes of 94 users)[4].

Compression Algorithms: To evaluate and compare the model performance against some popular and state-of-the-art lossy compression algorithms we considered: JPEG, the current ISO standard JPEG2000 (J2K), the H.265 derived BPG, the WEBP algorithms, and a deep learning based image compression model termed Conditional Probability Models for Deep Image Compression (CPDIC) [16]. The overall compression model consists of an encoder, a quantizer, and a decoder. The encoder $E : \mathbb{R}^d \to \mathbb{R}^m$ maps an input image to a latent representation y which is in form of a 3D feature map. The encoder architecture consists of convolution and ReLU layers combined with 15 Residual Blocks, with skip connection between every third layer. The quantizer $Q : \mathbb{R} \to C$ then discretized the coordinates of the latent representation (y) to the $L = |P|$ centers, which can then be losslessly encoded into the bit-stream. Specifically, given centers $P = \{p_1, \ldots, p_L\} \subset \mathbb{R}$, the quantizer uses nearest neighbor assignments to compute

$$\tilde{y}_i = Q(y_i) := argmin_j ||y_i - p_j||, \tag{1}$$

relying on the following differentiable soft quantization:

$$\tilde{y}_i = \sum_{j=1}^{L} \frac{exp(-\sigma||y_i - p_j||)}{\sum_{l=1}^{L} exp(-\sigma||y_i - p_l||)} p_j. \tag{2}$$

---

[3] http://www4.comp.polyu.edu.hk/~csajaykr/database.php.
[4] http://www.biometrics.idealtest.org.

Table 1. Selected compression parameters (par) and their corresponding compression performance in bits per pixel (bpp) for each algorithm.

Dataset	Casia4i				Casia5a				IITD				Notredame			
Method	par	bpp	par	bpp	par	bpp	par	bpp	par	bpp	par	bpp	par	bpp	par	bpp
DSSLIC	23	0.20	16	0.44	23	0.16	14	0.45	27	0.30	19	0.53	23	0.16	14	0.51
BPG	37	0.21	30	0.54	30	0.19	24	0.42	33	0.29	26	0.60	33	0.18	24	0.55
J2K	35	0.23	21	0.55	45	0.18	14	0.55	28	0.27	14	0.55	45	0.18	14	0.55
JPEG	23	0.20	57	0.50	12	0.19	57	0.51	17	0.30	57	0.53	09	0.18	57	0.58
WEBP	1	0.21	82	0.44	45	0.20	82	0.44	1	0.29	45	0.57	25	0.19	82	0.57
CPDIC	11	0.29	22	0.60	11	0.27	22	0.57	11	0.29	22	0.60	11	0.27	22	0.57
bpp	A (0.30)		B (0.60)		A (0.30)		B (0.60)		A (0.30)		B (0.60)		A (0.30)		B (0.60)	

The decoder D, which has a similar architecture as the encoder, forms the reconstructed image from the quantized latent representation, which is in turn (losslessy) decoded from the bit-stream

Metrics and Measures: To measure the compression performance: Peak Signal-to-Noise Ratio (PSNR), which is a mathematical measure of image quality based on the pixel difference between input images, and Multi-Scale Structural Similarity Index Measure (MS-SSIM) are used. Unlike in Structural Similarity Index Measure (SSIM), where variation in luminance, contrast and structure of "single-scale" input images are compared, MS-SSIM alliteratively down-samples the input images up to M scales. At each scale, the contrast comparison and the structure comparison are calculated. The luminescence comparison is computed only at scale M, and the final MS-SSIM evaluation is obtained by combining the measurements at different scales [26]. As an overall measure of biometric recognition performance the Equal Error Rate (EER) was chosen. It is the operation point on the receiver operating characteristic curse where the false non-match rate and the false match rate are equal.

Recognition Pipeline: We used the contrast adjusted Hough transform (CAHT) [18], and Osiris [17], for iris segmentation, local Gabor filters (LG) for feature extraction, and the Hamming distance with rotation correction for matching. Apart from the Osiris the algorithms from the USIT toolkit [19] were used.

5   Experiments and Analysis

To fit the fixed network dimensions all images are re-scaled to $256 \times 512 \times 1$. Since the networks are trained on RGB format we cloned each image two times to generate 3 channel (RGB) images ($256 \times 512 \times 3$). We applied a cross-fold scheme to train the model. First we partitioned each dataset into two equal parts and then trained and tested the model alternatively on each partition. Doing so, we tested the networks on all samples in each dataset without overlapping training

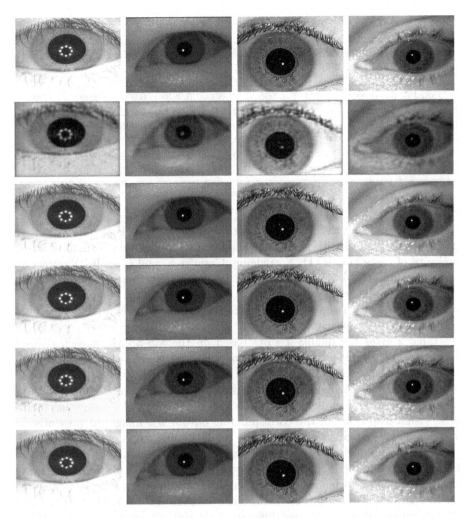

Fig. 3. Samples of highly (A) compressed iris images from the Casia4i, Casia5a, IITD, and Notredame datasets, per column respectively, using DSSLIC, CPDIC, BPG, J2K, JPEG and WEB algorithms per row respectively

and testing sets. We set the down-scaling factor $\alpha = 8$ to get the compact representation of the inputs. All models were jointly trained for 250 epochs with mini-batch stochastic gradient descent (SGD) and a mini-batch sizes of 2 and 8 respectively. To address the fixed bandwidth/storage compression limit requirement we set two bandwidth limits of 0.30 (A) and 0.60 (B), corresponding to the higher and the lower compression levels respectively, for each dataset in terms of bit-per-pixel (bpp). It should be noted that not all algorithms allow to set the exact output file size. Thus, we selected the compression parameter for each algorithm so that the achieved bpp of the resulting compressed images are

Table 2. Average MS-SSM scores using high (A) and low (B) compression levels

Dataset	Casia4i		Casia5a		IITD		Notredame	
Compress	B	A	B	A	B	A	B	A
DSSLIC	0.998	0.994	0.995	0.989	0.998	0.994	0.997	0.990
BPG	0.996	0.988	0.994	0.985	0.997	0.992	0.996	0.988
J2K	0.991	0.966	0.992	0.970	0.987	0.945	0.988	0.964
JPEG	0.993	0.950	0.988	0.931	0.994	0.957	0.991	0.949
WEBP	0.993	0.982	0.991	0.965	0.995	0.987	0.992	0.981
CPDIC	0.897	0.889	0.844	0.852	0.881	0.875	0.909	0.902

equal to or less than the fixed bandwidth/storage limit. It is also important to note that the resulting file sizes using the DSSLIC model are the smallest in the majority of cases (*i.e.* IITD, Notredame, Casia5a-A, and Casia4i-B) among all the algorithms. Table 1 shows the selected compression parameters (par) and the resulting bpps per algorithm and dataset. Samples of the compressed images in each dataset using the compression methods used are presented in Fig. 3 per column and row respectively.

Table 2 gives the quality results based on the MS-SSIM for each dataset (averaged over all images) for the different compression algorithms. The DSSLIC model shows superior performance over all other codecs for both compression levels considered. This is a quite remarkable result given that the files produces by the DSSLIC are smaller in size than files produces by the competing methods. Visual inspection of the corresponding output iris images as presented in the Fig. 3 (first column) shows that the model is able to preserve spatial precision and the uniqueness of the iris features very well. Across all datasets, and both compression settings, BPG is always the second-best and CPDIC is always the worst. The performance of the other three algorithms are varies depending on the dataset. The performance, in terms of rank, of the WEBP, JPEG and J2k algorithms also can vary for different compression levels (on Notredame and Casia4i). While the order of performance for the higher compression level (A) on these datasets is: WEBP, J2k, JPEG, the order of performance for the lower

Table 3. Average PSNR scores using high (A) and low (B) compression levels

Dataset	Casia4i		Casia5a		IITD		Notredame	
Compress	B	A	B	A	B	A	B	A
DSSLIC	49.1	44.0	45.2	41.6	45.5	41.3	45.7	40.3
BPG	44.5	39.8	44.0	40.9	44.7	40.5	43.5	40.0
J2K	41.8	35.5	43.1	37.9	40.5	34.4	41.1	35.5
JPEG	39.7	33.0	39.6	32.4	39.6	32.5	39.1	32.5
WEBP	41.0	37.0	41.8	37.5	41.5	37.6	41.0	37.2
CPDIC	16.1	16.0	18.7	18.7	17.8	17.8	16.8	16.4

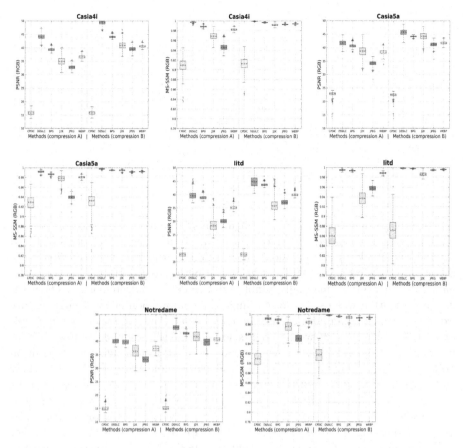

Fig. 4. Compression performance in terms of PSNR and MS-SSIM for the high (left side of the graphs) and low (right side of the graphs) compression levels

compression level (B) is: WEBP, JPEG, then J2k. Considering the average performance of each algorithm on the different dataset the order of performance (after DSSLIC and BPG) is: WEBP, J2k, and JPEG. Table 3 shows the corresponding results for each dataset (averaged over all images)in terms of PSNR. The superior performance of DSSLIC over the other algorithms is visible in these results too. Likewise, BPG ranks the second-best and CPDIC ranks the worst in terms of peak signal-to-noise ratio. Despite slight differences in the ranking orders (compared to those of the MS-SSM experiments) the other algorithms are also ranked the same when considering the average performance: WEBP, J2K, then JPEG. Figure 4 presents further details about the experimental results in the form of box-plots for each dataset. Unsurprisingly, the higher (left in the graphs) compression rate results in a decreases in performance over all datasets and algorithms (including DSSLIC).

Table 4. EERs for the different datasets using the CAHT algorithm

Dataset	Casia4i		Casia5a		IITD		Notredame	
Compress	B	A	B	A	B	A	B	A
DSSLIC	1.2	1.0	21.1	21.2	1.4	1.8	29.9	29.9
BPG	1.0	1.2	21.6	21.3	1.6	2.4	29.6	30.3
J2K	1.1	1.3	20.6	22.3	2.0	2.6	30.0	30.1
JPEG	1.2	2.8	20.6	26.1	1.9	2.5	29.9	32.4
WEBP	1.2	1.7	21.5	23.0	2.0	2.6	30.3	31.5
CPDIC	3.4	4.0	28.8	29.4	2.3	2.8	32.5	34.1

Next, we applied the biometric recognition system to all obtained compressed iris images and evaluated the biometric comparison accuracy, in terms of EER, for the two levels of compression. In addition to the two segmentation algorithms used, Osiris and CAHT, we used the perfect segmentation produced by manual segmentation (manually annotated segmentation drop masks). The manual segmentation was used to disentangle the compression effect on iris texture from the segmentation performance on compressed data, and their possible failures. Tables 4 and 5 show the results for the CAHT segmentation and manual segmentation respectively. When using the CAHT segmentation recognition does not work at all for the Casia5a and Notredame datasets. For the IITD and Casia4i data the DSSLIC compression frequently shows the best performance, especially for the high compression level. When using manual segmentation results (Table 5), recognition still does not work for Notredame data, while for the remaining datasets, DSSLIC results are never surpassed by any other compression scheme. Given the fact that the DSSLIC also produces the smallest actual files these results imply that DSSLIC compression is able to preserve iris texture very well. Certainly better than the other algorithms under test, as the segmentation effects can ruled out due to manual segmentation. Table 6 shows the results when the OSIRIS algorithm is used for segmentation. ecognition on the Notredame data does not work either, but otherwise the ranking of the

Table 5. EERs for the different datasets using manual masks

Dataset	Casia4i		Casia5a		IITD		Notredame	
Compress	B	A	B	A	B	A	A	B
DSSLIC	0.4	0.4	2.5	2.9	0.4	0.5	23.8	23.9
BPG	0.4	0.6	2.9	3.9	0.4	0.5	23.8	23.9
J2K	0.4	0.6	2.7	5.1	0.4	0.5	23.8	24.0
JPEG	0.5	1.7	3.0	14.0	0.4	0.5	23.8	25.7
WEBP	0.5	0.7	3.4	5.4	0.4	0.5	24.0	24.6
CPDIC	1.6	2.0	15.1	18.2	0.5	0.6	26.6	29.3

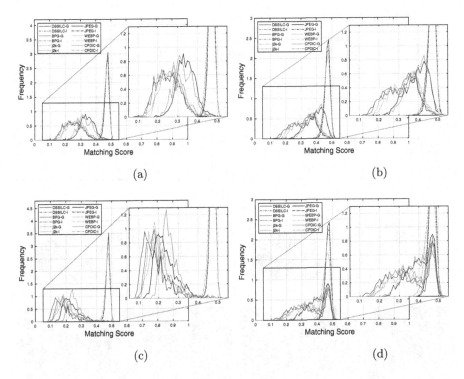

Fig. 5. Genuine and impostor distributions of the different compression methods for Casi4i (a), Casi5a (b), IITD (c), and Notredame (d) when applying the manual drop masks

algorithms is fairly different. DSSLIC is the best performer only for Casia5a, while it is actually the worst performing algorithm on the IITD dataset. When comparing CAHT and OSIRIS segmentation results it's clear that the segmentation methods, and the logic behind them, react quite differently to the artifacts in the compressed images, and thus deliver very different results considering identical compressed iris images. Overall, the clearly higher rate-distortion compression performance of the DSSLIC algorithm is **not** directly translated into best recognition accuracy, except where a manual segmentation is used.

It is also interesting that the recognition performance of CPDIC on Casi5a is much lower compared to other compression algorithms on the same dataset. When inspecting the iris images generated by this algorithm, along with their corresponding iris features extracted, we noticed some artifacts which were distributed uniformly over all the images in a block-like pattern. These artifacts are more severe and intense in areas of high texture, specifically the iris texture areas. For an example of this behavior see Fig. 6 where an image from the Notredame datasets is compared to an image from the Casia5a dataset. This effect seems to be due to the different performance of the encoder network on the input iris images when generating the latent representations combined with

Table 6. EERs for different the datasets using the Osiris algorithm

Dataset	Casia4i		Casia5a		IITD		Notredame	
Compress	B	A	B	A	B	A	A	B
DSSLIC	1.1	1.0	2.0	2.2	0.7	0.8	25.2	25.5
BPG	0.9	1.0	2.0	2.5	0.3	0.3	26.9	26.4
J2K	0.8	0.9	2.0	3.1	0.4	0.7	25.7	25.1
JPEG	0.8	1.8	2.4	9.7	0.5	0.6	24.7	24.7
WEBP	0.8	0.9	2.9	4.0	0.4	0.4	25.1	25.0
CPDIC	2.2	2.6	15.9	19.2	0.6	0.6	26.1	27.8

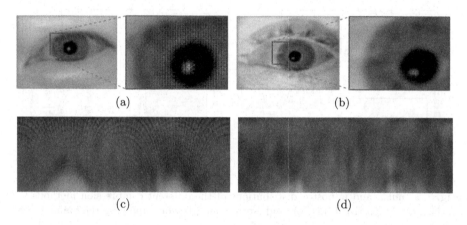

(a)   (b)

(c)   (d)

Fig. 6. A sample iris image in the Casia5a dataset (a) vs a sample image in the Notredame datasets (b), both generated by CPDIC algorithm, and their corresponding normalized outputs (c and d) respectively

the subsequent quantization technique. The persistence of these artifacts over all images of the Casia5a dataset clearly undermined the recognition performance.

In order to clarify how the quality of the images generated by different compression algorithms affect the actual recognition performance we analysed the distribution of the genuine and impostor scores obtained using each algorithm and dataset. Figure 5 shows the genuine and impostor distributions for the different compression methods for each dataset when using the manual drop masks (to exclude the influence of segmentation errors). Each pair of curves (genuine and impostor) are indicated by color while linetype distinguishes between impostor (dash-dotted) and genuine (solid). The impostor curves remains virtually unchanged, while the genuine curves fluctuate almost in all cases. This leads us to the argument that the compression process affects the genuine scores, by introducing artifacts into the iris images which alter the distinct patterns that are present in the genuine samples, making the compressed images more dissimilar. This effect appears as higher fluctuation in genuine scores, and thus EERs.

6   Conclusion

We investigated the performance of a deep learning model (DSSLIC) for iris image compression in terms of rate-distortion and recognition accuracy. The model showed superior compression performance over all other algorithms using different datasets and compression rates. Unlike the other algorithms, the DSSLIC model was able to cope with iris images with complex feature characteristic, and possessed stable performance on all different types of iris data. The results of the recognition experiments showed that the higher compression performance of the DSSLIC algorithm is directly translated into better recognition rates in majority of the cases. Yet, further experiments with an alternative segmentation algorithm (Osiris) revealed that the segmentation techniques, and the logic used in them, could react quiet differently to the compress images. In the case of Osiris the segmentation performance was degraded considerably. The results obtained using the manual drop masks supported this argument. The experiments also showed that an increase in compression results in reduction of recognition performance in aa majority of cases. Analysis of the genuine and the impostor scores indicated that compression process introduces artifacts into the iris images which alter the distinct patterns that are present in the genuine samples, making the compressed images more dissimilar. Overall, the results showed that the presented deep learning based model is capable of efficient iris image compression for the use in an iris biometric recognition system.

Acknowledgment. This project was partly funded from the FFG KIRAS project AUTFingerATM under grant No. 864785 and the FWF project "Advanced Methods and Applications for Fingervein Recognition" under grant No. P 32201-NBL.

References

1. Agustsson, E., et al.: Soft-to-hard vector quantization for end-to-end learned compression of images and neural networks. CoRR abs/1704.00648 (2017)
2. Agustsson, E., Tschannen, M., Mentzer, F., Timofte, R., Gool, L.V.: Generative adversarial networks for extreme learned image compression. In: Proceedings of the IEEE International Conference on Computer Vision, pp. 221–231 (2019)
3. Akbari, M., Liang, J., Han, J.: DSSLIC: deep semantic segmentation-based layered image compression. In: IEEE International Conference on Acoustics, Speech and Signal Processing (ICASSP), pp. 2042–2046. IEEE (2019)
4. Ballé, J., Laparra, V., P-Simoncelli, E.: End-to-end optimized image compression. In: International Conference on Learning Representations (ICLR), Toulon, France, April 2017
5. Daugman, J., Downing, C.: Effect of severe image compression on iris recognition performance. IEEE Trans. Inf. Forensics Secur. **3**(1), 52–61 (2008)

6. Goodfellow, I., et al.: Generative adversarial nets. In: Advances in Neural Information Processing Systems, pp. 2672–2680 (2014)

7. Grother, P.: Quantitative standardization of iris image formats. biometrics and electronic signatures (BIOSIG) (2009)

8. Horvath, K., Stögner, H., Uhl, A., Weinhandel, G.: Lossless compression of polar iris image data. In: Vitrià, J., Sanches, J.M., Hernández, M. (eds.) IbPRIA 2011. LNCS, vol. 6669, pp. 329–337. Springer, Heidelberg (2011). https://doi.org/10.1007/978-3-642-21257-4_41

9. Ives, R., Bishop, D., Du, Y., Belcher, C.: Iris recognition: The consequences of image compression. EURASIP J. Adv. Signal Process. (1) (2010)

10. Jalilian, E., Uhl, A.: Iris segmentation using fully convolutional encoder–decoder networks. In: Bhanu, B., Kumar, A. (eds.) Deep Learning for Biometrics. ACVPR, pp. 133–155. Springer, Cham (2017). https://doi.org/10.1007/978-3-319-61657-5_6

11. Jiang, F., Tao, W., Liu, S., Ren, J., Guo, X., Zhao, D.: An end-to-end compression framework based on convolutional neural networks. IEEE Trans. Circuits Syst. Video Technol. **28**(10), 3007–3018 (2017)

12. Johnston, N., et al.: Improved lossy image compression with priming and spatially adaptive bit rates for recurrent networks. In: Proceedings of the IEEE Conference on Computer Vision and Pattern Recognition, pp. 4385–4393 (2018)

13. Li, M., Zuo, W., Gu, S., Zhao, D., Zhang, D.: Learning convolutional networks for content-weighted image compression. In: Proceedings of the IEEE Conference on Computer Vision and Pattern Recognition, pp. 3214–3223 (2018)

14. Luo, S., Yang, Y., Yin, Y., Shen, C., Zhao, Y., Song, M.: DeepSIC: deep semantic image compression. In: Cheng, L., Leung, A.C.S., Ozawa, S. (eds.) ICONIP 2018. LNCS, vol. 11301, pp. 96–106. Springer, Cham (2018). https://doi.org/10.1007/978-3-030-04167-0_9

15. Matschitsch, S., Tschinder, M., Uhl, A.: Comparison of compression algorithms' impact on iris recognition accuracy. In: International Conference on Biometrics, pp. 232–241 (2007)

16. Mentzer, F., Agustsson, E., Tschannen, M., Timofte, R., Gool, L.V.: Conditional probability models for deep image compression. In: IEEE/CVF Conference on Computer Vision and Pattern Recognition, pp. 4394–4402 (2018)

17. Othman, N., Dorizzi, B., Garcia-Salicetti, S.: Osiris: an open source iris recognition software. Pattern Recogn. Lett. **82**, 124–131 (2016)

18. Rathgeb, C., Uhl, A., Wild, P.: Iris Recognition: From Segmentation to Template Security. Advances in Information Security, vol. 59. Springer, New York (2013). https://doi.org/10.1007/978-1-4614-5571-4

19. Rathgeb, C., Uhl, A., Wild, P., Hofbauer, H.: Design decisions for an iris recognition SDK. In: Bowyer, K.W., Burge, M.J. (eds.) Handbook of Iris Recognition. ACVPR, pp. 359–396. Springer, London (2016). https://doi.org/10.1007/978-1-4471-6784-6_16

20. Rippel, O., Bourdev, L.: Real-time adaptive image compression. In: Precup, D., Teh, Y.W. (eds.) Proceedings of the 34th International Conference on Machine Learning. Proceedings of Machine Learning Research, vol. 70. PMLR, International Convention Centre, Sydney, Australia, 06–11 August 2017, pp. 2922–2930 (2017)

21. Santurkar, S., Budden, D., Shavit, N.: Generative compression. In: 2018 Picture Coding Symposium (PCS), pp. 258–262 (2018)

22. Sneyers, J., Wuille, P.: FLIF: free lossless image format based on maniac compression. In: IEEE International Conference on Image Processing, pp. 66–70, September 2016

23. Theis, L., Shi, W., Cunningham, A., Huszár, F.: Lossy image compression with compressive autoencoders. In: International Conference on Learning Representations (2017)
24. Toderici, G., et al.: Variable rate image compression with recurrent neural networks. In: International Conference on Learning Representations (2016)
25. Wang, C., Han, Y., Wang, W.: An end-to-end deep learning image compression framework based on semantic analysis. Appl. Sci. $9(17)$, 3580 (2019)
26. Wang, Z., P-Simoncelli, E., C-Bovik, A.: Multiscale structural similarity for image quality assessment. In: The Thrity-Seventh Asilomar Conference on Signals, Systems & Computers, 2003, vol. 2, pp. 1398–1402. IEEE (2003)

IFEPE: On the Impact of Facial Expression in Head Pose Estimation

Carmen Bisogni$^{(\boxtimes)}$ and Chiara Pero

Department of Computer Science, University of Salerno,
Via Giovanni Paolo II, 132 Fisciano, Salerno, Italy
{cbisogni,cpero}@unisa.it

Abstract. The Head Pose Estimation (HPE) is the study of the angular rotations of the head along the Pitch, Yaw, and Roll axes. Widely used in facial involving methods, as face frontalization, driver attention and best surveillance frame selection, is strongly related to facial features. In this study we examine the impact of facial expressions (FE) on HPE and, in particular, we put in relation the axis more affected by the error when a specific facial expression is observable. The HPE method chosen for this purpose is based on the Partitioned Iterated Function System (PIFS). For its construction this method is dependent on the facial appearance and self-similarity. Basing on this, and using a FER network, we observed that there is an evident relation between facial expressions and pose errors. This relation go thought the facial keypoints distances and can be discriminated along the three axes, by providing an estimate of the percentages of variation in errors related to a percentage of variation in distances.

Keywords: Head pose estimation · Facial expressions · PIFS · Fractal encoding · CNN

1 Introduction

Head movements constitute an intrinsic characteristic of an individual and provide crucial information such as subject's intentions and attention. In the past decade, numerous applications have been related to Head Pose Estimation (HPE) analysis, i.e assisted technologies, video-surveillance or artificial intelligence. According to literature review, HPE analysis extrapolates a great amount of information from head gestures and improve the accuracy of recognition and expression of a subject. Indeed, like head orientation, an individual's facial expressions represent also an important component of non-verbal communication [3,21]. Emotional expressions define a facial action unit through which a human's mood/mental state is understood.

In this paper, our aim is to examine the impact of facial expressions on head position and orientation estimations. The main contributions of this study are:

- the analysis of the facial keypoints distances variations related to facial expressions;

A. Del Bimbo et al. (Eds.): ICPR 2020 Workshops, LNCS 12665, pp. 486–500, 2021.
https://doi.org/10.1007/978-3-030-68821-9_41

- the analysis of HPE error variations respect to facial expressions;
- the relationship between HPE error and distances variations.

The following Subsects. 1.1 and 1.2 analyze in details the state-of-art of HPE strategies and FER systems. Section 2 describes, in order, the method chosen to perform HPE, the algorithm adopted to develop the facial expression recognition and the datasets used in the experimental evaluation. Section 3 includes the obtained results and, consequently, the relationship between HPE and FER. Finally, Sect. 4 concludes our research and defines the future lines.

1.1 Head Pose Estimation

Head pose estimation represents an important aspect in computer vision field. Applications may include video surveillance, assisted living, advanced driver assistance systems (ADAS), etc. This analysis can also provide extra information in order to improve identity or expression recognition accuracy of a subject [37]. In HPE, the angles of head rotations can be defined in different forms. In literature, the most commonly representation adopted is the Euler angle. A 3D vector includes the head rotations and, in particular, the angles of *yaw*, *pitch* and *roll*. Figure 1 shows the x, y, and z-axis respectively. So, HPE from a sample frame or image essentially apply for learning a mapping among 2D and 3D spaces.

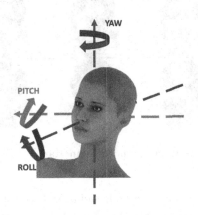

Fig. 1. Head rotation expressed in yaw, pitch and roll angles.

According to [26] and [10], there is a large amount of studies on HPE topic; most of the research has focused on machine learning approaches and, more specifically, on CNN models, particularly suited to image processing. Preliminary works [2,28] analyse, respectively, Gaussian processes and PLS Regression techniques performed on classifiers (i.e Support Vector Machines, SVMs). More recently, in [27] Ranjan et al. adopt a deep CNN model to extract and individuate keypoints locations from the region-of-interest, and, subsequently, predict the pose estimation and gender of an individual. As opposite to the above-mentioned CNN models, there are some works not based on deep learning approaches. In [1], the HPE is implemented thought a quad-tree based model; Barra et al. [5] detect the 68 facial landmarks and, after whose, they applies a web-shaped model in order to detect the specific face sector to which each landmark belongs. In this paper, the strategy chosen to estimate the head rotation, namely HP^{2}IFS, is the one proposed in [8] (See Sect. 2.1).

1.2   Facial Expression Recognition

In recent years, research in neuroscience has placed particular attention on the processing of *facial expressions*, which represent an important component of non-verbal communication. In the fields of Computer Vision and Pattern Recognition, various systems have been analyzed in order to obtain expression information from human facial representation. In 1971, P. Ekman and W. V. Friesen [12] asserted that anger, disgust, fear, happiness, sadness and surprise represented the six basic emotions of an individual (besides neutral); later they also included contempt. Figure 2 illustrates image samples from a public controlled benchmark for evaluating FER systems.

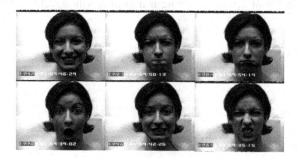

Fig. 2. Image samples from Extended Cohn–Kanade (CK+) database [23].

Characteristics such as face, speech and even text constitute important features to perform emotion recognition. Among these, facial expressions are the most examined, as they contain useful functions for recognition and it is possible to obtain a large set of data. FER systems can be divided into two main group: static 2D images and 3D dynamic image sequences. In the first case, the feature vector include only information of the current image sample. In dynamic sequences, the temporal information are used to identify the expression captured from one or more frames [22]. Earlier works on emotions recognition are characterized by a traditional approach, which can be divided into two phases: extraction of the characteristics from the reference images and the use of a classifier (for example SVM, Neural network, Random Forest) in order to detect emotions. The techniques adopted in preliminary studies include the

Histogram of Oriented Gradients (HOG) [15], Local Binary Patterns (LBP) [31], Gabor wavelets [6] and Haar features [35]. With the emergence of deep learning-based approaches, and in particular of convolutional neural networks for image classification, several studies have performed CNN models for facial expression recognition [17,19,24]; those approaches fuse the three phases of a FER system (learning, features selection and classification) in one single step. Recently, the researches for FER have also focused on uncontrolled environments (e.g. not frontal face, non-cooperative subjects, partial occlusions of facial region, and others), which is still a challenging problem. In fact, as regards the head pose estimation and non-frontal images, studies conducted have highlighted that the recognition rates decrease as a function of pitch and yaw angles [17,20].

2   Methods and Materials

To extract relevant experimental information from the relations between facial expression and head pose, we have chosen two methods. The HPE method is called HP^{2}IFS, and the facial expression method is called FMPN-FER. Both methods are recent (2020 and 2019, respectively) and reached high performances in literature when compared to the state of the art. Other reasons related to the choose of this two particular methods, are exposed in the following sections. In addition, we also present, in the following, the datasets used to perform the experiments of our study.

2.1   HP^{2}IFS for Head Pose Estimation

The method chosen to perform HPE is quite new and proposed in [8]. This method is based on the concept of Partition Iterated Function Systems (PIFS) and, consequently, on fractal compression. Fractal theory was introduced by Benoit B. Mandelbrot in early 1980s [4]. He starts from the observation that there are self-similarity structures in nature, called *fractals*, which have almost identical characteristics at any level of detail they are enlarged. Originally introduced in image compression tasks, PIFS allow to reconstruct an image using self-similarities in the image itself. So, they are adopted to evaluate the self-similarity of two pose images conducting to a similar head rotation. The main concept of PIFS are:

- Domain blocks, obtained splitting the original image in non-overlapping blocks of size $N \times N$, where we call R each block.
- Range blocks, obtained splitting the original image in overlapping blocks of size $2N \times 2N$, where we call D each block.
- Contractive transformation, defined as an affine transformation f obtained combining variation in rotation, translation, brightness and contrast. They are called contractive because the distance d between two points x, y became smaller after the transformation, following the rule:

$$d(f(x), f(y)) \leq kd(x, y) \tag{1}$$

with $0 < k < 1$.

From those basic definitions, an IFS can be defines as a set of affine transformation f_i that act as contractive functions. Their purpose is to match Domain Blocks in Range Blocks to perform the image compression. The descriptions storing of these transformations f_i constitute the result of fractal compression. In the case of HPE, the such obtained encode is used to compare head poses and to obtain the must similar one.

As can be seen in Fig. 3, the overall steps of the HP^{2}IFS method are:

1. *Face detection and landmark prediction.* The face is detected using the Viola-Jones algorithm [33], based on the AdaBoost algorithm. Then the landmarks are predicted on the face by the algorithm in [18], using HOG and SVM. The resulting 68 landmarks are used to build a mask of the face.
2. *Fractal encoding.* By the definitions previously introduced, the fractal encoding of the image is obtained, as a matrix, then converted in an array.
3. *Comparisons.* The fractal array is then compared with the ones stored, representing the reference model. The metric used in this case is the Hamming Distance [14].

The resulting angles are expressed in pitch, yaw and roll as usual.

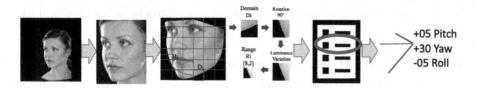

Fig. 3. Overall framework of HP^{2}IFS.

This algorithm has been tested on the two must popular HP annotated datasets in literature, BIWI and AFLW2000. BIWI [13] is a dataset registered under controlled condition. Its head pose were captured by a Kinect 1 for a total of 20 subjects and about 15K images. AFLW2000 [39] is a subset of AFLW of 2000 elements, with more accurate pose annotations. Differently from BIWI, AFLW2000 is a collection of face images publicly available and under uncontrolled environment. This means that BIWI does not contain facial expression variation in the majority of cases, and AFLW2000 contain facial expression variations in almost all cases.

To better understand and evaluate the behaviour of this algorithm, in Table 1 we report the mean errors on BIWI and AFLW, the Mean Absolute Error (MAE), and the percentage of faces with error less than fixed angular values.

As can be seen, this method has very low errors, for this reason has been chosen in this kind of analysis. In addition, since it is based on self-similarity, it will be of particular interest in the analysis of the errors variation depending on facial expression. Another characteristic of this method is that, even if the errors are in general low, there is a visible difference of errors along the axes.

Table 1. Errors of the HP²IFS algorithm on BIWI and AFLW. As can be seen, the mean errors reflect the behavior of the errors distribution along the axes.

Errors/Datasets	BIWI	AFLW
Err_Yaw(°)	4.05	6.28
Err_Pitch(°)	6.23	7.46
Err_Roll(°)	3.30	5.53
MAE(°)	4.52	6.42
Zero_Errors	55%Y-35%P-71%R	25%P-30%YR
Err_Yaw<10°	97%	87%
Err_Pitch<10°	95%	81%
Err_Roll<10°	99.9%	92%

Methods using DNNs, as in [34,36] and [16], reach in some cases few better performances, however for BIWI or AFLW2000 or both, they presents an angular error difference less than 1° along the three axis. For this reason, HP²IFS is preferable to enhance the axis error difference in our facial expression variation analysis.

2.2 FMPN-FER for Facial Expression Recognition

Differently from the HP²IFS algorithm, to perform the facial expression recognition, we prefer a DNN based algorithm. This is because it results more fast than the training-free algorithms and achieve better results. The method used is presented in [9]. FMPN-FER uses three networks:

- *Facial Motion Mask Generator (FMG).* The aim of FMG is to generate a mask that highlight the facial expression. Basing on the concept of muscle contraction, those moving area are compared with a neutral face, using the following formula:

$$I_m^{(k)} = f\left(\frac{1}{N_k}\sum_i^{N_k}|g(R_{e,i}^k) - g(R_{n,i}^k)|\right) \tag{2}$$

where $I_m^{(k)}$ is the ground truth mask, $R_n^{(k)}$ is the k-th expression face, N_k is the number of faces in the k-th expression and f(*) and g(*) are the pre-processing and post-processing functions. By this formula and using the Mean Square Error (MSE), this first network is trained to generate the facial expression masks.
- *Prior Fusion Net (PFN).* The aim of this network is to fuse the created mask with the original image. The fused output is obtained by the formula:

$$I_s = w_1 * I_{e'} + w_2 * (I_e \otimes f_G(I_e))) \tag{3}$$

where $I_{e'}$ is the RGB image, $\otimes$ is the element-wise multiplication between the face and the mask, and w_1 and w_2 are the weights updated during the training. The loss function used is the cross entropy loss.

- *Classification Net (CN)*. The last network is the CN itself. It is a typical CNN for feature extraction and classification.

This network was trained and tested on three different datasets. On the Extended Cohn-Kanade Dataset (CK+) [23], that is created in laboratory with 7 different expressions, the method outperform the previous facial expression methods, reaching 98.06% of accuracy. On the MMI dataset [32], also created in laboratory-controlled environment, with 6 expressions, the algorithm reached an accuracy of 82.74. On the AffectNet dataset [25], the newest and the larger one, collected in uncontrolled environment, for a total of 24530 images of subjects in 7 expressions, the algorithm reached 61.52% of accuracy. In each case, this method outperform the state of the art in the comparisons reported in [9] and, also contain in-the-wild training, that is particularly suitable for our purposes.

Fig. 4. Image samples from 300W-LP dataset.

2.3 Datasets

The 300W-LP dataset [41] is extended from 300W [30], which standardizes different face alignment benchmark with 68 landmark points, including AFW [40], LFPW [7], HELEN [38] and IBUG [29]. In 300W-LP, the face profile is used to generate 61225 image samples on large poses (1786 from IBUG, 5207 from AFW, 16556 from LFPW and 37676 from HELEN). The dataset is also extended to 122450 samples with yaw angle, as showed in Fig. 4. As can be highlights from this figure, digitally generated rotations does not respect all the dependencies between facial keypoints, for this reason, even if we will re-train the HPE method on this dataset, it is more than natural that the HPE errors along the three axes will results higher than the ones reported in [8].

3 Experiments and Results

To study the relations between the HPE and FE results, we started from a consideration about the changes in distances of relevant facial points during the expressions. We consider a subject of the dataset presented in [11], because of the high expression variation per subject. The 8 poses, 7 expressions and 1 neutral, are taken under consideration, as the pose classified by FMPN-FER and can be seen in Fig. 5 (a). Then, we detected the landmarks on those facial images, using the method described in [18], the same used by HP^{2}IFS, as can be seen in Fig. 5 (b). In particular, we are not interested in the presence of some misplaced points, because, since the landmark detector is the same, the same situation will be verified also in HPE.

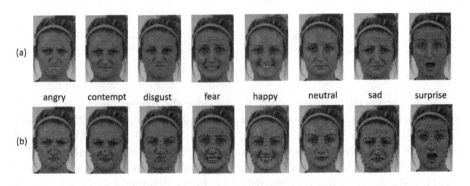

Fig. 5. Several expressions considered for the distances analysis (a) and their landmarks locations (b). Images from the dataset in [11].

Each landmark position is numbered and it is in a fixed array location, e.g. the nose is always in the 33th position of the array. From those arrays we evaluated some distances of particular interest in face recognition due to their variation during the facial expressions:

- Eye_l: the left eye opening, the distance between the landmark corresponding to the eyelid and the landmark corresponding to the bottom part of the eye.
- Eye_r: the right eye opening, computed the same as EL, on the right eye.
- H_Mouth: the horizontal opening of the mouth, calculated in the farthest horizontal points of the mouth.
- V_Mouth: the vertical opening of the mouth, as the distance between the higher and lower points of the mouth.
- Eyeb_l: the distance between the left eye and the left eyebrow (in the center).
- Eyeb_r: the distance between the right eye and the right eyebrow (in the center).
- Chin_Mouth: the distance between the chin, and the lower landmark of the mouth.

After we compute those distances, we evaluated their variation taking a neutral expression as a reference. Their increasing or decreasing are presented in percentage in Table 2.

Table 2. The percentages of increasing or decreasing of the distances respect to the facial expression. In red the decreasing.

Expr/Dist %	Eye_l	Eye_r	H_Mouth	V_Mouth	Eyeb_l	Eyeb_r	Chin_Mouth
Angry	−24,55	−25,58	−7,22	−10,97	−37,19	−36,75	11,60
Contempt	−25,58	−24,55	−2,46	−10,97	−36,26	−44,25	19,23
Disgust	−25,58	−37,98	−4,84	21,98	−12,28	−22,14	34,67
Fear	−0,77	0,00	23,76	98,78	−12,50	−16,61	−3,85
Happy	−37,98	−25,58	30,83	76,69	0,20	−5,70	3,92
Neutral	0,00	0,00	0,00	0,00	0,00	0,00	0,00
Sad	−25,58	−24,55	−0,08	−0,61	−12,28	−22,34	15,45
Surprise	24,65	24,65	−11,97	220,25	25,00	10,94	−11,54

To better visualize those values, we consider the histogram in Fig. 6. Some consideration can be drawn from this first graph. First of all, SURPRISE register the higher value in V_Mouth distance, followed by FEAR and HAPPY. In all cases, Eye_l and Eye_r decrease, with an exception for SURPRISE. ANGRY and CONTEMPT have a very similar behaviour. DISGUST has a behaviour similar to those two, however eyes distances change differently and the V_mouth is increasing. SAD results to be the emotion with less evident changes. Those considerations, and this histogram, in general, will be of great relevance to put in correspondence the HPE errors with the facial expressions in the following study.

At this point, we proceed considering the angular error values committed by the HPE method. Since the method of the head pose estimation was modeled over real head poses, and in 300W-LP heads are digitally rotated, we consider it appropriate to change the reference model, to choose a set of image in 300W-LP. In particular, each of the datasets contained in 300W-LP, AFW, HELEN, IBUG and LFPW was chosen in turn to be the reference model of the method. For the remaining images, we extracted the angular error committed along the three axis by HP²IFS. Then, the same set of images, has been classified by the subject's facial expressions using FMPM-FER. The result is a set of relative errors respect to the facial expressions, divided by the model chosen as reference. From those errors we evaluated, as for the distances, the increments or decrements, in percentage, of the errors respect to the neutral image, and created the new histograms in Fig. 7. In particular in the test set using IBUG as reference there are no detected DISGUST or FEAR expressions.

However, the test data such obtained, are not homogeneous respect to the number of images for each facial expressions. For this reasons, we evaluated the weighted mean relative errors in Fig. 8, that we are going to comment.

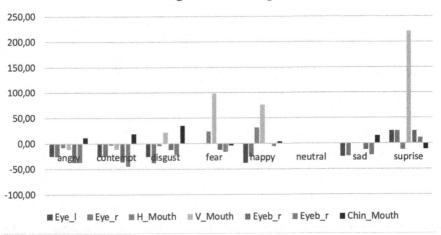

Fig. 6. Histogram of the increasing or decreasing in distances in different facial expressions.

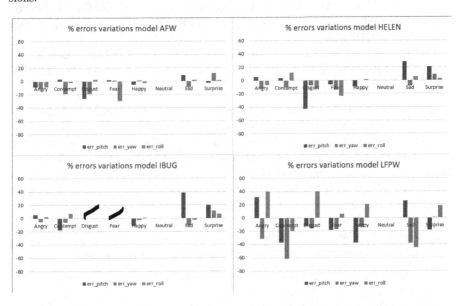

Fig. 7. Histogram of the % of error increasing or decreasing respect to the facial expressions, divided by the reference model.

Respect to the rotation axes we can claim that:

- The error in *pitch* is decreasing for the expressions CONTEMPT, FEAR, HAPPY and, in particular for DISGUST. The same is increasing for ANGRY, SAD and SURPRISE.

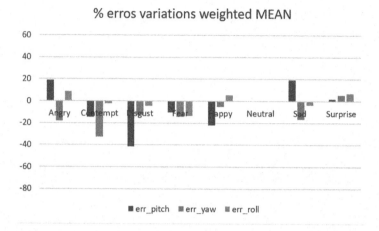

Fig. 8. Histogram of the % of mean weighted error increasing or decreasing, respect to the facial expressions.

- The error in *yaw* is decreasing for the expressions ANGRY, DISGUST, FEAR, HAPPY, SAD, and in particular for CONTEMPT. The same is increasing only for SURPRISE.
- The error in *roll* is decreasing for the expressions CONTEMPT, DISGUST, SAD, and in particular FEAR. The same is increasing for ANGRY, HAPPY and SURPRISE.

In the last step of our analysis we put in relation the graphs in Fig. 6 and Fig. 8 and the corresponding considerations made, highlighting the direct relations between the facial points distances and the relative errors. In doing so, we use as link the facial expressions. Our final aim is to connect the variations in distances to the variations in errors, providing a useful estimate to be used in error previsions of HPE methods. We evaluated the relations as *directly proportional* when an increasing of the distances implies an increasing of the errors, and vice versa. We evaluated the relations as *inversely proportional* when an increasing of the distances implies a decreasing of the errors, and vice versa.

After defining our criteria, the following final consideration can be made:

- The distances between eyes and eyebrows (Eyeb_l and Eyeb_r) are directly proportional to the errors in yaw.
- The vertical opening of the mouth (V_Mouth) is directly proportional to the errors in yaw.
- The horizontal opening of the mouth (H_Mouth) is inversely proportional to the errors in roll.
- The mouth variations (V_Mouth and H_Mouth), combined with an absence of eye variation (Eye_l, Eye_r, Eyeb_l and Eyeb_r), are inversely proportional to the errors in roll.
- The distance between mouth and chin (Chin_Mouth) *seems to be* related to pitch.

We are not sure about the relation between the Chin_Mouth and the errors in pitch because of the mismatching values obtained in the expressions ANGRY and CONTEMPT, that not allow us to understand if the relation is direct or inverse. This can be related to the HPE method chosen to perform the error evaluations. In fact, in its original form, HP^{2}IFS presents the higher error values right on pitch. In addition, along this axes, the error has a less homogeneous behaviour, since the presence of some outliers can be the cause of the higher error compared to yaw and roll.

Despite this, it is clear that there is a direct relation between the facial points distances and the errors committed by an Head Pose Estimation method. This relation can be well extracted by the facial expression estimation as the presented study confirm.

To further demonstrate this claiming, we selected the facial expression that presented the minimum mean error in the HPE methods along the overall dataset, the expression CONTEMPT. In Fig. 9 and Fig. 10, we shown the histograms of Fig. 6 and Fig. 8, respectively, considering the expression CONTEMPT as a reference. As can be seen, all the distances are increasing, as well as the errors. The only relevant exception, with overall distance increased by small values and eye distances decreasing, is represented by DISGUST expressions, that present a relevant pitch error decreasing.

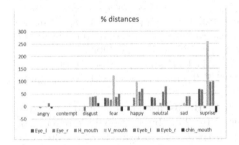 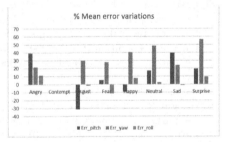

Fig. 9. Histogram of the % of distances increasing considering the expression CONTEMPT as reference.

Fig. 10. Histogram of the % of mean error increasing considering the expression CONTEMPT as reference.

4   Conclusions

Head pose estimation shows its utility in several application fields, especially in surveillance and security purposes. It is known that the facial expressions can impact on HPE evaluation errors, more if they originate from faces in uncontrolled environment. The presented paper highlights the quantitative relations between HPE errors and facial expressions, being a precursor in this kind of study. Starting from a HPE algorithm and a FE method, we examined the relations between facial expressions, head pose errors and facial keypoints distances.

As a result, we obtained a set of configurations that can help HPE methods authors to better predict and handle with HPE errors related to facial expressions in uncontrolled environment. We plan to extend this kind of analysis in future, also taking under consideration other HPE and FE methods. A study based on the robustness of several methods respect to the Facial Expressions variations can also be taken under consideration in future works.

References

1. Abate, A.F., Barra, P., Bisogni, C., Nappi, M., Ricciardi, S.: Near real-time three axis head pose estimation without training. IEEE Access **7**, 64256–64265 (2019). https://doi.org/10.1109/ACCESS.2019.2917451
2. Abdi, H.: Partial least square regression (pls regression). Encyclopedia Res. Methods Soc. Sci. **6**(4), 792–795 (2003)
3. Ariz, M., Villanueva, A., Cabeza, R.: Robust and accurate 2d-tracking-based 3d positioning method: application to head pose estimation. Comput. Vis. Image Underst. **180**, 13–22 (2019)
4. Barnsley, M.F., et al.: The Science of Fractal Images. Springer, New York (1988). https://doi.org/10.1007/978-1-4612-3784-6
5. Barra, P., Barra, S., Bisogni, C., De Marsico, M., Nappi, M.: Web-shaped model for head pose estimation: an approach for best exemplar selection. IEEE Trans. Image Process. **29**, 5457–5468 (2020)
6. Bartlett, M.S., Littlewort, G., Frank, M., Lainscsek, C., Fasel, I., Movellan, J.: Recognizing facial expression: machine learning and application to spontaneous behavior. In: 2005 IEEE Computer Society Conference on Computer Vision and Pattern Recognition (CVPR 2005), vol. 2, pp. 568–573. IEEE (2005)
7. Belhumeur, P.N., Jacobs, D.W., Kriegman, D.J., Kumar, N.: Localizing parts of faces using a consensus of exemplars. IEEE Trans. Pattern Anal. Mach. Intell. **35**(12), 2930–2940 (2013)
8. Bisogni, C., Nappi, M., Pero, C., Ricciardi, S.: Hp2ifs: head pose estimation exploiting partitioned iterated function systems. In: 25th International Conference on Pattern Recognition (ICPR2020) (2020). https://arxiv.org/abs/2003.11536
9. Chen, Y., Wang, J., Chen, S., Shi, Z., Cai, J.: Facial motion prior networks for facial expression recognition. In: 2019 IEEE Visual Communications and Image Processing, VCIP 2019, Sydney, Australia, December 1–4, 2019, pp. 1–4. IEEE (2019)
10. Czuprynski, B., Strupczewski, A.: High accuracy head pose tracking survey. In: Ślęzak, D., Schaefer, G., Vuong, S.T., Kim, Y.-S. (eds.) AMT 2014. LNCS, vol. 8610, pp. 407–420. Springer, Cham (2014). https://doi.org/10.1007/978-3-319-09912-5_34
11. Du, S., Tao, Y., Martinez, A.M.: Compound facial expressions of emotion. Proc. Natl. Acad. Sci. **111**(15), E1454–E1462 (2014). https://doi.org/10.1073/pnas.1322355111
12. Ekman, P., Friesen, W.V.: Constants across cultures in the face and emotion. J. Pers. Soc. Psychol. **17**(2), 124 (1971)
13. Fanelli, G., Weise, T., Gall, J., Van Gool, L.: Real time head pose estimation from consumer depth cameras. In: Joint Pattern Recognition Symposium (2011)
14. Hamming, R.W.: Error detecting and error correcting codes. Bell Syst. Tech. J. **29**(2), 147–160 (1950)

15. Hough, P.V.: Method and means for recognizing complex patterns (Dec 18 1962), uS Patent 3,069,654
16. Hsu, H.W., Wu, T.Y., Wan, S., Wong, W.H., Lee, C.Y.: Quatnet: quaternion-based head pose estimation with multiregression loss. IEEE Trans. Multimedia **21**(4), 1035–1046 (2018)
17. Jain, D.K., Shamsolmoali, P., Sehdev, P.: Extended deep neural network for facial emotion recognition. Pattern Recogn. Lett. **120**, 69–74 (2019)
18. Kazemi, V., Sullivan, J.: One millisecond face alignment with an ensemble of regression trees. In: Proceedings of the IEEE Conference on Computer Vision and Pattern Recognition, pp. 1867–1874 (2014)
19. Kim, J.H., Kim, B.G., Roy, P.P., Jeong, D.M.: Efficient facial expression recognition algorithm based on hierarchical deep neural network structure. IEEE Access **7**, 41273–41285 (2019)
20. Krizhevsky, A., Sutskever, I., Hinton, G.E.: Imagenet classification with deep convolutional neural networks. In: Advances in Neural Information Processing Systems, pp. 1097–1105 (2012)
21. Li, S., Deng, W.: Deep facial expression recognition: a survey. IEEE Trans. Affect. Comput. (2020)
22. Lopes, A.T., de Aguiar, E., De Souza, A.F., Oliveira-Santos, T.: Facial expression recognition with convolutional neural networks: coping with few data and the training sample order. Pattern Recogn. **61**, 610–628 (2017)
23. Lucey, P., Cohn, J.F., Kanade, T., Saragih, J., Ambadar, Z., Matthews, I.: The extended cohn-kanade dataset (ck+): a complete dataset for action unit and emotion-specified expression. In: 2010 IEEE Computer Society Conference on Computer Vision and Pattern Recognition-Workshops, pp. 94–101. IEEE (2010)
24. Meng, Z., Liu, P., Cai, J., Han, S., Tong, Y.: Identity-aware convolutional neural network for facial expression recognition. In: 2017 12th IEEE International Conference on Automatic Face & Gesture Recognition (FG 2017), pp. 558–565. IEEE (2017)
25. Mollahosseini, A., Hasani, B., Mahoor, M.H.: AffectNet: a database for facial expression, valence, and arousal computing in the wild. IEEE Trans. Affect. Comput. **10**(1), 18–31 (2019)
26. Murphy-Chutorian, E., Trivedi, M.M.: Head pose estimation in computer vision: a survey. IEEE Trans. Pattern Anal. Mach. Intell. **31**(4), 607–626 (2008)
27. Ranjan, R., Patel, V.M., Chellappa, R.: Hyperface: a deep multi-task learning framework for face detection, landmark localization, pose estimation, and gender recognition. IEEE Trans. Pattern Anal. Mach. Intell. **41**(1), 121–135 (2019). https://doi.org/10.1109/TPAMI.2017.2781233
28. Rasmussen, C.E.: Gaussian processes in machine learning. In: Bousquet, O., von Luxburg, U., Rätsch, G. (eds.) ML -2003. LNCS (LNAI), vol. 3176, pp. 63–71. Springer, Heidelberg (2004). https://doi.org/10.1007/978-3-540-28650-9_4
29. Sagonas, C., Antonakos, E., Tzimiropoulos, G., Zafeiriou, S., Pantic, M.: 300 faces in-the-wild challenge: database and results. Image Vis. Comput. **47**, 3–18 (2016)
30. Sagonas, C., Tzimiropoulos, G., Zafeiriou, S., Pantic, M.: 300 faces in-the-wild challenge: the first facial landmark localization challenge. In: Proceedings of the IEEE International Conference on Computer Vision Workshops, pp. 397–403 (2013)
31. Shan, C., Gong, S., McOwan, P.W.: Facial expression recognition based on local binary patterns: a comprehensive study. Image Vis. Comput. **27**(6), 803–816 (2009)

32. Valstar, M.F., Pantic, M.: Induced disgust, happiness and surprise: an addition to the mmi facial expression database. In: Proceedings of International Conference Language Resources and Evaluation, Workshop on EMOTION, Malta, 2019, May 2010, pp. 65–70 (2010)

33. Viola, P., Jones, M.: Rapid object detection using a boosted cascade of simple features. In: IEEE Conference on Computer Vision and Pattern Recognition, CVPR 2001. vol. 1, pp. I-I. IEEE (2001)

34. Wang, Y., Liang, W., Shen, J., Jia, Y., Yu, L.F.: A deep coarse-to-fine network for head pose estimation from synthetic data. Pattern Recogn. **94**, 196–206 (2019)

35. Whitehill, J., Omlin, C.W.: HAAR features for FACS au recognition. In: 7th International Conference on Automatic Face and Gesture Recognition (FGR06), pp. 5-pp. IEEE (2006)

36. Yang, T.Y., Chen, Y.T., Lin, Y.Y., Chuang, Y.Y.: Fsa-net: Learning fine-grained structure aggregation for head pose estimation from a single image. In: IEEE Conference on Computer Vision and Pattern Recognition, pp. 1087–1096 (2019)

37. Zhang, F., Zhang, T., Mao, Q., Xu, C.: Joint pose and expression modeling for facial expression recognition. In: Proceedings of the IEEE Conference on Computer Vision and Pattern Recognition, pp. 3359–3368 (2018)

38. Zhou, E., Fan, H., Cao, Z., Jiang, Y., Yin, Q.: Extensive facial landmark localization with coarse-to-fine convolutional network cascade. In: Proceedings of the IEEE International Conference on Computer Vision Workshops, pp. 386–391 (2013)

39. Zhu, X., Lei, Z., Shi, H., Liu, X., Li, S.Z.: Face alignment across large poses: a 3d solution. In: IEEE Conference on Computer Vision and Pattern Recognition (2016)

40. Zhu, X., Ramanan, D.: Face detection, pose estimation, and landmark localization in the wild. In: 2012 IEEE Conference on Computer Vision and Pattern Recognition, pp. 2879–2886. IEEE (2012)

41. Zhu, X., Lei, Z., Liu, X., Shi, H., Li, S.Z.: Face alignment across large poses: a 3d solution. In: Proceedings of the IEEE Conference on Computer Vision and Pattern Recognition, pp. 146–155 (2016)

Analysing and Exploiting Complexity Information in On-Line Signature Verification

Miguel Caruana, Ruben Vera-Rodriguez$^{(\boxtimes)}$, and Ruben Tolosana

BiDA Lab, School of Engineering, Universidad Autonoma de Madrid, Madrid, Spain
`miguel.caruana@estudiante.uam.es`, {`ruben.vera,ruben.tolosana`}`@uam.es`

Abstract. This paper proposes an in-depth analysis on how the complexity of signatures affects the performance in on-line signature verification. In signature verification there is a very wide range of signatures from some based on a simple flourish to very complex ones. In this work we consider three different complexity groups: low, medium and high. We carry out an analysis of performance evaluation for each complexity group for both random and skilled forgeries. Two verification systems are used for this analysis, a traditional one based on the popular DTW and a state-of-the-art one based on time aligned recurrent neural networks (TA-RNN) recently proposed. The experiments are carried out over the largest database available to date for on-line signature verification (Deep-SignDB). Then, we propose several approaches in order to exploit the information related to the signature complexity with the final aim of improving the signature verification system performance. Our best proposed approach is based on training a system with a balanced number of subjects regarding their type of signature complexity.

Keywords: On-line signature verification · Deep learning · Biometrics

1 Introduction

On-line handwritten signature verification is one of the most popular behavioral biometrics technologies. In the last 40 years, on-line signature verification has evolved very significantly and has proved to be one of the most reliable and convenient biometric systems in many relevant sectors. As a behavioral biometric trait, there are many factors that affect the performance of on-line signature such as the ergonomics, the quality of the acquisition device, device interoperability [23], usability factors [6], using the finger as the writing tool [16], the effect of aging [24], signature quality [9], signature complexity [22], the limited amount of public databases which has motivated the generation of synthetic signatures, etc. Most of these factors are reviewed in [3].

Complexity is an important factor in some traditional authentication systems such as those based on passwords, where a minimum complexity of the password is needed in order to ensure a minimum level of security. On-line dynamic signature verification systems may suffer from this problem as well. Analyzing the

© Springer Nature Switzerland AG 2021
A. Del Bimbo et al. (Eds.): ICPR 2020 Workshops, LNCS 12665, pp. 501–513, 2021.
https://doi.org/10.1007/978-3-030-68821-9_42

complexity of the signatures allows us to find out how the complexity of the signatures affects the performance of a verification system. In addition, it would be possible to warn users with vulnerable signatures in terms of their complexity, so they could modify their signature by another more robust one.

In this paper we focus on the effect of the signature complexity in the system performance, which has been shown to be a significant factor. In [2], Alonso-Fernandez et al. evaluated the effect of the complexity and legibility of the signatures for off-line signature verification (i.e., signatures with no available dynamic information) pointing out the differences in performance for several matchers.

Different approaches have been proposed to detect the complexity of dynamic handwritten signatures. Houmani et al. proposed an entropy measure based on local density estimation by a Hidden Markov Model (HMM) [8]. Miguel-Hurtado et al. investigated the creation of a novel mathematical model for the automatic assessment of the signature complexity [12]. A recent approach was carried out by Tolosona et al. in [22]. This study proposed a complexity detector based on using the number of strokes applying the well-known writing generation Sigma LogNormal model [5]. Then, once the signatures were classified into three levels of complexity (low, medium and high), optimal time functions associated with each specific complexity level were extracted. Finally, they measured the performance of a signature verification system based on Dynamic Time Warping (DTW) only using the optimal time functions for each complexity class. In this way, significant improvements in the system's performance were obtained compared to a DTW-based system using the same time functions for all signatures without taking into account their complexity level.

Recently, Vera-Rodriguez et al. proposed in [25] a new complexity detection system based on Deep Learning (DL) techniques. This system was developed through a semi-supervised process where an initial model was trained over a medium-size database (BioSecurID [4]), which was then used to classify the complexity of signatures of a much larger database (DeepSignDB [21]). Finally, based on these automatic labels they developed the complexity detection system, achieving results ca. 85% of accuracy compared to the manual labels. This system improved significantly the results of 64% of accuracy achieved previously in [22] in the same experimental conditions.

Deep learning is the state-of-the-art technology used nowadays in many other biometric recognition traits such as the face [14] or the voice [7]. However, most of the state-of-the-art signature verification systems are still based on traditional approaches such as DTW, HMM, and Support Vector Machines (SVM).

Very recently, some works that apply Deep Learning techniques, both based on Recurrent Neural Networks (RNNs) [1,10,11,17,20], but also based on Convolutional Neural Networks (CNNs) [15,26] have been published, obtaining promising results. In particular, the strategy proposed in [20] is based on using a large database of on-line signatures (DeepSignDB) with almost 1500 subjects in order to better train a RNN-based system achieving very good results both for skilled and random forgeries.

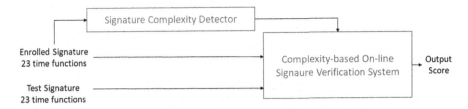

Fig. 1. Architecture of our proposed complexity-based on-line signature verification system.

In this work we first carry out an analysis of the on-line signature verification system performance using the publicly available DeepSignDB database in order to study the diversity of the subjects in terms of their signature complexity. Then, we carry out several experiments in order to exploit the signature complexity with the aim of improving the overall performance of a on-line signature verification system based on recurrent neural networks.

The remainder of the paper is organised as follows. Section 2 describes our proposed on-line verification system specific to signature complexity. Section 3 describes the DeepSignDB database considered in the experiments of this article. Section 4 describes the experimental protocol, Sect. 5 reports the results achieved using our proposed approach. Finally, Sect. 6 draws the final conclusions and points out some lines for future work.

2   Proposed Approach

This section describes our proposed approach based on detecting the complexity of the enrolled signatures and then applying a complexity-based on-line signature verification system, as shown in Fig. 1. The main idea of this work is to analyse how the complexity of the enrolled signatures affects the performance of a verification system and if it is possible to exploit that complexity information in order to develop a complexity-based on-line verification system that can improve its signature verification performance. In order to achieve that, we have defined a simple but effective architecture. In on-line signature verification we will have a test (unknown) signature that is going to be compared to an enrolled signature to verify its identity. First, the enrolled signature goes through a signature complexity detector which classifies the signature into one of three levels of complexity. Then, the two signatures together with the complexity label of the enrolled signature enter the complexity-based on-line verification system. Finally, the verification system provides an output score value (between 0 and 1), which states the similarity of the two signatures under comparison (a value close to 0 would be expected when the two signatures are genuine and a value close to 1 would be expected when the test signature is either a skilled or a random forgery). Next, we describe briefly the two technologies used both for signature complexity estimation and on-line signature verification.

Fig. 2. Examples of signatures of three complexity groups: low complexity (top), medium complexity (middle) and high complexity (bottom).

2.1 Signature Complexity Detector

The first stage of our proposed system consist of a signature complexity detector. For this we make use of the system proposed in [25]. This system classifies each signature into one of three levels of complexity considered: low, medium and high. Figure 2 shows examples of signatures in the three levels of complexity considered in this work.

For each signature, signals related to X and Y spatial coordinates and pressure are used to extract a set of 23 time functions [17], which are the input of the system. These time functions are preprocessed following a zero mean and unit standard deviation normalization. The network is composed of two Bidirectional Long Short-Term Memory (BLSTM) layers and a feed-forward layer with a softmax activation, which provides an output score for each of the three complexity levels considered. As described in [25], this system achieves 85% of accuracy of complexity level compared to a manual ground truth for an evaluation dataset from BiosecurID database [4].

2.2 On-Line Signature Verification System

We base our proposed complexity-based signature verification system on the TA-RNN system (Time-Aligned Recurrent Neural Networks) proposed in [19,20]. For the input of the system, we feed the network with the 23 time functions extracted from the signature, which are the same that are used for the complexity detection system. The TA-RNN architecture is based on two stages: i) a first stage based on time sequence alignment through DTW and ii) a second stage consisting of a neural network, specifically a RNN. The system developed in [20] was comprised of three layers. The first layer is composed of two Bidirectional Gated Recurrent Unit (BGRU) hidden layers with 46 memory blocks each, sharing the weights between them. The outputs of the first two parallel BGRU hidden layers are concatenated and serve as input to the second layer, which corresponds to a BGRU hidden layer with 23 memory blocks. Finally, a feed-forward neural network layer with a sigmoid activation is considered, providing an output score for each pair of signatures.

TA-RNN architecture is used in this paper as one of the baseline systems to compare the results achieved with our complexity-based signature verification system. In our complexity-based signature verification system we carried out different strategies to exploit the signatures complexity. In particular we considered three main approaches: i) training from scratch a specific DL model per complexity level, ii) training a specific DL model per complexity level but applying fine tuning from the general DeepSign model in [20], and iii) training just one model for all types of signatures, but balancing the complexity classes during the training. The different verification systems adapted to each complexity use the same architecture as the one described before. However, for certain experiments some changes in the architecture were made. These details are described in Sect. 4.

3   Database

The DeepSignDB database [21] comprises data from a total of 1526 subjects from four different well-known on-line signature databases: MCYT (330 subjects) [13], BiosecurID (400 subjects) [4], Biosecure DS2 (650 subjects) [9], eBioSign (65 subjects) [16] and a novel signature database comprised of 81 subjects. This database comprises more than 70 K signatures acquired using both stylus and finger inputs. Two acquisition scenarios are considered, office and mobile, with a total of 8 different devices. Additionally, different types of impostors and number of acquisition sessions are considered along the database. For the results presented in this work, only signatures performed with pen stylus are considered.

4   Experimental Protocol

The experimental protocol has been designed to analyse two main ideas: i) how the signatures complexity affects on the performance of an on-line signature verification system, and ii) how considering the signatures complexity in the training process can improve the performance of the signature verification system.

Five separate blocks of experiments have been carried out. First, in Exp. 1 we analyse the performance of the DTW and the TA-RNN baseline systems for each complexity group. In Exp. 2 we propose to train from scratch a specific system per each complexity group using the TA-RNN architecture. Then, in Exp. 3 we analyse a similar approach to Exp. 2 but modifying the system architecture per each complexity group. After this, in Exp. 4 we follow a similar approach to Exp. 2, but fine tuning each complexity group system from the baseline system instead of training from scratch. Finally, in Exp. 5 we followed a different approach, which is based on training just one global system, similar to the baseline, but with data from complexity balanced subjects.

DeepSignDB has been the database used for all the experiments reported in this work. We followed the experimental protocol from [20], and divided it into two different datasets, one for development and one for evaluation. The development set contains 70% of the subjects while the other 30% is the evaluation set. It is important to note that each dataset contains different subjects in order to avoid biased results.

From the original 1084 subjects contained in the development set, we applied the signature complexity detector proposed in [25] to all the genuine signatures. Then, we computed the mean complexity of each subject, taking all their genuine signatures complexity into account. Finally, we classified each subject into the complexity group closer to its mean complexity. At the end we obtained 230 high-complexity subjects, 637 medium-complexity subjects and 217 low-complexity subjects in the development set.

For system training, the development set has a total of 980 subjects. This set has been further divided into two different subsets, one for training (80%) and one for validation (20%).

As the first objective is to analyze the system performance for the three groups of complexity separately, the evaluation dataset was also divided into three subsets, one per each complexity group. This was done based on the complexity level of the enrolment genuine signature of the pairs of signatures under comparison, as Fig. 1 shows. In order to provide a global system performance the scores from the three evaluation sets were put together.

Two impostor scenarios have been considered, skilled and random forgeries. For the skilled forgery case, all available skilled forgery samples are included in the analysis whereas for the random forgery case, one genuine sample of each of the remaining subjects of the same database is considered. This way verification systems are tested with different types of presentation attacks [18]. It is worth noting that the evaluation results reported in this work are only based on one to one comparisons of signatures. Thus, only one enrolment genuine signature is considered per subject, which is an extreme case as normally more than just one signature is considered as enrolment.

The evaluation results are given as the performance of the system in terms of DET curves and Equal Error Rate (EER). The evaluation results are obtained over the three evaluation datasets, one per class, as well as over the complete evaluation dataset. In such a manner we can establish a comparative analysis of the results achieved for each class. Two different systems are used as a baseline to compare the results achieved in this work. We use a traditional approach, a DTW-based system, and a state-of-art system [20].

5   Experimental Work

5.1   Exp. 1 - Analysis of Complexity for Baseline Systems

In this experiment we carry out the analysis of the evaluation performance of the two baseline systems (DTW and TA-RNN) for the three signature complexity groups. This way we can obtain the performance of the baseline systems over the same evaluation datasets and carry out a comparative analysis with the following proposed approaches. Tables 1 and 2 show the performance of the system for each complexity group for the case of skilled and random forgeries comparisons respectively.

First of all it is worth noting the much superior performance of the TA-RNN system compared to the traditional DTW approach in particular for skilled forgeries. In both skilled and random forgeries cases the best performance is achieved for the medium complexity subjects and in both baseline systems, with 9.94% and 2.40% EER for the DTW system, and 3.32% EER and 1.19% EER for the TA-RNN system. This can be due to several factors. On the one hand, the number of medium complexity subjects is the highest in the development dataset so it is normal that the performance over this group is better, since it has almost twice as many subjects as the other two classes. On the other hand, the medium complexity signatures might be more stable and robust achieving a lower EER. Low complexity signatures can be easily confused with signatures of different subjects due to the low inter-class variability. High complexity signatures of the same subject can be quite different due to the high intra-class variability. The second best performance is achieved for high complexity signatures leaving the low complexity signatures with the worst performance.

In general terms, the global performance for the baseline systems is 11.13% EER for DTW and 4.20% EER for TA-RNN in skilled forgeries, and 2.62% EER for DTW and 1.51% EER for TA-RNN in random forgeries. Figure 3 also shows the DET curve for the global evaluation of the TA-RNN baseline system.

Table 1. Performance over skilled forgeries in terms of EER.

	Low	Med	High	Global
Exp. 1 - DTW baseline	13.27	9.94	11.53	11.13
Exp. 1 - TA-RNN baseline	5.88	3.32	4.60	4.20
Exp. 2–3 Models scratch	8.89	3.66	6.31	5.75
Exp. 3 - Different architecture	6.80	4.20	5.63	5.11
Exp. 4–3 Models fine tuning	6.03	3.30	4.60	4.23
Exp. 5 - Prop. 1 Model balanced	**5.63**	**3.27**	**3.89**	**3.92**

Table 2. Performance over random forgeries in terms of EER.

	Low	Med	High	Global
Exp. 1 - DTW baseline	2.62	2.40	2.86	2.62
Exp. 1 - TA-RNN baseline	2.08	1.19	1.84	1.51
Exp. 2–3 Models scratch	3.40	1.24	2.22	2.02
Exp. 3 - Different architecture	1.72	1.45	2.26	1.73
Exp. 4–3 Models Fine tuning	2.00	1.17	1.84	1.54
Exp. 5 - Prop. 1 Model balanced	**1.50**	**1.09**	**1.62**	**1.32**

5.2   Exp. 2 - Training from Scratch 3 Systems, One System per Complexity

From Exp. 1 it is clear that the system based on TA-RNN clearly outperforms the traditional system based on DTW. Therefore in the following experiments the aim is to exploit the signature complexity to try to improve the already very good performance of the TA-RNN system. As a first approach in order to exploit the signatures complexity in an on-line signature verification system we tried to train three different models from scratch using the TA-RNN architecture, one per complexity group. Each model was trained only using comparisons where the genuine signature belongs to the specific complexity class, but where the impostor signature can belong to any complexity group. It is important to mention that all the subjects available per class were used, so when evaluating the results it is worth taking this into account, as each complexity group has different subjects and therefore different amounts of data to be trained with. Specifically, 181 subjects were used to train the low complexity model, 502 subjects to train the medium complexity model and 184 to train the high complexity model. Tables 1 and 2 show the results achieved by each of the models trained in this experiment following the same evaluation protocol as the baseline systems shown in Exp. 1.

The results obtained in this experiment lead us to a similar conclusion to the previous one regarding the complexity groups as they follow similar trends. However, results achieved with this approach comprised of three systems, one per complexity group, are significantly worse compared to the ones achieved by the baseline TA-RNN system. This can be due to the baseline system having been trained with a much higher number of subjects, and it seems that the baseline system can make use of the information provided by the higher variability of subjects trained with, and provide better results. Only for the case of the medium complexity evaluation the EER of the baseline system and this approach are quite similar as the system with medium complexity has been trained with the highest number of subjects.

In general terms, the global performance for this approach is 5.75% EER for skilled forgeries and 2.02% EER for random forgeries, which is also worse than the performance of the baseline system reported in Exp. 1. Figure 3 also shows the DET curves with the global evaluation for this approach, showing the worst performance of all experiments carried out.

5.3   Exp. 3 - Training from Scratch and Changing the Baseline Architecture

This experiment was designed to see if any changes in the system's architecture from the original TA-RNN architecture could improve its performance against a particular group of complexity. Two different models were trained, one focused on low complexity signatures and the other focused on improving performance against high complexity signatures. Only these two groups were considered as these are the classes where the worst results were obtained in Exp. 2.

In the model for low complexity the second BGRU layer was removed in order to create a simpler model. The results we achieved using this system were really bad for all types of signatures, not just for low complexity ones. On the other hand, in the model focused on high complexity a third hidden BGRU layer was added before the feed forward layer. This new model trained just with high complexity subjects turned out to give reasonable results in general.

The second proposed architecture just trained with high complexity subjects did get better results. Tables 1 and 2 show the performance achieved by this system. As we can see the results obtained for the high complexity model improve the results obtained by the models of Exp. 2, both in high and low complexity. This can be also seen in general terms in the DET curves shown in Fig. 3.

Despite not being able to improve the results of the baseline system, this new architecture is promising as it achieves results closer to those of the baseline system even though it is trained with a much lower number of subjects.

5.4   Exp. 4 - Fine Tuning 3 Systems

In addition to changes in the architecture, in this experiment we also train three systems similar to Exp. 2 but instead of training from scratch we apply fine tuning from the baseline system in Exp. 1 to each complexity group system.

This experiment was designed to find out if the performance of the system could be improved for a particular complexity group by carrying out a fine-tuning of the baseline model using only the subjects of that complexity group. For each complexity, three types of fine-tuning were performed: training only the final layer (fully connected), training the last two layers (second BGRU and fully connected layers) and training all layers (the two BGRU and fully connected layers). Therefore, three different models per complexity group were trained.

Similar results were obtained by the different fine-tuning strategies. The best results were achieved by training only the fully connected layer. Tables 1 and 2 show the achieved results by the three models that apply this strategy.

We can see that there is hardly any difference with the performance of the baseline system. For low complexity signatures there is a small drop in the performance over skilled forgeries and a subtle improvement over random forgeries. Carrying out a fine-tuning with more subjects of low and high complexity might get better results. In addition, having a look at the DET curves in Fig. 3 we can see how the performance achieved with this approach is very similar to the one achieved by the TA-RNN baseline system in general terms.

5.5   Exp. 5 - Training a Global System with Balanced Classes

After having analysed many different approaches training specific systems per complexity group, then we decided to train just one system but using a balanced number of subjects (and samples) per complexity group.

One model was trained using the TA-RNN architecture. To train the system 181 subjects per class were used, in total 543. This way we used all the possible subjects maintaining a balanced number of subjects between the different groups of complexity. Different strategies were followed during the training process, i.e., training from scratch and fine tuning one, two and the three layers from the TA-RNN architecture. Best results were achieved when training the model from scratch.

Tables 1 and 2 show the performance of this approach. Despite having been trained with a small number of subjects when comparing with the baseline system (543 Vs. 1084 subjects), we observe that the system achieves better performance for all types of complexity and also in the general evaluation. Analysing the case of skilled forgeries, the improvement of performance for low and medium complexity is small. However, for high complexity there is a relative improvement of 15.44% EER compared to the TA-RNN baseline system. Regarding the global performance the relative improvement achieved with the proposed system is of 6.67% EER skilled forgeries.

Analysing the case of random forgeries, the improvement achieved is more significant compared to the case of skilled forgeries. Here, a very significant relative improvement of 27.89% EER is achieved for the case of low complexity with 1.50% EER. The relative improvements for medium and high complexity are 8.40% and 11.96% EER respectively. Regarding the global performance the relative improvement achieved with the proposed system is of 12.58% EER for random forgeries.

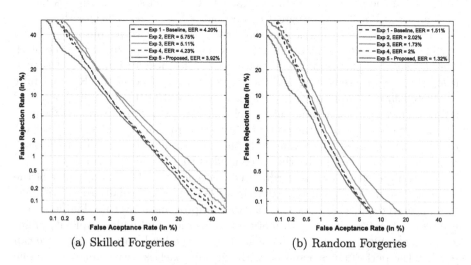

(a) Skilled Forgeries   (b) Random Forgeries

Fig. 3. System performance results of our experiments over the DeepSignDB evaluation dataset.

Finally, Fig. 3 shows the DET curves for the proposed system achieving the best system performance at all operating points of false rejection rate and false acceptance rate compared to all the experiments carried out and the baseline systems. This highlights the importance of having balanced classes in the training phase. Analysing the obtained results we can conclude that it is more important to have a balanced number of subjects per class than a high number of unbalanced subjects.

6   Conclusions and Future Work

This paper has proposed an in-depth analysis on how the complexity of signatures affects the performance of an on-line signature verification system. In particular, we have carried out an analysis of the system performance for three groups of subjects regarding their signature complexity: subjects with low, medium and high signature complexity. In general, based on two baseline systems (DTW and TA-RNN), subjects with medium signature complexity achieve the best system performance both for skilled and random comparisons, followed by high complexity users and finally low complexity users. The reason for this might be that low complexity signatures may have low inter-class variability, while high complexity signatures may have high intra-class variability. Medium complexity signatures are likely to have higher inter-class and lower intra-class variability compared to low and high complexity ones. This information could be taken into account to warn users with low or high complexity signatures, especially low complexity ones, as the system will perform worse over those types of signatures.

Then, different approaches have been proposed in order to exploit the information related to the signature complexity with the final aim of improving the signature verification system performance. In particular we have proposed training specific systems per complexity group following different strategies (training from scratch, trying different system architectures, or applying fine tuning), but none of them improved the performance of the TA-RNN baseline system. Finally, an approach based on training a global system with balanced subjects regarding their complexity has outperformed the TA-RNN baseline system with a relative improvement of 6.67% EER for skilled forgeries and a relative improvement of 12.58% EER for random forgeries. We can conclude that training with a balanced number of subjects regarding their type of signature complexity reduces the number of users needed to achieve a particular performance, thus making training more efficient.

There is still a lot of work to be conducted regarding the complexity of signatures. In this work, our experimental work has been based on using just one enrolled signature. In future works, the case of having access to more than just one enrolled signature will be considered. Also, we will study different types of deep learning architectures, not just based on RNNs, but also on CNNs.

Acknowledgment. This work has been supported by projects: PRIMA (MSCA-ITN-2019-860315), TRESPASS (MSCA-ITN-2019-860813), BIBECA (RTI2018-101248-B-I00 MINECO FEDER) and Cecabank. M. Caruana is supported by Ayudas para el fomento de la Investigación en Estudios de Máster-UAM 2019. R. Tolosana is supported by Comunidad de Madrid and Fondo Social Europeo.

References

1. Ahrabian, K., Babaali, B.: On usage of autoencoders and siamese networks for online handwritten signature verification. Neural Comput. Appl. (2017)
2. Alonso-Fernandez, F., Fairhurst, M., Fierrez, J., Ortega-Garcia, J.: Impact of signature legibility and signature type in off-line signature verification. In: Proceedings of IEEE Biometrics Symposium (2007)
3. Diaz, M., Ferrer, M.A., Impedovo, D., Malik, M.I., Pirlo, G., Plamondon, R.: A perspective analysis of handwritten signature technology. ACM Comput. Surv. **51**, 1–39 (2019)
4. Fierrez, J., Galbally, J., Ortega-Garcia, J., et al.: BiosecurID: a multimodal biometric database. Pattern Anal. Appl. **13**(2), 235–246 (2010)
5. Fischer, A., Plamondon, R.: Signature verification based on the kinematic theory of rapid human movements. IEEE Trans. Hum. Mach. Syst. **47**(2), 169–180 (2017)
6. Guest, R., Brockly, M., Elliott, S., Scott, J.: An assessment of the usability of biometric signature systems using the human-biometric sensor interaction model. Int. J. Comput. Appl. Technol. **53**(4), 336–347 (2016)
7. Heigold, G., Moreno, I., Bengio, S., Shazeer, N.: End-to-end text-dependent speaker verification. In: Proceedings of ICASSP, pp. 5115–5119 (2016)
8. Houmani, N., Garcia-Salicetti, S., Dorizzi, B.: A novel personal entropy measure confronted to online signature verification systems performance. In Proceedings of International Conference on Biometrics: Theory, Applications and System, BTAS pp. 1–6 (2008)
9. Houmani, N., et al.: BioSecure signature evaluation campaign (BSEC'2009): evaluating on-line signature algorithms depending on the quality of signatures. Pattern Recognition **45**(3), 993–1003 (2012)
10. Lai, S., Jin, L.: Recurrent adaptation networks for online signature verification. IEEE Trans. Inf. Forensics Secur. **14**, 1624–1637 (2019)
11. Li, C., et al.: A stroke-based RNN for writer-independent online signature verification. In: Proceedings of International Conference on Document Analysis and Recognition (ICDAR), pp. 526–532 (2019)
12. Miguel-Hurtado, O., Guest, R., Chatzisterkotis, T.: A new approach to automatic signature complexity assessment. In: Proceedings of IEEE International Carnahan Conference on Security Technology (ICCST), pp. 1–7 (2016)
13. Ortega-Garcia, J., et al.: MCYT baseline corpus: a bimodal biometric database. IEE Proc. Vis. Image Signal Proc. **150**(6), 395–401 (2003)
14. Parkhi, O.M., Vedaldi, A., Zisserman, A.: Deep face recognition. In: Proceedings of British Machine Vision Conference (2015)
15. Sekhar, C., Mukherjee, P., Guru, D.S., Pulabaigari, V.: OSVNet: convolutional Siamese network for writer independent online signature verification. In: Proceedings of International Conference on Document Analysis and Recognition (ICDAR) (2019)

16. Tolosana, R., Vera-Rodriguez, R., Fierrez, J., Morales, A., Ortega-Garcia, J.: Benchmarking desktop and mobile handwriting across COTS devices: the e-BioSign biometric database. PLoS ONE **12**, e0176792 (2017)

17. Tolosana, R., Vera-Rodriguez, R., Fierrez, J., Ortega-Garcia, J.: Exploring recurrent neural networks for on-line handwritten signature biometrics. IEEE Access **6**, 5128–5138 (2018)

18. Tolosana, R., Vera-Rodriguez, R., Fierrez, J., Ortega-Garcia, J.: Presentation attacks in signature biometrics: types and introduction to attack detection. In: Marcel, S., Nixon, M.S., Fierrez, J., Evans, N. (eds.) Handbook of Biometric Anti-Spoofing. ACVPR, pp. 439–453. Springer, Cham (2019). https://doi.org/10.1007/978-3-319-92627-8_19

19. Tolosana, R., Vera-Rodriguez, R., Fierrez, J., Ortega-Garcia, J.: BioTouchPass2: Touchscreen password biometrics using time-aligned recurrent neural networks. IEEE Trans. Inf. Forensics Secur. **5**, 2616–2628 (2020)

20. Tolosana, R., Vera-Rodriguez, R., Fierrez, J., Ortega-Garcia, J.: DeepSign: Deep on-line signature verification. arXiv preprint arXiv:2002.10119 (2020)

21. Tolosana, R., Vera-Rodriguez, R., Fierrez, R., Morales, A., Ortega-Garcia, J.: Do you need more data? the DeepSignDB on-line handwritten signature biometric database. In: Proceedings of 15th IAPR International Conference on Document Analysis and Recognition, ICDAR (2019)

22. Tolosana, R., Vera-Rodriguez, R., Guest, R., Fierrez, J., Ortega-Garcia, J.: Exploiting complexity in pen- and touch-based signature biometrics. Int. J. Doc. Anal. Recogn. **23**, 129–141 (2020)

23. Tolosana, R., Vera-Rodriguez, R., Ortega-Garcia, J., Fierrez, J.: Preprocessing and feature selection for improved sensor interoperability in online biometric signature verification. IEEE Access **3**, 478–489 (2015)

24. Tolosana, R., Vera-Rodriguez, R., Fierrez, J., Ortega-Garcia, J.: Reducing the template aging effect in on-line signature biometrics. IET Biometrics **8**(6), 422–430 (2019)

25. Vera-Rodriguez, R., et al.: DeepSignCX: Signature complexity detection using recurrent neural networks. In: Proceedings of 15th International Conference on Document Analysis and Recognition, ICDAR (September 2019)

26. Wu, X., Kimura, A., Iwana, B.K., Uchida, S., Kashino, K.: Deep dynamic time warping: end-to-end local representation learning for online signature verification. In: Proceedings of International Conference on Document Analysis and Recognition (ICDAR) (2019)

A Novel Ensemble Framework for Face Search

Shashank Vats$^{(\boxtimes)}$, Sankalp Jain, and Prithwijit Guha(iD)

Department of Electronics and Electrical Engineering
Indian Institute of Technology Guwahati, Assam, India
shashank.vats8@gmail.com, jainsankalp7913@gmail.com, pguha@iitg.ac.in

Abstract. This paper proposes an ensemble of different state-of-art algorithms for realizing a face search system aimed at achieving higher accuracies compared to any single algorithm. This is achieved by leveraging most promising deep networks (Facenet, OpenFace, DeepFace, and VGGFace – originally trained for face recognition) and different Approximate Nearest Neighbor Search (ANNS) algorithms (Annoy and LSHash). Face images in the database are subjected to feature extraction (embeddings computed by deep networks) and indexing (in set structure for faster search) by ANNS algorithms. An input face query image is processed in the following four stages. First, the face region is detected from the query image and appropriately aligned for further processing. Second, the facial features are extracted using multiple deep networks. Third, the ANNS algorithms perform fast search by efficiently shrinking the gallery size from millions to a few hundred faces. Fourth, a fine matching is performed using two different methods separately to produce the final search results. These are (a) cosine similarity and (b) score-based matching and re-ranking of results. The experimental results demonstrate the diversity in results obtained by use of multiple feature extractors and ANNS techniques and the accuracy achieved by using the proposed ensemble framework.

Keywords: Biometric analysis · Face search · Ensemble learning

1 Introduction

Images (and videos) are playing a more important role in our lives than ever before due to the increasing use of smartphones, media sharing sites, surveillance cameras (in public places), thereby leading to a surge in digital images (and videos). Estimates suggest that more than 1 trillion photos were taken in 2018. A large percentage of them contain humans. The recent success of deep convolutional neural networks in different fields of AI has established its necessity in visual information extraction from vast amounts of image data. These deep models can be deployed for the efficient extraction of different human-specific information from images. These are person's identity [1, 16, 20, 22], facial emotion, activities etc. Among these, face related information are of particular interest.

S. Vats and S. Jain—These authors have an equal contribution.

© Springer Nature Switzerland AG 2021
A. Del Bimbo et al. (Eds.): ICPR 2020 Workshops, LNCS 12665, pp. 514–528, 2021.
https://doi.org/10.1007/978-3-030-68821-9_43

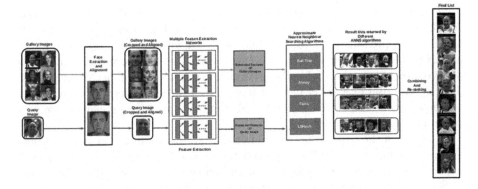

Fig. 1. The functional block diagram of the proposed framework. Multiple face specific deep networks are employed to extract features as real valued embeddings. Different approximate nearest neighbor search algorithms are employed to search for the features (embeddings) nearest to that of a query face.

Researchers in the vision and biometrics community have approached problems related to face detection, verification, recognition, emotion recognition, pose estimation, gender identification, age estimation, and search in databases. A detailed discussion of these individual problems is out of the scope of this work. Interested readers may refer to [18,27] for a detailed review of these topics. This work focuses on face search in databases. Here, a ranked list of top-k similar faces (from database) is returned in response to the query image submitted to the system. A well-designed face search system is optimized for searching in large databases in the minimal time while maximizing the correct number of hits in the top-k responses.

Ensemble methods in machine learning have demonstrated a reduction in error rates by combining multiple base classifiers (or regressors) learned from datasets generated by different diversity induction techniques. This motivated us to propose an ensemble of multiple deep networks and approximate nearest neighbor search (ANNS) techniques for the task of face search. The proposed framework has two distinct components – (a) face feature collection and (b) face query on database. This framework involves the following operations – (i) face extraction and alignment; (ii) face feature extraction using multiple deep networks; (iii) face indexing in the database through hashing techniques suitable for ANNS techniques; (iv) approximate nearest neighbor search to produce a gallery of similar-looking faces and combining results obtained from each network-ANNS combination; (v) fine matching for further reduction of search results using cosine distance or rank based score. Feature collection involves operations (i), (ii) and (iii) in order. On the other hand, query response generation involves operations (i),(ii),(iv), and (v) in order. The proposed approach is benchmarked on two standard datasets against baseline approaches using a combination of single deep network and ANNS algorithm. A strategy is discussed to determine a good value for the gallery size. Figure 1 depicts the process flow explained above.

The main contributions of this work can be summarized as follows. **First**, An ensemble approach for face search involving multiple faces specific deep networks and approximate nearest neighbor search algorithms. A deep network and an ANNS technique together form a *base search system*. **Second**, Combination of search results from individual base search systems to obtain a diverse gallery. **Third**, Proposal of a novel method to re-rank results obtained by using query responses from base search systems. This functions as the combiner for the proposed ensemble framework.

The rest of the paper is organized in the following manner. The related works are discussed in Sect. 2. The proposed framework is described in Sect. 3. The experimental results of our proposal are presented in Sect. 4. Finally, we conclude in Sect. 5 and outline the future extensions of present work.

2   Related Works

The face search system has three major components. These are (a) face detection and alignment, (b) face feature extraction, and (c) approximate nearest neighbor search algorithms. Related works in these domains are described in the following subsections.

2.1   Face Detection and Alignment

The first promising work on face detection was proposed by Viola et al. [23]. This is a general object detector that operates in real-time. However, a single detector is limited to frontal faces only, and multiple detectors are trained on profile faces to handle faces with a varying pose. This detector uses Haar-like features and speeds up computation using integral images. Further, it employs the AdaBoost algorithm to select strong features among the computed ones and uses a cascade approach for quick rejection of non-facial images.

Zhang et al. [27] have proposed the multi-purpose MTCNN network. MTCNN leverages a cascaded architecture with three stages of deep convolutional networks to predict face and landmark locations in a coarse-to-fine manner. It also proposes joint face detection and alignment and adopts carefully designed lightweight CNN architecture for real-time performance. The MTCNN also uses a cascaded approach to reject false positives quickly. The MTCNN is built upon a multi-task learning framework.

2.2   Face Feature Extraction

Researchers have proposed several approaches for face feature extraction. Such proposals range from handcrafted features to learned embeddings. Recent works have mostly focused on embeddings derived from deep networks trained in discriminative framework.

Taigman et al. proposed *DeepFace* [22] architecture in 2014. It employed an eight-layer neural network with over 120 million connection weights and was trained on over four million images uploaded by over 4000 Facebook users. A 3-channel (RGB) facial image of size 152×152 serves as the input, whereas the output is a 4096-dimensional embedding. The model minimizes cross-entropy loss for each training sample. Facebook researchers claimed human-level performance and state of the art accuracy of $97.35\% \pm 0.25\%$.

Table 1. Comparison of feature extraction models

Method	Public time	Loss	Architecture	Number of networks	Training set	Accuracy ± Std (%)
DeepFace	2014	Softmax	AlexNet	3	Facebook (4.4M, 4K)	97.35 ± 0.25
Facenet	2015	Triplet loss	GoogleNet-24	1	Google (500M, 10M)	99.63 ± 0.09
VGGFace	2015	Softmax	VGGNet-16	1	VGGFace (2.6M, 2.6K)	98.95
OpenFace	2016	Triplet loss	Inception-ResNet V1	1	CASIA-WebFace (495K, 10.5K) + FaceScrub(107K, 530)	92.92 ± 1.34

Schroff et al. proposed *Facenet* [20] in 2015. It is built on the inception-net model. A 3-channel (RGB) face image of size 160×160 serves as the input, whereas the output is a 128-dimensional embedding. The model is trained using triplet loss, where it minimizes the euclidean distance between the anchor and the positive sample and maximizes the euclidean distance between the anchor and the negative sample, for a given triplet. It is trained on Google's private dataset, which contains over 500 million face images of more than 10 million people. The paper reported state of the art accuracy of $99.63\% \pm 0.09\%$ on the LFW dataset.

Omkar et al. proposed *VGGFace* [16] in 2015. It employed a 22-layer convolutional neural network where it trains over 145 million parameters. It is trained on the VGGFace dataset consisting of over 2.6 million face images with 2622 different identities. A 3-channel (RGB) face image of size 224×224 serves as the input, whereas the output is a 2622-dimensional embedding. It adopts an empirical softmax log loss for feature learning. The paper reports 98.95% accuracy on the LFW dataset.

OpenFace [1] was proposed by Brandon et al. in 2016. This work is based on an earlier work on unified embeddings for face recognition and clustering [20]. This architecture builds on the Inception-Resnet-V1 network. A 3-channel (RGB) face image of size 96×96 is given as input, whereas the output is a 128-dimensional embedding. The model adopts triplet loss for feature learning and is trained on the combination of CASIA-Webface and the Face-scrub dataset. The paper reports 92.92% accuracy on the LFW dataset.

2.3   Approximate Nearest Neighbor Search (ANNS)

The approximate nearest neighbor search or similarity search aims to find the top-k nearest neighbors for the query face from a gallery dataset. The gallery dataset is structured in a specific way to facilitate fast search and generally consist of high-dimensional features. Algorithms performing an exact k-NN search can be slow for large databases and reduce the practicality of the system. An alternative is to use approximate k-NN search algorithms that are fast enough while maintaining good accuracy.

The approaches towards approximate neighbor search can be broadly categorized into two groups. These are quantization [11] and hashing [10]. Both these methods take advantage of the fact that the feature vectors generated by deep CNNs are fixed in length. Several new modifications like IMI [2], OPQ [6], LOPQ [12], Faiss [8] were proposed to the basic product quantization (PQ) known as IVFADC [11]. Previous works on face search, such as the ones proposed by Wang et al. [24] and Qi et al. [17], have adopted PQ and Faiss respectively for similarity search operations.

Hashing based methods such as LSH [4], multiple-feature LSH [21], and MIH [15] project n-dimensional deep features to a discriminative space of fewer dimensions, thereby reducing the searching time in comparison to the exhaustive linear search. Zou et al. [28] proposed two new GPU-hash and M-index-hash based searching techniques. Other approximate search methods mentioned in the work of Li et al. [13] can also be used for nearest neighbor search operations.

3   Proposed Framework

The proposed framework consists of the following three steps. First step is face detection from input image and the alignment of detected face image region for ensuring uniformity (Subsect. 3.1). Second step is multiple deep networks based feature extraction from aligned faces to obtain real-valued multi-dimensional embeddings (Subsect. 3.2). Further, we make a structured database to store these extracted features. Third, the generation of query response using features extracted from the query face. This feature is compared to the gallery image features stored in the database. Our goal is to return a list of faces from the gallery database, which are identified as sharing the same identity with the query image or being the most similar to the query image.

3.1   Face Detection and Alignment

The Viola-Jones face detector [9] is used to extract face regions from images. The OpenCV implementation for the same is used for this purpose. It uses a Haar classifier cascade with 68 facial landmarks. The detected face region is cropped and rotated such that the line joining the eyes becomes horizontal. The alignment is performed to maintain uniformity among the detected faces. This proposal uses four feature extraction networks, each of which takes input face images of different sizes. Thus, each detected face is cropped multiple times to satisfy the input specifications of a particular network.

3.2   Feature Extraction

The aligned faces are passed through four different networks to generate real-valued multi-dimensional embeddings. These networks contain a different number of layers and produce features with different dimensions. We adopt the ensemble method to reduce the effect of the bias formed by a single network by using multiple networks. Facenet [20] generates 128-dimensional embedding for 160×160 input face size while VGGFace [16] generates a 2622-dimensional embedding for a 224×224 input face size. OpenFace [1] also produces 128-dimensional embedding, but for a smaller 96×96 input face size, whereas Deep-Face [22] produces 4096-dimensional embedding for 152×152 input face size. These networks were chosen as they are among the most popular deep networks in the field of face recognition. These networks were trained on different datasets and had different backbone architecture. This ensures diversity in search results.

3.3   Face Search

The query image that acts as an input to the face search system is first subjected to face region detection and alignment, followed by feature extraction using all the four networks. The query face feature extracted from a network is matched against the gallery face features extracted by the same feature extraction network. As exact nearest neighbor search algorithms are slow and bulky, we use approximate nearest neighbor search (ANNS) algorithms to achieve low latency and less memory for larger gallery sizes. We have experimented with the following algorithms for ANNS.

The Ball Tree [14] is a binary tree, whose leaf nodes represent a set of points. At each non-leaf node, the set of points are divided according to their distance from the center points of child nodes. Points represented by a non-leaf node are divided into its children such that Eq. 1 and 2 are satisfied.

$$Points(Node.child1) \cap Points(Node.child2) = \varphi, \qquad (1)$$

$$Points(Node.child1) \cup Points(Node.child2) = Points(Node) \qquad (2)$$

Each node has a pivot and a radius. The pivot is either a point represented by the node or the centroid of all the points represented by the node. The radius is the maximum distance of any point represented by the node from the pivot of the node. Euclidean distance is adopted to decide the proximity of the point from pivot. Let, the query point be $\mathbf{q}$ and $\mathbf{x} \in Points(Node)$, where $Points(Node)$ is the set of points represented by the node. Thus, by using the triangle inequality we get the following expressions.

$$|\mathbf{x} - \mathbf{q}| \geq |\mathbf{q} - Node.Pivot| - Node.Radius \qquad (3)$$

$$|\mathbf{x} - \mathbf{q}| \leq |\mathbf{q} - Node.Pivot| + Node.Radius \qquad (4)$$

Using Eqs. 3 and 4, we can search for any query point $\mathbf{q}$ in $O(d \log N)$ time where N represents the number of total points in the dataset and d represents the dimensionality of feature vector. A similar strategy is used by KD-Tree [3]. However, a KD-Tree has an exponential dependence on the number of dimensions [5], while Ball tree has a linear dependence on the number of dimensions [14]. This proposal uses scikit-learn (Python library) implementation of Ball tree.

Locality Sensitive Hashing [4] utilizes a mapping function in which data points close to each other in some n-dimensional space have the same d-length hash value, whereas points far off have different hash values. Mathematically, a hash function h of LSH is such that,

$$P_r[h(x) = h(y)] \geq p_1, \text{ if } f(x, y) < r_1 \tag{5}$$

$$P_r[h(x) = h(y)] \leq p_2, \text{ if } f(x, y) > r_2, \tag{6}$$

where $f(x, y)$ is the distance between the points x and y. An approximate solution to nearest neighbor problem may be found by hashing the query embedding and scanning the buckets where the query embedding is hashed. This proposal uses the Python implementation of LSHash (lshash Python library). A hash size of 20 is used, and the number of hashtables is set to 500.

Annoy was developed by *spotify.com* to improve its music recommendation system. It constructs multiple hierarchical 2-means trees. Recursively partitioning the data space is the basis of the formation of trees, and all trees are independent of each other. At each iteration, two pivots are formed by running a simplified clustering algorithm on a subset of samples from the input data points. The two pivots help define a hyperplane that is equidistant from both the pivots. The data points are further partitioned into two sub-trees according to the hyperplane, and the algorithm builds the index on each sub-trees recursively. The search procedure uses a priority queue where nodes are pushed or popped out of the queue based on their respective key values. Initially, all tree roots are pushed with key values set to infinity. A node's key value is calculated as the minimum of its parent's key value and the negative of its distance to the hyperplane. The node with the maximum key value is chosen for exploration. This proposal uses the implementation provided by *spotify* and builds a forest of 1000 trees for this work.

Product Quantization (PQ) decomposes the original vector space into the Cartesian product of M lower-dimensional subspaces and quantizes them separately. By dividing the original dataspace into sub-spaces, we reduce the complexity of similarity matching. Search procedures are assisted by inverted indexing. A vector quantizer is a function q that maps a vector $q(\mathbf{x}) \in C$. Here $C = \{c_i; i \in I\}$, is a codebook and index set $I = \{0, \ldots (k-1)\}$. The *cell*, which is the set of vectors that are mapped to same index i is given by

$$V_i = \{\mathbf{x} \in \mathbb{R}^d : q(\mathbf{x}) = c_i\} \tag{7}$$

Thus, these k cells partition the d-dimensional space. But as the value of d increases, the value of optimal k increases exponentially. So we split the vector

$\mathbf{x}$ into m sub-vectors $\mathbf{v}_j, 1 \leq j \leq m$ of dimension $d^* = \dfrac{d}{m}$, where m is a factor of d. The sub-vectors are quantized using m different quantizers. So $\mathbf{x}$ is mapped as follows I = { 0 , ... (k−1) }

$$\underbrace{x_1, \ldots, x_{d^*}}_{v_1(x)}, \ldots, \underbrace{x_{d-d^*+1}, \ldots, x_d}_{v_m(x)} \rightarrow q_1(v_1(x)), \ldots q_m(v_m(x)) \qquad (8)$$

To compute distance between two vectors $\mathbf{x}$ and $\mathbf{y}$, we approximate the distance $d(\mathbf{x},\mathbf{y})$ as $\hat{d}(\mathbf{x},\mathbf{y})$, which is given by

$$\hat{d}(\mathbf{x},\mathbf{y}) = d(q(\mathbf{x}), q(\mathbf{y})) = \sqrt{\sum_j d(q_j(x), q_j(y))^2} \qquad (9)$$

This proposal uses Facebook's implementation of PQ, [8].

The above-mentioned four different ANNS algorithms are separately used for searching the nearest neighbors of the query face feature in each set of gallery face features. A set of gallery face features consists of features extracted from the same feature extraction network. Therefore, there are four gallery face feature sets. We compare the different ANNS algorithms on the following parameters. First, the average time it takes to perform a search for one query image. Second, the percentage (accuracy) that the correct identity face appears in the first position. The correct identity face share the same identity with the query face. The overlap of search results (faces) from different ANNS algorithms is also shown using a Venn diagram (Fig. 2).

Table 2. Accuracy at first rank comparison of ANNS algorithms for Facenet network (CASIA-WebFace)

ANNS algorithm	Accuracy (%)	Time complexity
Ball Tree	73.2	$\mathcal{O}(\log n)$
LSHash	73.6	$\mathcal{O}(Lk)$
Annoy	73.2	$\mathcal{O}(\log \log n)$
Faiss	73.4	$\mathcal{O}(\log n)$

As the accuracy in the first rank is near identical (Table 2) for all ANNS algorithms for a particular feature extraction network, we only include those ANNS algorithms in our ensemble framework which offer more diversity in the search result faces. We try to achieve higher accuracy by combining the results of multiple ANNS algorithms as they produce diverse, but correct results individually.

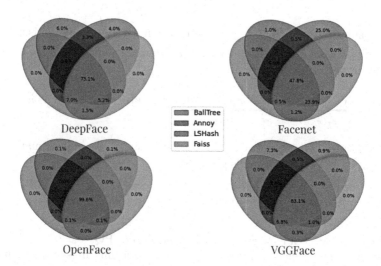

Fig. 2. Overlapping of result lists produced by different approximate nearest neighbor search algorithms

From Fig. 2, we conclude that ANNS algorithms like Annoy and LSHash approximately cover all of the results space. This implies that the other two algorithms do not offer any variety. Therefore, we proceed with only two algorithms, namely, Annoy and LSHash. The use of 4 feature extraction networks and 2 ANNS algorithms leads to $4 \times 2 = 8$ different base search systems for every possible combination of feature extraction network and ANNS algorithm. These systems produce eight result lists in response to a query image. By performing ANNS, we shrink the gallery size to a few hundred faces depending upon the list size k. It is noteworthy that these 8 result sets might have significant overlaps.

3.4   Fine Matching

List size of k leads to $8 \times k$ query results. Out of these, there are repetitions, relevant results, and false positives. The fine matching or re-ranking stage aims to improve search accuracy by identifying the repetitions and removing false positives. The following fine matching techniques are used in this proposal.

Cosine similarity based ranking - All query responses in eight lists are stored after the removal of duplicates (repetitions). The final set of results now acts as a smaller gallery to the query face. Due to fewer faces in the gallery, an exact nearest neighbor search can be performed to improve the accuracy. The cosine distance between the query face feature and the smaller gallery face features are measured to re-rank the gallery faces. Here, a lower distance implies a higher similarity between the faces. This re-ranked list of faces provides the news search result.

Score based Re-ranking - We devise a new scoring pattern for faces that incorporates their frequency of occurrence in the individual result lists and the ranks they get according to the ANNS algorithm. For a given list size k for every individual result list, the score S_i for the ith face is given as

$$S_i = \sum_j (k + 1 - rank_{ij}) \tag{10}$$

where, $rank_{ij}$ represents the rank of ith face in the jth result list. If a face i is not present in a particular result list j, then $rank_{ij} = k+1$. This makes the term $(k + 1 - rank_{ij})$ equal to zero for that particular j. A particular face can occur at various ranks in different search lists. We sort the faces in descending order with respect to their scores to form the final result list.

4   Experiments and Results

This proposal is benchmarked on two standard face datasets. First, the Labelled Faces in Wild (LFW) [7] consists of 13,233 face images of 5,749 persons, of which 1,680 people have two or more images in the dataset. These images are generated from news articles on the web and are further filtered using the Viola-Jones detector, eliminating the side, bottom, and top views of faces. Second, the CASIA-WebFace [26] dataset consists of 494,414 images of 10,575 subjects. CASIA-WebFace images are collected from the IMDb website. The faces were detected with a multi-view face detector. This proposal is evaluated against baseline search systems consisting of a single deep network (with pre-trained weights) and a nearest neighbor search algorithm. For individual search systems, a query result list size is taken to be $k = 50$.

This work does not train a new feature extraction network. Thus, the proposed system can not be evaluated based on the standard face recognition protocols. Individual accuracies of the feature extraction networks used are presented in Table 1. For the evaluation of individual networks in the face search domain, we choose 1001 random images of identities having multiple images in the gallery. After face detection and alignment, features are extracted by the networks. We use Annoy for face search on all different features extracted from networks. We calculate the accuracy at the first rank of the system consisting of a single face extraction network followed by Annoy in Table 3.

The diversity in results offered by these individual feature extraction networks is also shown using the Venn diagram in Fig. 3. It can be observed from Fig. 3 that these networks possess minimal similarity in their search results and hence, offer high diversity. This finding incentivizes the idea to use an ensemble method to achieve higher accuracy.

Similarly, the accuracies at the first rank for different combinations of ANNS algorithm and re-ranking technique applied to the ensemble framework are estimated. The proposed system achieves the highest 98.20% accuracy on CASIA-WebFace when adopting an ensemble network with Annoy & LSHash and applying score based re-ranking. Similarly, for LFW, we achieve the highest accuracy

Table 3. Accuracy at first rank comparison of feature extraction networks for Annoy algorithm (CASIA-WebFace)

Feature extraction network	Accuracy (%)
Facenet	68.83
DeepFace	29.07
VGGFace	68.23
OpenFace	9.29
ResNet50	8.6

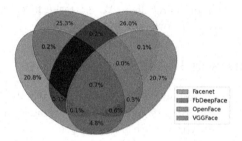

Fig. 3. Overlapping of result lists produced by different feature extraction networks

of 86.31% for our proposed ensemble framework. Also, the proposed network outperforms any singular feature extraction network as evident from the data in Table 3 and Table 4.

For reference, we also report the accuracy achieved by related works in face search. Zou et al. have reported an accuracy of 72.5% in [28]. They have used re-trained Resnet network, hashing based on PCA and binerization, and 2-stage matching. Wang et al. have used their own deep network for feature generation and 2-stage matching in [24]. They report 98.02% accuracy under the standard protocol and 88.03% accuracy under BLUFR protocol on LFW database. Sadovnik et al. have developed a deep network targeted towards face similarity rather than face recognition in [19]. They have reported an accuracy of 92.44% for rank under 5 and 33.2% at rank 1. Qi et al. have used a retrained Norm-Face network [25] and Product Quantization in [17] and reported an accuracy of 86.18%.

The average rank of faces of the same identity in result lists and the average time taken per query using different combinations of approximate nearest neighbor search algorithms and re-ranking techniques are listed in Table 5. We calculate average rank by averaging all ranks in the result list of a query face at which images with the same identity occur. The average time taken consists of searching and re-ranking operations.

Sample final result lists using cosine similarity based re-ranking and score based re-ranking are shown in Fig. 4 and Fig. 5 respectively.

Table 4. Accuracy comparison between different systems for face search (CASIA-WebFace)

System	Re-ranking technique	Accuracy (%)
Ensemble network + Annoy	Cosine similarity	79.62
Ensemble method + Annoy	Score	74.52
Ensemble network + LSH	Cosine similarity	78.62
Ensemble network + LSH	Score	97.60
Ensemble network + (Annoy and LSH)	Cosine similarity	92.92
Ensemble network + (Annoy and LSH)	Score	98.20

Table 5. Average rank of faces of same identity and average time taken in one query using different combinations of ANNS algorithms (CASIA-WebFace)

ANNS algorithms	Strategy	Avg. rank of face of the same identity	Avg. time per query (s)
Annoy	Cosine similarity	3.658	0.178
Annoy	Score based	5.687	0.140
LSHash	Cosine similarity	8.374	107.627^a
LSHash	Score based	1.147	107.589^a
Annoy + LSHash	Cosine similarity	1.968	107.800^a
Annoy + LSHash	Score based	1.275	107.728^a

a These results were produced when the search operation was running on the CPU as LSHash library does not have a GPU implementation.

Fig. 4. Sample final result list for a query face using cosine similarity based re-ranking. Note the similarity in the search results. This can be attributed to the operation of cosine distance which enforces the inclusion of only (very) similar images while probably rejecting the variations in images of the same person.

We also plot the number of correct identity faces (correct hits) present in the result list while varying the result list's length. We find that the number of correct identity faces saturates as the result list's length increases, as shown in Fig. 6. An optimum choice for result list length could be the size where saturation starts.

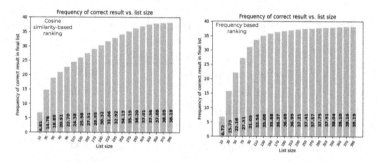

Fig. 5. Sample final result list for a query face using score based re-ranking. Note the diversity in the search results. The results contain variations in face alignments, illumination conditions etc. of the same person while maintaining the accuracy for the same gallery size as in Fig. 4.

Fig. 6. Number of correct result in result list vs result list length

5   Conclusion

An ensemble of deep feature extraction networks (DeepFace, Facenet, OpenFace, and VGGFace) and approximate nearest neighbor search algorithms (Annoy and LSHash) is proposed for the task of face search. A pairing of a deep network and an ANNS algorithm forms a base search system. The ensemble contains eight base search systems whose search results are combined using a score based re-ranking scheme.

The following results are experimentally demonstrated. First, the ensemble framework achieves higher accuracy compared to any base search system. Second, the score based re-ranking scheme outperforms cosine distance-based ranking scheme as it leverages the rankings of the results produced by individual windows and scores accordingly. In contrast, the cosine distance-based re-ranking scheme does not give weightage to the image's previous ranks but re-ranks all images based on cosine-distance with the query image. Third, we confer that Annoy and LSHash give better diversity out of the four ANNS algorithms. However, LSHash takes more time to compute the results with similar accuracy. Fourth, the diversity in the results of base search systems can be attributed to the face feature extraction networks. Using a multitude of ANNS algorithms is less beneficial as the ANNS algorithms give similar results for a single face feature extraction network.

The present work has only considered images from standard datasets. In the future, different types of images from different sources e.g., surveillance cameras, scanned images from newspapers and magazines, and hand-made sketches for investigative purposes, can be used to construct the dataset as well as the query. Also, parallel implementations and faster ANNS algorithms can be explored for reducing latency in the face search system.

References

1. Amos, B., Ludwiczuk, B., Satyanarayanan, M., et al.: Openface: a general-purpose face recognition library with mobile applications. CMU School Comput. Sci. **6**(2) (2016)
2. Babenko, A., Lempitsky, V.: The inverted multi-index. IEEE Trans. Pattern Anal. Mach. Intell. **37**(6), 1247–1260 (2014)
3. Bentley, J.L.: Multidimensional binary search trees used for associative searching. Commun. ACM, 509–517 (1975)
4. Datar, M., Immorlica, N., Indyk, P., Mirrokni, V.S.: Locality-sensitive hashing scheme based on p-stable distributions. In: Twentieth Annual Symposium on Computational Geometry, pp. 253–262 (2004)
5. Friedman, J.H., Bentley, J.L., Finkel, R.A.: An algorithm for finding best matches in logarithmic expected time. ACM Trans. Math. Softw. **3**, 209–226 (1977)
6. Ge, T., He, K., Ke, Q., Sun, J.: Optimized product quantization. IEEE Trans. Pattern Anal. Mach. Intell. 744–755
7. Huang, G.B., Mattar, M., Berg, T., Learned-Miller, E.: Labeled faces in the wild: a database for studying face recognition in unconstrained environments. In: Workshop on Faces in 'Real-Life' Images: Detection, Alignment, and Recognition, October 2008
8. Johnson, J., Douze, M., Jégou, H.: Billion-scale similarity search with gpus. IEEE Trans. Big Data 1 (2019)
9. Jones, M.J., Viola, P.A.: Fast multi-view face detection. CTIT Technical Reports Series (2003)
10. Junjie Yan, Zhen Lei, Dong Yi, Li, S.Z.: Towards incremental and large scale face recognition. In: 2011 International Joint Conference on Biometrics, pp. 1–6 (2011)
11. Jégou, H., Douze, M., Schmid, C.: Product quantization for nearest neighbor search. IEEE Trans. Pattern Anal. Mach. Intell. 117–128 (2011)
12. Kalantidis, Y., Avrithis, Y.: Locally optimized product quantization for approximate nearest neighbor search. In: IEEE Conference on Computer Vision and Pattern Recognition, pp. 2321–2328 (2014)
13. Li, W., Zhang, Y., Sun, Y., Wang, W., Zhang, W., Lin, X.: Approximate nearest neighbor search on high dimensional data - experiments, analyses, and improvement (v1.0). CoRR abs/1610.02455 (2016)
14. Liu, T., Moore, A.W., Gray, A.: New algorithms for efficient high-dimensional nonparametric classification. J. Mach. Learn. Res. 1135–1158, June 2006
15. Norouzi, M., Punjani, A., Fleet, D.J.: Fast exact search in hamming space with multi-index hashing. IEEE Trans. Pattern Anal. Mach. Intell. **6**, 1107–1119 (2014)
16. Parkhi, O.M., Vedaldi, A., Zisserman, A.: Deep face recognition. In: British Machine Vision Conference, pp. 41.1–41.12, September 2015

17. Qi, C., Liu, Z., Su, F.: Accurate and efficient similarity search for large scale face recognition. CoRR abs/1806.00365 (2018)
18. Ranjan, R., Patel, V.M., Chellappa, R.: Hyperface: a deep multi-task learning framework for face detection, landmark localization, pose estimation, and gender recognition. IEEE Trans. Pattern Anal. Mach. Intell. **41**, 121–135 (2017)
19. Sadovnik, A., Gharbi, W., Vu, T., Gallagher, A.: Finding your lookalike: measuring face similarity rather than face identity. In: 2018 IEEE/CVF Conference on Computer Vision and Pattern Recognition Workshops, pp. 2408–24088 (2018)
20. Schroff, F., Kalenichenko, D., Philbin, J.: Facenet: a unified embedding for face recognition and clustering. In: IEEE Conference on Computer Vision and Pattern Recognition, pp. 815–823, June 2015
21. Song, J., Yang, Y., Huang, Z., Shen, H.T., Hong, R.: Multiple feature hashing for real-time large scale near-duplicate video retrieval. In: 19th ACM International Conference on Multimedia, pp. 423–432 (2011)
22. Taigman, Y., Yang, M., Ranzato, M., Wolf, L.: Deepface: closing the gap to human-level performance in face verification. In: 2014 IEEE Conference on Computer Vision and Pattern Recognition, pp. 1701–1708 (2014)
23. Viola, P., Jones, M.: Rapid object detection using a boosted cascade of simple features. In: IEEE Computer Society Conference on Computer Vision and Pattern Recognition. CVPR 2001. vol. 1, p. I (2001)
24. Wang, D., Otto, C., Jain, A.K.: Face search at scale. IEEE Trans. Pattern Anal. Mach. Intell. **6**, 1122–1136 (2017)
25. Wang, F., Xiang, X., Cheng, J., Yuille, A.L.: Normface: L_2 hypersphere embedding for face verification. CoRR abs/1704.06369 (2017)
26. Yi, D., Lei, Z., Liao, S., Li, S.Z.: Learning face representation from scratch. CoRR abs/1411.7923 (2014)
27. Zhang, K., Zhang, Z., Li, Z., Qiao, Y.: Joint face detection and alignment using multitask cascaded convolutional networks. IEEE Sig. Process. Lett. **23**(10), 1499–1503 (2016)
28. Zou, F., et al.: Fast large scale deep face search. Pattern Recogn. Lett. 83–90 (2020)

Real-Time Thermal Face Identification System for Low Memory Vision Applications Using CNN

Rami Reddy Devaram[1], Alessandro Ortis[1]($\boxtimes$) (iD), Sebastiano Battiato[1] (iD),
Arcangelo R. Bruna[2], and Valeria Tomaselli[2]

[1] Department of Mathematics and Computer Science, University of Catania,
Viale A. Doria, 6, 95125 Catania, Italy
ramireddy.devaram@phd.unict.it,
{alessandro.ortis,sebastiano.battiato}@unict.it
[2] STMicroelectronics, Catania 95121, Italy
{arcangelo.bruna,valeria.tomaselli}@st.com

Abstract. Image based face identification systems have attained optimal performance. However, the design of such systems often involves some issues related to extreme light conditions and privacy protection, among others. Since several years, Face Identification (FI) based on thermal images using deep neural networks (DNN) has received significant attention. Yet, the majority of the FI systems developed through DNN's need huge computational power; those systems are not suitable for the devices with memory limitations. In this paper, we proposed a new CNN framework based on depthwise separable convolutions for real-time face identification for low memory vision applications. The lack of publicly available thermal datasets makes very hard the research and developing of new techniques. In this work, we further present a new large-scale thermal face database called "ST_UNICT_Thermal_Face". As per our analysis, the evaluation of the learnt model using the data obtained in the single-day (without temporal variations), it might not stable over time. One of the main reasons behind the development of this database for the real-time evaluation of the proposed model depends on the fact that most thermal face identification systems are not stable over time and climate due to insufficient time data. The evaluation results exhibit that the proposed framework is suitable for the devices having limited memory and which is stable over time and different indoor environmental conditions.

Keywords: Thermal face identification · Thermal images ·
Convolutional neural networks

1 Introduction

Over the last two decades, Face Identification or Recognition, based on surveillance and traditional images obtained in the visible spectrum, have reached a

© Springer Nature Switzerland AG 2021
A. Del Bimbo et al. (Eds.): ICPR 2020 Workshops, LNCS 12665, pp. 529–543, 2021.
https://doi.org/10.1007/978-3-030-68821-9_44

significant level of advancement among various disciplines [5]. It has applied to many real world applications such as security and transportation. Although a face identification system based on visual images performs under controlled illumination conditions and there is a possibility to recognize faces of corpses, such system is not entirely suitable for the security applications. Nevertheless, in literature, we have a reliable biometric technology based on human physical or behavioural feature and can be used to identify human-beings such as fingerprint effect. There are various biometric systems based on fingerprints such as iris patterns, signatures, palm-prints, and voice. However, such systems require the involvement of the subject [18]. Among these, Thermal Face Identification based biometric technology has been attracting significant attention due to its various advantages, such as ease of handling with low-resolution images and robust to ambience illumination, economic friendly hardware and high recognition accuracy and privacy preserving. To address the limitations of the above-mentioned biometrics systems, we were motivated to develop a face identification system based on thermal Vision. In the processes to overcome the aforementioned matters, there are huge works for many years to learn some usual innovations that can be transferred across various recognition tasks. Accompanying this direction, Deep Convolutional Neural Networks (DCNN) have attained enormous progress in grabbing various tasks of computer vision problems [10,17]. However, since such algorithms require high computational and memory resources, proper strategies must be employed [1]. In this paper, we focused on a novel CNN model for mobile or embedded vision applications, the one of the goal is the learned model must fit into the low-memory portable device like STM32F7 Family Microcontrollers, which includes limited memory, in terms of RAM and Flash Memory.

The convolutional neural network itself having a dense computational model, a large number of parameters, heavy computing load, and excess memory access leads to large power consumption, which makes the task more challenging to embed the learnt model into mobile or other portable devices with limited hardware resources (fixed memory). The motivation behind the development of the proposed work that previous works reveal that the compression of large networks according to the tasks attains the significant results, such as SqueezeNet [8] which is based on fire module and ShuffleNet [27] modified from the residual structure with group pointwise convolution and channel shuffle operation.

First we performed attempts to retrain state of the art models such as ResNet50 and MobileNet on the publicly available dataset from scratch, in order to assess how these models perform on the thermal vision domain in terms of performance and the computational complexity. Although these models consumed huge memory and showing significant performance. However, to be adequately applied to real-time applications and low-memory portable devices like STM32F7 Family Microcontrollers having limited memory, we selected MobileNet architecture as the best alternative to meet the requirements of the task by compress and accelerate the network to reduce parameters, computation, ad the power consumption of the model. MobileNet is a lightweight network compared with

ResNet in terms of the number of parameters, and the performance is nearly similar with both models. Though, parameters and computational burden reduced by the implementation of depthwise separable convolutions.

2 Materials and Data

2.1 Thermal Camera

The proposed Thermal Image Database called "ST-UNICT-Thermal-Face" has been acquired using a PureThermal-2 FLIR Lepton Radiometric LWIR camera equipped with Smart I/O STM32F412CGU6 microcontroller and 50-degree field view module including stutter for automatic calibration. It is pre-configured to operate plug and play UVC 1.0 USB. The 'thermal image' acquired using a thermal camera can be handled as a Grayscale Image (2D-array @16bpp). Each value is related to the absolute temperature of the corresponding area. During acquisition, the camera can be configured to operate in a High gain state, which provides lower Noise Equivalent Differential Temperature and lower intra-scene range. It is using a focal-plane array of 160×120 active pixels. Integrated digital thermal image processing functions capable of filtering and compensation for environmental issues. The radiometric Lepton captures accurate, calibrated, non-contact temperature data in every pixel of each image with the thermal sensitivity of less then 50 millikelvin, Radiometric accuracy (35 °C blackbody) at High gain: ±5 °C @ 25 °C, at Low gain ±10 °C @ 25 °C and scene dynamic range at High gain is −10 °C to +140 °C and at Low gain is −10 °C to +400 °C. It scans 8 to 14 μm wavelength bands to generate uniform thermal images at up to 9 frame/s.

2.2 Microcontroller

With the help of STM32CubeMX extension AI conversion tool which is STM32Cube.AI, it is simple and effective interoperability with modern Deep Learning training tools broadly used by the AI developer can be directly imported into the STM32Cube.AI. In this research, to embed the pre-trained model, we utilized STM32F767 Microcontroller, it has a new set of AI solutions to map and run pre-trained ANN models on the board. Since, STM32F767 includes fixed high-speed embedded memories with a Flash memory up to 2 MB, 512 KB of SRAM. The objective of this research is the development of the smallest CNN model for vision applications, which adequately fit into such STM32F767 Microcontroller. Moreover, this device is incorporate high-performance Arm Cortex-M7 32 bit RISC core processor operating at up to 216 MHz, and it is enabled with Floating point unit (FPU) which supports double and single precision data processing instructions and data types.

2.3 Datasets

Development of a thermal face identification system requires input data to test and validate the performance of the system. Datasets are required to train deep

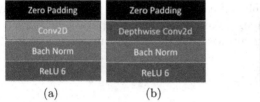 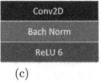

| (a) | (b) | (c) |

Fig. 1. CNN Blocks. (a). Standard Convolution Block, (b). Depthwise Convolution Block, (c). Pointwise Convolution Block

Table 1. Train, Validation and Test data distribution of Dataset-1

# Subjects	# Train	# Validation	# Test
12 Subjects	500	200	100
Total Samples	6000	2400	1200

learning models as well as to evaluate system performance. Proposed ST-UNICT-THERMAL-FACE DATABASE been obtained different states of ambience and the subject - a small Orientation of faces for flexible real-time system. It is very useful to obtain diverse data including various scenarios and to utilize the freely available sets to analyse the results of the experiments. Research Community frequently offered substantial datasets with respect to the various tasks. To evaluate the proposed model, we employed 5 Thermal Face datasets, including, public domain datasets. Since, unavailability of the subject, freely available data is not relevant to real-time evaluation. However, we proposed the following new benchmark datasets to evaluate the system in real-time. The description of all datasets we used in this research as follows.

Dataset-1. This dataset developed for the competition of Benchmark/Test Datasets by IEEE OTCBVS Workshop series [3]. The images have been captured using a long wave Raytheon L-3 Thermal-Eye 2000AS thermographic camera. The camera produces a resolution of 320 × 240 pixels of infrared images and this has been the final resolution chosen to evaluate the proposed model. It contains 20 subjects, and due to unbalanced classes distribution, we selected 12 subjects of 9600 images Table 1. The data acquired in different acquisition modalities, such as face orientation, ambience and occlusions. The images captured with Front, Right and Left orientations of a video with 20 frames in each acquisition. Moreover, the data obtained in indoor/outdoor conditions and various face occlusions including with and without Eye Glasses and Hat. The whole dataset is pre-processed and stored in 8-bit Grayscale JPEG format.

Table 2. Train, Validation and Test data distribution of Dataset-2

# Subjects	# Train	# Validation	# Test
29 Subjects	100	≈50	≈50
Total Samples	2900	1303	1305

Dataset-2. The images were captured using a PureThermal-2 Radiometric camera Sect. 2.1. The dataset developed to evaluate the proposed model in real-time. It contains 29 male and female subjects/people of 6405 images Table 2 with the resolution of 160 × 120 pixels. Each subject has been recorded in a single day as both snapshots and continues images (Videos) for further analysis. The whole dataset was captured in indoor (room) environment with different viewpoints Fig. 2 and accessories (Eyeglass, Cap, free and tied hair for women) Fig. 4 under uniform lighting and climate conditions. Each subject was asked to look at a fixed view-point continuously to 9 equidistant positions Fig. 3 making an estimated semi-circle around the camera with each accessory. The average time required for the whole acquisition process per individual subject has been 3 to 5 min. Moreover, the distance between the face of the subject and the camera is approximately between 120 cm to 150 cm to minimize the inherent parallax error. Finally, for the later advances, the entire data was saved in RAW-16bit TIFF format and further pre-processed to 8-bit JPEG visible grayscale image format to train and test the CNN model.

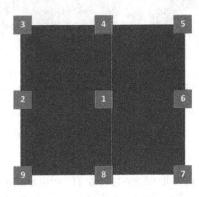

Fig. 2. Structure of head postures

Dataset-3. The whole dataset has been obtained with the same device and modalities used to as the Dataset-2 [2.3]. However, after the one-hold evaluation of the proposed model on the test set of the Dataset-2 [2.3], the system obtained optimal performance. Yet, due to temporal thermal variations between data used for training and real-time testing, the system performance is not optimal.

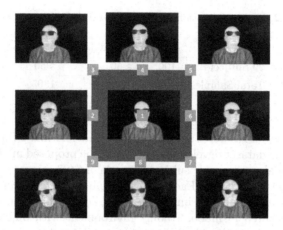

Fig. 3. Head Postures

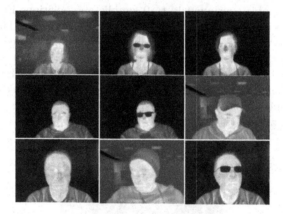

Fig. 4. Samples from the dataset

However, we acquired new data over multiple sessions and with a diverse environments (background) due to develop the system robust to background and its artifacts.

The dataset eventually developed with 11 subjects, a total of 14740 images acquired in 6 distinctive days between 10 to 20 days period, including the data from dataset-2 [2.3]. The data distribution for the train, Validation and testing of this dataset presented in Table 3.

Note: The Final Dataset available in public domain soon.

Table 3. Train, Validation and Test data distribution of Dataset-3

# Subjects	# Train	# Validation	# Test
11 Subjects	1000	200	140
Total Samples	11000	2200	1540

Dataset - 4. The Carl Database is one of the benchmark datasets obtained in three different scenarios such as visible, NIR and Thermal domain under various illumination conditions. In this paper, we utilise one the dataset from Carl-database, which is the dataset obtained in the thermal domain by using thermographic camera TESTO 880-3, it contains 41 subjects/people and 60 images/subject with the resolution of 320 × 240 pixels. In [4] provides the complete description of the dataset. However, the Carl thermal images dataset divided into two datasets. Such as the dataset contains the images with and without background (segmented). We evaluate the proposed model on both datasets to investigate is the background matters. In the following sections, we named dataset-4.1 and Dataset-4.2 for the images with background and without background respectively Table 4.

Table 4. Train, Validation and Test data distribution of Dataset-4A and Dataset-4B

# Subjects	# Train	# Validation	# Test
41 Subjects	40	10	10
Total Samples	1640	410	410

3   Related Works

Face Identification (FI) technologies are used in security related applications, it needs to be analysed well before going to deploy, such analysis well described in [6]. However, most of the technologies are utilized images obtained in the visible spectrum. Since the huge availability of thermal imagery technology, FI system based on thermal imagery seems more secured and robust compare with the FI system based on visible images. However, the features of skin colour and texture, often exploited to make inferences on face images [23], are not present in the thermal images, which are mainly determined by the absolute temperature values of the face. There are well traditional feature extraction or appearance based methods works for images acquired in the thermal domain, yet in [24] analysed and explored the conflicts by utilizing those approaches. Moreover, to extract thermal features in [15] performed Fast Independent Component Analysis and Gabor Wavelet Transformation, but it does not improve the recognition rate. Certainly, face identification in the thermal domain has been relatively limited compare with the visual domain. However, [11] explains the comparisons, benefits

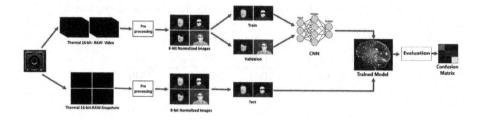

Fig. 5. Training and Testing Pipeline

and weaknesses of various thermal face recognition methods. [21,22] explores a relative study on the performance of various approaches for the FI system using both thermal and visual images and in authors in [9] provides an opinion on most of the research implemented on the face recognition approaches in both IR and Visible spectrum. Deep Learning methods might be an alternative to robust and real-time face identification system. In literature, many experiments showing great interest in the thermal domain. In [19] employed a standard pre-trained CNN based model to identify the person in thermal images. [13] works to develop a face recognition system by fusion of both CNN and SVM, but this approach needs huge computation power. In [25] proposed a multilayer CNN architecture, since the evaluation results are optimal, since those obtained on the data taken the same day as data used for training. In [16] proposed TIRFaceNet based on CNN, it takes extracted features from both visible and thermal images to train the network. Compare with all the previous works proposed approach is more convenient in terms of computational cost and temporal variations.

To improve the performance of the model with respect to their task, authors of [2,12,14,20,26] modified the state of the art models in terms of hyperparameters, size of the kernels and the architecture.

4   Proposed CNN Architecture

In this paper, we introduced a small and robust model based on CNN which is described in Fig. 6 for thermal face identification system, with advantages of the Depthwise Separable Convolution (DWSC) and modality of the MobileNet [7]. The architecture, presents an efficient tradeoff between complexity and performance of the system. It is typically designed for the devices with a shortage of computational power such as mobile or embedded based vision applications. The main goal of the proposed model is to significantly reduce the number of parameters by reducing the multiplication of the total number of floating-points. Proposed modernised architecture Fig. 6, employed two types layers such as standard convolution Fig. 1(a) and depthwise separable convolution. Depthwise separable convolution is divided into depthwise convolutions Fig. 1(b) followed by pointwise convolution Fig. 1(c). However, standard convolution built only on the top of the network, and the whole network remains work with only depthwise separable convolutions. Proposed topology having one standard convolution, eight depthwise convolutional layers followed by pointwise convolution layer each, one fully connected and a softmax classifier at the end of the network respectively. All the layers are followed by Batch Normalization and ReLU non-linearity except final softmax layer. To improve the performance by preserving the spatial information at the boarders after convolution operation we used Zeropadding in both standard and DWSC layers. One dropout layer is implanted at the end of the fully connected layer. To reduce the spatial resolution to one a final global average pooling used before the fully connected layer. Initially, the top layer of the network which is standard convolution layer gets the input. The input is a thermal image of dimensions $H \times W \times C$. The Conv2d layer holds all the pixel values and computes the output of the neuron and passes them to the following layer. The parameter of the layer is composed of a set of learnable kernels. Kernels or filters are convolved across dimensions of the input and enlarging with its depth, with the implementation of the dot product between input values and kernels. It outputs a two-dimensional activation map of the kernel. The network learns the kernels thought the features from the input spatial position. The ReLU perform an elementwise activation function, it activates and only grows linearly with positive values, but there is no impact on the size of the volume. Then it passes the output values to the following depthwise separable convolution layer.

Depthwise convolution is a spatial convolution based on the number of channels, each of the filters only computes on a single input channel to do convolution. In thermal images are having a single channel, in such case 1×1 spatial convolutions and integrate depthwise convolution outputs linearly with the help of 1×1 pointwise convolution. The computational operations using depthwise separable convolutions are much lesser than the standard convolutions. As like MobileNet, we have two hyperparameters such as width multiplier α and depth multiplier σ, both parameters are chosen as 1. In this work, we did not use any pooling operation except before the fully connected layer. In proposed topology we have designed a unique structure. Our goal is to reduce the complexity of the network, since, the complexity of the network depends on the size of the output feature maps of each layer. The size of the feature map influenced by three important parameters, such as size of the kernel, stride and zero padding.

To find the key features from the input data, the size of the kernel plays an important role. Large kernels may overlook at the features it leads to loss essential features, since small size kernel may find more information it may lead to over fitting. However, it is very hard task to find the optimal size of the kernel, it may depends on the task. In this paper, we proposed, instead of finding optimal size of the kernel, we would fix the size of the kernel to the entire network, we increase the number of kernels with small difference in each of the following layer, it prevents the confusion with more information. However, Strides also actually influences on the number of steps that moves the kernel on the input image, and also the size and volume of the output feature maps.

The entire training processes implemented in Keras following TensorFlow backend, for fast computation we employed NVIDIA Graphic Processing Unit having 12 GB of RAM. All the training process implemented from scratch.

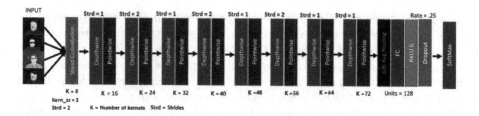

Fig. 6. Proposed CNN Architecture

Fig. 7. Real-Time Testing Phase Pipeline

The proposed model having total 29,798 parameters and it consumes 335.17 KB and 117.14 KB of RAM and FLASH memory respectively and which obtained optimal performance on five thermal face datasets, three of them are publicly available dataset-1, dataset-4&5 and datasets-2 and dataset-3 are developed by ourselves to test the learnt model in real-time.

5 Algorithm Pipeline

The algorithm pipeline to train the network with the proposed datasets is described in Fig. 5. We have acquired 16-bit RAW thermal Videos and Images (snapshots). Further, we extracted all the frames from the videos, then we preprocessed those 16-bit RAW non-visible IR Images into 8-bit visible grayscale images by the implementation of Min-Max Normalization (Eq. 1) using Python-OpenCV. Those Normalized images are randomly shuffled and split into train and validation sets. To train the proposed CNN, those train and validation datasets are given as an input to the model. However, we obtain 16-bit RAW thermal images as snapshots rather than the videos to test the learnt model. We have implemented the same preprocessing approach to test set shown in Fig. 5.

The preprocessing, such conversion of 16-bit image to 8-bit image by the following Min-Max Normalization equation.

$$\widehat{I}(x,y) = round(\frac{I(x,y) - min(I)}{max(I) - min(I)}) * 255) \tag{1}$$

Where I is the input image, min(I), max(I) are, respectively, the minimum and maximum value of the image I pixel values. Where $\widehat{I}$ is the input to the CNN.

Table 5. Evaluation results of proposed model

Dataset	# Persons	# Training	# Validation	# Testing	Avg. validation accuracy (%)	Avg. test accuracy(%)
Dataset- 1	12	6000	2400	1200	100	100
Dataset- 2	29	2885	1303	1046	99.61	97.57
Dataset- 3	11	11000	2200	1755	99.95	99.96
Dataset- 4A	41	4140	410	410	93.90	95.12
Dataset- 4B	41	4140	410	410	100	100

Table 6. Complexity of the proposed architecture compare with state of the art models

Models	Number of parameters	RAM memory consumption	FLASH memory consumption
ResNet50	23,794,333	4.30 MB	94.96 MB
MobileNet-V1	3,342,341	1.32 MB	13.32 MB
Proposed Model	29,798	335.17 KB	117.14 KB

6 Experimental Analysis and Results

In this section we describe all the experimental analysis has been implemented to obtain the optimal performance of the real-time thermal face identification system. However, all the obtained results are described in the Table 5 and complexity of the proposed model compared with the state of the models are described in the Table 6.

Experiment - 1
Initially, we have analysed several state of the art CNN topologies with publicly available dataset-1, such as ResNet50, MobileNet to find the suitable networks in terms of low memory consumption. However, ResNet50 and MobileNet are consuming huge computation power. ResNet50 has 23,794,33 parameter and it need minimum of 5 MB and 100 MB of RAM and FLASH memory respectively. Compare with ResNet50, MobileNet-V1 consumes very less memory Table 6.

However, as we decided by utilizing the advantages of MobileNet, we designed the small proposed CNN topology especially for the devices having low computational power, which described in Fig. 6 and confusion matrix of evaluation presented in Fig. 8.

Experiment - 2
To development of Face Identification system, we trained the proposed model with 12 subjects having total of 9600 images selected from the dataset-1. We split the dataset as train, validation and test of 500, 200 and 100 images per subject respectively; the distribution of the data is described in Table 1. We evaluate learnt model on both validation and test sets, we obtain the maximum results, presents in the Table 5.

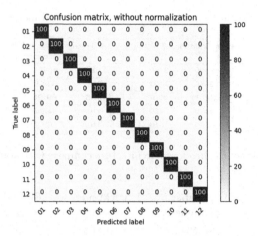

Fig. 8. Confusion Matrix of Test Set of Dataset-1

Experiment - 3

Due to unavailability of subject, we are not able evaluate learnt model in real-time. However, we developed a new dataset described in 'Sect. 2.3' and trained the network from scratch. The distribution of the data to train the network described in the Table 2. The proposed model shows optimal performance on both validation and test sets presented in Table 5 and evaluation confusion matrix shown in Fig. 10. However, the performance of real-time testing is poor. Thermal images contain absolute temperature values of the face surface, yet temperature may changes with emotions, ambience and/or time.

Experiment - 4

To address the drawbacks in the previous experiments, such as the model expects having data with temporal variations. However, we acquired a new dataset in several distinct days, which is described in Sect. 3. The evaluation of the proposed model on the dataset-4 showing optimal performance on the both train and test sets presented in Table 5 and also showing significant performance on the real-time test. The pipeline of the real-time evaluation described in Fig. 7 and Fig. 9 is the real-time identified image.

Experiment - 5

In order to improve the analysis, we evaluate our model with another publicly available dataset described in Sect. 2.3. This dataset having two type of images, such as segmented (without background) and original (with background) images. The evaluation results Table 5 reveals that the recognition rate may improve by removing the background.

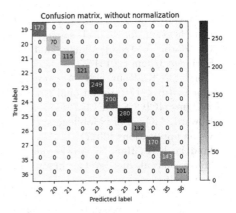

Confusion matrix, without normalization

Fig. 9. Identified Image in Real-Time

Fig. 10. Confusion Matrix of Test Set of Dataset-3

7 Conclusion

In this work we addressed the problem of the complexity of CNN for low memory portable devices and real-time evaluation. The proposed framework which includes data acquisition modalities and a new CNN topology based on depthwise separable convolution makes the model more efficient for real-time thermal face identification. Despite that already high performance achieved by various previous works, yet those systems evaluate the learnt model only with validation or test data. Our method performs well to identify the person from thermal images. Based on this research in future works, hopefully by the analysis of proper prepossessing techniques may improve the performance and robustness of the system.

References

1. Battiato, S., Conoci, S., Leotta, R., Ortis, A., Rundo, F., Trenta, F.: Benchmarking of computer vision algorithms for driver monitoring on automotive-grade devices. In: 2020 AEIT International Conference of Electrical and Electronic Technologies for Automotive (AEIT AUTOMOTIVE), pp. 1–5 (2020)
2. Chen, L., Peng, L., Yao, G., Liu, C., Zhang, X.: A modified inception-ResNet network with discriminant weighting loss for handwritten chinese character recognition. In: 2019 International Conference on Document Analysis and Recognition (ICDAR). IEEE, September 2019, https://doi.org/10.1109/icdar.2019.00197
3. Davis, J.W.: Otcbvs benchmark dataset collection, http://vcipl-okstate.org/pbvs/bench/
4. Espinosa-Duró, V., Faundez-Zanuy, M., Mekyska, J.: A new face database simultaneously acquired in visible, near-infrared and thermal spectrums. Cogn. Comput. **5**, 119–135 (2013). https://doi.org/10.1007/s12559-012-9163-2

5. Farinella, G.M., Farioli, G., Battiato, S., Leonardi, S., Gallo, G.: Face re-identification for digital signage applications. In: Distante, C., Battiato, S., Cavallaro, A. (eds.) Video Analytics for Audience Measurement, pp. 40–52. Springer, Cham (2014)

6. Gondhi, N.K., Kour, E.N.: A comparative analysis on various face recognition techniques. In: 2017 International Conference on Intelligent Computing and Control Systems (ICICCS). IEEE (2017). https://doi.org/10.1109/iccons.2017.8250626

7. Howard, A.G., et al.: Mobilenets: efficient convolutional neural networks for mobile vision applications (2017)

8. Iandola, F.N., Han, S., Moskewicz, M.W., Ashraf, K., Dally, W.J., Keutzer, K.: Squeezenet: alexnet-level accuracy with $50\times$ fewer parameters and <0.5 mb model size (2016)

9. Kong, S.G., Heo, J., Abidi, B.R., Paik, J., Abidi, M.A.: Recent advances in visual and infrared face recognition—a review. Comput. Vis. Image Understanding **97**(1), 103–135 (2005). https://doi.org/10.1016/j.cviu.2004.04.001

10. krishna, M., Neelima, M., Mane, H., Matcha, V.: Image classification using deep learning. Int. J. Eng. Technol. **7**, 614 (2018). https://doi.org/10.14419/ijet.v7i2.7.10892

11. Kristo, M., Ivasic-Kos, M.: An overview of thermal face recognition methods. In: 2018 41st International Convention on Information and Communication Technology, Electronics and Microelectronics (MIPRO). IEEE, May 2018. https://doi.org/10.23919/mipro.2018.8400200

12. Li, X., Li, W., Xu, X., Du, Q.: Cascadenet: Modified resnet with cascade blocks. In: 2018 24th International Conference on Pattern Recognition (ICPR), pp. 483–488 (2018)

13. Lin, S.D., Chen, K.: Thermal face recognition under disguised conditions. In: 2019 International Conference on Machine Learning and Cybernetics (ICMLC). IEEE, July 2019. https://doi.org/10.1109/icmlc48188.2019.8949194

14. Liu, S., Deng, W.: Very deep convolutional neural network based image classification using small training sample size. In: 2015 3rd IAPR Asian Conference on Pattern Recognition (ACPR). IEEE, November 2015. https://doi.org/10.1109/acpr.2015.7486599

15. Majumder, G., Bhowmik, M.K.: Gabor-fast ICA feature extraction for thermal face recognition using linear kernel support vector machine. In: 2015 International Conference on Computational Intelligence and Networks. IEEE, January 2015. https://doi.org/10.1109/cine.2015.14

16. Manssor, S.A.F., Sun, S.: TIRFaceNet: thermal IR facial recognition. In: 2019 12th International Congress on Image and Signal Processing, BioMedical Engineering and Informatics (CISP-BMEI). IEEE, October 2019. https://doi.org/10.1109/cisp-bmei48845.2019.8966066

17. Mateen, M., Wen, J., Nasrullah, D., Song, S., Huang, Z.: Fundus image classification using VGG-19 architecture with PCA and SVD. Symmetry **11**, 1 (2018). https://doi.org/10.3390/sym11010001

18. Santarcangelo, V., Farinella, G.M., Battiato, S.: Gender recognition: methods, datasets and results. In: 2015 IEEE International Conference on Multimedia Expo Workshops (ICMEW), pp. 1–6 (2015). https://doi.org/10.1109/ICMEW.2015.7169756

19. Sayed, M., Baker, F.: Thermal face authentication with convolutional neural network. J. Comput. Sci. **14**(12), 1627–1637 (2018). https://doi.org/10.3844/jcssp.2018.1627.1637

20. Sheng, T., Feng, C., Zhuo, S., Zhang, X., Shen, L., Aleksic, M.: A quantization-friendly separable convolution for MobileNets. In: 2018 1st Workshop on Energy Efficient Machine Learning and Cognitive Computing for Embedded Applications (EMC2). IEEE (2018). https://doi.org/10.1109/emc2.2018.00011
21. Socolinsky, D., Selinger, A.: A comparative analysis of face recognition performance with visible and thermal infrared imagery. In: Object recognition supported by user interaction for service robots. IEEE Comput. Soc. https://doi.org/10.1109/icpr.2002.1047436
22. Socolinsky, D.A., Selinger, A., Neuheisel, J.D.: Face recognition with visible and thermal infrared imagery. Computer Vision and Image Understanding **91**(1–2), 72–114 (2003). https://doi.org/10.1016/s1077-3142(03)00075-4
23. Trenta, F., Conoci, S., Rundo, F., Battiato, S.: Advanced motion-tracking system with multi-layers deep learning framework for innovative car-driver drowsiness monitoring. In: 2019 14th IEEE International Conference on Automatic Face Gesture Recognition (FG 2019), pp. 1–5 (2019). https://doi.org/10.1109/FG.2019.8756566
24. Vigneau, G.H., Verdugo, J.L., Castro, G.F., Pizarro, F., Vera, E.: Thermal face recognition under temporal variation conditions. IEEE Access **5**, 9663–9672 (2017). https://doi.org/10.1109/access.2017.2704296
25. Wu, Z., Peng, M., Chen, T.: Thermal face recognition using convolutional neural network. In: 2016 International Conference on Optoelectronics and Image Processing (ICOIP). IEEE, June 2016. https://doi.org/10.1109/optip.2016.7528489
26. Yuan, A., Bai, G., Jiao, L., Liu, Y.: Offline handwritten english character recognition based on convolutional neural network. In: 2012 10th IAPR International Workshop on Document Analysis Systems. IEEE, March 2012. https://doi.org/10.1109/das.2012.61
27. Zhang, X., Zhou, X., Lin, M., Sun, J.: Shufflenet: An extremely efficient convolutional neural network for mobile devices (2017)

MADiMa 2020 - 6th International Workshop on Multimedia Assisted Dietary Management

Preface

We are delighted to welcome you to the 6th International Workshop on Multimedia Assisted Dietary Management – MADiMa2020. After the success of the past MADiMa workshops, we would like to present to you the MADiMa2020 to be virtually held with ICPR2020 in Milano, Italy. The workshop provides a platform, in which researchers, students, and industry players can meet in order to explore and discuss state of the art in research and technology, to investigate the challenges faced during the design and development of multimedia assisted dietary management systems, as well as to exchange ideas in future research trends.

The call for papers attracted submissions from Asia, Europe and America. The workshop had in total nine (9) submissions. The review was double blind and each paper was reviewed by at least two reviewers. All the nine papers were accepted in this year's program. The workshop was complemented by two invited speakers. Dr. Benny Lo from Imperial College London, UK, presented the results of the Bill and Melinda Gates Foundation funded research project on the development of a passive dietary monitoring system for people living in low-or-middle income countries. He presented an overview of the project and introduced some of the innovative approaches developed to address challenges faced in collecting/analyzing data and estimating the individual dietary intake from the data acquired in field studies in Africa. Prof. Anastasios N. Delopoulos from Aristotle University of Thessaloniki, Greece, presented the results of the H2020 funded project on the collection and analysis of big data on behavioral and living environments against childhood obesity. The presentation was accompanied by the validation results at different pilots across Europe.

We would like to deeply thank the authors for submitting the results of their research to the MADiMA2020 workshop. We are grateful to the program committee, and the reviewers, who worked very hard in reviewing papers and providing feedback for authors.

We do hope that this year's workshop was interesting, rewarding and enjoyable for all participants. We expect that MADiMa2020 will support the expansion of the researcher's community working on multimedia assisted dietary management all over the world, and that it will facilitate cross-disciplinary research collaboration towards innovative solutions in the related fields.

November 2020

Stavroula Mougiakakou
Giovanni Maria Farinella
Keiji Yanai
Dario Allegra

Organization

Workshop Chairs

Giovanni Maria Farinella   University of Catania, Italy
Stavroula Mougiakakou   University of Bern, Switzerland
Keiji Yanai   The University of Electro-Communications, Japan

Publication Chair

Dario Allegra   University of Catania, Italy

Program Committee

Oliver Amft   University of Erlangen-Nuremberg, Germany
Jingjing Chen   Fudan University, China
Anastasios Delopoulos   Aristotle University of Thessaloniki, Greece
Touradj Ebrahimi   EPFL, Switzerland
Ichiro Ide   Nagoya University, Japan
Ya Lu   University of Bern, Switzerland
Alessandro Mazzei   Università di Torino, Italy
Paolo Napoletano   University of Milan-Bicocca, Italy
Chong-Wah Ngo   City University of Hong Kong, Hong Kong
Petia Radeva   Universitat de Barcelona, Spain
Edward Sazonov   University of Alabama, USA
Raimondo Schettini   University of Milan-Bicocca, Italy
Ingmar Weber   Qatar Computing Research Institute, Quatar
Yoko Yamakata   University of Tokyo, Japan

Additional Reviewer

Lorenzo Di Silvestro   University of Catania, Italy

Assessing Individual Dietary Intake in Food Sharing Scenarios with Food and Human Pose Detection

Jiabao Lei[1,2], Jianing Qiu[1,3(✉)], Frank P.-W. Lo[1,2], and Benny Lo[1,2]

[1] The Hamlyn Centre, Imperial College London, London SW7 2AZ, UK
{j.lei19,po.lo15,benny.lo}@imperial.ac.uk
[2] Department of Surgery and Cancer, Imperial College London,
London SW7 2AZ, UK
[3] Department of Computing, Imperial College London, London SW7 2AZ, UK
jianing.qiu17@imperial.ac.uk

Abstract. Food sharing and communal eating are very common in some countries. To assess individual dietary intake in food sharing scenarios, this work proposes a vision-based approach to first capturing the food sharing scenario with a 360-degree camera, and then using a neural network to infer different eating states of each individual based on their body pose and relative positions to the dishes. The number of bites each individual has taken of each dish is then deduced by analyzing the inferred eating states. A new dataset with 14 panoramic food sharing videos was constructed to validate our approach. The results show that our approach is able to reliably predict different eating states as well as individual's bite count with respect to each dish in food sharing scenarios.

Keywords: Dietary intake assessment · 360-degree video · Food detection · Human pose estimation

1 Introduction

With recent advances in deep learning and computer vision, a new range of methods have been proposed for food recognition [1,3,11,13,16,19] and volume estimation [9,10,12], aiming to provide objective and accurate measurements of dietary intake. However, most approaches developed to date are mainly for western cultures, and not much research has been conducted to address the problem of dietary intake measurement in communal eating or shared plate scenarios, which are very common in typical Asian or African households. In nutritional epidemiological studies, analyzing individual intake in a communal eating or shared plate setting is one of the major challenges.

To estimate the individual dietary intake in a food sharing scenario, a system shall be able to monitor all movements of the individuals who are sharing the

Supported by the Innovative Passive Dietary Monitoring Project funded by the Bill & Melinda Gates Foundation (Opportunity ID: OPP1171395).

A. Del Bimbo et al. (Eds.): ICPR 2020 Workshops, LNCS 12665, pp. 549–557, 2021.
https://doi.org/10.1007/978-3-030-68821-9_45

food. To capture such information, multiple cameras are often required, but the needed set up, calibration and fusion greatly hinder the use of such approach for epidemiological studies. Through combining 2 cameras with wide angle lenses, 360 cameras can capture everything around in close proximity of the camera, and therefore, it is particularly suitable for capturing eating in shared plate and communal eating settings. This work proposes to use a 360 camera (Samsung's Gear 360) to capture the entire episode of a meal in which multiple people are sharing a number of dishes together, and a neural network is then applied to infer the eating states of each individual based on their body pose and position to dishes. The number of bites each person has taken of each dish is then deduced from the inferred eating states throughout the meal. From the number of bites taken, it is then possible to estimate the volume of food an individual has eaten.

2   Related Work

Most vision-based approaches proposed for dietary intake assessment are either constrained to laboratory environments or only targeted for a single subject having a meal alone [4,8,15,18,20]. Assessing dietary intake in food sharing scenarios have been rarely researched. A recent work in [14] proposes to use food detection, face recognition, and hand tracking to quantify individual dietary intake in food sharing scenarios pre-recorded by a 360-degree camera. In their recorded food sharing videos, 2–3 subjects were sharing food, such as sushi and pizza, together. In [17], a 360-degree camera was set up to record communal eating scenarios in which 4 people have meals together. However, in their settings, each individual eats their own meal on a plate placed in front of them. Therefore, by cropping out the subject and his/her plate, the dietary intake assessment process becomes similar to those common assessment scenarios (i.e., assessing single subject having a meal alone). In this work, we also use a 360-degree camera to record the entire episode of multiple people eating together. Unlike [17], our work aims to quantify individual intake in shared food scenarios in a typical household setting and the data was collected in the subjects' own home. Our setting is closer to [14] (i.e., people share dishes from different plates), but our technical solutions differ from [14] in that we integrate human pose and dish detection, and use a neural network to infer the eating states of each individual to estimate which dishes each subject has eaten and how many bites of each dish they have taken.

3   Method

Figure 1 illustrates the framework of our proposed approach. A neural network is designed to infer three different eating states (i.e., grabbing the food, eating, and others). The network estimates each individual's state on the basis of their interaction with each dish on the table. Specifically, interactions are modeled using individual's body pose and the location of each dish on the table. We introduce techniques used in each module of our framework in the following.

Fig. 1. The framework of our proposed approach, which includes dish detection, body pose estimation, a neural network for estimating the eating state of each individual (i.e., grabbing, eating and others), and a bite counting step, for assessing individual dietary intake in food sharing scenarios.

3.1 Dish Detection

Mask R-CNN [5] is one of the most widely used methods for instance segmentation and it is able to detect dishes accurately (i.e., localize and recognize dishes) on the dinning table once fine-tuned with a dish dataset. However, due to the wide variety of prepared dishes in this work, and the limited available data of each dish, we therefore did not resort to fine-tuning Mask R-CNN but instead we used the Mask R-CNN model pretrained on the COCO dataset [7] to detect plates and bowls as the proxy for the associated dishes. Recognizing dish types will be addressed in our future work as our dataset expands. At the current stage of this work, though the method does not recognize the type of each dish on the dinning table, it can detect the location of the dishes, which is sufficient to model subject-dish interactions. Every dish in each video is assigned with a pseudo dish type based on their location (e.g., dishes A, B, and C from left to right). Our approach then utilizes the pseudo dish types and the bounding boxes of the detected food containers for the subsequent dietary intake assessment for each individual. Specifically, for the location of each dish, the x and y coordinates of the top-left and bottom-right corners of the plate/bowl bounding boxes are used.

3.2 Human Pose Estimation

OpenPose [2] is an accurate tool for estimating body pose from video images, and it is used in this work to estimate the body poses of each individual during the meal for capturing the subject-dish interactions. Specifically, we use it to detect 25 body keypoints, which returns 75 values (x, y, c where x and y indicate the location of a keypoint and c indicates the detection confidence).

3.3 Eating State Estimation

A 4-layer feed-forward neural network is designed to infer the eating state of each individual with regard to each dish on the basis of dish location and individual's body pose. The dimension of each layer of the network is as follows: 79-60-40-20-3 (input, 3 hidden, and output layers). The input of the network is a 79 dimensional vector composed of 4 elements of the location of

state 0: grabbing   state 1: eating

state 2: others

Fig. 2. Illustration of the three states (left subject in each image) during a meal. The estimated body poses and detected dish bounding boxes and masks are overlaid on top of the images.

one targeted dish and 75 elements of body keypoints. Therefore, given a frame with N subjects and M dishes, for each subject, M number of 79-D vectors are constructed to infer the subject's interactions with all M dishes. Each 79-D vector has a ground truth label of one of the three eating states. We define these three states as follows: 1) `state 0` (grabbing): the subject reaches out to grab the food associated with the vector (recall the vector has 4 elements that are the food location) and then gradually moves his/her hand close to the face; 2) `state 1` (eating): following grabbing the food associated with the vector, the subject's hand is near his/her face area until the subject puts down his/her hand; 3) `state 2` (others): the rest situations are treated as others (i.e., there is no interaction between the food associated with the vector and the subject). Figure 2 shows some examples of these three states.

3.4 Bite Counting

Based on the inferred states of each individual throughout the meal, we then count how many bites each individual has taken of each dish. Starting from the first predicted `eating` state (`state 1`) of that dish, which is counted as the first bite, the second bite is the next predicted `eating` state that has at least 4 predicted `non-eating` states in between it and the first predicted `eating` state. This then continues to count the bites based on the condition that at least 4 `non-eating` states exist in between 2 predicted `eating` states.

4 Experiments

4.1 Dataset

Data Collection and Pre-processing. 14 videos of a household in north-western China eating shared food were collected using a 360-degree camera. 4 subjects participated and consented to be recorded while having their self-cooked meals with their family members. They were asked to eat as they normally do and were free to converse with each other during the meal. Among 14 recorded videos, the longest one lasts for 13 m 58 s, and the shortest one lasts for 5 m 36 s, with the average length being 10 m 49 s. Each video has 2–3 subjects sitting around the table sharing 3–4 dishes. All videos were then downsampled to 2 frames per second for later dietary intake assessment. For each frame, one annotator labelled each subject's states with regard to all dishes present.

Dataset Preparation. Leave-one-out cross-validation (LOOCV) is chosen to evaluate eating state estimation and the bite counting method. As we observe the number of 79-D vectors labelled as state 2 (i.e., others) is far more than that of the other two states, In each fold, the training set is therefore balanced to have its 50% of data as state 2 and 25% each as state 0 and 1. For the test set, we test the network with both the balanced set (i.e., state 0, 1, and 2 account for 25%, 25%, and 50% respectively), and the full unbalanced set (i.e., all vectors from the downsampled frames of the test video).

4.2 Results

Eating State Estimation. Table 1 summarizes the results of the eating state estimation. In each fold of LOOCV, The network was trained for 20 epochs with cross entropy loss. Adam optimization [6] was used with a learning rate of 0.001. The average top-1 testing accuracy on the balanced test sets is 87.7%. The average accuracy on the unbalanced sets is lower than that of the balanced sets. This is because each unbalanced set has more state 2 samples than its balanced counterpart, which increases the likelihood of state 2 samples being mis-recognized, as some of them appear to be similar to grabbing or eating. In addition, in determining the eating state (state 1), the body pose plays a more important role and the dish location has less impact, but in a frame in which a subject is eating, only the vector associated with the food being eaten is labelled as state 1, his/her other vectors are labelled as state 2. This may confuse the network as the body pose is the same in these vectors. As the unbalanced set has more such vectors than its balanced counterpart, this may also explain its accuracy is lower than its balanced counterpart's (in 13 out of 14 test videos, the accuracy on the unbalanced set is lower than its balanced counterpart).

Table 1. The results of eating state estimation (Top-1 Accuracy). V1 to V14 are the recorded video sequences, each used as a test set during LOOCV.

Dataset	V01	V02	V03	V04	V05	V06	V07	V08	V09	V10	V11	V12	V13	V14	Avg.
Balanced	93.3	94.0	87.3	70.2	90.8	89.3	46.7	92.2	94.5	94.8	93.5	93.3	94.3	93.2	**87.7**
Unbalanced	59.0	47.1	42.9	60.8	47.8	48.9	52.1	54.4	70.7	51.7	54.2	54.4	59.3	52.2	**54.0**

Bite Counting. Based on the results of eating state estimation on the unbalanced sets (i.e., full sets), we then count bites for each individual. We first report the sum of predicted bites of all individuals in each test video, and the difference between it and ground truth. Table 2 shows the results. On average, the predicted number has 39.0 less bites than ground truth (106.8 vs 145.8 bites). The bite error percentage after averaging across 14 videos is 26.2%. An example is shown in Fig. 3, which illustrates the predicted and ground truth bites of three different subjects in video 8. It can be seen that in this particular example, most predicted bites are exactly at the same time point as their ground truth bite occurs. While there are some bites not predicted as occurring in the cases of subjects I (Fig. 3a) and II (Fig. 3b), the predicted number of bites and their occurring time points are exactly the same as ground truth in the case of subject III (Fig. 3c).

We then show the bite error percentage of each subject with respect to each dish in each video. Table 3 summarizes the results. In 12 videos, 3 subjects shared 4 dishes. In 81 out of 158 possible subject-dish associations, the predicted number of bites matches exactly with the number of ground truth bites (bite error percentage shown as 0.0 in Table 3). An example of bite prediction of each individual with regard to each dish is shown in Fig. 4. Despite in the case of subject I having dish A, where no bite is successfully predicted, most predicted bites in other cases match their corresponding true bites.

Table 2. The number of bites all subjects in a video have taken. G.T. bites are the ground truth data of each video sequence, Pred. bites are the predicted number of bites in each respective video sequence, △ bites are the difference between the ground truth and the predicted bite counts, and Bite err. % is the error percentage calculated as △ bites/G.T. bites.

	V01	V02	V03	V04	V05	V06	V07	V08	V09	V10	V11	V12	V13	V14	Avg.
G.T. bites	168	333	354	104	107	197	124	84	89	134	87	69	84	107	**145.8**
Pred. bites	130	279	195	49	94	162	98	61	78	97	74	56	29	93	**106.8**
△ bites	38	54	159	55	13	35	26	23	11	37	13	13	55	14	**39.0**
Bite err. %	22.6	16.2	44.9	52.9	12.1	17.8	21.0	27.4	12.4	27.6	14.9	18.8	65.5	13.1	**26.2**

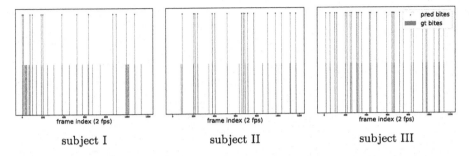

subject I   subject II   subject III

Fig. 3. The predicted and ground truth bites of 3 different subjects in video 8. Zoom in for details and best viewed in color.(Color figure online)

Table 3. Bite error percentage (each subject with respect to each dish in a video sequence), calculated as △ bites/G.T. bites where △ bites are the difference between the predicted number of bites a subject has taken of a specific dish and the respective ground truth (G.T. bites). Subjects are represented as capital roman numerals, and dishes are indicated using capital letters (i.e., I-A refers to subject I with respect to dish A in a video sequence. I and A can be different subjects and dishes in different videos.)

Err. %	I-A	I-B	I-C	I-D	II-A	II-B	II-C	II-D	III-A	III-B	III-C	III-D	Avg.
V01	100.0	19.4	66.7	10.5	0.0	0.0	6.7	0.0					**25.4**
V02	100.0	1.6	6.7	7.4	100.0	0.0	0.0	0.0	2.2	0.0	2.8	0.0	**18.4**
V03	87.5	20.0	33.3	0.0	100.0	55.6	72.9	86.5	6.3	3.8	0.0	0.0	**38.8**
V04	7.1	0.0	0.0	0.0	100.0	100.0	100.0	100.0	100.0	50.0	100.0	33.3	**57.5**
V05	50.0	0.0	0.0	0.0	46.2	0.0	0.0	15.4	0.0	0.0	0.0	0.0	**9.3**
V06	100.0	8.7	0.0	0.0	100.0	5.1	0.0	0.0	14.3	8.3	0.0	3.6	**20.0**
V07	100.0	100.0	100.0	33.3	100.0	5.0	0.0	7.1	7.7	0.0	5.9	16.7	**39.6**
V08	100.0	66.7	55.6	42.9	83.3	0.0	0.0	0.0	0.0	0.0	0.0	0.0	**29.0**
V09	100.0	0.0	0.0		0.0	6.9	12.5						**19.9**
V10	0.0	0.0	75.0	84.6	14.3	0.0	10.5	0.0	0.0	0.0	0.0	0.0	**15.4**
V11	100.0	0.0	0.0	0.0	0.0	0.0	0.0	0.0	54.5	0.0	0.0	0.0	**12.9**
V12	100.0	0.0	0.0	0.0	0.0	0.0	0.0	0.0	77.8	14.3	0.0	0.0	**16.0**
V13	100.0	0.0	0.0	100.0	75.0	80.0	100.0	0.0	0.0	100.0	58.3	92.3	**58.8**
V14	100.0	10.0	0.0	0.0	0.0	0.0	0.0	0.0	0.0	0.0	0.0	0.0	**9.2**

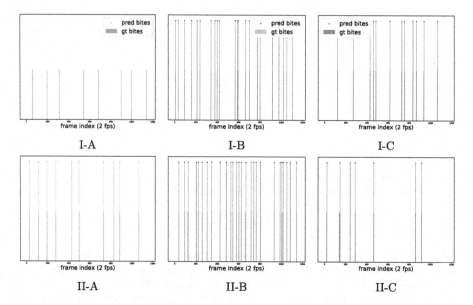

Fig. 4. The predicted and ground truth bites subjects I and II have taken of dishes A, B, and C in video 9. Zoom in for details and best viewed in color. (Color figure online)

5   Conclusion

A novel vision and neural network-based approach for assessing individual dietary intake in food sharing scenarios has been proposed. Based on an individual's body poses and their relative positions to each dish, the network estimates the eating states of each individual throughout the meal. The resulting estimated states are then used to count the number of bites each individual has taken of each dish. Experiments have shown that the proposed approach is promising in assessing individual dietary intake in Chinese food sharing scenarios. Evaluating the performance of the proposed approach on more diverse communal eating and food sharing scenarios is planned in future work.

References

1. Bossard, L., Guillaumin, M., Van Gool, L.: Food-101 – Mining discriminative components with random forests. In: Fleet, D., Pajdla, T., Schiele, B., Tuytelaars, T. (eds.) ECCV 2014. LNCS, vol. 8694, pp. 446–461. Springer, Cham (2014). https://doi.org/10.1007/978-3-319-10599-4_29
2. Cao, Z., Hidalgo Martinez, G., Simon, T., Wei, S., Sheikh, Y.A.: Openpose: real-time multi-person 2D pose estimation using part affinity fields. IEEE Trans. Pattern Anal. Mach. Intell. (2019)
3. Chen, J., Ngo, C.W.: Deep-based ingredient recognition for cooking recipe retrieval. In: Proceedings of the 24th ACM International Conference on Multimedia, pp. 32–41 (2016)

4. Doulah, A., Ghosh, T., Hossain, D., Imtiaz, M.H., Sazonov, E.: Automatic ingestion monitor version 2–a novel wearable device for automatic food intake detection and passive capture of food images. IEEE J. Biomed. Health Informatics (2020)
5. He, K., Gkioxari, G., Dollár, P., Girshick, R.: Mask R-CNN. In: Proceedings of the IEEE International Conference on Computer Vision, pp. 2961–2969 (2017)
6. Kingma, D.P., Ba, J.: Adam: A method for stochastic optimization. arXiv preprint arXiv:1412.6980 (2014)
7. Lin, T.-Y., et al.: Microsoft COCO: common objects in context. In: Fleet, D., Pajdla, T., Schiele, B., Tuytelaars, T. (eds.) ECCV 2014. LNCS, vol. 8693, pp. 740–755. Springer, Cham (2014). https://doi.org/10.1007/978-3-319-10602-1_48
8. Liu, J., et al.: An intelligent food-intake monitoring system using wearable sensors. In: 2012 Ninth International Conference on Wearable and Implantable Body Sensor Networks, pp. 154–160. IEEE (2012)
9. Lo, F.P.W., Sun, Y., Qiu, J., Lo, B.: Food volume estimation based on deep learning view synthesis from a single depth map. Nutrients 10(12), 2005 (2018)
10. Lo, F.P.W., Sun, Y., Qiu, J., Lo, B.P.: Point2volume: a vision-based dietary assessment approach using view synthesis. IEEE Trans. Ind. Informatics 16(1), 577–586 (2019)
11. Martinel, N., Foresti, G.L., Micheloni, C.: Wide-slice residual networks for food recognition. In: 2018 IEEE Winter Conference on Applications of Computer Vision (WACV), pp. 567–576. IEEE (2018)
12. Meyers, A., et al.: Im2calories: towards an automated mobile vision food diary. In: Proceedings of the IEEE International Conference on Computer Vision, pp. 1233–1241 (2015)
13. Min, W., Liu, L., Luo, Z., Jiang, S.: Ingredient-guided cascaded multi-attention network for food recognition. In: Proceedings of the 27th ACM International Conference on Multimedia, pp. 1331–1339 (2019)
14. Qiu, J., Lo, F.P.W., Lo, B.: Assessing individual dietary intake in food sharing scenarios with a 360 camera and deep learning. In: 2019 IEEE 16th International Conference on Wearable and Implantable Body Sensor Networks (BSN), pp. 1–4. IEEE (2019)
15. Qiu, J., Lo, F.P.W., Jiang, S., Tsai, C., Sun, Y., Lo, B.: Counting bites and recognizing consumed food from videos for passive dietary monitoring. IEEE J. Biomed. Health Informatics (2020)
16. Qiu, J., Lo, F.P.W., Sun, Y., Wang, S., Lo, B.: Mining discriminative food regions for accurate food recognition. In: British Machine Vision Conference (2019)
17. Rouast, P.V., Adam, M.T.: Learning deep representations for video-based intake gesture detection. IEEE J. Biomed. Health Informatics 24(6), 1727–1737 (2019)
18. Sun, M., et al.: An exploratory study on a chest-worn computer for evaluation of diet, physical activity and lifestyle. J. Healthcare Eng. 6(1), 1–22 (2015)
19. Yanai, K., Kawano, Y.: Food image recognition using deep convolutional network with pre-training and fine-tuning. In: 2015 IEEE International Conference on Multimedia and Expo Workshops (ICMEW), pp. 1–6. IEEE (2015)
20. Zhu, F., Bosch, M., Khanna, N., Boushey, C.J., Delp, E.J.: Multiple hypotheses image segmentation and classification with application to dietary assessment. IEEE J. Biomed. Health Informatics 19(1), 377–388 (2014)

Recognition of Food-Texture Attributes Using an In-Ear Microphone

Vasileios Papapanagiotou[1]([✉]) [iD], Christos Diou[1,2] [iD], Janet van den Boer[3] [iD], Monica Mars[4] [iD], and Anastasios Delopoulos[1] [iD]

[1] Multimedia Understanding Group, Department of Electrical and Computer Engineering, Faculty of Engineering, Aristotle University of Thessaloniki, Thessaloniki, Greece
vassilis@mug.ee.auth.gr, adelo@eng.auth.gr
[2] Department of Informatics and Telematics, Harokopio University of Athens, Kallithea, Greece
cdiou@hua.gr
[3] Department of Biomedical Signals and Systems, Faculty of Electrical Engineering, Mathematics and Computer Science, University of Twente, Enschede, The Netherlands
j.h.w.vandenboer@utwente.nl
[4] Division of Human Nutrition and Health, Wageningen University, Wageningen, The Netherlands
monica.mars@wur.nl

Abstract. Food texture is a complex property; various sensory attributes such as perceived crispiness and wetness have been identified as ways to quantify it. Objective and automatic recognition of these attributes has applications in multiple fields, including health sciences and food engineering. In this work we use an in-ear microphone, commonly used for chewing detection, and propose algorithms for recognizing three food-texture attributes, specifically crispiness, wetness (moisture), and chewiness. We use binary SVMs, one for each attribute, and propose two algorithms: one that recognizes each texture attribute at the chew level and one at the chewing-bout level. We evaluate the proposed algorithms using leave-one-subject-out cross-validation on a dataset with 9 subjects. We also evaluate them using leave-one-food-type-out cross-validation, in order to examine the generalization of our approach to new, unknown food types. Our approach performs very well in recognizing crispiness (0.95 weighted accuracy on new subjects and 0.93 on new food types) and demonstrates promising results for objective and automatic recognition of wetness and chewiness.

Keywords: Food texture · Dietary monitoring · Wearables

Part of this work has been presented in the first author's Ph.D. thesis [20].
The work leading to these results has received funding from (a) the European Community's ICT Programme under Grant Agreement No. 610746, 01/10/2013–30/09/2016 https://splendid-program.eu/, and (b) the European Community's Health, demographic change and well-being Programme under Grant Agreement No. 727688, 01/12/2016–30/11/2020 https://bigoprogram.eu.

A. Del Bimbo et al. (Eds.): ICPR 2020 Workshops, LNCS 12665, pp. 558–570, 2021.
https://doi.org/10.1007/978-3-030-68821-9_46

1   Introduction

Chewing is one of the main ways of how we perceive food texture [25]. While there is a huge variety of products with different food textures (e.g. crispy products like potato chips, hard and moist products like apples and cucumbers), some textures are generally perceived as more pleasant and desirable than others [11]. It is clear from several studies that food texture and structure are becoming more important in understanding eating behavior, especially in food intake regulation and weight management [1,17,29,31]. Taking food structure into account in dietary advice can may support the prevention and dietary treatment of overweight and obesity [6,9,14]. However, the effects still need to be supported by longer-term studies outside the laboratory. The current, existing dietary assessment methods, such as diaries and recalls, rely on memory and do not provided detailed information about the texture of foods [7].

Currently, there is a strong effort in creating automated tools for dietary monitoring, in the context of understand and preventing obesity and eating disorders [22,27]. One of the first approaches has been to automatically detect chewing based on the audio captured by an in-ear microphone [4]. Such audio signals have also been used to extract information such as the food type [3,23]. There are also alternative types of approaches for identifying food types; for example, leveraging photos that people take with their mobile phones can be used to detect food-relevant photos and then subsequently to perform image segmentation and identify the food type [10,13,18]. Alternatively, user input can be requested when an automatic eating detection system detects eating activity [5].

Identifying food-content–relevant information such as food type from audio signals is commonly formulated as a multi-class problem where each class is a different food type from a list of pre-determined food types [2,4]. The selection of food types is usually aimed at creating a diverse set with different textures, such as crispy and non-crispy food types; crispiness, however, is only one of the attributes of texture. In the early work of [19], a set of texture reference scales were introduced that include multiple attributes. Table 1 presents three groups of attributes: attributes related to surface attributes and springiness, attributes assessed during mastication (chewing), and those assessed during manual manipulation. Out of the three groups, the attributes assessed during mastication are the ones of interest to this work. The more recent work of [30] presents a more extensive and complete review of the state of knowledge for food texture. According to that work, it is commonly accepted that "texture is the sensory and functional manifestation of the structural, mechanical and surface properties of foods detected through the senses of vision, hearing, touch and kinesthetics". As a result, no single modality sensor (such as a microphone) can completely identify texture.

It is worth mentioning that there are additional, non-medical fields where research in understanding human eating behavior is also useful. More specifically, in the field of food design and engineering, understanding how people perceive certain attributes of food (such as crispiness) has been found to correlate with freshness (in particular for the case of apples [12,24]) which in turn is the most

Table 1. Food-texture attributes as presented and organized in [19], and their correspondance with the food-attributes used in this work.

Attributes	Crisp	Wet	Chewy
Attributes related to surface attributes and springiness			
Wetness	✗	✓	✗
Adhesiveness to lips	✗	✗	✗
Roughness	✓	✗	✗
Self-adhesiveness	✗	✗	✓
Springiness	✓	✗	✗
Attributes assessed during mastication			
Cohesiveness of mass	✓	✗	✗
Moisture absorption	✗	✓	✗
Adhesiveness to teeth	✗	✗	✓
Attributes assessed during manual manipulation			
Manual adhesiveness	✗	✗	✗

important factor in consumer's choices [16,26]. Thus, providing tools that can objectively measure such food attributes cannot only help to assess eating behavior and food intake, but can also help food technologists to design food with more desirable and pleasant characteristics.

In this work we use an in-ear microphone that is part of the wearable, prototype sensor developed in the context of the SPLENDID project and focus on the audio captured during chewing in order to recognize three attributes of food texture from a variety of food types. The three attributes are crispiness, wetness, and chewiness. Each one corresponds to each of the attributes "assessed during mastication" according to [19] (Table 1). The attributes "related to surface attributes and springiness" can also be loosely mapped to these three attributes. The attributes that are "assessed during manual manipulation" are not of interest to this work (but are only included in the table for completeness).

We propose an algorithm for recognizing each of the three food-texture attributes of this work (i.e. crispiness, wetness, and chewiness) given a single chew based on three individual binary SVMs (one for each attribute). We also propose a modified version of the algorithm that operates on entire chewing bouts. We evaluate the generalization both in new subjects and in new food types.

2   Attribute Recognition Algorithms

The algorithms presented in this work require audio of at least 8 kHz sampling rate. The original audio recordings of the dataset used in this work (see Sect. 3) have been sampled at 48 kHz. We have experimented with down-sampled versions of the signal, in particular 2, 4, 8, 16, 32, as well as the original 48 kHz. We have observed that down-sampling as low as 8 kHz does not cause any noticeable drop in recognition effectiveness (by repeating the experiments presented in this paper for all different sampling frequencies), however, down-sampling lower than 8 kHz does. In all the following, we use the 8 kHz down-sampled versions of the audio signals.

We also apply a high-pass Butterworth filter to the down-sampled signal to remove low frequency components. The filter is of 9-th order with a cut-off frequency at approximately 20 Hz. We propose two algorithms: the first recognizes attributes for each chew individually, while the second one for entire chewing bouts.

2.1 Chew-Level Algorithm

A feature vector is first extracted from each chew; note that start and stop time-moment annotations for chews have been made available by manual extraction based on acoustic and visual observation of the captured audio signals (in a fully automated application, a chew-detection algorithm such as [22] can be used to obtain them). The extracted features consist of signal energy in 11 log-scale frequency bands based on time-varying spectrum (TVS) estimation, fractal dimension (FD), condition number (CN) of the auto-correlation matrix, and higher order statistics (i.e. third and fourth-order moments). These features have been used in [22] for chewing detection and are thus a good starting point for food-texture–attribute recognition. Since the audio sampling frequency is only 2 kHz in [22] (compared to 8 kHz of this work) we have added two more bands in the TVS, in particular 2 to 4 and 4 to 8 kHz. It is also worth noting that each chew has different duration (average of 0.56 s and standard deviation of 0.15 s in the data-set used in this work) in contrast to windows of fixed length often used in signal processing. The features we have selected, however, are invariant to the length of the audio segment used to extract them.

Before the classification stage each feature is standardized by subtracting the mean and then dividing by the standard deviation (the mean and standard deviation of each feature are estimated over the available training set for each case). The multi-label classifier we use is an array of three binary SVMs; each SVM is related to one of the three food-texture attributes: crispiness, wetness, and chewiness. We use a radial-basis function (RBF) kernel. Parameters C and γ are selected automatically using 5-fold cross-validation on the training set. The optimal values are chosen using Bayesian optimization [15]; care to escape local minima of the objective function is also taken using a threshold for the standard deviation of the posterior objective function [8,28].

As a result, each chew can be classified individually for each of the three attributes. As the food type does not change within a bout, we can obtain one decision per bout based on the chews that belong to it. One way to do so is to use majority voting across the chews of a bout (for each attribute). Another way is to consider only the first n chews of a bout, since processing of the food in the mouth transforms it into a wet bolus, thus altering the attributes of the food in its unprocessed state. All these evaluation methods are presented in Sect. 4.

2.2   Chewing-Bout–Level Algorithm

Chewing-bout–level detection shares the same pre-processing steps with chew-level detection: the audio signal is down-sampled and the same high-pass is applied to remove low-frequency components.

Bout segments are then obtained based on the chews that belong to each bout. A bout audio segment starts at the start time of its first chew and stops at the stop time of its last chew. The average bout duration in the data-set used in this work is 15.22 s with a standard deviation of 10.7 s. Since bouts are significantly longer than chews and also contain non-chewing sounds between each chew (see Fig. 1) we do not directly extract the features over the entire bout duration. Instead, we obtain overlapping windows of 0.5 s length and 0.1 s step from each bout and extract the features from each window separately. Thus, we obtain one list of feature vectors for each bout; each list contains, in general, a different amount of vectors.

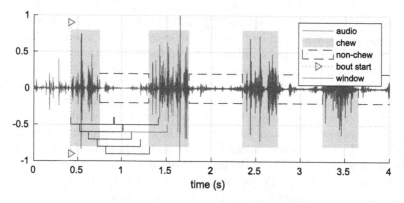

Fig. 1. An example of a chewing bout. The first four chews are marked by the gray rectangles. When entire chewing bouts are used, the audio between two successive chews is also used.

We then use a bag-of-words (BoW) approach to obtain a single feature vector of fixed length for each bout. In particular, given a set of bouts, we obtain all of the feature vectors from each bout and use k-means to select a set of k centroid vectors. Once we obtain the k centroid vectors we can transform any new bout into a feature vector of fixed length (equal to k) by computing the normalized histogram of the bout's feature vectors against the set of k centroid vectors. Each feature vector is assigned to one of the k centroid (i.e. hard assignment).

Using the BoW approach offers many advantages. It allows to use the same features of the previous, chew-level algorithm (Sect. 2.1) on short windows (with similar duration to that of chews). In addition it allows to extract feature vectors of fixed length from audio segments with (highly) varying length. Finally, it also allows to handle the non-chewing sounds that occur between successive chews within each bout: window-based feature vectors that correspond to such in-between audio segments will likely be similar and will be clustered together; corresponding cluster centers are equally present in signals of different food types and the SVM models are expected to learn to ignore them.

The BoW features are then standardized similarly to Sect. 2.1. Classification is performed in exactly the same way as in chew-level recognition: we use an array of three binary SVM classifiers with RBF kernel and hyper-parameter selection using Bayesian optimization.

3   Data-Set and Evaluation Metrics

The data-set used to evaluate the proposed algorithms has been collected at Wageningen University, Netherlands, in the context of the EU-funded SPLENDID project[1] and is the same data-set as the one we use in [21]. The recording apparatus is an in-ear microphone (FG-23329-D65 model manufactured by Knowles) connected via wire to a computer audio interface. The sensor housing and recording has been done by CSEM S.A. [22]. In this work, the first version of the SPLENDID sensor is used; more details about this version and the future versions of the sensor can be found in [5]. In total, 21 subjects were enrolled for the data collection trials, however, signals from only 9 could be used in this work due to problems with data acquisition (such as incorrect sensor placement or corrupted audio due to hardware/software malfunction). Each subject consumed a variety of food types (complete list can be found in [5]).

We have selected 9 different food types that we can clearly annotate their attributes. Not all 9 subjects have consumed all 9 food types. Table 2 lists these food types along with their attribute values we have assigned them. This data-set of 9 participants and 9 food types is the one we use to evaluate this work.

Table 2. List of food types and their attributes for the evaluation data-set.

	Crispy	Wet	Chewy
Apple	✓	✓	✗
Banana	✗	✓	✗
Bread	✗	✗	✗
Candy bar	✗	✗	✓
Cookie	✓	✗	✗
Lettuce	✓	✓	✗
Potato chips	✓	✗	✗
Strawberry	✗	✓	✗
Toffee	✗	✗	✓

For this evaluation data-set, we have manually created ground truth on chew and chewing bout levels (with start and stop time-moments) based on the available experimental logs as well as audio and visual inspection of the captured

---

[1] https://splendid-program.eu/.

signals. It contains 4, 989 chews with a total duration of 46.31 min which belong to 238 chewing bouts; total duration of bouts is almost 1 h and is greater than total duration of chews because bouts also contain the audio segments between each successive pair of chews. Tables 3 and 4 show duration statistics for the chews and chewing bouts.

Table 3. Statistics of chews duration across the food types for the evaluation data-set.

	Instances	Total (min)	Average (s)	Std (s)
Apple	1, 091	9.74	0.54	0.13
Banana	294	2.67	0.54	0.16
Bread	1, 260	11.72	0.56	0.13
Candy bar	415	4.26	0.62	0.17
Cookie	359	3.07	0.51	0.14
Lettuce	492	4.06	0.50	0.11
Potato chips	386	3.45	0.54	0.12
Strawberry	236	2.04	0.52	0.13
Toffee	456	5.30	0.70	0.17
Total	4, 989	46.31	0.56	0.15

Table 4. Statistics of bouts duration across the food types for the evaluation data-set.

	Instances	Total (min)	Average (s)	Std (s)
Apple	48	12.12	15.15	5.23
Banana	25	3.57	8.58	2.91
Bread	37	15.03	24.37	15.69
Candy bar	22	5.51	15.02	7.97
Cookie	16	4.03	15.10	5.31
Lettuce	28	5.31	11.38	5.39
Potato chips	29	4.40	9.11	3.12
Strawberry	17	2.63	9.30	5.82
Toffee	16	6.23	23.35	11.37
Total	238	58.83	14.83	9.84

We evaluate each food attribute, namely crispiness, wetness, and chewiness, as binary classification problems. We regard crispy, wet, and chewy as the positive classes, and non-crispy, dry, and non-chewy as the negative ones respectively.

To account for class imbalance, which is particularly large for chewiness, we calculate weighted accuracy as

$$\frac{w \cdot TP + TN}{w \cdot (TP + FN) + TN + FP} \tag{1}$$

where $w = (TN + FP)/(TP + FN)$ is the ratio of priors.

4   Evaluation and Results

The chew-level algorithm can also be modified to operate on bout-level by taking into account each bout's chews. We explore how the bout-level decision is affected by the number of chews that are taken into account. We train models both in the typical leave-one-subject-out (LOSO) fashion as well as in leave-one-food-type-out (LOFTO) fashion. In both types of experiments we use the entire available training data (from the non–left-out subjects or food types) to both obtain the BoW centroid vectors and train the SVM classifiers.

Table 5 presents per-chew classification results for each of the three attributes; the BoW centroids, SVM models, and SVM hyper parameters have been trained in LOSO fashion. Crispiness is the attribute that the algorithm identifies more effectively. The majority voting approach consistently improves results by 2 to 5%.

While it makes sense to assume that food type as such does not change during a bout, the attributes of the food within the mouth do as food is grinded and lubricated during oral processing/chewing. Given that we are interested in identifying the attributes that the food has in its unprocessed form, we can consider only the first few chews of each bout in the majority voting stage, during which the food type's original attributes are still retained to some degree. Figure 2 shows the recognition effectiveness for each attribute when considering only the first n chews of each bout for $n = 1$ to 20. Recognition of crispiness exhibits high effectiveness, however, the highest (weighted) accuracy is obtained by considering the first 6 to 10 chews. Almost the same range of 5 to 10 chews seems to be the best choice for recognizing wetness as well. Chewiness results are somewhat different since considering only the first few chews seems to yield erratic effectiveness. The situation improves as more chews are taken into account.

Table 6 presents results for the LOFTO experiments. Crispiness is the most easily recognizable attribute again, however, wetness does not generalize well across different food types. Majority voting improves results for crispiness and chewiness only. Looking at Fig. 2, the highest effectiveness for wetness is achieved by considering only a few chews (6 to 7 chews).

Table 7 presents LOSO and LOFTO results for the bout-level algorithm. Comparing these results with chew-level results we can see that the bout-level algorithm achieves almost similar results for LOSO: slightly lower weighted accuracy for crispiness (but still quite high), and almost the same for wetness. Recognition accuracy for chewiness is worse.

Table 5. LOSO results for chew-level recognition.

	Prior	Weighted accuracy	w
Chew level			
Crispy (avg)	0.4707	0.9068	1.1968
Crispy (sum)	0.4666	0.9017	1.1430
Wet (avg)	0.4280	0.7516	1.4588
Wet (sum)	0.4235	0.7503	1.3611
Chewy (avg)	0.1741	0.5994	4.9418
Chewy (sum)	0.1746	0.6212	4.7279
Majority voting per bout			
Crispy (avg)	0.4943	0.9519	1.1141
Crispy (sum)	0.5063	0.9496	0.9752
Wet (avg)	0.4850	0.7978	1.1018
Wet (sum)	0.4937	0.7900	1.0254
Chewy (avg)	0.1666	0.6296	5.9804
Chewy (sum)	0.1632	0.6154	5.1282

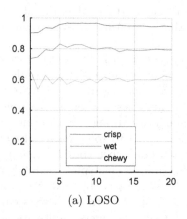

(a) LOSO

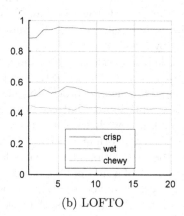

(b) LOFTO

Fig. 2. Weighted accuracy for each attribute for the LOSO and LOFTO experiments.

Table 6. LOFTO results for chew-level recognition.

	Prior	Weighted accuracy	w
Chew-level			
Crispy (sum)	0.4666	0.8987	1.1430
Wet (sum)	0.4235	0.5481	1.3611
Chewy (sum)	0.1746	0.3957	4.7279
Majority voting per bout			
Crispy (sum)	0.4957	0.9446	1.0172
Wet (sum)	0.4829	0.5046	1.0708
Chewy (sum)	0.1667	0.4179	5.0000

On the other hand, the bout-level algorithm seems to be able to better generalize across different food types. Looking at the results of the LOFTO experiment, the algorithm achieves only slightly lower weighted accuracy (compared to the chew-level algorithm with majority voting) for crispiness and improves significantly for wetness and chewiness.

Table 7. Results for bout-level recognition.

	Prior	Weighted accuracy	w
LOSO			
Crispy (avg)	0.4967	0.9541	1.1030
Crispy (sum)	0.5084	0.9534	0.9669
Wet (avg)	0.4869	0.7865	1.0880
Wet (sum)	0.4958	0.7900	1.0169
Chewy (avg)	0.1625	0.5200	6.0749
Chewy (sum)	0.1597	0.5238	5.2632
LOFTO			
Crispy (sum)	0.5084	0.9288	0.9669
Wet (sum)	0.4958	0.6422	1.0169
Chewy (sum)	0.1597	0.4970	5.2632

5   Conclusions

In this work we have proposed two algorithms for automatically and objectively recognizing three attributes of food texture from audio signals captured by an in-ear microphone. The algorithms combine feature extraction and binary SVMs and operate both for single chews and entire chewing bouts. We have examined their ability to generalize not only to new subjects (LOSO) but also to new food types (LOFTO). With the use of these algorithms, the SPLENDID sensor was able to recognize 3 important food-texture attributes affecting eating behavior. In particular, crispiness was recognized with weighted accuracy of at least 0.9 across all experiments. Results for recognizing wetness and chewiness are promising but there is a large margin for improvement: introducing more suitable features in the algorithms could possibly help improve the overall effectiveness of the proposed algorithms. Including more food types in the training set could also potentially improve recognition, however, certain food types with attributes that are not easy to annotate (e.g. food types that are neither completely dry nor wet) might not be suitable for a crisp-label classification problem and thus require alternative methods. As a result, this type of digital devices will make it possible to further study the objective exposure to different food textures in relation to eating behavior and longer term outcomes, such as weight change, in a real life setting.

References

1. Aguayo-Mendoza, M.G., Ketel, E.C., van der Linden, E., Forde, C.G., Piqueras-Fiszman, B., Stieger, M.: Oral processing behavior of drinkable, spoonable and chewable foods is primarily determined by rheological and mechanical food properties. Food Qual. Pref. **71**, 87–95 (2019). https://doi.org/10.1016/j.foodqual.2018.06.006
2. Amft, O., Kusserow, M., Troster, G.: Bite weight prediction from acoustic recognition of chewing. IEEE Trans. Biomed. Eng. **56**(6), 1663–1672 (2009)
3. Amft, O.: A wearable earpad sensor for chewing monitoring. In: SENSORS, 2010 IEEE, pp. 222–227 (2010). https://doi.org/10.1109/ICSENS.2010.5690449
4. Amft, O., Stäger, M., Lukowicz, P., Tröster, G.: Analysis of chewing sounds for dietary monitoring. In: Beigl, M., Intille, S., Rekimoto, J., Tokuda, H. (eds.) UbiComp 2005. LNCS, vol. 3660, pp. 56–72. Springer, Heidelberg (2005). https://doi.org/10.1007/11551201_4
5. van den Boer, J., et al.: The splendid eating detection sensor: development and feasibility study. JMIR Mhealth Uhealth, p. e170. (2018). https://doi.org/10.2196/mhealth.9781
6. van den Boer, J., Werts, M., Siebelink, E., de Graaf, C., Mars, M.: The availability of slow and fast calories in the dutch diet: the current situation and opportunities for interventions. Foods **6**(10), 87 (2017). https://doi.org/10.3390/foods6100087
7. Brouwer-Brolsma, E.M., et al.: Dietary intake assessment: from traditional paper-pencil qestionnaires to technology-based tools. In: Athanasiadis, I.N., Frysinger, StP, Schimak, G., Knibbe, W.J. (eds.) ISESS 2020. IAICT, vol. 554, pp. 7–23. Springer, Cham (2020). https://doi.org/10.1007/978-3-030-39815-6_2
8. Bull, A.D.: Convergence rates of efficient global optimization algorithms. arXiv e-prints arXiv:1101.3501 (2011)
9. Campbell, C.L., Wagoner, T.B., Foegeding, E.A.: Designing foods for satiety: the roles of food structure and oral processing in satiation and satiety. Food Structure **13**, 1–12 (2017). https://doi.org/10.1016/j.foostr.2016.08.002
10. Christodoulidis, S., Anthimopoulos, M., Mougiakakou, S.: Food recognition for dietary assessment using deep convolutional neural networks. In: Murino, V., Puppo, E., Sona, D., Cristani, M., Sansone, C. (eds.) ICIAP 2015. LNCS, vol. 9281, pp. 458–465. Springer, Cham (2015). https://doi.org/10.1007/978-3-319-23222-5_56
11. Cox, D.N., et al.: Sensory and hedonic judgments of common foods by lean consumers and consumers with obesity. Obesity Res. **6**, 438–447 (1998). https://doi.org/10.1002/j.1550-8528.1998.tb00376.x
12. Daillant-Spinnler, B., MacFie, H.J.H., Beyts, P.K., Hedderley, D.: Relationships between perceived sensory properties and major preference directions of 12 varieties of apples from the southern hemisphere. Food Qual. Pref. **7**(2), 113–126 (1996). https://doi.org/10.1016/0950-3293(95)00043-7

13. Dehais, J., Anthimopoulos, M., Mougiakakou, S.: Food image segmentation for dietary assessment. In: Proceedings of the 2nd International Workshop on Multimedia Assisted Dietary Management. MADiMa '16, ACM, New York, NY, USA, pp. 23–28 (2016). /DOIurl10.1145/2986035.2986047

14. Forde, C.G.: From perception to ingestion; the role of sensory properties in energy selection, eating behaviour and food intake. Food Qual. Pref. **66**, 171–177 (2018). https://doi.org/10.1016/j.foodqual.2018.01.010

15. Gelbart, M.A., Snoek, J., Adams, R.P.: Bayesian optimization with unknown constraints. arXiv e-prints arXiv:1403.5607 (2014)

16. Harker, R.F., Gunson, A.F., Jaeger, S.R.: The case for fruit quality: an interpretive review of consumer attitudes, and preferences for apples. Postharvest Biol. Technol. **28**(3), 333–347 (2003). https://doi.org/10.1016/S0925-5214(02)00215-6

17. Lasschuijt, M.P., Mars, M., Stieger, M., Miquel-Kergoat, S., De Graaf, C., Smeets, P.A.M.: Comparison of oro-sensory exposure duration and intensity manipulations on satiation. Physiol. Behav. **176**, 76–83 (2017). https://doi.org/10.1016/j.physbeh.2017.02.003

18. Lu, Y., Allegra, D., Anthimopoulos, M., Stanco, F., Farinella, G.M., Mougiakakou, S.: A multi-task learning approach for meal assessment. arXiv e-prints arXiv:1806.10343 (2018)

19. Muñoz, A.M.: Development and application of texture reference scales. J. Sens. Stud. **1**(1), 55–83 (1986). https://doi.org/10.1111/j.1745-459X.1986.tb00159.x

20. Papapanagiotou, V.: Modeling and automatically measuring human eating behavior. Ph.D. thesis, Department Electrical and Computer Engineering, Faculty of Engineering, Aristotle University of Thessaloniki (2019)

21. Papapanagiotou, V., Diou, C., Lingchuan, Z., van den Boer, J., Mars, M., Delopoulos, A.: Fractal nature of chewing sounds. In: Murino, V., Puppo, E., Sona, D., Cristani, M., Sansone, C. (eds.) ICIAP 2015. LNCS, vol. 9281, pp. 401–408. Springer, Cham (2015). https://doi.org/10.1007/978-3-319-23222-5_49

22. Papapanagiotou, V., Diou, C., Zhou, L., van den Boer, J., Mars, M., Delopoulos, A.: A novel chewing detection system based on PPG, audio and accelerometry. IEEE J. Biomed. Health Inform. **21**(3), 607–618 (2017). https://doi.org/10.1109/JBHI.2016.2625271

23. Päßler, S., Wolff, M., Fischer, W.: Food intake monitoring: an acoustical approach to automated food intake activity detection and classification of consumed food. Physiol. Meas. **33**(6), 1073–1093 (2012). https://doi.org/10.1088/0967-3334/33/6/1073

24. Péneau, S., et al.: Relating consumer evaluation of apple freshness to sensory and physico-chemical measurements. J. Sens. Stud. **22**(3), 313–335 (2007). https://doi.org/10.1111/j.1745-459X.2007.00112.x

25. Pereira, L.J., van der Bilt, A.: The influence of oral processing, food perception and social aspects on food consumption: a review. J. Oral Rehabil. **43**(8), 630–648 (2016). https://doi.org/10.1111/joor.12395

26. Péneau, S., Hoehn, E., Roth, H.R., Escher, F., Nuessli, J.: Importance and consumer perception of freshness of apples. Food Qual. Pref. **17**(1), 9–19 (2006). https://doi.org/10.1016/j.foodqual.2005.05.002

27. Sazonov, E.S., Makeyev, O., Schuckers, S., Lopez-Meyer, P., Melanson, E.L., Neuman, M.R.: Automatic detection of swallowing events by acoustical means for applications of monitoring of ingestive behavior. IEEE Trans. Biomed. Eng. **57**(3), 626–633 (2010). https://doi.org/10.1109/TBME.2009.2033037

28. Snoek, J., Larochelle, H., Adams, R.P.: Practical bayesian optimization of machine learning algorithms. arXiv e-prints arXiv:1206.2944 (2012)

29. StribiȚcaia, E., Evans, C.E.L., Gibbons, C., Blundell, J., Sarkar, A.: Food texture influences on satiety: systematic review and meta-analysis. Sci. Rep. **10**(1), 12929 (2020). https://doi.org/10.1038/s41598-020-69504-y

30. Szczesniak, A.S.: Texture is a sensory property. Food Qual. Pref. **13**(4), 215–225 (2002). https://doi.org/10.1016/S0950-3293(01)00039-8

31. Zijlstra, N., de Wijk, R., Mars, M., Stafleu, A., de Graaf, C.: Effect of bite size and oral processing time of a semisolid food on satiation. Am. J. Clin. Nutr. **90**(2), 269–275 (2009). https://doi.org/10.3945/ajcn.2009.27694

Visual Aware Hierarchy Based Food Recognition

Runyu Mao[iD], Jiangpeng He[iD], Zeman Shao[iD], Sri Kalyan Yarlagadda[iD], and Fengqing Zhu[(✉)][iD]

Purdue University, West Lafayette, IN 47907, USA
{mao111,he416,shao112,yarlagad,zhu0}@purdue.edu

Abstract. Food recognition is one of the most important components in image-based dietary assessment. However, due to the different complexity level of food images and inter-class similarity of food categories, it is challenging for an image-based food recognition system to achieve high accuracy for a variety of publicly available datasets. In this work, we propose a new two-step food recognition system that includes food localization and hierarchical food classification using Convolutional Neural Networks (CNNs) as the backbone architecture. The food localization step is based on an implementation of the Faster R-CNN method to identify food regions. In the food classification step, visually similar food categories can be clustered together automatically to generate a hierarchical structure that represents the semantic visual relations among food categories, then a multi-task CNN model is proposed to perform the classification task based on the visual aware hierarchical structure. Since the size and quality of dataset is a key component of data driven methods, we introduce a new food image dataset, VIPER-FoodNet (VFN) dataset, consists of 82 food categories with $15k$ images based on the most commonly consumed foods in the United States. A semi-automatic crowdsourcing tool is used to provide the ground-truth information for this dataset including food object bounding boxes and food object labels. Experimental results demonstrate that our system can significantly improve both classification and recognition performance on 4 publicly available datasets and the new VFN dataset.

Keywords: Food image recognition · Multi-task learning · Convolutional neural network · Hierarchical structure

1 Introduction

Many chronic diseases including cancer, diabetes, and heart disease, can be linked to diet. However, accurate assessment of dietary intake is an open and challenging problem. Conventional assessment methods including food records, 24-h dietary recall, and food frequency questionnaires (FFQ) are prone to biased measurement and are burdensome to use [45,48,51,59,66]. In the last decade, there has been a growing popularity of using mobile and wearable computing

© Springer Nature Switzerland AG 2021
A. Del Bimbo et al. (Eds.): ICPR 2020 Workshops, LNCS 12665, pp. 571–598, 2021.
https://doi.org/10.1007/978-3-030-68821-9_47

devices to monitor diet-related behaviors and activities [6,75,92]. At the same time, advances in computer vision and machine learning has enabled the development of image-based dietary assessment systems [26,33,58,91] that can analyze food images captured by mobile and wearable devices to provide an estimate of dietary intake. Accurate estimation of dietary intake relies on the system's ability to distinguish foods from the image background (i.e., localization), to identify (or label) food items (i.e., classification), to estimate food portion size, and to understand the context of the eating event. Although there are promising advancements, many challenges still remain in automating the assessment of dietary intake from images.

Recently, a series of breakthroughs in computer vision have been led by deep learning [49] techniques such as Convolutional Neural Networks (CNNs) [47] using data-driven approaches. The success of deep learning methods depends largely on the quantity and quality of data. The increased availability of online food images shared on social media and review forum has made the collection of large food image dataset possible. However, high quality ground-truth labels are equally, if not more important, for improving the performance of image-based dietary assessment systems. In this paper, we selected the most frequently consumed foods in the United States [2] as the food categories to build a new food image dataset, Viper FoodNet (VFN) Dataset. A semi-automatic image collection system and a web-based crowdsourcing tool [71] are implemented to collect and annotate those food images for the VFN Dataset.

Food classification [37,43,54,55,85,88] is the task of labeling food items in an image, which assumes the input image contains only a single food item. Thus, there is no need to output the pixel location of the foods in an image. Others have worked on food detection [5,42,43], which determines whether an image contains food or not. However, it is common for food images to contain multiple foods. In this paper, we define food recognition as the task of simultaneously localize and label foods present in an image. This task also provides value to subsequent tasks such as estimating food volume and portion size. Recently, [9] proposed a method to generate bounding boxes for food localization. However, the process is quite complex and many hand-crafted parameters are required, it is difficult to generalize to larger foods datasets or real-life food images.

In this work, we propose a two-step food recognition system that can localize and label multiple foods in an image and generalize to other food image datasets. Our system consists of food localization and food classification to handle multi-food images which are prevalent in daily life. Since many single food images also contain non-food objects such as human hands, menus, and tables, a well-designed food localization process can also remove background clutters to improve classification performance. Given the success of Faster R-CNN [65] for face detection [40] and hand detection [22], we implemented a version of it for the food localization task.

Labeling food categories for each region selected by food localization is a typical classification task. Many existing methods [36,38] have shown good performance for image classification of general objects. However, different food categories contain many hidden relations. For example, pancake and waffle are closely related compared to pancake and pork chop based on semantic meaning. In [85], instead of treating food classification as a flat fine-grained classification problem, a semantic-based hierarchical structure for food categories is proposed to improve the performance of classification. However, it is time-consuming and impossible to manually build such a hierarchical structure given that there are thousands of food categories in the world. It is also impractical to build a specific hierarchical structure for each available food image dataset since the same food may have different names or the same name may represent different foods in different regions of the world. In this paper, we proposed a method to automatically cluster visually similar foods and build a hierarchical structure for the food categories. We classify food regions by leveraging the hierarchical structure in a multi-task manner.

In summary, the contribution of this paper is twofold. We developed an image-based food recognition system consisting of food localization and hierarchical food classification, which can be used as building blocks for image-based automatic dietary assessment applications. We designed and constructed a new food image dataset, VIPER-FoodNet (VFN) dataset, which contains 15k real-life multi-food images of most frequently consumed foods in the United State. This dataset along with other publicly available food image datasets are used for evaluating the performance of our food recognition system.

The rest of the paper is organized as follows. In Sect. 2, we discuss and summarize related works to different components of our system. We discuss the design and construction of the VFN dataset in Sect. 3. Details of the food recognition system are presented in Sect. 4. In Sect. 5, we discuss experimental results on different datasets and compare our method to other food localization and classification methods. Discussion and Conclusion is provided in Sect. 6 and 7.

2   Related Work

2.1   Image-Based Dietary Assessment

With the development of mobile and wearable technologies, a wide range of approaches using food images captured at the eating scenes have been proposed to assess dietary intake [11]. Many image-based approaches have been integrated into sensor systems and mobile devices with the goal of automating dietary assessment by reducing human input, e.g., mFR [92], eButton [75], FRapp [13], NuDAM [67], and [61]. The broad range of approaches can be classified into two main categories: active capture and passive capture.

Active capture requires the participant or a data collector to operate the device and capture images of food being consumed. A mobile device is typically used for image capturing. In addition to images, some methods include other forms of inputs. For example, FRapp [13] captures text and voice as additional information. NuDAM [67] includes voice recording from the participant about the food consumed, leftovers, information about the meal occasion, and a follow-up call in the next day for making the adjustment. On the contrary, the mFR

[4,92] provides an end-to-end solution based on capturing a pair of before and after eating scene images from a mobile device camera as the sole input to estimate food consumption using image analysis techniques [26,83,84,91].

Passive capture takes pictures or videos automatically in real time or semi-automatically at intervals. Compared to active capture, it may be more challenging to process collected data due to uncertainty of how food consumption is captured, and possible concerns about privacy. The eButton [75] is a chest-worn device that takes images at a preset rate during eating occasions. Food-specific models are used to estimate food volume [39]. Another approach [61] estimates food intake based on video of the eating scenario captured by a 360 camera. Mask R-CNN [34] is used to detect people and 13 food categories.

2.2   Food Detection and Food Localization

Food detection, which refers to the presence of foods in an image, is a binary classification problem [28,42,43,46,62,74]. On the other hand, Food localization aims to detect where the food is located in an image, commonly indicated by bounding boxes or pixel-level segmentation masks. It is also known as food region detection [57]. To avoid terminology confusion, we use food localization throughout this paper with more details about our method described in Sect. 4.1. Although we can extract spatial information about the foods in the image, localization will not return food categories associated with the spatial information. In this section, we will illustrate previous works of both food detection and food localization.

Food detection, traditionally, is solved based on handcrafted features, e.g., scale-invariant feature transform (SIFT) [52] and speeded up robust features (SURF) [7] for feature representations. Support vector machine (SVM) [20] is then used to do binary classification. A food logging system proposed in [46] performs automated food/non-food classification based on global features [29], e.g. circles detected by Hough transforms and the average value in color space. In 2015, a one-class SVM [14] for food detection was proposed in [28]. Without non-food images in the training dataset, this method still achieved promising performance. Given the success of Convolutional Neural Networks (CNNs) for image classification, authors in [28,42,43,74] fine-tuned existing CNN models for food detection by treating it as a binary classification task.

Food localization requires more information since its goal is to locate regions in a food image that corresponds to food. Local handcraft features [76] are adopted since it can provide more spatial information than global feature representation [29]. In [57], the Bag-of-Features representation [41] and local color features [76] are used to generate feature representations of the input image. The 2-class SVM [20] and Histogram Intersection [76] is then trained and applied for food localization. Class Activation Map (CAM) [90] proposed in 2016 showed that CNNs trained for classification can also coarsely highlight objects' positions in the image. A food activation map (FAM) [9] is proposed in 2017, which is a kind of CAM that is sensitive to food images based on modified GoogLeNet [78] for food localization.

2.3   Food Image Recognition

Food recognition plays a key role in image-based dietary assessment. The goal is to automatically detect pixels in an image corresponding to foods and label the type of foods. Food image recognition is similar to the task of object detection. However, it is much more challenging since it requires fine-grain recognition of different foods. Moreover, many foods have similar visual appearance and foods are generally non-rigid. There are two main categories of food recognition: single-food recognition and multiple-food recognition.

Single food recognition assumes that only one food is present in the image. Therefore, the problem can be viewed as food image classification. Unlike the general image classification problem, food classification is much more challenging due to intra-class variation and inter-class confusion [54]. Also, depending on personal preference, recipe used, and the availability of ingredients, the same food may have very different visual appearance. On the other hand, using the same cooking method may cause different foods to have a similar appearance, e.g., fried chicken breast and fried pork.

Earlier work [37] focuses on fusing different image features including SIFT, Gabor, and color histograms to classify food categories. Due to the success of using CNNs for feature representation, several groups have proposed different CNN backbone models that are pre-trained on ImageNet dataset [69], and fine-tuned these models for food image classification. For example, AlexNet [47] is used in [43], the Network in Network model [50] is fine-tuned in [79], and the Wide residual networks [89] is modified in [54]. Although the performance of food classification has been improved since, these methods use the same underlying concept, that is relying on one CNN model to extract image feature and perform classification.

In 2016, Wu *et al.* proposed a new concept that uses semantic hierarchy to learn the relationship between food categories [85]. The advantage of this method is the classifier can make a better mistake, which has closer semantic meaning to the actual food category. However, the semantic hierarchical structure is manually generated and is designed for a specific dataset. Therefore, this hierarchical structure cannot be generalized to different food image datasets. In addition, the same food may have different names or the same name may represent different foods in different cultures. Thus, building a good and adaptive semantic hierarchical structure is quite challenging.

Multiple food recognition analyzes food images containing multiple foods which are more close to real-life scenario. Matsuda *et al.* proposed a two-step solution which consists of regions proposal and region classification based on hand-crafted features [56]. Following this concept, a CNN-based two-step recognition system is developed in [72] which is assisted by Selective Search [80], bounding box clustering [72], and GrabCut [68]. The Selective Search and bounding box clustering are used to propose region candidates. Saliency maps corresponding to candidate proposals are estimated from a pre-trained CNN model by back-propagating loss to input images. Segments, generated by GrabCut based on saliency maps, were unified and integrated. A bounding box is adjusted to one segment as a final region proposal and the region inside is provided to another CNN model to generate a class label. The performance of this method is limited by the threshold used for the saliency map, and the quality of segmentation generated by GrabCut.

CNN features are used to generate a Food Activation Map (FAM) in [9], which places more weights to the food regions. The candidate regions are proposed based on the FAM and are fed to the other CNNs for classification. The size of FAM is 14×14. Although it can provide some spatial information to localize foods, much useful information may be lost using such a low resolution activation map. In addition, the food region generation depends on three parameters manually determined by cross-validation on UEC-256 [44] and EgocentricFood [9]. Thus, it is difficult to generalize the performance of the method on other datasets.

Unlike the two-step method mentioned above, YOLO v2 [64] is used in [3] to recognize multiple foods in an image. To further improve the result, segmentation masks generated by the Fully Convolutional Neural Network (FCN) and the Non-maximum Suppression technique are used to remove wrong predictions. However, the test dataset, UNIMIB2016 [19], used in this work has fixed settings where each image includes a tray with several foods placed on plates. Faster R-CNN [65] was adopted in [23] for multiple food recognition. It is also a one-step method where the Faster R-CNN generates both bounding boxes and food labels simultaneously. The UEC-100 dataset [56] is used for evaluation. However, the Faster R-CNN training process is not supervised by multiple food images since only single food images are used for training. The multiple food images, which is a small portion (9.2%) of UEC-100, are used for inference.

2.4   Food Image Datasets

The success of deep learning methods depends largely on the quantity and quality of data. Therefore, a large quantity and good quality of training data would, in general, improve the accuracy of training-based methods. Several publicly available food image datasets, as shown in Table 1, have been widely used to assess dietary intake based on deep learning approach.

Table 1 summarizes the characteristics of different datasets for both single food recognition and multiple food recognition. We report the size of each dataset (i.e. number of food images and food categories). To better understand the advantages and limitations of each dataset, we also report the food types included in the dataset and collection method (e.g., **Free-living** for unconstrained image capturing environment, or **Controlled** settings for fixed lighting conditions, dinnerware such as plates, glasses, and silverwares). Many datasets do not specify the food type selection process and use constrained environments for image acquisition. The annotation can be categorized into three types: image-level label only, bounding boxes, and polygonal areas. Datasets contain image-level label only are designed for single food classification. For multiple food recognition datasets, we also report the percentage of multi-food images.

Although these datasets contain a large number of food images, they do not always meet the needs of different applications. The food categories in PFID [16] and Menu-Match [8] are limited to popular fast foods and foods from specific restaurant menus. Food-101 [10] and UPMC-101 [82] contain many noisy images which have incorrect food labels. Recipe1M [70], Recipe1M+ [53], and Vireo-172 [15] are three large image datasets designed for recipe retrieval and UNICT-FD889 [27] and FooDD [60] are designed for food classification. All of these datasets have no food location (i.e., bounding boxes or pixels corresponding to foods) information. UEC-100 [56] is collected from popular foods in Japan. Similarly, UEC-256 [44], the expansion of UEC-100, focus on asian foods only. Although both datasets have food location and category information, only small portion of them are multiple food images. In UNIMIB2015 [18] and UNIMIB2016 [19], food images are captured under controlled environment using the same canteen tray and plates. The Mixed-Dish [21] is a recently published dataset containing 164 different asian foods in Singapore restaurants. It is worth mentioning that all the category names in the datasets we've mentioned above are defined by their authors. Therefore, it is challenging to establish the associations between those semantic food categories and standard food nutrition database such as the FNDDS [1].

Table 1. Food datasets used in the literature

Dataset name	# of Images	# of Cat.	Food type	Study type	Annotation	% of Multi-food
PFID [16]	4,545	101	Fast food	Controlled	Label	–
Chen [17]	5,000	50	–	Free-living	Label	–
Food-101 [10]	101,000	101	–	Free-living	Label	–
UNICT-FD889 [27]	3,583	889	–	Free-living	Label	–
UPMC-101 [82]	90,840	101	–	Free-living	Label	–
FooDD [60]	3,000	23	–	Free-living	Label	–
Menu-Match [8]	646	41	Restaurants	Free-living	Label	–
Recipe1M [70]	887,706	1,047	–	Free-living	Label	–
Recipe1M+ [53]	13,735,679	1,047	–	Free-living	Label	–
Vireo-172 [15]	110,241	172	Chinese	Free-living	Label	–
UEC-100 [56]	12,740	100	Japanese	Free-living	BBox	9.2%
UEC-256 [44]	28,897	256	Asian	Free-living	BBox	6.4%
UNIMIB2015 [18]	2,000	15	–	Controlled	Poly	100%
UNIMIB2016 [19]	1,027	73	–	Controlled	Poly	100%
Mixed-Dish [21]	9,246	164	Asian	Free-living	BBox	100%
VFN[1]	14,991	82	American	Free-living	BBox	26.1%

[1] https://lorenz.ecn.purdue.edu/~vfn/.

3   VIPER-FoodNet (VFN) Dataset

3.1   Food Categories

What We Eat In America (WWEIA) [2] provides two days of 24-h dietary recall data which are collected through an initial in-person interview and a follow-up phone interview. It also shows the intake frequency of each food category during two-day 24-h recall interviews. We selected food categories with high intake frequency to create a food image dataset that represents the most frequently consumed foods in the United States. These food categories have associated food codes created by the United States Department of Agriculture (USDA), which can be used to retrieve nutrient information through standard food nutrition database such as the FNDDS [1]. We selected 82 food categories from the WWEIA database, and used them as food categories in our VFN dataset.

3.2 Semi-automatic Food Image Collection and Annotation

Collecting food images with proper annotations in a systematic way can be very time-consuming and tedious using existing tools (e.g. Amazon Mechanical Turk [12]). Therefore, we implemented a semi-automatic data collection system to efficiently collect large sets of relevant online food images [25].

Online sharing of food images has gained popularity in recent years on websites such as Facebook, Flickr, Instagram for social networking and Yelp, Pinterest for product review and recommendation. There are also websites dedicated to the sharing of food images, such as yummly[1] and foodgawker[2]. There are hundred-thousands of food images uploaded by smartphone users to these websites. Online food images also provide valuable contextual information which is not directly produced by the visual appearance of food in the image, such as the users' dietary patterns and food combinations [83]. To quickly collect a large number of online food images, we implemented a web crawler to automatically search on the Google Image website based on selected food labels and download the retrieved images according to the relevant ranking on the Google Image.

However, some of these retrieved images are considered as noisy images which do not contain relevant foods. Following the method described in [71], we trained a Faster R-CNN [65] for food region detection to remove non-food images. Food images passed automatic noisy image removal step are assigned for further confirmation and food item localization in the online crowdsourcing tool. The crowds are asked to draw a bounding box around each food item in the image, and select the food category associated with each bounding box. Using this semi-automatic crowdsourcing tool, We created the VIPER-FoodNet (VFN) dataset which contains 82 food categories, 14,991 online food images and 22,423 bounding boxes.

4   Food Recognition System

Dietary assessment, which collects what an individual eats during the course of a day, can be time-consuming, tedious, and error-prone using traditional methods that rely solely on human memories and/or recordings. To improve the efficiency and accuracy of dietary assessment, we propose an automated image-based food recognition system shown in Fig. 1. Our system consists of two parts:

---

[1] https://www.yummly.com/.
[2] https://foodgawker.com/.

food localization and food classification. The goal of food localization is to locate each individual food region in an image with a bounding box. Pixels within the bounding box are assumed to represent a single food, which is the input to the food classification. Food localization serves as a pre-processing step since it is common for food images in real-life to contain multiple foods. In addition, food localization can remove non-food background in the image to improve the classification performance. Without this step, the food classification task is much more challenging. Different from existing CNN based food classification systems, the visual-aware hierarchical structure is embedded in a multi-task CNN model in our food classification method. Our method first clusters visually similar food categories based on learned features, and then leverages the hierarchical structure and a multi-task CNN model to embed visual relations between different food categories and improve the classification performance. We describe the details of each component of our system in this section.

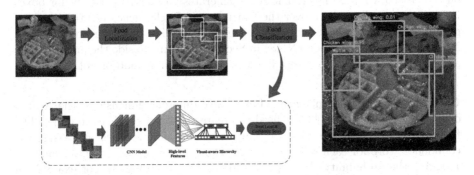

Fig. 1. Our proposed food recognition system. The food localization step, trained on Faster R-CNN, selects regions in an input image that contain food item. The selected regions, resized to 224 × 224, are fed into the food classification system. The visual-aware hierarchical structure is built based on the features extracted from a CNN model. Food label, cluster label and associated confidence scores can then be predicted for each selected region in a multi-task manner. The final output includes the bounding box and food label for each food in the input image.

4.1 Food Localization

We are interested in finding regions in a food image that contain foods, in particular, each region should contain just one food. Deep learning based methods such as Faster R-CNN [65] and YOLO [63] have shown success in many computer vision applications. Most mainstream CNN architectures such as VGG [73] and ResNet [35] can be used as the backbone structure for these methods. In our method, we use Faster R-CNN with VGG-16 as the backbone for food localization.

Faster R-CNN proposes potential regions that may contain the object with bounding boxes. It also assigns a confidence score to each bounding box. In our system, we call this confidence score the "foodness" score since it is the confidence score of food regions in the image. A high "foodness" score indicates a high likelihood that the region contains food. In our implementation, we estimate the "foodness" score threshold based on validation dataset's performance. Regions with "foodness" score above that threshold is fed into the food classification step. To train the Faster R-CNN, all different food categories in the dataset is treated as one category, i.e., food. For each food dataset, we selected 70% of the images as training data, the rest 10% is used for validation to determine the optimal hyper-parameter in Sect. 5.1, and 20% for testing the performance of food localization. The Faster R-CNN method consists of a Region Proposal Network (RPN) and a Classifier. A Non-Maximum Suppression (NMS) threshold is also selected to remove redundant regions.

Region Proposal Network (RPN). This network is used to suggest foreground object regions in the image. Before RPN, feature map is generated based on the last convolution layer. The RPN generates 9 different sized anchor boxes by sliding a small network over the feature map. Each anchor returns the foreground object confidence score and a set of bounding box coordinates. After Non-Maximum Suppression (NMS) in Sect. 4.1, features inside the anchor boxes are used by a classifier to determine whether it contains food or not.

Classifier. Since different anchor boxes have different dimensions, the Region of Interest (RoI) pooling [31] is used to create the fixed size feature maps. The fully-connected layer, the classifier, will predict the generic labels and assign the confidence score for each selected region. The confidence score ranges from 0 to 1, and is the probability of the predicted label for each region. For example, if our system assigns 0.65 to a region of the input image, that means our system believes this region has 65% probability of containing food. In our case, this is a binary classification task, which identifies whether a region contains food or not. We label this confidence score as the "foodness" score. Ideally, the classifier should assign high "foodness" score to food regions and low score to non-food regions.

Non-Maximum Suppression (NMS). The RPN may propose regions that are highly overlapped. An example is shown in Fig. 2. We adopt Non-Maximum Suppression (NMS) to select the bounding box with the highest "foodness" score and remove other bounding boxes with significant overlap. Intersection Over Union (IoU) is used to measure how significant the overlap is. As shown in Eq. 1, B1 and B2 correspond to two bounding boxes. Following [65], we set the IoU threshold to 0.7. In our implementation, if there are several bounding boxes with IoU value larger than 0.7, we retain the bounding box with the largest "foodness" score.

$$IoU = \frac{B_1 \cap B_2}{B_1 \cup B_2} \tag{1}$$

Fig. 2. An example of applying Non-Maximum Suppression (NMS) to proposed food regions. In the left image, all three regions have high confidence scores and the IoU is larger than 0.7. In the right image, NMS selects the region with the highest confidence score.

4.2 Food Classification

Convolutional Neural Networks (CNNs) have been widely used in image classification applications. Instead of training a flat CNN structure using food image datasets, we propose a hierarchical structure to further improve the accuracy and to make better mistakes. For vanilla CNN-based image classification method, the feature map will densely connect to the top layer, whose length equal to the number of categories. Each ground-truth label will be encoded in the one-hot sequence for computing cross-entropy loss. One-hot representation of N class will have N binary bits with one single high (1) bit and all the others low (0). One-hot encoding makes the L_p distances between different category label equally. In other words, the distance between label "Bagel" and "Bread" is the same as that between "Bagel" and "Pork chop" in encoding space. To reduce the information loss in this encoding process, we proposed to embed the hierarchical structure to represent visual relationships between food categories. In [85], a pre-defined semantic hierarchical tree is proposed, which contains food clusters with semantic similar food categories. Results showed that using the hierarchical structure can improve the accuracy of classification and make better mistakes. However, the hierarchy is defined manually, and customized for Food-101 [10] and 5-Chain [85]. Most existing food image datasets [10,44,56,86] contain different food categories. As a result, the semantic-aware hierarchical structure need to be rebuilt for different datasets. It is worth mentioning that same food may have different names, e.g. courgette and zucchini, and same word may refer to different foods, e.g. muffin in England and in America are different. It would be very time-consuming to define a specific semantic-aware hierarchical structure for each dataset. In this paper, we propose a method to cluster visually similar food categories and automatically generate a hierarchical structure to improve CNN based food classification.

Food Similarity Measure. Many existing methods can cluster similar categories based on semantics. However, food categories with high semantic relations do not always share similar visual features. In addition, food categories vary in different regions of the world. The same food may have different names in different cuisine. Manually record each food category and compute semantic relation is expensive and not feasible for large datasets. Therefore, semantics structure is hard to build and the semantics correlation may mislead visual-feature based training process if semantic similar categories have distinctive visual appearances. CNNs are commons used in image classification to extract visual features. These visual features can be used to identify correlations between different food categories. Based on the feature map of the convolutional layer, we can compute the visual similarity between food categories and cluster similar categories automatically.

In our system, we choose DenseNet-121 [38] model as our visual feature extractor. It consists of convolutional layers and full-connected layers. Convolutional layers are used to extract features from input images. Fully-connected layers are used to perform the classification task based on the features generated by convolutional layers. The output of the last convolution layer is treated as the feature map for each food image. Our feature map for each input image is a 1×1024 space vector and represents one data point in the $1,024$ dimensional feature space. We used the pre-trained model on the ImageNet [69] dataset and use a small learning rate to fine-tuning the pre-trained model to reduce training time. The learning rate is set to 0.0001. The model is flat trained on the food dataset and we used the cross-entropy loss as the loss function.

$$Cross\ Entropy\ Loss = -\sum_{i=1}^{N} y_i log(p_i) \tag{2}$$

As shown in Eq. 2, N is the total number of classes, y_i and p_i correspond to the ith element in **y** and **p**, whose length are N. **y**, the ground truth label, is encoded as one-hot sequence, and **p** is the confidence scores of each category predicted by networks. Once the loss is converged, the model then has the ability to extract meaningful visual features for food classification. If the model is well trained, as

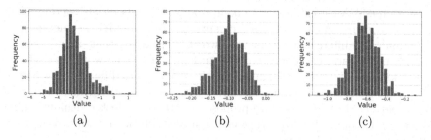

Fig. 3. The feature map of the input image is a 1×1024 vector represents 1024 feature dimensions. Different food categories have different feature distributions. This figure shows histograms of 3 of 1024 feature dimensions for all training images of apple pie. All three features exhibit Gaussian-like distribution.

show in Fig. 3, each dimension of the feature map of one food category should have a Gaussian-like distribution. Therefore, we can generate a 1D Gaussian Probability Density Function to fit the distribution and compute their Overlap Coefficient (OVL) [81].

As shown in Fig. 4, the OVL refers to the area under two probability density functions. It is a measure of the agreement between two distributions. Therefore, if two food categories have high OVL in one dimension of the feature map, that means both food categories are similar with respect to this feature dimension. As a result, we compute the OVLs in all 1,024 dimensions and normalize them to generate the similarity matrix. Figure 5a shows the similarity matrix of the Food-101 dataset food categories. We select three categories, as shown in Fig. 5b, to show an example of the similarity measure between different food categories. For instance, baby back rib and prime rib show higher similarity (0.53) compared to apple pie (0.42).

As shown in Eq. 2, cross-entropy uses one-hot sequence to encode the ground truth label. Due to the nature of one-hot encoding, each pair of labels has the same L^p distance and there is no visual relations embedded. However, visually similar food categories obtain higher similarity score in our similarity matrix in Fig. 5. We propose to cluster those similar categories and build a hierarchy to express their relations in the explicit way.

Food Clustering and Hierarchical Structure. Hierarchical structure can represent the relations between food categories. In addition, it is the key to build the multi-task model for further improving the performance of the classification task. To generate the hierarchical structure for our system, we need to cluster similar food categories first. Based on the similarity matrix calculated above, many clustering methods can be applied. Although the existing method, such as

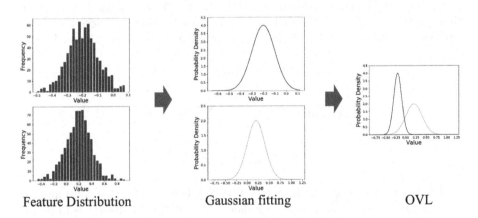

Feature Distribution   Gaussian fitting   OVL

Fig. 4. The left two plots are distributions of two different food categories in one specific high-level feature. We fit Gaussian Probability Density Function (PDF) over this distribution. The overlap coefficient (OVL) is the overlapped area between the two PDFs.

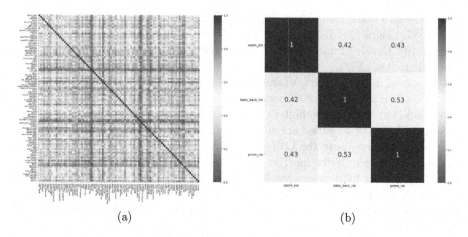

(a)   (b)

Fig. 5. Similarity matrix: (a) shows the entire similarity matrix of the Food-101 dataset. In (b), we select three categories: Apple pie, Baby back rib, and Prime rib. Apple pie is quite different from the other two categories. Prime rib and Baby back rib are visually similar, which indicated by higher similarity scores.

K-means, can partition a dataset into K clusters efficiently and find the centroids of the K clusters accurately, it requires pre-defined number of clusters, k. Unlike K-means, Affinity propagation (AP) [30] does not need to know the number of clusters a priori, instead, it can determine the optimal cluster number. In our implementation, we use AP to cluster the similar food category and generate a 2-level hierarchical structure. AP treats all food categories as candidates and selects m candidates as exemplars to represent m clusters separately. It iteratively refines the selection until it reaches the optimal solution. The input of AP is the similarity matrix (s) calculated in Sect. 4.2. We first define two matrices "Responsibility" (r) and "Availability" (a). Initially, both matrices are set to zero. Both matrices are then updated alternately as shown in Eq. 3 and Eq. 4.

$$r(i, k) = s(i, k) - \max_{k' \neq k}(a(i, k') + s(i, k')) \qquad (3)$$

$$a(i, k)_{i \neq k} = \min\left(0, r(k, k) + \sum_{i' \notin \{i, k\}} \max(0, r(i', k))\right)$$

$$a(k, k) = \sum_{i' \neq k} \max(0, r(i', k)) \qquad (4)$$

The three matrix: s, a, r, have size N × N, where N refers the total number of categories. In Eq. 3, $r(i, k)$ quantify how well-suited k^{th} category is to be the exemplar for i^{th} category, relative to other candidate exemplars. It is the information propagated from i^{th} category to k^{th} category. In Eq. 4, $a(i, k)$ quantify how appropriate for i^{th} category to pick k^{th} category as its exemplar, which is a feedback propagated from k^{th} category. If $r(i, i) + a(i, i) > 0, x_i$ is selected as the exemplar. Each following iteration will update the selected exemplars. If the selection does not change for more than 15 iterations, the result is said to reach the optimal solution. Once we formed the stable clusters, we can build a hierarchical structure based on the clustering result. Using the same strategy, similar clusters can be further grouped for generating three or higher-level hierarchy.

Multi-task Learning for Deep Neural Networks. Multi-task models are employed for obtaining predictions for several related tasks simultaneously. Suppose the hierarchical structure generated from Sect. 4.2 has two levels, then there are two related tasks assigned to the multi-task model, i.e. 1st-level category predication and 2nd-level cluster prediction. As shown in Fig. 6, the multi-task deep learning model proposed in this paper contains two parts: feature extraction layers and output layers. Unlike the visual feature extractor trained by regular cross-entropy loss as described in Sect. 4.2, the feature extraction layers for joint feature learning are trained by multi-task loss back-propagated from output layers. The number of the output layers is equal to the number of levels in the hierarchy. The nodes in each layer correspond to labels of that level. All the output layers are fully-connected to the high-level features learned from joint feature learning for predictions.

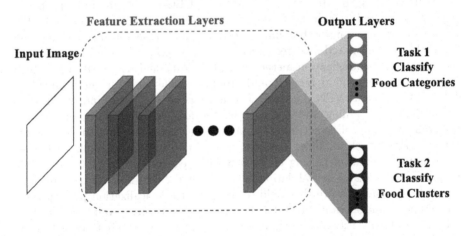

Fig. 6. A two-level multi-task CNN architecture: The feature extraction layers for joint feature learning output the high-level features. Two separated output layers are fully connected to those features for category prediction (Task 1) and cluster prediction (Task 2)

Suppose we have a hierarchical structure $\psi = \{Y^{(t)}\}_{t=1}^T$ with T levels, where $\{Y^{(t)}\}$ represent the tth level's label set of the given T-level hierarchical structure. Each node in each level will be assigned a label, e.g. $\{y_i^{(1)}\}_{i=1}^{N_1}$ represents the original category set and $\{y_i^{(2)}\}_{i=1}^{N_2}$ represent the label set for the cluster in the second level. Thus the multi-task loss function is formulated as

$$L(\mathbf{w}) = \sum_{t=1}^{T} \lambda_t \sum_{i=1}^{N_t} -logp(y_i^{(t)}|\mathbf{x}_i, \mathbf{w}_0, \mathbf{w}^{(t)}) \qquad (5)$$

where $y_i^{(t)} \in Y^{(t)}$ is the corresponding class/cluster label for the tth hierarchical level. $\mathbf{w}^{(t)}$ represent the network parameters for the tth output layer, and $\mathbf{w}_0$ compose the parameters for feature extraction layers. λ_t is the hyperparameter that controls the weight of the tth level contribution in the given hierarchical structure. During the training process, the weights of the shared feature extraction layers are initialized using the values of the corresponding network pre-trained on ImageNet dataset [47], while the parameter $\mathbf{w}^{(t)}$ for the tth output layer are learned from scratch. In addition, for the two-level hierarchy proposed in this paper, we set $\lambda_1 = \lambda_2 = 0.5$ in the multi-task loss.

5   Experimental Results

Our food recognition system consists of food localization and food classification. In this section, we first evaluated the performance of food localization and food classification separately, and then test the overall performance of the food recognition system. The datasets we used for our experiments include Food-101 [10], UPMC-101 [86], UEC-100 [56], UEC-256 [44] and our proposed VFN datasets. It is worth mentioning that only UEC-100, UEC-256, and VFN datasets contain bounding box information for food images, which can be used for food localization and food recognition evaluation. For classification task, our hierarchy-based classification method is tested on Food-101, UPMC-101, which contain only single food images, and cropped single food images from UEC-100, UEC-256, and VFN datasets. The authors of Food-101 and UPMC-101 established the training and testing sets. We followed their splits and report the standard multi-class accuracy on each testing set. Following the setting for the recognition task in [9], we applied a random 70%/10%/20% split of images for training/validation/testing on each food category for UEC-100, UEC-256, and VFN datasets. The validation set of each dataset is used to determine the best "foodness" score threshold to optimize food localization performance. The cropped images from these datasets are used as training/validation/testing images for classification. Since testing sets are not revealed to both classification and localization, there is no overfitting occurred during the recognition evaluation. Although UEC-100 is the predecessor of UEC-256, which means it is a subset of UEC-256, many previous works [32,72,87] were evaluated on UEC-100, and the expanded 156 categories made UEC-256 quite different from UEC-100. Therefore, we evaluated our system on both datasets for comparison.

5.1   Food Localization

As mentioned in Sect. 4.1, food localization is trained on the training set of each food image datasets, i.e., UEC-100, UEC-256, and VFN datasets. The "foodness" score threshold is determined by the validation set. Localization performance on the testing sets of each dataset is reported in Table 2.

Precision and recall are the most common performance metrics used for localization evaluation. We define four related terminologies: True Positive (TP) means a food region is correctly detected; False Positive (FP) means a non-food region is incorrectly detected as a food region; True Negative (TN) means a non-food region is correctly detected; False Negative (FN) means a food region is incorrectly detected as a non-food region. We define a region is correctly detected if the IoU, defined in Eq. 1, between it and the ground-truth is larger than 0.5. Based on these definitions, we can calculate precision (Eq. 6) and recall (Eq. 7).

$$Precision = \frac{TP}{TP + FP} \tag{6}$$

$$Recall = \frac{TP}{TP + FN} \tag{7}$$

As shown in Fig. 7, we evenly sampled 21 points as "foodness" score thresholds in the range [0.0, 1.0] and plot precision and recall for each threshold. High precision usually corresponds to low recall. In order to find the optimal combination of precision and recall, F-measure (Eq. 8), which is the harmonic mean of precision and recall, is introduced. In Fig. 7, we plot F-measure for each threshold and mark the highest value in black.

$$F - measure = 2 \times \frac{Precision \times Recall}{Precision + Recall} \tag{8}$$

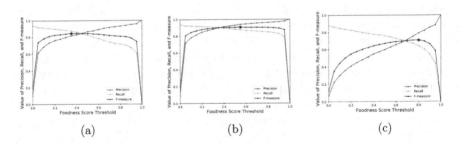

Fig. 7. Precisions, Recall, and F-Measure corresponding to different "foodness" score threshold: (a) UEC-100 dataset has the highest F-Measure when "foodnes" score threshold = 0.35. (b) UEC-256 dataset has the highest F-Measure when "foodness" score threshold = 0.55. (c) VFN dataset has the highest F-Measure when "foodness" score threshold = 0.80.

As shown in the Table 2, we report the selected "foodness" score threshold and all three performance metrics on the testing set of each food dataset. Precision measures the proportion of positive detection that is actually correct, and recall calculates the proportion of actual positives that is detected correctly. Therefore, we expect our system to have both high values in precision and recall. The VFN datasets has higher precision but relatively low recall. It is worth mentioning that about 6.4% of images in UEC-256 dataset and 9.2% of UEC-100 contain more than 2 bounding boxes, while the VFN dataset has more than 26% images with multiple bounding boxes, making it much more challenging. Due to these multiple food regions, False Negative is higher for the VFN dataset which causes lower recall.

Table 2. Performance of food localization on different food image datasets

Dataset	UEC-100	UEC-256	VFN
Foodness score threshold	0.35	0.55	0.80
Precision	0.8159	0.9388	0.7926
Recall	0.8604	0.8764	0.6372
F-Measure	0.8376	0.9065	0.7064

5.2 Food Classification

In our system, classification is performed on food regions identified by food localization. Ideally, each food region should contain only one food item. We selected Food-101, UPMC-101, UEC-100, UEC-256, and VFN to evaluate the performance of proposed food classification. Among these datasets, Food-101 and UPMC-101 contain only single food images. Since the images in UEC-100, UEC-256, and VFN datasets contain multiple food items, we cropped food regions based on ground-truth bounding box information to generate single food images to evaluated the performance of proposed food classification. We follow the selection of training and testing data as provided by the Food-101 and UPMC-101 datasets. For other three datasets, we select 70% for training, 10% for validation, and 20% for testing as standard practice. We report multi-class accuracy, the percentage of correctly classified images, on the testing set of each dataset.

There are many powerful deep learning models developed for food classification. It is worth mentioning that the use of more complicated Neural Networks models, such as Inception [77], ResNet [35] and DenseNet [38], can achieve higher accuracy. However, our proposed method is agnostic about the underlying CNN model used, so we want to show the improvement of the classification accuracy based on a hierarchical structure of the class labels. Therefore, the term flat classification is referred to tuning a CNN model for food classification, and hierarchical classification means a hierarchical structure generated by visual semantics among class labels is used for food classification.

We used DenseNet-121 as our backbone CNN model for this evaluation. The evaluation of classification task consists of three experiments. We trained the selected CNN model for flat classification (CNN-FC) at the learning rate of 0.0001, the same CNN model for hierarchical classification (CNN-HC) with the same learning rate at 0.0001, and fine-tuning the same CNN model for hierarchical classification (CNN-HC-FT) at a smaller learning rate of 0.00001. As discussed earlier, it is possible to replace DenseNet-121 with other CNN models to improve the performance of the baseline method, i.e., flat classification. Our CNN model is initialized with pre-trained weights on ImageNet, and uses batch size of 20.

To generate the hierarchical structure, we first train the DenseNet-121 for flat classification. Once the accuracy and loss converge, we extract the feature maps from each training image and compute the similarity score (OVL) among all categories to generate clusters using Affinity Propagation. As shown in Table 3, each dataset has a different number of clusters. We designed a 2-level hierarchical structure based on these clusters, i.e., the 1st-level (bottom-level) is food category and the 2nd-level (top-level) is food cluster.

Table 3. Category and cluster numbers in different datasets

	Food-101	UPMC-101	UEC-100	UEC-256	VFN
Category no.	101	101	100	256	82
Cluster no.	17	18	15	33	14

There are two tasks assigned to our multi-task model, one is to classify the food cluster, and the other is to classify the food category. As shown in the Table 4, with fixed learning rate and batch size, hierarchical classification achieves better performance for top-1 accuracy. After fine-tuning the multi-task model with a smaller learning rate, the accuracy can be further improved.

Table 4. Single food image classification top-1 accuracy

	Food-101	UPMC-101	UEC-100	UEC-256	VFN
CNN-FC	0.7531	0.6483	0.7823	0.6708	0.6520
CNN-HC	0.7625	0.6601	0.7940	0.6857	0.6784
CNN-HC-FT	0.7978	0.6926	0.8081	0.7236	0.7181

From a nutrient perspective, visually similar foods may contain similar nutrition content, e.g., fried chicken and fried pork. Therefore, our proposed recognition system can minimize the impact of a mistake by clustering visually similar foods together. It is worth mentioning that top-5 accuracy is another performance metric often used in the classification task. However, top-5 accuracy cannot reflect how good or bad a mistake is. As a result, We define a new performance metric called "Cluster Top-1" accuracy to measure whether our system made a good or bad mistake. The proposed visual-aware hierarchical structure contains many clusters (top level) that consist of several visually similar foods (2nd level). Therefore, if the top-1 decision is a member of the cluster that the correct category belongs to, we consider it a correct "Cluster Top-1" decision. As shown in Table 5, the visual-aware hierarchical structure not only improves the top-1 accuracy, but can also improve the cluster top-1 accuracy. In other words, our proposed system is able to make a better mistake than flat classification methods.

Table 5. Single food image classification cluster top-1 accuracy

	Food-101	UPMC-101	UEC-100	UEC-256	VFN
CNN-FC	0.8506	0.7426	0.8895	0.7839	0.7986
CNN-HC	0.8512	0.7607	0.8944	0.8049	0.8217
CNN-HC-FT	0.8782	0.7873	0.9020	0.8337	0.8481

There are many food images in UEC-100, UEC-256, and VFN datasets contain only a single food. As mentioned in Sect. 4, food localization can help remove the non-food background pixels to improve the classification performance. To show this benefit, we selected the single food images from UEC-100, UEC-256 and VFN datasets and compose two new datasets: (1) original images which contain single food and background (2) cropped images which contain food region cropped from single food images without background. Our split for these two datasets is under the constraint that each training/validation/testing image of (2) is cropped from corresponding image in (1). To compare the classification performances of these two dataset, we trained vanilla DenseNet-121 (flat classification) under the experiment settings mentioned at the beginning of this section for these datasets. As shown in Table 6, cropping the food regions in the image indeed improves the classification accuracy, especially for more complex images such as those in the VFN dataset.

Table 6. Classification accuracy of original food images and food regions

	UEC-100	UEC-256	VFN
Original image	0.7621	0.6354	0.5542
Cropped image	0.7847	0.6560	0.6385

5.3   Food Recognition

In this section, we report the evaluation of our overall system by combining the food localization and food recognition. For single food images, localization can help remove irrelevant background pixels. For multi-food images, localization can detect all food regions. Since UEC-100, UEC-256, and VFN datasets have ground-truth bounding box information, we use their test images to evaluate the performance of our food recognition system.

Since it is impossible for predicted bounding boxes from food localization to match exactly to the ground-truth, we followed the most common standards of practice for recognition task using precision and recall, which are described in Sect. 5.1. The difference is that we have multiple category labels instead of food/non-food. For example, the predicted bounding box is treated as True Positive (TP) when it is assigned the correct food label and the IoU between the predicted and ground-truth bounding box is larger than 0.5. Precision (Eq. 6) and recall (Eq. 7), are calculated the same way as illustrated in Sect. 5.1. For comparison, we also calculate the accuracy (Eq. 9) defined in [9], which is different from the definition of multi-class accuracy for classification in Sect. 5.2.

$$Accuracy = \frac{TP}{TP + FP + FN} \tag{9}$$

As shown in Table 7, we compare our method with [9] on UEC-256 dataset. Reported precision, recall, and accuracy are solely based on label correctness and IoU metric, they do not consider the confidence score of each bounding box assigned by the localization step. Both precision and recall of our method are much higher than those reported in [9]. The reasons for the improvements include (1) the food localization step in our system is fully-supervised by bounding-box level annotations, which is stronger than the image level supervision used in [9] for region proposal. (2) the classification backbone network used in our system, DenseNet-121, is more powerful than GoogleNet [78] in [9]. (3) the hierarchical structure based on visual similarity further improves the classification performance as indicated in Sect. 5.2.

Table 7. Comparison with other method on UEC-256 dataset

	Precision	Recall	Accuracy
Other method [9]	0.5433	0.5086	0.3684
Our method	0.6560	0.6124	0.4635

Table 8. Precision, recall, accuracy, and mAP of our method on three datasets

	Precision	Recall	Accuracy	mAP
UEC-100	0.6309	0.6654	0.4790	0.6063
UEC-256	0.6560	0.6124	0.4635	0.5673
VFN	0.5655	0.4546	0.3369	0.4006

We also evaluated our system's performance on all three datasets as shown in Table 8. To provide a more accurate and fair evaluation, we follow the mean Average Precision (mAP) metric used in PASCAL Visual Object Classes [24] and report our experimental results in Table 8. As we illustrated in Sect. 5.1, precision and recall vary as we change the confidence score threshold. Average Precision (AP) for each category is the average precision value for recall value over 0 to 1 for each food category, and mAP is the mean value of all APs of all categories.

6   Discussion

We evaluated the performance of various components of our system in Sect. 5. Table 3 shows that the proposed method of building the two-level hierarchical structure is applicable for different datasets. Table 4 and Table 5 shows that by using the same CNNs model and the same learning rate, our proposed method can improve both top-1 accuracy and cluster top-1 accuracy. After fine-tuning with smaller learning rate, the result can be further improved. In addition, Table 6 illustrates that even for single food image, food localization can remove non-food background pixels and improve classification accuracy. Localization is particularly useful for complex images with background clutters such as those in the VFN dataset as indicated by the larger improvement. It is worth mentioning that for the results in both Table 4 and Table 6, the performance on VFN is lower than other public datasets due to several reasons. First, the VFN dataset contains many visually similar food categories, e.g. milk, ice cream, and yogurt. In addition, many categories in this dataset contain around 100 images, which is far less than other public datasets, e.g. Food-101 has 1000 images per category. In our future work, we plan to expand the VNF dataset by increasing the number of images per category.

Since UEC-100, UEC-256, and VFN datasets contain bounding box information, we use these datasets to test the performance of the overall recognition system. Our proposed system significantly outperforms previous method [9] as shown in Table 7. Table 8 shows that the mAP of VFN is lower than that of the other two datasets. Since the mAP highly depends on the confidence score of the class label assigned to the food region by the classification, the lower classification result of VFN leads to the low mAP value which is another indication that VFN is a more challenging dataset. Without taking into consideration the confidence score, Table 8 also reports our proposed method achieved high precision, recall and accuracy results on UEC-100 and UEC-256, and a reasonable performance results on VFN dataset. The low recall of the VFN is mainly caused by the errors in food localization, which may not detect all the food regions in images. This is a main challenge of the VFN dataset which contains significantly more multiple food images than the UEC-100 and UEC-256 datasets as described in Table 1.

7   Conclusion

In this paper, we developed a recognition system consisting of a food localization step to detect food regions in an image and a hierarchical food classification step that can cluster visually similar food categories to improve classification performance. We also introduced a high quality and challenging dataset, VIPER-FoodNet (VFN) dataset, which is based on the most commonly consumed foods in the United States and the images are sourced from the Internet including social media platforms such that they are closely related to daily life food images.

Our food recognition system is evaluated on several public datasets, including the new VFN dataset and showed improved performance. We also discussed opportunities to further improve the system performance on challenging dataset such as the VFN. As part of our future work, we will expand the VNF dataset by obtaining additional images for the existing categories, as well as adding more categories to the dataset.

References

1. USDA food and nutrient database for dietary studies 2015–2016. Agricultural Research Service, Food Surveys Research Group (2018)
2. What we eat in america, nhanes 2015–2016
3. Aguilar, E., Remeseiro, B., Bolaños, M., Radeva, P.: Grab, pay, and eat: semantic food detection for smart restaurants. IEEE Trans. Multimed. **20**, 3266–3275 (2017)
4. Ahmad, Z., et al.: A mobile food record for integrated dietary assessment. In: Proceedings of the 2nd International Workshop on Multimedia Assisted Dietary Management, Amsterdam, Netherlands, pp. 53–62, October 2016
5. Aizawa, K., Maruyama, Y., Li, H., Morikawa, C.: Food balance estimation by using personal dietary tendencies in a multimedia Food Log. IEEE Trans. Multimed. **15**(8), 2176–2185 (2013)
6. Alharbi, R., Pfammatter, A., Spring, B., Alshurafa, N.: Willsense: adherence barriers for passive sensing systems that track eating behavior. In: Proceedings of the 2017 CHI Conference Extended Abstracts on Human Factors in Computing Systems, pp. 2329–2336 (2017). https://doi.org/10.1145/3027063.3053271
7. Bay, H., Ess, A., Tuytelaars, T., Gool, L.V.: Speeded-up robust features (SURF). J. Comput. Vis. Image Underst. **110**(3), 346–359 (2008)
8. Beijbom, O., Joshi, N., Morris, D., Saponas, S., Khullar, S.: Menu-match: restaurant-specific food logging from images. In: 2015 IEEE Winter Conference on Applications of Computer Vision, pp. 844–851 (2015)
9. Bolaños, M., Radeva, P.: Simultaneous food localization and recognition. In: 2016 23rd International Conference on Pattern Recognition (ICPR), pp. 3140–3145 (2016)
10. Bossard, L., Guillaumin, M., Gool, L.V.: Food-101 - mining discriminative components with random forests. In: Proceedings of European Conference on Computer Vision, Zurich, Switzerland, vol. 8694, pp. 446–461, September 2014
11. Boushey, C.J., Spoden, M., Zhu, F.M., Delp, E.J., Kerr, D.A.: New mobile methods for dietary assessment: review of image-assisted and image-based dietary assessment methods. Proc. Nutr. Soc. **76**(3), 283–294 (2017)
12. Buhrmester, M., Kwang, T., Gosling, S.D.: Amazon's mechanical Turk: a new source of inexpensive, yet high-quality data? (2016)
13. Casperson, S.L., Sieling, J., Moon, J., Johnson, L.K., Roemmich, J.N., Whigham, L.D.: A mobile phone food record app to digitally capture dietary intake for adolescents in a free-living environment: usability study (2015)
14. Chang, C.C., Lin, C.J.: LIBSVM: a library for support vector machines. ACM Trans. Intell. Syst. Technol. **2**(3), 27 (2011)

15. Chen, J., Ngo, C.W.: Deep-based ingredient recognition for cooking recipe retrieval. In: Proceedings of the 24th ACM International Conference on Multimedia, pp. 32–41 (2016)

16. Chen, M., Dhingra, K., Wu, W., Yang, L., Sukthankar, R., Yang, J.: PFID: Pittsburgh fast-food image dataset. In: Proceedings of the IEEE International Conference on Image Processing, Cairo, Egypt, pp. 289–292, November 2009

17. Chen, M., et al.: Automatic Chinese food identification and quantity estimation. In: Proceedings of SIGGRAPH Asia Technical Briefs, Singapore, Singapore, pp. 29:1–29:4 (2012)

18. Ciocca, G., Napoletano, P., Schettini, R.: Food recognition and leftover estimation for daily diet monitoring. In: New Trends in Image Analysis and Processing - ICIAP 2015 Workshops, pp. 334–341 (2015)

19. Ciocca, G., Napoletano, P., Schettini, R.: Food recognition: a new dataset, experiments and results. IEEE J. Biomed. Health Inform. **21**(3), 588–598 (2017). https://doi.org/10.1109/JBHI.2016.2636441

20. Cortes, C., Vapnik, V.: Support-vector networks. Mach. Learn. **20**(3), 273–297 (1995)

21. Deng, L., et al.: Mixed-dish recognition with contextual relation networks. In: Proceedings of the 27th ACM International Conference on Multimedia, pp. 112–120 (2019)

22. Deng, X., et al.: Joint hand detection and rotation estimation using CNN. IEEE Trans. Image Process. **27**(4), 1888–1900 (2017)

23. Ege, T., Yanai, K.: Estimating food calories for multiple-dish food photos. In: 2017 4th IAPR Asian Conference on Pattern Recognition (ACPR), pp. 646–651 (2017)

24. Everingham, M., Van Gool, L., Williams, C.K.I., Winn, J., Zisserman, A.: The pascal visual object classes (VOC) challenge. Int. J. Comput. Vis. **88**(2), 303–338 (2010)

25. Fang, S., Liu, C., Khalid, K., Zhu, F., Boushey, C., Delp, E.J.: CTADA: the design of a crowdsourcing tool for online food image identification and segmentation. In: Proceedings of the IEEE Southwest Symposium on Image Analysis and Interpretation, Las Vegas, NV, April 2018 (2018)

26. Fang, S., Shao, Z., Kerr, D.A., Boushey, C.J., Zhu, F.: An end-to-end image-based automatic food energy estimation technique based on learned energy distribution images: protocol and methodology. Nutrients **11**(4), 877 (2019)

27. Farinella, G.M., Allegra, D., Stanco, F.: A benchmark dataset to study the representation of food images. In: Agapito, L., Bronstein, M.M., Rother, C. (eds.) ECCV 2014. LNCS, vol. 8927, pp. 584–599. Springer, Cham (2015). https://doi.org/10.1007/978-3-319-16199-0_41

28. Farinella, G.M., Allegra, D., Stanco, F., Battiato, S.: On the exploitation of one class classification to distinguish food vs non-food images. In: Murino, V., Puppo, E., Sona, D., Cristani, M., Sansone, C. (eds.) ICIAP 2015. LNCS, vol. 9281, pp. 375–383. Springer, Cham (2015). https://doi.org/10.1007/978-3-319-23222-5_46

29. Fei-Fei, L., Perona, P.: A Bayesian hierarchical model for learning natural scene categories. In: IEEE Conference on Computer Vision and Pattern Recognition, vol. 2, pp. 524–531 (2005)

30. Frey, B.J., Dueck, D.: Clustering by passing messages between data points. Science **315**(5814), 972–976 (2007)

31. Girshick, R.: Fast R-CNN. In: Proceedings of the IEEE International Conference on Computer Vision, pp. 1440–1448, December 2015

32. Hassannejad, H., Matrella, G., Ciampolini, P., De Munari, I., Mordonini, M., Cagnoni, S.: Food image recognition using very deep convolutional networks. In: Proceedings of the 2nd International Workshop on Multimedia Assisted Dietary Management, pp. 41–49 (2016). https://doi.org/10.1145/2986035.2986042

33. He, J., Shao, Z., Wright, J., Kerr, D., Boushey, C., Zhu, F.: Multi-task image-based dietary assessment for food recognition and portion size estimation. arXiv preprint arXiv:2004.13188 (2020)

34. He, K., Gkioxari, G., Dollar, P., Girshick, R.: Mask R-CNN. In: Proceedings of the IEEE International Conference on Computer Vision, Venice, Italy, pp. 2980–2988, October 2017

35. He, K., Zhang, X., Ren, S., Sun, J.: Deep residual learning for image recognition. In: Proceedings of the IEEE Conference on Computer Vision and Pattern Recognition, Las Vegas, NV, pp. 770–778, June 2016

36. He, K., Zhang, X., Ren, S., Sun, J.: Deep residual learning for image recognition. In: The IEEE Conference on Computer Vision and Pattern Recognition (CVPR), June 2016

37. Hoashi, H., Joutou, T., Yanai, K.: Image recognition of 85 food categories by feature fusion. In: 2010 IEEE International Symposium on Multimedia, pp. 296–301, December 2010. https://doi.org/10.1109/ISM.2010.51

38. Huang, G., Liu, Z., Van Der Maaten, L., Weinberger, K.Q.: Densely connected convolutional networks. In: Proceedings of the IEEE Conference on Computer Vision and Pattern Recognition, pp. 4700–4708 (2017)

39. Jia, W., Yue, Y., Fernstrom, J.D., Zhang, Z., Yang, Y., Sun, M.: 3D localization of circular feature in 2D image and application to food volume estimation. In: 2012 Annual International Conference of the IEEE Engineering in Medicine and Biology Society, pp. 4545–4548 (2012)

40. Jiang, H., Learned-Miller, E.: Face detection with the faster R-CNN. In: IEEE International Conference on Automatic Face & Gesture Recognition, pp. 650–657 (2017)

41. Joutou, T., Yanai, K.: A food image recognition system with multiple kernel learning. In: Proceedings of the IEEE International Conference on Image Processing, Cairo, Egypt, pp. 285–288, October 2009

42. Kagaya, H., Aizawa, K.: Highly accurate food/non-food image classification based on a deep convolutional neural network. In: Murino, V., Puppo, E., Sona, D., Cristani, M., Sansone, C. (eds.) ICIAP 2015. LNCS, vol. 9281, pp. 350–357. Springer, Cham (2015). https://doi.org/10.1007/978-3-319-23222-5_43

43. Kagaya, H., Aizawa, K., Ogawa, M.: Food detection and recognition using convolutional neural network. In: Proceedings of the 22nd ACM International Conference on Multimedia, Orlando, Florida, USA, pp. 1085–1088 (2014)

44. Kawano, Y., Yanai, K.: Automatic expansion of a food image dataset leveraging existing categories with domain adaptation. In: Proceedings of European Conference on Computer Vision Workshops, Zurich, Switzerland, pp. 3–17, September 2014

45. Kirkpatrick, S.I., et al.: Performance of the automated self-administered 24-hour recall relative to a measure of true intakes and to an interviewer-administered 24-h recall. Am. J. Clin. Nutr. 100(1), 233–240 (2014)

46. Kitamura, K., Yamasaki, T., Aizawa, K.: Foodlog: capture analysis and retrieval of personal food images via web. In: Proceedings of the ACM Multimedia Workshop on Multimedia for Cooking and Eating Activities, Beijing, China, pp. 23–30, November 2009

47. Krizhevsky, A., Sutskever, I., Hinton, G.E.: ImageNet classification with deep convolutional neural networks. In: Proceedings of Advances in Neural Information Processing Systems, pp. 1097–1105, December 2012
48. Larsson, C.L., Westerterp, K.R., Johansson, G.K.: Validity of reported energy expenditure and energy and protein intakes in Swedish adolescent vegans and omnivores. Am. J. Clin. Nutr. **75**(2), 268–274 (2002)
49. LeCun, Y., Bengio, Y., Hinton, G.: Deep learning. Nature **521**, 436–444 (2015)
50. Lin, M., Chen, Q., Yan, S.: Network in network. arXiv preprint arXiv:1312.4400 (2013)
51. Livingstone, M.B.E., Robson, P.J., Wallace, J.M.W.: Issues in dietary intake assessment of children and adolescents. Br. J. Nutr. **92**, S213–S222 (2004)
52. Lowe, D.: Distinctive image features from scale-invariant keypoints. Int. J. Comput. Vis. **2**(60), 91–110 (2004)
53. Marin, J., et al.: Recipe1m+: a dataset for learning cross-modal embeddings for cooking recipes and food images. IEEE Trans. Pattern Anal. Mach. Intell. (2019)
54. Martinel, N., Foresti, G.L., Micheloni, C.: Wide-slice residual networks for food recognition. In: 2018 IEEE Winter Conference on Applications of Computer Vision (WACV), pp. 567–576, March 2018. https://doi.org/10.1109/WACV.2018.00068
55. Martinel, N., Piciarelli, C., Micheloni, C., Foresti, G.L.: A structured committee for food recognition, pp. 484–492, December 2015. https://doi.org/10.1109/ICCVW.2015.70
56. Matsuda, Y., Hoashi, H., Yanai, K.: Recognition of multiple-food images by detecting candidate regions. In: Proceedings of IEEE International Conference on Multimedia and Expo, Melbourne, Australia, pp. 25–30, July 2012
57. Miyano, R., Uematsu, Y., Saito, H.: Food region detection using bag-of-features representation and color feature. VISAPP (2012)
58. Myers, A., et al.: Im2Calories: towards an automated mobile vision food diary. In: Proceedings of the IEEE International Conference on Computer Vision, Santiago, Chile, December 2011
59. Poslusna, K., Ruprich, J., de Vries, J.H., Jakubikova, M., van't Veer, P.: Misreporting of energy and micronutrient intake estimated by food records and 24 hour recalls, control and adjustment methods in practice. Br. J. Nutr. **101**(S2), S73–S85 (2009)
60. Pouladzadeh, P., Yassine, A., Shirmohammadi, S.: FooDD: food detection dataset for calorie measurement using food images. In: Murino, V., Puppo, E., Sona, D., Cristani, M., Sansone, C. (eds.) ICIAP 2015. LNCS, vol. 9281, pp. 441–448. Springer, Cham (2015). https://doi.org/10.1007/978-3-319-23222-5_54
61. Qiu, J., Lo, F.P., Lo, B.: Assessing individual dietary intake in food sharing scenarios with a 360 camera and deep learning. In: 2019 IEEE 16th International Conference on Wearable and Implantable Body Sensor Networks (BSN), pp. 1–4, May 2019. https://doi.org/10.1109/BSN.2019.8771095
62. Ragusa, F., Tomaselli, V., Furnari, A., Battiato, S., Farinella, G.M.: Food vs nonfood classification. In: Proceedings of the 2nd International Workshop on Multimedia Assisted Dietary Management, pp. 77–81 (2016). https://doi.org/10.1145/2986035.2986041
63. Redmon, J., Divvala, S., Girshick, R., Farhadi, A.: You only look once: unified, real-time object detection. In: Proceedings of the IEEE Conference on Computer Vision and Pattern Recognition, pp. 779–788 (2016)
64. Redmon, J., Farhadi, A.: Yolo9000: better, faster, stronger. In: The IEEE Conference on Computer Vision and Pattern Recognition (CVPR), July 2017

65. Ren, S., He, K., Girshick, R., Sun, J.: Faster R-CNN: towards real-time object detection with region proposal networks. In: Proceedings of Advances in Neural Information Processing Systems, pp. 91–99, December 2015

66. Rockett, H.R., Berkey, C.S., Colditz, G.A.: Evaluation of dietary assessment instruments in adolescents. Curr. Opin. Clin. Nutr. Metab. Care **6**(5), 557–562 (2003)

67. Rollo, M., Ash, S., Lyons-Wall, P., Russell, A.: Evaluation of a mobile phone image-based dietary assessment method in adults with type 2 diabetes. Nutrients **7**(6), 4897–4910 (2015)

68. Rother, C., Kolmogorov, V., Blake, A.: GrabCut: interactive foreground extraction using iterated graph cuts. ACM Trans. Graph. **23**(3), 309–314 (2004)

69. Russakovsky, O., et al.: ImageNet large scale visual recognition challenge. Int. J. Comput. Vis. **115**(3), 211–252 (2015)

70. Salvador, A., Hynes, N., Aytar, Y., Marin, J., Ofli, F., Weber, I., Torralba, A.: Learning cross-modal embeddings for cooking recipes and food images. In: Proceedings of the IEEE Conference on Computer Vision and Pattern Recognition, pp. 3020–3028 (2017)

71. Shao, Z., Mao, R., Zhu, F.: Semi-automatic crowdsourcing tool for online food image collection and annotation. In: 2019 IEEE International Conference on Big Data, pp. 5186–5189, December 2019

72. Shimoda, W., Yanai, K.: CNN-based food image segmentation without pixel-wise annotation. In: Murino, V., Puppo, E., Sona, D., Cristani, M., Sansone, C. (eds.) ICIAP 2015. LNCS, vol. 9281, pp. 449–457. Springer, Cham (2015). https://doi.org/10.1007/978-3-319-23222-5_55

73. Simonyan, K., Zisserman, A.: Very deep convolutional networks for large-scale image recognition. arXiv preprint arXiv:1409.1556 (2014)

74. Singla, A., Yuan, L., Ebrahimi, T.: Food/non-food image classification and food categorization using pre-trained GoogLeNet model. In: Proceedings of the 2nd International Workshop on Multimedia Assisted Dietary Management, pp. 3–11 (2016). https://doi.org/10.1145/2986035.2986039

75. Sun, M., et al.: ebutton: a wearable computer for health monitoring and personal assistance. In: Proceedings of the 51st Annual Design Automation Conference, pp. 1–6 (2014)

76. Swain, M.J., Ballard, D.H.: Color indexing. Int. J. Comput. Vis. **7**, 11–32 (1991)

77. Szegedy, C., Ioffe, S., Vanhoucke, V., Alemi, A.A.: Inception-v4, inception-ResNet and the impact of residual connections on learning. In: Thirty-First AAAI Conference on Artificial Intelligence (2017)

78. Szegedy, C., et al.: Going deeper with convolutions. In: Proceedings of the IEEE Conference on Computer Vision and Pattern Recognition, pp. 1–9 (2015)

79. Tanno, R., Okamoto, K., Yanai, K.: DeepFoodCam: a DCNN-based real-time mobile food recognition system. In: Proceedings of the 2nd International Workshop on Multimedia Assisted Dietary Management, pp. 89–89 (2016). https://doi.org/10.1145/2986035.2986044

80. Uijlings, J.R., van de Sande, K.E., Gevers, T., Smeulders, A.W.: Selective search for object recognition. Int. J. Comput. Vis. **104**(2), 154–171 (2013)

81. Vijaymeena, M., Kavitha, K.: A survey on similarity measures in text mining. Mach. Learn. Appl. Int. J. **3**(2), 19–28 (2016)

82. Wang, X., Kumar, D., Thome, N., Cord, M., Precioso, F.: Recipe recognition with large multimodal food dataset. In: 2015 IEEE International Conference on Multimedia & Expo Workshops (ICMEW), pp. 1–6 (2015)

83. Wang, Y., He, Y., Boushey, C.J., Zhu, F., Delp, E.J.: Context based image analysis with application in dietary assessment and evaluation. Multimed. Tools Appl. **77**(15), 19769–19794 (2018)
84. Wang, Y., Zhu, F., Boushey, C.J., Delp, E.J.: Weakly supervised food image segmentation using class activation maps. In: 2017 IEEE International Conference on Image Processing (ICIP), pp. 1277–1281, September 2017. https://doi.org/10.1109/ICIP.2017.8296487
85. Wu, H., Merler, M., Uceda-Sosa, R., Smith, J.R.: Learning to make better mistakes: semantics-aware visual food recognition. In: Proceedings of the 24th ACM International Conference on Multimedia, pp. 172–176 (2016)
86. Xin Wang, Kumar, D., Thome, N., Cord, M., Precioso, F.: Recipe recognition with large multimodal food dataset. In: 2015 IEEE International Conference on Multimedia Expo Workshops (ICMEW), pp. 1–6, June 2015. https://doi.org/10.1109/ICMEW.2015.7169757
87. Yanai, K., Kawano, Y.: Food image recognition using deep convolutional network with pre-training and fine-tuning. In: Proceedings of the IEEE International Conference on Multimedia & Expo Workshops, pp. 1–6, July 2015
88. Yang, S., Chen, M., Pomerleau, D., Sukhankar, R.: Food recognition using statistics of pair-wise local features. In: Proceedings of the International Conference on Computer Vision and Pattern Recognition, pp. 2249–2256, June 2010
89. Zagoruyko, S., Komodakis, N.: Wide residual networks. arXiv preprint arXiv:1605.07146 (2016)
90. Zhou, B., Khosla, A., A., L., Oliva, A., Torralba, A.: Learning deep features for discriminative localization. In: Proceedings of the IEEE International Conference on Computer Vision and Pattern Recognition, June 2016
91. Zhu, F., Bosch, M., Khanna, N., Boushey, C., Delp, E.: Multiple hypotheses image segmentation and classification with application to dietary assessment. IEEE J. Biomed. Health Inf. **19**(1), 377–388 (2015)
92. Zhu, F., et al.: The use of mobile devices in aiding dietary assessment and evaluation. IEEE J. Sel. Top. Signal Process. **4**(4), 756–766 (2010)

Analysis of Chewing Signals Based on Chewing Detection Using Proximity Sensor for Diet Monitoring

Nur Asmiza Selamat[1,2]($\boxtimes$) and Sawal Hamid Md. Ali[1]

[1] Department of Electric, Electronics and System Engineering, Faculty of Engineering and Built Environment, Universiti Kebangsaan Malaysia (UKM), 43600 Bangi, Malaysia
`sawal@ukm.edu.my`
[2] Faculty of Electrical Engineering, Universiti Teknikal Malaysia Melaka (UTeM), Hang Tuah Jaya, Durian Tunggal, 76100 Melaka, Malaysia
`nurasmiza@utem.edu.my`

Abstract. This paper presents chewing data analysis based on the new approach of chewing detection for diet monitoring applications. The proposed approach is based on chewing detection using a proximity sensor in capturing the temporalis muscle movement during chewing. The aim is to support the development of non-contact-based chewing detection. A wearable device of eyeglass is used with the sensor mounted at the right side of the eyeglass temple using a 3D printed housing. The main activity involved in this study is resting and eating, three test food that represents different food hardness (carrot, banana, and apple) with a portion of one spoonful. Several upper cut-off frequencies (f_{c2}) of bandpass filters were used during the analyses. The signals were evaluated using accuracy and F1-score for classification and the absolute mean of error for chewing count estimation. In the classification stage, using the setting of a 10-fold cross-validation method and a 3 s segmented window, f_{c2} of 6 Hz gives the highest accuracy with 97.6%, while, 2.5 Hz gives the lowest accuracy of 92.6%. However, in the chewing count estimation stage, which is based on a 240 s segmented window, 2.4 Hz able to give a smaller percentage absolute error of 2.69%, compare to 6 Hz with 12.11%. It can be concluded that the chewing frequency was under 2.5 Hz, but, the self-reporting labeling approach used in this study reduced the accuracy of the system as f_{c2} equal to 2.5 Hz is used. Further analysis of chewing count shows that might in relating the total chewing count with different food hardness.

Keywords: Proximity sensor · Chewing detection · Temporalis muscle · Chewing classification · Chewing count · Chewing rate

1 Introduction

Food intake monitoring is used to help a person in keeping track of the details of the consumed food, especially for those with overweight problems and health issues. The conventional way of food intake monitoring requires an approach of self-reporting which

© Springer Nature Switzerland AG 2021
A. Del Bimbo et al. (Eds.): ICPR 2020 Workshops, LNCS 12665, pp. 599–616, 2021.
https://doi.org/10.1007/978-3-030-68821-9_48

the implementation is less suitable in this modern era [1]. Along with the advancement of technology, development of automatic, objective, accurate, robust, and reliable food intake detection system have been initiated. While more research had been done to complete the system from as simple as food detection to as complicated as volume estimation [2], specifically for dietary monitoring applications.

The use of a single sensing approach might not be enough for the development of comprehensive automatic food intake monitoring; it is however could provide an important input to perfecting the system. Several methods can be used to capture the food intake detection such as hand-to-mouth (HtM) movement, bite, chew, and then swallow. However, chewing shows good potential as it occurs repeatedly in sequence. The commonly used sensors for food intake monitoring specifically based on chewing activity are acoustic [3], piezoelectric [4], electromyography (EMG) [5], and accelerometers [6]. The sensors were placed to the preferred location by either using a wearable device or direct attachment.

During food intake, chewing will provide a sequential movement that involves muscle movement of the masseter, the temporalis, the medial pterygoid, and the lateral pterygoid muscles. The temporalis movement had captured the researcher's attention as it has the capability in providing significant chewing signals. Sensors that are used to capture chewing activity based on the temporalis movement are piezoelectric, EMG, and accelerometer. The piezoelectric sensors have been used by [4] and [7] for chewing detection based on the temporalis muscle movement, where the sensors are attached to the temporalis muscle by using medical tape and the wearable device, respectively. EMG sensors used to capture the temporalis muscle movement by using the wearable device of eyeglass which used dry EMG electrode [8] and stainless steel dry electrode [5]. The implementation of an accelerometer in capturing the temporalis movement has been done by [9] and [6], by attaching the sensor to the headband and eyeglass. However, some of the disadvantages of using EMG and the piezoelectric sensor are the requirement of direct attachment of the sensor which might be not suitable for all, such as people with allergies. While for accelerometer, eventhough the user does not require a direct attachment to the skin, the signals are impacted by the physical activities. The use of non-contact sensor-based has been proposed by researchers such as photoplethysmography (PPG) sensor [10], a photo sensor [11], a proximity sensor [12, 13], and a doppler sonar sensor [14]. Most of the listed research which proposed a non-contact sensor based on capturing the chewing activity used the jaw movement body sensing [12, 13, 14]. The distance-based sensors are placed around the neck area by using a necklace-based wearable device at which its performance might affect by physical activity. In a condition of controlled environment or laboratory, the previously discussed sensor of the temporalis movement-based detection gives a F1-score of 80% [8], 91.5% [6], 94.2% [5], and 99.85% [4], while for the non-contact-based detection gives F1-score of 91.9% [12] and accuracy of 91.4% [14].

This study used the new approach of non-contact-based detection to capture the movement of temporalis muscle during food consumption. The proposed method is based on a proximity sensor that will be attached to the temple of eyeglass by using 3D printed housing. The objective is to provide a new option in detecting chewing activities for food intake monitoring or diet monitoring applications. The chewing count estimation and the chewing rate data were also extracted. The analyses were then extended, to study the possibility of relating or differentiating the chewing count and chewing rate of different food hardness. The labeling of the chewing, chewing episode and chewing count are based on self-reporting where the subject requires to push the pushbutton.

2 Hardware Design

In this study, the chewing activity was captured based on the movement of the temporalis muscle during food consumption. A wearable sensor is designed using a click board of proximity 9 clicks from Mikro-Elektronika (MikroE) that equip with a VCNL4040 proximity sensor (by Vishay semiconductor). The sensor is a combination of proximity and an ambient light sensor that capable of measuring the ambient light, white light, and proximity within the range of 20 cm. For this study, the proximity function is used, where the sensor was mounted at the right temple of a wearable device of eyeglass using a 3D printed housing. Generally, the sensor works by emitting continuous infrared light and the amount of reflected light is used to measure the distance. The sensor could detect an object within the range of 20 cm, however, the measured distance is based on the qualitative measurement or change of the object distance from the last reading not based on quantitative distance readings. Hence, for this study, the temporalis muscle acts as the targeted object to be measured. During chewing, the temporalis muscle movement causes the change in distance between the sensor and the temporalis muscle, the collective distance changes represent the chewing pattern which then captures by the sensor.

The data from the sensor transferred to a microprocessor (Arduino Uno board) using a sampling rate of 50 Hz. Besides the chewing sensor and microcontroller, two pushbuttons were included in the chewing detection system. Each of the pushbuttons is used for validation purposes to provide separated labeling or ground truth for eating activity and chewing activity respectively. Figure 1 shows the implementation of a wearable sensor for capturing the temporalis muscle movement.

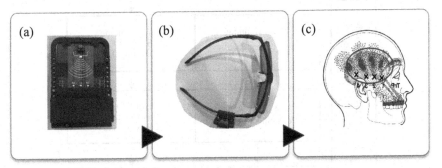

Fig. 1. Chewing detection system: (a) the proximity sensor into the 3D printed housing, (b) Attachment of wearable sensor to the eyeglass, (c) Temporalis muscle position.

3 Methodology

3.1 Data Collection

The summary of the methodology used in this study is shown in Fig. 2. A total of ten set data were taken from a single subject. The data were collected in a controlled environment where only eating and resting activity were considered. For eating activity, the subject requires to eat three test foods with different hardness. The foods are banana, apple, and carrot which represent food hardness of soft, medium, and hard respectively as used by [7]. The portion for each intake was based on 1 spoonful which also represents by 9 g. The relation between 1 spoonful and 9 g of the test food was achieved by cutting the test food into small pieces, placed it in a measuring spoon, and weighted using a food scale. All test food gives a weight of 9 g. The test food served to the subject in the form of cylindrical shape with the same thickness (±15 mm), diameter (±27 mm), and weight (9 g). Figure 3 shows the food test preparation.

The subject performed a total of ten sets of the same activity sequence of resting for 15 s, eating carrot for about 90 s, eating a banana in 30 s, eating an apple in 30 s with 30 s resting in between food intake, and 15 s after the last foods are taken. Each set of

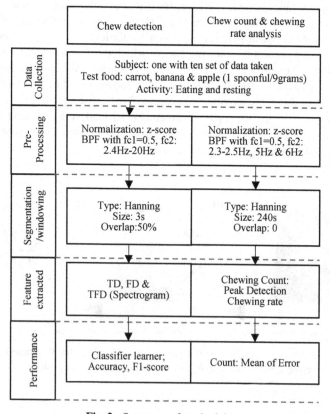

Fig. 2. Summary of methodology

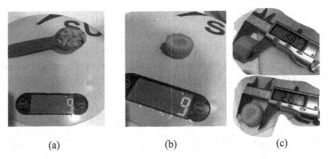

(a)   (b)   (c)

Fig. 3. Test food portion preparation and measurement: (a) one spoonful of test food being weighted, a cylindrical test food being (b) weight, and (c) measure.

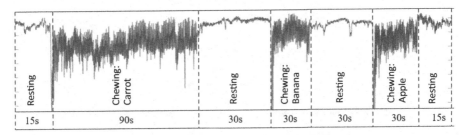

Fig. 4. The sequence of activity for each of the data

data takes 240 s and a total of the 2400 s are required to complete data collection for ten sets of data. The sequence for a set of activities is shown in Fig. 4. While performing the activities, the subject requires to label the activities of chewing and chewing episodes using pushbuttons.

3.2 Chewing Detection

Data Pre-processing

In this stage, the dataset of the raw sensor signal will be prepared to be used in the classification stage. A suitable pre-processing method will help to amplify the desired signal by removing the unwanted signal or noise. In determining the method, the raw data will be first observed by either using time, frequency, or time-frequency representation or combinations. Then, depending on the application, the pre-processing methods such as normalization, detrend, smoothing, down-sample, and filtering could be used to obtain the desired signal.

Based on the observation of the raw data shown in Fig. 5 (a) and the spectrogram as shown in Fig. 6, the normalization and bandpass filter will be used in pre-processing the signals. The normalization is required to eliminate the amplitude variation due to a variety of factors such as the position of the sensor and the distance between the sensor and the temporalis muscle. Several methods can be used as the normalization such as z-score normalization, minimum to maximum normalization, and signals to median normalization. Additionally, the researchers in [15] believe that the normalization method could improve the classification accuracy. The z-score normalization that represents in (1) is used. Next, the bandpass filter is used to preserve the desired signal. The lower cut-off frequency, f_{c1} used to remove the DC component and the high cut-off frequency, f_{c2} used to keep the signal in the range of chewing frequency. Previous studies had defines the frequency range of 0.94 Hz to 2.17 Hz [16], 1.25 Hz to 2.5 Hz [17], and 0.5 Hz to 2.5 Hz

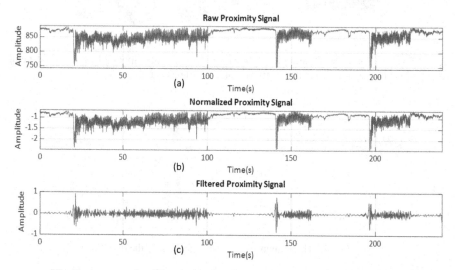

Fig. 5. An example of Proximity signal: (a) Raw (b) Normalized (c) Filtered

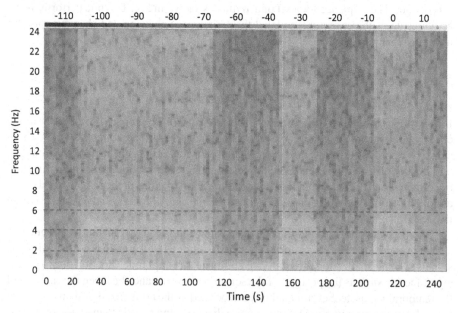

Fig. 6. Time-Frequency representation (Spectrogram) of the raw signal

[9]. Then, the Time-Frequency distribution is observed by using the spectrogram as in Fig. 6. Based on the signal distributions, it shows that the high-power spectral density in the range of 3 Hz and 5 Hz. Hence, this study will analyze the chewing classification using f_{c1} of 0.5 Hz and ranges of f_{c2} of 2.5 Hz to 10 Hz. Additionally, the effect of setting up the f_{c2} to 15 Hz and 20 Hz was also observed.

$$z = \frac{x - \bar{x}}{S} \tag{1}$$

Where, x = sample data, $\bar{x}$ = mean of the sample, and S = standard deviation of the sample.

Segmentation and Feature Extraction

In extracting the features of the signal, the pre-processed signal will be segmented into an appropriate window type, size or length, and overlap length. The selection of the segmentation parameter are depending on the signal application where it is used to capture the energy envelope of the signal. For chewing detection, there is no standard size [18], however, the most commonly used time resolution were 3 s [3, 4, 19], 4 s [20], 5 s [12, 21–23], 15 s [24] and 30 s [17].

This study will extract features from the Time-domain (TD), Frequency-domain (FD), and Time-Frequency domain (TFD). In TD and TF, the features will be directly extracted with the segmentation setting of 3 s and 50% overlap. For TFD, the segmented TD will be multiplying with the Hanning window and converted to TFD by using Fast Fourier Transform (FFT). Since the FFT is based on the segmentation of the window, the process is known as a short-time Fourier transform (STFT). The STFT is usually represented by using a spectrogram, where the information of the magnitude values of STFT and power spectral density (PSD) for 0 to half of the sampling frequency can be obtained. The features extracted for chewing classification is based on the significant features that have been applied by [12–14, 18, 19], was computed in this study. A total

Table 1. Extracted features

Features category	Features (features no. if more than 1)	No. of features
Time-domain	Min., max., max-min, RMS, median, variance, standard deviation, skewness, kurtosis, interquartile range	10
Frequency-domain	Mean frequency, power bandwidth, median frequency	3
Time-frequency domain	Amplitude: ranges of frequency between 1 Hz to 3 Hz (6), kurtosis & skewness, concentration measure PSD: Min. max., mean, median, standard deviation, kurtosis, & skewness Energy: sum, min, max, mean, energy in four bands of frequency (4)	27

of 40 features has been extracted, which includes 10 features from TD, 3 features from FD, and 27 features from TFD. The list of features extracted is shown in Table 2.

Classification and Evaluation

The final stage is to classify the candidate segmented signal to either chewing or non-chewing. The classification model is first required to be trained and validated. In training and validation, the signal references are required for each segmented signal. Where in this study the self-reporting signal labeling by using pushbuttons is used to indicates the chewing episodes (food intake) activity and chewing activity. For the chewing episodes, the subject is required to push the chewing episodes pushbuttons to mark the starting and ending point of each food consumption. While, for the chewing label, the subject is required to push the chew label pushbutton during each chew. For the computation of the signal references for the training and validation, only chewing label signals will be used. The chewing label will be first segmented according to the chewing signal segmentation setting. Then, taking the average of the segmented chew label, the signal references will be label as chew ($C = +1$) if the average is more than 0, otherwise, it will label as non-chew ($C = -1$). An example of the chewing label and chewing count as ground truth is given in Fig. 7.

All chewing features and labels will be feed to the Classifier learner application in MATLAB 2020 (from Mathworks, Inc) for classification and evaluation. The classifier was trained using the k-fold cross-validation (CV) method. The k-fold cross-validation method divides the training and testing data according to the parameter "k". This study used a cumulative duration-based evaluation, where an individual set of data (240 s) with a total of ten sets, will combine to form datasets (2400 s). The dataset will partition according to the individual dataset duration (240 s) which leads to the "k" parameter in k-fold CV is set to 10. The dataset will be validated it will iteratively "k" times and the final evaluation is the average of evaluated performance metrics. The classifier performance is based on the accuracy and F1-score value where the calculation is based on (2), (3), (4), and (5), where, TP, TN, FP, and FN denote true positives, true negatives, false positives, and false negatives, respectively.

$$Precision = \frac{TP}{TP + FP} \tag{2}$$

$$Recall = \frac{TP}{TP + FN} \tag{3}$$

$$F_1\ score = \frac{2 * Precision * Recall}{Precision + Recall} \tag{4}$$

$$Accuracy = \frac{TP + TN}{TP + TN + FP + FN} \tag{5}$$

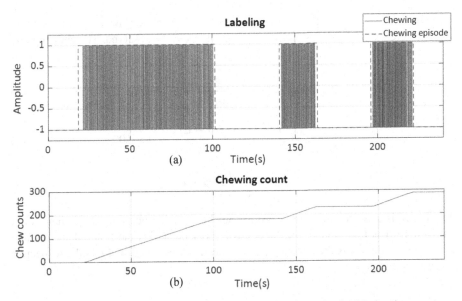

Fig. 7. Ground truth: (a) Labeling of chewing and chewing episode, (b) chewing count

3.3 Chewing Analysis

Chewing Count

In chewing count analysis, the pre-processes signal with upper cut-off frequency, f_{c2} of 2.5 Hz, 5 Hz, and 6 Hz is used for estimating the chew count. The selection of the f_{c2} was based on the results of the classification stage. The 5 Hz and 6 Hz selected as it gives the highest classifier performance compared to other frequencies. Meanwhile, eventhough 2.5 Hz gives the lowest accuracy, it was chosen as researchers agreed that the chewing frequency was in the under the range of 2.5 Hz. To further analyze the effect of f_{c2} on the estimation of chew count analyses, f_{c2} of 2.3 Hz and 2.4 Hz were also analyzed. The window was segmented to 240 s and the number of peaks was computed for each segment. For f_{c2} of 2.3 Hz, 2.4 Hz, and 2.5 Hz, only the number of peaks that were in the range of chewing label episodes (refer to Fig. 7 (a)) and peaks value greater than 0 will be counted. For 5 Hz and 6 Hz, an additional restriction of minimum peak prominence of 0.33 and 0.35 was implemented, respectively. The value of minimum peak prominence is based on trial and error which contributes to the smallest total error.

This study used to test food with different hardness and chewing time. Hence, instead of estimating the chew count for the whole segmented window, estimation of the chewing counts was based on the chewing episodes. For this analysis, the counted number of peaks from the chewing signals were compared with the number of peaks counted from the chewing label as in Fig. 7 (b). The capability of the chewing detection approach in estimating the chewing counts were evaluated using the percentage of error based on each chewing episodes and total chewing for each set of data. The percentage of absolute error for the individual chewing episode and mean percentage of absolute error of chewing episodes was calculated using (6) and (7), respectively. Besides that, the effect of the different food hardness on the chewing rate was also observed. The chewing rate is calculated using (8).

$$|\% \ Error| = \left| \frac{C_{Act}(n) - C_{Est}(n)}{C_{Act}(n)} \right| \times 100 \tag{6}$$

$$|\% \ Error| = \frac{1}{M} \sum_{n=1}^{M} \left| \frac{C_{Act}(n) - C_{Est}(n)}{C_{Act}(n)} \right| \times 100 \tag{7}$$

$$C_R = \frac{C_{Act}(n)}{C_T(n)} \times 100 \tag{8}$$

Where C_{Act} is actual chew count based on the chew count label, C_{Est} is the chew count estimation, M is the numbers of the chewing episode, C_T is the time taken for each chewing episode, C_R is the chewing rate or chewing frequency, and n is the respective chewing episodes.

4   Results

4.1   Chewing Detection

The chewing activity approach used in this study was first evaluated based on its capability of classifying the chewing activity. The upper cut-off frequency, f_{c2} was varied in the range of 2.5 Hz to 20 Hz. The accuracy and F1-score were computed for each f_{c2} of 2.5 Hz, 3 Hz, 3.5 Hz, 4 Hz, 5 Hz, 5.5 Hz, 6 Hz, 6.5 Hz, 7 Hz, 8 Hz, 9 Hz, 10 Hz, 15 Hz, and 20 Hz, where the result is shown in Table 3 along with the classifier. The performances of the classifier were then plotted and compared in the form of a graph as is Fig. 8. Based on the results, accuracy and F1-score show significantly the same trend. Then, by comparing the performance, 2.5 Hz gives the lowest accuracy of 92.6% using Medium Gaussian Support Vector Machine (SVM), while 6 Hz gives the highest accuracy value of 97.4% using Quadratic SVM classifier. The accuracies of the classifier decrease with a constant rate and maintain in the range of ±97% as the f_{c2} increase.

Table 2. Classifier and its performance for variation of the upper cutoff frequency

Fc1 (Hz)	Fc2 (Hz)	Classifier	Accuracy (%)	F1-score (%)
0.5	2.5	SVM: Medium gaussian	92.6	92.48
0.5	3	Ensemble: Boosted tree	93.9	93.79
0.5	3.5	SVM: Medium gaussian	94.8	94.71
0.5	4	SVM: Quadratic	95.3	95.25
0.5	4.5	SVM: Quadratic	96.7	96.66

(*continued*)

Table 2. (*continued*)

Fc1 (Hz)	Fc2 (Hz)	Classifier	Accuracy (%)	F1-score (%)
0.5	5	SVM: Quadratic	97.4	97.35
0.5	5.5	SVM: Medium gaussian	97.1	97.04
0.5	**6**	**Ensemble: Boosted tree**	**97.6**	**97.60**
0.5	6.5	SVM: Quadratic	97.4	97.36
0.5	7	SVM: Quadratic	97.2	97.21
0.5	8	SVM: Quadratic	96.9	96.97
0.5	9	SVM: Quadratic	97.1	97.16
0.5	10	Ensemble: Boosted tree	97.0	97.01
0.5	15	SVM: Quadratic	96.7	96.70
0.5	20	Ensemble: Boosted tree	96.8	96.75

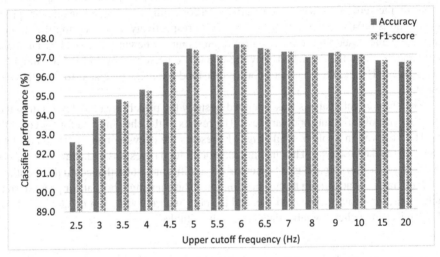

Fig. 8. Classifier performance for a different upper cutoff frequency of bandpass filter

4.2 Chew Count Estimation

The estimation of the chew count analysis is solely based on the number of peaks of the sensor signal. Signals with different upper cut-off frequencies were considered and only peaks that were in the range of chewing episode labels will be considered. In each chewing episode, the number of peaks was counted and compared with the chew count algorithm, which's developed based on the automatic chew label. Each segmented window consists of three chewing episodes based on three different test foods.

The results of the average chew count estimation and its absolute error, when compared to the actual chew count (based on chew label), is shown in Table 3. The plot of absolute error for each test foods is shown in Fig. 9. Based on the results mean absolute error of the total chew count estimation for f_{c2} of 2.3 Hz to 2.5 Hz gives the error less than 4.0% when compared to f_{c2} equal to 5 Hz and 6 Hz which gives the error of 11.77% and 12.11%, respectively. Among the three frequencies, 2.3 Hz gives the smallest error when chewing the banana with 5%, 2.4 Hz gives an error of 6.41% when chewing the apple, and 2.5 Hz the smallest error of 2.9% when chewing the carrot. However, based on the total error, 2.4 Hz gives the smallest error of 2.69%, compared to 2.3 Hz and 2.5 Hz that give the total error of 3.90% and 3.21%, respectively.

Since, f_{c2} equal to 2.4 Hz provides the smallest error in chewing count estimation, the details of the chewing count estimation, means, standard deviation, percentage of error, and absolute error for each chewing episode of a dataset is shown in Table 4. The collected dataset consisted of 2635 chewing count from 30 chewing episodes, were 1713 from chewing a carrot, 429 from chewing a banana, and 520 from chewing an apple. The mean of the chewing count for 10 sets of data was given by 171.3, 42.20, and 52 with a standard deviation of 19.36, 10.10, and 12.95 for test food of carrot, banana, and apple, respectively. While the distribution of the mean absolute error is shown in Fig. 10. Next, the evaluation of the chewing counts was based on the sum of the chewing count of all 10 sets of data, and the results are shown in Table 5. The percentage of error based on the sum of chewing count estimation for eating a carrot, a banana, an apple, and a total is 0.94%, 6.72%, 2.99%, and 0.76%, respectively. By observing the sum of chewing count based on food test, carrot requires more chewing, followed by an apple and banana where the estimated chewing count is represented by 1713, 520, and 429, respectively. Hence, there is a possibility that food hardness is related to the chewing count.

The chew count analysis was extended to study the possibility of differentiating the chewing rate of different food hardness. The results of the chewing rate for f_{c2} equal to 2.4 Hz are given in Table 5, while Fig. 11 presents the chewing rate of 10 sets of data according to the food type. The chewing rate for all food types was in the range of 1.7 Hz to 2.3 Hz. By observing the graph, there is no significant pattern that could differentiate the food hardness according to the chewing rate. The chewing label data or ground truth data of chewing count, chewing time, and the chewing rate was given in Table 6, while, the details of the chewing label data are given in Table 7.

Table 3. Mean absolute error of chewing count estimation

F_{c2}	Chewing episodes											
	Carrot			Banana			Apple			Total		
	Mean			Mean			Mean			Mean		
	C_{Est}	%error	|%error|	C_{Est}	%error	|%error|	C_{Est}	%error	|%error|	C_{Est}	%error	|%error|
2.3	168.5	0.14	3.91	41.00	−2.16	**5.00**	49.20	7.70	11.38	258.70	1.46	3.90
2.4	171.30	−1.52	3.16	42.2	−4.54	6.02	52	2.79	**6.41**	265.50	−1.04	**2.69**
2.5	172.20	−2.03	**2.90**	42.90	−6.66	7.25	54.30	−1.11	6.90	269.40	−2.41	3.21
5	177.10	−5.11	14.13	37.50	7.36	9.61	48.70	9.04	18.17	263.30	−0.23	11.77
6	175	−3.92	13.62	37.5	7.56	9.42	51.50	3.56	14.99	264	−0.43	12.11

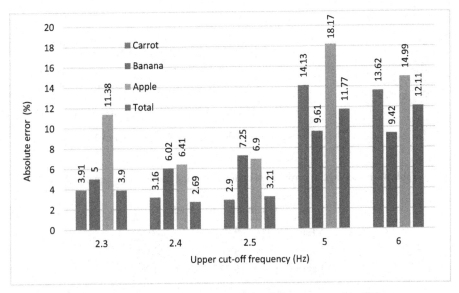

Fig. 9. The absolute error of chewing count for different upper cut-off frequency

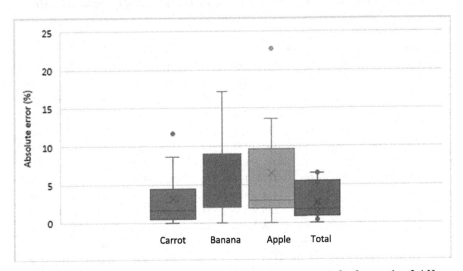

Fig. 10. Distribution of mean absolute error of the chewing count for f_{c2} equal to 2.4 Hz

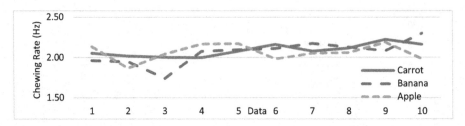

Fig. 11. The chewing rate based on food type for f_{c2} equal to 2.4 Hz

Table 4. Percentage of error based on total chewing count for f_{c2} equal to 2.4 Hz

	Carrot	Banana	Apple	Total
C_{Est}	1713	429	520	2655
C_{Act}	1697	402	536	2635
|%error|	0.94	6.72	2.99	0.76

Table 5. The details of the chew count estimation in a dataset for f_{c2} equal to 2.4 Hz

Data	Chewing episodes											
	Carrot			Banana			Apple			Total		
	C_{Est}	%error	|%error|	C_{Est}	%error	|%error|	C_{Est}	%error	|%error|	C_{Est}	%error	|%error|
1	153	−11.68	11.68	37	0.00	0.00	72	0.00	0.00	262	−6.50	6.50
2	126	−8.62	8.62	35	−2.94	2.94	35	−2.94	2.94	196	−6.52	6.52
3	167	−3.09	3.09	25	7.41	7.41	49	−2.08	2.08	241	−1.69	1.69
4	173	2.81	2.81	41	−17.14	17.14	73	−2.82	2.82	287	−1.06	1.06
5	178	1.66	1.66	36	−5.88	5.88	44	22.81	22.81	258	5.15	5.15
6	196	1.01	1.01	52	0.00	0.00	35	7.89	7.89	283	1.74	1.74
7	178	1.66	1.66	58	−11.54	11.54	52	−8.33	8.33	288	−2.49	2.49
8	180	0.55	0.55	47	−4.44	4.44	56	1.75	1.75	283	0.00	0.00
9	182	0.55	0.55	38	−2.70	2.70	53	−1.92	1.92	273	−0.37	0.37
10	180	0.00	0.00	53	−8.16	8.16	51	13.56	13.56	284	1.39	1.39
Sum	1713			429			520			2655		
Mean	171.30	−1.52	3.16	42.20	−4.54	6.02	52.00	2.79	6.41	265.50	−1.04	2.69
STD	19.36	4.86	3.88	10.10	6.77	5.33	12.95	9.34	7.09	28.83	3.59	2.45

Table 6. The chewing rate for f_{c2} equal to 2.4 Hz

Data	Chewing rate (Signal)					
	Carrot		Banana		Apple	
	C_T (s)	C_R (Hz)	C_T (s)	C_R (Hz)	C_T (s)	C_R (Hz)
1	74.52	2.05	18.86	1.96	33.72	2.14
2	62.42	2.02	17.98	1.95	18.74	1.87
3	83.44	2.00	14.40	1.74	24.00	2.04
4	86.54	2.00	19.74	2.08	33.70	2.17
5	85.62	2.08	17.18	2.10	20.26	2.17
6	90.62	2.16	24.64	2.11	17.68	1.98
7	85.68	2.08	26.68	2.17	25.36	2.05
8	85.00	2.12	22.08	2.13	27.20	2.06
9	81.80	2.23	18.26	2.08	24.20	2.19
10	83.28	2.16	23.04	2.30	25.76	1.98
Mean	**81.89**	**2.09**	**20.28**	**2.06**	**25.06**	**2.06**
SD	**7.98**	**0.08**	**3.75**	**0.15**	**5.52**	**0.10**

Table 7. The chewing label data

Data	Chewing rate (ground truth)								
	Carrot			Banana			Apple		
	C_{Act}	C_T (s)	C_R (Hz)	C_{Act}	C_T (s)	C_R (Hz)	C_{Act}	C_T (s)	C_R (Hz)
1	137	63.66	2.15	37	16.14	2.29	72	30.90	2.33
2	116	54.42	2.13	34	14.98	2.27	34	15.56	2.19
3	162	72.18	2.24	27	11.82	2.28	48	21.34	2.25
4	178	82.94	2.15	35	16.86	2.08	71	30.86	2.30
5	181	83.02	2.18	34	15.14	2.25	57	18.14	3.14
6	198	88.92	2.23	52	22.56	2.30	38	15.36	2.47
7	181	83.26	2.17	52	23.76	2.19	48	21.10	2.27
8	181	82.38	2.20	45	19.82	2.27	57	25.02	2.28
9	183	79.84	2.29	37	15.36	2.41	52	21.14	2.46
10	180	79.38	2.27	49	20.22	2.42	59	23.68	2.49
Sum	**1697**			**402**		**536**	**2635**		
Mean	**169.70**	**77.00**	**2.20**	**40.20**	**17.67**	**2.28**	**53.60**	**22.31**	**2.42**
SD	**24.83**	**10.58**	**0.05**	**8.68**	**3.78**	**0.10**	**12.41**	**5.49**	**0.27**

5 Discussions

The works presented a new approach to chewing detection and classification based on the proximity sensor. The proposed approach aims to support the development of non-contact-based chewing detection that could guarantee the users' comfort while maintaining its reliability. The proximity sensor of VCNL4040 in a form click board manufactured by Mikro-Elektronika (MikroE) was used. The sensor was placed in 3D printed housing, which then attaches to the temple of eyeglass near the temporalis muscle to capture the temporalis muscle movement. The labeling or ground truth of chewing, chewing episodes, and chewing count are based on the self-reporting using pushbuttons.

In chewing classification, several upper cutoff-frequency of a bandpass filter with the segmented window of 3 s were used. Based on the results the use of f_{c2} equal to 6 Hz gives the highest accuracy of 97.4% using Quadratic SVM classifier compared to f_{c2} equal to 2.5 Hz with an accuracy of 92.6% using Medium Gaussian Support Vector Machine (SVM). Evethough, the previous study agreed that the chewing frequency is in the range of under 2.5 Hz, however, for this study the accuracy of the 2.5 Hz does not gives comparable accuracy with 6 Hz as the f_{c2}. As this study only considered chewing food and resting, the signal noise due to the motion artifacts could be neglected.

The chewing signals were then further analyzed in terms of chewing count and chewing rate. The windows were segmented based on a set of data that is equal to 240 s. For chewing count estimation only features of peak count were extracted and the chewing count estimation is based on the chewing episodes and total chewing in segmented windows. Similarly, the significance of the f_{c2} value was selected based on the classification accuracy. By referring to the results of the chew count estimation, f_{c2} of 2.4 Hz gives the smallest total absolute error of 2.69% compared to other f_{c2}. The total absolute error obtained is comparable or even smaller compared to the previous study 8.09 ± 7.16% [25], 10.4% ± 7.0% [21], 9.66% [26], 3.83% [27], and 12.2% [9] which using method of the peak detection algorithm, histogram-peak detection algorithm, multiple regression model, multivariate regression model, and maximum frequency component (MFC), respectively.

Eventhough, f_{c2} of 6 Hz gives the highest accuracy during the classification stage, yet it does not give a good percentage of error in chewing count estimation. Additionally, the use of 6 Hz required a restriction during peak extraction, when compared to 2.4 Hz which does not the use of restriction during its peak extractions. By focusing on the use of f_{c2} of 2.4 Hz and 6 Hz and referring to the classification stage results and chewing count estimation results, an inference can be made that the chewing frequency is in the range of 2.5 Hz. However, the 2.5 Hz does not give good accuracy in the classification stage as the labeling of the chewing signal is based on the self-reporting (using pushbutton). There chewing signal and the chewing label does not tally, due to delay in pushing the pushbutton or during data collection (obtaining the label data) as the self-reporting label approach was used. The unsynchronized data and label would affect when shorter window segmentation was used as the chewing data wrongly label. This was proven as the chewing classification stage used a shorter window of 3 s compared to the chewing count estimation of 240 s.

Next, the analyses of finding the relation between the food hardness with the chewing count and chewing rate. Based on the work done, the total chewing count could be used to differentiate the food hardness. However, the chewing rate does not show an obvious pattern during chewing food with different hardness.

6   Conclusion

The analyses of the new approach of chewing detection were done. The proposed system was able to give high accuracy with 97.6% and F1-score of 97.6% of chewing detection using f_{c2} equal to 6 Hz in its bandpass filter. Eventhough, as f_{c2} is set to 2.5 Hz the accuracy reduced to 92.6%, however, the percentage of mean absolute error gives a good value of 3.21% compared to 6 Hz with 12.11%. The f_{c2} was then changed to f_{c2} of 2.4 Hz aiming to find the optimal f_{c2}, and the results do improve with the percentage of error of 2.69%. While the results of relating the chewing count with the different food hardness show a potential and could be further investigated. The results suggest that the proposed approach could be used in characterizing the chewing activity. However, further modification of labeling methods by either using manual or improving the current self-reporting labeling method is required. Besides that, more data will be collected with different subjects in proving the effectiveness of the systems.

Acknowledgment. This work was supported by Universiti Kebangsaan Malaysia and Ministry of Education Malaysia, under the Grant Code FRGS/1/2018/TK04/UKM/02/2 and Universiti Teknikal Malaysia Melaka (UTeM).

References

1. Subhi, M.A., Ali, S.M.: A deep convolutional neural network for food detection and recognition. In: 2018 IEEE-EMBS Conference on Biomedical Engineering and Sciences (IECBES), pp. 284–287 (2018)
2. Subhi, M.A., Ali, S.H., Mohammed, M.A.: Vision-based approaches for automatic food recognition and dietary assessment: a survey. IEEE Access **7**, 35370–35381 (2019)
3. Bi, S., et al.: Auracle: detecting eating episodes with an ear-mounted sensor. In: Proceedings of the ACM on Interactive, Mobile, Wearable, and Ubiquitous Technologies, vol. 2, no. 3, p. 27 (2018)
4. Farooq, M., Sazonov, E.: A novel wearable device for food intake and physical activity recognition. Sensors (Switz.) **16**(1067), 13 (2016)
5. Zhang, R., Amft, O.: Monitoring chewing and eating in free-living using smart eyeglasses. IEEE J. Biomed. Heal. Informatics **22**(1), 23–32 (2018)
6. Farooq, M., Sazonov, E.: Accelerometer-based detection of food intake in free-living individuals. IEEE Sens. J. **18**(9), 3752–3758 (2018)
7. Hossain, D., Imtiaz, M.H., Sazonov, E.: Comparison of wearable sensors for estimation of chewing strength. IEEE Sens. J. **1748**, 9 (2020)
8. Zhang, R., Bernhart, S., Amft, O.: Diet eyeglasses: recognising food chewing using EMG and smart eyeglasses. In: BSN 2016-13th Annual Body Sensor Networks Conference, pp. 7–12 (2016)
9. Wang, S., et al.: Eating detection and chews counting through sensing mastication muscle contraction. Smart Heal. **9–10**, 179–191 (2018)

10. Papapanagiotou, V., Diou, C., Zhou, L., Van Den Boer, J., Mars, J., Delopoulos, A.: A novel approach for chewing detection based on a wearable PPG sensor. In: Proceedings of the Annual International Conference of the IEEE Engineering in Medicine and Biology Society, EMBS, pp. 6485–6488 (2016)
11. Taniguchi, K., Chiaki, H., Kurosawa, M., Nishikawa, A.: A novel earphone type sensor for measuring mealtime: consideration of the method to distinguish between running and meals. Sensors (Switz.) 17(252), 14 (2017)
12. Chun, K.S., Bhattacharya, S., Thomaz, E.: Detecting eating episodes by tracking jawbone movements with a non-contact wearable sensor. In: Proceedings of the ACM on Interactive, Mobile, Wearable and Ubiquitous Technologies, vol. 2, no. 1, p. 21 (2018)
13. Zhang, S., et al.: NeckSense: a multi-sensor necklace for detecting eating activities in free-living conditions. In: Proceedings of the ACM on Interactive, Mobile, Wearable and Ubiquitous Technologies, vol. 1, no. 1 (2019)
14. Lee, K.: Food intake detection using ultrasonic doppler sonar. IEEE Sens. J. 17(18), 6056–6068 (2017)
15. Farooq, M., Sazonov, E.: Detection of chewing from piezoelectric film sensor signals using ensemble classifiers. In: Proceedings of the Annual International Conference of the IEEE Engineering in Medicine and Biology Society, EMBS, pp. 4929–4932 (2016)
16. Po, J.M.C., Kieser, J.A., Gallo, L.M., Tésenyi, A.J., Herbison, P., Farella, M.: Time-frequency analysis of chewing activity in the natural environment. J. Dent. Res. 90(10), 1206–1210 (2011)
17. Sazonov, E.S., Fontana, J.M.: A sensor system for automatic detection of food intake through non-invasive monitoring of chewing. IEEE Sens. J. 12(5), 1340–1348 (2012)
18. Selamat, N.A., Ali, S.H.M.: Automatic food intake monitoring based on chewing activity: a survey. IEEE Access 8, 48846–48869 (2020)
19. Chung, J., Chung, J., Oh, W., Yoo, Y., Lee, W.G., Bang, H.: A glasses-type wearable device for monitoring the patterns of food intake and facial activity. Sci. Rep. 7, 8 (2017)
20. Nyamukuru, M.T., Odame, K.M.: Tiny eats: eating detection on a microcontroller. In: 2020 IEEE Second Workshop on Machine Learning on Edge in Sensor Systems (SenSys-ML), p. 5 (2020)
21. Farooq, M., Sazonov, E.: Automatic measurement of chew count and chewing rate during food intake. Electronics 5(62), 14 (2016)
22. Farooq, M., Sazonov, E.: Real time monitoring and recognition of eating and physical activity with a wearable device connected to the eyeglass. In: Proceedings of the International Conference on Sensing Technology, ICST, p. 6 (2017)
23. Papapanagiotou, V., Diou, C., Delopoulos, A.: Chewing detection from an in-ear microphone using convolutional neural networks. In: Proceedings of the Annual International Conference of the IEEE Engineering in Medicine and Biology Society, EMBS, pp. 1258–1261 (2017)
24. Fontana, J.M., Sazonov, E.S.: A robust classification scheme for detection of food intake through non-invasive monitoring of chewing. In: Proceedings of the Annual International Conference of the IEEE Engineering in Medicine and Biology Society, EMBS, pp. 4891–4894, August 2012
25. Farooq, M., Sazonov, E.: Comparative testing of piezoelectric and printed strain sensors in characterization of chewing. In: Proceedings of the Annual International Conference of the IEEE Engineering in Medicine and Biology Society, EMBS, pp. 7538–7541 (2015)
26. Farooq, M., Sazonov, E.: Linear regression models for chew count estimation from piezoelectric sensor signals. In: 2016 Tenth International Conference on Sensing Technology Linear, p. 5 (2016)
27. Farooq, M., Sazonov, E.: Segmentation and characterization of chewing bouts by monitoring temporalis muscle using smart glasses with piezoelectric sensor. IEEE J. Biomed. Heal. Informatics 21(6), 1495–1503 (2017)

Food Recognition in the Presence of Label Noise

Ioannis Papathanail[1], Ya Lu[1], Arindam Ghosh[2], and Stavroula Mougiakakou[1(✉)]

[1] ARTORG Center for Biomedical Engineering Research, University of Bern, Bern, Switzerland
stavroula.mougiakakou@artorg.unibe.ch
[2] Oviva S.A., Zurich, Switzerland

Abstract. The objective of multi-label image classification is to recognise several objects that appear within a single image. In the current paper, we consider the task of multi-label food recognition, where the images contain foods for which the labels in the training set are noisy, as they are annotated by inexperienced annotators. We now propose that a noise adaptation layer should be appended to a pretrained baseline model, in order to make it possible to learn from these noisy labels. From the baseline model, predictions are made on the training set and a confusion matrix is created from these predictions and the noisy labels. This confusion matrix is used to initialise the weights of the noise layer and the full model is retrained on the training set. The final predictions for the testing set are made from the baseline model, after its weights have been readjusted by the noise layer. We show that the final model significantly improves performance on noisy datasets.

Keywords: Multi-label image classification · Noisy data

1 Introduction

Recent estimations of the World Health Organisation (WHO) [1], show that more than 1.9 billion and 650 million people worldwide live with excess adiposity and clinical obesity, respectively. Moreover, around 422 million people live with diabetes. According to the American Centers for Disease Control and Prevention (CDC) [2], a healthy diet can not only prevent overweight and obesity, but also lower the risk of numerous chronic diseases, such as type 2 diabetes, heart disease and some forms of cancer. Adherence to a healthy diet must be based on proper dietary assessment by monitoring dietary habits.

Continuous dietary assessment has traditionally been performed using instruments such as food diaries and 24-h dietary recall [3]. One major challenge of such subjective assessment methods is self-reporting errors due to inability to estimate the correct portion sizes. With the development of Artificial Intelligence (AI) and computer vision, dietary assessment can now be performed automatically, with a smartphone camera, and this procedure is very accurate and efficient. Several methods have been proposed for the automatic estimation of the nutritional content of an image [4–7] and the procedure usually consists of the following three steps i) food recognition, ii) food segmentation and iii) volume estimation and calculation of nutrient content.

© Springer Nature Switzerland AG 2021
A. Del Bimbo et al. (Eds.): ICPR 2020 Workshops, LNCS 12665, pp. 617–628, 2021.
https://doi.org/10.1007/978-3-030-68821-9_49

Food recognition is the fundamental step of dietary assessment. Hand-engineered features and traditional image classifiers were initially used for food recognition [8–10], while deep learning algorithms have recently improved the accuracy of food recognition tasks significantly [4–6, 11].

Most of the existing approaches in food recognition focus on the single-food recognition task, i.e. each input image corresponds only to a single food label [12, 13]. However, it is common in a real scenario for a food image to contain more than one food label.

In multi-label food recognition, the image is first segmented into parts that contain a single food category, followed by classification of the individual segments [11, 14, 15]. Although these methods can yield satisfactory results, they require additional computation time for food segmentation. In [14] and [16], a "sigmoid" layer is applied at the end of a classification network, in order to predict the multi-label food categories that appear in an image. Even though these methods tend to have better results, they depend on large-scale databases [10, 17] with pure annotations. Collecting expert label data with pure annotations is an extremely time-consuming task and low inter-annotator agreement is a fundamental characteristic of any such task.

In this paper, we propose a simple but effective approach to deal with noisy labels in the training set in multi-label food recognition. Thus, we have built a Confusion Matrix (CM) that represents the distribution of label noise in the training set. The CM is used to initialise the weights of a Noise Layer (NL) that connects the correct labels with the noisy labels and is subsequently removed, so that predictions can be made on a clean testing set. The NL therefore has no negative effect on the computation time. The dataset that is used in our method contains images from real end-users, so that it is easily applicable to real-world problems. Finally, the training set does not have a subset of images with clean labels that could possibly help the training process.

2 Related Work

2.1 Food Recognition

In [8], the proposed method first detects candidate regions that probably include foods and then estimates the probability of each region belonging to every food category. A similar approach is used in [9] and [10], where the bag of features model was adopted to represent an image as a collection of local features. These methods make use of hand-engineered features like colour histograms, scale invariant feature transforms or a combination of these [18] and simple architectures, like support vector machines, in order to classify the images. More recently, with the advance of deep learning, more complicated architectures like Convolutional Neural Networks (CNN) [4–6, 11] have been used for food recognition and these have tended to outperform the above approaches. These methods often use networks like GoogleNet [19], ResNet [20] or InceptionV3 [21] that are pretrained on large image datasets like ImageNet - which contains 1.2 million images with 1000 classes. These networks are then fine-tuned for the food recognition task.

The methods reviewed in this section depend on large databases, like the UEC-FOOD100 [8, 10] or the UEC-FOOD256 [22], where the labels of the images are free of noise. In practice, it may be costly and time-consuming to rely on human experts to annotate a dataset that does not contain label noise. Although the Food-101 dataset [17] contains some label noise, it incorporates 101,100 images divided equally into 101 classes. Therefore, the dataset can be used only for single-food recognition and, also, has the same number of samples for each category, thus facilitating the training process. In this paper, we use a dataset that contains images from real end-users and, thus, contains label noise. The classes are imbalanced and each image can contain multiple food categories.

2.2 Noisy Labels

The presence of noise in the labels of the training set can strongly influence the results of food recognition. Zhang *et al.* [23] showed that deep neural networks can overfit noisy labels and generalise poorly on a clean testing set. An in-depth survey was conducted in 2013 [24], that addressed the different types of noise, the effects of label noise and different methods of dealing with label noise, such as: label noise-cleansing, noise-robust methods or algorithms that try to model label noise during training. These methods are often used in tandem to improve the results.

The label noise-cleansing method aims to improve the quality of the data by either relabelling the samples that are likely to be mislabelled [25, 26], pruning them [27] or applying sample weights to the examples, based on the likelihood that their labels are correct [28, 29]. In [30] and [31], a small set of clean samples is used in conjunction with a much larger dataset that contains noisy labels, in order to assist in the training process. A method called "curriculum learning" has been increasingly successful in addressing the problem of learning from noisy data [28, 32], and is based on the idea that networks can benefit if they start learning with easy examples and progressively move to more complex ones. However, the above techniques either assume that there is a subset that contains clean labels, can sometimes discard useful data or adopt a complex method that can increase the computational time.

Other methods propose building models that are robust to label noise [33, 34]. Natarajan *et al.* [33], provided a way to modify a given loss function for binary classification, so that it is more robust to label noise. In [34], the CNN learns visual features by being trained on millions of weakly-labelled images. Nevertheless, the label noise is not actually being considered in these cases.

Finally, there are methods that try to estimate the noise transition matrix between the noisy labels and the true, hidden labels. Sukhbaatar *et al.* [35] suggested appending a linear layer on top of the baseline CNN that can be interpreted as the noise-transition matrix. However, in their method, the noise depends only on the true labels and not on the images themselves. In [36], a similar approach is used, but the output of the baseline CNN is fully connected to the noisy-label layer, and the noise also depends on the image features.

Our approach is similar to that of [36], but we extend the problem to the case of multi-label classification. Moreover, the noisy labels in the training set are not specifically assigned to classes but have a probability of belonging to each class, that is equal to the average of the annotations performed by the different annotators. In comparison to other methods [30, 31], this approach does not rely on a subset of clean labels that can assist in the training process and does not affect the computation time.

3 Method

Our goal is to train a multi-label classifier that can distinguish the food categories that appear in a single RGB image. The labels of the training dataset are noisy, in the sense that they are annotated by inexperienced annotators.

In our method, a baseline image classification model (BM) is trained first, in order to give some preliminary results. For the BM, any prevalent network architectures such as GoogleNet [19], InceptionV3 [20] or ResNet [21] can be used. We have now used the ResNet-101 and the InceptionV3 as BM, as they perform well in image classification [37]. The BM is used to make predictions on the training set and the CM is built out of these predictions and the noisy labels. The CM is a simple, yet valid, representation of the dataset's noise. On top of the BM, a NL is added, using the values of the CM as its weights, and with the aim of predicting the noisy labels. The final predictions on a clean testing set are implemented by the model, after removing the NL used to learn the noise distribution in the training set. The architecture of the full model (FM) is depicted in Fig. 1.

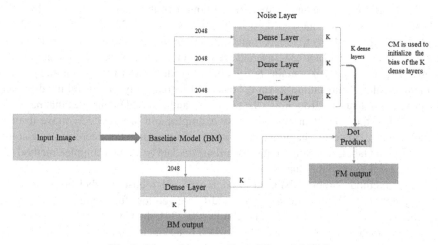

Fig. 1. The architecture of our full model (FM)

3.1 Confusion Matrix (CM) Building

Assume that the training dataset contains N images that belong to one or more classes, out of K classes in total. Let $x_i \in X \subset R^d$ be the feature vector of the ith image ($i \leq N$) and $z_i = \{Z_{i1}, \ldots, Z_{iK}\} \in [0, 1]^K$, where Z_{ir} is the average of the annotations for the ith image and the rth class. However, $\mathbf{z}$ is just a noisy version of the true, hidden labels $\mathbf{y}$, which are unknown.

In the first step, the BM is trained on the noisy dataset $D = \{(x_1, z_1), \ldots, (x_N, z_N)\}$. Instead of using the BM to make predictions on the testing set, it is used to predict the labels of the training set. The predictions are $P = \{p_1, \ldots, p_N\}$, where $p_i = \{P_{i1}, \ldots, P_{iK}\} \in [0, 1]^K$ are the probabilities that image i contains labels 1 to

K. Thus, we can observe which classes are confidently assigned to the annotated classes and which differ from them, which implies that they are correctly or probably incorrectly annotated, respectively.

From the predictions P and the noisy annotations $Z = \{z_1, \ldots, z_N\}$, a $CM \in R^{K \times K}$ is built, bearing in mind that the problem is multi-label. In addition, the noisy labels are the probabilities that every image belongs to each class, which is equal to the average of the annotations. The rows of the CM depict the predictions of the BM (that can be treated as an estimation of the true hidden labels $\mathbf{y}$) and the columns depict the noisy labels. For each pair (p_i, z_i) the CM is updated as described below.

Initially, the classes that are apparent in both p_i and z_i are identified. If, for a class $\alpha \in K$, $P_{i\alpha} > th_\alpha$ and $Z_{i\alpha} > 0$, then in the αth row and α^{th} column of the CM, the value $Z_{i\alpha}$ is added. The threshold for predicting class α, th_α, is calculated so that the number of images with $P_{ia} > th_a$ is equal to the number of images with $Z_{ia} > 0$. In other words, if A is the number of images that at least one annotator has assumed to contain class α, then the A images with the highest predicted probabilities for class α are assigned to the class α.

Assuming μ classes appear in z_i but not in p_i and v classes appear in p_i but not in z_i, if $P_{i\beta} > th_\beta$ and $Z_{i\gamma} > 0$ (β and γ are classes that do not appear in the other list), then the element in the βth row and γ^{th} column of CM is increased by $\frac{Z_{i\gamma}}{(\mu*v)}$.

If μ or v are equal to 0, then the classes that appear in both lists are taken instead. Figure 2 shows an example of how the CM is built based on the predictions of the BM and the noisy labels.

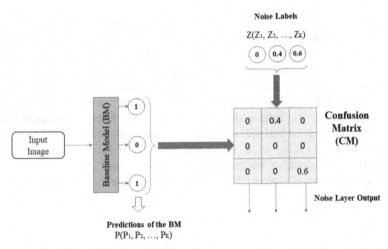

Fig. 2. An outline of the CM calculation. In such case, $\mu = 1$, since only one category (category 2) appears in Z but not in P; $v = 1$ in a similar way.

3.2 Noise Layer

The CM is used here, since it is generally a simple and highly accurate approach to estimate the label noise and the relationships between the classes. For each of the K outputs of the BM, a dense layer with K units is added. For the kth output of the BM, the appended dense layer is initialised with bias equal to the kth row of the CM. Each column, j, of the kth row of CM represents the probability that the kth output of the BM will go to the jth output of the NL - as shown in Fig. 2.

The FM, which contains the BM and the NL, is then retrained on the training set. It is worth noting here that the weights of the BM that gave the best results were transferred to this FM. The NL is used to re-adjust the weights of the BM, by trying to estimate the noise distribution. The predictions for the testing set are therefore based on the output of the BM.

If the CM were diagonal, each BM output would only connect to the NL that depicts the same class. However, this is not the case. By connecting each BM output to several NL outputs, a correlation between these classes is also considered. If the element in the ith row and j^{th} column of the CM is high, then the relation between the ith BM output and the jth NL is also high, which means that there is a chance that label i could possibly be mislabelled as class j.

4   Experimental Results

4.1   Dataset

The dataset we used contains in total 5778 RGB food images, which were taken under free living conditions by the end users of Oviva [38]. The database was annotated into 31 food categories by 5 inexperienced annotators and each image may contain more than one food category. For each food category in an image, the mean of the annotations is taken. To quantitatively measure the noise level of the database, we randomly selected 200 food images from the database and conducted a consistency study among 5 annotators. According to the study, the Intersection over Union (IoU) of different annotators is around 0.8. We split the database into training and testing sets, with 5485 and 293 food images, respectively. For the testing set, an additional experienced dietitian was commissioned to correct the annotations, so that the testing labels were much cleaner than those of the training set. Examples of images taken from the database are shown in Fig. 3, along with the annotations.

Fig. 3. Example images of the training set (upper row) and the testing set (lower row) of the database along with their annotations.

4.2 Evaluation Metrics

The mean Average Precision (mAP) is typically used for the evaluation of multi-label classification tasks. mAP is calculated as described below:

$$mAP = \frac{1}{K} \sum_{k=1}^{K} mean\left(\max\left(P_R^k\right)\right), \tag{1}$$

where K is the number of classes and $\max\left(P_R^k\right)$ is the maximal precision for each recall value of category k.

The per-class Average Precision (AP) is also considered; for each class K this is the $mean\left(\max\left(P_R^k\right)\right)$.

4.3 Results

We used the ResNet-101 and the InceptionV3 as BMs, which were pretrained on the images of ImageNet. With the addition of a Dense layer with K = 31 units, the BMs were used to predict the probability of every image belonging to each class. For both BMs, the Stochastic Gradient Descent was preferred as the optimizer, with learning rate set to 0.01, momentum 0.9 and decay 10^{-5}. The BMs were supervised with a binary cross-entropy loss for 30 epochs and with a batch size equal to 8. The BM achieved an mAP of 0.466 on the testing set for the ResNet-101 and outperformed the InceptionV3, that achieved an mAP of 0.416.

After the BM had been trained, it was used again to make predictions on the training set, in order to build the CM as suggested in Sect. 3.1. The NL was then appended to the BM. The same optimizer was used to train the FM for a batch size equal to 16 on 2 NVIDIA GeForce GTX TITAN X GPUs for another 30 epochs. The learning rate was set to 0.01 for the first 10 epochs and 0.005 for the rest. Changing the hyperparameters of the optimizer or the learning rate had minimal effects on the output of the model.

Table 1 shows a comparison between the two BMs and their respective FMs with the addition of the NL. The FM with the InceptionV3 as a BM reached its highest mAP of 0.499 at the 20th epoch and the FM with the ResNet-101 as a BM at the 10th epoch with mAP of 0.507. This is an 8.3% increase in mAP for the InceptionV3 model and a 4.1% increase for the ResNet-101 model.

Table 1. Comparison of mAP between the FM and the BM for the InceptionV3 and the ResNet-101 architecture.

Model	mAP
InceptionV3	0.416
InceptionV3 with NL	0.499
ResNet-101	0.466
ResNet-101 with NL	**0.507**

A comparison between the per-class AP of the BM and the FM for each category of the dataset is presented in Table 2, for both architectures. The foods are placed in order, so that the first category, "Vegetables", has the most samples in the training set, while the last category has the fewest. The first column of Table 2 shows the 31 food categories. The second and third columns show the AP for the BM and the FM, respectively. The fourth and fifth columns show the numbers of samples that appear in the training and testing sets, respectively. The last (sixth) column lists the differences in the AP between FM and the BM. This appears with a white background if there is no difference between these two, in green if the AP is increased with the FM and in red if the AP is actually worse with the FM. In general, we observe that the AP for the ResNet-101 is increased in 19 out of 31 food categories after the addition of the NL; for the InceptionV3, the AP is increased in 24 out of 31 food categories. Therefore, the FM can predict the most common food categories with greater consistency. In particular, the results indicate that the FM can distinguish between red meat and white meat better than the BM can. Moreover, the FM can more accurately predict the class yoghurt, which is considered a "difficult" category. For both models, the AP is increased for most drinks, which are generally harder to recognise and often include label noise. In general, in food categories where the annotators disagree, AP tends to increase with the FM, implying that the NL can effectively learn the noise distribution. For the food categories for which the annotators tend to agree, the results may vary, so that further investigation is needed.

Table 2. The 31 food categories (first column), the AP for each class for the BM and the FM (second and third columns), the samples of each class in the training and the testing sets (fourth and fifth columns) and the difference between the AP for the FM and the BM, when using the ResNet-101 and the InceptionV3 architectures. Green colouring indicates improved performance with FM, while red colouring indicates poorer performance with FM.

Class	AP for BM		AP for FM		# of samples in the training set	# of samples in the testing set	Difference in AP between the FM and BM	
	ResNet-101	Incep-tionV3	ResNet-101	Incep-tionV3			ResNet-101	Incep-tionV3
Vegetables	0.95	0.90	0.95	0.93	2505	140	0.00	0.03
Red meat	0.61	0.45	0.63	0.60	896	51	0.02	0.15
Sweets	0.61	0.55	0.57	0.66	863	36	-0.04	0.11
Yoghurt	0.33	0.45	0.40	0.55	832	22	0.07	0.10
Fruits	0.80	0.64	0.80	0.76	808	38	0.00	0.12
Cheese	0.67	0.62	0.72	0.59	707	40	0.05	-0.03
Non-white bread	0.74	0.64	0.64	0.71	652	31	-0.10	0.07
White meat	0.15	0.24	0.20	0.41	571	16	0.05	0.17
White bread	0.61	0.50	0.59	0.62	507	51	-0.02	0.12
Breaded food	0.10	0.07	0.10	0.11	442	8	0.00	0.04
Milk coffee	0.26	0.24	0.27	0.23	378	7	0.01	-0.01
Legumes	0.17	0.23	0.22	0.35	375	9	0.05	0.12
Eggs	0.72	0.52	0.70	0.74	315	25	-0.02	0.22
Water	0.36	0.19	0.47	0.34	309	5	0.11	0.15
White pasta	0.57	0.58	0.60	0.58	308	21	0.03	0.00
Milk	0.43	0.42	0.47	0.51	279	10	0.04	0.09
Sweet drink	0.56	0.43	0.61	0.57	257	14	0.05	0.14
Non-fried potatoes	0.30	0.27	0.39	0.33	243	8	0.09	0.06
White rice	0.72	0.75	0.68	0.81	232	22	-0.04	0.06
Fish	0.19	0.20	0.26	0.21	224	15	0.07	0.01
Nuts	0.62	0.65	0.72	0.65	223	5	0.10	0.00
Unprocessed cereal	0.41	0.31	0.48	0.33	167	6	0.07	0.02
Non-white pasta	0.20	0.17	0.24	0.25	132	12	0.04	0.08
Fried potatoes	0.26	0.15	0.22	0.31	123	8	-0.04	0.16
Non-white rice	0.14	0.14	0.31	0.12	116	6	0.17	-0.02
Processed cereal	0.51	0.57	0.47	0.62	110	9	-0.04	0.05
Tea	0.46	0.47	0.50	0.67	96	6	0.04	0.20
Coffee	0.59	0.53	0.61	0.46	74	15	0.02	-0.07
Liquor	0.00	0.00	0.00	0.00	42	0	0.00	0.00
Wine	0.07	0.33	1.00	0.50	31	1	0.93	0.17
Beer	0.83	0.25	0.40	0.50	27	2	-0.43	0.25

Figure 4 compares the results of the BM and the FM for the ResNet-101 architecture with different testing sets.

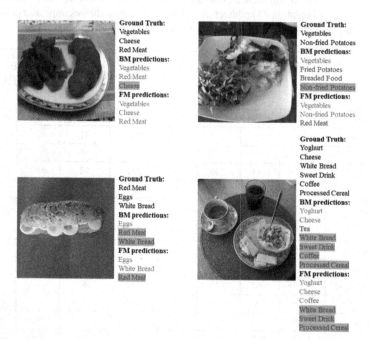

Fig. 4. Examples of images in the testing set along with predictions from the BM and FM using the ResNet-101 architecture. The categories appear in green, red and red with grey background for correct, wrong and missing predictions, respectively.

5   Conclusions

In this paper we propose a method to deal with multi-label datasets containing label noise, where the noise distribution is unknown. We showed that by constructing a CM, the relations between the different classes, and therefore the existence of noise, can be ascertained. The FM consists of the BM and the NL and yields an 8.3% increase in mAP compared to the BM when using the InceptionV3 architecture and a 4.1% increase when using ResNet-101.

The NL was only used during the training phase, and is not needed in the testing phase, so that the proposed approach does not increase the computational time. We plan to evaluate our proposed method on much larger datasets.

Acknowledgments. This work was funded by Innosuisse under agreement n° 33780.1 IP-LS [www.innosuisse.ch] and it is a part of the medipiatto project [www.go-food.tech].

References

1. World Health Organization (WHO). https://www.who.int/. Accessed 15 Oct 2020
2. Centers for Disease Control and Prevention (CDC). https://www.cdc.gov/. Accessed 15 Oct 2020
3. Thompson, F.E., Subar, A.F.: Dietary assessment methodology. In: Nutrition in the Prevention and Treatment of Disease, pp. 5–48. Academic Press (2017)
4. Meyers, A., et al.: Im2Calories: towards an automated mobile vision food diary. In: Proceedings of the IEEE International Conference on Computer Vision, pp. 1233–1241 (2015)
5. Chang Liu, Y., Cao, Y., Chen, G., Vokkarane, V., Ma, Y.: Deepfood: deep learning-based food image recognition for computer-aided dietary assessment. In: Chang, C.K., Lorenzo Chiari, Y., Cao, H.J., Mokhtari, M., Aloulou, H. (eds.) ICOST 2016. LNCS, vol. 9677, pp. 37–48. Springer, Cham (2016). https://doi.org/10.1007/978-3-319-39601-9_4
6. Christodoulidis, S., Anthimopoulos, M., Mougiakakou, S.: Food recognition for dietary assessment using deep convolutional neural networks. In: Murino, V., Puppo, E., Sona, D., Cristani, M., Sansone, C. (eds.) ICIAP 2015. LNCS, vol. 9281, pp. 458–465. Springer, Cham (2015). https://doi.org/10.1007/978-3-319-23222-5_56
7. Dehais, J., Anthimopoulos, M., Shevchik, S., Mougiakakou, S.: Two-view 3D reconstruction for food volume estimation. IEEE Trans. Multimedia 19(5), 1090–1099 (2016)
8. Matsuda, Y., Hoashi, H., Yanai, K.: Recognition of multiple-food images by detecting candidate regions. In: 2012 IEEE International Conference on Multimedia and Expo, pp. 25–30. IEEE (2012)
9. Anthimopoulos, M.M., Gianola, L., Scarnato, L., Diem, P., Mougiakakou, S.G.: A food recognition system for diabetic patients based on an optimized bag-of-features model. IEEE J. Biomed. Health Inform. 18(4), 1261–1271 (2014)
10. Kawano, Y., Yanai, K.: Foodcam: a real-time food recognition system on a smartphone. Multimedia Tools Appl. 74(14), 5263–5287 (2015)
11. Lu, Y., et al.: goFOODTM: an artificial intelligence system for dietary assessment. Sensors 20(15), 4283 (2020)
12. Kagaya, H., Aizawa, K., Ogawa, M.: Food detection and recognition using convolutional neural network. In: Proceedings of the 22nd ACM International Conference on Multimedia, pp. 1085–1088 (2014)
13. Martinel, N., Foresti, G.L., Micheloni, C.: Wide-slice residual networks for food recognition. In: 2018 IEEE Winter Conference on Applications of Computer Vision (WACV), pp. 567–576. IEEE (2018)
14. Anthimopoulos, M., Dehais, J., Diem, P., Mougiakakou, S.: Segmentation and recognition of multi-food meal images for carbohydrate counting. In: 13th IEEE International Conference on BioInformatics and BioEngineering, pp. 1–4. IEEE (2013)
15. Aguilar, E., Remeseiro, B., Bolaños, M., Radeva, P.: Grab, pay, and eat: semantic food detection for smart restaurants. IEEE Trans. Multimedia 20(12), 3266–3275 (2018)
16. Bolaños, M., Ferrà, A., Radeva, P.: Food ingredients recognition through multi-label learning. In: Battiato, S., Farinella, G.M., Leo, M., Gallo, G. (eds.) ICIAP 2017. LNCS, vol. 10590, pp. 394–402. Springer, Cham (2017). https://doi.org/10.1007/978-3-319-70742-6_37
17. Bossard, L., Guillaumin, M., Gool, L.: Food-101 – mining discriminative components with random forests. In: Fleet, D., Pajdla, T., Schiele, B., Tuytelaars, T. (eds.) ECCV 2014. LNCS, vol. 8694, pp. 446–461. Springer, Cham (2014). https://doi.org/10.1007/978-3-319-10599-4_29
18. Martinel, N., Piciarelli, C., Micheloni, C., Luca Foresti, G.: A structured committee for food recognition. In: Proceedings of the IEEE International Conference on Computer Vision Workshops, pp. 92–100 (2015)

19. Szegedy, C., et al.: Going deeper with convolutions. In Proceedings of the IEEE Conference on Computer Vision and Pattern Recognition, pp. 1–9 (2015)
20. He, K., Zhang, X., Ren, S., Sun, J.: Deep residual learning for image recognition. In: Proceedings of the IEEE Conference on Computer Vision and Pattern Recognition, pp. 770–778 (2016)
21. Szegedy, C., Vanhoucke, V., Ioffe, S., Shlens, J., Wojna, Z.: Rethinking the inception architecture for computer vision. In: Proceedings of the IEEE Conference on Computer Vision and Pattern Recognition, pp. 2818–2826 (2016)
22. Kawano, Y., Yanai, K.: Automatic expansion of a food image dataset leveraging existing categories with domain adaptation. In: Agapito, L., Bronstein, M.M., Rother, C. (eds.) ECCV 2014. LNCS, vol. 8927, pp. 3–17. Springer, Cham (2015). https://doi.org/10.1007/978-3-319-16199-0_1
23. Zhang, Z., Sabuncu, M.: Generalized cross entropy loss for training deep neural networks with noisy labels. In: Advances in Neural Information Processing Systems, pp. 8778–8788 (2018)
24. Frénay, B., Verleysen, M.: Classification in the presence of label noise: a survey. IEEE Trans. Neural Netw. Learn. Syst. **25**(5), 845–869 (2013)
25. Reed, S., Lee, H., Anguelov, D., Szegedy, C., Erhan, D., Rabinovich, A.: Training deep neural networks on noisy labels with bootstrapping. arXiv preprint arXiv:1412.6596 (2014)
26. Tanaka, D., Ikami, D., Yamasaki, T., Aizawa, K.: Joint optimization framework for learning with noisy labels. In: Proceedings of the IEEE Conference on Computer Vision and Pattern Recognition, pp. 5552–5560 (2018)
27. Northcutt, C.G., Jiang, L., Chuang, I.L.: Confident learning: Estimating uncertainty in dataset labels. arXiv preprint arXiv:1911.00068 (2019)
28. Jiang, L., Zhou, Z., Leung, T., Li, L.J., Fei-Fei, L.: Mentornet: learning data-driven curriculum for very deep neural networks on corrupted labels. In: International Conference on Machine Learning, pp. 2304–2313 (2018)
29. Ren, M., Zeng, W., Yang, B., Urtasun, R.: Learning to reweight examples for robust deep learning. arXiv preprint arXiv:1803.09050 (2018)
30. Veit, A., Alldrin, N., Chechik, G., Krasin, I., Gupta, A., Belongie, S.: Learning from noisy large-scale datasets with minimal supervision. In: Proceedings of the IEEE Conference on Computer Vision and Pattern Recognition, pp. 839–847 (2017)
31. Lee, K.H., He, X., Zhang, L., Yang, L.: Cleannet: transfer learning for scalable image classifier training with label noise. In: Proceedings of the IEEE Conference on Computer Vision and Pattern Recognition, pp. 5447–5456 (2018)
32. Chen, X., Gupta, A.: Webly supervised learning of convolutional networks. In: Proceedings of the IEEE International Conference on Computer Vision, pp. 1431–1439 (2015)
33. Natarajan, N., Dhillon, I.S., Ravikumar, P.K., Tewari, A.: Learning with noisy labels. In Advances in Neural Information Processing Systems, pp. 1196–1204 (2013)
34. Joulin, A., Van Der Maaten, L., Jabri, A., Vasilache, N.: Learning visual features from large weakly supervised data. In: Leibe, B., Matas, J., Sebe, N., Welling, M. (eds.) ECCV 2016. LNCS, vol. 9911, pp. 67–84. Springer, Cham (2016). https://doi.org/10.1007/978-3-319-464 78-7_5
35. Sukhbaatar, S., Fergus, R.: Learning from noisy labels with deep neural networks, vol. 2, no. 3, p. 4. arXiv preprint arXiv:1406.2080 (2014)
36. Goldberger, J., Ben-Reuven, E.: Training deep neural-networks using a noise adaptation layer (2016)
37. Ciocca, G., Napoletano, P., Schettini, R.: CNN-based features for retrieval and classification of food images. Comput. Vis. Image Underst. **176**, 70–77 (2018)
38. Oviva S.A., Zurich, Switzerland. https://oviva.com/global/

S2ML-TL Framework for Multi-label Food Recognition

Bhalaji Nagarajan[1]([envelope])[ID], Eduardo Aguilar[1,2][ID], and Petia Radeva[1,3][ID]

[1] Dept. de Matemàtiques i Informàtica, Universitat de Barcelona, Barcelona, Spain
{bhalaji.nagarajan,petia.ivanova}@ub.edu
[2] Departamento de Ingeniería de Sistemas y Computación,
Universidad Católica del Norte, Antofagasta, Chile
eaguilar02@ucn.cl
[3] Computer Vision Center, Cerdanyola, Barcelona, Spain

Abstract. Transfer learning can be attributed to several recent break-throughs in deep learning. It has shown upbeat performance improvements, but most of the transfer learning applications are confined towards fine-tuning. Transfer learning facilitates the learnability of the networks on domains with less data. However, learning becomes a difficult task with complex domains, such as multi-label food recognition, owing to the shear number of food classes as well as to the fine-grained nature of food images. For this purpose, we propose S2ML-TL, a new transfer learning framework to leverage the knowledge learnt on a simpler single-label food recognition task onto multi-label food recognition. The framework is further enhanced using class priors to tackle the dataset bias that exists between single-label and multi-label food domains. We validate the proposed scheme with two multi-label datasets on different backbone architectures and the results show improved performance compared to the conventional transfer learning approach.

Keywords: Food recognition · Multi-label · Class priors

1 Introduction

Food is not just a source of energy, but is a cultural expression. It is central to the regular and pleasure activities of day-to-day life. Food habits directly affect the lifestyle and healthcare of individuals. Consuming a well-balanced healthy diet averts a wide range of noncommunicable diseases and conditions such as diabetes and obesity [43]. Growing emphasis on well-maintained food habits has given rise to a large number of automated food intake monitoring systems [42,48,66] that help in regulating food intake. Food computing is possible through different forms of data - images, texts, tables, etc. of which images are more prevalent due to the large number of social media posts. Automated food recognition is vital to any food journal because of the ease it gives to the users and is integral to several modern dietary applications [15]. However, food recognition is a very complex computer vision task, due to the nature of images [60]. Food images

© Springer Nature Switzerland AG 2021
A. Del Bimbo et al. (Eds.): ICPR 2020 Workshops, LNCS 12665, pp. 629–646, 2021.
https://doi.org/10.1007/978-3-030-68821-9_50

are often mixed or composed of many items in a single platter. Moreover, high intra-class and low inter-class variance make it difficult to work for any food recognition model.

Deep Learning has been vital in improving the performance of several tasks. However, a well-developed model requires large volumes of training data. Collecting huge volumes of data and annotating them are both costly and time intensive. This data dependency is addressed using Transfer Learning (TL), the ability of deep networks to transfer knowledge from one domain or task to another [54]. Automated food recognition using deep networks takes advantage of TL, as there are insufficient large-scale food datasets [38]. The common food recognition datasets, such as ETH Food101 [8] and VireoFood172 [11] are quite small and do not represent wide range of diverse classes. Food recognition falls under fine-grained recognition task, where the latent features are less separable, making it difficult to establish a well-trained network. These factors make food recognition a challenging research problem, but most of the existing literature until today, are often done on single-label datasets. However, the food images in real world are often not single-labelled by nature [60]. Single-label recognition is an easier task, because the final activation function (softmax) is bound to get exactly one output whereas in a multi-label scenario, possible solutions are larger (allowing to activate 0, 1 or many final labels), thus making the probability error much higher. In spite of all the challenges it presents, tacking food recognition in a multi-label perspective would bring the problem closer to the real-world.

High success of TL in visual recognition is due to its capacity to extract shared low-level features such as edges and curves across different image domains [58]. However, as the layers go deeper, they become more task-specific. Multi-stage TL has been widely used in classification tasks of high complexity [16]. Using this approach, an ImageNet-trained network is often used to fine-tune on common datasets, which in turn, would be used to fine-tune on more complex datasets. This forces the deeper layers to learn intermediate representations that would allow better learning of the complex task. It has to be also noted that TL does not always result in improvements. When weights are transferred from similar domains, the learning of layers is faster and more accurate, whereas, when the two domains are dissimilar, the learning could give inaccurate results, known as Negative transfer [10,62]. However, there are a lot of open questions regarding when negative transfer appears and how to avoid it [44]. A typical heuristic solution to avoid negative transfer is to train only on samples that are nearer to the target domain and avoid those samples that are far away from the source domain [46]. Choice of positive samples thus becomes an important aspect. However, there is no existing mechanism to determine if the particular sample would result in positive or negative transfer [44].

The recent success in single-label food classifiers can be largely attributed to the ease in training such models. We therefore hypothesise to utilize the learning ability of single-label classifiers into a more complex task: multi-label recognition. In this work, we propose Single to Multi-label Transfer Learning (S2ML-TL) framework, using single-label recognition as an intermediate task to achieve multi-label recognition. As we will show, this allows the model to generalize better and improve its learnability. We further enhance the framework by using class priors that helps in selection of positive samples for better transferability. We organize the paper as follows: In Sect. 2, we review the recent literature on food recognition. We provide details of the proposed scheme in Sect. 3 and show the experimental details and results in Sect. 4. We present the concluding remarks in the last section.

2   Related Works

Food recognition is increasingly popular because of the advancements in intelligent health applications in dietary management, food perception, recommendation and health analysis [36]. With the development of deep networks, food recognition has become on par with human performance and have out-performed hand-crafted feature based classifiers [21,23,65]. Different architectures have been applied on the food recognition tasks: GoogLeNet [28,63], Network-In-Networks [55], Inception V3 [18], ResNet50 [39], Ensemble NN [40], Wide Residual Networks [31], and CleanNet [27]. The base architectures were also modified to enhance the learning task, such as modifying Alexnet in NutriNet [34]. However, most of the popular benchmark datasets [8,11,13,25] do not offer a diverse representation of food classes. They are confined to either a certain region or to a certain representation. With the explosion of images in social platforms, recent datasets involve a large number of food images [12,24]. With increased computational capabilities, ensemble of various models is a common approach [2,45,56]. An integration of local and flat classifiers [4] and fusion of slice network and residual network [31] have also been effective. Preceding the classification with a detection network is another common approach [35]. Faster R-CNN based detection was used to find the candidate regions before classification [22]. Recent architecture advances include using teacher-student learning [67], knowledge distillation [20], attention network [37] and incremental learning [53].

Real world food images are often multi-labelled in nature, ie. more than one food class is present in an image. Compared with single-label food recognition, there have been much fewer works in multi-label food recognition. A general approach is to detect the location of food and then recognize each class in the image [6]. Multi-task based learning methods [3,68] and multi-scale region-based classifier [61] have also improved the performance. Using segmentation networks before recognition [49] has also been effective. Region proposal based candidate region detection [5,32,50] has helped in improving the recall rate. Using additional information such as ontology [14] has also assisted in improving the multi-label performance. However, there is still a big difference in the performance between single-label and multi-label recognition tasks, owing to the complexity of the data and also to the difficulty in learning such tasks.

In the proposed S2ML-TL framework, we use single-label models to improve the learning of multi-label models for multi-label food recognition, which up to our knowledge is the first such approach. Additionally, we propose to enhance the model with specially designed class priors for better recognition performance, which is used to tackle the covariate shift problem. The complexity and

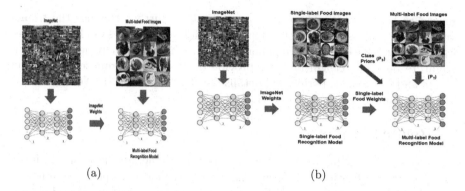

(a)   (b)

Fig. 1. Traditional TL (fine-tuning) (a) vs. S2ML-TL framework (b)

fine-grained nature of the food images, coupled with increased performance in multi-stage frameworks in other domains are primary reasons in our proposed methodology.

3   Proposed Methodology

Supervised fine-tuning in two-stages, using datasets similar to the target domain in the first stage, yields better results than a single stage fine-tuning [41]. The advantage of using such a framework is that the models are generalized as they go deeper in the stages and also the learning is made possible with smaller number of more complex images compared to the earlier stages. With this underlying premise, we propose the S2ML-TL framework. Figure 1 shows the proposed scheme against the traditional TL methodology.

3.1   S2ML-TL Framework

Let us consider a domain, $D = \{x, P(X)\}$ consisting of feature space x and marginal probability distribution $P(X)$, where $X = \{x_1, ..., x_n\} \in x$. A task, $T = \{y, f(x)\}$ consists of a label space y and a target prediction function $f(x)$. $f(x)$ determines the conditional probability function $P(y|x)$. Given a learning task T_t based on D_t, transfer learning aims at increasing the learning performance by leveraging the knowledge used in another learning task T_s based on domain D_s. The deep network learns the latent features using the transferred knowledge from D_s and T_s, where $D_s \neq D_t$ and/or $T_s \neq T_t$. In addition, in most cases, the size of D_s is much larger than the size of D_t.

As discussed previously, TL has been successfully applied on various food datasets. However, when multi-label food recognition is considered, knowledge transfer becomes much harder. To overcome such a scenario, we hypothesise S2ML-TL framework. Let us consider two tasks T_{t1} and T_{t2} on domains D_{t1} and D_{t2}, where D_{t1} and D_{t2} are similar domains, but the task T_{t2} (e.g. multi-label recognition) is more complex than T_{t1} (e.g. single-label recognition).

In this scenario, transferring knowledge from the source task, T_s on domain D_s to the target task T_{t2} (multi-label) on domain D_{t2} could be achieved using the task T_{t1} (single-label) on domain D_{t1} as an intermediate transfer. The deep network trained on the simpler domain D_{t1} learns the latent space better from the source and then when it is used on the more complex domain D_{t2}, the network is better equipped to learn the more complex multi-label space.

The impact of TL can be seen in one or combination of the following three aspects: a higher performance at the very beginning of learning, a steeper slope in the learning curve, and a higher asymptote [57]. With the first two cases, it is evident that the learning is happening faster and with the last one, it is known that the performance of TL is better. However, transferring knowledge between two completely different tasks might also result in a negative transfer, that is, decreasing in performance of the target deep network, which makes the selection of task/domain a very important factor. In most of the tasks, transfer of knowledge is performed through mapping of characteristics of the source and target tasks [57]. The correspondence between tasks is automatically performed during TL or is induced by a mapping. In this work, the performance of the TL framework is further enhanced using class priors, which acts as mapping between the simpler and the complex task.

3.2 Class Priors for Improved Transferability of Food Recognition

Covariate shift [1,47] is a common phenomenon in TL where the input and output relationships are the same, but the distributions of training and test sets are different. The dataset bias or the domain shift makes the generalization of deep networks a difficult task [59]. Importance-weighting [9,17,51] has been a common solution to this problem. The distribution of samples in a domain is a direct representation of the nature of the domain. In this work, we use this information as a prior knowledge, that would enable the algorithms to be robust to shifts.

The priors of both domains would be different due to overlapping classes, under-sampled classes, unevenly distributed classes or classes that are more similar to each other. All these situations give rise to an uncertainty in the model which makes prior-induced learning important. Class priors are computed for the simpler (the single-label) domain D_{t1} and are used in the training of the more complex (the multi-label) domain D_{t2}. The class priors of the target domain (D_{t2}), P_T and the source domain (D_{t1}), P_S are computed as a function of the samples that represent a certain class. The ratio of the class priors, P_T/P_S is thus used to establish the mapping between domains. However, it has to be noted that it is not always necessary that the classes present in both domains need to be the same. In this particular food recognition problem, the information of the ingredients present in classes of both domains are used when the classes are not matching.

In the multi-label setting, for the domain $D = \{x, P(X)\}$, with the number of classes as C, we would have $P(X) = [y_1, y_2, ..., y_C]$. The most commonly used loss function to train a multi-label classification model is the Binary Cross-Entropy (BCE) loss:

$$l(x, y) = \frac{1}{C} \sum_{c=1}^{C} [\, y_i log(p(y_i)) + (1 - y_i) log(1 - p(y_i))\,] \tag{1}$$

where y_i is the label for the class i and $p(y_i)$ is the corresponding predicted probability.

The ratio of priors, P_T/P_S, is added to the loss computation to enhance the transferability of the domain knowledge. This means that when P_S is smaller, the classes has to be learnt from the data which is available with the target domain. However, when P_S is larger, the learning can be achieved from the source model. During TL, the training of the target domain starts with initialization of weights from the source domain. At this point, the weights of the network are more suitable for the source domain than the target domain. Over iterations, the network learns the underlying target domain distribution until convergence so that the learning of the target domain is complete. In this way the learning would gradually forget the source domain and adapt better to the target domain. This gradual learning process is replicated in the impact of source distribution over the target distribution using the prior impact factor, r_i:

$$r_i = \alpha \frac{P_T}{P_S} + (1 - \alpha) P_T \tag{2}$$

where $0 \leq \alpha \leq 1$. As we can see, higher target priors denote the importance of that particular class in the domain. During the beginning of the training, α is set to maximum and is gradually decayed along the training process. However, the value of weights may scale the loss value, which in turn can increase the difficulty of optimization. In order to make the optimization process stable, a correction constant, β is used, which will ensure that the prior impact factor r_i, falls under proper range of values. The balanced prior impact factor, r_i^b, is given as follows:

$$r_i^b = \beta \left[\alpha \frac{P_T}{P_S} + (1 - \alpha) P_T \right] \tag{3}$$

where $\beta \geq 0$. Finally, the prior-induced loss function is as in Eq. (4):

$$l_p(x, y) = \frac{1}{C} \sum_{c=1}^{C} [\, y_i.log(p(y_i)) + (1 - y_i).log(1 - p(y_i))\,] * r_i^b \tag{4}$$

This prior-induced loss function has shown optimal performance in transferring knowledge from the source to target domain, as it will be validated in the next section.

Prior Computation. The next objective is to compute the ratio of priors, $P(T)/P(S)$, between the single-label (source) and multi-label datasets (target). $P(T_i)$ for the target datasets defines the probability of each class, i, in the multi-label datasets:

$$P(T_i) = \frac{1}{N_t} \sum_{n=1}^{N_t} y_i^n \tag{5}$$

where N_t is the total number of training samples in the target domain.

It is also possible that there could be more than one class of the source dataset where the target class is present. In this case, $P(S)$ is computed as the sum of probabilities of all classes, where the target class is present. For the classes, i present in the target domain, the mapping in the source domain is computed as follows:

$$P(S_i) = \frac{1}{N_s} \sum_{i} \sum_{j=1}^{N_s} y_j, \ j \in \{all\ source\ classes\ containing\ i\} \tag{6}$$

where N_s is the total number of the training samples in the source domain.

4 Validation

In this section, we brief the datasets, evaluation metrics and the implementation details of the deep networks. We also show the computation of priors and the selection of hyper-parameters. Finally, we show the experimental results and the inferences made from those results.

4.1 Datasets

In order to validate the proposed framework, we use two multi-label food datasets, Food201 [33] and Combo-plates. Food201 is a public dataset, whereas Combo-plates is an in-house dataset. We use Food101 [8] as the single-label dataset. Figure 2 shows sample images of each of the dataset used in the validation.

Food101. Food101 is one of the most popular single-label food datasets. It contains 101 food classes of international cuisines with 1000 images each. The dataset is divided into 75% training and the remaining as test images. The dataset is annotated for the class names only.

Food201. Food201 is a multi-label dataset that can be considered as an extension to the Food101 class labels. The images from Food101, although, single-labelled, contain images that have more than one class. This behaviour was leveraged to create the Food201 dataset and resulted in around 35k training images and 15k test images. These images were re-annotated for a new 100 classes in addition to the ones in Food101.

(a)   (b)   (c)

Fig. 2. Sample images from Food101 (a), Food201 (b) Combo-plates (c)

Combo-Plates. There are a very few public multi-label food datasets, of which, the multi-label datasets are primarily targeted towards ingredient detection [11] or category detection [14]. One popular multi-label food recognition dataset is UNIMIB2016 [13], which is actually a tray-based dataset, where each tray would again contain spatially separated classes in different plates inside the tray. However, these images are confined to a very particular type of presentation. With very few public datasets available and moreover the aim of having resemblance with the real-world food representations, we decided to annotate a new dataset (Combo-plates).

We created the Combo-plates dataset from web-scrapped images. Initially, we constructed a list of 75 commonly consumed European foods and created search queries using different combination of the classes and crawled the candidate images from different search engines. The candidate images were cleaned using a food detector network, so that the non-food images are removed and then we annotated the filtered food images. We further filtered the images during annotation, in such a way that all the images are multi-labelled in nature, placed in a single platter and the classes had a distinguishable boundary between them. The annotation was done independent of the search queries and there is no fixed combination or fixed number of the classes in each image. The dataset is split into 75% train, 10% validation and 15% test images.

Prior Computation. For both Food201 and Combo-plates, we compute $P(T_i)$ using Eq. (5), which is the probability of each class. As we explained previously, not all classes are present in both the source and target and we use the ingredient information to create the associated mapping. The ingredients information is already available for Food101 dataset via the Ingredients101 [7] dataset. For a single class in Food201 and Combo-plates, there are more than one class in Food101. For example, for the class, *avocado* present in Combo-plates, it is present in *guacamole* and *ceviche* classes of Food101. In this case, we compute $P(S)$ using Eq. (6). Since Food101 is a balanced dataset, the probabilities of each source class would be the same. Calculating priors of Food201 from Food101 is a simpler case, as the 101 primary classes are a direct overlapping information. The priors are computed only for the classes that are present in both datasets.

We then fit the computed source and target priors into Eq. (3) to compute the balanced prior impact factor r_i^b.

4.2   Evaluation Metrics

We use Precision, Recall and F1-Score to evaluate the proposed hypothesis. Accuracy is not a good measure for the essence of the problem, due to the multi-label and multi-class nature of the dataset and also due to the class imbalance in both datasets. We perform 'Micro' averaging to compute the overall F1-Score for each model.

4.3   Implementation Details

We use Resnet50 [19] and InceptionResnetV2 [52] as backbone architectures. For single-label training, we used the pre-trained ImageNet models and trained with the standard data splits available in Food101. For multi-stage transfer learning, we initialized the weights of single-label models. For all the models, we removed the classification layer and the fully connected layer from the base models and replaced with a fully connected layer of 2048 neurons, followed by the classification layer of n neurons, where n is the number of classes in each dataset. For single-label training, we used a softmax activation, whereas for multi-label training, we used a sigmoid activation. For all the models, we trained the entire network. As pre-processing, we resized all the images to 224×224. As far as the training parameters are concerned, we used Adadelta optimizer with an initial learning rate of 1 and we used a batch size of 24. We trained all the models in Keras framework with Tensorflow backend.

Hyper-parameter Selection. There are two parameters that we define in our proposed scheme, α and β, which affect the impact of source distribution on the target distribution. We show the selection of these parameters using the experiments performed using InceptionResnetV2 trained on Combo-plates using Food101 as the source domain.

In order to evaluate the impact of α, we considered α values at 0, 0.25, 0.5, 0.75 and 1. When $\alpha = 1$, the first term of r_i^b is only active, ie. the loss function is impacted by the ratio of priors, whereas, when $\alpha = 0$, it is similar to applying class weights during the model training. The values in Fig. 3(a) show that the models in between the limits outperform the models at the extremes. This prompted us to use a decaying function on α based on the number of epochs. We investigate this, by using a decay of 0.1 every 5 epochs and 0.1 every 10 epochs. It can be inferred from the Fig. 3(a) that the decayed α works better rather than a fixed α. We attribute this to the learning of the model, where the model has minimum or no influence from the source domain during the later stages of the model training. Out of the two decay networks, the one with larger decay performs better. This also shows the importance of target distribution weights on the training of the models.

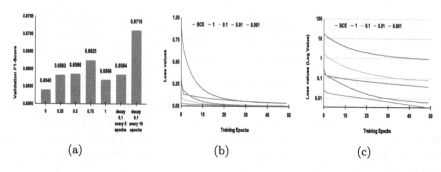

(a)   (b)   (c)

Fig. 3. Performance of models with different α values (a); loss curves of models with varying β values at $\alpha = 0$ (b); and $\alpha = 0.75$ (c).

We use the training loss curves to study the smoothing parameter, β using the optimal value of α. Figure 3(b) shows the curves with fixed $\alpha = 0$ and the Fig. 3(c) shows the loss curves with fixed $\alpha = 0.75$. The loss curves of BCE is taken as a reference curve and β is set to bring the curves closer to the reference loss curve. This is performed in order to induce higher performance during early training steps and also to have steeper slope in the learning curve. We empirically select the values of β as 0.1 and 0.003 for transferring Food101 to Combo-plates and Food201 respectively.

Comparing Methods. We establish standard BCE loss with single transfer learning scheme as the baseline. For this, we use an ImageNet pre-trained model directly on the multi-label datasets. We compare this baseline with different strategies: (1) Empirical risk minimization (ERM): The plain multi-stage framework with standard BCE loss. (2) Kullback–Leibler Divergence (KL): We replace the prior computation with the KL entropy values. (3) Priors: We compute the ratio of priors as in Eq. (3) and use Eq. (4) for the loss computation. KL-Divergence is a relative entropy score that defines how one probability distribution is different from another distribution [29]. KL-divergence based loss function is used to improve the similarity of the latent distributions to the original distribution. KL-divergence has been used in generative adversarial networks [64], Prior Networks [30] and Density fixing Regularization methods [26]. The main intuition in using KL-divergence as a comparing method is its effectiveness in providing the entropy between distributions. Since there is no prior results on Food201 multi-label recognition, we compare it against the above methods only.

4.4 Results and Discussion

We show the overall precision, recall and F1-score for the validation and test splits of both multi-label datasets to study the effectiveness of the proposed

Table 1. Model performance of InceptionResnetV2 on Combo-plates

Model	Validation data			Test data		
	Precision	Recall	F1-score	Precision	Recall	F1-score
Standard TL	0.7209	0.5865	0.6468	0.7152	0.5840	0.6430
ERM	0.6991	0.5667	0.6260	0.6900	0.5700	0.6200
KL	0.7030	0.6212	0.6596	0.6984	0.6173	0.6553
Priors	0.7045	0.6229	**0.6612**	0.7000	0.6200	**0.6600**

framework. We show the performance of InceptionResnetV2 and Resnet50 models on Combo-plates dataset in Table 1 and Table 2 respectively, while the performance of InceptionResnetV2 and Resnet50 models on Food201 dataset are shown in Table 3 and Table 4.

Comparison with SoA Methods. From the tables showing the overall performance of the experiments, it can be seen that except for the InceptionResnetV2 model on Food201 (decreased by 1.6% on the test set), all the other experiments show improvements with simple multi-stage transfer learning using BCE loss. However, it can be seen in all experiments that the recall has increased compared to the baseline method. Higher recall is particularly noted because it would result in lesser false negatives. When we use Food101 dataset in computing the KL-Divergence and in Priors to enhance the loss function further, the performance is boosted further. Since the priors are a direct representation of the classes, it is also necessary to infer the class-wise performance of the models. We compute the difference in F1-score of BCE loss and prior-induced loss for each class and denote the positive or negative transfer of the model, which we call it as degree of transfer. Figure 4 shows the histogram of the degree of transfer for all the four experiments. It can be inferred that in all the models, most of the classes have a positive transfer. However, the histogram also shows that classes have a negative transfer.

What Are the Possible Reasons for Negative Transfer in Some Classes? In order to answer this question, we study the relationship between the validation F1-score and the number of training samples of each class where priors were applied. We study this relationship using the experiments with InceptionResnetV2 as shown in Fig. 5. For the experiments using combo-plates, it is clearly evident that the classes having fewer training examples (<100) were not enhanced in the training. Also, with the corresponding scatter plot, it is evident that the validation F1-score is very low in these classes. Lacking of training data can be attributed to this performance. However, the performance of Food201 is showing mixed results. Classes that are showing a negative trend are classes that are difficult to classify (such as *ketchup* and *mustard*) or that has a larger variation inside the same class (such as *potatoes*, where there is also a *boiled*

Table 2. Model performance of Resnet50 on Combo-plates

Model	Validation data			Test data		
	Precision	Recall	F1-score	Precision	Recall	F1-score
Standard TL	0.7250	0.5581	0.6307	0.7200	0.5582	0.6289
ERM	0.7268	0.5590	**0.6320**	0.7223	0.5616	0.6319
KL	0.6956	0.5473	0.6126	0.6933	0.5491	0.6128
Priors	0.6861	0.5783	0.6276	0.6882	0.5886	**0.6345**

Table 3. Model performance of InceptionResnetV2 on Food201

Model	Validation data			Test data		
	Precision	Recall	F1-score	Precision	Recall	F1-score
Standard TL	0.6800	0.4595	0.5485	0.6997	0.5001	0.5833
ERM	0.7936	0.5354	0.6394	0.7895	0.5563	**0.6527**
KL	0.7521	0.4755	0.5826	0.7567	0.5044	0.6053
Priors	0.8189	0.6176	**0.7041**	0.7464	0.5550	0.6366

Table 4. Model performance of Resnet50 on Food201

Model	Validation data			Test data		
	Precision	Recall	F1-score	Precision	Recall	F1-score
Standard TL	0.7204	0.4215	0.5319	0.7322	0.4636	0.5678
ERM	0.7518	0.4546	0.5666	0.7493	0.4800	0.5852
KL	0.7918	0.4317	0.5587	0.7740	0.4370	0.5586
Priors	0.7767	0.5877	**0.6691**	0.7313	0.5400	**0.6213**

potatoes class present in the dataset). The performance of such classes may be due to the fine-grained nature of the dataset and also due to the close inter-class variance with other classes. In general, with the histograms in Fig. 4, it can be seen that there is a general positive trend in the performance.

4.5   Ablation Study

Finally we show the importance of each term in the proposed framework using Table 5. When $\alpha = 1$, the ratio of class probabilities is constant throughout the training process and the decay curve proves to improve the performance compared to the constant α. P_T uses only the target probabilities as weighting factor. Results using source distribution alone and using target distribution alone show both are equally important and the final proposed term gives a cumulative performance improvement. In all the experiments using β, the performance increases, showing the importance of scaling of the loss value.

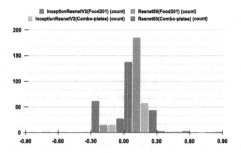

Fig. 4. Histogram showing the degree of transfer.

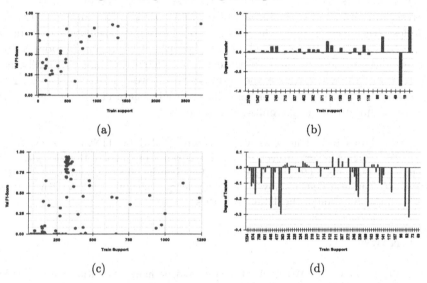

(a)   (b)

(c)   (d)

Fig. 5. Degree of transfer with respect to the train support. Train support vs. Val F1-score of InceptionResnetV2 on Combo-plates (a), Degree of transfer (b), Inception-ResnetV2 on Food201 (c), Degree of transfer (d)

Table 5. Ablation study

Model	$\alpha * \frac{P_T}{P_S}$	P_T	β	Validation data			Test data		
				Prec.	Recall	F1 Sc.	Prec.	Recall	F1 Sc.
$\alpha = 1$ (w/o β)	x	-	-	0.7537	0.5685	0.6481	0.7394	0.5666	0.6415
$\alpha = 1$ (w β)	x	-	x	0.7237	0.6012	0.6568	0.7200	0.6000	0.6500
Decayed α (w/o β)	x	-	-	0.7281	0.5958	0.6553	0.7112	0.5932	0.6469
Decayed α (w β)	x	-	x	0.7118	0.6094	0.6567	0.6963	0.6086	0.6495
Target priors (w/o β)	-	x	-	0.6972	0.6238	0.6585	0.6811	0.6140	0.6458
Target priors (w β)	-	x	x	0.7092	0.6068	0.6540	0.7050	0.5994	0.6479
Proposal (w/o β)	x	x	-	0.6996	0.6034	0.6480	0.7045	0.6069	0.6521
Proposal (w β)	x	x	x	0.7114	0.6349	**0.6710**	0.7011	0.6127	**0.6539**

5   Conclusions

Transfer learning has been an active means of transferring knowledge from tasks of one domain to another. In this work, we use S2ML-TL framework for multi-label food recognition by transferring knowledge from an intermediate simpler domain to a more complex domain. We validated the proposed framework on two multi-label food datasets, using single-label food dataset as an intermediate in two backbone architectures. We showed that utilizing single-label recognition tasks will further increase the learning ability of the multi-label recognition tasks. We also showed that the recognition performance could be further boosted by using class priors. We further analyzed the results using class-wise performance analysis and also studied the impact of transfer based on the number of training samples. We have validated the selection of the hyper-parameters used in the proposed approach. We observed that the proposed approach provides a good performance in most of the classes across different experiments. Finally, as a future work, we will advance the proposed framework to tackle the long-tail data problem, which is common for any multi-label dataset, thereby easing the process of annotating large multi-label datasets.

Acknowledgements. This work was partially funded by TIN2018-095232-B-C21, SGR-2017 1742, Nestore project of the European Commission Horizon 2020 programme (Grant no. 769643), Validithi EIT Health program and CERCA Programme/Generalitat de Catalunya. We acknowledge the support of NVIDIA Corporation with the donation of the Titan Xp GPUs.

References

1. Adel, T., Zhao, H., Wong, A.: Unsupervised domain adaptation with a relaxed covariate shift assumption. In: Thirty-First AAAI Conference on Artificial Intelligence (2017)
2. Aguilar, E., Bolaños, M., Radeva, P.: Food recognition using fusion of classifiers based on CNNs. In: Battiato, S., Gallo, G., Schettini, R., Stanco, F. (eds.) ICIAP 2017. LNCS, vol. 10485, pp. 213–224. Springer, Cham (2017). https://doi.org/10.1007/978-3-319-68548-9_20
3. Aguilar, E., Bolaños, M., Radeva, P.: Regularized uncertainty-based multi-task learning model for food analysis. J. Vis. Commun. Image Represent. **60**, 360–370 (2019)
4. Aguilar, E., Radeva, P.: Uncertainty-aware integration of local and flat classifiers for food recognition. Pattern Recogn. Lett. **136**, 237–243 (2020)
5. Aguilar, E., Remeseiro, B., Bolaños, M., Radeva, P.: Grab, pay, and eat: semantic food detection for smart restaurants. IEEE Trans. Multimedia **20**(12), 3266–3275 (2018)
6. Anzawa, M., Amano, S., Yamakata, Y., Motonaga, K., Kamei, A., Aizawa, K.: Recognition of multiple food items in a single photo for use in a buffet-style restaurant. IEICE Trans. Inf. Syst. **102**(2), 410–414 (2019)

7. Bolaños, M., Ferrà, A., Radeva, P.: Food ingredients recognition through multi-label learning. In: Battiato, S., Farinella, G.M., Leo, M., Gallo, G. (eds.) ICIAP 2017. LNCS, vol. 10590, pp. 394–402. Springer, Cham (2017). https://doi.org/10.1007/978-3-319-70742-6_37

8. Bossard, L., Guillaumin, M., Van Gool, L.: Food-101 – mining discriminative components with random forests. In: Fleet, D., Pajdla, T., Schiele, B., Tuytelaars, T. (eds.) ECCV 2014. LNCS, vol. 8694, pp. 446–461. Springer, Cham (2014). https://doi.org/10.1007/978-3-319-10599-4_29

9. Byrd, J., Lipton, Z.: What is the effect of importance weighting in deep learning? In: International Conference on Machine Learning, pp. 872–881 (2019)

10. Cao, Z., Long, M., Wang, J., Jordan, M.I.: Partial transfer learning with selective adversarial networks. In: CVPR, pp. 2724–2732 (2018)

11. Chen, J., Ngo, C.W.: Deep-based ingredient recognition for cooking recipe retrieval. In: Proceedings of the 24th ACM International Conference on Multimedia, pp. 32–41 (2016)

12. Chen, X., Zhou, H., Zhu, Y., Diao, L.: ChineseFoodNet: a large-scale image dataset for Chinese food recognition. arXiv preprint arXiv:1705.02743 (2017)

13. Ciocca, G., Napoletano, P., Schettini, R.: Food recognition: a new dataset, experiments, and results. IEEE J. Biomed. Health Inform. **21**(3), 588–598 (2016)

14. Donadello, I., Dragoni, M.: Ontology-driven food category classification in images. In: Ricci, E., Rota Bulò, S., Snoek, C., Lanz, O., Messelodi, S., Sebe, N. (eds.) ICIAP 2019. LNCS, vol. 11752, pp. 607–617. Springer, Cham (2019). https://doi.org/10.1007/978-3-030-30645-8_55

15. El Khoury, C.F., Karavetian, M., Halfens, R.J., Crutzen, R., Khoja, L., Schols, J.M.: The effects of dietary mobile apps on nutritional outcomes in adults with chronic diseases: a systematic review and meta-analysis. J. Acad. Nutr. Diet. **119**(4), 626–651 (2019)

16. Godasu, R., El-Gayar, O., Sutrave, K.: Multi-stage transfer learning system with light-weight architectures in medical image classification (2020)

17. Grover, A., et al.: Bias correction of learned generative models using likelihood-free importance weighting. In: NIPS, pp. 11058–11070 (2019)

18. Hassannejad, H., Matrella, G., Ciampolini, P., De Munari, I., Mordonini, M., Cagnoni, S.: Food image recognition using very deep convolutional networks. In: Proceedings of the 2nd International Workshop on Multimedia Assisted Dietary Management, pp. 41–49 (2016)

19. He, K., Zhang, X., Ren, S., Sun, J.: Deep residual learning for image recognition. corr abs/1512.03385 (2015)

20. Hinton, G., Vinyals, O., Dean, J.: Distilling the knowledge in a neural network. arXiv preprint arXiv:1503.02531 (2015)

21. Horiguchi, S., Amano, S., Ogawa, M., Aizawa, K.: Personalized classifier for food image recognition. IEEE Trans. Multimedia **20**(10), 2836–2848 (2018)

22. Jiang, L., Qiu, B., Liu, X., Huang, C., Lin, K.: DeepFood: food image analysis and dietary assessment via deep model. IEEE Access **8**, 47477–47489 (2020)

23. Kagaya, H., Aizawa, K., Ogawa, M.: Food detection and recognition using convolutional neural network. In: Proceedings of the 22nd ACM International Conference on Multimedia, pp. 1085–1088 (2014)

24. Kaur, P., Sikka, K., Wang, W., Belongie, S., Divakaran, A.: FoodX-251: a dataset for fine-grained food classification. arXiv preprint arXiv:1907.06167 (2019)

25. Kawano, Y., Yanai, K.: Automatic expansion of a food image dataset leveraging existing categories with domain adaptation. In: Agapito, L., Bronstein, M.M., Rother, C. (eds.) ECCV 2014. LNCS, vol. 8927, pp. 3–17. Springer, Cham (2015). https://doi.org/10.1007/978-3-319-16199-0_1

26. Kimura, M., Izawa, R.: Density fixing: simple yet effective regularization method based on the class prior. arXiv preprint arXiv:2007.03899 (2020)

27. Lee, K.H., He, X., Zhang, L., Yang, L.: CleanNet: transfer learning for scalable image classifier training with label noise. In: CVPR, pp. 5447–5456 (2018)

28. Liu, C., Cao, Yu., Luo, Y., Chen, G., Vokkarane, V., Ma, Y.: DeepFood: deep learning-based food image recognition for computer-aided dietary assessment. In: Chang, C.K., Chiari, L., Cao, Yu., Jin, H., Mokhtari, M., Aloulou, H. (eds.) ICOST 2016. LNCS, vol. 9677, pp. 37–48. Springer, Cham (2016). https://doi.org/10.1007/978-3-319-39601-9_4

29. MacKay, D.J., Mac Kay, D.J.: Information Theory, Inference and Learning Algorithms. Cambridge University Press, Cambridge (2003)

30. Malinin, A., Gales, M.: Predictive uncertainty estimation via prior networks. In: Advances in Neural Information Processing Systems, pp. 7047–7058 (2018)

31. Martinel, N., Foresti, G.L., Micheloni, C.: Wide-slice residual networks for food recognition. In: 2018 IEEE WACV, pp. 567–576. IEEE (2018)

32. Matsuda, Y., Yanai, K.: Multiple-food recognition considering co-occurrence employing manifold ranking. In: Proceedings of the 21st International Conference on Pattern Recognition (ICPR 2012), pp. 2017–2020. IEEE (2012)

33. Meyers, A., et al.: Im2Calories: towards an automated mobile vision food diary. In: ICCV, pp. 1233–1241 (2015)

34. Mezgec, S., Seljak, B.K.: Using deep learning for food and beverage image recognition. In: 2019 IEEE International Conference on Big Data (Big Data), pp. 5149–5151. IEEE (2019)

35. Miasnikov, E., Savchenko, A.: Detection and recognition of food in photo galleries for analysis of user preferences. In: Campilho, A., Karray, F., Wang, Z. (eds.) ICIAR 2020. LNCS, vol. 12131, pp. 83–94. Springer, Cham (2020). https://doi.org/10.1007/978-3-030-50347-5_9

36. Min, W., Jiang, S., Liu, L., Rui, Y., Jain, R.: A survey on food computing. ACM Comput. Surv. (CSUR) 52(5), 1–36 (2019)

37. Min, W., Liu, L., Luo, Z., Jiang, S.: Ingredient-guided cascaded multi-a ention network for food recognition (2019)

38. Min, W., et al.: ISIA Food-500: a dataset for large-scale food recognition via stacked global-local attention network. arXiv preprint arXiv:2008.05655 (2020)

39. Ming, Z.-Y., Chen, J., Cao, Yu., Forde, C., Ngo, C.-W., Chua, T.S.: Food photo recognition for dietary tracking: system and experiment. In: Schoeffmann, K., et al. (eds.) MMM 2018. LNCS, vol. 10705, pp. 129–141. Springer, Cham (2018). https://doi.org/10.1007/978-3-319-73600-6_12

40. Nag, N., Pandey, V., Jain, R.: Health multimedia: lifestyle recommendations based on diverse observations. In: Proceedings of the 2017 ACM on International Conference on Multimedia Retrieval, pp. 99–106 (2017)

41. Ng, H.W., Nguyen, V.D., Vonikakis, V., Winkler, S.: Deep learning for emotion recognition on small datasets using transfer learning. In: Proceedings of the 2015 ACM on International Conference on Multimodal Interaction, pp. 443–449 (2015)

42. Oka, R., et al.: Study protocol for the effects of artificial intelligence (AI)-supported automated nutritional intervention on glycemic control in patients with type 2 diabetes mellitus. Diabetes Ther. 10(3), 1151–1161 (2019)

43. World Health Organization, et al.: Healthy diet. Technical report, World Health Organization. Regional Office for the Eastern Mediterranean (2019)
44. Pan, S.J., Yang, Q.: A survey on transfer learning. IEEE Trans. Knowl. Data Eng. **22**(10), 1345–1359 (2009)
45. Pandey, P., Deepthi, A., Mandal, B., Puhan, N.B.: FoodNet: recognizing foods using ensemble of deep networks. IEEE Sig. Process. Lett. **24**(12), 1758–1762 (2017)
46. Peng, Z., Zhang, W., Han, N., Fang, X., Kang, P., Teng, L.: Active transfer learning. IEEE Trans. Circ. Syst. Video Tech. **30**(4), 1022–1036 (2019)
47. Sakai, T., Shimizu, N.: Covariate shift adaptation on learning from positive and unlabeled data. In: Proceedings of the AAAI Conference on Artificial Intelligence, vol. 33, pp. 4838–4845 (2019)
48. Selamat, N.A., Ali, S.H.M.: Automatic food intake monitoring based on chewing activity: a survey. IEEE Access **8**, 48846–48869 (2020)
49. Joachims, T.: Text categorization with support vector machines: learning with many relevant features. In: Nédellec, C., Rouveirol, C. (eds.) ECML 1998. LNCS, vol. 1398, pp. 137–142. Springer, Heidelberg (1998). https://doi.org/10.1007/BFb0026683
50. Shimoda, W., Yanai, K.: Foodness proposal for multiple food detection by training of single food images. In: Proceedings of the 2nd International Workshop on Multimedia Assisted Dietary Management, pp. 13–21 (2016)
51. Stojanov, P., Gong, M., Carbonell, J.G., Zhang, K.: Low-dimensional density ratio estimation for covariate shift correction. In: Proceedings of Machine Learning Research, vol. 89, p. 3449 (2019)
52. Szegedy, C., Ioffe, S., Vanhoucke, V., Alemi, A.A.: Inception-v4, inception-ResNet and the impact of residual connections on learning. In: Thirty-First AAAI Conference on Artificial Intelligence (2017)
53. Tahir, G.A., Loo, C.K.: An open-ended continual learning for food recognition using class incremental extreme learning machines. IEEE Access **8**, 82328–82346 (2020)
54. Tan, C., Sun, F., Kong, T., Zhang, W., Yang, C., Liu, C.: A survey on deep transfer learning. In: Kůrková, V., Manolopoulos, Y., Hammer, B., Iliadis, L., Maglogiannis, I. (eds.) ICANN 2018. LNCS, vol. 11141, pp. 270–279. Springer, Cham (2018). https://doi.org/10.1007/978-3-030-01424-7_27
55. Tanno, R., Okamoto, K., Yanai, K.: DeepFoodCam: a DCNN-based real-time mobile food recognition system. In: Proceedings of the 2nd International Workshop on Multimedia Assisted Dietary Management, pp. 89–89 (2016)
56. Tasci, E.: Voting combinations-based ensemble of fine-tuned convolutional neural networks for food image recognition. Multimed. Tools Appl. **79**, 30397–30418 (2020). https://doi.org/10.1007/s11042-020-09486-1
57. Torrey, L., Shavlik, J.: Transfer learning. In: Handbook of Research on Machine Learning Applications and Trends: Algorithms, Methods, and Techniques, pp. 242–264. IGI Global (2010)
58. Wang, M., Deng, W.: Deep visual domain adaptation: a survey. Neurocomputing **312**, 135–153 (2018)
59. Wang, X., Li, L., Ye, W., Long, M., Wang, J.: Transferable attention for domain adaptation. In: Proceedings of the AAAI Conference on Artificial Intelligence, vol. 33, pp. 5345–5352 (2019)
60. Wang, Y., Chen, J.J., Ngo, C.W., Chua, T.S., Zuo, W., Ming, Z.: Mixed dish recognition through multi-label learning. In: Proceedings of the 11th Workshop on Multimedia for Cooking and Eating Activities, pp. 1–8 (2019)

61. Wang, Y., Chen, J.J., Ngo, C.W., Chua, T.S., Zuo, W., Ming, Z.: Mixed dish recognition through multi-label learning. In: Proceedings of the 11th Workshop on Multimedia for Cooking and Eating Activities, CEA 2019, p. 1–8. Association for Computing Machinery, New York (2019)
62. Wang, Z., Dai, Z., Póczos, B., Carbonell, J.: Characterizing and avoiding negative transfer. In: CVPR, pp. 11293–11302 (2019)
63. Wu, H., Merler, M., Uceda-Sosa, R., Smith, J.R.: Learning to make better mistakes: semantics-aware visual food recognition. In: Proceedings of the 24th ACM International Conference on Multimedia, pp. 172–176 (2016)
64. Wu, J., Huang, Z., Thoma, J., Acharya, D., Van Gool, L.: Wasserstein divergence for GANs. In: Proceedings of ECCV, pp. 653–668 (2018)
65. Yanai, K., Kawano, Y.: Food image recognition using deep convolutional network with pre-training and fine-tuning. In: 2015 IEEE ICMEW, pp. 1–6. IEEE (2015)
66. Zhang, Y., Parker, A.G.: Eat4Thought: a design of food journaling. In: Extended Abstracts of the 2020 CHI Conference on Human Factors in Computing Systems, pp. 1–8 (2020)
67. Zhao, H., Yap, K.H., Kot, A.C., Duan, L.: JDNet: a joint-learning distilled network for mobile visual food recognition. IEEE J. Sel. Top. Sig. Process. **14**(4), 665–675 (2020)
68. Zhou, B., Khosla, A., Lapedriza, A., Oliva, A., Torralba, A.: Learning deep features for discriminative localization. In: CVPR, pp. 2921–2929 (2016)

UEC-FoodPix Complete: A Large-Scale Food Image Segmentation Dataset

Kaimu Okamoto and Keiji Yanai[✉]

The University of Electro-Communications,
Tokyo 1-5-1 Chofugaoka, Chofu-shi, Tokyo 182-8585, Japan
{okamoto-ka,yanai}@mm.inf.uec.ac.jp

Abstract. Currently, many segmentation image datasets are open to the public. However, only a few open segmentation image dataset of food images exists. Among them, UEC-FoodPix is a large-scale food image segmentation dataset which consists of 10,000 food images with segmentation masks. However, it contains some incomplete mask images, because most of the segmentation masks were generated automatically based on the bounding boxes. To enable accurate food segmentation, complete segmentation masks are required for training. Therefore, in this work, we created "UEC-FoodPix Complete" by refining the 9,000 segmentation masks by hand which were automatically generated in the previous UEC-FoodPix. As a result, the segmentation performance was much improved compared to the segmentation model trained with the original UEC-FoodPix. In addition, as applications of the new food segmentation dataset, we performed food calorie estimation using the food segmentation models trained with "UEC-FoodPix Complete", and food image synthesis from segmentation masks.

Keywords: Semantic segmentation · Food image · Calorie estimation · Food image synthesis

1 Introduction

Nowadays the accuracy of image recognition has dramatically improved due to the development of deep learning, and excellent results have been achieved in various tasks such as image generation and semantic region segmentation. In supervised semantic segmentation by deep learning, a large-scale mask image dataset annotated for each pixel is required for training of segmentation models. PASCAL VOC 2012 [9] and MS COCO [13] are widely used as large-scale segmentation datasets, in which the annotated objects are generic objects such as animals and vehicles. MS COCO includes only a limited number of food categories.

Although there exists many food image datasets such as Food-101 [3] and VIREOFood-172 [4], most of them have only food category labels on each of the images. A few datasets have bounding box annotation or segmentation

ⓒ Springer Nature Switzerland AG 2021
A. Del Bimbo et al. (Eds.): ICPR 2020 Workshops, LNCS 12665, pp. 647–659, 2021.
https://doi.org/10.1007/978-3-030-68821-9_51

mask annotation. For example, UECFood-100 [15] has bounding box annotation for each of all the dishes. As a dataset annotated on segmentation masks, UEC-FoodPix [8] has been created by adding segmentation mask annotation to 10,000 images of UECFood-100 by Ege et al. However, UEC-FoodPix has the problem that it contains incomplete segmenation masks because they are semi-automatically annotated by GrabCut [20] based on the bounding boxes annotated in the UECFood-100 dataset. To enable accurate food segmentation, complete segmentation masks are desirable for training. Therefore, in this paper, we have updated UEC-FoodPix by manually modifying the incomplete segmentation masks. We call the updated food image segmentation dataset as "UEC-FoodPix Complete" (Fig. 1).

By using the new food segmentation dataset, "UEC-FoodPix Complete" for training of the state-of-the-art semantic segmentation model, DeepLabV3+ [5], the segmentation performance was improved by 0.14 mIoU compared to the segmentation model trained with the original UEC-FoodPix. In addition, as applications of the new food segmentation dataset, we performed region-based food calorie estimation using the food segmentation models trained with "UEC-FoodPix Complete", and food image synthesis from segmentation masks employing SPADE [18].

Fig. 1. UECFood-100 images overlaid with segmentation masks annotated in "UEC-FoodPix Complete."

2   Related Work

As bechmark datasets for semantic segmentation, PASCAL VOC 2012 [9] and MS COCO [13] are commonly used. PASCAL VOC is the dataset used in the competition held from 2005 to 2012, and the 2012 edition includes 9,993 images of 22 classes including airplanes and bicycles. MS COCO is a dataset provided by Microsoft and includes 330,000 images in 80 classes. Only 10 food classes such as pizza and hot dogs are included in the COCO category. Therefore, it is not suitable as a training dataset for food image segmentation models.

Currently, there are a few large-scale open food image datasets with segmentation masks. The UNIMIB2016 dataset [7] provides food region information as polygons which are equivalent to segmentation masks. However, its scale is not so large (1027 multiple-dish images with 73 food categories), and the food images in UNIMIB2016 are biased and not unconstrained since all the food images were taken at the same canteen.

Lu et al. [14] proposed a food volume estimation method by extending Mask R-CNN [11] which extracts food regions from a given RGB-D image. To train the proposed model, they used the MADiMa17 dataset [1] which consists of 21 food categories with segmentation masks. However, all the images in the MADiMa17 dataset were taken in the laboratory environment which was different from uncontrolled real situations.

Okamoto et al. proposed a region-based food calorie estimation system running on a mobile phone [17]. They employed food image segmentation and estimated food calories based on the size of the reference card and food regions. However, at that time, no food image segmentation dataset on uncontrolled food images is available. Instead of the segmentation method which requires training data, they used GrabCut [20], which was a hand-crafted segmentation method that divides the foreground and background by graph-based reasoning.

To change this situation, Ege et al. created a large-scale food image segmentation dataset, which was called "the UEC-FoodPix dataset" [8]. They added pixel-wise annotation to 10,000 food images included in the UECFood-100 dataset [15]. Regarding 1,000 food images for testing, they added pixel-wise labels by hand, while for the other 9,000 images they created pixel-wise labels automatically by applying GrabCut [20] on each of the bounding boxes originally annotated in the UECFood-100 dataset. Before applying GrabCut, they verified if the bounding box annotations were enough correct one by one, and revised them if needed. In addition, Ege et al. [8] proposed a method to estimate actual size of foods without a reference card for estimating food calorie amounts of uncontrolled food images. To do that, they proposed to estimate actual size of foods in the image by using the size of rice grains as reference objects. Although this methods can be applied to food images containing rice, we can estimate real size of foods and their calories by combining food region segmentation without a reference card with this method.

However, since the UECFoodPix created by Ege et al. [8] generated pixel-wise annotations semi-automatically, it may contain noisy annotations, which is expected to be harmful for training of CNN models. Therefore, in this paper, we improve the UECFoodPix dataset for more accurate food image segmentation.

As the other dataset for unconstrained food images, Google Food-201 [16], SUEC Food Dataset [10], and Food segmentation benchmark [2] have been released so far. Food-201 [16] was created for the Im2Calories project by Google, and released to the public several years after the paper was published. They annotated 201 pixel-level labels to parts of the images in the ETH Food-101 dataset [3] with the help of the crowd-sourcing workers. SUEC Food Dataset [10] was created by GrabCut [20] based on the bounding box annotation of UEC-Food256 [12]. The dataset for segmentation benchmark created by the UMINIB group [2] contains 5,000 segmentation masks for all the images of 50-category Chinese food image dataset [6]. We listed the current public food segmentation datasets on unconstrained food images in Table 1.

Table 1. A list of the public food segmentation datasets on unconstrained food images.

Dataset name	Release	#image	#class	Annotation	Original dataset
Google Food-201 [16]	2017	12,093	208	Crowdworker	ETH Food101 [3]
SUEC Food Dataset [10]	2019	28,897	256	Auto (GrabCut)	UEC-Food256 [12]
Food segmentation benchmark [2]	2020	5,000	50	Controlled	Chinese food 50 categories [6]
UEC-FoodPix [8]	2020	10,000	102	Auto (GrabCut)	UEC-Food100 [15]
UEC-FoodPix Complete (this paper)	2021	10,000	102	Controlled	UEC-Food100 [15]

3   Dataset Construction

Currently, many meal image datasets are open to the public, such as Food-101 [3], VIREO Food-172 [4], UECFood-100 [15] and UECFood-256 [12], for food image classification. They are commonly used as standard benchmark datasets. Only a few, such as UECFood-100/256, have bounding box annotations on food regions in all the images.

As a large-scale food image dataset with a segmentation mask, UEC-FoodPix [8] created by Ege et al. exists. However, the UEC-FoodPix dataset contains some incomplete segmentation masks on the boundaries of the food regions, since they were generated automatically from the bounding box annotations. Therefore, in this study, we created "**UECFoodPix Complete**" as a higher quality dietary image segmentation dataset by updating UECFoodPix manually.

We used the Web-based pixel-wise annotation tool implemented by Pongsate et al. [22]. This tool allows easy synthesis and separation of food regions with super-pixels. To make the annotation higher quality and more reliable, we did not used crowd-sourcing, instead he shared the jobs among the lab members and hired a limited number of bachelor students. To keep annotation quality, we set annotation rules on how to create food region masks for each of the food categories. After working with several people, the first author himself made the final confirmation of all of the food region masks of 10,000 images to keep annotation consistency in the dataset. The working period took about 4 months.

We show some examples modification on food region masks between UEC-FoodPix and UEC-FoodPix Complete in Fig. 2. In the first row of the figure, in UEC-FoodPix (show in the second column) the region of "salad" was annotated as a "pork cutlet" region. We divides them into "salad" and "pork cutlet" regions in UEC-FoodPix Complete (showin in the third column). In the second rows, the "corn soup" region was incorrect in UEC-FoodPix, since its boundary is not circular. We revised it in UEC-FoodPix Complete.

4 Evaluation

The updated food image segmentation dataset is entitled "UEC-FoodPix Complete," and consists of 9000 training images and 1000 validation/testing images. We trained the state-of-the-art semantic segmentation method, DeepLab V3+ [5], to compare the model performance trained with the original UEC-FoodPix and the updated UEC-FoodPix Complete. In addition, we trained the DeepLab V3+ model with 2,000 UEC-FoodPix Complete images and 7,000 UEC-FoodPix images together as well. We evaluated both trained models with accuracy and mean Intersection over Union (mIoU).

The experimental results are shown in Table 2. The evaluation scores were improved by about 0.1 in Accuracy and about 0.14 in mIoU. In case of using 2,000 Complete images, the improvement was very limited. In fact, it was one of the reasons why we decided to update annotation on all the images. Figure 3 shows some segmentation results by both the UEC-FoodPix model. The results by the Complete model (shown in the fourth column) are similar to the groundtruth (shown in the second column), while the results by the original UEC-FoodPix were apparently irrelevant except for the first row.

Table 2. The accuracy and mean IoU scores on the three food segmentation models.

Training dataset	Acc	mIoU
UEC-FoodPix (all automatic)	0.560	0.416
Partial UEC-FoodPix Complete (2000 hand annotation)	0.597	0.436
UEC-FoodPix Complete (all 9000 hand annotation)	0.668	0.555

5 Application 1: Region-Based Food Calorie Estimation

In this section, as one of the applications of UEC-FoodPix Complete, we explain the results applying region-based food calorie estimation method using rice grain as reference objects proposed by Ege et al. [8], and compare the results between the cases of using both segmentation models.

Fig. 2. The differences on segmentation masks in the both datasets. (1st column: food images image, 2nd column: the corresponding segmentation masks in the orginal UEC-FoodPix, 3rd column: the corresponding segmentation masks in the renewed UEC-FoodPix Complete.)

5.1   Method

As a utilization of the created dataset, food calorie amounts are estimated from the estimated food regions. In order to estimate the calorie amounts in consideration of the area of dishes, calorie values are estimated from the regression equation after estimating the dish category, extracting the food region, and estimating the actual size of the food region based on rice grains. The procedure is as follows, following Ege et al. [8].

1. Detect food bounding box using Faster-RCNN [19] from an input image.
2. Estimate food regions by using Deeplab V3+ [5] in the bounding box.

Fig. 3. Segmentation results by Deeplab V3+. (1st column: input images, 2nd column: groundtruth region masks, 3rd column: estimated masks by the model trained with "UECFoodPix," 4th column: results by the model trained with "UEC-FoodPix-COMPLETE.")

3. Estimate the area of each of the detected food items by using the rice grain based system from the estimated food region of the cooked rice portion.
4. Estimate the calorie by using the calorie/area-regression formula created in advance for the estimated region.

5.2 Experimental Results

First, a comparison was made up to area estimation. 51 images containing both actual rice and a reference card were used in the experiments. Since the actual size of the reference car is known, the actual size of the food region was annotated.

Table 3. Evaluation on region-based food calorie estimation.

	area(rice)		area(multiple food)	
Dataset	abs.err(cm^2)	rel.err(%)	abs.err(cm^2)	rel.err(%)
UECFoodPix [8]	7.21	8.73	**30.0**	**14.2**
COMPLETE	**3.03**	**3.67**	44.7	20.7

The evaluation was performed by both absolute and relative errors, and was performed only on images in which food was correctly detected. The experimental results are shown in Table 3 and in Fig. 4. As a result, when comparing the areas using only rice, the accuracy was improved by $4.18\,cm^2$ in absolute error and 5.06% in relative error. In addition, from Fig. 4, it was found that when UECFoodPix was used, accurate area estimation was not possible for some testing images, since the model failed to detect the region of streamed rice correctly. However, when comparing multiple dishes, both absolute and relative errors of the original UEC-FoodPix were lower. This is because the actual size estimation part has a greater influence on the area size estimation than the region estimation part. When the cooked rice mask estimated by Deeplab V3+[5] trained by UECFoodPix was used for the actual size estimation, it tended to estimate larger regions than actual food regions. Therefore, even if the other meal area than rice is somewhat lacking, a value close to the correct answer value is calculated. Therefore, it is necessary to improve the accuracy by improving the actual size estimation part.

Next, we estimated the calorie amounts from the size of food items and calorie density per unit size in the same way as Ege et al. [8]. The images were similarly performed using a reference card, and were estimated with the food regions estimated by the segmentation model trained with UEC-FoodPix Complete. The result is shown in Fig. 5. Since the values close to the actual calories were calculated, it was shown that it can be fully utilized for application to calorie content estimation.

6   Application 2: Mask-Based Image Synthesis

As the second application of "UEC-FoodPix Complete," we performed mask-based image synthesis employing the state-of-the-art mask-based image generation method, SPADE [18]. SPADE is a GAN-based model for generating images from mask images, which spatially adapts the scaling and bias terms based on the given mask to reflect the semantic information effectively. Training of the SPADE model was performed using 9000 trained images and 1000 validation/test images.

Figure 6 shows the synthesized images in which the first and third rows represent input region mask images and the second and fourth rows represent the corresponding generated images. Rice bowls, noodles, and Japanese combo meals which look realistic were successfully generated. Interestingly, dish plates

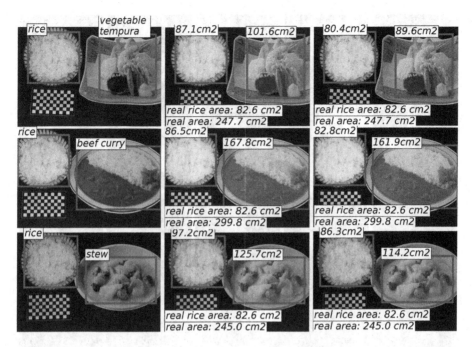

Fig. 4. Estimated results on the area size. (left: input images with food category labels, center: estimated results by "UECFoodPix," right: estimated results by "UEC-FoodPix Complete.")

Fig. 5. The estimated result of food calorie amounts. (All the results were estimated from the segmentation masks produced by the segmentation model trained with "UEC-FoodPix Complete.")

were generated around food regions naturally, although no region masks on plates were given. That is why distorted plates or bowls were sometimes generated like the images on 4th rows and 3th and 4th columns. In the case on 4th rows and 3rd column which was a tempura rice bowl, the generated bowl were deformed along the shrimp tempura, although the shrimp tempura is expected to stick out of the bowl. To solve this problem, pixel-wise plate region annotation is needed. In the case on 4th rows and 4th column which represents bread rolls, two pieces of bread rolls were concatenated, since input masks cannot represents multiple different instances of the same food category.

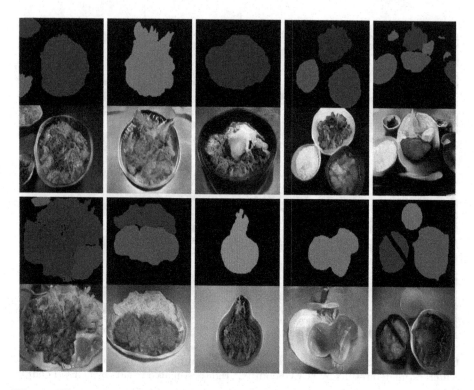

Fig. 6. The results of mask-based food image synthesis. (1st and 3rd rows:0mask images, 2nd and 3rd rows: generated images by SPADE)

In the next experiments, we synthesized food images from the same mask images with different class labels. Figure 7 shows the results. In the second row, we generated a beef rice bowl, a chicken rice bowl, a chilled ramen noodle, and a ramen noodle from the same mask input. In the third row, we generated four multiple dish food images by changing only one dish on the left-bottom with the same food categories as the second row. In the fifth row, we generated multiple dish images as well by changing two dishes at the same time on the dishes on the left-bottom and middle-top. We confirmed that mask-based food image synthesis worked well even for multiple dish food images, although the shape of plates and bowls sometime were distorted and look unnatural.

Overall, we found that food image synthesis from region masks was possible. However, since our dataset, "UEC-FoodPix Complete" has no pixel-wise annotation on plate regions, we cannot control the shape of plates which are usually generated around food regions. Therefore, distorted plates tend to be generated, which made the synthesized images look unnatural. For future work, we think we need to add pixel-wise plate region annotation to the dataset for more natural food image synthesis. We plan to obtain plate annotation employing the unsupervised plate region estimation method [21] for the time being.

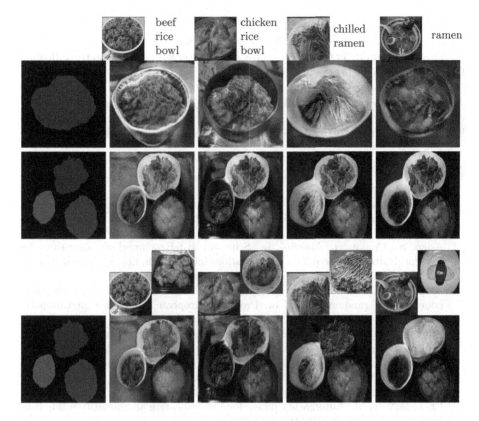

Fig. 7. Food image synthesis from the same region masks with different food category labels. (1st and 4th rows: class label images. 2nd row: single dish images. 3rd and 5th rows: multiple dish images.)

7   Conclusions

In this study, we created a new dataset, "UEC-FoodPix Complete," by updating the existing the food image segmentation dataset, "UEC-FoodPix [8]." We evaluated improvement on food semantic segmentation with the state-of-the-art segmentation model, DeepLabV3+ [5]. As a result of segmentation using the updated dataset, mean IoU was improved by 0.14 compared to the original dataset. In addition, as applications of the new food segmentation dataset, we performed region-based food calorie estimation using the food segmentation models trained with "UEC-FoodPix Complete" and food image synthesis from segmentation masks employing SPADE [18].

In fact, our motivation on updating the UEC-FoodPix dataset is to estimate food calories more accurately. Therefore, we like to improve region-based food calorie estimation. Our future works include improving the accuracy of actual size estimation using cooked rice, improving the regression equation to a more robust estimation, and dealing with images that do not contain cooked rice. In addition, as further development, we plan to introduce CNN-based architecture for the part of the calorie amount estimation as well.

The "UEC-FoodPix Complete" dataset can be downloaded from the following URL: http://mm.cs.uec.ac.jp/uecfoodpix/.

Acknowledgments. We would like to thank all those who worked on pixel-wise annotation for creating "UEC-FoodPix Complete." This work was supported by JSPS KAKENHI Grant Number 17J10261, 15H05915, 17H01745, and 19H04929.

References

1. Allegra, D., et al.: A multimedia database for automatic meal assessment systems. In: Proceedings of the ICIAP Workshop on Multimedia Assisted Dietary Management (2017)
2. Aslan, S., Ciocca, G., Mazzini, D., Schettini, R.: Benchmarking algorithms for food localization and semantic segmentation. Int. J. Mach. Learn. Cybern. **11**(12), 2827–2847 (2020). https://doi.org/10.1007/s13042-020-01153-z
3. Bossard, L., Guillaumin, M., Van Gool, L.: Food-101 - mining discriminative components with random forests. In: Proc. of European Conference on Computer Vision (2014)
4. Chen, J., Ngo, C.W.: Deep-based ingredient recognition for cooking recipe retrieval. In: Proceedings of ACM International Conference Multimedia (2016)
5. Chen, L., Zhu, Y., Papandreou, G., Schroff, F., Adam, H.: Encoder-decoder with atrous separable convolution for semantic image segmentation. In: Proceedings of European Conference on Computer Vision (2018)
6. Chen, M.Y., et al.: Automatic Chinese food identification and quantity estimation. In: Proceedings of SIGGRAPH Asia (2012)
7. Ciocca, G., Napoletano, P., Schettini, R.: Food recognition: a new dataset, experiments and results. IEEE J. Biomed. Health Informat. **21**(3), 588–598 (2017)
8. Ege, T., Yanai, K.: A new large-scale food image segmentation dataset and its application to food calorie estimation based on grains of rice. In: Proceedings of ACM MM Workshop on Multimedia Assisted Dietary Management (2019)
9. Everingham, M., Eslami, S., Van Gool, L., Williams, C., Winn, J., Zisserman, A.: The pascal visual object classes challenge: a retrospective. Int. J. Comput. Vision **88**(2) (2010)
10. Gao, J., Tan, W., Ma, L., Wang, Y., Tang, W.: MUSEFood: multi-sensor-based food volume estimation on smartphones. arXiv:1903.07437 (2019)
11. He, K., Gkioxari, G., Dollar, P., Girshick, R.: Mask R-CNN. In: Proceedings of IEEE International Conference on Computer Vision (2017)
12. Kawano, Y., Yanai, K.: Automatic expansion of a food image dataset leveraging existing categories with domain adaptation. In: Proc. of ECCV Workshop on Transferring and Adapting Source Knowledge in Computer Vision (TASK-CV) (2014)
13. Lin, T., et al.: Microsoft coco: common objects in context. In: Proceedings of European Conference on Computer Vision (2014)
14. Lu, Y., Allegra, D., Anthimopoulos, M., Stanco, F., Farinella, G.M., Mougiakakou, S.: A multi-task learning approach for meal assessment. In: Proceedings of the IJCAI Joint Workshop on Multimedia for Cooking and Eating Activities and Multimedia Assisted Dietary Management, pp. 46–52 (2018)

15. Matsuda, Y., Hajime, H., Yanai, K.: Recognition of multiple-food images by detecting candidate regions. In: Proceedings of IEEE International Conference on Multimedia and Expo, pp. 25–30 (2012)
16. Myers, A., et al.: Im2Calories: towards an automated mobile vision food diary. In: Proceedings of IEEE International Conference on Computer Vision, pp. 1233–1241 (2015)
17. Okamoto, K., Yanai, K.: An automatic calorie estimation system of food images on a smartphone. In: Proceedings of ACM MM Workshop on Multimedia Assisted Dietary Management (2016)
18. Park, T., Liu, M., Zhu, J.: Semantic image synthesis with spatially-adaptive normalization. In: Proceedings of IEEE Computer Vision and Pattern Recognition (2019)
19. Ren, S., He, K., Girshick, R., Sun, J.: Faster R-CNN:towards real-time object detection with region proposal networks. IEEE Trans. Pattern Anal. Mach. Intell. **39**(6), 1137–1149 (2017)
20. Rother, C., Kolmogorov, V., Blake, A.: "GrabCut": interactive foreground extraction using iterated graph cuts. ACM Trans. Graph. **23**(3), 309–314 (2004)
21. Shimoda, W., Yanai, K.: Predicting plate regions for weakly-supervised food image segmentation. In: Proceedings of IEEE International Conference on Multimedia and Expo (2020)
22. Tangseng, P., Wu, Z., Yamaguchi, K.: Looking at outfit to parse clothing. arXiv:1703.01386 (2017)

Event Mining Driven Context-Aware Personal Food Preference Modelling

Vaibhav Pandey$^{(\boxtimes)}$, Ali Rostami$^{(\boxtimes)}$, Nitish Nag, and Ramesh Jain

University of California, Irvine, CA, USA
vaibhap1@uci.edu

Abstract. A personal food model (PFM) is essential for high-quality food recommendation systems to enhance health and enjoyment. We can build such models using food logging platforms that capture the users' food events. As proposed in the Westermann and Jain event model, capturing six facets of multi-modal data provides a holistic view of any event. Five of these facets are captured during the event (temporal, structural, informational, experiential, spatial), while the sixth facet is related to the *causality* of the event. This causal facet is needed to build a robust PFM if all the other relevant information in the aforementioned five facets are captured. Any food logger and subsequent processing should collect all this data in the food event. Ultimately, we want to know what caused this person to eat this food and what changes this food event causes in the person's health state. In this paper, we identify details of the food event model that may help build a causal understanding in PFM to address the first aspect of the causality, what may be the contextual factors that cause a certain food event to occur for a user. We utilize an event mining approach to determine the causal relationships to build a contextual understanding of the PFM. We generate data using a food event simulator that can generate needed food event data for a person with known PFM. The event mining results uncover this hidden PFM and demonstrate the greater efficacy of this approach than a traditionally designed PFM.

Keywords: Food computing · Personal Health Navigation · Health State Estimation · Multimedia

1 Introduction

According to the World Health Organization, Noncommunicable diseases (NCDs) kill 41 million people each year, equivalent to 71% of all deaths globally. Cardiovascular diseases account for most NCD deaths, followed by cancers, respiratory diseases, and diabetes. An unhealthy diet is one of the major causes of NCD deaths. Our dietary patterns affect not only our health but also have a huge impact on our environment and economy (Fig. 1). The food and meat industry is one of the largest contributors to green house gas emissions [12]. Clearly, there are multiple stakeholders in the food ecosystem and eventually, computational systems should strive to improve our understanding of each of these layers and

© Springer Nature Switzerland AG 2021
A. Del Bimbo et al. (Eds.): ICPR 2020 Workshops, LNCS 12665, pp. 660–676, 2021.
https://doi.org/10.1007/978-3-030-68821-9_52

devise more efficient operational paradigms that minimize resource and food waste while maximizing health and enjoyment.

Food serves many functions at an individual level. It provides us with the energy and building blocks to sustain our lives while also serving as a source of personal fulfillment and social glue. Our taste and sensory preferences are a significant causal factor behind our food decisions and affect our health. For this reason, there is a rapidly growing need for personalized food services that guide users towards a healthier lifestyle while also ensuring the food's enjoyment. With the advancement of technology, especially in the recommendation and sensing fields, it is possible to guide users towards a healthier lifestyle by understanding their underlying taste profile and their daily lifestyles to provide healthier recommendations that still appeal to the user's tastes [22]. Food is an essential part of our lives, and advancements in applications such as food logging platforms and recipe recommendations can help us identify and improve our eating behavior.

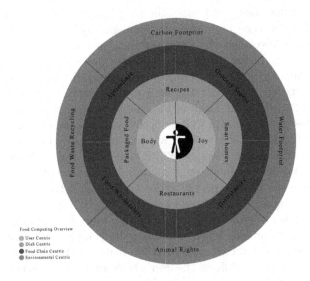

Fig. 1. Personal food computing overview and relevant proposed layers.

At the heart of these personalized food services lies the Personal Food Model [34]. As shown in Fig. 1, it (PFM) has two main components: 1) the biological component and 2) the preferential component. The biological component determines how different food items interact with our biology and health [20,23]. In contrast, the preferential component captures how different contextual and environmental factors impact our food preferences and, in turn, affect our choices. There has been a lot of work done on context-aware preference modeling and recommendations. However, the current approaches are still far from truly personalizing these recommendations. Especially for health and food-related applications, the contextual factors can be captured by different multi-modal devices and applications. Typically, these applications store individual data in their silos, which do not interact with other applications. We propose a comprehensive food event model that could provide a mechanism for these applications to cross-utilize each other's data. We also demonstrate how we could utilize the data collected using such applications to create a user preference model and how it varies with different contextual factors such as stress and temperature. We use event mining principles to model the contextual relationships in an unsupervised manner.

2   Related Research

We first take a look at current food models and services. Diet and chronic diseases are closely correlated [40]. A Western diet characterized by a high intake of energy-dense and processed food is a risk factor for many chronic diseases, including diabetes, obesity, and cardiovascular diseases [39]. A significant hurdle towards maintaining a healthy diet is the draw towards pleasure (rather than health) from eating. Tasty and palatable food is often linked to chronic health risks. According to some interesting experiments by [31], the more unhealthy dish items are perceived to have better taste and are enjoyed more during actual consumption. Thus, future meals have a greater preference for it, especially for tasks when a hedonic goal is more salient. However, this is not necessarily true. Many other instances show that a healthy option can be tasty. A good example is discussed in [3], where the result of the study shows that not only organic food has a great positive impact on well-being but can also be pleasurable. Furthermore, the Mediterranean diet, which appears to be tasty to many, is linked to the prevention of Chronic Diseases [33]. It may seem that delicious foods must be unhealthy and healthy foods must be dull, but this is not the case. Since the taste preference of different people varies considerably based on many factors such as environmental, cultural, and genetics [32], it is impossible to manually come up with a healthy diet that would appear tasty to everyone. People have their personal taste profile, which could be quite complex and changes with the context. Personalized food services need to create the PFM of the user, which understands how the food affects the user's body and the user's taste profile and what kind of food the user enjoys [34]. But there aren't any concrete methods to create the user's taste profile since taste digitization and quantification are challenging. [34] presents a novel US4B taste model as a unified model to capture taste. While this model is very promising, there is still no precise method to obtain the taste value of different food items. That's why most food models and recommendation services completely ignore the pleasure aspect of the food and purely focus on health and nutrition like [1,9,24].

Some other works have recognized preference as an important factor and have tried to create a simple preference model. For example, [16] considers the spiciness of the food as the cue for its taste and as a reference point, which is an interesting improvement. Still, the spiciness alone is not adequate to model the taste profile. [11] proposes a recipe recommendation method based on similar ingredients in the dishes with a high rating from the user. Ingredient-similarity-based methods like [25] are a significant step towards finding healthier options that the user can enjoy. However, they are still limited to replacing one or two ingredients, and the gap to understanding the taste profile of the food remains.

There are many methods for providing foods with suitable nutritional content, as reviewed in [41]. However, food is more than just refueling energy; it is an experience. Therefore it is essential to capture all the aspects of the experience to have enough information to create the personal food model. Different aspects of a food event can change the impact on the body and affect the enjoyment aspect. [2] brings good intuition that stress has a strong correlation with food. Time of eating is also an important factor in how the food affects the body [7]. [34] uses food events to capture many different aspects of a meal such as location, time, and amount, but a standard food event model doesn't exist. The causal aspect of events poses an interesting problem as compared to the other aspects [42]. It requires events from other sources as well and finding the causal contextual factors. But the personalized causal aspect of the food events have not been studied to date. Some population studies have explored the causal aspect of specific diets and their relation with age and weight like [17], but these insights do not generalize to every individual.

Some studies have explored the causal aspect modelling in other health related applications such as health state estimation [23] and context-driven nutrition recommendation [22]. The eventual goal of causal aspect modelling, especially for food events, is to enable context-driven health state navigation [21] that would help individuals achieve their health-related goals.

There are multiple statistical techniques available for causal and context-driven modelling. There has been an increase in embedding causal relationships within recommendation systems [6]. We have adopted an event driven approach and utilize event mining [14] for finding causal relationships between different lifestyle events [27]. This approach utilizes principles from Pearl's *do-calculus* [30] and tests for causal relationships in different bins of confounding factors. This approach results in relationships between events, and such insights are inherently interpretable, which is a desirable quality for personal models[38]. This approach would also be able to fully leverage the benefits of a comprehensive event model.

3   Food Event Model

A single food event has multiple facets captured by different applications. The food being eaten, the time of the day, the amount of food, the location type, the ambience, the person eating the food, and other people involved in that event are some examples. If we capture sufficient contextual information about the food event, it will be possible to find what caused the food event. Furthermore, collecting information about the body's response to the food event opens the door to understanding the biological responses to the food event. Inspired by the multimedia event model described by Westermann and Jain [42], we propose a unified food event model that contains all the factors defining the food event, as shown in Fig. 2. The food event model consists of 6 main aspects: **spatial, experiential, informational, structural, temporal** and **causal** aspect. Each of these

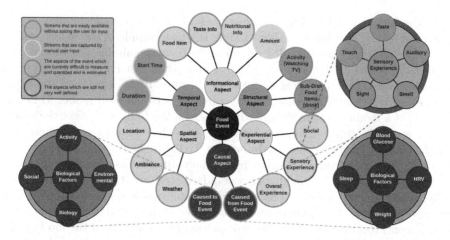

Fig. 2. Food Event Model: It is essential to capture all the different aspects that a food event contains in order to build powerful models. The causal aspect of a food event is especially challenging to capture. In the bottom right and left corners, we see prior events that cause food events to occur on the bottom left (such as a user's taste model), and we see what future events the food event is responsible for affecting (such as a user's health).

aspects has sub-components, as illustrated in Fig. 2. Some of these aspects have been studied extensively and are widely captured, such as location and time. We can capture the biological aspects in free-living conditions thanks to the advances in Internet-of-Things (IoT) and wearable technologies such as sleep monitoring [4]. Physiological data-streams such as Electrocardiography (ECG) and Photoplethysmography (PPG) are non-invasive and low-cost techniques and enable continuous health and well-being data collection [15,19]. However, some other sub-components are challenging to collect as they are not understood very well, such as the sensory experience. Auditory and visual information are the only exceptions and are well understood in the multimedia field; however, no such model exists for the sense of taste and smell. The taste information of a food event is crucial for building the preferential side of the personal food model, but to the best of our knowledge, there is currently no method to map food items to ingredients to taste information. In this paper, we propose a novel approach to capture information about the taste experience of a dish driven by the informational aspect discussed in detail in the Experiment Design section.

3.1   The Causal Aspect

Identifying an event's cause(s) is not an easy question to answer even in trivial cases. Numerous factors could affect a food event, such as physical activity, social gathering, weather, or the time of the day. Modeling this aspect of a food event is extremely challenging using current methods; however, it is critical for building a Personal Model. As shown in Fig. 2, the causal aspect has two sub-components: events that caused the food event and events that the food event has caused. Events caused by a food event are mostly reflected in the biological impact of food. This includes changes in heart rate variability, sleep quality, and other effects on the individual's body and health. On the other hand, the events that caused a food event could be more complicated, as external factors could also influence and initiate a food event. These include social events, environmental factors, and weather conditions. Many environmental and biological factors have been known to affect a food event. Some biological factors may be easier to model, for example, age and weight, which are shown to affect the food decision making process [17]. Psychological aspects may be more challenging to measure, like mental stress; however, many studies have shown that it can be measured using wearable devices and even social media usage [36,37]. [2] brings excellent intuition on how stress can have a strong influence on food choice. A food event also depends on environmental factors such as the weather [13]. Complex environmental causal factors are often missed, which can bring substantial help in the context reconstruction. For example, a pandemic, such as the COVID-19, can drastically affect the food habits of populations. [18] shows that for geographical regions with higher numbers of daily COVID-19 cases, the historical trends in search queries related to bars and restaurants are strongly correlated with re-openings happening in those areas. Therefore the environmental knowledge is an essential factor in the causal aspect of the food. In this paper, we picked two important causal factors: stress and weather, to demonstrate how the context can change the user's food preference profile and analyze how they affect the dietary choices, which will be discussed in the following sections.

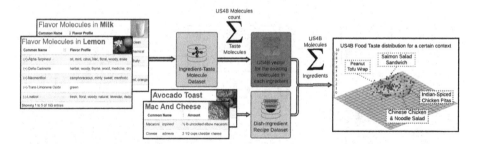

Fig. 3. Taste Space Generation: This figure illustrates our approach to map the food items to a corresponding US4B vector in the taste space using the taste information associated with the present molecules in each ingredient.

4   Food Preference Space: Taste Space

The taste of food items can be very complex. The taste sensory aspect has not been modeled as robustly as the visual and auditory senses, which have standard models such as the RGB color space model. In [34], the authors demonstrated how a unified and robust taste space model is required to create a preferential personal food model. They presented the US4B taste space, which includes six dimensions: umami, salty, sweet, sour, spicy, and bitter. However, that work was the initial step and did not provide any actual taste dataset or concrete approach to build such a dataset. There is currently no available method that could approximate the US4B values of a set of dishes using available resources. We provide a novel approach that uses the taste molecules to estimate a dish's US4B taste space using its ingredients. FlavorDB [10] is the only existing publicly available extensive data set on food taste that contains the list of taste molecules associated with each food item, and a list of taste and smell attributes to each molecule. However, we could not derive the US4B values for dish items directly from flavorDB as there are a few limitations to this data set. This dataset only has the information for ingredients and lacks the information for dish items and recipes. The dataset does not have any information about the intensity of the taste for different molecules. As shown in Fig. 3, we start by counting the taste molecules associated with each element of the US4B taste model and create a taste vector for each ingredient item. Then we use a recipe data set containing a list of ingredient items for each dish and use the calculated US4B vector for ingredients in the previous step to calculate a US4B value for each dish based on adding the taste vectors of the ingredients. The taste values for dishes create the personal food model based on the food items they consume in different situations. We used this approach to create a taste profile of 60 different dishes. We picked 20 dish recipes for each meal type: breakfast, lunch, dinner. Each meal type has ten dishes for a heavy meal option and 10 dishes for a light meal option. This data is fed to a randomized markov-chain event generator, described in the following section, to create a randomized events log, including food events.

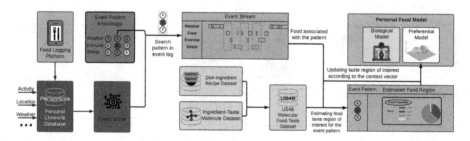

Fig. 4. Causal Preferential Model Architecture: The food logging platform captures the different aspects of the food events. We use event mining to find contextual patterns and build a taste profile for each pattern and update the preferential subsection of the personal food model.

5   Experimental Design

We present a novel food preference model that considers causal factors to estimate the taste preferences in a particular context. The food model captures the user's preferred taste region, which could change with context. Figure 4 illustrates the overall architecture of the preferential food model. Food logger [35] collects information about the food event and stores in the Personicle. The Personicle is a database containing different data streams about the user over a long time in one place[26]. We apply event mining operators on the user's personicle [27,28] to identify contextual factors that impact food preferences. We create event patterns relating different contextual factors with the meal events and find all occurrences of these contextual event patterns in the event streams. This allows us to find food items consumed in different contexts. We can then aggregate the corresponding taste vectors to find the contextual taste preference

We opted to utilize synthesized data for the experiments because we can use the ground truth of contextual factors' impact on taste to validate the model, just like in many other works such as [5]. By using synthesized training data, the dataset size can be significantly increased with little human labor [8]. [29] introduces a system that automatically creates synthetic data to enable data scientists. [29] suggests that synthetic data can successfully replace original data for data science if it meets two requirements: First, it must somewhat resemble the original data statistically to ensure realism and keep problems engaging for data scientists. Second, it must also formally and structurally resemble the original data so that any software written on top of it can be reused.

We designed a rich event stream database, and the occurrences and parameters of these events depend on the contextual factors such as time of the day, temperature, and stress. We use the novel US4B taste estimation method to estimate the taste-related molecules' quantity in a dish as the taste cue for the personal model. We showcase multiple experiments on our rich event stream data set generated using a randomized Markov-chain based event generator.

We created five different lifestyle profiles, which would determine the generated events for five different people over a period of 500 days with approximately three food events a day for a total 7373 food events (Fig. 5). The lifestyle profiles consist of the parameters needed for the Markov-chain model to generate the event streams. These parameters include the probability distribution of each event occurrence based on the previous event, designed to imitate a natural event stream. These events include food events that are controlled by contextual variables such as stress and weather. Research shows that stress correlates with eating more palatable and delicious food [2]. Even though the relationship could be both ways, either overeating or not eating as much depending on the person. We designed the parameters associated with the stress-related causal aspect of a food choice based on the available findings such that if a person had a stressful day, it would impact their food choice towards more palatable foods for some subjects and towards less appetite for others. Accordingly, some of our synthetic subjects have a higher probability of having a stressful day than the others to achieve a greater variety within the dataset. The causal relation of

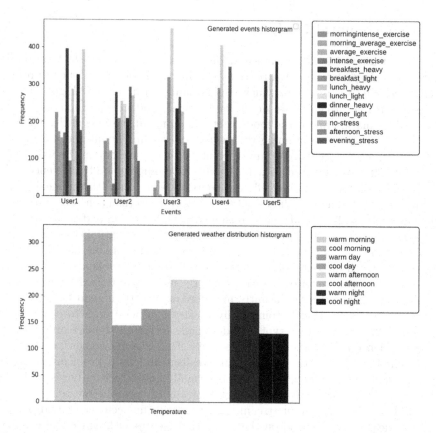

Fig. 5. Dataset Summary: This figure displays a summary of our events dataset. This includes the frequency distribution for the different events that are present in the events log for the five people in our dataset. The event relationships were encoded as probabilistic transitions in a Markov-chain model. Concurrent and past contextual events also affect the parameters of the lifestyle events.

weather context with food choice has also been studied. [13] shows that combining weather context in food profile modeling yields better results. We also have distribution parameters regarding the weather condition and parameters that affect each subject's food choice based on the weather context. We then use event mining operators to find causal relationships between contextual factors and meal events in the generated data. The underlying causal relationships in the synthetic data were hidden from the event mining system and the person doing the analysis.

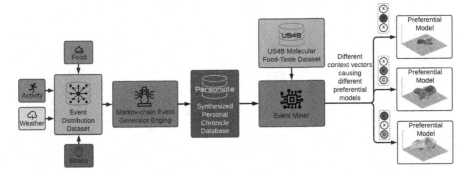

Fig. 6. Experimental Design: This figure illustrates how we perform hypothesis testing using synthetic data. The events dataset contains the list of event types which are to be generated such as food and activity. The events must resemble the real data statistically so the parameters are carefully selected and are fed to the Markov-chain event generator engine to create the synthesized dataset. Then we use event mining to apply our model to the dataset and test its viability in action.

6   Results

We attempted to answer three research questions (RQ) in our experiments:

1. How does the individual taste preference vector change with changes in contextual parameters?
2. How does adding context-awareness change the predictive performance of the preference model?
3. How much data is needed to create a stable model?

6.1   RQ1: Contextual Variation in Taste Profile

Figure 7 shows the variation in the preferred taste profile with different contextual variables for the five individuals in our dataset. We created the individuals' contextual taste profile by averaging the US4B taste vectors for meals consumed in different contextual situations. Thus, every individual has nine contextual preference vectors (3 temperature levels * 3 stress levels) for every meal (breakfast, lunch, and dinner). The contextual preference vectors are compared against the average preference vector for the three meals in the radar-plots in Fig. 7. We have included the radar plots for two users. We can see that **user5** has an increased preference for umami flavored food for dinner when it's cool outside, but that preference goes down with an increase in temperature, and **user1**'s preference for sweet, bitter, and umami flavors during lunch goes down with increase in temperature.

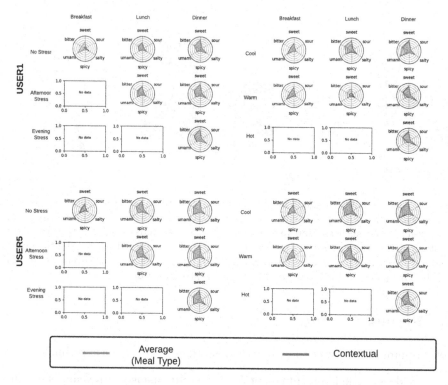

Fig. 7. Variation in taste preferences with context. This figure shows how the preferences for different taste aspects change with context. We can see that for User1, the preference for sweet, bitter, and umami flavors during lunch goes down with increase in temperature.

6.2   RQ2: Comparison of Prediction Performance

We compared the context-aware preference model's predictive performance against the "No-Context" preference model using Top-5 accuracy as our performance measure. We used an 80-20 train-test split while maintaining the chronological order (test set samples were from a period after the training set samples) and report the models' performance on the test set. We used a nearest-neighbor approach to match an individual's preference vector with the available food items using cosine similarity. We predicted the five most likely food items for every meal event in the test set and compared the predictions against the meal event's actual dish.

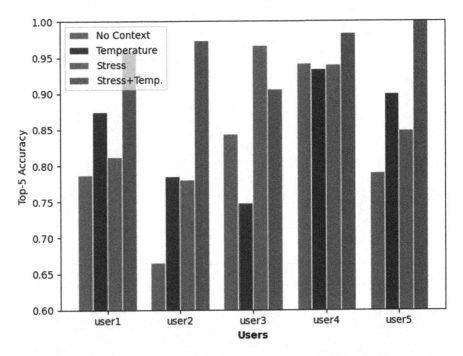

Fig. 8. Model performance using Top-5 predictions accuracy. We can see that for all users adding all contextual factors (Stress+Temperature) leads to a better model than no contextual information.

Figure 8 compares the performance of models with different levels of contextual information. As we expected, adding contextual information leads to a better performance than the "No-Context" model for all five individuals in our dataset.

6.3 RQ3: Model Accuracy with Training Data Volume

We also performed experiments to find how the model accuracy varies with the amount of training data. We used a fixed test set containing events data for 100 days. The training set size was varied on a logarithmic scale from 4 to 400 (with a factor of 2). We used the top-5 accuracy metric, and the results are reported in Fig. 9 for all users. We observe that initially, the non-contextual model outperforms the context-aware model. This could be due to a lack of data in different contextual situations. This explanation is supported by the observation that as the size of the training dataset increases, the context-aware model outperforms the non-contextual model. The accuracy graph starts flattening at 128 days; thus, we believe that we would need to collect about 100 days of events to train and use this model effectively.

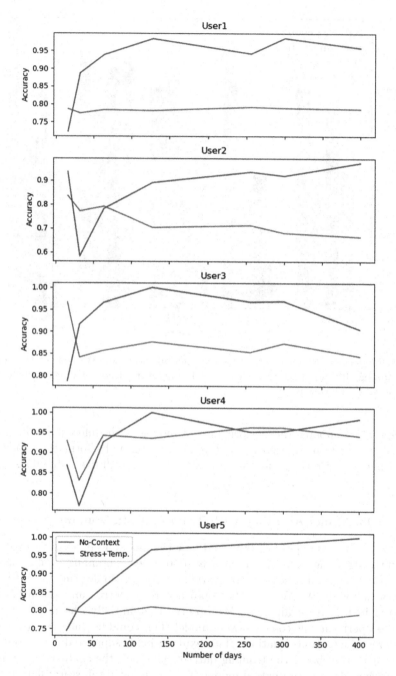

Fig. 9. Model accuracy vs training data volume. The context-aware model appears to stabilize at 128 days as mentioned in Sect. 6.3. As expected, initially the non-contextual model outperforms the context-aware model, but with more training data, the context-aware model has the higher accuracy.

7   Conclusion and Future Work

We presented a novel approach which extends a new door of possibilities in multimedia research. Our dataset is available open-source to help with further investigation of this topic. The results demonstrate the importance of the causal aspect of food events and the estimation of the taste preference model by regarding food as media and more advanced mapping of the food items to the US4B taste space. This observation suggests much stronger future work on the study of the food event's causality by studying more complex factors involved in the causal aspect. Furthermore, studies with rich data streams from real users, including individuals differing in biological status and living-lab environments, will be invaluable to unravel the causal factors that shape food decisions.

References

1. Abhari, S., et al.: A systematic review of nutrition recommendation systems: with focus on technical aspects. J. Biomed. Phys. Eng. **9**(6), 591–602 (2019). https://doi. org/10.31661/jbpe.v0i0.1248, www.ncbi.nlm.nih.gov/pmc/articles/PMC6943843/

2. Adam, T.C., Epel, E.S.: Stress, eating and the reward system. Physiol. Behav. **91**(4), 449–458 (2007). https://doi.org/10.1016/j.physbeh.2007.04.011

3. Apaolaza, V., Hartmann, P., D'Souza, C., López, C.M.: Eat organic - feel good? the relationship between organic food consumption, health concern and subjective wellbeing. Food Qual. Prefer. **63**, 51–62 (2018). https://doi.org/10.1016/j. foodqual.2017.07.011

4. Asgari Mehrabadi, M., et al.: Sleep validation of commercially available smart ring and watch against medical-grade actigraphy in everyday settings (Preprint). JMIR mHealth and uHealth (2020). https://doi.org/10.2196/20465, https://pubmed. ncbi.nlm.nih.gov/33038869/

5. Barnard, K., Cardei, V., Funt, B.: A comparison of computational color constancy algorithms - Part I: methodology and experiments with synthesized data. IEEE Trans. Image Process. **11**(9), 972–984 (2002). https://doi.org/10.1109/TIP.2002. 802531

6. Bonner, S., Vasile, F.: Causal embeddings for recommendation. In: RecSys 2018– 12th ACM Conference on Recommender Systems. Association for Computing Machinery Inc, New York, NY, USA, pp. 104–112 (2018). https://doi.org/10.1145/ 3240323.3240360, https://dl.acm.org/doi/10.1145/3240323.3240360

7. Chaix, A., Manoogian, E.N., Melkani, G.C., Panda, S.: Time-restricted eating to prevent and manage chronic metabolic diseases. Ann. Rev. Nutr. **39**, 291–315 (2019). https://doi.org/10.1146/annurev-nutr-082018-124320, https://doi.org/10. 1146/annurev-nutr-082018-

8. Chen, Q., Qiu, W., Zhang, Y., Xie, L., Yuille, A.: SampleAhead: online classifier-sampler communication for learning from synthesized data. British Machine Vision Conference 2018, BMVC 2018 arXiv preprint arXiv:1804.00248 (2018)

9. Drescher, L.S., Thiele, S., Mensink, G.B.: A new index to measure healthy food diversity better reflects a healthy diet than traditional measures. J. Nutr. **137**(3), 647–651 (2007). 10.1093/jn/137.3.647, https://academic.oup.com/jn/article/137/ 3/647/4664681

10. Garg, N., et al.: FlavorDB: a database of flavor molecules. Nucleic Acids Res. **46**(D1), D1210–D1216 (2018). https://doi.org/10.1093/nar/gkx957, https://pubmed.ncbi.nlm.nih.gov/29059383/

11. Harvey, M., Ludwig, B., Elsweiler, D.: You are what you eat: learning user tastes for rating prediction. In: Kurland, O., Lewenstein, M., Porat, E. (eds.) SPIRE 2013. LNCS, vol. 8214, pp. 153–164. Springer, Cham (2013). https://doi.org/10.1007/978-3-319-02432-5_19

12. Hedenus, F., Wirsenius, S., Johansson, D.J.A.: The importance of reduced meat and dairy consumption for meeting stringent climate change targets. Climatic Change **124**(1), 79–91 (2014). https://doi.org/10.1007/s10584-014-1104-5

13. Ito, T., Fukazawa, Y., Zhu, D., Ota, J.: Modeling weather context dependent food choice process. J. Inf. Process. **26**, 386–395 (2018). https://doi.org/10.2197/ipsjjip.26.386, https://www.jstage.jst.go.jp/article/ipsjjip/26/0/26_386/_article

14. Jalali, L.: Interactive event-driven knowledge discovery from data streams (2016)

15. Kasaeyan Naeini, E., Shahhosseini, S., Subramanian, A., Yin, T., Rahmani, A.M., Dutt, N.: An edge-assisted and smart system for real-time pain monitoring. In: Proceedings - 4th IEEE/ACM Conference on Connected Health: Applications, Systems and Engineering Technologies, CHASE 2019. Institute of Electrical and Electronics Engineers Inc., pp. 47–52 (2019). https://doi.org/10.1109/CHASE48038.2019.00023

16. Li, X., et al.: Application of intelligent recommendation techniques for consumers' food choices in restaurants. Front. Psychiatry **9**, 415 (2018). https://doi.org/10.3389/fpsyt.2018.00415, https://www.frontiersin.org/article/10.3389/fpsyt.2018.00415/full

17. van Meer, F., Charbonnier, L., Smeets, P.A.M.: Food decision-making: effects of weight status and age. Current Diabetes Reports **16**(9), 1–8 (2016). https://doi.org/10.1007/s11892-016-0773-z

18. Mehrabadi, M.A., Dutt, N., Rahmani, A.M.: The causality inference of public interest in restaurants and bars on COVID-19 daily cases in the US: a google trends analysis. http://arxiv.org/abs/2007.13255 (2020)

19. Naeini, E.K., Azimi, I., Rahmani, A.M., Liljeberg, P., Dutt, N.: A real-time PPG quality assessment approach for healthcare Internet-of-Things. In: Procedia Computer Science. vol. 151, pp. 551–558. Elsevier B.V. (2019). https://doi.org/10.1016/j.procs.2019.04.074

20. Nag, N.: Health state estimation. http://arxiv.org/abs/2003.09312 (2020)

21. Nag, N., Jain, R.: A navigational approach to health: actionable guidance for improved quality of life. Computer **52**(4), 12–20 (2019). https://doi.org/10.1109/MC.2018.2883280

22. Nag, N., Pandey, V., Jain, R.: Live personalized nutrition recommendation engine. In: MMHealth 2017 - Proceedings of the 2nd International Workshop on Multimedia for Personal Health and Health Care, co-located with MM 2017. Association for Computing Machinery Inc, New York, New York, USA, pp. 61–68 (2017). https://doi.org/10.1145/3132635.3132643, http://dl.acm.org/citation.cfm?doid=3132635.3132643

23. Nag, N., Pandey, V., Putzel, P.J., Bhimaraju, H., Krishnan, S., Jain, R.: Cross-modal health state estimation. In: MM 2018 - Proceedings of the 2018 ACM Multimedia Conference. Association for Computing Machinery Inc, New York, New York, USA, pp. 1993–2002 (2018). https://doi.org/10.1145/3240508.3241913, http://dl.acm.org/citation.cfm?doid=3240508.3241913

24. Namgung, K., Kim, T.H., Hong, Y.S., Nazir, S.: Menu recommendation system using smart plates for well-balanced diet habits of young children. Wireless Commun. Mob. Comput. **2019** (2019). https://doi.org/10.1155/2019/7971381

25. Nirmal, I., Caldera, A., Bandara, R.D.: Optimization framework for flavour and nutrition balanced recipe: a data driven approach. In: 5th IEEE Uttar Pradesh Section International Conference on Electrical, Electronics and Computer Engineering, UPCON 2018. Institute of Electrical and Electronics Engineers Inc. (2018). https://doi.org/10.1109/UPCON.2018.8596886

26. Oh, H., Jain, R.: From multimedia logs to personal chronicles. In: MM 2017 - Proceedings of the 2017 ACM Multimedia Conference. Association for Computing Machinery Inc, New York, New York, USA, pp. 881–889 (2017). https://doi.org/10.1145/3123266.3123375, http://dl.acm.org/citation.cfm?doid=3123266.3123375

27. Pandey, V., Deepak Upadhyay, D., Nag, N., Jain, R.: Personalized user modelling for context-aware lifestyle recommendations to improve sleep. Tech. rep. (2020)

28. Pandey, V., Nag, N., Jain, R.: Ubiquitous event mining to enhance personal health. In: UbiComp/ISWC 2018 - Adjunct Proceedings of the 2018 ACM International Joint Conference on Pervasive and Ubiquitous Computing and Proceedings of the 2018 ACM International Symposium on Wearable Computers. Association for Computing Machinery Inc, New York, New York, USA, pp. 676–679 (2018). https://doi.org/10.1145/3267305.3267684, http://dl.acm.org/citation.cfm?doid=3267305.3267684

29. Patki, N., Wedge, R., Veeramachaneni, K.: The synthetic data vault. In: Proceedings - 3rd IEEE International Conference on Data Science and Advanced Analytics, DSAA 2016. Institute of Electrical and Electronics Engineers Inc., pp. 399–410 (2016). https://doi.org/10.1109/DSAA.2016.49

30. Pearl, J.: Causal inference in statistics: an overview. Stat. Surv. **3**, 96–146 (2009). https://doi.org/10.1214/09-SS057. http://projecteuclid.org/euclid.ssu/1255440554

31. Raghunathan, R., Naylor, R.W., Hoyer, W.D.: The unhealthy = tasty intuition and its effects on taste inferences, enjoyment, and choice of food products. J. Mark. **70**(4), 170–184 (2006). https://doi.org/10.1509/jmkg.70.4.170. http://journals.sagepub.com/doi/10.1509/jmkg.70.4.170

32. Risso, D.S., et al.: A bio-cultural approach to the study of food choice: the contribution of taste genetics, population and culture. Appetite **114**, 240–247 (2017). https://doi.org/10.1016/j.appet.2017.03.046

33. Romagnolo, D.F., Selmin, O.I.: Mediterranean diet and prevention of chronic diseases. Nutrition Today **52**(5), 208–222 (2017). https://doi.org/10.1097/NT.0000000000000228. www.ncbi.nlm.nih.gov/pmc/articles/PMC5625964/

34. Rostami, A., Pandey, V., Nag, N., Wang, V., Jain, R.: Personal food model. In: Proceedings of the 28th ACM International Conference on Multimedia, pp. 4416–4424 (2020). https://doi.org/10.1145/3394171.3414691, http://arxiv.org/abs/2008.12855

35. Rostami, A., Xu, B., Jain, R.: Multimedia food logger. In: Proceedings of the 28th ACM International Conference on Multimedia. ACM, New York, NY, USA, pp. 4548–4549 (2020). https://doi.org/10.1145/3394171.3414454, https://dl.acm.org/doi/10.1145/3394171.3414454

36. Saha, K.: Modeling stress with social media around incidents of gun violence on college campuses. In: Proceedings of the ACM on Human-Computer Interaction, 1(CSCW), pp. 1-27 (2017). https://doi.org/10.1145/3134727

37. Saha, K., et al.: A social media study on the effects of psychiatric medication use. Tech. rep. (2019), www.aaai.org

38. Schäfer, H., et al.: Towards health (Aware) recommender systems. In: ACM International Conference Proceeding Series. vol. Part F128634, Association for Computing Machinery, New York, New York, USA, pp. 157–161 (2017). https://doi.org/10.1145/3079452.3079499, http://dl.acm.org/citation.cfm?doid=3079452.3079499
39. Shi, Z.: Gut microbiota: an important link between western diet and chronic diseases. Nutrients **11**(10), 2287 (2019). 10.3390/nu11102287, https://www.mdpi.com/2072-6643/11/10/2287
40. Shivappa, N.: Diet and chronic diseases: is there a mediating effect of inflammation? Nutrients **11**(7), 1639 (2019). https://doi.org/10.3390/nu11071639. https://www.mdpi.com/2072-6643/11/7/1639
41. Trang Tran, T.N., Atas, M., Felfernig, A., Stettinger, M.: An overview of recommender systems in the healthy food domain. J. Intell. Inf. Syst. **50**(3), 501–526 (2018). https://doi.org/10.1007/s10844-017-0469-0. http://www.who.int
42. Westermann, U., Jain, R.: Toward a common event model for multimedia applications. IEEE Multimedia **14**(1), 19–29 (2007). https://doi.org/10.1109/MMUL.2007.23

Analysis of Traditional Italian Food Recipes: Experiments and Results

Maria Teresa Artese[1]●, Gianluigi Ciocca[2](✉)●, and Isabella Gagliardi[1]●

[1] IMATI - CNR (National Research Council), Milan, Italy
{teresa,isabella}@mi.imati.cnr.it
[2] Universitá degli Studi di Milano-Bicocca, 20126 Milan, Italy
gianluigi.ciocca@unimib.it

Abstract. Traditional recipes are among those elements that UNESCO included in its Intangible Cultural Heritage for safeguarding. Traditional recipes are passed down from one generation to the other, and offer strong links with a particular territory. Driven by the important role of food recipes in the cultural heritage domain, we have create CookIt, a web portal with the aim to collect, disseminate and safeguard the knowledge of typical Italian recipes and the Mediterranean diet which is a significant part of the Italian cuisine. In this paper we present some preliminary results in recipe analysis to be used within our web portal to support innovative ways to navigate and browse them. We developed some processing and visualization tools to support the analysis and the presentation of the recipes. Our tools are tailored for the Italian language although they can be generalized.

Keywords: Italian cuisine · Cultural heritage · Recipe analysis · Natural language processing · Visualization tools

1 Introduction

Intangible cultural heritage is an integral part of our identity and of what each of us identifies as part of our own culture and being as individuals [4]. Food, with its traditions of preparation and consumption, are a legitimate part of intangible cultural assets. The way food is prepared, the occasions in which food is consumed, the ingredients linked to the seasons and traditions, are handed down from generation to generation. Food today receives special attention from government organizations with the twofold objective of preserving historical roots and cultural identification, and improving the quality of life, and reducing ailments, obesity, and an unbalanced diet.

Cooking recipes provide ingredients and step-by-step instructions for preparing a dish, and thousands of recipes are available. Discovering patterns of use of cooking actions and ingredients is important to understand how to prepare a healthy and safe meal.

© Springer Nature Switzerland AG 2021
A. Del Bimbo et al. (Eds.): ICPR 2020 Workshops, LNCS 12665, pp. 677–690, 2021.
https://doi.org/10.1007/978-3-030-68821-9_53

In this paper we present some preliminary results of some tools that we are developing for recipe analysis. These tools are intended to be used to augment the traditional browsing modalities of the recipes within our web portal CookIT[1] [2]. This is a web portal on Traditional Italian Recipes aimed at preserving, safeguarding, and disseminating them. The portal is designed to support a multimodal navigation and browsing of the recipes. It offers standard search interfaces, and is designed to support different visualization strategies of the retrieved items to engage the user in the exploration of the different aspects of the Italian cuisine.

Here we use the CookIt portal as a source of textual recipes with ingredients and detailed cooking procedures, and as a test-bed for the implemented tools. Specifically, we are developing some recipe processing tools for the analysis and interpretation of recipes, to identify terms able to describe ingredients, actions, and order of actions, using tools specific to Natural Language Processing (NLP). A further processing step is the classification of candidate terms as belonging/not belonging to the food domain performed using machine learning approaches. By analysing the recipes we can retrieve the overall recipe structure in terms of ingredients, actions, and output products.

We formalized a recipe structure in a document type definition with which we are able to produce a structured document with all the recipe's procedures. This document contains all the information of the recipe and can be used in different ways. For example, it could allow the identification of patterns that traditional recipes followed, to retrieve similar recipes by method, number of steps or total time. It could makes it possible to provide for the replacement of classic cooking methods with new, healthier, and faster ones, or the replacement of ingredients with others that do not cause food intolerance or sensitization and to learn how to cook balanced and healthy meals, in line with traditions.

Here we show how we exploited it to design a novel way to show a recipe to users using an interactive, graph-based, interface that allow the users to navigate and follow, step-by-step, the recipe. The prototype visualization application allows the user to easily access every step of the recipe procedure while having an overall overview of its components. By adding editing tools to the visualization application, we can also exploit it as a annotation tools for the creation of training data to be used for the development of the recipe analysis tools as well. This is greatly important since there is a lack of annotated data for Italian recipes.

The article is structured as follows. Section 2 gives an overview of the current works related to Natural Language Processing (NLP) tools and to methods to classify terms as generic/domain specific. Section 3 describes the recipe analysis steps, the NLP processing tools and classification methods designed and implemented, together with some preliminary results. Then, in Sect. 4 the recipe visualization tool is presented. The navigation/retrieval tools of the CookIT portal are illustrated in Sect. 5. Finally, future developments and conclusions are presented in Sect. 6.

---

[1] http://arm.mi.imati.cnr.it/cookIT.

2   Related Works

In this work, we are interested in choosing a publicly available NLP library that is widely used, can be used for the Italian language, and has a python implementation or wrapper. For the English language, well known and consolidated tools are available, such as Stanford's core NLP suite[14], or the NLTK package [19] with PENN Treebank [15,24] as a POS tagger and tokenizer. Other tools have been developed specifically for the Italian language, for example, the Italian version of Snowball, Pattern python pack-age specific for Italian (Pattern clips 2.6), Polyglot, Tint [5] or Opennlp.

Many of these tools for Italian produce results not useful due to the presence of too many errors and inaccuracies, both for the POS tagging and for the lemmatization, unless you do not customize it very accurately, which requires time and in-depth knowledge. TreeTagger [22], spaCy, and Stanza [21] have proven to provide the best results for the Italian language, for the different features involved in this experiment, as detailed below. The TreeTagger is a tool for annotating text with part-of-speech and lemma information. Stanza is based on Stanford's CoreNLP and, like spaCy, uses neural network components that also allow a re-training and evaluation with own annotated data, if the results obtained are not optimal.

The ability to define whether a term is general or it belongs to a specific domain is gaining great importance, both for applications in specific environments and the creation of glossaries or thesauri to be used to query cultural heritage archives, to exploit their full potential. Wang et al. [25] propose a learning-based approach for the automatic construction of domain glossary. Arora [1] presents a tool-supported approach for extracting candidate glossary terms from natural language requirements and grouping these terms into clusters based on relatedness. To extract domain-specific terms, different strategies have been tested and adopted: machine learning algorithms [13], different architectures of featureless deep learning approaches, including both supervised and semi-supervised models [12] or deep learning approach [23].

RecipeScape [7] provides an interactive visual interface to browse, compare and display recipes, using a computational pipeline able to extract ingredients and actions from Web-scraped recipes in English. The recipes are then corrected and validated by human annotators. Other papers, such as [11,17], are concerned with recipe analysis and food recognition from images or videos, starting from public annotated datasets, in the English language.

To the best of our knowledge, this is the first experiment on recipe analysis that focuses on traditional recipes written in Italian.

3   Recipe Analysis

One of the aims of the project is to identify the structure of the recipes and to visualize them in a user-friendly way. This is achieved by starting with the automatic or semi-automatic identification, within each recipe, of the constituent elements of the food-making process. In the specific case, the elements considered essential in the recipes are:

- ingredients (flour, oil, almonds, eggplants, ...);
- cooking utensils (bowl, knife, ...);
- actions (cut, mix, join, ...);
- duration of actions (let it rest for 30 min, ...);
- conditional actions (if the dough is too hard , ... otherwise, ...);
- order in which the actions are executed;
- whether the actions are (almost) simultaneously performed.

The process of automatic identification of ingredients, kitchen utensils, and actions is an NLP (Natural Language Processing) complex problem, requiring methods and tools able to perform syntactic and semantic analysis of the text. The steps to be performed by the NLP are:

- Tokenization;
- Annotation with POS tagging;
- Normalization: Lemmatization and stemming;
- Dependency parsing.

Tokenization is the process of decomposing a text, considered as a continuous set of words, into a set of terms, composed of a single or compound words. In Italian, for example, the apostrophe is a character of division of words. It is obligatory in case of elisions, such as a "bell'amico" (good friend) or "quest'alunna" (this (girl) student). In these cases, two distinct words should be identified.

POS (part-of-speech) tagging is the process of associating the corresponding grammatical category to every single word. This process requires understanding the structure of the sentence because, in Italian as in English, the same word can belong to different grammatical categories (e.g. be an adjective, a noun, or a verb) depending on the composition of the sentence.

Normalization: the process of lemmatization/stemming reduces the words to the lemma or stem. The Porter algorithm is the most widespread stemmer for the English language. For Italian, there are no similar "universal" algorithms.

Dependency parser is the tool able to identify the dependencies of a sentence, representing its grammatical structure and defining the relationships between "head" words and words, which modify those heads. The result of dependency parsing is a graph of words and relations (dependencies) between them within a sentence.

The data used in this experiment have two characteristics that impact on the instruments to be used and that greatly influence the results:

- the language in which the texts are written: Italian language;
- the writing style: food recipes are often written using a colloquial and informal language, where directions and instruction are regulatory texts, with verbs in the imperative form.

```
For each recipe in CookIT:
    for each sentence:
        tokens are identified
        tokens are POS tagged
        tokens are dependency parsed
        for each token they are identified:
            compound nouns (mainly nouns and adjectives)
            compound verbs
            expressions of time
            conditional expressions
    Post processing:
        harmonize compound words/verbs/expression of time
        classify terms as belong/not belonging to the food domain
```

Fig. 1. Steps of the recipe analysis.

Figure 1 illustrates the steps designed to be performed on a raw text to obtain a set of ingredients, materials, actions. To perform the typical NLP processes (tokenization, POS tagging and dependency parsing), we used and integrated different tools. Specifically, spaCy is used to identify tokens and find rule-based components. Then, Stanza is used for its good results in tokenization, POS tagging and dependency parsing. Moreover, Stanza allows to improve the performance, by using your own annotated data. TreeTagger, although its lack of the dependency parsing functionality, has been used as a lemmatizer and POS tagger: using the standard Italian tagset, it has proved to give the best results. Time expressions have been identified with spaCy's built-in tools, using a rule-based matcher, along with POS tagging and dependency parser.

To fully understand the recipes and interpret them correctly, we have to cope with the fact that most of the ingredients/utensils are usually noun groups, composed of nouns and adjectives, for example, "olio extra vergine d'oliva" (Extra Virgin olive oil), and verbs can be composed of two or more words, for example "[il forno] si sta scaldando" ([the oven] is heating). So a procedure to merge two or more single terms to form a compound term has been designed able to take into account the specificity of the Italian language. Different methods have been tested, either building compound words based only on the results of the dependency parser or using rule-based grammar, or a combination of the twos. These methods depend largely on the correctness of the POS tagger, because both in the case of nouns and verbs, the erroneous attribution to a different category leads to false positives (creation of non-existent n-grams) or false negatives (lack of identification of compound terms).

Once identified the (compound) terms, a further step is required to discard those terms that are too generic or noisy to be useful for the recipe graph. To automatically evaluate the belonging/not belonging of terms to the food domain, a machine learning approach has been implemented and used [3]. It uses standard classification methods (KNN and Logistic–Regression) working on the word embedding models - the semantic representation of candidate terms

Table 1. Classification results for food/non food text on the training set.

Training set		Precision	Recall	F1 score	Accuracy
Logistic regression	Food	0.92	0.93	0.92	0.914
	Non food	0.91	0.90	0.91	
KNN (k = 2)	Food	0.89	0.96	0.92	0.914
	Non food	0.95	0.86	0.90	
KNN (k = 3)	Food	0.92	0.94	0.93	0.921
	Non food	0.93	0.90	0.91	
KNN (k = 5)	Food	0.89	0.94	0.91	0.900
	Non food	0.92	0.85	0.89	

Table 2. Classification results of the food/non food text on the test set.

Test set		Precision	Recall	F1 score	Accuracy
Logistic regression	Food	0.91	0.91	0.91	0.896
	Non food	0.88	0.89	0.88	
KNN (k = 2)	Food	0.86	0.95	0.90	0.881
	Non food	0.92	0.80	0.86	
KNN (k = 3)	Food	0.88	0.92	0.90	0.884
	Non food	0.89	0.84	0.86	
KNN (k = 5)	Food	0.86	0.93	0.89	0.876
	Non food	0.90	0.81	0.85	

able to capture the semantics of words and their context [16,20]. For training and testing the classifiers, we used a data set created ad-hoc by scraping Wikipedia web pages and collecting data from the 9 root categories, plus the food category. Starting from each category, the scraper tool extracted titles and abstracts of all pages of that category, recursively, for a depth of k level (for this experiment, k was set to 2, a balanced compromise between the total number of documents to be processed and the variety of terms to consider). The dataset has been created to have approximately the same number of labelled entries for the two classes, food and non food.

The classifiers use the word embedding vectors for both titles and abstract of the Wikipedia dataset: each abstract/title is calculated as the average of the vectors of all terms present, except stop-words, and returns a vector that is used by the classifiers. Here the pre-trained word2vec embedding model [16] for Italian has been used[2]. Table 1 and Table 2 report the classification results using

---

[2] https://wikipedia2vec.github.io/wikipedia2vec/pretrained/.

Table 3. Classification results of the food and non food text on the n-gram terms set.

N-gram terms set		Precision	Recall	F1 score	Accuracy
Logistic regression	Food	0.81	0.97	0.88	0.820
	Non food	0.87	0.45	0.60	
KNN (k = 2)	Food	0.75	0.99	0.85	0.757
	Non food	0.85	0.20	0.33	

Logistic Regression and KNN (with k = 2, k = 3, and k = 5) algorithms, on the training set and the test set respectively.

The models have then been further tested on a set formed by human-created lists of n-gram terms containing ingredients, tools, and actions, taken from the web and manually integrated with missing terms. Again, for n-grams the average of the vectors of the terms present is calculated and used. Table 3 presents the results of the classification algorithms on the n-gram terms set to which words not belonging to the domain have been added. We can note that, for both classifiers, the recall on food class is very close to 1 (all terms related to food have been correctly classified), while the precision is lower, indicating that also n-grams labeled as non-food have been classified as food. For the classification of non-food terms, the situation is more critical, struggling to correctly classify many terms. One of the reasons why the models do not generalize well may be the difference between the two datasets. As stated before, the dataset used for training and testing the classifiers is composed of the titles and abstracts scraped from Wikipedia on different subjects, starting from the root categories, with an average length of each entry of approximately 75 words. While, the lists of n-grams, used for further testing, instead are composed on average of 1.7 words. Since the purpose of the classifiers is to distinguish generic terms from specific terms, further work will be done to improve the precision of the food class, and in general, the performance of the non-food class.

Figure 2 shows an excerpt of the "Caponata" recipe, with ingredients highlighted in green, utensils in cyan, and actions in yellow. In light gray the terms discarded by the classification algorithm. We formalize the information extracted from the recipes with a Document Type Definition (DTD) as shown in Fig. 3).

The ingredients are identified by name and quantity (QUANTITY). Each action has ingredients in input (PRE), in a specific quantity for that action (USED_QUANTITY), and can produce some processed products (POST), in an defined time (DURABLE), and in conditional mode (CONDITION). The recipes are a succession of actions (ORDER_RELATION), which can sometimes be performed simultaneously (SIMULTANEITY_RELATION). The DTD is used to produce an XML file that store the recipe structure.

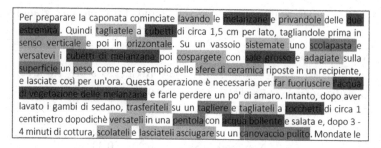

Fig. 2. Excerpt of the "Caponata" recipe. Ingredients are highlighted in green, utensils in cyan, and actions in yellow. Light gray terms are those discarded by the classifier. (Color figure online)

```
<!DOCTYPE Recipe [
<!ELEMENT RECIPE (INGREDIENT+, ACTION+, ORDER_RELATION*)>.
<!ELEMENT INGREDIENT (INGREDIENT_NAME, QUANTITY?)>
<!ELEMENT INGREDIENT_NAME (#PCDATA)>
<!ELEMENT QUANTITY (#PCDATA)>
<!ELEMENT ACTION (ACTION_NAME, PRE*, POST*, DURABLE?, CONDITION?)>
<!ELEMENT ORDER_RELATION (#PCDATA)>
<!ELEMENT SIMULTANEITY_RELATION (#PCDATA)>.
<!ELEMENT ACTION_NAME (#PCDATA)>
<!ELEMENT PRE (INGREDIENT+, USED_QUANTITY*)>.
<!ELEMENT POST (INGREDIENT+, USED_QUANTITY*)>.
<!ELEMENT DURABLE(#PCDATA)>
<!ELEMENT CONDITION (#PCDATA)>
<!ELEMENT USED_QUANTITY (#PCDATA)>.

<!ATTLIST INGREDIENT_ID ID #REQUIRED>
<!ATTLIST ACTION_ID ID #REQUIRED>
<!ATTLIST ORDER_RELATION ID_ACTION Prec IDREF #REQUIRED>
<!ATTLIST ORDER RELATION ID_ACTION Succ IDREF #REQUIRED>
<!ATTLIST SIMULTANEITY_RELATION ID_ACTION DURABLE IDREF #REQUIRED>
<!ATTLIST SIMULTANEITY_RELATION ID_ACTION IDREF CONDITION #REQUIRED>
<!ATTLIST USED_QUANTITY INGREDIENT_ID IDREF #REQUIRED>
]>
```

Fig. 3. DTD for a recipe.

An example is shown in Fig. 4. The file have been obtained by applying the NLP pre-trained tools (spaCy and Stanza) and the compound terms were identified based on the dependency parser.

4   Recipe Visualization Application

The output of the recipe analysis contains all the information about a recipe: ingredients, tools, actions, and intermediate products. All these elements are connected to form a graph of the whole recipe. We call this graph a recipe graph. The nodes of the graph are ingredients, tools, and intermediate products. The arcs of the graph are the actions to be performed. We developed a prototype application to visualize the recipe graph that can be navigated and edited. This application has been designed with different tasks in mind. First, it could be used

Fig. 4. Information extracted from the "Caponata" recipe rendered as an XML file following the devised DTD.

by the end-user who wants to step-by-step follow the recipe. They can visualize the overall procedure and see if there are some concurrent steps in the recipe or have an overall idea of the recipe complexity by looking at the structure of the graph. They may select nodes and arcs to have detailed information about the specific element.

Another use of this application is for creating a ground truth of recipes that can be used in the analysis modules. The output of the recipe analysis is often not completely correct and there are errors in the identification of ingredients and tools but mostly in the recognition of the cooking actions and their sequences. The application can be used to manually correct these errors. In this way, we can obtain reference recipes that can be used to refine the analysis modules.

Figure 5 (top) shows the main page of the application. The processed recipe, "Caponata", is shown both as text and as a step-by-step recipe graph. On the left, there is a menu with which the user can see all the detailed information about the recipe. The graph can be also edited by adding and/or removing elements. The Graph can be navigated and zoomed as necessary as it is shown in Fig. 5 (bottom). Each node of the graph can be analyzed. In the figure information, about five nodes are shown. The recipe graph application is currently under development and it lacks some functionalities and a more appealing user

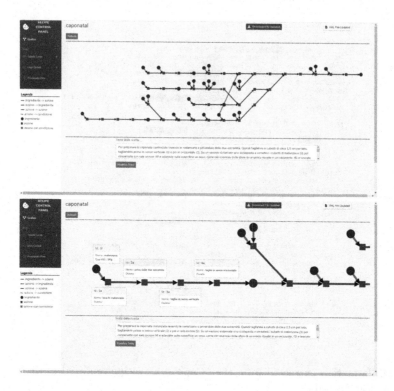

Fig. 5. A screenshot of the recipe visualization tool. The recipe is shown as a graph with nodes indicating ingredients, implements, and actions. The different branches also suggest that some procedures can be executed in parallel.

interface. It is a web app and can be used by multiple users concurrently working on different recipes.

5   CookIt Portal

The portal aims to promote awareness of Italian cuisine recipes and the Mediterranean diet, of which Italian cuisine is an important element. The portal focuses only on traditional food recipes, considered the core and heart of Italian cuisine, to preserve the typical ones, also considering local variations.

For the purposes of this paper, only the information and the search/browse tools are described.

CookIT portal stores multimedia information describing, in the Italian language, the traditional recipes of each Italian region, handed down from generation to generation. Two different types of information, to be used for search and visualization purposes, have been identified:

1. Recipes: they are the kernel of the portal and are defined by title, description, ingredients, variants, place, date, tags ..., integrated with images and videos.

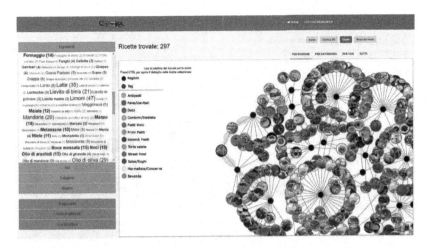

Fig. 6. 2D elastic visualization. The links among the recipes have been highlighted in yellow. (Color figure online)

The recipes can be linked together, because they are variants of the same food, are prepared on the occasion of the same celebration, or share some common background.

2. Ingredients/nutrients: data are taken from or linked to authoritative ingredients/nutrient databases, including open linked data. They consist of ingredient name (and its variations), nutrients, colors, calories, class, ...

The data have been inserted in the CookIT portal, through a semi-automatic procedure that scraped the contents from those websites that have the following characteristics: to be authoritative, also internationally recognized as containers of recipes following the tradition; to have implemented a schema for recipes (the most used is the schema.org/recipe standard, supported by Google, Bing, and Yahoo).

Navigation and retrieval for the CookIT Portal have been designed and implemented focusing on the multimodal nature of collected data. CookIT offers a standard retrieval interface that allows the users to perform searches in two steps, to reduce the results to more targeted results.

Recipes are retrieved combining different keys: tags, co-occurrence of words related to recipes, localization, etc. and results are offered as a list, as a mosaic, as points in a map, as points in a calendar, as a graph to show how recipes are related to ingredients, categories, tags and any other.

Figure 6 shows the recipes using a 2D elastic visualization, organized by Italian regions (Lombardy, Piedmont, Sicily, ...). The links among the recipes have been highlighted. The query results can be narrowed by clicking on the indices, on the left. Other views include the arrangement of recipes on Cartesian axes, using colors, calories, categories, and other attributes as axes. Figure 7 shows an example of the visualization of the recipes on a 2D graph. The graph

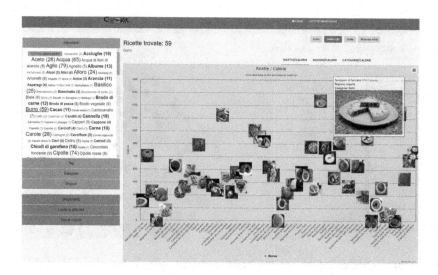

Fig. 7. Example of 2D graph visualization. Recipes containing butter are displayed according to their calories per portion.

displays the selected recipes according to their calories per portion. On the left the list of ingredients can be used to narrow down the search. Recipes can be browsed, by moving the mouse, and a double click opens the detail view.

At the moment, the CookIT site contains 297 traditional recipes, including pizza and some typical dishes of the Mediterranean diet, intangible heritage included in the UNESCO Representative List of the Intangible Cultural Heritage of Humanity. Other 300 traditional Italian recipes have been identified for inclusion.

6   Future Works and Conclusions

In this paper, we presented a set of tools for automatically analyzing and modeling cooking procedures to be used in the CookIt portal. The CookIT portal, designed for the conservation and preservation of traditional Italian recipes, has been used as a source of textual recipes with ingredients and detailed cooking procedures and as a test-bed for the implemented tools. It has been also designed to be a research sandbox in which to experiment with new algorithms of visualization and search of content, images and texts [8,9,18].

The process of automatic identification of ingredients, kitchen utensils, and actions has required NLP methods and tools able to perform syntactic and semantic analysis of the text. A further step of classification of candidate terms as belonging/not belonging to the food domain has been performed using a machine learning approach. Preliminary results of the recipe analysis steps are quite satisfactory for the automatic identification of ingredients, tools, and duration, while the identification of actions and their order in the execution of the recipe requires further refinement, especially concerning actions started and then resumed after some time. The DTD proved itself able to catch most of the relations between actions and ingredients. However the classification results on the n-gram terms are not yet satisfactory. The models do not generalize well on the n-gram dataset. More experiments are needed to evaluate how the performance are improved both by inserting in the training/test dataset more n-grams, and by fine tuning the classifiers, to obtain better recall and precision of food and non-food classes.

The designed graph-based recipe visualization tool allow the users to navigate and browse the recipe in an easy way. The tool can be also exploited as a recipe annotation tool to create new recipe datasets that can be exploited by researched to design more robust NLP algorithms for food recipes. In the future, we plan to study the use of LSTM and RCNN deep learning frameworks to analyze and process texts in Italian, tailored for food recipes in order to recognize food-specific terms [6]. Moreover, we plan to develop more analysis tools such as the comparison between recipes by defining new distances taking into account different properties of the recipe graph and of food images [10]. In addition, we intend to use the structure of the graphs to automatically gain information about some features of the recipes that could be interesting for possible users such as recipe complexity in terms of procedures and time.

References

1. Arora, C., Sabetzadeh, M., Briand, L., Zimmer, F.: Automated extraction and clustering of requirements glossary terms. IEEE Trans. Software Eng. **43**(10), 918–945 (2016)
2. Artese, M.T., Ciocca, G., Gagliardi, I.: Cookit: a web portal for the preservation and dissemination of traditional Italian recipes. Int. J. Humanit. Soc. Sci. **13**(2), 171–176 (2019)
3. Artese, M.T., Gagliardi, I.: Automatic identification of domain terms: an approach for Italian. In: Digital Preservation and Presentation of Cultural and Scientific Heritage, pp. 251–257 (2020)
4. Brulotte, R.L., Di Giovine, M.A.: Edible Identities: Food as cultural heritage. Routledge, London (2016)
5. Cabrio, E., Mazzei, A., Tamburini, F.: Tint 2.0: an all-inclusive suite for NLP in Italian. In: Proceedings of the Fifth Italian Conference on Computational Linguistics CLiC-it, vol. 10, p. 12 (2018)
6. Carvalho, M., Cadène, R., Picard, D., Soulier, L., Thome, N., Cord, M.: Cross-modal retrieval in the cooking context: learning semantic text-image embeddings. In: The 41st International ACM SIGIR Conference on Research & Development in Information Retrieval, pp. 35–44 (2018)
7. Chang, M., Guillain, L.V., Jung, H., Hare, V.M., Kim, J., Agrawala, M.: RecipeScape: an interactive tool for analyzing cooking instructions at scale. In: Proceedings of the 2018 CHI Conference on Human Factors in Computing Systems, pp. 1–12 (2018)
8. Ciocca, G., Napoletano, P., Schettini, R.: Food recognition: a new dataset, experiments, and results. IEEE J. Biomed. Health Inf. **21**(3), 588–598 (2016)

9. Ciocca, G., Napoletano, P., Schettini, R.: CNN-based features for retrieval and classification of food images. Comput. Vis. Image Underst. **176**, 70–77 (2018)

10. Ciocca, G., Napoletano, P., Schettini, R., Gagliardi, I., Artese, M.T.: Analyzing color harmony of food images. In: Color and Imaging Conference, pp. 369–374. Society for Imaging Science and Technology (2019)

11. Herranz, L., Min, W., Jiang, S.: Food recognition and recipe analysis: integrating visual content, context and external knowledge. arXiv preprint arXiv:1801.07239 (2018)

12. Khosla, K., Jones, R., Bowman, N.: Featureless deep learning methods for automated key-term extraction (2019)

13. Kulkarni, A., Smith, R.: Automated glossary construction of a biology textbook (2018)

14. Manning, C., Surdeanu, M., Bauer, J., Finkel, J., Bethard, S., McClosky, D.: Stanford coreNLP a suite of core NLP tools (2014)

15. Marcus, M., Santorini, B., Marcinkiewicz, M.A.: Building a large annotated corpus of english: The penn treebank (1993)

16. Mikolov, T., Sutskever, I., Chen, K., Corrado, G.S., Dean, J.: Distributed representations of words and phrases and their compositionality. In: Advances in Neural Information Processing Systems, pp. 3111–3119 (2013)

17. Min, W., Bao, B.K., Mei, S., Zhu, Y., Rui, Y., Jiang, S.: You are what you eat: exploring rich recipe information for cross-region food analysis. IEEE Trans. Multimedia **20**(4), 950–964 (2017)

18. Mori, S., Sasada, T., Yamakata, Y., Yoshino, K.: A machine learning approach to recipe text processing. In: Proceedings of the 1st Cooking with Computer Workshop, pp. 29–34 (2012)

19. NLTK: Natural language toolkit NLTK 3.0 documentation (2016). http://www.nltk.org. Accessed 27 Sept 2020

20. Pennington, J., Socher, R., Manning, C.D.: Glove: global vectors for word representation. In: Proceedings of the 2014 Conference on Empirical Methods in Natural Language Processing (EMNLP), pp. 1532–1543 (2014)

21. Qi, P., Zhang, Y., Zhang, Y., Bolton, J., Manning, C.D.: Stanza: a python natural language processing toolkit for many human languages. In: Proceedings of the 58th Annual Meeting of the Association for Computational Linguistics: System Demonstrations, pp. 101–108, Jul 2020

22. Schmid, H.: Treetagger-a language independent part-of-speech tagger (1994). http://www.ims.uni-stuttgart.de/projekte/corplex/TreeTagger/

23. Singh, M., Boggess, M.: Automatic extraction of textbook glossaries using deep learning (2019)

24. Taylor, A., Marcus, M., Santorini, B.: The penn treebank: an overview. In: Abeille, A. (ed.) Treebanks, pp. 5–22. Springer, Dordrecht (2003). https://doi.org/10.1007/978-94-010-0201-1_1

25. Wang, C., et al.: A learning-based approach for automatic construction of domain glossary from source code and documentation. In: Proceedings of the 2019 27th ACM Joint Meeting on European Software Engineering Conference and Symposium on the Foundations of Software Engineering, pp. 97–108 (2019)

Author Index

Printed in the United States
By Bookmasters